The Many Faces of Philosophy

The Many Faces of Philosophy

Reflections from Plato to Arendt

Edited by
Amélie Oksenberg Rorty

OXFORD
UNIVERSITY PRESS

2003

OXFORD
UNIVERSITY PRESS

Oxford   New York
Auckland   Bangkok   Buenos Aires
Cape Town   Chennai   Dar es Salaam   Delhi   Hong Kong   Istanbul
Karachi   Kolkata   Kuala Lumpur   Madrid   Melbourne   Mexico City   Mumbai
Nairobi   São Paulo   Taipei   Tokyo   Toronto

Copyright © 2003 by Oxford University Press, Inc.

Published by Oxford University Press, Inc.
198 Madison Avenue, New York, New York 10016

Oxford is a registered trademark of Oxford University Press

ISBN 0-19-513402-8

Printed in the United States of America

In gratitude to

Matthew Carmody
ὁ ἰατρός

Genevieve Lloyd
ἡ φιλόσοφος

Jay Rorty
ὁ φίλος

Contents

Preface

The philosophers represented in this collection have, for better or worse, influenced the way philosophy is practiced. They have formed the canon that presently defines the field, guides apprentices, and sets standards of authority. The scope of their meditative self-presentations nevertheless suggests that philosophy has not formed a specific genre of writing or argumentation. Philosophical credos, manifestos, and programs are found in letters, prefaces, journals, diaries, interviews. Moreover, the aims, the stylistic conventions, and the audiences of such self-conscious self-mirrorings vary historically. Many of Augustine's reflections were formulated as prayers. Montaigne's *Essais* are exercises: expansive, concentric attempts to present himself to his intimate friends, as if he were speaking to himself. Other autobiographies—those of Al Ghazali, Maimonides, and Descartes—follow a narrative form, a reconstructed story of an intellectual quest that moves them from sensory experience through skepticism toward an affirmation of the consonance of faith and science. Later philosophical autobiographies—for instance, those by Hobbes and Hume—introduce a different narrative mode of self-examination. Rousseau's artful attempts at spontaneity announce a new form of autobiographical writing. And when self-conscious intellectual autobiographies are continuous with philosophical polemics—as they are with Heidegger, Russell, and Carnap—the genre "philosophical autobiography" yet again takes a different style, agenda, and audience.

The modes of philosophy are as various as those of autobiography. As their aims, issues, and audiences vary, philosophers experiment with different argumentative rhetorical and literary genres. In doing so, they often realign themselves: sometimes they keep company with theologians, sometimes with scientists or historians, sometimes with statesmen and educators, journalists and citizens of the republic of letters. Most recently, philosophy has become an academic profession, an exclusive, self-selective, and self-perpetuating guild with strict rules of apprenticeship and membership, a guild that regulates acceptable philosophic publication.

The Many Faces of Philosophy marks the intersection between continuously transforming genres. The introduction questions the rigid distinctions between "philosophy," "autobiography," "literary essays," and "political argumentation," distinctions that emerged from the practical necessities of library and publishers' catalogues—and from the departmental politics of university organization. It presents philosophers' meditations on the nature and tasks of philosophy, their reflections on the contribution that their "strictly" philosophic work makes to their other activities and commitments as political or spiritual advisers, as scientists and educators. Those self-searching meditations include materials culled from letters, prefaces, memoirs, political tracts, replies to critics. They also include a few excerpts from contemporary biographies (Baillet on Descartes, Aubrey on Hobbes, Fox Bourne on Locke, Adam Smith on Hume, Engels on Marx).

I have not included technical philosophical discussions (Spinoza on the vortex; Leibniz on the infinite). Nor I have I included personal letters, letters of condolence, love letters ("Darling, our marriages are out of town, meet me at l'Hôtel d'Amour"), letters of recommendation ("Schmuel Potsdam is the best student we've had since Leibniz"), pleas for money or patronage ("Greatest Protector of Learning, please send money") or ordinary whining ("Did you see the disgusting mis-review of my latest book by that envious idiot?").

I have omitted well-known, carefully crafted philosophical autobiographies— for instance, those of Marcus Aurelius, Augustine, Boethius, Rousseau, Mill, Sartre, and Russell. They are readily available in inexpensive paperback editions, and it would be a travesty to edit such works. Instead I have included shorter, less well known works by many of these authors.

There are glaring omissions. Aristotle: we only have his will and a poem honoring Plato, neither of philosophical interest. Aquinas: to the best of my knowledge, we unfortunately have no autobiographical scraps of any kind. Asian and African philosophers: it would require another book to present them, one prepared by scholars specialized in those rich and varied traditions.

Knowledgeable readers of a book of this kind will inevitably regret some selections: why Seneca rather than Cicero? why so much of Augustine's correspondence with St. Jerome and so little of his reflections on political theory? surely there are better passages from Rousseau, from Hegel? And I, too, as I read proofs, thought: "Oh, if I could only have included some delicious material from Plotinus or from Boethius!" I can only hope that our shared disappointments send us to the originals, each of us editors of a book we would have preferred.

Peter Ohlin, our editor at Oxford University Press, rightly thought we should introduce each philosopher with a brief biographical note. In despair at doing justice to the subject, I turned for help to a team of expert colleagues, who (understandably enough) preferred to remain anonymous. On behalf of our readers, I am grateful to them for their resourceful and conscientious work in writing the headnotes.

The initial skeletal table of contents was circulated with a request for comments and suggestions, additions and editions to colleagues, specialists in ancient and medieval philosophy (Myles Burnyeat, Steven Harris, Simon Harrison, Matthew Kraus), in early modern philosophy (Frederick Beiser, Daniel Garber, Stephen Gendzier, Genevieve Lloyd, Terence Pinkard, James Schmidt, Sally Sedgwick, Jacqueline Taylor, Kenneth Winkler, Arnulf Zweig), in contemporary analytic and continental philosophy (Seyla Benhabib, William Bristow, James Dwyer, Juliet Floyd, Mary Mothersill, Ronald de Sousa). Several colleagues (Seyla Benhabib, Sissela Bok, Tracy Kosman, Mary Mothersill, Sara Ruddick, William Ruddick, Sally Sedgwick) insisted on the inclusion of at least some women philosophers. Sissela Bok generously showed me her "Autobiography as Moral Background." Jacob Dreyfack let me use his translation of Bailliet. I am grateful to Jeffrey Michels, Charles McKinley, and Scott Ruescher for their bibliographical and technical help, and to Peter Ohlin for his editorial acumen. Byron Good of the Department of Social Medicine at Harvard University, Williams College and the members of its philosophy department offered me ideal conditions for study and writing. In truth, a work of this kind is a cooperative enterprise that draws on the expertise of a host of generous and helpful colleagues. Without their knowledge and their critical and empathic imagination, and without their collaboration in preparing biographical notes, this book would not exist.

Introduction
Witnessing Philosophers

Philosophy has been—and been perceived as—a dangerous activity. In raising fundamental questions, examining basic assumptions, revising received views, philosophers undertook immense risks. Even when philosophers took themselves to be engaged in the constructive work of rationalizing World Systems, their interpretations of religious doctrines were seen as subversive, their analyses of social and political practices were frequently thought disloyal if not actually seditious, their reconstructions of morality were often perceived as potentially corrupting. Athenians saw Socratic questioning as a threat to the stability and morality of public order; Roman emperors feared Seneca; theologians censored Abelard; Scottish universities were apprehensive of Hume's skeptical influence. Voltaire and Diderot were briefly imprisoned for their views, Kant was temporarily prohibited from publishing his works on religion. Nor have recent philosophers fared much better: Marx was effectively exiled; Husserl and Russell were dismissed from their university positions for political reasons.

Philosophers themselves often suffered from the turn of their reflections, uncertain of where their meditations and arguments might lead them. Like Hume, they were sometimes in despair at where their arguments brought them. Even when Voltaire and Rousseau questioned the pretensions of unsupported rationalism, they struggled to avoid what they feared might be nihilistic skepticism. In a more strictly philosophical mode, Schopenhauer and Wittgenstein, each in his own way, endeavored to overcome the destructive tenor of their work by stressing its liberating character. Different as they were, radically critical philosophical figures like Nietzsche, Marx and Sartre thought it necessary to present their attacks on superstition and tyranny as ushering in a freer, more exuberant mode of life.

Even at their most meditative, autobiographers actively try to persuade someone of something. Witness St. Teresa of Avila (1515–1582): "I write about my way of prayer . . . I beg anyone who reads this account of my life to bear in mind how wicked it has been . . . May it lead my confessors to know me better, so they may help my weakness" (*The Life of St. Teresa of Avila*);[1] Thomas de Quincy (1785–1859): "I present to you, courteous reader, with the record of a remarkable period of my life. I trust that it will prove not merely an interesting record, but, in a considerable degree, useful and instructive" (*Confessions of an Opium Eater*);* Joseph Priestly (1733–1804): "I hope this account of myself will not be without use . . . especially in promoting virtue and piety" (*Memoirs of Dr. Joseph Priestly Written by Himself*).*

Like most rhetoricians, autobiographers claim trust by announcing artless truthfulness. Witness Montaigne (1533–1592): "I want to be seen here in my simple, natural, ordinary fashion, without straining or artifice." Lord Herbert of

Cherbury (1583–1648): "I have thought fit to relate to my posterity those passages of my life which I conceive may best declare me, and be useful to them, in the delivery of which I profess to write with all truth and sincerity, as scorning ever to deceive or speak false" (*The Life of Edward, Lord Herbert of Cherbury*);* Lev Tolstoy (1828–1910): "When a man writes his life, he should write the whole and exact truth" (*Autobiography*); John Ruskin (1828–1900): "I have written these sketches of effort and incident in former years . . . frankly, garrulously . . . without endeavor to conceal . . . very carefully of what I think may be useful for others to know" (*Praeterita*).* J.-J. Rousseau (1712–1778): "I undertake a project which has never before been attempted, and which cannot ever be imitated. I wish to display a man in every way true to nature; and this man will be myself. Myself alone. I feel my own heart . . . I am not like any other whom I know . . . [I shall disguise nothing] and speak of what is good and what is bad with equal frankness" (*Confessions*); Mohandas Gandhi (1869–1948): "I simply want to tell the story of my numerous experiments with truth . . . I am not going to conceal or understate any ugly things that must be told" (*Autobiography: My Experiments with Truth*).

Of course we know better than to take what people say at face value, least of all when they are talking about themselves. Secret diaries without apparent rhetorical purpose—the self artlessly talking to itself and for itself at sixteen, at twenty-five, at thirty-three, at fifty, and reflecting on it all at seventy-five—enact an internal dialogue, one part of the self presenting itself to another, often exhibiting a singular lack of cohesion, even when there is continuity of style. Like the last thoughts before sleep, introspective self-revelation expresses the images of the day. Witness Leslie Stephen (1832–1904): "The autobiographer . . . is writing about a topic in which he is keenly interested . . . It [is] a special felicity that an autobiography may be more valuable in proportion to the amount of misrepresentation which it contains . . . It is always curious to see how a man contrives to give a false testimonial to himself . . . [casting] his own shadow upon the discolored and distorting mists of memory."* Going beyond Stephen—himself a biographer never shy about encapsulating lives—we know better than to imagine that a life can be summarized, let alone evaluated by an omniscient observer. Not even the portraits of close witnesses—the person as seen by parents, friends, colleagues, lovers, students, patrons, enemies, children, all actively intent on their own concerns—can be projected to form a coherent composite picture. And what is true for the subject, is true for the interpreter: readers of self-presentations bring their own active preoccupations to their reading. If autobiography cannot be taken at face value, if friends and relations have their own directions, if scholarly biographers have their preoccupations, then certainly we latter-day curious and casual readers are also carried by our own currents.

For all of that, we understand one another reasonably well, at least for practical purposes; and perhaps, when we are lucky, we also have reasonably reliable self-knowledge.[2] Except for dramatically dark moments when the near and dear seem incomprehensible, moments that are not necessarily more truthful for being momentous, we do not, in ordinary life, treat one another as if we—our real selves—were ineffable, unfathomable, inscrutable souls, beyond kenning. If that were so, there could be no common world, no serious conversation, no deeply shared projects, no advice, either to one another or to our future selves. To the extent that we swerve to a mode of life, an occupation, a partner, our major decisions would flounder (even more hopelessly than they seem to do) if we were unable to understand ourselves and our fellows. We would have died of hunger and misery long ago if we were unable to discern one another's characters, to distinguish desire from refusal, trustworthy friends from unreliable louts, talented colleagues from pretentious frauds. Failures of understanding stand out against the steady background hum of ordinary understanding. Indeed the question, "Did I misunderstand?" only makes sense on the assumption of considerable success. The rhetorical overstated proclamation—"Isn't it obvious? We can never understand one another"—undermines itself. Though we tend to find ourselves in what we read—through identification or antagonism—we hold ourselves to stand corrected.

The ability to discern the lineaments of character extends beyond ourselves and our contemporaries, beyond the necessities of mutual understanding for the basic activities of life. We are capable of refined discriminations: we readily distinguish the style and mentality of Augustine from that of Plato, Rousseau from Leibniz, Heidegger from Hume, Russell from de Beauvoir. To be sure, there are uncertainties (was the Seventh Letter written by Plato?); there are serious mistakes (perhaps James I should not have appointed Francis Bacon, even in his persona as Verulam, to be lord chancellor of the realm); and we are not all equally skilled in the art of reading character (imagine Heidegger trying to understand Hume; consider Russell trying to understand himself). What's more, we gloss over dramatic differences in mentality: in the name of intellectual charity, we crudely (re)interpret what seems strange in order to preserve what seems to us consistent and true. So, for instance, many scholars, incredulous that Hobbes could have sincerely intended to set an argument for a Christian commonwealth right at the heart of the *Leviathan* (2.31–pt. 4: "Of the Kingdom of God by Nature" "Of a Christian Commonwealth," and "Of the Kingdom of Darkness"), treat it as a prudently self-protective mask or as a recommendation to the sovereign, a pragmatic tactic designed to promote security and civility.[3]

Despite our limitations, we persevere in our curiosity, our passion for understanding our ancestors, for imitating heroes and reviling villains. All this attests to a working conviction that past lives do not disappear into vanishing points, that they are not mosaic mirror fragments set at odd angles, reflecting only a bit of the observer's face. Attempts to deconstruct the self quickly move to incoherence: Who's doing the bulldozing? On what ground does the bulldozer find its purchase point?

"Interpreter": the etymology derives from Latin, *inter pres;* it refers to a go-between, a negotiator, a broker. A practical rather than contemplative activity. Later metaphors for interpretive activity move to observation and perspective, surface appearances and underlying structure, signs and their meaning. Unlike the original implication of commercial transaction, these later metaphors seem to pose a dilemma: either there is a basic fact of the matter about a person's character, or descriptions of persons are no more than shadows cast (on what?) by a beholder (what beholder?). Best avoid the hopeless heroics of facing such dilemmas. Take a detour around those metaphors; they branch to dead ends in all directions.

Other metaphors may serve us better, carry us further. In solitary reflection, even in summary self-assessment, we are not omniscient introspective authorities, but actors in a fragmented drama. Authors try to make the drama of their lives into a coherent story. Because Monica prayed that her son would accept Christ, he became . . . Because Sartre was brought up by a single mother living in her parents' stern and literary household, he . . . Because Virginia Woolf was mauled by her stepbrothers, she . . . Even philosophers seem to have a tenacious need to represent ourselves as living in the center of a coherent life, managing or healing it, with an imprint of style if not of purpose. Such a patterned form provides a sense of contained continuity, enabling us to choose in character, from stable habits, entrenched modes of thought and desires. But in truth, accident and chance—an unexpected encounter, an illness, war and exile, sudden wealth or sudden poverty—are major players in our lives. They fragment us: they break what had seemed the continuous arc line of our lives. To be sure, we remain recognizably ourselves in these accidental encounters and upheavals: we meet them in characteristic ways, evasively, stoically, belligerently, humorously, or inventively. For all of that, we are transformed—indeed formed—by accidents. The autobiographer attempts to weave these accidents into a patterned tapestry of a life, a comfort of closure, of explanation or justification.

We play different roles as we are cast into different situations with different acting partners. We improvise, artfully cooperating in the activities that constitute our lives. The actions and outcomes of the drama are not planned; a thoughtful motion does not always foresee its successor. We attempt to conciliate ancestors and reconcile our descendants with our contemporaries; we are sustained by friends and enemies, and also blocked by friends and enemies; we are bounded by stark necessity, and transformed by accidents and illness. If you ask, "Who is this active/passive we?" you too have become an actor in the drama, and we shall together improvise the answer as best we can, given our respective situations and mutual understanding.

Autobiography: graphic self-revelation. But in truth "autobiography" does not form a single genre: its aims and conventions, its formality or intimacy, its vernacular and audience vary contextually. The style of even the most apparently naive heartfelt moments of self-disclosure is unself-consciously governed by the rhetoric of the time. "Self-revelation" was transformed by Augustine, yet again by Montaigne, again by Rousseau, again and again by contemporary public interviews and the politics of disclosure. The Stoic writing for his son, a great lady whispering to another about the foibles of her philosopher friends are no less formally and stylistically shaped than are the self-portraits of Titian, Rembrandt, Bonnard, Bacon, or Kitaj.[4] Self-revelation can appear in memoirs, letters, prefaces, interviews, journals. It may take the form of apology, manifesto, credo, meditation, confession, tale of adventure or tribulation, a testimonial, a fantasy, a disputation, a consolation, a traveler's guide, a detective story, a self-promoting hagiography . . . and most likely, a combination of these. The author inadvertently reveals—or craftily presents—a persona. (For reasons that will become clear, I must reluctantly use the masculine pronoun throughout.) He is Everyman, or an impassioned and outraged reformer, a defender and protector of tradition, a searcher, a judge, a petitioner or a patron; he is the Eternal Mind, a sinner, a rogue, a victim, a penitent . . . and most likely, a masked and multiheaded hydra composed of these. He addresses posterity, ancestors, political or religious authority, intimate friends, divinity, enemies or allies, his future self, or an imagined aspect of himself . . . and most likely, a fused combination of these. Witness Timur the Lame (a.k.a. Tamerlane the Great) (1336–1405): "I have written my memoirs in order that . . . my posterity may, by divine aid, succeed to [the] sovereignty which I obtained by labor, toil, marches and wars, so that they may put in practice those rules and regulations by which their . . . Dominion may be pre-served" (*Memoirs of Timur*).*

"Autobiography," "philosophy," "the lyric," and "the novel" are relatively ar-bitrary distinguished categories, useful for libraries, bookstores, and university course catalogs. But all these "genres" are alive, in the constant transformations of imitation, of borrower, beggar, and donor. All are (among other things) engaged in dynamic, dramatic activity. Like all activities, they are effectively unfinished interactions. Like all writing, autobiography engages an implicit conversation, set at a specific time and place. The author foresees a moment of incredulity and responds in the next sentence; he envisages a gesture or a query, and moves to reply in the next paragraph. Like all performers, the autobiographer rarely does only one thing at a time. He addresses different audiences for different reasons. He has several things in view, several purposes in mind, hopes and habits as well as motives or interests. There is a project that organizes his life: educating a ruler or showing humankind the way to divinity or freeing it from superstition, setting us on the road to high science, high morality, democratic art, or enlight-ened politics. His current preoccupations guide his reflections: he is exiled or misunderstood, hungers for salvation or forgiveness; longs to counsel his de-scendants; he is intent on unmasking pretense; he envisages a revolution. He advises a struggling young philosopher, a forlorn widow; he writes letters of recommendation for ambitious young men, indignant replies to bumptious re-viewers, flattering and pleading letters to powerful patrons, affectionate or testy criticism to close colleagues, endless proposals for political or academic reforms, momentous or trivial. Letters of gossip evaluating public figures and the passing scene, letters from every kind of battlefront, remarks on conic sections or the vortex; notes on the latest translations of Pauline letters or the latest production of *Parsifal*.

We are torn. On the one hand, we suspect that all these bits and shards—these oddly slanted mosaics of words and works—cannot, without distortion, be con-structed/reconstructed onto a flat, linear plane, the consecutive narrative of a subject/object: the person. Attempting to trace patterns in the perspectival mir-rorings, the accidents and coincidences that impel a life seems a grotesque megalomaniac presumption. That's on the one hand. On the other, as we are honest scholars, we know full well that we are directed to discover and recover (and not to impose) the experience—the constraints—of lives that (in their shape, experience, and suffering) were by no means endlessly open to the accidents of self-creation or even choice. There is (to put it crudely) biology, the physical constitution and health of a person; there are the deep features of early child-hood; there were the formative books and teachers, the friends and colleagues. These features of our lives makes the illusion of open-ended Olympian interpre-tation and reinterpretation seem grotesque, laughable, and even cruel. We expe-rience our lives as fragmented and disordered . . . and at the same time suspect (and even recognize) patterns of repetition. We have the sense of choice . . . and at the same time reflect that sense to be an illusion. Somehow, tucked in the heart of all of the accidents and perspectives, all the fragments and fragmenta-tions of life, revelatory autobiography lives and shines, shedding dim, often over-shadowed light on philosophical activity. "Sheds light" is certainly an exasper-atingly evasive phrase. But "explains" or even "interprets" would be too bold, too reductive. Let the banal metaphor stand, surrounded by its reservations.

I

Why read philosophers' autobiographical writing? After all, even if an autobiography indicates the origins of a philosophical work, it cannot provide an interpretive guide or a translation manual. The genealogy of a work need not reveal its meaning. A philosopher may be unaware of his assumptions; he may be so deeply focused on the details of his task that he does not place it in a larger context. Spinoza's letters do not construe a difficult proposition in the *Ethics*, any more than van Gogh's letters provide an analysis of the compositional structure of one his paintings. Nor does the philosophical work usually illuminate the travails or dark passages of a life. It would be naive and vulgar—an insult to the craft that goes into a philosopher's writing—to force it through a sieve of his autobiographical activities, and vice versa.

But autobiographical reflections are not on that account merely sheer self-deceptive fabrications, nothing more than masks or propaganda. Preferring a method of demonstration to a narrative of discovery, philosophers rarely present their motivations—the obsessions and preoccupations that implicitly guide their arguments—in the body of the treatises that we consider their primary philosophical work. Philosophers' autobiographical reflections are of more than antiquarian or voyeuristic interest: they often indicate their philosophical aims and passions. A letter from Kant about the relation of religious awe to critical philosophy shows that his conception of philosophy—its aims and import—differs from that of most contemporary Anglo-American philosophers.[5] Difference must affect our understanding of the structure of Kant's critical enterprise. A journal entry by Berkeley: "My end is . . . to deliver metaphysiques . . . in some measure to accommodate them to the Sciences & shew how they may be useful in Optiques, Geometry &c." indicates that his conception of metaphysics—as an instrument of the sciences—is dramatically different from that of Augustine, Al Ghazali, or Maimonides. His theory of knowledge is correspondingly designed to serve a specific function, a function radically different from that envisaged by Augustine, when he was trying to understand how a fallen soul can know and follow divine law. The stamp of the person, moments of self-revelation, advice to princes and kings (Leibniz to the House of Hanover, Bentham to Czar Alexander), to penitents (Augustine, Pascal), expressions of gratitude (Bacon to James I, Arendt to Jaspers) or irritable responses to critics (Descartes to Gasendi, Nietzsche to all comers) are all blended and fused with philosophical preoccupations, without a dominant direction from Life to Thought or Thought to Life. The philosophical is the political and the personal, all in the same act. Sometimes the impetus of a philosophical investigation appears in a dedication or a preface (Bacon, Locke, Arendt), sometimes in letters (Spinoza, Hegel), and of course sometimes in a reflective autobiography (Mill, Russell, Sartre). Even when he writes in an intensely personal manner, the autobiographer-as-philosopher—the 'I' of Augustine's *Confessions* and of Pascal's *Pensées*—speaks for, as well as to, the reader. By presenting himself, he intends the reader to discover himself. Moving in the opposite direction, Al Ghazali, Maimonides, and Descartes present a reconstructed intellectual autobiography of a fictionalized persona whose meditative, formulaic narrative is designed to retrace the steps that move from the personal to the universal Mind.

Philosophic theories are Janus-faced. As directed to their contemporaries, they work within the frame of inherited assumptions and use an inherited idiom. But in the interest of convincing any and all comers, they attempt to abstract from those immediate concerns, to offer considerations that (they believe) should convince Everyone Everywhere. Witness Hobbes, speaking of *Leviathan* and echoing his translation of Thucydides: "My design being not to shew what is Law here, and there, but what is Law in general" (*Leviathan*, chap. 26).

Philosophers undertake a double task, each laden with tensions: the first is that of weaving together various strands in their inheritance (Al Ghazali, interpreting the Koran in Neoplatonic terms; Maimonides, interpreting the Talmud in an Aristotelian frame; Kant, writing his ethics under the influence of the Stoics and Rousseau). The second is that of addressing but transforming the specific interests of their contemporaries. For instance, a good deal of political philosophy has its origins in specific concerns: What establishes a legitimate political regime after a revolution? What should determine legislation about contested, principle-based practices like abortion and euthanasia in a pluralistic democracy? To address those issues effectively, political theories typically work with— but not entirely or exclusively within—the frame of current assumptions about the aims of political systems, about the domain and limits of individual rights and liberties. To persuade their audience, they must acknowledge their preoccupations; but since they are often carried by indignation or by a vision of a possible good, they attempt to redirect them. Similarly, epistemologists begin with a reigning stellar example of knowledge—divine revelation or mathematics or a present sensation. They set their task within a frame that they reinterpret and sometimes entirely redefine. Witness Descartes's subtle shift of the emphasis on knowledge of divine providence to knowledge of divine mathematics.

The problems that arise from the tension between—and the fusion of—contextually situated philosophical projects and their ambitious generalized aims are rarely explicitly explored within the main body of a philosophical work, but they are often the focus of reflective autobiographical writing (Diderot, Fichte, Nietzsche, Kierkegaard). A potter's notes on the blend of clay and sand, the pigments of his glaze, the heat of his kiln does not tell us anything about the shape or strength of his pots, but it does tell us a good deal about his craft. Similarly, autobiographies can shed light on a philosopher's craft, on how he approaches the many tensions inherent in the work of philosophy. It can reveal the philosopher-as-diplomat, negotiating to reconcile apparently opposed objectives. Interpretation needs whatever help it can get: if laundry lists and library lists, marginal notes in much-thumbed books, theater ticket stubs, and dream notes help us understand our fellows, autobiographies may provide some guidance to self-contained philosophical writing, particularly when we have forgotten or abandoned its original problems and assumptions.

II

Well then, what can we learn from philosophers' autobiographies? Beyond the pleasures of developing an acquaintance with a person who had previously only been approached as a mind, there are unexpected discoveries. Here, in outline telegraphic form, is what I think seems to emerge:

(1) Philosophy has always been, and remains, a dialogical and collaborative activity. Like scientists, philosophers begin with a rigorous apprenticeship, controlled by the masters of their guild; they announce programs of research; they depend on the judgment of their colleagues. Like craftsmen and artists, they

engage in sibling rivalry; they argue and form factions. They work within one another's purview, evaluate the latest improvisations. They have a common frame of reference: they set one another's vocabulary and agenda. (Compare logical positivists, phenomenologists, moral realists with the Impressionists, British Romantic poets, Surrealist painters, jazz musicians.)

Even comparatively otherworldly meditative philosophers—Augustine, Spinoza, Pascal, and Wittgenstein—were members of a select republic of letters; they engaged in mutually critical correspondence with a wide range of learned colleagues, relatives, old school friends. Even a reclusive philosopher immersed in (what we have come to isolate as) his technical philosophical work actively imagines the objections, the demands for clarification, the rebuttals of colleagues. He replies to their questions, accepts or rejects their proposed modifications. Augustine engaged the Manicheans . . . and the Manichean within. Pascal has the Jesuits constantly in mind; Leibniz consulted with Huygens and argued with Newton; Berkeley studied Molyneux's experiments. Notoriously, Kant was aghast at Fichte presuming to present critical transcendental philosophy to the world; and each in his distinctive way, Kierkegaard and Russell battled the Hegelians of their time. Even a crusty, evasive, and defensive figure like Descartes willingly engaged in discussion with the likes of Hobbes, Arnauld, Gassendi, Mersenne, and (even!) Princess Elizabeth. He solicited objections, responded with elaborate clarifications, and allowed the exchanges to be circulated and published. A close reader can discern the interplay of multiple voices, many of them embattled with one another, as Descartes attempts to integrate his responses within the development of his own systematic views.

All this discourse—autobiography, letters, technical philosophy—takes place in a forum that is more or less public. Prefaces, dedicatory letters—and more recently, footnotes and acknowledgments—indicate the audience, the categories, and agenda of a work. Their rhetoric is designed to seduce the reader and placate the critic. When, in the main body of his work, a philosopher attempts to represent the truth as he sees it, he chooses a persuasive idiom, in extreme cases that of outright combat (Nietzsche) or irony (Kierkegaard). As in war, polemical philosophy—and philosophy is always implicitly polemical—a warrior crafts his strategy and chooses his weapons in response to his enemy's situation and strength. No matter how visionary and revolutionary he may be, he remains partially in enemy territory. Although each war introduces tactical and technological inventions, the history of combat remains latent within every encounter.

(2) Philosophers were, in the largest sense of the term, politically—and therefore didactically—engaged. Princes and legislators turned to them for advice (Plato, Bacon, Locke, Leibniz); they, for their part, proposed searching reforms (Bentham, Mill, Kant) and wrote endless letters of recommendation, attempting to place the right person in the right place (Cicero, Augustine, Russell). Although prudence often counseled discretion, they were at least partly aware of the far-reaching implications of their conceptual changes, as these might affect the sciences (and therefore education) and morality (and therefore the range of institutions and practices that channel motives and mentality).

Bacon and Hobbes, Leibniz and Spinoza thought that epistemology and logic should influence education; that moral and political theory should influence social planning. As Bishop of Hippo, Augustine was an administrator, a pastor, a preacher, a theologian. He corresponded with Jerome about the problems of translating Paul's letters; he wrote sermons, admonitions, letters of recommendation.

Leibniz was an active counsellor and historian of the court of Hanover, where his advice ranged from proposing engineering plans to attempting a reconciliation between Catholics and Protestants. Bentham tried to persuade Czar Alexander of Russia to adopt an enlightened penal code; Locke wrote a report on the conditions of paupers. Although Spinoza declined an academic appointment in order to concentrate on his philosophic writing, he had an active correspondence with physicians and with endangered political liberals. Bacon and Diderot knew everyone worth knowing and told them all how to run their affairs. Mill's correspondence and journalistic writing runs to volumes; it includes detailed proposals for electoral reform and views on the secret ballot. Dewey participated in a review of the Trotsky trials, claiming that his doing so was a direct consequence of his philosophic views; Russell wrote to Kennedy and Khrushchev about the dangers of nuclear arsenals.

(3) Philosophers were reformer-revolutionaries in the broadest sense of that term. Even when the likes of Hobbes and Burke were politically conservative, they developed radically new ways of seeing and conceiving the world. Their discoveries and articulations often involved marked changes in conceptual categories, and so also in the conventional territorial divisions between "subjects." When is philosophy no longer either a part of natural science or moral science? As reformers, philosophers were usually sensitive to problems of persuasion, of rhetoric, language, and genre. How to pour new wine in old bottles; how to clothe revisionary thoughts in traditional language? Philosophic writing embeds implicit, usually unreflective views about perspicuous as well as sound persuasion, about the methods and techniques of demonstration. The craft of exposition assumes beliefs about the direction of readers' interests, the scope of their knowledge, their modes of reasoning. Philosophers as dramatically different from one another as Plato, Maimonides, and Pascal think that persuasive philosophic writing is inevitably ambiguous. Indeed, Maimonides provides a code manual for the esoteric layers of *The Guide for the Perplexed*. By contrast, most authors of contemporary Anglo-American journal articles and books preselect their readers—the initiated who are already familiar with their agenda and terminology. But even when it introduces technical terms, philosophic reasoning is not transparent. It must be crafted to address different types of readers: to speak with the vulgar and think with the learned; to use the vocabulary of the past, while changing the meaning of that vocabulary; to imagine the concerns of the future. Even more difficult: it must—at its best—also appeal to quite different aspects of each reader's mind.

Philosophy does not form a single genre. It has differed in its aims and conventions, in its methods and rhetoric. It has differed in its accepted cannon. Sometimes Cicero and Seneca were major philosophic figures, sometimes not; sometimes Bacon, Erasmus, Montaigne were central, sometimes marginal. Sometimes Voltaire and d'Alembert were the major philosophers of the age; sometimes they were read as literature.

In both their autobiographies and in (what we think of as) their more narrowly philosophic writing, philosophers were engaged in experiments of genre presentation: dialogues, meditations, treatises, articles, proofs in mathematical form, thought experiments, genealogies, real and imaginary histories. Descartes presents the *Meditations* and the *Discourses* as pseudo-autobiographies; Spinoza begins his *Treatise on the Emendation of the Intellect* with a standard moment in the genre of intellectual autobiography, a catalogue of the illusions and errors from which he hopes to free himself. Hobbes wrote his reflective chronicle twice, once in the first person in Latin verse and once in the third person in English prose. Toward the end of his life, Hume essayed a brief, wry self-examination; much earlier, he voiced a poignant moment of philosophical despair in a crucial transitional passage of the *Treatise*. Hobbes, Hume, and Leibniz wrote large-scope histories: Leibniz, *A History of the House of Brunswick;* Hume, *The History of England.* Augustine, Hobbes, Berkeley, and Hume wrote dialogues that surveyed the field of opinion without explicitly revealing their own. In his preface to the *Encyclopédie*, Diderot explains the necessity of a collective effort: he and his colleagues engaged craftsmen and artisans as well as scholars in the work of tracing the growth of science from its sources in practical problems. Leibniz and Spinoza, each in his distinctive way, offered demonstrations in mathematical form; Hobbes, Locke, Hume, Rousseau, and Nietzsche, each in his distinctive way, presented historical and pseudo-historical thought experiments and gene-alogies of all kinds. Bentham and Mill wrote articles for political and literary journals. Diderot, Rousseau, Russell, and Sartre wrote fiction. Russell, Sartre, and Isaiah Berlin gave interviews to the popular literary press. And now, of course, we have journal articles, a genre whose origins and assumptions derive from scholastic and legal disputations.

(4) A good deal of the past is more distant and more difficult to recover than we often like to suppose. As a result, we often mistakenly read our predecessors as if they were our contemporaries.[6] Finding some of the concerns of the past alien, and thinking that what is alien to us must have been alien to (those whom we see as) kindred spirits, we detach our favorite philosophic passages from their political and emotional contexts. Our eyes tend to gloss over the lively presence of ancestral traditions, the remnants of Stoic and medieval preoccupations, as-sumptions, and vocabulary. We read our predecessors much as we might examine a few selected cells under a microscope, without any knowledge of the organism in which they functioned.[7] But with the strong exception of Hume, Voltaire, and Diderot, the mentality and preoccupations of early modern philosophers were in some respects dramatically different from our own.

Let's sketch a fairly familiar example of a tangential misreading. Because we consider the philosophical projects of the early modern period continuous with (what remains of) our confidence in scientific and human progress, we ignore the intense fervor with which Descartes, Spinoza, Leibniz, Kant, Fichte, and Hegel attempt to reconcile their metaphysics and epistemology with the religious the-ology of the time. We treat their (varied) discussions of divine providence either as clever ways of deflecting charges of politically dangerous atheism, or as meta-physical strategies—say, those directed against skepticism—emotionally on a par with the distinction between primary and secondary qualities, or as philosoph-ically irrelevant accidents on a par with a neurotic obsession with health rather than as desperate attempts to preserve the conviction that the world is well-ordered.

Leibniz represents the direct seriousness of the general tenor of the time.[8] Writing to the Landgrave E. von Hessen Rheinfels in 1686, he says, "I have writ-ten a discourse on metaphysics [*A Discourse on Metaphysics*, 1686] . . . Ques-tions on grace, God's concourse with creatures, the nature of miracles, the cause of sin and the origin of evil, the immortality of the soul . . . are touched on in a manner which seems to provide new openings capable of illuminating some very great difficulties" [*G*. 2. 11]. He might be describing a work in theology instead of a treatise on metaphysics with strong implications for a mathematically based science. Although writing from quite a different perspective, Berkeley similarly insists "The principles which . . . I endeavor to propagate [intend] that atheism and scepticism . . . be utterly destroyed." (*Three Dialogues between Hylas and Philonous*, 1713). As disparate figures as Descartes and Spinoza, as diverse philosophers as Kant, Fichte, and Hegel, all protest again and again that they are not atheists.

Many philosophers nevertheless had good reason to be wary. Despite their protestations to the contrary, many of our witnesses were perceived as threats to religion and civic order. Consider the history of philosophic exile, censorship, and imprisonment starting with Socrates. Seneca was exiled by Caligula, and Nero imposed his suicide. Abelard's work "On the Divine Unity and Trinity" was burned in 1121; and he was condemned at the Council of Sens in 1141. Bacon and Hobbes performed political gymnastics to remain in the good graces of sovereigns. A parliamentary committee scrutinized Hobbes' *Leviathan* for signs of atheism. Voltaire's anti-clerical essays prompted his exile to Holland in 1713; he was imprisoned in the Bastille in 1717, and again exiled in 1726. Locke followed the Earl of Shaftesbury into exile in the Netherlands. Hume was refused appointments at the University of Edinburgh and at the University of Glasgow in 1745 and in 1752 on suspicion of his religious skepticism. Diderot was briefly imprisoned after the 1747 publication of *The Skeptic's Walk*. Kant was prohibited from publishing work on religion after the appearance of *Religion within the Limits of Reason Alone*. Charged with atheism and nihilism, Fichte was forced to resign his chair at the University of Jena. Marx found himself effectively exiled from Prussia for his radical views. Russell was dismissed from Trinity College, Cambridge, for unorthodoxy, imprisoned in Britain for his pacifism, and refused an appointment at City University because he was considered an enemy of religion and morality. And that's not even beginning to cite the self-censorship of such figures as Descartes and Spinoza, and the reluctance of Hume, Spinoza, and Mill to publish work they feared might be too controversial.

To be sure, some autobiographers—perhaps Maimonides, certainly Descartes and Spinoza—had good reasons to be cautious, good reason to placate powerful ecclesiastical authority. But political prudence did not require them to go as far as they did in giving divinity a central, major metaphysical role. They may have been keen to assure suspicious censors that a deist divinity who preserves cosmic order is the first person of the Trinity. Each, in his own way, may have feared to be a latter-day Socrates, substituting a new divinity for the gods of the city. Although Descartes is obviously a defensive mind, he could readily have protected himself without assigning such far-reaching, complex roles to divinity. And it's hard to believe Spinozistic pantheism is a cover for atheism, hard to believe that the author of his letters is a sarcastic ironist covering his tracks. Kant ends both critiques in reverence, with the conviction that a divine plan orders the world, and that the transcendental project of articulating the conditions that make morality possible also make it necessary, actually binding. Hard to believe he was merely satisfying the formalities of his university appointment. Reading the fervent protestations of those early modern philosophers, it is difficult to believe that they were solely made for self-protective political reasons. There is good reason to suppose that they themselves were not always sure how far their revisionary thinking would carry them. They had, after all, been formed by the same books, the same world as their censors. And they had a good deal at stake in wanting to ensure that the world was safe for rationality. Postulating that the world expressed what religion chose to identify as the work of a rational Creator seemed a provisionally useful way of getting on with their philosophic work.

There was more at stake in early modern discussions of providential divinity than a philosophically ingenious strategy designed to refute academic skepticism. Extreme dogmatic skepticism is manifestly incoherent. A more modest notional epistemological variety ("can we trust the grounds of belief?") might seem to endanger the progressive science and morality that post-Cartesian philosophers envisioned. For philosophers living in a world permeated by theological categories and convictions, piecemeal epistemological skepticism was a side effect, a symptom of what Descartes and many of his successors saw as a far more basic ontological terror: Is the world reliably well-ordered? Descartes' polarized opposition between a rational divinity and a malignant demon was no mere rhetorical expository trope: It went to the heart of the question that haunted the period. Early modern philosophers after Descartes were educated by their readings of the ancient Stoics; they placed the challenges of skepticism within a context that moved to a version of a Stoic re-affirmation. The cosmos is a providentially ordered, unified whole that sustains both science and morality. But the Stoicism of the early modern period—a Stoicism that occurs within a Christian setting—faces a special problem: How far does ordered providential determination go? For science: Does divine providence rest with the general laws of nature or does it extend to individual particulars? (Leibniz, Berkeley) For epistemology: What is the relation between the primary essential attributes of objects and standard, normal perceptions? (Descartes, Locke) For morality: What room is there for the kind of individual free will that at least some forms of Christianity seems to require? (Spinoza, Kant) For both science and morality: Does divinity watch over—does divinity intend the fate of—every fallen sparrow, every secondary quality? For philosophers of this period, these were not merely academic or political questions: they pervaded a way of being-in-the-world.

There were, to be sure, some exceptions. Whatever their remnant vocabularies, their reservations and hesitations, neither Voltaire nor Hume—and eventually neither Bentham nor Mill—appear to have been plagued by religious agony, as it was commonly understood. They were certainly not engaged in reconciling the ways of God to man. Although Hume and Mill thought it prudent to postpone publication of their anticlerical writing, they seemed unable (as we now find it natural to do) to ignore theology and religious practice, as on a par with astrology and alchemy, not worth serious philosophic attention. As the last of the early modern Enlightenment philosophers, utilitarians might have laid these concerns to rest, but the anxiety remained—and culminated—in the anguish of many Victorians (Sidgwick, Jowett) about whether they lost their faith, or whether in losing faith they lost anything worth losing. To the extent that such anguish affected philosophical work—and it is difficult to believe that it did not—bracketing such concerns as historical oddities, political prudence, or neurotic symptoms correspondingly misconstrues the role that those anxieties played in the philosophy of the period.

We would understand our predecessors more clearly if we saw their aims in their own terms. Where did they hope to bring their audience? To see Divinity as beyond questioning or as a benign Hidden Hand? To substitute mathematical science for theology as a form of genuinely pious inquiry? To accept and participate in a new form of political life? To join a specific research program? We—

living in different circumstances, with different preoccupations and a dramatically different education—must try to imagine the dramatic action that an autobiography and a philosophic project once expressed. (Consider the difference between a contemporary education largely formed by the assumptions of popularized science and a classical education focused on reading Greek and Roman authors. Those differences form distinctive expectations and ambitions; they constrain the interpretive imagination. Reading the past, we must set ourselves to imagine beyond our pieties and recover the original occasions and audiences, the envisioned outcomes.)

Of course it is always possible, without the special insights of historical attentiveness, to benefit from a "read and raid" approach that treats phrases and notions as suggestive, appropriating them out of context without attempting to understand their original meaning. After all, why not? Picasso turned the handles and seat of a bicycle into the head of a bull. Why shouldn't our contemporaries turn Stoic *prolepseis* into intuitions about "what we would say"?

Fine. Brilliant. Now let's see what comes of it. But why pretend that an improvisation is a faithful interpretation of the past? There might have been good reason for presenting critical or revolutionary ideas as commentaries on a master or a sacred text when appeal to tradition or authority carries primary weight and conviction, but (whatever may actually be the case) we do not believe that ours is such an age.

(5) Why are there so few women philosophers, so late? Yes, there were Christine de Pisan, Mme. d'Epinay, Mme. du Châtelet, Sophie d'Houdetot, Harriet Taylor, Princess Elizabeth of Bohemia, Lady Masham, Mary Astell, Mary Wollstonecraft, Christine Ladd Franklin. The tragedy of their absence—the loss of the philosophic contributions they might have made—goes beyond their work not being recognized or published, excluded from courses and textbooks. It goes to the very heart of the conditions of their intellectual development. By and large, they wrote as correspondents of Descartes, Rousseau, Voltaire, Mill. They asked subtle and penetrating questions, sometimes made bold and original suggestions; but they did not present their own views systematically. Princess Elizabeth's questions to Descartes were as astute, as trenchant as those of Hobbes and Mersenne, but she did not develop the metaphysical or psychological theory that her questions suggest. Harriet Taylor's *The Enfranchisement of Women*, Mary Wollstonecraft's *A Vindication of the Rights of Women* are brilliant, courageous, radical. They presuppose and imply—but do not develop or articulate—an ethics and a theory of human nature. They are, in genre and spirit, closer to Voltaire and Diderot than to Bentham and J. S. Mill . . . but they did not organize an *Encyclopedia*.

The harm done to women went far deeper than the failure to recognize their work. Our candidate women philosophers manifest a talented intelligence comparable to that of their male counterparts; their contemporary admirers—Voltaire, Hume, Rousseau, Mill—certainly thought them subtle and perceptive. Why then did they not produce the kind of works that their men friends wrote? It was not because they lacked libraries or academic appointments; most men also lacked them. They had rooms of their own, and time and money at their command; many were patronesses of philosophers (Queen Christiana, the Comtesse de Boufflers; Mme. du Châtelet). They were not excluded from the company of men of learning and letters, indeed many of them organized the salons in which intellectual and political life took place. Were they uneducated? Many had tutors, but few were taught mathematics and science, Latin and Greek, and (until relatively recently) that would have affected their participation in learned discussions. But many of the men were essentially self-educated. Did the women lack the self-confidence that bursts from most of the usual male suspects? Perhaps. Although the women write deferentially, often hesitantly, they nevertheless persevere; they manifest (a brave show of) assurance and authority.

An important part of the explanation is to be found in the tone, in the rhetoric and stance of the letters of (even such feminist philosophers as) Hume and Mill to their respected women colleagues. We need only compare Leibniz's letters to Arnauld with those to Elizabeth, Hume's letters to Adam Smith with those to the Comtesse de Boufflers, Diderot's to Rousseau with those to Sophie Volland, Mill's letters to Carlyle with those to Harriet Taylor, Peirce's letters to William James with his letters to Christine Ladd Franklin. The men criticize one another "man to man." They fence "point to point," each challenging the other. By contrast, the women raise self-deprecating questions to which the men respond; they suggest ideas that the men gratefully accept. The asymmetry of the exchange is marked; the metaphors are revealing. The women are maternal: they nurture; the men are fraternal: they challenge and wrestle. Women philosophers are not pressed, not expected to develop their views. While the men manifestly respected the acumen and originality of their women correspondents, they tread gingerly on (imagined) sensibilities. When the men write to their philosophically minded women friends, they defer, protect, placate, flatter rather than challenge. Their delicacy stretches beyond a lover's awkward gallantry or a suppliant's diplomatic tact to a patroness. No matter how affectionate or respectful, the distance is evident. To be sure, men flatter their patrons (Bacon to the bishop of Winchester and to virtually every lord and king of the land, Bentham to Lord Lansdowne); they are careful of one another's foibles and sensibilities (Augustine to Jerome); they write with fatherly advice (Cicero to his son Marcus) or with gentle affection (Spinoza writing to de Blyenbergh: "To my unknown friend, I gather from [your letter asking for an explanation of divine providence] that you are deeply devoted to the truth . . . Of all things not under my control, what I most value is the bond of friendship with sincere lovers of truth . . . I shall grant without stint . . . to answer [your] questions"). But even when they are forwarding their ambitions, they are, within the bounds of the manners and literary genres of their time, frank and critical.

All serious intellectual development—and certainly the discipline required for substantive and complex philosophy—takes place in an atmosphere of candid exchange in which disagreement is expected and expressed, inconsistencies are exposed, requests for more details are made, in which criticism and response are the natural mode. Even such touchy members of the republic of letters as Descartes, Rousseau, and Fichte know they'll survive and thrive on critical exchange. By contrast, women are (at best) seen as brilliant and profound, but with a distinctive and somewhat mysterious set of intuitively intellectual talents. Witness Mill (of all people): "The special . . . mental capacities . . . of women of talent . . . fit them for practice . . . A woman's capacity of intuitive perception [is] a rapid and correct insight into present fact. [Her] gravitation to the present, to the real, to actual fact . . . has nothing to do with general principles" (*The Subjection of Women*, chap. 3). Women were seen as nurturing and generous, but perhaps demanding beyond the possibility of satisfaction ("what do women want?") and so best placated; at best they are found (ahem) exciting and stimulating, but perhaps dangerous. In any case, Other, but not other selves.[9]

III

Is there anything distinctive about philosophers' autobiographical writing? Does it set philosophers apart from poets, painters, mathematicians, scientists, politicians, historians, everybody's grandparents? Yes and no.

No: anyone who knows any philosophers knows that they do not have any distinctive talent for self-knowledge. They differ from one another in the usual ways, some apparently extremely acute (Augustine), others remarkably dense (Russell). And this seems to hold as much for their explanations of their philosophical aims and obsessions, as for their affections and enmities. Like other reflective self-revelation, philosophers' autobiographical writing is rhetorically designed to persuade a real or imaginary audience; like other such writing, it has an implicit agenda.

Yes: philosophical autobiography is set apart by the expectations of some of its authors and some of its readers. Some philosophers—and some of their readers—expect exceptional insight, candor, and transparency from the work of philosophy. Others, in the grip of a chronic distrust of intellectual pretensions of any kind, search for hidden psychological or political motives. Unfortunately many philosophers often set themselves up for these reactions. Like scientists and mathematicians, some philosophers announce grand if not actually grandiose ambitions, but they tend not to define or limit those ambitions. Nothing less than the truth about God, reality, knowledge, the right and the good. By contrast, other philosophers announce an apparently minor task: to correct X's views about the significance of the inverted spectrum on the presumed distinction between primary and secondary qualities. Initiates understand that this modest refutation is meant to demolish an entire metaphysical system.

Read aright, philosophical autobiographies help correct both misapprehensions. They reveal the work of philosophers in attempting to forge—and to understand—their undertaking. Like poets and painters, philosophers are engaged in defining—usually redefining—their craft (or denying that it is a craft). Philosophers' autobiographies help demystify claims to a special access to truthful insight. They express hesitations, uncertainties, appeals for help, struggles to find an appropriate method of discovery or a persuasive rhetorical genre. They reveal the risks and plight of all serious inquiry; but they also express—often in an encoded, indirect, hesitant way—a philosopher's struggle to think, to define and exhibit the process of thinking.

NOTES

1. Rather than select among the many editions and translations of well-known, readily available autobiographies (e.g., St. Teresa of Avila's *Life*, Rousseau's *Confessions*, Mill's *Autobiography*, Augustine's *Confessions*, Pascal's *Pensées*, Descartes's *Meditations*, Hobbes's *Leviathan*, and so on), I have left the choice of edition and translation to the reader.

All quotations and references marked with an asterisk (*) are to be found in the *University Library of Autobiography*, ed. Charles Bushnell (New York: F. Tyler

Daniels Company, 1918). This is a series of fifteen volumes, each "edited with introductions, essays, and appreciations by leading scholars and educators." I recommend this extraordinary collection.

2. See Amélie Rorty, "Understanding Others," in *Other Intentions*, ed. Lawrence Rosen (Santa Fe, N.M.: School of American Research Press, 1995), pp. 203–233.

3. For a vigorous attack on attempts to psychologize Hobbes, see Quentin Skinner, *Reason and Rhetoric in the Philosophy of Hobbes* (Cambridge, 1996).

4. See Patricia Spacks, *Gossip* (New York: Knopf, 1985).

5. For a wonderfully detailed account of Kant's attempt to integrate the various strands in his intellectual inheritance, see J. B. Schneewind, *The Invention of Autonomy: A History of Modern Moral Philosophy* (Cambridge: Cambridge University Press, 1998); for a model review essay on Schneewind's book, see Susan James, "Kant through the Looking Glass of History," *Times Literary Supplement*, December 18, 1998, p. 9.

6. See Richard Rorty, J. B. Schneewind, and Quentin Skinner, eds., *Philosophy in History* (Cambridge: Cambridge University Press, 1985).

7. For exceptions to the philosophical practices of "read and enjoy misreading" (e.g., Jacques Derrida and Richard Rorty), "read and raid" (e.g., Barbara Herman and Christine Korsgaard), and "read and destroy" (e.g., G. A. Cohen), see the "read and reconstruct" writings of Myles Burnyeat, Knut Haakonssen, J. B. Schneewind, Quentin Skinner, Bernard Williams, and Margaret Wilson.

8. See James, "Kant through the Looking Glass."

9. For a remarkable account of the sources of the ambivalence and the fearful deference with which women are regarded, see Dorothy Dinnerstein, *The Mermaid and the Minotaur* (New York: Harper & Row, 1976).

SUGGESTIONS FOR FURTHER READING

Balibar, Renée. *Les Français fictifs*. Paris: Hachette, 1974.

Bruss, Elizabeth. *Autobiographical Acts*. Baltimore: Johns Hopkins University Press, 1976.

Courcelle, Pierre. *Les Confessions d'Augustine and la tradition littéraire*. Paris, 1963.

Eakin, Paul. *Fictions in Autobiography*. Princeton: Princeton University Press, 1985.

Fleishman, Avrom. *Figures of Autobiography*. Berkeley: University of California Press, 1983.

Huizinga, Johan. *Men and Ideas*. New York: Meridian, 1959.

Kaplan, Louis, et al. *A Bibliography of American Autobiographies*. Madison: University of Wisconsin Press, 1961.

Lejeune, Philippe. *L'Autobiographie en France*. Paris, 1971.

———. *On Autobiography*. Minneapolis: University of Minnesota Press, 1989.

———. *Lire Leiris, Autobiographie et langage*. Paris: Klinksiek, 1975.

———. *Le Pacte autobiographique*. Paris: Seuil, 1975.

Matthews, William. *British Autobiographies*. Berkeley: University of California Press, 1960.

Misch, Georg. *A History of Autobiography in Antiquity*. 2 vols. London, 1950. English translation of the first two volumes of *Geschichte der Autobiographie*, 8 vols. (Frankfurt, 1949–1969).

Introduction   xxix

Olney, James. *Autobiography: Essays Theoretical and Critical.* Princeton: Princeton University Press, 1980.

———. *Metaphors of the Self: The Meaning of Autobiography.* 1972.

Pascal, Roy. *Design and Truth in Autobiography.* Cambridge: Harvard University Press, 1960.

Pilling, John. *Autobiography and Imagination: Studies in Self-Scrutiny.* London: Routledge & Kegan Paul, 1981.

Porter, Roger, and H. R. Wolf. *The Voice Within.* New York: Knopf, 1973.

Shumaker, Wayne. *English Autobiography.* Berkeley: University of California Press, 1954.

Smith, Sidonie. *A Poetics of Women's Autobiography and the Fictions of Self-Representation.* Bloomington: Indiana University Press, 1987.

Spengemann, William. *The Forms of Autobiography.* New Haven: Yale University Press, 1980.

University Library of Autobiography. 15 vols. New York: F. Tyler Daniels, 1918.

Warner, Martin. "Philosophical Autobiography." In *Philosophy and Literature.* Edited by A. Phillips Griffith. Cambridge: Cambridge University Press, 1984.

Weintraub, Karl Jacob. *The Value of the Individual: Self and Circumstance.* Chicago: University of Chicago Press, 1978.

Wollheim, Richard. *The Thread of Life.* Cambridge: Harvard University Press, 1984.

FROM PLATO TO MAIMONIDES

PLATO
A Philosopher Educates a Tyrant

Plato (427–347/348 B.C.) came from an aristocratic and largely antidemocratic Athenian family. Had he not come under the influence of Socrates, he might well have been active in Athenian political life. After the condemnation and execution of Socrates in 399, Plato retreated to Megara, and then traveled to Egypt and Sicily. During this period, he became acquainted with the major philosophical schools of the time: Heracleiteans, Pythagoreans, Protagorean relativists, and Democritean atomists. He returned to Athens in 387–386 to found the Academy as a center of philosophic study, where—with the exception of several disastrous visits to Syracuse—he taught and wrote until his death. At the request of Dion of Syracuse, he went to Syracuse in 367–366 and again in 361–360 in hopes of educating and influencing the younger Dionysius. Finding Dion exiled and Dionysius a vicious despot, he returned to the Academy and to philosophy. His dialogues—some twenty in number—ranged from representations of Socratic discussions on logical and moral issues, to the vast construction of *The Republic*, a work that systematically connects political and ethical questions with the central problems of metaphysics, epistemology, rhetoric, the philosophy of education and the arts. The intricate and presumptively "later" dialogues formulated and pursued problems in cosmology, the philosophy of logic and language.

While there is no proof of the authenticity of the thirteen *Epistles* often attributed to him, the Seventh Letter—which is excerpted here—chronicles reflections on his Syracusan experiment in political education.

Letter VII

When I was a young man I had the same ambition as many others: I thought of entering public life as soon as I came of age. And certain happenings in public affairs favored me, as follows. The constitution we then had, being anathema to many, was overthrown; and a new government was set up consisting of fifty-one men, two groups—one of eleven and another of ten—to police the market place and perform other necessary duties in the city and the Piraeus respectively, and above them thirty other officers with absolute powers. Some of these men happened to be relatives and acquaintances of mine, and they invited me to join them at once in what seemed to be a proper undertaking. My attitude toward them is not surprising, because I was young. I thought that they were going to lead the city out of the unjust life she had been living and establish her in the path of justice, so that I watched them eagerly to see what they would do. But as I watched them they showed in a short time that the preceding constitution had been a precious thing. Among their other deeds they named Socrates, an older friend of mine whom I should not hesitate to call the wisest and justest man of that time, as one of a group sent to arrest a certain citizen who was to be put to death illegally, planning thereby to make Socrates willy-nilly a party to their actions. But he refused, risking the utmost danger rather than be an associate in their impious deeds. When I saw all this and other like things of no little consequence, I was appalled and drew back from that reign of injustice. Not long afterwards the rule of the Thirty was overthrown and with it the entire constitution; and once more I felt the desire, though this time less strongly, to take part in public and political affairs. Now many deplorable things occurred during those troubled days, and it is not surprising that under cover of the revolution too many old enmities were avenged; but in general those who returned from exile acted with great restraint. By some chance, however, certain powerful persons brought into court this same friend Socrates, preferring against him a most shameless accusation, and one which he, of all men, least deserved. For the prosecutors charged him with impiety, and the jury condemned and put to death the very man who, at the time when his accusers were themselves in misfortune and exile, had refused to have a part in the unjust arrest of one of their friends.

The more I reflected upon what was happening, upon what kind of men were active in politics, and upon the state of our laws and customs, and the older I grew, the more I realized how difficult it is to manage a city's affairs rightly. For I saw it was impossible to do anything without friends or sheer good luck, since our city was no longer guided by the customs and practices of our fathers, while to train up new ones was anything but easy. And the corruption of our written laws and our customs was proceeding at such amazing speed that whereas at first I had been full of zeal for public life, when I noted these changes and saw how unstable everything was, I became in the end quite dizzy; and though I did not cease to reflect how an improvement could be brought about in our laws and in the whole constitution, yet I refrained from action, waiting for the proper time. At last I came to the conclusion that all existing states are badly governed and the condition of their laws practically incurable, without some miraculous remedy and the assistance of fortune; and I was forced to say, in praise of true philosophy, that from her height alone was it possible to discern what the nature of justice is, either in the state or in the individual, and that the ills of the human race would never end until either those who are sincerely and truly lovers of wisdom come into political power, or the rulers of our cities, by the grace of God, learn true philosophy.

Such was the conviction I had when I arrived in Italy and Sicily for the first time. When I arrived and saw what they call there the "happy life"—a life filled with Italian and Syracusan banquets, with men gorging themselves twice a day and never sleeping alone at night, and following all the other customs that go with this way of living—I was profoundly displeased. For no man under heaven who has cultivated such practices from his youth could possibly grow up to be wise—so miraculous a temper is against nature—or become temperate, or indeed acquire any other part of virtue. Nor could any city enjoy tranquillity, no matter how good its laws; when its men think they must spend their all on excesses, and be easygoing about everything except the feasts and the drinking bouts and the pleasures of love that they pursue with professional zeal. These cities are always changing into tyrannies, or oligarchies, or democracies, while the rulers in them will not even hear mention of a just and equitable constitution.

When one is advising a sick man who is living in a way injurious to his health, must one not first of all tell him to change his way of life and give him further counsel only if he is willing to obey? If he is not, I think any manly and self-respecting physician would break off counseling such a man, whereas anyone who would put up with him is without spirit or skill. So too with respect to a city: whether it be governed by one man or many, if its constitution is properly ordered and rightly directed, it would be sensible to give advice to its citizens concerning what would be to the city's advantage. But if it is a people who have wandered completely away from right government and resolutely refuse to come back upon its track and instruct their counselor to leave the constitution strictly alone, threatening him with death if he changes it, and order him instead to serve their interests and desires and show them how they can henceforth satisfy them in the quickest and easiest way—any man, I think, who would accept such a role as adviser is without spirit, and he who refuses is the true man. These are my principles; and whenever anyone consults me on a question of importance in his life, such as the making of money, or the care of his body or soul, if it appears to me that he follows some plan in his daily life or is willing to listen to reason on the matters he lays before me, I advise him gladly and don't stop with merely discharging my duty. But a man who does not consult me at all, or makes it clear that he will not follow advice that is given him—to such a man I do not take it upon myself to offer counsel; nor would I use constraint upon him, not even if he were my own son. Upon a slave I might force my advice, compelling him to follow it against his will; but to use compulsion upon a father or mother is to me an impious act, unless their judgment has been impaired by disease. If they are fixed in a way of life that pleases them, though it may not please me, I should not antagonize them by useless admonitions.

Do not subject [a] state to the despotism of men, but to the rule of laws; this at least is my doctrine. For despotic power benefits neither rulers nor subjects, but is an altogether deadly experience for themselves, their children, and their children's children; and no one grasps at the prizes it offers except petty and illiberal souls who know nothing of the divine and human goods that are now and for all time good and just. It is altogether noble and right to suffer whatever may come while aiming at the highest for oneself or one's city. None of us can avoid death, nor if any man could would he be happy, as people think; for there is nothing worth mentioning that is either good or bad to creatures without souls, but good and evil exist only for a soul, either joined with a body or separated from it. And we must always firmly believe the sacred and ancient words declaring to us that the soul is immortal, and when it has separated from the body will go before its judges and pay the utmost penalties. Therefore we must count it a lesser evil to suffer great wrongs and injustices than to do them, though this is a saying that the avaricious man, who is poor in the goods of the soul, will not give ear to; or if he does, laughs it into silence, as he thinks, and goes about like a wild beast snatching from every quarter whatever he thinks will furnish him meat or drink or the satisfaction of that slavish and graceless pleasure incorrectly called after Aphrodite. He is blind and does not see what defilement his plunderings involve, nor how great an evil attaches to each wicked act—a defilement which the evildoer necessarily drags with him as he goes up and down the earth and follows his dishonorable and utterly wretched path to the world below.

If a state is hard-pressed by many and diverse factions, . . . then anyone to whom the gods have given a modicum of right opinion must know that there can be no end to the evils of faction until the party that has gained the victory in these battles and in the exiling and slaughtering of fellow citizens forgets its wrongs and ceases trying to wreak vengeance upon its enemies. If it controls itself and enacts laws for the common good, considering its own interests no more than those of the vanquished, the defeated party will be doubly constrained, by respect and by fear, to follow the laws—by fear because the other party has demonstrated its superior force, and by respect because it has shown that it is able and willing to conquer its desires and serve the law instead. In no other way can a city that is rent by factions bring its disorders to an end, but it will continue to be divided within itself by strife and enmity, hatred and distrust.

Whenever, then, the victors desire to save their city, they must enter into counsel with themselves and first of all select the most eminent Greeks they can discover—old men, with wives and children at home, descended from a long line of illustrious ancestors and each of them possessing a fair amount of property (fifty such men will be enough for a city of ten thousand)—and these they must induce, by personal entreaties and by all the honors at their disposal, to leave home and come to their aid; and when they have come they must direct them to make laws, binding them upon oath to award no more to the victors than to the vanquished, but to consider only the equal and common good of the whole city. And then when the laws have been laid down everything depends upon this. If the victors show themselves more eager than the vanquished to obey the laws, then everything will be safe, happiness will abound, and all these evils will take their flight.

When I arrived, I thought my first task was to prove whether Dionysius was really on fire with philosophy, or whether the many reports that came to Athens were without foundation. Now there is a certain way of putting this to the test, a dignified way and quite appropriate to tyrants, especially to those whose heads are full of half-understood doctrines, which I saw at once upon my arrival was particularly the case with Dionysius. You must picture to such men the extent of the undertaking, describing what sort of inquiry it is, with how many difficulties it is beset, and how much labor it involves. For anyone who hears this, who is a true lover of wisdom, with the divine quality that makes him akin to it and worthy of pursuing it, thinks that he has heard of a marvelous quest that he must at once enter upon with all earnestness, or life is not worth living; and from that time forth he pushes himself and urges on his leader without ceasing, until he has reached the end of the journey or has become capable of doing without a guide and finding the way himself. This is the state of mind in which such a man lives; whatever his occupation may be, above everything and always he holds fast to philosophy and to the daily discipline that best makes him apt at learning and remembering, and capable of reasoning soberly with himself; while for the opposite way of living he has a persistent hatred. Those who are really not philosophers but have only a coating of opinions, like men whose bodies are tanned by the sun, when they see how much learning is required, and how great the labor, and how orderly their daily lives must be to suit the subject they are pursuing, conclude that the task is too difficult for their powers; and rightly so, for they are not equipped for this pursuit. But some of them persuade themselves that they have already heard enough and need make no further effort. Now this is a clear and infallible test to apply to those who love ease and are incapable of strenuous labor, for none of them can ever blame his teacher, but only himself, if he is unable to put forth the efforts that the task demands.

There is no writing of mine about these matters, nor will there ever be one. For this knowledge is not something that can be put into words like other sciences; but after long-continued intercourse between teacher and pupil, in joint pursuit of the subject, suddenly, like light flashing forth when a fire is kindled, it is born in the soul and straighway nourishes itself. And this too I know: if these matters are to be expounded at all in books or lectures, they would best come from me. Certainly I am harmed not least of all if they are misrepresented. If I thought they could be put into written words adequate for the multitude, what nobler work could I do in my life than to compose something of such great benefit to mankind and bring to light the nature of things for all to see? But I do not think that the "examination," as it is called, of these questions would be of any benefit to men, except to a few, i.e., to those who could with a little guidance discover the truth by themselves. Of the rest, some would be filled with an ill-founded and quite unbecoming disdain, and some with an exaggerated and foolish elation, as if they had learned something grand.

Let me go into these matters at somewhat greater length, for perhaps what I am saying will become clearer when I have done so. There is a true doctrine that confutes anyone who has presumed to write anything whatever on such subjects, a doctrine that I have often before expounded, but it seems that it must now be said again. For every real being, there are three things that are necessary if knowledge of it is to be acquired: first, the name; second, the definition; third, the image; knowledge comes fourth, and in the fifth place we must put the object itself, the knowable and truly real being. To understand what this means, take a particular example, and think of all other objects as analogous to it. There is something called a circle, and its name is this very word we have just used. Second, there is its definition, composed of nouns and verbs. "The figure whose extremities are everywhere equally distant from its center" is the definition of precisely that to which the names "round," "circumference," and "circle" apply. Third is what we draw or rub out, what is turned or destroyed; but the circle itself to which they all refer remains unaffected, because it is different from them. In the fourth place are knowledge (*epistēmē*), reason (*nous*), and right opinion (which are in our minds, not in words or bodily shapes, and therefore must be taken together as something distinct both from the circle itself and from the three things previously mentioned); of these, reason is nearest the fifth in kinship and likeness, while the others are further away. The same thing is true of straight-lined as well as of circular figures; of color; of the good, the beautiful, the just; of body in general, whether artificial or natural; of fire, water, and all the elements; of all living beings and qualities of souls; of all actions and affections. For in each case, whoever does not somehow grasp the four things mentioned will never fully attain knowledge of the fifth.

These things, moreover, because of the weakness of language, are just as much concerned with making clear the particular property of each object as the being of it. On this account no sensible man will venture to express his deepest thoughts in words, especially in a form which is unchangeable, as is true of written outlines. Let us go back and study again the illustration just given. Every circle that we make or draw in common life is full of characteristics that contradict the "fifth," for it everywhere touches a straight line, while the circle itself, we say, has in it not the slightest element belonging to a contrary nature. And we say that their names are by no means fixed; there is no reason why what we call "circles" might not be called "straight lines," and the straight lines "circles," and their natures will be none the less fixed despite this exchange of names. Indeed the same thing is true of the definition: since it is a combination of nouns and verbs, there is nothing surely fixed about it. Much more might be said to show that each of these four instruments is unclear, but the most important point is what I said earlier: that of the two objects of search—the particular quality and the being of an object—the soul seeks to know not the quality but the essence, whereas each of these four instruments presents to the soul, in discourse and in examples, what she is not seeking, and thus makes it easy to refute by sense perception anything that may be said or pointed out, and fills everyone, so to speak, with perplexity and confusion. Now in those matters in which, because of our defective training, we are not accustomed to look for truth but are satisfied with the first image suggested to us, we can ask and answer without making ourselves ridiculous to one another, being proficient in manipulating and testing these four instruments. But when it is "the fifth" about which we are compelled to answer questions or to make explanations, then anyone who wishes to refute has the advantage, and can make the propounder of a doctrine, whether in writing or speaking or in answering questions, seem to most of his listeners completely ignorant of the matter on which he is trying to speak or write. Those who are listening sometimes do not realize that it is not the mind of the speaker or writer which is being refuted, but these four instruments mentioned, each of which is by nature defective.

By the repeated use of all these instruments, ascending and descending to each in turn, it is barely possible for knowledge to be engendered of an object naturally good, in a man naturally good; but if his nature is defective, as is that of most men, for the acquisition of knowledge and the so-called virtues, and if the qualities he has have been corrupted, then not even Lynceus could make such a man see.[9] In short, neither quickness of learning nor a good memory can make a man see when his nature is not akin to the object, for this knowledge never takes root in an alien nature; so that no man who is not naturally inclined and akin to justice and all other forms of excellence, even though he may be quick at learning and remembering this and that and other things, nor any man who, though akin to justice, is slow at learning and forgetful, will ever attain the truth that is attainable about virtue. Nor about vice, either, for these must be learned together, just as the truth and error about any part of being must be learned together, through long and earnest labor, as I said at the beginning. Only when all of these things—names, definitions, and visual and other perceptions—have been rubbed against one another and tested, pupil and teacher asking and answering questions in good will and without envy—only then, when reason and knowledge are at the very extremity of human effort, can they illuminate the nature of any object.

For this reason anyone who is seriously studying high matters will be the last to write about them and thus expose his thought to the envy and criticism of men. What I have said comes, in short, to this: whenever we see a book, whether the laws of a legislator or a composition on any other subject, we can be sure that if the author is really serious, this book does not contain his best thoughts; they are stored away with the fairest of his possessions. And if he has committed these serious thoughts to writing, it is because men, not the gods, "have taken his wits away."

2

SENECA
Philosophy as a Guide to Life

Born in Cordova, Lucius Annaeus Seneca (4 B.C.–65 C.E.) was educated in Rome, where he was strongly influenced by his discussions with Stoic philosophers. He became a prominent rhetorician, advocate and essayist. Charged with having a politically dangerous liaison with Caligula's sister, he was banished to Corsica in 41, where he devoted himself to writing tragedies. Agrippina recalled him to Rome in 49, and charged him to serve as the tutor to Nero. He rose to the influential position of praetor during the early part of Nero's reign, working to achieve a balance of power between the emperor and the Senate. When his popularity cost him Nero's favor and patronage, he retired from public life, spending his last years traveling and writing philosophical essays. Anticipating assassination, he committed suicide in 65.

Seneca's formulations of Stoicism—the practical advice of his *Morales*—inspired the style and thought of Bacon and Montaigne; his conception of philosophy as a guide to life became the watchword of popular conceptions of stoicism; and Elizabethan dramatists like Marlowe and Kydd imitated his powerful psychological melodramas.

Letters to Lucilius

LETTER V

I view with pleasure and approval the way you keep on at your studies and sacrifice everything to your single-minded efforts to make yourself every day a better man. I do not merely urge you to persevere in this; I actually implore you to. Let me give you, though, this one piece of advice: refrain from following the example of those whose craving is for attention, not their own improvement, by doing certain things which are calculated to give rise to comment on your appearance or way of living generally. Avoid shabby attire, long hair, an unkempt beard, an outspoken dislike of silverware, sleeping on the ground and all other misguided means to self-advertisement. The very name of philosophy, however modest the manner in which it is pursued, is unpopular enough as it is: imagine what the reaction would be if we started dissociating ourselves from the conventions of society. Inwardly everything should be different but our outward face should conform with the crowd. Our clothes should not be gaudy, yet they should not be dowdy either. We should not keep silver plate with inlays of solid gold, but at the same time we should not imagine that doing without gold and silver is proof that we are leading the simple life. Let our aim be a way of life not diametrically opposed to, but better than that of the mob. Otherwise we shall repel and alienate the very people whose reform we desire; we shall make them, moreover, reluctant to imitate us in anything for fear they may have to imitate us in everything. The first thing philosophy promises us is the feeling of fellowship, of belonging to mankind and being members of a community; being different will mean the abandoning of that manifesto. We must watch that the means by which we hope to gain admiration do not earn ridicule and hostility. Our motto, as everyone knows, is to live in conformity with nature: it is quite contrary to nature to torture one's body, to reject simple standards of cleanliness and make a point of being dirty, to adopt a diet that is not just plain but hideous and revolting. In the same way as a craving for dainties is a token of extravagant living, avoidance of familiar and inexpensive dishes betokens insanity. Philosophy calls for simple living, not for doing penance, and the simple way of life need not be a crude one. The standard which I accept is this: one's life should be a compromise between the ideal and the popular morality. People should admire our way of life but they should at the same time find it understandable.

'Does that mean we are to act just like other people? Is there to be no distinction between us and them?' Most certainly there is. Any close observer should be aware that we are different from the mob. Anyone entering our homes should admire us rather than our furnishings. It is a great man that can treat his earthenware as if it was silver, and a man who treats his silver as if it was earthenware is no less great. Finding wealth an intolerable burden is the mark of an unstable mind.

But let me share with you as usual the day's small find. . . . Limiting one's desires actually helps to cure one of fear. 'Cease to hope and you will cease to fear.' 'But how,' you will ask, 'can things as diverse as these be linked?' Well, the fact is that they are bound up with one another, unconnected as they may seem. Widely different though they are, the two of them march in unison like a prisoner and the escort he is handcuffed to. Fear keeps pace with hope. Nor does their so moving together surprise me; both belong to a mind in suspense, to a mind in a state of anxiety through looking into the future. Both are mainly due to projecting our thoughts far ahead of us instead of adapting ourselves to the present. Thus it is that foresight, the greatest blessing humanity has been given, is transformed into a curse. Wild animals run from the dangers they actually see, and once they have escaped them worry no more. We however are tormented alike by what is past and what is to come. A number of our blessings do us harm, for memory brings back the agony of fear while foresight brings it on prematurely. No one confines his unhappiness to the present.

LETTER XLVIII

. . . . Friendship creates a community of interest between us in everything. We have neither successes nor setbacks as individuals; our lives have a common end. No one can lead a happy life if he thinks only of himself and turns everything to his own purposes. You should live for the other person if you wish to live for yourself. The assiduous and scrupulous cultivation of this bond, which leads to our associating with our fellow-men and believes in the existence of a common law for all mankind, contributes more than anything else to the maintenance of the more intimate bond of friendship. A person who shares much with a fellow human being will share everything with a friend.

What I should like those subtle thinkers—you know the ones I mean, my peerless Lucilius—to teach me is this: what my duties are to a friend and to a man, rather than the number of senses in which the expression "friend" is used and how many different meanings the word "man" has. Before my very eyes wisdom and folly are taking their separate stands: which shall I join? whose side am I to follow? For one person "man" is equivalent to "friend," for another "man" and "friend" are far from being identified, and in making a friend one man will be seeking an asset while another will be making himself an asset to the other; and in the midst of all this, what you people do for me is pull words about and cut up syllables. One is led to believe that unless one has constructed syllogisms of the craftiest kind, and reduced fallacies to a compact form in which a false conclusion is derived from a true premise, one will not be in a position to distinguish what one should aim at and what one should avoid. It makes one ashamed—that men of our advanced years should turn a thing as serious as this into a game. . . .

Shall I tell you what philosophy holds out to humanity? Counsel. One person is facing death, another is vexed by poverty, while another is tormented by wealth—whether his own or someone else's; one man is appalled by his misfortunes while another longs to get away from his own prosperity; one man is suffering at the hands of men, another at the hands of the gods. What's the point of concocting whimsies for me of the sort I've just been mentioning? This isn't the place for fun—you're called in to help the unhappy. You're pledged to bring succour to the shipwrecked, to those in captivity, to the sick, the needy and men who are just placing their heads beneath the executioner's uplifted axe. Where are you off to? What are you about? The person you're engaging in word-play with is in fear—go to his aid. . . . All mankind are stretching out their hands to you on every side. Lives that have been ruined, lives that are on the way to ruin are appealing for some help; it is to you that they look for hope and assistance. They are begging you to extricate them from this awful vortex, to show them in their doubt and disarray the shining torch of truth. Tell them what nature has made necessary and what she has made superfluous. Tell them how simple are the laws she has laid down, and how straightforward and enjoyable life is for those who follow them and how confused and disagreeable it is for others who put more trust in popular ideas than they do in nature. All right if you can point out to me where those puzzles are likely to bring such people relief. Which of them removes cravings or brings them under control? If only they were simply unhelpful! They're actually harmful. I'll give you the clearest proof whenever you like of their tendency to weaken and enfeeble even eminent talents once applied to such quibbles. And when it comes to saying how they equip people proposing to do battle with fortune and what weapons they offer them, one hangs one's head with shame. Is this the way to our supreme ideal? Do we get there by means of all that "if X, Y, or if not Y, Z" one finds in philosophy? And by means of quibbles that would be shameful and discreditable even among persons occupying themselves with law reports? When you're leading the person you're questioning into a trap, aren't you just making it look as if he has lost his case on a purely technical point of pleading? . . . Why do philosophers like you abandon the magnificent promises you have made? After assuring me in solemn terms that you will see to it that my eyes shall no more be overwhelmed by the glitter of gold than by the glitter of a sword, that I shall spurn with magnificent strength of purpose the things all other men pray for and the things all other men are afraid of, why do you have to descend to the schoolroom ABC? What do you say?

Is this the way to the heavens?*

---

*Virgil, *Aeneid*, IX: 641.

For that is what philosophy has promised me—that she will make me God's equal. That's the invitation and that's what I've come for; be as good as your word.

Keep clear, then, my dear Lucilius, as far as you can, of the sort of quibbles and qualifications I've been mentioning in philosophers. Straightforwardness and simplicity are in keeping with goodness. Even if you had a large part of your life remaining before you, you would have to organize it very economically to have enough for all the things that are necessary; as things are, isn't it the height of folly to learn inessential things when time's so desperately short! . . .

Philosophy has the single task of discovering the truth about the divine and human worlds. The religious conscience, the sense of duty, justice and all the rest of the close-knit, interdependent "company of virtues," never leave her side. Philosophy has taught men to worship what is divine, to love what is human, telling us that with the gods belongs authority, and among human beings fellowship. That fellowship lasted for a long time intact, before men's greed broke society up—and impoverished even those she had brought most riches; for people cease to possess everything as soon as they want everything for themselves. . . .

What has the philosopher investigated? What has the philosopher brought to light? In the first place, truth and nature (having, unlike the rest of the animal world, followed nature with more than just a pair of eyes, things slow to grasp divinity); and secondly, a rule of life, in which he has brought life into line with things universal. And he has taught us not just to recognize but to obey the gods, and to accept all that happens exactly as if it were an order from above. He has told us not to listen to false opinions, and has weighed and valued everything against standards which are true. He has condemned pleasures an inseparable element of which is subsequent regret, has commended the good things which will always satisfy, and for all to see has made the man who has no need of luck the luckiest man of all, and the man who is master of himself the master of all.

The philosophy I speak of is not the one* which takes the citizen out of public life and the gods out of the world we live in, and hands morality over to pleasure, but the philosophy which thinks nothing good unless it is honorable, which is incapable of being enticed astray by the rewards of men or fortune, and the very pricelessness of which lies in the fact that it cannot be bought at any price. And I do not believe that this philosophy was in existence in that primitive era in which technical skills were still unknown and useful knowledge was acquired through actual practical experience, or that it dates from an age that was happy, an age in which the bounties of nature were freely available for the use of all without discrimination, before avarice and luxury split human beings up and got them to abandon partnership for plunder. The men of that era were not philosophers, even if they acted as philosophers are supposed to act.† No other state of man could cause anyone greater admiration; if God were to allow a man to fashion the things of this earth and allot its peoples their social customs, that man would not be satisfied with any other system than the one which tradition says existed in those people's time, among whom

> No farmers tilled ploughed fields; merely to mark
> The line of boundaries dividing land

*Epicureanism.
†i.e 'in accordance with nature'.

> Between its owners was a sin; men shared
> Their findings, and the earth herself then gave
> All things more freely unsolicited.*

What race of men could be luckier? Share and share alike they enjoyed nature. She saw to each and every man's requirements for survival like a parent. What it all amounted to was undisturbed possession of resources owned by the community. I can surely call that race of men one of unparalleled riches, it being impossible to find a single pauper in it.

Into this ideal state of things burst avarice, avarice which in seeking to put aside some article or other and appropriate it to its own use, only succeeded in making everything somebody else's property and reducing its possessions to a fraction of its previously unlimited wealth. Avarice brought in poverty, by coveting a lot of possessions losing all that it had. This is why although it may endeavour to make good its losses, may acquire estate after estate by buying out or forcing out its neighbours, enlarge country properties to the dimensions of whole provinces, speak of "owning some property" when it can go on a long tour overseas without once stepping off its own land, there is no extension of our boundaries that can bring us back to our starting point. When we have done everything within our power, we shall possess a great deal: but we once possessed the world.

The earth herself, untilled, was more productive, her yields being more than ample for the needs of peoples who did not raid each other. With any of nature's products, men found as much pleasure in showing others what they had discovered as they did in discovering it. No one could outdo or be outdone by any other. All was equally divided among people living in complete harmony. The stronger had not yet started laying hands on the weaker; the avaricious person had not yet started hiding things away, to be hoarded for his own private use, so shutting the next man off from actual necessities of life; each cared as much about the other as about himself. Weapons were unused; hands still unstained with human blood had directed their hostility exclusively against wild beasts.

Protected from the sun in some thick wood, living in some very ordinary shelter under a covering of leaves preserving them from the rigours of winter or the rain, those people passed tranquil nights with never a sigh. We in our crimson luxury toss and turn with worry, stabbed by needling cares. What soft sleep the hard earth gave those people! They had no carved or panelled ceilings hanging over them. They lay out in the open, with the stars slipping past above them and the firmament silently conveying onward that mighty work of creation as it was carried headlong below the horizon in the magnificent pageant of the night sky. And they had clear views by day as well as by night of this loveliest of mansions, enjoying the pleasure of watching constellations falling away from the zenith and others rising again from out of sight beneath the horizon. Surely it was a joy to roam the earth with marvels scattered so widely, around one. You now, by contrast, go pale at every noise your houses make, and if there is a creaking sound you run away along your frescoed passages in alarm. Those people had no mansions on the scale of towns. Fresh air and the untrammelled breezes of the open spaces, the unoppressive shade of a tree or rock, springs of crystal clarity, streams which chose their own course, streams unsullied by the work of man, by pipes

*Virgil, *Georgics,* I: 125–8.

or any other interference with their natural channels, meadows whose beauty owed nothing to man's art, that was the environment around their dwelling places in the countryside, dwelling places given a simple countryman's finish. This was a home in conformity with nature, a home in which one enjoyed living, and which occasioned neither fear of it nor fears for it, whereas nowadays our own homes count for a large part of our feeling of insecurity.

But however wonderful and guileless the life they led, they were not wise men; this is a title that has come to be reserved for the highest of all achievements. All the same, I should be the last to deny that they were men of exalted spirit, only one step removed, so to speak, from the gods. There can be no doubt that before this earth was worn out it produced a better type of offspring. But though they all possessed a character more robust than that of today, and one with a greater aptitude for hard work, it is equally true that their personalities fell short of genuine perfection. For nature does not give a man virtue: the process of becoming a good man is an art. Certainly they did not go in search of gold or silver or the various crystalline stones to be found in the nethermost dregs of the earth. They were still merciful even to dumb animals. Man was far and away from killing man, not out of fear or provocation, but simply for entertainment. They had yet to wear embroidered clothing, and had yet to have gold woven into robes, or even mine it. But the fact remains that their innocence was due to ignorance and nothing else. And there is a world of difference between, on the one hand, choosing not to do what is wrong and, on the other, not knowing how to do it in the first place. They lacked the cardinal virtues of justice, moral insight, self-control and courage. There were corresponding qualities, in each case not unlike these, that had a place in their primitive lives; but virtue only comes to a character which has been thoroughly schooled and trained and brought to a pitch of perfection by unremitting practice. We are born for it, but not with it. And even in the best of people, until you cultivate it there is only the material for virtue, not virtue itself.

3

AUGUSTINE
Two Cities: Two Roads to Knowledge

Augustine (354–430) was born in Thagaste (now in Algeria), the son of a pagan father and a devoutly Christian mother. Distinguishing himself as an exceptionally brilliant, questioning intellectual, he first went to Carthage and then to Rome and Milan to study rhetoric. He describes his spiritual struggles and his dramatic conversion to Christianity in his autobiographical work, *The Confessions* (397–400). Augustine was initially attracted to the Manichean view that the world is a battleground between the forces of good and evil, and that man is a battleground between the claims of the soul and the body. As he tells it, he was liberated from that heresy by reading Plotinus and by the influence of the Neoplatonic circles in Milan. His philosophical and theological work henceforward concentrated on reconciling—indeed fusing—Christian beliefs with Platonism. Returning to North Africa in 391, he was appointed Bishop of Hippo in 395. His vast outpouring of philosophic, theological, and pastoral writing formed and transformed Christian doctrine (*De Trinitate* 399–412), *On Genesis* (40). Besides being a compendium of reflections on the relation between eternity and historical time, divine benevolence and frailty, *The City of God* (413–26) set the frame and topics for subsequent discussions of the sources of political legitimacy, the respective powers and roles of secular and religious authorities. Augustine also formulated many of the canonical topics of philosophy: is the will free? (*De Libero Arbitrio* 388–391; how do we learn? (*De Magister* 389); what is living and what is dead in skepticism? (*Contra Academicos* 386.) His correspondence with St. Jerome defined criteria for biblical interpretation, a theological version of the principle of charity: preserve the truth-claims of the texts.

Writing for many different audiences, Augustine used his rhetorical talents to explore a variety of literary genres. His correspondence with St. Jerome and his pastoral letters show a keen empathic sensibility; his tightly argued polemical writings manifest a sharp combative intelligence; his dialogues (e.g., *De Ordine*, 386) reveal a dramatic and satirical flair.

The Happy Life

Does reason teach those approaching and entering upon philosophy that they should fear any mountain more than the proud pursuit of empty glory? For within it there is nothing substantial or solid and, with a cracking of the ground-crust beneath, it collapses and swallows up those walking above, puffed up with themselves, and, as they tumble headlong into darkness, it withdraws from them the gleaming dwelling place just barely seen. . . .

At the age of nineteen, when in the school of rhetoric I came upon Cicero's book *Hortensius*, I was inflamed with such enthusiasm for philosophy that I thought of devoting myself to it immediately.

But there was no lack of mist to confuse my course and for some time, I confess, I followed stars falling into the ocean and so I was led astray. For a kind of childish superstition caused me to cringe before inquiry itself, and when having become self-reliant, I dispelled that mist and persuaded myself to submit to those who teach rather than to those who command, I met men by whom the light seen by the eyes was beheld as that which was an object of highest and even divine veneration. I did not agree, but I thought they were concealing within those veils some important secret which at some time they would divulge.

But when I shook off those men and escaped, especially after I had crossed this sea, for some time the Academics held the tiller of my ship as, surrounded by waves, it battled all winds. Then I came to this land. Here I have learned to know the North Star to which I entrusted myself.

Often I noticed in the sermons of our priest, that when there was consideration of God or of the soul, which is nearest to God, there was to be no thought at all of anything corporeal. The enticements of a woman and of fame kept holding me back, I confess, from flying immediately into philosophy's embrace, so that not until I had satisfied my desire for these did I—and this has been granted only to the most fortunate few—under full sail and with all oars pulling make that harbor quickly and there find rest. But having read a few books of Plotinus, of whom I understand that you are a zealous student, and having compared them, as well as I could, with the authority of those who have handed down the divine mysteries, I was so inflamed that I would have cast off all those anchors holding me if my esteem for certain men had not restrained me. What then remained except that a storm which seemed ill luck should come to my rescue as I hesitated, occupied with unnecessary cares? And so such a violent chest ailment seized me that, unable to bear the burden of my profession, by which perhaps I was sailing to the Sirens, I threw everything overboard and brought my ship, battered and weary, to the desired resting place.

Therefore, you see the philosophy in which, as in a port, I am now sailing. But even the port itself lies wide open; although its great size presents less danger, yet it does not entirely exclude error. For I am not at all aware to what part of the land I should move—that part which alone is really happy—and how I should reach it. For what do I hold as firm, since up to now the question about the soul is still wavering and uncertain? Wherefore I entreat you through your virtue, through your kindness, through the spiritual bond and fellowship between us, that you extend your helping right hand, for this means that you love me and that you may believe that I in turn love you and hold you dear. If I obtain this request, I shall arrive very easily and with slight effort at that happy life in which I presume you already share.

But that you may know what I am doing and how I am gathering my dear ones at the port, and from this more completely understand my mind—for I cannot find any other signs by which to reveal myself to you—I thought that one of my discussions which seemed to me more religious in character and especially worthy of your fame should be addressed to you and dedicated to your name.

This is surely most appropriate for together we have inquired concerning the happy life, and I know nothing else which should rather be called a gift of God. I am not frightened by your eloquence, for whatever I love I cannot fear, although I may not attain it; much less am I frightened by the height of your good fortune. For, although it is great, it is truly secondary in your consideration because it puts in second place the very ones whom it dominates. But now please listen to what I say.

Against the Academicians
Book 2, Second Dedicatory Introduction

If it were as inevitable to find wisdom when searching for it as it is to be unable to be wise without discipline and the knowledge of wisdom, then surely the trickery, obstinacy, and persistence of the Academicians—or, as I sometimes think, their policy—which were suitable to the times would then have been interred with those times. Yet it happens that knowledge is cultivated rarely and by only a few. This is due to either (a) the many different upheavals of this life, as you, Romanianus, have learned though experience; (b) some thickness or laziness or sluggishness of our dulled minds; (c) our despair at finding [wisdom], since the star of wisdom doesn't appear to our minds as easily as the light does to our eyes; or (d) the common error that men, having found a false opinion, do not search diligently for the truth if they search at all, and even turn away from the desire for searching.

So it happens that the weapons of the Academicians, when one joins issue with them, seem invincible. It is as if they were forged by Vulcan. They seem this way not only to insignificant men, but to learned and acute men. Accordingly, while one should row against the winds and waves of fortune with the oars of whatever virtues are available, one should first implore divine assistance with all devotion and piety, so that the resolute application of oneself to good studies holds to its course and no chance drives it astray from reaching the secure and pleasant harbor of philosophy.

This is your first responsibility, and I fear for you on this score. I want you to be set free from it. I don't stop praying for favorable winds for you in my daily prayers. If only I were worthy enough to bring it to pass! I pray to the power and wisdom itself of God the Highest.[1] What else is He whom the mysteries reveal to us as the Son of God?

You'll help me a great deal while I'm praying for you if you don't despair of our being able to be heard, and if you exert yourself with us, not only with your prayers but also with your will and the natural profundity of that mind of yours. It is on account of your mind that I seek you out: it gives me exceptional delight and I always admire it. But alas! Your mind is like a thunderbolt that is wrapped up in clouds of domestic matters. It is hidden from most people; indeed, almost from all. Yet it can't be hidden from me, or from one or two of your intimate friends. We have often listened attentively to your rumblings, and in addition we have seen a few of the flashes that announce the thunderbolt. For the time being I'll recall just a single case and keep quiet about the rest. Who has ever suddenly thundered and shone the light of his mind so greatly that, with a single thunderclap of his reason and a brilliant flash of restraint, he killed off in a single day a passion that had been most fierce the day before? Will that power of yours, then, not burst forth at some point and turn the jeers of many who had given up hope into consternation and bewilderment? Will it not speak in this world some 'signs,' as, it were, of future events, and then cast off the burden of the whole body and return again to Heaven?[2] Has Augustine said these things about Romanianus in vain? No! He to Whom I have wholly given myself, He Whom I have now begun to know a little again, will not allow it!

Therefore, come with me to philosophy. In it there is everything that is wont to move you wonderfully whenever you're anxious and thrown into doubt. I have no fears on the score of moral looseness or the dullness of your wit! When you were allowed to take a little time off [from work], who showed himself more alert than you in our conversations, or more penetrating? Shall I not fully repay your favors to me? Do I perhaps owe you only a very little?

When I was an impoverished young man setting out on my studies away from home, you welcomed me into your house, into your munificence, and, what is much more, into your spirit.[3] You comforted me with your friendship when I lost my father, encouraged me with your counsel, and helped me with your wealth. You made me nearly as renowned and important in our own town as yourself by your patronage, familiarity, and reception of me in your home. You alone were the one, when I returned to Carthage to get a more advantageous position, to whom I confided my plan and my hopes, not anyone in my family.[4] Though you hesitated for a little while out of love for your home town, since I was already teaching there, when you weren't able to overcome a young man's ambition for things that seemed better you turned your opposition into support, with admirable self-control and benevolence. You furnished all that was necessary for my venture. You watched over the cradle and, so to speak, the nest of my studies, and you again now supported my first efforts in daring to fly. When I sailed away in your absence and without your knowledge, you weren't at all angry that I didn't communicate with you, as I usually did. Suspecting anything but defiant behavior, you remained unshaken in your friendship. You worried no more about your children, who had been deserted by their teacher, than you did about the purity and innermost depths of my mind.

Finally, you are the one who has inspired, advanced, and brought about whatever I now enjoy in my retirement—that I've escaped from the chains of superfluous desires; that in putting down the burdens of mortal cares I breathe, come to my senses, return to myself;[5] that I'm searching for the truth most eagerly; that I'm now beginning to find it; that I'm confident about arriving at its highest degree.[6] Whose assistant you were, however, I still conceive by faith rather than apprehend by reason. When we were face to face, I set out the inner turmoils of my mind. I declared earnestly many times that no fortune would seem good to me except what would provide leisure for doing philosophy, and that no life would seem happy except one in which I might live in philosophy. Yet I was held back by the heavy burden of my dependents whose life was supported by my job, and by many expenses, be they due to propriety or to the embarrassing circumstances of my dependents. You were elevated by so great a joy, so inflamed by a holy zeal for this kind of life, that you told me that if you could somehow extricate yourself from the chains of your troublesome lawsuits you would break all the chains holding me, even to the extent of sharing your patrimony with me.[7]

Therefore, when you departed after the tinder had been sparked in us, we never stopped yearning for philosophy. Nor did we think about anything except that way of life, a way of life both appropriate and suitable for us. We thought about it constantly. Yet we weren't as passionate as we might have been, despite our thinking we were passionate enough. We hadn't yet been touched by the greatest flame, the flame that was to consume us. We thought that the flame with which we were burning slowly was really the greatest flame. But look! When certain books[8] *brimming full* (as Celsinus[9] says) wafted their exotic scents[10] to us, and when a few drops of their precious perfume trickled onto that meager flame, they burst into an unbelievable conflagration—unbelievable, unbelievable, and beyond what perhaps even you believe of me—what more shall I say?—even beyond what I believe of myself!

What honor attracted me then? What human pomp moved me? What desire for empty fame? What comforts or chains that belong to this mortal life? I was quickly returning to myself as a complete whole. Now I confess that I looked back on the religion implanted in us as boys, binding us from the marrow, as though from a long journey's end. Yet it was actually drawing me to itself without my realizing it. And so stumbling, hastening, hesitating I snatched up the Apostle Paul.[11] Truly, I declared, the [apostles] would not have been able to do such great deeds, nor would they have lived as they clearly did live, if their books and arguments were opposed to so great a good. I read all of it with the greatest attention and the greatest care.

Then, no matter how little the light was that had already been cast by the visage of philosophy, it now appeared so great to me that if I could show it to—I don't say "to you," Romanianus, since you always burned with the hunger for it, despite your not yet knowing it, but instead I say "to your adversary" (I don't know whether he's more of an annoyance than a hindrance to you)—if I could show it to your adversary, he would rush to its beauty as a passionate and holy lover, admiring and breathless and exhilarated. He would forsake and abandon his fashionable resorts, his pleasant orchards, his luxurious and elegant banquets, his household performing troupe; and, in the end, he would shun whatever strongly inclines him to all kinds of pleasures. We should admit that even your adversary has a certain beauty of spirit—or rather we should admit that he has a seed of beauty, so to speak. It's straining to blossom forth into true beauty, but it sends forth only twisted and misshapen shoots among the rough underbrush of vices and the brambles of fallacious opinions.[12] Yet it continues to bloom and to exhibit itself, as far as it is able, to those who peer keenly and intently into the thicket. From this source comes his hospitality; the civility that seasons his banquets; his elegance, charm, sophisticated taste in all things; and his urbanity that everywhere sprinkles all things with traces of loveliness.

This is commonly called 'philocaly.' Don't condemn the name because it's common! Philocaly and Philosophy are nearly the same names[13] and they want to be seen as members of the same family, as in fact they are. What is Philosophy? The love of wisdom. What is Philocaly? The love of beauty. (Just ask the Greeks!) What, then, is wisdom? Is it not true beauty itself? Hence they are sisters born of the same father.[14] Although Philocaly was dragged down from her heights by the birdlime[15] of lust and kept in an ordinary cage, she retains the close resemblance in her name to remind the birdcatcher not to despise her. Her sister, flying freely, often sees her in a debased and needy condition with her wings clipped. She rarely sets her free. Philocaly does not know from what origin she springs; only Philosophy knows that.

(This whole fable—I've suddenly become an Aesop!—will be recounted to you more pleasantly in a poem by Licentius. He's close to being an accomplished poet.)[16]

If your adversary, then, who is a lover of false beauty, could look upon true beauty through eyes that were open and healthy, even for a moment, with what pleasure would he take refuge in the bosom of philosophy! How he would embrace you there, knowing you as his true brother!

You're surprised at these things. Maybe you're laughing at them. What if I could explain them as I should like? What if you could hear the voice of philosophy even without yet seeing its visage? You would surely be surprised, but you wouldn't laugh at or despair of [your adversary]. Believe me, we should never despair of anyone, and least of all of such men. There are many examples. This kind of bird easily escapes and flies away again, while many others are caged and look on in great astonishment.

Let's return to ourselves—let us, I say, devote our attention to philosophy, Romanianus. I should like to thank you: your son is beginning to do philosophy. I'm restraining him so that he may proceed with more strength and vigor after first getting the necessary training. You yourself need not be afraid because you lack this training. Knowing you so well, I only wish for you to have a favorable opportunity. What can I say about your natural abilities? If only they were not so uncommon among men as they are constant in you!

There remain two defects and obstacles to finding truth. I don't have much fear for you on their account. Still, I'm afraid that (i) you may underrate yourself and despair of your ever finding the truth; or (ii) you believe yourself to have found it.[17]

Now if you're hindered by the first of these obstacles, perhaps our discussion will remove it for you. You have often been angry at the Academicians: the more severely, in fact, the less knowledgeable you were about them; the more gladly, because you were led on by your love of the truth. Therefore, I'll now join battle with Alypius, under your patronage, and easily persuade you of my views—only as plausible views, however, since you won't see the truth itself unless you give yourself over completely to philosophy.

As for the second obstacle, namely that you perhaps assume that you have found some truth, despite the fact that you were searching and doubting when you left us—if any superstition has returned to your mind, it will surely be cast out once I've sent you a discussion among ourselves concerning religion[18] or once I talk many things over with you in person.

For my part, I'm doing nothing at present except purging myself of futile and harmful opinions, so I'm undoubtedly better off than you are.

How I Came to the Episcopacy
(Sermon 355.2, trans. Vernon Bourke)

I, whom by God's favor you observe as your bishop, came as a young man to this City [Hippo], as many of you know. I was looking for a place to establish a monastery and to live together with my brethren. Of course, I had abandoned my worldly ambition and refused to be what I might have been; in fact, I did not seek to become what I am now. "I have chosen to be an abject in the house of my God, rather than to dwell in the tabernacles of sinners." [Ps. 83:11] I dissociated myself from those who love the world, and made no effort to be on the level of those who rule the people. Nor did I choose a higher place at my Lord's table but a lower one, much removed. And it pleased Him to say to me: Go up higher. At that point, I was so much afraid of the office of bishop that, since my reputation had begun to be of some importance among God's servants, I would not visit any place that I knew to be without a bishop. I took this precaution and did as much as I could to achieve salvation in a low position, lest I run into danger in a high one. As I have said, however, the servant should not contradict his master.

I came to this City to see a friend whom I thought I might win over for God and have him with us in the monastery: I felt safe, because this place had a bishop. I was caught and made a priest; then, through this step, I reached the episcopate. I brought nothing: I came to this church with nothing more than the clothes that I wore at the time. Since I had this intention to live in a monastery with my brethren, the venerable [Bishop] Valerius of happy memory, who knew my plan and desire, gave me this garden in which the monastery is now located. I started to assemble brethren who were well-disposed as my colleagues, men who possessed nothing, as I had nothing, and who followed my example. Thus, as I sold my meager little estate and gave it to the poor, so also did those who wished to live with me; our purpose was to live in common: indeed, what was common to us was that great and most rewarding prize, God Himself.

I reached the episcopate and saw that it is necessary for a bishop to provide continuous hospitality for various visitors and travelers, and if I did not do this as a bishop, I would have been deemed discourteous. However, if this sort of behavior were permitted in a monastery, it would have been unfitting. Consequently, I decided to maintain a community of priests with me in this episcopal house.

Notice how we live. In our community, no one is permitted to own anything, though possibly some do. It is permitted to no one: if some do own property, they do so without permission. However, I think well of my own brethren, and since I always maintain this good opinion, I have omitted any inquiry into this matter, for to ask would have given the impression that I suspected some evil. In fact, I know, and all who live with me know, what our objective is and what is the rule of our life. . . .

Augustine on His Own Writings
(*Retractions*, Prologue 1.1–3, trans. Vernon Bourke)

For some time, I have been thinking over and considering the task which I am now beginning with the help of God . . . for I do not feel that I should put off reviewing with judicial severity my works, whether in the form of books, letters or treatises, and noting like a censor anything that displeases me. For, except for an imprudent person, no one will dare to criticize me because I am criticizing my own errors. However, if he says that I should not have uttered things that would later displease me, he is right and in agreement with me. In fact, he is criticizing the same things that I do, for I would not have to criticize them, if I had written what I ought.

However, let each person interpret what I am doing, as he wills. For myself, the Apostle's view of this matter merits attention, where he says, "If we judged ourselves, we might not be judged by God." [I Cor. 11:31] There is also the text, "In the multitude of words, you will not escape sin." [Prov. 10:19] which frightens me a good deal. Not because I have written much, or because many things that I have said have been copied down even though I did not dictate them (far be it from me to regard as verbosity what has to be said, even though the result is a large and prolix quantity of words), yet I cringe from this text of Scripture because there is no doubt that from many of my discussions a good many things could be gathered which, if not false, might definitely appear, or even might be proved, unnecessary. What one of the faithful did not Christ frighten, when He said, "For every idle word that men shall speak, they shall render an account on the day of judgment." [Matt. 12:36] Hence, on this point the Apostle James said, "Let every man be swift to hear but slow to speak"; [Jas. 1:19] and elsewhere he said, "Be ye not many masters, my brethren, knowing that you receive the greater judgment. All of us offend in many things. If any man offend not in word, the same is a perfect man." [Jas. 3:1ff] As for myself, I do not now lay claim to such perfection, even now that I am elderly; how much less, when I began as a young man to write or speak to the people. So much notoriety was then accorded me that, wherever I found myself, I had to speak to the people; rarely could I keep silent and listen to others and be "quick to hear but slow to speak." As a result, I judge myself before the one Master Whose judgment of my offenses I desire to avoid. I think there can be many teachers when there are plural views that are diversified and mutually opposed. But when all say the same thing and speak the truth, they do not depart from the teaching of one true Teacher. They sin, on the other hand, not when they say a good deal in agreement with Him but when they add their own notions. This is how they fall from much speaking into false speaking.

Now I was glad to write this work, so that I might put it in the hands of those men from whom I could not recall and correct the books that I had already produced. Nor, indeed, do I pass over those things that I wrote while still a catechumen, when I had abandoned the earthly expectations that I had formerly held but was still filled with the literary affectations of this world. In fact, these writings did come to the attention of copyists and readers, and they can be read with some profit, provided one is prepared to ignore their several faults, or if one cannot ignore the mistakes at least one can pay no attention to them. So, let all those who will read this work imitate me not in my errors but in my progress toward the better. For, whoever will read my little works in the order in which they were written, will perhaps discover how much progress I made in writing. To enable the reader to do this, I shall take care in this work to inform him as to this order, as much as I can.

Authority and Reason
(*Against the Academics* 3.20.43)[19]

. . . And now—that you may grasp my whole meaning in a few words—whatever may be the nature of human wisdom, I see that I have not yet understood it. Nevertheless, although I am now in the thirty-third year of my life, I do not think that I ought to despair of understanding it some day, for I have resolved to disregard all the other things which mortals consider good, and to devote myself to an investigation of it. And, whereas the reasonings of the Academics used to deter me greatly from such an undertaking, I believe that through this disputation I am now sufficiently protected against those reasonings. Certainly, no one doubts that we are impelled toward knowledge by a twofold force: the force of authority and the force of reason. And I am resolved never to deviate in the least from the authority of Christ, for I find none more powerful. But, as to what is attainable by acute and accurate reasoning, such is my state of mind that I am impatient to grasp what truth is—to grasp it not only by belief, but also by comprehension. Meanwhile, I am confident that I shall find among the Platonists what is not in opposition to our Sacred Scriptures.

Two Ways to Knowledge
(*De Ordine* 2.9.26–27)[18]

It remains for me to declare how instruction is to be imparted to the studious youths who have resolved to live after the manner described above. Likewise, with regard to the acquiring of knowledge, we are of necessity led in a twofold manner: by authority and by reason. In point of time, authority is first; in the order of reality, reason is prior. What takes precedence in operation is one thing; what is more highly prized as an object of desire is something else. Consequently, although the authority of upright men seems to be the safer guide for the uninstructed multitude, reason is better adapted for the educated. Furthermore, since no one becomes learned except by ceasing to be unlearned, and since no unlearned person knows in what quality he ought to present himself to instructors or by what manner of life he may become docile, it happens that for those who seek to learn great and hidden truths authority alone opens the door. But, after one had entered, then without any hesitation he begins to follow the precepts of the perfect life. When he has become docile through these precepts, then at length he will come to know: (a) how much wisdom is embodied in those very precepts that he has been observing before understanding; (b) what reason itself is, which he—now strong and capable after the cradle of authority—follows and comprehends; (c) what intellect is, in which all things are, or rather, which is itself the sum total of all things; (d) and what, beyond all things, is the source of all things. To this knowledge, few are able to arrive in this life; even after this life, no one can exceed it.

As to those who are content to follow authority alone and who apply themselves constantly to right living and holy desires, while they make no account of the liberal and fine arts, or are incapable of being instructed in them—I know not how I could call them happy as long as they live among men. Nevertheless, I firmly believe that, upon leaving the body, they will be liberated with greater facility or difficulty according as they have lived the more virtuously or otherwise.

Authority is, indeed, partly divine and partly human, but the true, solid and sovereign authority is that which is called divine. In this matter there is to be feared the wonderful deception of invisible beings that, by certain divinations and numerous powers of things pertaining to the senses, are accustomed to deceive with the utmost ease those souls that are engrossed with perishable possessions, or eagerly desirous of transitory power, or overawed by meaningless prodigies.

We must, therefore, accept as divine that Authority which not only exceeds human power in its outward manifestations, but also, in the very act of leading a man onward, shows him to what extent It has debased Itself for his sake, and bids him not to be confined to the senses, to which indeed those things seem wondrous, but to soar upward to the intellect. At the same time It shows him what great things It is able to do, and why It does them, and how little importance It attaches to them. For, it is fitting that by deeds It show Its power; by humility, Its clemency; by commandment, Its nature. And all this is being delivered to us so distinctly and steadily by the sacred rites into which we are now being initiated: therein the life of good men is most easily purified, not indeed by the circumlocution of disputation, but by the authority of the mysteries.

But human authority is very often deceiving. Yet it rightly seems to show itself at its best in those men who propose various proofs for their teachings, insofar as the mind of the unlearned can grasp them, and who do not live otherwise than how they prescribe that one ought to live. If certain goods of fortune accrue to these men, they reveal themselves great men in the use of those things, but still greater in their contempt of them; and then it is most difficult to lay blame on anyone who puts trust in those men when they enunciate principles of right living.

Letter to Zenobius

I think we agree that nothing our bodily senses come into contact with can remain the same, even for a moment. These things pass away without our noticing; they disappear; their present being doesn't last. To put it bluntly, they don't exist. Accordingly, true and divine philosophy urges us to restrain our love of them, as this love is destructive and the cause of much suffering. Then even while the soul is still ruling this body, it can wholly devote itself to what is always the same, what doesn't please us with its merely passing charm.

Although this is so, and although my mind sees you as you are, a true and simple being whom I can love without anxiety, still I must confess that when you are absent in body and separated from me by distance, I long to meet you, to see you. This fault I believe, if I know you as well as I think, you like in me; and even if you wish everything good for your closest friends, you don't want them cured of it. If your mind is strong enough to recognize this snare, and you are able to smile at those who are caught in it, you are a great man and very different from me. For my part, while I am missing anyone, I want that person to miss me. But all the same I keep watch, as well as I can, and make an effort not to love anything that can be taken away from me against my will.

Letter to Valerius, His Bishop

Above everything else I ask you to consider this: during our life on earth, and especially in our own day, nothing is easier, pleasanter, and more likely to win people's respect than the office of bishop or priest or deacon, if it is performed negligently and with a view to securing their approval; but in God's sight there is nothing more sorrowful, miserable, and deserving of condemnation. Again, there is nothing in this present life, and especially now, more difficult, toilsome, and perilous than these offices if they are carried out in the way our Lord commands; but, at the same time, nothing is more blessed in God's sight. But this "way our Lord commands"—this I failed to learn either as a boy or young man; and when I had started to learn it, I was compelled because of my sins (this is the only way I can explain it) to take the second place in your diocese—to help guide the boat, without knowing how to handle an oar!

I know it was the Lord's will to correct me in this way. I was presuming to point out to many sailors their faults, as if I were better and more learned than they, before I had experience in their work. After I was sent in among them, I began to feel how rash my faultfinding had been; though even before this experience, I had judged their ministry to be a very dangerous one. That is why I was so troubled at the time of my ordination as priest. Many people noticed this, but they didn't know the cause of my distress. They did what they could to console me, but their words didn't apply to my trouble even though their intention was good. But now I have wider and deeper experience in these things than I had when I used to ponder them. I haven't discovered any new waves or storms, nothing I didn't know before, or hadn't heard or read or thought of. But at that time I had no idea of my own skill or strength to avoid them or to put up with them. I thought they were of some value! But the Lord has laughed at me; he's revealed me to myself by means of these experiences.

Now, it may be that God has done this not in judgment but in mercy. At least that is my hope. Now that I know my weakness I feel I must search through all the remedies his Scriptures contain and give myself to prayer and reading, so that my soul may be given enough strength for its responsible work. This I haven't yet done because I haven't had the time. It was just when I, together with some others, was planning to devote a period of leisure to getting to know the holy Scriptures that I was ordained. Our intention was to arrange things so that we could be unoccupied for the sake of this occupation. At that time I was still ignorant of how unfit I was for such a work as this one that now worries me and wears me down. But now that I've learned by experience what is required to minister to others God's Word and sacrament, I find that I cannot obtain what I know I do not possess. I know that you love both me and the Church to which you intend me to minister, unqualified as I am. You think me qualified; I know myself better, but I wouldn't have come to know myself if experience hadn't taught me.

Perhaps you'll answer that you want to know what is lacking in my education in the faith? There are so many things—I could more easily say what I have than what I want to have.

This I will say: I know, and unreservedly believe, what concerns my own salvation. My difficulty lies in this: how am I to use this for the salvation of others, not seeking what is helpful to myself but to the many, so that they can be saved? There may be—no, there most certainly *are*—counsels written in the sacred books which, if a man of God knows and understands them, will enable him to carry out his duties in the Church in a more orderly way; or at least to live among the unrighteous, or to die among them, with a righteous conscience, and not lose that life for which every humble and meek Christian heart longs. But how can this be done except as the Lord tells us, by asking, seeking, and knocking—that means by praying, reading, and weeping for our sins? It is for this purpose that I have, through my brethren, made the request for a little time, say until Easter, and this request I now want to renew with this letter.

Letter to St. Jerome

You ask—rather you demand, with the confidence of charity—that we play together in the fields of Scripture without harming one another. I myself would prefer that we approach these matters in earnest, not in play. But if this word pleases you, because it suggests effortlessness, I tell you frankly that I am looking for something more from your gifts of great ability, educated good sense, and the diligence you have exercised without hindrance over so many years, with enthusiasm and acuteness. The Holy Spirit not only gives you all these gifts, but challenges you to offer your help; they are not given to one who is playing with great and demanding questions in the fields of Scripture, but to one toiling across mountains.

If you chose the words "let us play" because of the good humor friends ought to have when discussing these things, whether the subject be plain and clear or hard and troublesome, I ask you to teach me how I may be able to achieve it. Say that I encounter something which, not from lack of attention but because of my slow understanding, seems to me unproven, and I venture to assert the opposite. If I do this with a kind of unguarded frankness, I shouldn't be suspected of childish conceit—as if I were seeking to boost my reputation by attacking illustrious men, as you say. If I can't keep from bringing out something harsh to refute an argument, and I surround it with mild expressions to make it more acceptable, let me not be judged to be wielding a "honeyed sword." Or is there perhaps a way I can guard against both of these faults, or of being suspected of them, when I am arguing with a friend who is better educated than I am? Must I assent to whatever he says, and not put up even a little resistance, even for the sake of asking a question?

In this way we might play in the fields of Scripture without any fear of offense—but I wonder if I wouldn't be being played with. I tell you frankly, I have learned to confer this kind of respect and esteem only on the books of Scripture we describe as "canonical." I firmly believe that no author of these books committed any error in writing. If I find any mistakes in them, anything that appears contrary to the truth, I am in no doubt that either the text is faulty, or the translator has not grasped what was said, or I have misunderstood it. When reading other authors, no matter how distinguished they are in holiness and doctrine, I do not consider anything true because it is their opinion; they have to be able to persuade me, either by means of the canonical authors themselves, or by a likely reason, that their opinion is compatible with the truth.

I don't suppose that you think differently, my brother. In fact, I don't believe that you want your own books read as we read those of the prophets and apostles. To doubt their books, which are free from all error, would be irreverent. I'm sure this is far from your holy humility and your just estimate of yourself! Without these gifts you could not have said, "How I wish I could receive your embrace, and that by friendly conversation we might teach each other, and learn from one another."

Look into yourself a little, if you are willing—I mean into yourself as regards me. Recall or, if you have it in writing, reread your words in the short letter you sent me by our brother, now my colleague, Cyprian. When you had earnestly charged me with having done something against you, you added with genuine, brotherly, and loving affection, "By such conduct friendship is wounded and the bonds of intimacy broken. Let us not appear to be fighting like children, giving grounds of contention to our supporters and detractors." I take these words as coming not only from a kind heart, but from a kind heart that is seeking my good. Then you add what would have been evident even if you had not added it, "I write this because I want to love you with a pure and Christian love, and I would not keep in my heart anything that is not in accord with my words."

You holy man, as God sees my soul I love you with a true heart! What you set down in your letter, what I do not doubt you feel toward me, is (I believe) what the Apostle Paul felt, not toward a particular person, but toward Jews and Greeks and toward all his Gentile children, whose father he became in the Gospel, with whom he was in travail, and to the numberless faithful Christians who were to come. For them he committed his letter to writing, that he might keep nothing in his heart which was not in accord with his words.

You put yourself in my place, not by cunning deception but by loving compassion, when you considered that you should not leave me in the error into which you thought I had slipped, even as you would not wish me to leave you there if you had slipped in the same way. I give thanks for your kind intention toward me. At the same time, I ask you not to become angry with me if when something in your treatises disturbs me, I call it to your attention. I want everyone to treat me as I treat you. Then people will not offer me false praise for anything in my works they think should be rejected, nor criticize me to others while they say nothing to my face. To do this, it seems to me, is to wound friendship and to break the bonds of intimacy. I doubt whether we should consider those friendships Christian in which the common saying, "Flattery creates friends but truth begets hatred," takes precedence over the scriptural one, "More trustworthy are the wounds of a friend than the willing kisses of an enemy."

Let us earnestly set an example for the friends who sincerely wish us well in our work, so that they may know that among dear friends one may contradict the opinion of the other without love being diminished, and without having the truth due to friendship beget hatred. Whether what is contradicted is the truth or some uncertain thing spoken by a true heart doesn't matter, as long as they keep nothing in their hearts that is not in accord with their words.

Concerning your translation, you have persuaded me as to your purpose in wanting to translate from the Hebrew, which is to bring to our attention those things the Jews have omitted or misrepresented. But I ask you to be good enough to tell which Jews did this. Was it done by those who made their translations before the Lord's coming? In that case, by what one or what group of them was it done? Or was it by those who came after, whom we can then consider to have suppressed or misrepresented things in their Greek translations so that their testimony to the Christian faith should not prove them wrong. I see no reason why those before Christ would have done this.

Send us, please, your translation of the Septuagint. I did not know you had published it. I would like very much to read your book on the best method of translating, which you mentioned. I want to know how a translator is to balance his knowledge of the language against the interpretation of those who have studied Scripture and commented on it. Although they were all of the one true faith, the obscurity of many passages made it inevitable that they would produce various readings. This variety in readings is not in the least inconsistent with the unity of the faith—just as a single commentator can explain a certain passage in two different ways, both of them in accord with his faith, because the obscurity of the passage allows it.

I want your translation of the Septuagint so that we may be freed as much as possible from the incompetence of the Latin translators who, with various qualifications, have attempted it. Then those who think me envious of your useful labors should finally understand, if they can, my reason for objecting to having your translation from the Hebrew read in our churches. If against the authority of the Septuagint we present something that seems new we will seriously scandalize Christ's people. Their ears and hearts have been accustomed to listening to the translation approved by the apostles. If then the plant in the Book of Jonah is in Hebrew neither ivy nor gourd, but some unknown plant that stands upright on its trunk unsupported by any prop, I would prefer that it be called "gourd" in all the Latin versions. I do not think that the Septuagint translator would have set this down pointlessly, unaware that the plant was similar to a gourd.

Yet, let us decide to maintain between us not only the charity but also the liberty of friendship. Then you will not refrain from telling me, nor I from telling you, whatever in brotherly love disturbs us in our letters to each other, in that spirit that does not displease God. But if you think we cannot do this without harming our love, let us not do it. The charity I would like to have between us is certainly greater; but less is better than none.

Letter to St. Jerome
(394–395)

To Jerome, his most beloved lord, and brother and fellow-presbyter, worthy of being honoured and embraced with the sincerest affectionate devotion, Augustin sends greeting.

Never was the face of any one more familiar to another, than the peaceful, happy, and truly noble diligence of your studies in the Lord has become to me. For although I long greatly to be acquainted with you, I feel that already my knowledge of you is deficient in respect of nothing but a very small part of you,—namely, your personal appearance; and even as to this, I cannot deny that since my most blessed brother Alypius (now invested with the office of bishop, of which he was then truly worthy) has seen you, and has on his return been seen by me, it has been almost completely imprinted on my mind by his report of you; nay, I may say that before his return, when he saw you there, I was seeing you myself with his eyes. He is the truer friend who by his censure heals me, than the one who by flattery anoints my head. I find the greatest difficulty in exercising a right judgment when I read over what I have written, being either too cautious or too rash. For I sometimes see my own faults, but I prefer to hear them reproved by those who are better able to judge than I am; lest after I have, perhaps justly, charged myself with error, I begin again to flatter myself, and think that my censure has arisen from an undue mistrust of my own judgment.

We therefore, and with us all that are devoted to study in African churches, beseech you not to refuse to devote care and labour to the translation of the books of those who have written in the Greek language most able commentaries on our Scriptures. You may thus put us also in possession of these men, and especially of that one whose name you seem to have singular pleasure in sounding forth in your writings [Origen]. But I beseech you not to devote your labour to the work of translating into Latin the sacred canonical books, unless you follow the method in which you have translated Job, viz. with the addition of notes. . . .

I have been reading also some writings, ascribed to you, on the Epistles of the Apostle Paul. In reading your exposition of the Epistle to the Galatians, that passage came to my hand in which the Apostle Peter is called back from a course of dangerous dissimulation. To find there the defence of falsehood undertaken, whether by you, a man of such weight, or by any author (if it is the writing of another), causes me, I must confess, great sorrow, until at least those things which decide my opinion in the matter are refuted, if indeed they admit of refutation. For it seems to me that most disastrous consequences must follow upon our believing that anything false is found in the sacred books: that is to say, that the men by whom the Scripture has been given to us, and committed to writing, did put down in these books anything false. It is one question whether it may be at any time the duty of a good man to deceive; but it is another question whether it can have been the duty of a writer of Holy Scripture to deceive: nay, it is not another question—it is no question at all. For if you once admit into such a high sanctuary of authority one false statement as made in the way of duty,[21] there will not be left a single sentence of those books which, if appearing to any one difficult in practice or hard to believe, may not by the same fatal rule be explained away, as a statement in which, intentionally, and under a sense of duty, the author declared what was not true.

For if the Apostle Paul did not speak the truth when, finding fault with the Apostle Peter, he said: "If thou, being a Jew, livest after the manner of Gentiles, and not as do the Jews, why compellest thou the Gentiles to live as do the Jews?"—if, indeed, Peter seemed to him to be doing what was right, and if, notwithstanding, he, in order to soothe troublesome opponents, both said and wrote that Peter did what was wrong;[22]—if we say thus, what then shall be our answer when perverse men such as he himself prophetically described arise, forbidding marriage,[23] if they defend themselves by saying that, in all which the same apostle wrote in confirmation of the lawfulness of marriage,[24] he was, on account of men who, through love for their wives, might become troublesome opponents, declaring what was false,—saying these things, forsooth, not because he believed them, but because their opposition might thus be averted? It is unnecessary to quote many parallel examples. For even things which pertain to the praises of God might be represented as piously intended falsehoods, written in order that love for Him might be enkindled in men who were slow of heart; and thus nowhere in the sacred books shall the authority of pure truth stand sure. Do we not observe the great care with which the same apostle commends the truth to us, when he says: "And if Christ be not risen, then is our preaching vain, and your faith is also vain: yea, and we are found false witnesses of God; because we have testified of God that He raised up Christ; whom He raised not up, if so be that the dead rise not."[25] If any one said to him, "Why are you so shocked by this falsehood, when the thing which you have said, even if it were false, tends very greatly to the glory of God?" would he not, abhorring the madness of such a man, with every word and sign which could express his feelings, open clearly the secret depths of his own heart, protesting that to speak well of a falsehood uttered on behalf of God, was a crime not less, perhaps even greater, than to speak ill of the truth concerning Him? We must therefore be careful to secure, in order to our knowledge of the divine Scriptures, the guidance only of such a man as is imbued with a high reverence for the sacred books, and a profound persuasion of their truth, preventing him from flattering himself in any part of them with the hypothesis of a statement being made not because it was true, but because it was expedient, and making him rather pass by what he does not understand, than set up his own feelings above that truth. For, truly, when he pronounces anything to be untrue, he demands that he be believed in preference, and endeavours to shake our confidence in the authority of the divine Scriptures.

For my part, I would devote all the strength which the Lord grants me, to show that every one of those texts which are wont to be quoted in defence of the expediency of falsehood ought to be otherwise understood, in order that everywhere the sure truth of these passages themselves may be consistently maintained. For as statements adduced in evidence must not be false, neither ought they to favour falsehood.

Letter to Jerome
(405)

To Jerome, my lord beloved and honoured in the bowels of Christ, my holy brother and fellow-presbyter, Augustin sends greeting in the Lord.

... For I confess to your Charity that I have learned to yield respect and honour only to the canonical books of Scripture: of these alone do I most firmly believe that the authors were completely free from error. And if in these writings I am perplexed by anything which appears to me opposed to truth, I do not hesitate to suppose that either the MS. is faulty, or the translator has not caught the meaning of what was said, or I myself have failed to understand it. As to all other writings, in reading them, however great the superiority of the authors to myself in sanctity and learning, I do not accept their teaching as true on the mere ground of the opinion being held by them; but only because they have succeeded in convincing my judgment of its truth either by means of these canonical writings themselves, or by arguments addressed to my reason. I believe, my brother, that this is your own opinion as well as mine. I do not need to say that I do not suppose you to wish your books to be read like those of prophets or of apostles, concerning which it would be wrong to doubt that they are free from error. Far be such arrogance from that humble piety and just estimate of yourself which I know you to have, and without which assuredly you would not have said, "Would that I could receive your embrace, and that by converse we might aid each other in learning!"

I have written at great length, which may perhaps have been tedious to you, as you, although approving of the statements now made, do not expect to be addressed as if you were but learning truths which you have been accustomed to teach to others. If, however, there be anything in these statements—not in the style of language in which they are expounded, for I am not much concerned as to mere phrases, but in the substance of the statements—which your erudite judgment condemns, I beseech you to point this out to me in your reply, and do not hesitate to correct my error. For I pity the man who, in view of the unwearied labour and sacred character of your studies, does not on account of them both render to you the honour which you deserve, and give thanks unto our Lord God by whose grace you are what you are. Wherefore, since I ought to be more willing to learn from any teacher the things of which to my disadvantage I am ignorant, than prompt to teach any others what I know, with how much greater reason do I claim the payment of this debt of love from you, by whose learning ecclesiastical literature in the Latin tongue has been, in the Lord's name, and by His help, advanced to an extent which had been previously unattainable. Especially, however, I ask attention to the sentence: "Whosoever shall keep the whole law, and offend in one point, is guilty of all." If you know any better way, my beloved brother, in which it can be explained, I beseech you by the Lord to favour us by communicating to us your exposition.

NOTES

1. I Corinthians 1:24: "[We preach] Christ, the power of God and the wisdom of God, to the Jews and the Greeks." See *The Teacher* 11.38.48–49, where Au-

gustine alludes to "the unchangeable power and everlasting wisdom of God." See also *The Happy Life* 4.34: "We have it on divine authority that the Son of God is nothing other than God's wisdom."

2. "And then cast off the burden of the whole body and return again to Heaven": Augustine uses a similar phrase in 2.9.22.21, emended in *Revisions* 1.1.3.

3. *Confessions* 2.3.5: "When I was sixteen years old my studies were interrupted; I was brought back home from Madauros, the nearby town wherein I had already begun my residence in order to learn about literature and oratory, while funds were gathered for a longer residence at Carthage, a venture for which my father had more enthusiasm than cash." Romanianus apparently began to subsidize Augustine's education at this point, making it possible for him to pursue his studies in Carthage.

4. *Confessions* 4.7.12: "I fled from my home town . . . and from the town of Thagaste I came to Carthage."

5. "I breathe, come to my senses, return to myself": *respiro resipisco redeo ad me*. There is an echo of this passage in *Confessions* 7.10.16: "I was thereby counselled to return to my own self," *et inde admonitus redire ad memet ipsum*.

6. The 'highest measure' of truth is God, as Augustine explains in *The Happy Life* 4.34: "The fact that truth exists happens through some highest measure, from which it proceeds and toward which it turns itself when perfected. Furthermore, no other measure is imposed on this highest measure: if the highest measure is a measure through a highest measure, then it is a measure through itself; the highest measure must be a true measure; therefore, just as truth is begotten from measure, so too measure is known by truth. Therefore, truth has never existed without measure, and measure has never existed without truth. Who is the Son of God? He has been called 'Truth' [John 14:16]. Who is there who doesn't have a father? Who else but the highest measure? Therefore, whoever comes to the highest measure through the truth is happy. In the case of souls, this is the possession of God, *i.e.*, to enjoy God completely."

7. In *Confessions* 6.14.24 Augustine describes a plan to retreat from the world for a life of contemplation, with communal living and communal resources, where the tranquility of all would be safeguarded by the appointment of two 'magistrates' each year to see to all necessary business: "Anything we could raise would be placed in common and we would create a single household treasury, so that in genuine friendship there wouldn't be any private property for one or another person, but what had become one from all the contributions would belong as a whole to each and every person: everything would belong to everyone. . . . Some among us were extremely wealthy, especially Romanianus from our home town, who had come to the [Imperial] court because of serious problems involving his property. He had been a close friend of mine from my youth. He lent great support to this project and carried great weight in it, since his financial resources far outstripped anyone else's." Augustine is likely referring to this plan when he speaks of Romanianus's "holy zeal for this kind of life" and his offer to share his patrimony.

8. These books were neoplatonist treatises: see *Confessions* 7.9.13 (*quosdam platonicorum libros*), where Augustine says that these books were translations from Greek into Latin; *Confessions* 7.20.26 (*lectis platonicorum illis libris*); and *Confessions* 8.2.3 (*quosdam libros platonicorum*), where Augustine says that the

translations were made by Marius Victorinus. In *The Happy Life* 1.4 (Appendix 1), Augustine identifies them as books written by Plotinus (*lectis autem Plotini paucissimis libris*). Plotinian authorship would be consistent with Augustine's characterization of the books as 'platonist,' since Augustine says in *The City of God* 8.12 that the most note-worthy of the modern platonists are Plotinus, Iamblichus, and Porphyry, writing in Greek, and Apuleius, writing in Latin and Greek. In a similar vein, Augustine says that Plato has come to life again in Plotinus: 3.18.41.45–46. Some scholars, however, have argued that Augustine did not mean to exclude Porphyry, and the relative influence of Plotinus and Porphyry on Augustine's thought is a debated topic, as indeed is the question precisely which treatises by Plotinus (or Porphyry) Augustine is referring to here. See O'Donnell [1992], vol. 2, pp. 421–24 for a clear account of the scholarly debates and the secondary literature on these issues.

9. Most likely (Aulus) Cornelius Celsus, the first-century encyclopedist who wrote a six-volume work collecting the opinions of famous philosophers: Augustine refers to him by name in his *Soliloquies* 1.12.21 and describes his work in the prologue to his *Treatise on Heresies*.

10. "Wafted their exotic scents to us": *bonas res Arabicas ubi exhalarunt in nos*, an echo of Plautus, *cepere urbem in Arabia/ plenam bonarum rerum* (*Persa* 4.3.36–37).

11. "And so stumbling, hastening, hesitating I snatched up the Apostle Paul": *itaque titubans properans haesitans arripio apostolum Paulum*, a partial echo of Cicero, *Tusculan Disputations* 1.30.73, *itaque dubitans circumspectans haesitans multa adversa reverens*. For the events described here see *Confessions* 7.21.27 (*arripui . . . apostolum Paulum*) and 8.12.29 (*codicem apostoli [Pauli] . . . arripiui, aperui, et legi*), and the discussion in O'Meara [1992], Ch. 2.

12. "The brambles of fallacious opinions": *inter opinionum fallacium dumeta*, an echo of Cicero, *Academica* 2.35.112, *Stoicorum dumeta*. Augustine uses the same image in *Letter* 1.1 (*umbroasa et spinosa dumeta*), translated in Appendix 3.

13. Augustine writes *prope similiter cognominatae sunt*, which may be read 'are near-perfect synonyms' and 'are closely similar in their (sur)names.'

14. In *Revisions* 1.1.3 (Appendix 11) Augustine calls his allegory of Philosophy and Philocaly "completely inept and tasteless."

15. See *The Teacher* 10.32.82: birdlime and reeds were used to catch birds.

16. Writing to Licentius in 395 (*Letter* 26), Augustine quotes some poetry Licentius had sent to him for his approval, the only sample of Licentius's poetry we have—154 hexameters of dreadful verse. Augustine spends most of the letter castigating Licentius for not being a proper Christian, taking less care for his soul than for the metrical accuracy of his verses.

17. The difficulties given here as (i) and (ii) are the final two obstacles mentioned in 2.1.1.9–14, namely (c) and (d): Augustine has already acknowledged (a), and his remarks throughout 2.1.2 and in 2.2.3.3–5 address (b). In the present passage, in (ii), Augustine is referring to his (correct) suspicion that Romanianus may yet be a Manichaean. See below, where he refers to Manichaeanism as a 'superstition.'

18. Most likely *The True Religion*, dedicated to Romanianus but not completed until 390: see *Letter* 15.1 (Augustine to Romanianus) of that year: "I have written something about the Catholic religion, as far as the Lord found it worth-

while to grant to me; I want to send it to you before my arrival if I don't run out of paper in the meantime." The clear implication is that he has only recently finished *The True Religion*.

19. © *Fathers of the Church* (1948), 1: 220.
20. © *Fathers of the Church* (1948) 1.
21. *Officiosum mendacium*.
22. Gal. ii: 11–14.
23. I Tim. iv: 3.
24. I Cor. vii: 10–16.
25. I Cor. xv: 14, 15.

4

AL GHAZALI
My Life

Abu Hamid Muhammad Al Ghazali (1058–1111) was born in Tus (now in Iran). His autobiography, *The Deliverer from Error*, chronicles a spiritual crisis that led him to abandon a successful and influential position as a professor of law and theology in Baghdad and to become an ascetic and mystic, wandering to religious centers in Mecca, Damascus, Jerusalem, and Hebron. After eleven years of traveling, he returned to teaching and writing, primarily in classical Arabic and occasionally in Persian. *The Quickening of Religious Knowledge*, a comprehensive work on Muslim devotional practices, included treatises on ritual forms of worship, the perils of the soul, and the means of salvation. Although he attacked the program of rationalizing religious beliefs in *The Incoherence of Philosophers*, he was equally critical of the mystical practices of Sufism. He attempted to define an intermediate course, arguing for the subordinate utility of reason in clarifying the deliverances of revelation.

The Rescuer from Error

IN THE NAME OF THE MOST MERCIFUL GOD

Glory be to God, whose praise should precede every writing and every speech! May the blessings of God rest on Mohammed, his Prophet and his Apostle, on his family and companions, by whose guidance error is escaped!

You have asked me, O brother in the faith, to expound the aim and the mysteries of religious sciences, the boundaries and depths of theological doctrines. You wish to know my experiences while disentangling truth lost in the medley of sects and divergencies of thought, and how I have dared to climb from the low levels of traditional belief to the top-most summit of assurance. You desire to learn what I have borrowed from scholastic theology; and why I have been led to reject philosophic systems; and finally, what I have accepted of the doctrine of the Sufis, and the sum total of truth which I have gathered in studying every variety of opinion. Convinced as I am of the sincerity which prompts your inquiries, I proceed to answer them, invoking the help and protection of God.

Know then, my brothers (may God direct you in the right way), that the diversity in beliefs and religions, and the variety of doctrines and sects which divide men, are like a deep ocean strewn with shipwrecks, from which very few escape safe and sound. Each sect, it is true, believes itself in possession of the truth and of salvation, "each party," as the Koran saith, "rejoices in its own creed"; but as the chief of the apostles, whose word is always truthful, has told us, "My people will be divided into more than seventy sects, of whom only one will be saved." This prediction, like all others of the Prophet, must be fulfilled.

From the period of adolescence, that is to say, previous to reaching my twentieth year to the present time when I have passed my fiftieth, I have ventured into this vast ocean; I have fearlessly sounded its depths, and like a resolute diver, I have penetrated its darkness and dared its dangers and abysses. I have interrogated the beliefs of each sect and scrutinized the mysteries of each doctrine, in order to disentangle truth from error and orthodoxy from heresy. I have never met one who maintained the hidden meaning of the Koran without investigating the nature of his belief, nor a partisan of its exterior sense without inquiring into the results of his doctrine. There is no philosopher whose system I have not fathomed, nor theologian the intricacies of whose doctrine I have not followed out.

Sufism has no secrets into which I have not penetrated; the devout adorer of Deity has revealed to me the aim of his austerities; the atheist has not been able to conceal from me the real reason of his unbelief. The thirst for knowledge was innate in me from an early age; it was like a second nature implanted by God, without any will on my part. No sooner had I emerged from boyhood than I had already broken the fetters of tradition and freed myself from hereditary beliefs.

Having noticed how easily the children of Christians become Christians, and the children of Moslems embrace Islam, and remembering also the traditional saying ascribed to the Prophet, "Every child has in him the germ of Islam, then his parents make him Jew, Christian, or Zoroastrian," I was moved by a keen desire to learn what was this innate disposition in the child, the nature of the accidental beliefs imposed on him by the authority of his parents and his masters, and finally the unreasoned convictions which he derives from their instructions.

Struck with the contradictions which I encountered in endeavoring to disentangle the truth and falsehood of these opinions, I was led to make the following reflection: "The search after truth being the aim which I propose to myself, I ought in the first place to ascertain what are the bases of certitude." In the next place I recognized that certitude is the clear and complete knowledge of things, such knowledge as leaves no room for doubt nor possibility of error and conjecture, so that there remains no room in the mind for error to find an entrance. In such a case it is necessary that the mind, fortified against all possibility of going astray, should embrace such a strong conviction that, if, for example, anyone possessing the power of changing a stone into gold, or a stick into a serpent, should seek to shake the bases of this certitude, it would remain firm and immovable. Suppose, for instance, a man should come and say to me, who am firmly convinced that ten is more than three, "No; on the contrary, three is more than ten and, to prove it, I change this rod into a serpent," and supposing that he actually did so, I should remain nonetheless convinced of the falsity of his assertion, and although his miracle might arouse my astonishment, it would not instil any doubt into my belief.

I then understood that all forms of knowledge which do not unite these conditions (imperviousness to doubt, etc.) do not deserve any confidence, because they are not beyond the reach of doubt, and what is not impregnable to doubt can not constitute certitude.

THE SUBTERFUGES OF THE SOPHISTS

I then examined what knowledge I possessed, and discovered that in none of it, with the exception of sense-perceptions and necessary principles, did I enjoy that degree of certitude which I have just described. I then sadly reflected as follows: "We can not hope to find truth except in matters which carry their evidence in themselves—that is to say, in sense-perceptions and necessary principles; we must therefore establish these on a firm basis. Is my absolute confidence in sense-perceptions and on the infallibility of necessary principles analogous to the confidence which I formerly possessed in matters believed on the authority of others? Is it only analogous to the reliance most people place on their organs of vision, or is it rigorously true without admixture of illusion or doubt?"

I then set myself earnestly to examine the notions we derive from the evidence of the senses and from sight in order to see if they could be called in question. The result of a careful examination was that my confidence in them was shaken. Our sight, for instance, perhaps the best practiced of all our senses, observes a shadow, and finding it apparently stationary pronounces it devoid of movement. Observation and experience, however, show subsequently that a shadow moves not suddenly, it is true, but gradually and imperceptibly, so that it is never really motionless.

Again, the eye sees a star and believes it as large as a piece of gold, but mathematical calculations prove, on the contrary, that it is larger than the earth. These notions, and all others which the senses declare true, are subsequently contradicted and convicted of falsity in an irrefragable manner by the verdict of reason.

Then I reflected in myself: "Since I cannot trust to the evidence of my senses, I must rely only on intellectual notions based on fundamental principles, such as the following axioms: 'Ten is more than three. Affirmation and negation cannot coexist together. A thing cannot both be created and also existent from eternity, living and annihilated simultaneously, at once necessary and impossible.' " To this the notions I derived from my senses made the following objections: "Who can guarantee you that you can trust to the evidence of reason more than to that of the senses? You believed in our testimony till it was contradicted by the verdict of reason, otherwise you would have continued to believe it to this day. Well, perhaps, there is above reason another judge who, if he appeared, would convict reason of falsehood, just as reason has confuted us. And if such a third arbiter is not yet apparent, it does not follow that he does not exist."

To this argument I remained some time without reply; a reflection drawn from the phenomena of sleep deepened my doubt. "Do you not see," I reflected, "that while asleep you assume your dreams to be indisputably real? Once awake, you recognize them for what they are—baseless chimeras. Who can assure you, then, of the reliability of notions which, when awake, you derive from the senses and from reason? In relation to your present state they may be real; but it is possible also that you may enter upon another state of being which will bear the same relation to your present state as this does to your condition when asleep. In that new sphere you will recognize that the conclusions of reason are only chimeras."

This possible condition is, perhaps, that which the Sufis call "ecstasy" (hal), that is to say, according to them, a state in which, absorbed in themselves and in the suspension of sense-perceptions, they have visions beyond the reach of intellect. Perhaps also Death is that state, according to that saying of the prince of prophets: "Men are asleep; when they die, they wake." Our present life in relation to the future is perhaps only a dream, and man, once dead, will see things in direct opposition to those now before his eyes; he will then understand that word of the Koran, "Today we have removed the veil from thine eyes and thy sight is keen."

Such thoughts as these threatened to shake my reason, and I sought to find an escape from them. But how? In order to disentangle the knot of this difficulty, a proof was necessary. Now a proof must be based on primary assumptions, and it was precisely these of which I was in doubt. This unhappy state lasted about two months, during which I was, not, it is true, explicitly or by profession, but morally and essentially, a thorough-going skeptic.

God at last deigned to heal me of this mental malady; my mind recovered sanity and equilibrium, the primary assumptions of reason recovered with me all their stringency and force. I owed my deliverance, not to a concatenation of proofs and arguments, but to the light which God caused to penetrate into my heart—the light which illuminates the threshold of all knowledge. To suppose that certitude can be only based upon formal arguments is to limit the boundless mercy of God.

My object in this account is to make others understand with what earnestness we should search for truth, since it leads to results we never dreamed of. Primary assumptions have not got to be sought for, since they are always present to our minds; if we engage in such a search, we only find they persistently elude our grasp. But those who push their investigation beyond ordinary limits are safe from the suspicion of negligence in pursuing what is within their reach.

THE DIFFERENT KINDS OF SEEKERS AFTER TRUTH

When God in the abundance of his mercy had healed me of this malady, I ascertained that those who are engaged in the search for truth may be divided into three groups.

I. Scholastic theologians, who profess to follow theory and speculation.

II. The philosophers, who profess to rely upon formal logic.

III. The Sufis, who call themselves the elect of God and possessors of intuition and knowledge of the truth by means of ecstasy.

"The truth," I said to myself, "must be found among these three classes of men who devote themselves to the search for it. If it escapes them, one must give up all hope of attaining it. Having once surrendered blind belief, it is impossible to return to it, for the essence of such belief is to be unconscious of itself. As soon as this unconsciousness ceases it is shattered like a glass whose fragments cannot be again reunited except by being cast again into the furnace and refashioned." Determined to follow these paths and to search out these systems to the bottom, I proceeded with my investigations in the following order: Scholastic theology; philosophical systems; and, finally Sufism.

THE AIM OF SCHOLASTIC THEOLOGY AND ITS RESULTS

Commencing with theological science, I carefully studied and meditated upon it. I read the writings of the authorities in this department and myself composed several treatises. I recognized that this science, while sufficing its own requirements, could not assist me in arriving at the desired goal. In short, its object is to preserve the purity of orthodox beliefs from all heretical innovation. God, by means of his apostle, has revealed to his creatures a belief which is true as regards their temporal and eternal interests; the chief articles of it are laid down in the Koran and in the traditions. Subsequently, Satan suggested to innovators principles contrary to those of orthodoxy; they listened greedily to his suggestions, and the purity of the faith was menaced. God then raised up a school of theologians and inspired them with the desire to defend orthodoxy by means of a system of proofs adapted to unveil the devices of the heretics and to foil the attacks which they made on the doctrines established by tradition.

Such is the origin of scholastic theology. Many of its adepts, worthy of their high calling, valiantly defended the orthodox faith by proving the reality of prophecy and the falsity of heretical innovations. But, in order to do so, they had to rely upon a certain number of premises, which they accepted in common with their adversaries, and which authority and universal consent or simply the Koran and the traditions obliged them to accept. Their principal effort was to expose the self-contradictions of their opponents and to confute them by means of the premises which they had professed to accept. Now a method of argumentation like this has little value for one who only admits self-evident truths. Scholastic theology could not consequently satisfy me nor heal the malady from which I suffered.

I do not, however, deny that it has had a more satisfactory result for others; on the contrary, I admit that it has; but it is by introducing the principle of authority in matters which are not self-evident. Moreover, my object is to explain my own mental attitude and not to dispute with those who have found healing for themselves. Remedies vary according to the nature of the disease; those which benefit some may injure others.

PHILOSOPHY

I proceeded from the study of scholastic theology to that of philosophy. It was plain to me that, in order to discover where the professors of any branch of knowledge have erred, one must make a profound study of that science; must equal, nay surpass, those who know most of it, so as to penetrate into secrets of it unknown to them. Only by this method can they be completely answered, and of this method I can find no trace in the theologians of Islam. In theological writings devoted to the refutation of philosophy I have only found a tangled mass of phrases full of contradictions and mistakes, and incapable of deceiving, I will not say a critical mind, but even the common crowd. Convinced that to dream of refuting a doctrine before having thoroughly comprehended it was like shooting at an object in the dark, I devoted myself zealously to the study of philosophy; but in books only and without the aid of a teacher. I gave up to this work all the leisure remaining from teaching and from composing works on law. There were then attending my lectures three hundred of the students of Baghdad. With the help of God, these studies, carried on in secret, so to speak, put me in a condition to thoroughly comprehend philosophical systems within a space of two years. I then spent about a year in meditating on these systems after having thoroughly understood them. I turned them over and over in my mind till they were thoroughly clear of all obscurity. In this manner I acquired a complete knowledge of all their subterfuges and subtleties, of what was truth and what was illusion in them.

SUFISM

When I had finished my examination of philosophy I applied myself to the study of Sufism. I saw that in order to understand it thoroughly one must combine theory with practice. The aim which the Sufis set before them is as follows: to free the soul from the tyrannical yoke of the passions, to deliver it from its wrong inclinations and evil instincts, in order that in the purified heart there should only remain room for God and for the invocation of his holy name.

I acquired a thorough knowledge of their researches, and I learned all that was possible to learn of their methods by study and oral teaching. It became clear to me that the last stage could not be reached by mere instruction, but only by transport, ecstasy, and the transformation of the moral being.

In the same way there is a considerable difference between knowing renounce-ment, comprehending its conditions and causes, and practicing renouncement and detachment from the things of this world. I saw that Sufism consists in experiences rather than in definitions, and that what I was lacking belonged to the domain, not of instruction, but of ecstasy and initiation.

The researches to which I had devoted myself, the path which I had traversed in studying religious and speculative branches of knowledge, had given me a firm faith in three things—God, Inspiration, and the Last Judgment. These three fundamental articles of belief were confirmed in me, not merely by definite ar-guments, but by a chain of causes, circumstances, and proofs which it is impos-sible to recount. I saw that one can only hope for salvation by devotion and the conquest of one's passions, a procedure which presupposes renouncement and detachment from this world of falsehood in order to turn toward eternity and meditation on God. Finally, I saw that the only condition of success was to sac-rifice honors and riches and to sever the ties and attachments of worldly life.

Coming seriously to consider my state, I found myself bound down on all sides by these trammels. Examining my actions, the most fair-seeming of which were my lecturing and professorial occupations, I found to my surprise that I was engrossed in several studies of little value, and profitless as regards my salvation. I probed the motives of my teaching and found that, in place of being sincerely consecrated to God, it was only actuated by a vain desire of honor and reputation. I perceived that I was on the edge of an abyss, and that without an immediate conversion I should be doomed to eternal fire. In these reflections I spent a long time. Still a prey to uncertainty, one day I decided to leave Baghdad and to give up everything; the next day I gave up my resolution. I advanced one step and immediately relapsed. In the morning I was sincerely resolved only to occupy myself with the future life; in the evening a crowd of carnal thoughts assailed and dispersed my resolutions. On the one side the world kept me bound to my post in the chains of covetousness, on the other side the voice of religion cried to me, "Up! Up! Thy life is nearing its end, and thou hast a long journey to make. All thy pretended knowledge is naught but falsehood and fantasy. If thou dost not think now of thy salvation, when wilt thou think of it? If thou dost not break thy chains today, when wilt thou break them?" Then my resolve was strength-ened, I wished to give up all and flee; but the Tempter, returning to the attack, said, "You are suffering from a transitory feeling; don't give way to it, for it will soon pass. If you obey it, if you give up this fine position, this honorable post exempt from trouble and rivalry, this seat of authority safe from attack, you will regret it later on without being able to recover it."

Thus I remained, torn asunder by the opposite forces of earthly passions and religious aspirations, for about six months from the month Rajab of the year A.D. 1096. At the close of them my will yielded and I gave myself up to destiny. God caused an impediment to chain my tongue and prevented me from lecturing. Vainly I desired, in the interest of my pupils, to go on with my teaching, but my mouth became dumb. The silence to which I was condemned cast me into a violent despair; my stomach became weak; I lost all appetite; I could neither swallow a morsel of bread nor drink a drop of water.

The enfeeblement of my physical powers was such that the doctors, despairing of saving me, said, "The mischief is in the heart, and has communicated itself to the whole organism; there is no hope unless the cause of his grievous sadness be arrested."

Finally, conscious of my weakness and the prostration of my soul, I took refuge in God as a man at the end of himself and without resources. "He who hears the wretched when they cry" (Koran, xxvii. 63) deigned to hear me; He made easy to me the sacrifice of honors, wealth, and family. I gave out publicly that I intended to make the pilgrimage to Mecca, while I secretly resolved to go to Syria, not wishing that the Caliph (may God magnify him) or my friends should know my intention of settling in that country. I made all kinds of clever excuses for leaving Baghdad with the fixed intention of not returning thither. The Imams of Irak criticized me with one accord. Not one of them could admit that this sacrifice had a religious motive, because they considered my position as the highest attainable in the religious community. "Behold how far their knowledge goes!" (Koran. liii. 31). All kinds of explanations of my conduct were forthcoming. Those who were outside the limits of Iraq attributed it to the fear with which the government inspired me. Those who were on the spot and saw how the authorities wished to detain me, their displeasure at my resolution and my refusal of their request, said to themselves, "It is a calamity which one can only impute to a fate which has befallen the Faithful and Learning!"

At last I left Baghdad, giving up all my fortune. Only, as lands and property in Iraq can afford an endowment for pious purposes, I obtained a legal authorization to preserve as much as was necessary for my support and that of my children; for there is surely nothing more lawful in the world than that a learned man should provide sufficiently to support his family. I then betook myself to Syria, where I remained for two years, which I devoted to retirement, meditation, and devout exercises. I only thought of self-improvement and discipline and of purification of the heart by prayer in going through the forms of devotion which the Sufis had taught me. I used to live a solitary life in the Mosque of Damascus, and was in the habit of spending my days on the minaret after closing the door behind me.

From thence I proceeded to Jerusalem, and every day secluded myself in the Sanctuary of the Rock, [in the Mosque of Omar] After that I felt a desire to accomplish the pilgrimage, and to receive a full effusion of grace by visiting Mecca, Medina, and the tomb of the Prophet. After visiting the shrine of the Friend of God (Abraham), I went to the Hedjaz. Finally, the longings of my heart and the prayers of my children brought me back to my country, although I was so firmly resolved at first never to revisit it. At any rate I meant, if I did return, to live there solitary and in religious meditation; but events, family cares, and vicissitudes of life changed my resolutions and troubled my meditative calm. However irregular the intervals which I could give to devotional ecstasy, my confidence in it did not diminish; and the more I was diverted by hindrances, the more steadfastly I returned to it.

Ten years passed in this manner. During my successive periods of meditation there were revealed to me things impossible to recount. All that I shall say for the edification of the reader is this: I learned from a sure source that the Sufis are the true pioneers on the path of God; that there is nothing more beautiful than their life, nor more praiseworthy than their rule of conduct, nor purer than their morality. The intelligence of thinkers, the wisdom of philosophers, the knowledge of the most learned doctors of the law would in vain combine their efforts in order to modify or improve their doctrine and morals; it would be impossible. With the Sufis, repose and movement, exterior or interior, are illumined with the light which proceeds from the Central Radiance of Inspiration.

And what other light could shine on the face of the earth? In a word, what can one criticize in them? To purge the heart of all that does not belong to God is the first step in their cathartic method. The drawing up of the heart by prayer is the keystone of it, as the cry *"Allahu Akbar"* (God is great) is the keystone of prayer, and the last stage is the being lost in God. I say the last stage, with reference to what may be reached by an effort of will; but, to tell the truth, it is only the first stage in the life of contemplation, the vestibule by which the initiated are privileged to enter.

From the time that they set out on this path, revelations commence for them. They come to see in the waking state angels and souls of prophets; they hear their voices and wise counsels. By means of this contemplation of heavenly forms and images they rise by degrees to heights which human language cannot reach, which one cannot even indicate without falling into great and inevitable errors.

This state, then, can be revealed to the initiated in ecstasy, and to him who is incapable of ecstasy, by obedience and attention, on condition that he frequents the society of Sufis till he arrives, so to speak, at an imitative initiation. Such is the faith which one can obtain by remaining among them, and intercourse with them is never painful.

But even when we are deprived of the advantage of their society, we can comprehend the possibility of this state (revelation by means of ecstasy) by a chain of manifest proofs. We have explained this in the treatise entitled "Marvels of the Heart," which forms part of our work, "The Revival of the Religious Sciences." The certitude derived from proofs is called "knowledge"; passing into the state we describe is called "transport"; believing the experience of others and oral transmission is "faith." Such are the three degrees of knowledge, as it is written, "The Lord will raise to different ranks those among you who have believed and those who have received knowledge from him" (Koran, lviii. 12).

But behind those who believe comes a crowd of ignorant people who deny the reality of Sufism, hear discourses on it with incredulous irony, and treat as charlatans those who profess it. To this ignorant crowd the verse applies: "There are those among them who come to listen to thee, and when they leave thee, ask of those who have received knowledge, 'What has he just said?' These are they whose hearts God has sealed up with blindness and who only follow their passions."

Among the number of convictions which I owe to the practice of the Sufi rule is the knowledge of the true nature of inspiration.

To prove the possibility of inspiration is to prove that it belongs to a category of branches of knowledge which cannot be attained by reason. It is the same with medical science and astronomy. He who studies them is obliged to recognize that they are derived solely from the revelation and special grace of God. Some astronomical phenomena only occur once in a thousand years; how then can we know them by experience?

We may say the same of inspiration, which is one of the branches of intuitional knowledge. Further, the perception of things which are beyond the attainment of reason is only one of the features peculiar to inspiration, which possesses a great number of others. The characteristic which we have mentioned is only, as it were, a drop of water in the ocean, and we have mentioned it because people experience what is analogous to it in dreams and in the sciences of medicine and astronomy. These branches of knowledge belong to the domain of prophetic miracles, and reason cannot attain to them.

We now come to deal with doubts relative to the inspiration of a particular prophet. We shall not arrive at certitude on this point except by ascertaining, either by ocular evidence or by reliable tradition, the facts relating to that prophet. When we have ascertained the real nature of inspiration and proceed to the serious study of the Koran and the traditions, we shall then know certainly that Mohammed is the greatest of prophets. After that we should fortify our conviction by verifying the truth of his preaching and the salutary effect which it has upon the soul. We should verify in experience the truth of sentences such as the following: "He who makes his conduct accord with his knowledge receives from God more knowledge"; or this, "God delivers to the oppressor him who favors injustice"; or again, "Whosoever when rising in the morning has only one anxiety (to please God), God will preserve him from all anxiety in this world and the next."

When we have verified these sayings in experience thousands of times, we shall be in possession of a certitude on which doubt can obtain no hold. Such is the path we must traverse in order to realize the truth of inspiration.

[But] the supernatural should be only one of the constituents which go to form our belief, without our placing too much reliance on this or that detail. We should rather resemble a person who, learning a fact from a group of people, cannot point to this or that particular man as his informant, and who, not distinguishing between them, cannot explain precisely how his conviction regarding the fact has been formed.

Such are the characteristics of scientific certitude. As to the transport which permits men to see the truth and, so to speak, to handle it, it is only known to the Sufis. What I have just said regarding the true nature of inspiration is sufficient for the aim which I have proposed to myself.

5

ABELARD AND HELOISE
Calamities and Credos

Peter Abelard (1079–1142), educated to follow in his father's footsteps as an ad-viser to the Count of Brittany, would have studied the trivium (Latin grammar and literature, and dialectical logic), the quadrivium (geometry, arithmetic, as-tronomy, and music), and theology. He showed little interest in the sciences but a great talent in logic. After traveling from school to school, he distinguished himself as a master of the techniques of *disputatio*. In 1113, Abelard began teach-ing in Paris. Tutor to Heloise (?1100/1–1163/4), the seventeen-year-old niece of Canon Fulbert, he began a notorious and passionate love affair that ended when he was castrated at the instigation of Fulbert. Abelard's *Historia Calamitatum* (1132) tells the story of his affair with Heloise, including the birth of their child and the conspiracies against him. He retreated to the Abbey of St. Denis, but shortly quarreled with the monks there. After a period as abbot of the monas-tery of St. Gildas de Rhys, he established the Oratory of the Paraclete in 1125. That Foundation became a powerful and influential convent, to which Heloise retired. As abbess for thirty years, she made it a powerful and influential center of learning. Abelard returned to lecture in Paris in 1136, where, despite his com-bative ways, he attracted many students. His version of metaphysical concep-tualism was intended to bypass both the extreme realism of William of Cham-peaux and the strong nominalism of Jean Roscelin. Influenced by Augustine, Abelard's ethics focused on the direction of an agent's will rather than on the character of an action or its consequences. Even a malevolent intention might be pardonable if the will did not assent to the intention. (*Know Thyself; A Dia-logue between a Christian, a Philosopher, and a Jew*). A dialectical figure, defining his position by opposition, Abelard withstood the burning of his "On the Divine Unity and Trinity" at an ecclesiastical council at Soissons in 1121. He attacked the powerful Bernard of Clairvaux, who instituted Abelard's condemnation at the Council of Sens in 1141. Abelard spent his last years at the Abbey of Cluny, where he died in 1142. Peter the Venerable brought Abelard's body to the convent of the Paraclete in 1144. Heloise was buried with him at her death (1163/4).

In the midst of a turbulent life, Abelard was extremely prolific, writing in a variety of genres and styles. Besides his early autobiography, his disputation *Sic et Non*, his commentaries on Aristotle's *Categories* and on Porphyry's *Isagoge*, his biblical commentary on *Paul's Letter to the Romans*, and several works on Christian theology, there are hymns, bawdy songs, and a vast correspondence.

Heloise to Abelard

To her master, or rather her father, husband, or rather brother; his handmaid, or rather his daughter, wife, or rather sister; to Abelard, Heloise.

Not long ago, my beloved, by chance someone brought me the letter of consola-tion you had sent to a friend. I saw at once from the superscription that it was yours, and was all the more eager to read it since the writer is so dear to my heart. I hoped for renewal of strength, at least from the writer's words which would picture for me the reality I have lost. But nearly every line of this letter was filled, I remember, with gall and wormwood, as it told the pitiful story of our entry into religion and the cross of unending suffering which you, my only love, continue to bear.

In that letter you did indeed carry out the promise you made your friend at the beginning, that he would think his own troubles insignificant or nothing, in comparison with your own. First you revealed the persecution you suffered from your teachers, then the supreme treachery of the mutilation of your person, and then described the abominable jealousy and violent attacks of your fellow-students. You did not gloss over what at their instigation was done to your distinguished theological work or what amounted to a prison sentence passed on yourself. Then you went on to the plotting against you by your abbot and false brethren, the serious slanders spread against you and the scandal stirred up among many people because you had acted contrary to custom in naming your oratory after the Paraclete. You went on to the incessant, intolerable persecutions which you still endure at the hands of that cruel tyrant and the evil monks you call your sons, and so brought your sad story to an end.

No one, I think, could read or hear it dry-eyed; my own sorrows are renewed by the detail in which you have told it, and redoubled because you say your perils are still increasing. All of us here are driven to despair of your life, and every day we await in fear and trembling the final word of your death. And so in the name of Christ, who is still giving you some protection for his service, we beseech you to write as often as you think fit to us who are his handmaids and yours, with news of the perils in which you are still storm-tossed. We are all that are left you, so at least you should let us share your sorrow or your joy.

It is always some consolation in sorrow to feel that it is shared, and any burden laid on several is carried more lightly or removed. And if this storm has quietened down for a while, you must be all the more prompt to send us a letter which will be the more gladly received. But whatever you write about will bring us no small relief in the mere proof that you have us in mind. Letters from absent friends are welcome indeed.

You know, beloved, as the whole world knows, how much I have lost in you, how at one wretched stroke of fortune that supreme act of flagrant treachery robbed me of my very self in robbing me of you; and how my sorrow for my loss is nothing compared with what I feel for the manner in which I lost you. Surely the greater the cause for grief the greater the need for the help of consolation, and this no one can bring but you; you are the sole cause of my sorrow, and you alone can grant me the grace of consolation. You alone have the power to make me sad, to bring me happiness or comfort; you alone have so great a debt to repay me, particularly now when I have carried out all your orders so implicitly that when I was powerless to oppose you in anything, I found strength at your command to destroy myself. I did more, strange to say—my love rose to such heights of madness that it robbed itself of what it most desired beyond hope of recovery, when immediately at your bidding I changed my clothing along with my mind, in order to prove you the sole possessor of my body and my will alike. God knows I never sought anything in you except yourself; I wanted simply you, nothing of yours. I looked for no marriage-bond, no marriage portion, and it was not my own pleasures and wishes I sought to gratify, as you well know, but yours.

The name of wife may seem more sacred or more binding, but sweeter for me will always be the word mistress, or, if you will permit me, that of concubine or whore. I believed that the more I humbled myself on your account, the more gratitude I should win from you, and also the less damage I should do to the brightness of your reputation.

For a man's worth does not rest on his wealth or power; these depend on fortune, but worth on his merits. And a woman should realize that if she marries a rich man more readily than a poor one, and desires her husband more for his possessions than for himself, she is offering herself for sale. Certainly any woman who comes to marry through desires of this kind deserves wages, not gratitude, for clearly her mind is on the man's property, not himself, and she would be ready to prostitute herself to a richer man, if she could.

These are saintly words which are more than philosophic; indeed, they deserve the name of wisdom, not philosophy. It is a holy error and a blessed delusion between man and wife, when perfect love can keep the ties of marriage unbroken not so much through bodily continence as chastity of spirit. But what error permitted other women, plain truth permitted me.

What king or philosopher could match your fame? What district, town or village did not long to see you? When you appeared in public, who did not hurry to catch a glimpse of you, or crane his neck and strain his eyes to follow your departure? Every wife, every young girl desired you in absence and was on fire in your presence; queens and great ladies envied me my joys and my bed.

You had besides, I admit, two special gifts whereby to win at once the heart of any woman—your gifts for composing verse and song, in which we know other philosophers have rarely been successful. This was for you no more than a diversion, a recreation from the labours of your philosophic work, but you left many love-songs and verses which won wide popularity for the charm of their words and tunes and kept your name continually on everyone's lips. The beauty of the airs ensured that even the unlettered did not forget you; more than anything this made women sigh for love of you. And as most of these songs told of our love, they soon made me widely known and roused the envy of many women against me. For your manhood was adorned by every grace of mind and body, and among the women who envied me then, could there be one now who does not feel compelled by my misfortune to sympathize with my loss of such joys? Who is there who was once my enemy, whether man or woman, who is not moved now by the compassion which is my due? Wholly guilty though I am, I am also, as you know, wholly innocent. It is not the deed but the intention of the doer which makes the crime, and justice should weigh not what was done but the spirit in which it is done. What my intention towards you has always been, you alone who have known it can judge. I submit all to your scrutiny, yield to your testimony in all things.

Tell me one thing, if you can. Why, after our entry into religion, which was your decision alone, have I been so neglected and forgotten by you that I have neither a word from you when you are here to give me strength nor the consolation of a letter in absence? Tell me, I say, if you can—or I will tell you what I think and indeed the world suspects. It was desire, not affection which bound you to me, the flame of lust rather than love. So when the end came to what you desired, any show of feeling you used to make went with it. This is not merely my own opinion, beloved, it is everyone's. There is nothing personal or private about it; it is the general view which is widely held. I only wish that it *were* mine alone, and that the love you professed could find someone to defend it and so comfort me in my grief for a while. I wish I could think of some explanation which would excuse you and somehow cover up the way you hold me cheap.

I beg you then to listen to what I ask—you will see that it is a small favour which you can easily grant. While I am denied your presence, give me at least through your words—of which you have enough and to spare—some sweet semblance of yourself. It is no use my hoping for generosity in deeds if you are grudging in words. Up to now I had thought I deserved much of you, seeing that I carried out everything for your sake and continue up to the present moment in complete obedience to you. It was not any sense of vocation which brought me as a young girl to accept the austerities of the cloister, but your bidding alone, and if I deserve no gratitude from you, you may judge for yourself how my labours are in vain. I can expect no reward for this from God, for it is certain that I have done nothing as yet for love of him. When you hurried towards God I followed you, indeed, I went first to take the veil. Your lack of trust in me over this one thing, I confess, overwhelmed me with grief and shame. I would have had no hesitation, God knows, in following you or going ahead at your bidding to the flames of Hell. My heart was not in me but with you, and now, even more, if it is not with you it is nowhere; truly, without you it cannot exist. See that it fares well with you, I beg, as it will if it finds you kind, if you give grace in return for grace, small for great, words for deeds. If only your love had less confidence in me, my dear, so that you would be more concerned on my behalf! But as it is, the more I have made you feel secure in me, the more I have to bear with your neglect.

I have denied myself every pleasure in obedience to your will, kept nothing for myself except to prove that now, even more, I am yours. Consider then your injustice, if when I deserve more you give me less, or rather, nothing at all, especially when it is a small thing I ask of you and one you could so easily grant. And so, in the name of God to whom you have dedicated yourself, I beg you to restore your presence to me in the way you can—by writing me some word of comfort, so that in this at least I may find increased strength and readiness to serve God. When in the past you sought me out for sinful pleasures your letters came to me thick and fast, and your many songs put your Heloise on everyone's lips, so that every street and house echoed with my name. Is it not far better now to summon me to God than it was then to satisfy our lust? I beg you, think what you owe me, give ear to my pleas, and I will finish a long letter with a brief ending: farewell, my only love.

Abelard to Heloise

To Heloise, his dearly beloved sister in Christ, Abelard her brother in Christ.

If since our conversion from the world to God I have not yet written you any word of comfort or advice, it must not be attributed to indifference on my part but to your own good sense, in which I have always had such confidence that I did not think anything was needed; God's grace has bestowed on you all essentials to enable you to instruct the erring, comfort the weak and encourage the fainthearted, both by word and example, as, indeed, you have been doing since you first held the office of prioress under your abbess. So if you still watch over your daughters as carefully as you did previously over your sisters, it is sufficient to make me believe that any teaching or exhortation from me would now be wholly superfluous. If, on the other hand, in your humility you think differently, and you feel that you have need of my instruction and writings in matters pertaining to God, write to me what you want, so that I may answer as God permits me. Meanwhile thanks be to God who has filled all your hearts with anxiety for my desperate, unceasing perils, and made you share in my affliction; may divine mercy protect me through the support of your prayers and quickly crush Satan beneath our feet. To this end in particular, I hasten to send the psalter you earnestly begged from me, my sister once dear in the world and now dearest in Christ, so that you may offer a perpetual sacrifice of prayers to the Lord for our many great aberrations, and for the dangers which daily threaten me.

Abelard to Heloise: To the Bride of Christ, Christ's Servant

I come at last to what I have called your old perpetual complaint, in which you presume to blame God for the manner of our entry into religion instead of wishing to glorify him as you justly should. I had thought that this bitterness of heart at what was so clearly an act of divine mercy had long since disappeared. The more dangerous such bitterness is to you in wearing out body and soul alike, the more pitiful it is and distressing to me. If you are anxious to please me in everything, as you claim, and in this at least would end my torment, or even give me the greatest pleasure, you must rid yourself of it. If it persists you can neither please me nor attain bliss with me. Can you bear me to come to this without you—I whom you declare yourself ready to follow to the very fires of hell? Seek piety in this at least, lest you cut yourself off from me who am hastening, you believe, towards God; be the readier to do so because the goal we must come to will be blessed, and our companionship the more welcome for being happier. Remember what you have said, recall what you have written, namely that in the manner of our conversion, when God seems to have been more my adversary, he has clearly shown himself kinder. For this reason at least you must accept his will, that it is most salutary for me, and for you too, if your transports of grief will see reason. You should not grieve because you are the cause of so great a good, for which you must not doubt you were specially created by God. Nor should you weep because I have to bear this, except when our blessings through the martyrs in their sufferings and the Lord's death sadden you. If it had befallen me justly, would you find it easier to bear? Would it distress you less? In fact if it had been so, the result would have been greater disgrace for me and more credit to my enemies, since justice would have won them approval while my guilt would have brought me into contempt. And no one would be stirred by pity for me to condemn what was done.

However, it may relieve the bitterness of your grief if I prove that this came upon us justly, as well as to our advantage, and that God's punishment was more properly directed against us when we were married than when we were living in sin. After our marriage, when you were living in the cloister with the nuns at Argenteuil and I came one day to visit you privately, you know what my uncontrollable desire did with you there, actually in a corner of the refectory, since we had nowhere else to go. I repeat, you know how shamelessly we behaved on that occasion in so hallowed a place, dedicated to the most holy Virgin. Even if our other shameful behaviour was ended, this alone would deserve far heavier punishment. Need I recall our previous fornication and the wanton impurities which preceded our marriage, or my supreme act of betrayal, when I deceived your uncle about you so disgracefully, at a time when I was continuously living with him in his own house? Who would not judge me justly betrayed by the man whom I had first shamelessly betrayed? Do you think that the momentary pain of that wound is sufficient punishment for such crimes? Or rather, that so great an advantage was fitting for such great wickedness? What wound do you suppose would satisfy God's justice for the profanation such as I described of a place so sacred to his own Mother? Surely, unless I am much mistaken, not that wound which was wholly beneficial was intended as a punishment for this, but rather the daily unending torment I now endure.

You know too how when you were pregnant and I took you to my own country you disguised yourself in the sacred habit of a nun, a pretence which was an irreverent mockery of the religion you now profess. Consider, then, how fittingly divine justice, or rather, divine grace brought you against your will to the religion which you did not hesitate to mock, so that you should willingly expiate your profanation in the same habit, and the truth of reality should remedy the lie of your pretence and correct your falsity. And if you would allow consideration of our advantage to be an element in divine justice, you would be able to call what God did to us then an act not of justice, but of grace.

See then, my beloved, see how with the dragnets of his mercy the Lord has fished us up from the depth of this dangerous sea, and from the abyss of what a Charybdis he has saved our shipwrecked selves, although we were unwilling, so that each of us may justly break out in that cry: 'The Lord takes thought for me'. Think and think again of the great perils in which we were and from which the Lord rescued us; tell always with the deepest gratitude how much the Lord has done for our souls. Comfort by our example any unrighteous who despair of God's goodness, so that all may know what may be done for those who ask with prayer, when such benefits are granted sinners even against their will. Consider the magnanimous design of God's mercy for us, the compassion with which the Lord directed his judgement towards our chastisement, the wisdom whereby he made use of evil itself and mercifully set aside our impiety, so that by a wholly justified wound in a single part of my body he might heal two souls. Compare our danger and manner of deliverance, compare the sickness and the medicine. Examine the cause, our deserts, and marvel at the effect, his pity.

You know the depths of shame to which my unbridled lust had consigned our bodies, until no reverence for decency or for God even during the days of Our Lord's Passion, or of the greater sacraments could keep me from wallowing in this mire. Even when you were unwilling, resisted to the utmost of your power and tried to dissuade me, as yours was the weaker nature I often forced you to consent with threats and blows. So intense were the fires of lust which bound me to you that I set those wretched, obscene pleasures, which we blush even to name, above God as above myself; nor would it seem that divine mercy could have taken action except by forbidding me these pleasures altogether, without future hope. And so it was wholly just and merciful, although by means of the supreme treachery of your uncle, for me to be reduced in that part of my body which was the seat of lust and sole reason for those desires, so that I could increase in many ways; in order that this member should justly be punished for all its wrongdoing in us, expiate in suffering the sins committed for its amusement, and cut me off from the slough of filth in which I had been wholly immersed in mind as in body. Only thus could I become more fit to approach the holy altars, now that no contagion of carnal impurity would ever again call me from them. How mercifully did he want me to suffer so much only in that member, the privation of which would also further the salvation of my soul without defiling my body nor preventing any performance of my duties! Indeed, it would make me readier to perform whatever can be honourably done by setting me wholly free from the heavy yoke of carnal desire.

Come too, my inseparable companion, and join me in thanksgiving, you who were made my partner both in guilt and in grace. For the Lord is not unmindful also of your own salvation, indeed, he has you much in mind, for by a kind of holy presage of his name he marked you out to be especially his when he named you Heloise, after his own name, Elohim. In his mercy, I say, he intended to provide for two people in one, the two whom the devil sought to destroy in one; since a short while before this happening he had bound us together by the indissoluble bond of the marriage sacrament. At the time I desired to keep you whom I loved beyond measure for myself alone, but he was already planning to use this opportunity for our joint conversion to himself. Had you not been previously joined to me in wedlock, you might easily have clung to the world when I withdrew from it, either at the suggestion of your relatives or in enjoyment of carnal delights. See then, how greatly the Lord was concerned for us, as if he were reserving us for some great ends, and was indignant or grieved because our knowledge of letters, the talents which he had entrusted to us, were not being used to glorify his name.

Abelard's Confession of Faith

Heloise my sister, once dear to me in the world, now dearest to me in Christ, logic has made me hated by the world. For the perverted, who seek to pervert and whose wisdom is only for destruction, say that I am supreme as a logician, but am found wanting in my understanding of Paul. They proclaim the brilliance of my intellect but detract from the purity of my Christian faith. As I see it, they have reached this judgement by conjecture rather than weight of evidence. I do not wish to be a philosopher if it means conflicting with Paul, nor to be an Aristotle if it cuts me off from Christ. For there is no other name under heaven whereby I must be saved. I adore Christ who sits on the right hand of the Father. I embrace in the arms of faith him who acts divinely in the glorious flesh of a virgin which he assumed from the Paraclete. And so, to banish fearful anxiety and all uncertainties from the heart within your breast, receive assurance from me, that I have founded my conscience on that rock on which Christ built his Church. What is written on the rock I will testify briefly.

I believe in the Father, the Son and the Holy Spirit; the true God who is one in nature; who comprises the Trinity of persons in such a way as always to preserve Unity in substance. I believe the Son to be co-equal with the Father in all things, in eternity, power, will and operation. I do not hold with Arius, who is driven by perverted intellect or led astray by demoniac influence to introduce grades into the Trinity, laying down that the Father is greater and the Son less great, forgetting the injunction of the Law, 'You shall not mount up to my altar by steps.' He mounts up to the altar of God by steps who assigns first and second place in the Trinity. I bear witness that in everything the Holy Spirit is consubstantial and co-equal with the Father and the Son, and is he who, as my books often declare, is known by the name of Goodness. I condemn Sabellius, who, in holding that the person of the Father is the same as that of the Son, asserts that the Passion was suffered by the Father—hence his followers are called *Patripassiani*.

I believe that the Son of God became the Son of Man in such a way that one person is of and in two natures; that after he had completed the mission he had undertaken in becoming man he suffered and died and rose again, and ascended to heaven whence he will come to judge the living and the dead. I also declare that in baptism all offenses are remitted, and that we need grace whereby we may begin on good and persevere in it, and that having lapsed we may be restored through penitence. But what need have I to speak of the resurrection of the body? I would pride myself on being a Christian in vain if I did not believe that I would live again.

This then is the faith on which I rest, from which I draw my strength in hope. Safely anchored on it, I do not fear the barking of Scylla, I laugh at the whirlpool of Charybdis, and have no dread of the Sirens' deadly songs. The storm may rage but I am unshaken, though the winds may blow they leave me unmoved; for the rock of my foundation stands firm.

6

MOSES MAIMONIDES
Why I Write...and How I Write

Maimonides (Moses ben Maimon, 1135–1204) was born into an eminent Spanish rabbinical family. When Cordova was conquered by an Islamic sect, the family first fled to Morocco and then, in 1165, to Egypt. While remaining the head of the Jewish community in Cairo, Maimonides became a physician and eventually the personal physician of the Vizier of Saladin. Among his ten treatises of medicine, his *Regimen of Health* is extended discussion of preventive medicine. He wrote texts on logic but also published commentaries on the Talmud (*Commentary on the Mishnah*), on the 613 biblical commandments (*The Book of Commandments*), and a codification of Jewish law (the *Mishneh Torah*). Like his other treatises, his major philosophic work, *The Guide for the Perplexed* (c. 1190), was originally written in Arabic but soon translated into Hebrew and then Latin. Although he knew Aristotle only indirectly through his reading of Al-Farabi and Avicenna, Maimonides used Aristotelian philosophy to attack astrology and naive literal readings of biblical texts, many of which he interpreted as anthropomorphic allegorical expressions of a more profound, systematically developed metaphysical and theological system. The *Guide* treats a wide range of topics: the creation, the divine attributes, Providence and responsibility, the independent rationality of Jewish law. The work exhibits and articulates an elaborate theory of language, which licenses polysemous writing directed to different audiences with different levels of understanding.

A Teacher to a Student

The Guide for the Perplexed, Dedication
In the name of the Lord, God of the World

My honored pupil *Rabbi Joseph, may the Rock guard you, son of Rabbi Judah, may his repose be in Paradise.* When you came to me, having conceived the intention of journeying from the country farthest away in order to read texts under my guidance, I had a high opinion of you because of your strong desire for inquiry and because of what I had observed in your poems of your powerful longing for speculative matters. This was the case since your letters and compositions in rhymed prose came to me from Alexandria, before your grasp was put to the test. I said however: perhaps his longing is stronger than his grasp. When thereupon you read under my guidance texts dealing with the science of astronomy and prior to that texts dealing with mathematics, which is necessary as an introduction to astronomy, my joy in you increased because of the excellence of your mind and the quickness of your grasp. I saw that your longing for mathematics was great, and hence I let you train yourself in that science, knowing where you would end. When thereupon you read under my guidance texts dealing with the art of logic, my hopes fastened upon you, and I saw that you are one worthy to have the secrets of the prophetic books revealed to you so that you would consider in them that which perfect men ought to consider.

Thereupon I began to let you see certain flashes and to give you certain indications. Then I saw that you demanded of me additional knowledge and asked me to make clear to you certain things pertaining to divine matters, to inform you of the intentions of the Mutakallimūn in this respect, and to let you know whether their methods were demonstrative and, if not, to what art they belonged. As I also saw, you had already acquired some smattering of this subject from people other than myself; you were perplexed, as stupefaction had come over you; your noble soul demanded of you to *find out acceptable words*. Yet I did not cease dissuading you from this and enjoining upon you to approach matters in an orderly manner. My purpose in this was that the truth should be established in your mind according to the proper methods and that certainty should not come to you by accident. Whenever during your association with me a [biblical] *verse* or some text of the *Sages* was mentioned in which there was a pointer to some strange notion, I did not refrain from explaining it to you. Then when God decreed our separation and you betook yourself elsewhere, these meetings aroused in me a resolution that had slackened. Your absence moved me to compose this Treatise, which I have composed for you and for those like you, however few they are. I have set it down in dispersed chapters. All of them that are written down will reach you where you are, one after the other. Be in good health.

How to Read
(The Guide for the Perplexed, Introduction, Part I)

> Cause me to know the way wherein I should walk,
> For unto Thee have I lifted my soul.

> Unto you, O men, I call,
> And my voice is to the sons of men.

> Incline thine ear, and hear the words of the wise,
> And apply thy heart unto my knowledge.

The first purpose of this Treatise is to explain the meanings of certain terms occurring in books of prophecy. Some of these terms are equivocal; hence the ignorant attribute to them only one or some of the meanings in which the term in question is used. Others are derivative terms; hence they attribute to them only the original meaning from which the other meaning is derived. Others are amphibolous terms, so that at times they are believed to be univocal and at other times equivocal. It is not the purpose of this Treatise to make its totality understandable to the vulgar or to beginners in speculation, nor to teach those who have not engaged in any study other than the science of the Law—I mean the legalistic study of the Law. For the purpose of this Treatise and of all those like it is the science of Law in its true sense. Or rather its purpose is to give indications to a religious man for whom the validity of our Law has become established in his soul and has become actual in his belief—such a man being perfect in his religion and character, and having studied the sciences of the philosophers and come to know what they signify. The human intellect having drawn him on and led him to dwell within its province, he must have felt distressed by the externals of the Law and by the meanings of the above-mentioned equivocal, derivative, or amphibolous terms, as he continued to understand them by himself or was made to understand them by others. Hence he would remain in a state of perplexity and confusion as to whether he should follow his intellect, renounce what he knew concerning the terms in question, and consequently consider that he has renounced the foundations of the Law. Or he should hold fast to his understanding of these terms and not let himself be drawn on together with his intellect, rather turning his back on it and moving away from it, while at the same time perceiving that he had brought loss to himself and harm to his religion. He would be left with those imaginary beliefs to which he owes his fear and difficulty and would not cease to suffer from heartache and great perplexity.

This Treatise also has a second purpose: namely, the explanation of very obscure parables occurring in the books of the prophets, but not explicitly identified there as such. Hence an ignorant or heedless individual might think that they possess only an external sense, but no internal one. However, even when one who truly possesses knowledge considers these parables and interprets them according to their external meaning, he too is overtaken by great perplexity. But if we explain these parables to him or if we draw his attention to their being parables, he will take the right road and be delivered from this perplexity. That is why I have called this Treatise "The Guide for the Perplexed."

I do not say that this Treatise will remove all difficulties for those who understand it. I do, however, say that it will remove most of the difficulties, and those of the greatest moment. A sensible man thus should not demand of me or hope that when we mention a subject, we shall make a complete exposition of it, or that when we engage in the explanation of the meaning of one of the parables, we shall set forth exhaustively all that is expressed in that parable. An intelligent man would be unable to do so even by speaking directly to an interlocutor. How then could he put it down in writing without becoming a butt for every ignoramus who, thinking that he has the necessary knowledge, would let fly at him the shafts of his ignorance? And even those are not set down in order or arranged in coherent fashion in this Treatise, but rather are scattered and entangled with other subjects that are to be clarified. For my purpose is that the truths be glimpsed and then again be concealed, so as not to oppose that divine purpose which one cannot possibly oppose and which has concealed from the vulgar among the people those truths especially requisite for His apprehension. As He has said: *The secret of the Lord is with them that fear Him.* Know that with regard to natural matters as well, it is impossible to give a clear exposition when teaching some of their principles as they are. For you know the saying of [the Sages], *may their memory be blessed: The Account of the Beginning ought not to be taught in the presence of two men.* Now if someone explained all those matters in a book, he in effect would be *teaching* them to thousands of men. Hence these matters too occur in parables in the books of prophecy. The *Sages, may their memory be blessed,* following the trail of these books, likewise have spoken of them in riddles and parables, for there is a close connection between these matters and the divine science, and they too are secrets of that divine science.

You should not think that these great *secrets* are fully and completely known to anyone among us. They are not. But sometimes truth flashes out to us so that we think that it is day, and then matter and habit in their various forms conceal it so that we find ourselves again in an obscure night, almost as we were at first. We are like someone in a very dark night over whom lightning flashes time and time again. Among us there is one for whom the lightning flashes time and time again, so that he is always, as it were, in unceasing light. Thus night appears to him as day. That is the degree of the great one among the prophets, to whom it was said: *But as for thee, stand thou here by Me,* and of whom it was said: *that the skin of his face sent forth beams, and so on.* Among them there is one to whom the lightning flashes only once in the whole of his night; that is the rank of those of whom it is said: *they prophesied, but they did so no more.* There are others between whose lightning flashes there are greater or shorter intervals. Thereafter comes he who does not attain a degree in which his darkness is illumined by any lightning flash. It is illumined, however, by a polished body or something of that kind, stones or something else that give light in the darkness of the night. And even this small light that shines over us is not always there, but flashes and is hidden again, as if it were the *flaming sword which turned every way.* It is in accord with these states that the degrees of the perfect vary. As for those who never even once see a light, but grope about in their night, of them it is said: *They knew not, neither do they understand; They go about in darkness.* The truth, in spite of the strength of its manifestation, is entirely hidden from them, as is said of them: *And now men see not the light which is bright in the skies.* They are the vulgar among the people. There is then no occasion to mention them here in this Treatise.

Know that whenever one of the perfect wishes to mention, either orally or in writing, something that he understands of these *secrets,* according to the degree of his perfection, he is unable to explain with complete clarity and coherence even the portion that he has apprehended, as he could do with the other sciences whose teaching is generally recognized. Rather there will befall him when teaching another that which he had undergone when learning himself. I mean to say that the subject matter will appear, flash, and then be hidden again, as though this were the nature of this subject matter, be there much or little of it. For this reason, all the Sages possessing knowledge of God the Lord, knowers of the truth, when they aimed at teaching something of this subject matter, spoke of it only in parables and riddles. They even multiplied the parables and made them different in species and even in genus. In most cases the subject to be explained was placed in the beginning or in the middle or at the end of the parable; this happened where a parable appropriate for the intended subject from start to finish could not be found. Sometimes the subject intended to be taught to him who was to be instructed was divided—although it was one and the same subject—among many parables remote from one another. Even more obscure is the case of one and the same parable corresponding to several subjects, its beginning fitting one subject and its ending another. Sometimes the whole is a parable referring to two cognate subjects within the particular species of science in question. The situation is such that the exposition of one who wishes to teach without recourse to parables and riddles is so obscure and brief as to make obscurity and brevity serve in place of parables and riddles. The men of knowledge and the sages are drawn, as it were, toward this purpose by the divine will just as they are drawn by their natural circumstances. Do you not see the following fact? God, may His mention be exalted, wished us to be perfected and the state of our societies to be improved by His laws regarding actions. Now this can come about only after the adoption of intellectual beliefs, the first of which being His apprehension, may He be exalted, according to our capacity. This, in its turn, cannot come about except through divine science, and this divine science cannot become actual except after a study of natural science. This is so since natural science borders on divine science, and its study precedes that of divine science in time as has been made clear to whoever has engaged in speculation on these matters. Hence God, may He be exalted, caused His book to open with the *Account of the Beginning*, which, as we have made clear, is natural science. And because of the greatness and importance of the subject and because our capacity falls short of apprehending the greatest of subjects as it really is, we are told about those profound matters—which divine wisdom has deemed necessary to convey to us—in parables and riddles and in very obscure words. As [the Sages], *may their memory be blessed*, have said: *It is impossible to tell mortals of the power of the Account of the Beginning. For this reason Scripture tells you obscurely: In the beginning God created, and so on.* They thus have drawn your attention to the fact that the above-mentioned subjects are *obscure*. You likewise know *Solomon's* saying: *That which was is far off, and exceeding deep; who can find it out?* That which is said about all this is in equivocal terms so that the multitude might comprehend them in accord with the capacity of their understanding and the weakness of their representation, whereas the perfect man, who is already informed, will comprehend them otherwise.

We also saw that if an ignoramus should engage in speculation on [The] *Midrash*, he would find nothing difficult in them, inasmuch as a rash fool, devoid of any knowledge of the nature of being, does not find impossibilities hard to accept. If, however, a perfect man of virtue should engage in speculation on them, he cannot escape one of two courses: either he can take the speeches in question in their external sense and, in so doing, think ill of their author and regard him as an ignoramus—in this there is nothing that would upset the foundations of belief; or he can attribute to them an inner meaning, thereby extricating himself from his predicament and being able to think well of the author whether or not the inner meaning of the saying is clear to him. With regard to the meaning of prophecy, the exposition of its various degrees, and the elucidation of the parables occurring in the prophetic books, another manner of explanation is used in this Treatise. In view of these considerations, we have given up composing these two books in the way in which they were begun. We have confined ourselves to mentioning briefly the foundations of belief and general truths, while dropping hints that approach a clear exposition, just as we have set them forth in the great legal compilation, *Mishneh Torah*.

My speech in the present Treatise is directed, as I have mentioned, to one who has philosophized and has knowledge of the true sciences, but believes at the same time in the matters pertaining to the Law and is perplexed as to their meaning because of the uncertain terms and the parables. We shall include in this Treatise some chapters in which there will be no mention of an equivocal term. Such a chapter will be preparatory for another, or it will hint at one of the meanings of an equivocal term that I might not wish to mention explicitly in that place, or it will explain one of the parables or hint at the fact that a certain story is a parable. Such a chapter may contain strange matters regarding which the contrary of the truth sometimes is believed, either because of the equivocality of the terms or because a parable is taken for the thing being represented or vice versa.

Know that the key to the understanding of all that the prophets, peace be on them, have said, and to the knowledge of its truth, is an understanding of the parables, of their import, and of the meaning of the words occurring in them. You know what God, may He be exalted, has said: *And by the ministry of the prophets have I used similitudes.*

Know that the prophetic parables are of two kinds. In some of these parables each word has a meaning, while in others the parable as a whole indicates the whole of the intended meaning. In such a parable very many words are to be found, not every one of which adds something to the intended meaning. They serve rather to embellish the parable and to render it more coherent or to conceal further the intended meaning; hence the speech proceeds in such a way as to accord with everything required by the parable's external meaning. Understand this well.

An example of the first kind of prophetic parable is the following text: *And behold a ladder set up on the earth, and so on.* In this text, the word *ladder* indicates one subject; the words *set up on the earth* indicate a second subject; the words *and the top of it reached to heaven* indicate a third subject; the words *and behold the angels of God* indicate a fourth subject; the word *ascending* indicates a fifth subject; the words *and descending* indicate a sixth subject; and the words *And behold the Lord stood above it* indicate a seventh subject. Thus every word occurring in this parable refers to an additional subject in the complex of subjects represented by the parable as a whole.

An example of the second kind of prophetic parable is the following text: *For at the window of my house I looked forth through my lattice; And I beheld among the thoughtless ones, I discerned among the youths, A young man void of understanding, Passing through the street near her corner, And he went the way to her house; In the twilight, in the evening of the day, In the blackness of night and the darkness. And, behold, there met him a woman With the attire of a harlot, and wily of heart. She is riotous and rebellious, and so on. Now she is in the streets, now in the broad places, and so on. So she caught him, and so on. Sacrifices of peace-offerings were due from me, and so on. Therefore came I forth to meet thee, and so on. I have decked with coverlets, and so on. I have perfumed my bed, and so on. Come, let us take our fill of love, and so on. For my husband is not at home, and so on. The bag of money, and so on. With her much fair speech she causeth him to yield. With the blandishment of her lips she enticeth him away.* The outcome of all this is a warning against the pursuit of bodily pleasures and desires. Accordingly he [Solomon] likens matter, which is the cause of all these bodily pleasures, to a *harlot* who is also a *married woman*. In fact his entire book is based on this allegory. And we shall explain in various chapters of this Treatise his wisdom in likening matter *to a married harlot*, and we shall explain how he concluded this book of his with a eulogy of the *woman* who is not a *harlot* but confines herself to attending to the welfare of her household and husband. For all the hindrances keeping man from his ultimate perfection, every deficiency affecting him and every disobedience, come to him from his matter alone, as we shall explain in this Treatise. This is the proposition that can be understood from this parable as a whole. I mean that man should not follow his bestial nature; I mean his matter, for the proximate matter of man is identical with the proximate matter of the other living beings. And as I have explained this to you and disclosed the secret of this parable, you should not hope [to find some signification corresponding to every subject occurring in the parable] so that you could say: what can be submitted for the words, *Sacrifices of peace-offerings were due from me; this day have I paid my vows?* What subject is indicated by the words, *I have decked my couch with coverlets?* And what subject is added to this general proposition by the words, *For my husband is not at home?* The same holds good for the other details in this *chapter.* For all of them only figure in the consistent development of the parable's external meaning, the circumstances described in it being of a kind typical for adulterers. Also the spoken words and other such details are of a kind typical of words spoken among adulterers. Understand this well from what I have said for it is a great and important principle with regard to matters that I wish to explain.

When, therefore, you find that in some chapter of this Treatise I have explained the meaning of a parable and have drawn your attention to the general proposition signified by it, you should not inquire into all the details occurring in the parable, nor should you wish to find significations corresponding to them. For doing so would lead you into one of two ways: either into turning aside from the parable's intended subject, or into assuming an obligation to interpret things not susceptible of interpretation and that have not been inserted with a view to interpretation. The assumption of such an obligation would result in extravagant fantasies such as are entertained and written about in our time by most of the sects of the world, since each of these sects desires to find certain significations for words whose author in no wise had in mind the significations wished by them. Your purpose, rather, should always be to know, regarding most parables, the whole that was intended to be known. In some matters it will suffice you to gather from my remarks that a given story is a parable, even if we explain nothing more; for once you know it is a parable, it will immediately become clear to you what it is a parable of. My remarking that it is a parable will be like someone removing a screen from between the eye and a visible thing.

INSTRUCTION WITH RESPECT TO THIS TREATISE

If you wish to grasp the totality of what this Treatise contains, so that nothing of it will escape you, then you must connect its chapters one with another; and when reading a given chapter, your intention must be not only to understand the totality of the subject of that chapter, but also to grasp each word that occurs in it in the course of the speech, even if that word does not belong to the intention of the chapter. For the diction of this Treatise has not been chosen at haphazard, but with great exactness and exceeding precision, and with care to avoid failing to explain any obscure point. And nothing has been mentioned out of its place, save with a view to explaining some matter in its proper place. You therefore should not let your fantasies elaborate on what is said here, for that would hurt me and be of no use to yourself. You ought rather to learn everything that ought to be learned and constantly study this Treatise. For it then will elucidate for you most of the obscurities of the Law that appear as difficult to every intelligent man. I adjure—by God, may He be exalted!—every reader of this Treatise of mine not to comment upon a single word of it and not to explain to another anything in it save that which has been explained and commented upon in the words of the famous Sages of our Law who preceded me. But whatever he understands from this Treatise of those things that have not been said by any of our famous Sages other than myself should not be explained to another; nor should he hasten to refute me, for that which he understood me to say might be contrary to my intention. He thus would harm me in return for my having wanted to benefit him and would *repay evil for good*. All into whose hands it falls should consider it well; and if it slakes his thirst, though it be on only one point from among the many that are obscure, he should thank God and be content with what he has understood. If, on the other hand, he finds nothing in this Treatise that might be of use to him in any respect, he should think of it as not having been composed at all. If anything in it, according to his way of thinking, appears to be in some way harmful, he should interpret it, even if in a far-fetched way, in order to *pass a favorable judgment*. For as we are enjoined to act this way toward our vulgar ones, all the more should this be so with respect to our erudite ones and Sages of our Law who are trying to help us to the truth as they apprehend it. I know that, among men generally, every beginner will derive benefit from some of the chapters of this Treatise, though he lacks even an inkling of what is involved in speculation. A perfect man, on the other hand, devoted to Law and, as I have mentioned, perplexed, will benefit from all its chapters. How greatly will he rejoice in them and how pleasant will it be to hear them! But those who are confused and whose brains have been polluted by false opinions and misleading ways deemed by them to be true sciences, and who hold themselves to be men of speculation without having any knowledge of anything that can truly be called science, those will flee from many of its chapters. Indeed, these chapters will be very difficult for them to bear because they cannot apprehend their meaning and also because they would be led to recognize the falseness of the counterfeit money in their hands—their treasure and fortune held ready for future calamities. God, may He be exalted, knows that I have never ceased to be exceedingly apprehensive about setting down those things that I wish to set down in this Treatise. For they are concealed things; none of them has been set down in any book—written in the religious community in these times of *Exile*—the books composed in these times being in our hands. How then can I now innovate and set them down? However, I have relied on two premises, the one being [the Sages'] saying in a similar case, *It is time to do something for the Lord, and so on*, the second being their saying, *Let all thy acts be for the sake of Heaven*. Upon these two premises have I relied when setting down what I have composed in some of the chapters of this Treatise.

To sum up: I am the man who when the concern pressed him and his way was straitened and he could find no other device by which to teach a demonstrated truth other than by giving satisfaction to a single virtuous man while displeasing ten thousand ignoramuses—I am he who prefers to address that single man by himself, and I do not heed the blame of those many creatures. For I claim to liberate that virtuous one from that into which he has sunk, and I shall guide him in his perplexity until he becomes perfect and he finds rest.

FROM BACON TO HUME

7

FRANCIS BACON
How to Think Well

Francis Bacon (Baron Verulam, Viscount St. Albans, 1561–1626) was the youngest son of Sir Nicholas Bacon, a counsellor to Queen Elizabeth. Protean in his interests and activities, Bacon was a successful advocate, statesman, essayist, and philosopher of logic and science. Bacon argued that the aim of science is the mastery of nature, rather than the explanation of its order. Instead of relying on a priori arguments or deductions from metaphysical principles, scientific method should be inductive and experimental. Before the sciences could be established on a secure, empirical basis, it is first necessary to attack the four "idols" of inquiry: the anthropomorphic teleological projection of purposes onto nature ("idols of the tribe"), idiosyncratic individual opinions ("idols of the cave"), verbal disputes arising from confused and misleading language ("idols of the marketplace"), and the received mistaken theories, particularly those of Aristotelian and scholastic philosophy ("idols of the theater"). *The Advancement of Learning* (1605) and the master plan of the *Great Instauration* with the *Novum Organum* (1620) outlined an elaborate taxonomy of the branches of knowledge. The utopian society that Bacon sketched in *The New Atlantis* (1624) projected the establishment of learned societies to advance cooperative research. While none of his recommendations were adopted in his lifetime, they provided the model for the Royal Society. His *Essays* range from standard topics of reflection ("Of Parents and Children," "Of Anger," "Of Fortune," "Of Friendship") to topics more closely focused on issues of the time ("Of Sedition and Troubles," "Of Masques and Triumphs," "Of Ceremonies and Respects").

Bacon's friend and patron, the Earl of Essex, unsuccessfully attempted to procure a Court appointment for Bacon. To the consternation of his friends, Bacon was instrumental in bringing Essex to trial when he fell out of favor with Elizabeth. Popularly charged with perfidy, Bacon attempted to justify himself by arguing that the security of a strongly centralized dominant monarchy should take precedence over personal loyalties.

With the accession of James I, Bacon advanced to positions of increasing power and responsibility. Appointed lord chancellor in 1618, he again suffered disgrace for accepting bribes and was removed from office in 1621. Upon his retirement, he concentrated on his philosophic writing and scientific experiments. He died of complications from a chill he developed while conducting an experiment designed to discover a method for refrigerating food.

The Great Instauration
Proemium

Francis of Verulam reasoned thus with himself, and judged it to be for the interest of the present and future generations that they should be made acquainted with his thoughts.

Being convinced that the human intellect makes its own difficulties, not using the true helps which are at man's disposal soberly and judiciously, whence it follows manifold ignorance of things, and by reason of that ignorance, innumerable mischiefs, he thought all trial should be made whether that commerce between the mind of man and the nature of things (which is more precious than anything on earth, or at least than anything that is of the earth) might by any means be restored to its perfect and original condition or, if that may not be, yet reduced to a better condition than that in which it now is. Now that the errors which have hitherto prevailed, and which will prevail forever, should (if the mind be left to go its own way), either by the natural force of the understanding or by help of the aids and instruments of logic, one by one correct themselves, was a thing not to be hoped for because the primary notions of things which the mind readily and passively imbibes, stores up, and accumulates (and it is from them that all the rest flow) are false, confused, and over hastily abstracted from the facts. Nor are the secondary and subsequent notions less arbitrary and inconstant. Whence it follows that the entire fabric of human reason which we employ in the inquisition of nature is badly put together and built up and like some magnificent structure without any foundation. For while men are occupied in admiring and applauding the false powers of the mind, they pass by and throw away those true powers which, if it be supplied with the proper aids and can itself be content to wait upon nature instead of vainly affecting to overrule her, are within its reach.

There was but one course left, therefore, to try the whole thing anew upon a better plan, and to commence a total reconstruction of sciences, arts, and all human knowledge raised upon the proper foundations. And this, though in the project and undertaking it may seem a thing infinite and beyond the powers of man, yet when it comes to be dealt with it will be found sound and sober, more so than what has been done hitherto. For of this there is some issue, whereas in what is now done in the matter of science there is only a whirling round about, and perpetual agitation, ending where it began. And although he was well aware how solitary an enterprise it is, and how hard a thing to win faith and credit for, nevertheless he was resolved not to abandon either it or himself, nor to be deterred from trying and entering upon that one path which is alone open to the human mind. For better it is to make a beginning of that which may lead to something, than to engage in a perpetual struggle and pursuit in courses which have no exit. And certainly the two ways of contemplation are much like those two ways of action, so much celebrated, in this; that the one, arduous and difficult in the beginning, leads out at last into the open country, while the other, seeming at first sight easy and free from obstruction, leads to pathless and precipitous places.

Moreover, because he knew not how long it might be before these things would occur to any one else, judging especially from this, that he has found no man hitherto who has applied his mind to the like, he resolved to publish at once so much as he has been able to complete. The cause of which haste was not ambition for himself, but solicitude for the work, that in case of his death there might remain some outline and project of that which he had conceived and some evidence likewise of his honest mind and inclination towards the benefit of the human race. Certain it is that all other ambition whatsoever seemed poor in his eyes compared with the work which he had in hand; seeing that the matter at issue is either nothing, or a thing so great that it may well be content with its own merit, without seeking other recompense.

The Great Instauration

To our most gracious and mighty prince and lord
JAMES
by the grace of God of Great Britain, France and Ireland King,
Defender of the Faith, etc.

Most Gracious and Mighty King,

Your Majesty may perhaps accuse me of larceny, having stolen from your affairs so much time as was required for this work. I know not what to say for myself. For of time there can be no restitution, unless it be that what has been abstracted from your business may perhaps go to the memory of your name and the honor of your age, if these things are indeed worth anything. Certainly they are quite new; totally new in their very kind; and yet they are copied from a very ancient model—even the world itself and the nature of things and of the mind. And to say truth, I am wont for my own part to regard this work as a child of time rather than of wit; the only wonder being that the first notion of the thing (and such great suspicions concerning matters long established) should have come into any man's mind. All the rest follows readily enough. And no doubt there is something of accident (as we call it) and luck as well in what men think as in what they do or say. But for this accident which I speak of, I wish that if there by any good in what I have to offer, it may be ascribed to the infinite mercy and goodness of God, and to the felicity of your Majesty's times, to which as I have been an honest and affectionate servant in my life, so after my death I may yet perhaps, through the kindling of this new light in the darkness of philosophy, be the means of making this age famous to posterity. Surely to the times of the wisest and most learned of kings belongs of right the regeneration and restoration of the sciences. Lastly, I have a request to make—a request no way unworthy of your Majesty, and which especially concerns the work in hand; namely, that you who resemble Solomon in so many things (in the gravity of your judgments, in the peacefulness of your reign, in the largeness of your heart, in the noble variety of the books which you have composed) would further follow his example in taking order for the collecting and perfecting of a Natural and Experimental History, true and severe (unencumbered with literature and book-learning), such as philosophy may be built upon—such, in fact, as I shall in its proper place describe, so that at length, after the lapse of so many ages, philosophy and the sciences may no longer float in air, but rest on the solid foundation of experience of every kind, and the same well examined and weighed. I have provided the machine, but the stuff must be gathered from the facts of nature. May God Almighty long preserve your Majesty!

Your Majesty's most bounden and devoted Servant,
Francis Verulam
Chancellor

Preface

That the state of knowledge is not prosperous nor greatly advancing and that a way must be opened for the human understanding entirely different from any hitherto known and other helps provided in order that the mind may exercise over the nature of things the authority which properly belongs to it.

It seems to me that men do not rightly understand either their store or their strength, but overrate the one and underrate the other. Hence it follows that either from an extravagant estimate of the value of the arts which they possess they seek no further, or else from too mean an estimate of their own powers they spend their strength in small matters and never put it fairly to the trial in those which go to the main. These are as the pillars of fate set in the path of knowledge; for men have neither desire nor hope to encourage them to penetrate further. And since opinion of store is one of the chief causes of want, and satisfaction with the present induces neglect of provision for the future, it becomes a thing not only useful, but absolutely necessary, that the excess of honor and admiration with which our existing stock of inventions is regarded be in the very entrance and threshold of the work, and that frankly and without circumlocution, stripped off and men be duly warned not to exaggerate or make too much of them. For let a man look carefully into all that variety of books with which the arts and sciences abound, he will find everywhere endless repetitions of the same thing, varying in the method of treatment but not new in substance, insomuch that the whole stock, numerous as it appears at first view, proves on examination to be but scanty.

And for its value and utility it must be plainly avowed that that wisdom which we have derived principally from the Greeks is but like the boyhood of knowledge, and has the characteristic property of boys: it can talk, but it cannot generate, for it is fruitful of controversies but barren of works. So that the state of learning as it now is appears to be represented to the life in the old fable of Scylla, who had the head and face of a virgin, but her womb was hung round with barking monsters, from which she could not be delivered. For in like manner the sciences to which we are accustomed have certain general positions which are specious and flattering, but as soon as they come to particulars, which are as the parts of generation, when they should produce fruit and works, then arise contentions and barking disputations, which are the end of the matter and all the issue they can yield. Observe also, that if sciences of this kind had any life in them, that could never have come to pass which has been the case now for many ages—that they stand almost at a stay, without receiving any augmentations worthy of the human race, insomuch that many times not only what was asserted once is asserted still, but what was a question once is a question still, and instead of being resolved by discussion is only fixed and fed. And all the tradition and succession of schools is still a succession of masters and scholars, not of inventors and those who bring to further perfection the things invented.

In the mechanical arts we do not find it so. They, on the contrary, as having in them some breath of life, are continually growing and becoming more perfect. As originally invented they are commonly rude, clumsy, and shapeless. Afterwards they acquire new powers and more commodious arrangements and constructions, in so far that men shall sooner leave the study and pursuit of them and turn to something else, than they arrive at the ultimate perfection of which they are capable. Philosophy and the intellectual sciences, on the contrary, stand like statues, worshipped and celebrated, but not moved or advanced. Nay, they sometimes flourish most in the hands of the first author, and afterwards degenerate. For when men have once made over their judgments to others' keeping, and (like those senators whom they called *Pedarii*) have agreed to support some one person's opinion, from that time they make no enlargement of the sciences themselves, but fall to the servile office of embellishing certain individual authors and increasing their retinue.

And let it not be said that the sciences have been growing gradually till they have at last reached their full stature, and so (their course being completed) have settled in the works of a few writers; and that there being now no room for the invention of better, all that remains is to embellish and cultivate those things which have been invented already. Would it were so! But the truth is that this appropriating of the sciences has its origin in nothing better than the confidence of a few persons and the sloth and indolence of the rest. For after the sciences had been in several parts perhaps cultivated and handled diligently, there has risen up some man of bold disposition, and famous for methods and short ways which people like, who has in appearance reduced them to an art, while he has in fact only spoiled all that the others had done. And yet this is what posterity likes, because it makes the work short and easy, and saves further inquiry, of which they are weary and impatient.

And if any one take this general acquiescence and consent for an argument of weight, as being the judgment of Time, let me tell him that the reasoning on which he relies is most fallacious and weak. For, first, we are far from knowing all that in the matter of sciences and arts has in various ages and places been brought to light and published, much less, all that has been by private persons secretly attempted and stirred; so neither the births nor the miscarriages of Time are entered in our records. Nor, secondly, is the consent itself and the time it has continued a consideration of much worth. For however various are the forms of civil polities, there is but one form of polity in the sciences; and that always has been and always will be popular. Now the doctrines which find most favor with the populace are those which are either contentious and pugnacious, or specious and empty, such, I say, as either entangle assent or tickle it. And therefore no doubt the greatest wits in each successive age have been forced out of their own course, men of capacity and intellect above the vulgar having been fain, for reputation's sake, to bow to the judgment of the time and the multitude. And thus if any contemplations of a higher order took light anywhere, they were presently blown out by the winds of vulgar opinions. So that Time is like a river which has brought down to us things light and puffed up, while those which are weighty and solid have sunk. Nay, those very authors who have usurped a kind of dictatorship in the sciences and taken upon them to lay down the law with such confidence, yet when from time to time they come to themselves again, they fall to complaints of the subtlety of nature, the hiding-places of truth, the obscurity of things, the entanglement of causes, the weakness of the human mind; wherein nevertheless they show themselves never the more modest, seeing that they will rather lay the blame upon the common condition of men and nature than upon themselves. And then whatever any art fails to attain, they ever set it down upon the authority of that art itself as impossible of attainment; and how can art be found guilty when it is judge in its own case? So it is but a device for exempting ignorance from ignominy.

Now for those things which are delivered and received, this is their condition: barren of works, full of questions; in point of enlargement slow and languid; carrying a show of perfection in the whole, but in the parts ill filled up; in selection popular, and unsatisfactory even to those who propound them; and therefore fenced round and set forth with sundry artifices. And if there be any who have determined to make trial for themselves, and put their own strength to the work of advancing the boundaries of the sciences, yet have they not ventured to cast themselves completely loose from received opinions or to seek their knowledge at the fountain. But they think they have done some great thing if they do but add and introduce into the existing sum of science something of their own; prudently considering with themselves that by making the addition they can assert their liberty, while they retain the credit of modesty by assenting to the rest. But these mediocrities and middle ways so much praised, in deferring to opinions and customs, turn to the great detriment of the sciences. For it is hardly possible at once to admire an author and to go beyond him; knowledge being as water, which will not rise above the level from which it fell. Men of this kind, therefore, amend some things but advance little, and improve the condition of knowledge but do not extend its range. Some, indeed, there have been who have gone more boldly to work, and taking it all for an open matter and giving their genius full play, have made a passage for themselves and their own opinions by pulling down and demolishing former ones. And yet all their stir has but little advanced the matter since their aim has been not to extend philosophy and the arts in substance and value, but only to change doctrines and transfer the kingdom of opinions to themselves; whereby little has indeed been gained, for though the error be the opposite of the other, the causes of erring are the same in both.

And if there have been any who, not binding themselves either to other men's opinions or to their own, but loving liberty, have desired to engage others along with themselves in search, these, though honest in intention, have been weak in endeavor. For they have been content to follow probable reasons, and are carried round in a whirl of arguments, and in the promiscuous liberty of search have relaxed the severity of inquiry. There is none who has dwelt upon experience and the facts of nature as long as is necessary. Some there are indeed who have committed themselves to the waves of experience, and almost turned mechanics, yet these again have in their very experiments pursued a kind of wandering inquiry, without any regular system of operations. And besides they have mostly proposed to themselves certain petty tasks, taking it for a great matter to work out some single discovery—a course of proceeding at once poor in aim and unskillful in design. For no man can rightly and successfully investigate the nature of anything in the thing itself; let him vary his experiments as laboriously as he will, he never comes to a resting place, but still finds something to seek beyond. And there is another thing to be remembered: namely, that all industry in experimenting has begun with proposing to itself certain definite works to be accomplished, and has pursued them with premature and unseasonable eagerness. It has sought, I say, experiments of Fruit, not experiments of Light; not imitating the divine procedure, which in its first day's work created light only and assigned to it one entire day; on which day it produced no material work, but proceeded to that on the days following.

As for those who have given the first place to logic, supposing that the surest helps to the sciences were to be found in that, they have indeed most truly and excellently perceived that the human intellect left to its own course is not to be trusted; but then the remedy is altogether too weak for the disease; nor is it without evil in itself. For the logic which is received, though it be very properly applied to civil business and to those arts which rest in discourse and opinion, is not nearly subtle enough to deal with nature; and in offering at what it cannot master, has done more to establish and perpetuate error than to open the way to truth.

Upon the whole, therefore, it seems that men have not been happy hitherto either in the trust which they have placed in others or in their own industry with regard to the sciences; especially as neither the demonstrations nor the experiments as yet known are much to be relied upon. But the universe to the eye of the human understanding is framed like a labyrinth, presenting as it does on every side so many ambiguities of way, such deceitful resemblances of objects and signs, natures so irregular in their lines, and so knotted and entangled. And then the way is still to be made by the uncertain light of the sense, sometimes shining out, sometimes clouded over, through the woods of experience and particulars; while those who offer themselves for guides are (as was said) themselves also puzzled, and increase the number of errors and wanderers. In circumstances so difficult neither the natural force of man's judgment nor even any accidental felicity offers any chance of success. No excellence of wit, no repetition of chance experiments, can overcome such difficulties as these. Our steps must be guided by a clue, and the whole way from the very first perception of the senses must be laid out upon a sure plan.

Not that I would be understood to mean that nothing whatever has been done in so many ages by so great labors. We have no reason to be ashamed of the discoveries which have been made, and no doubt the ancients proved themselves in everything that turns on wit and abstract meditation, wonderful men. But as in former ages when men sailed only by observation of the stars, they could indeed coast along the shores of the old continent or cross a few small and Mediterranean seas; but before the ocean could be traversed and the new world discovered, the use of the mariner's needle, as a more faithful and certain guide, had to be found out. In like manner the discoveries which have been hitherto made in the arts and sciences are such as might be made by practice, meditation, observation, argumentation—for they lay near to the senses and immediately beneath common notions—but before we can reach the remoter and more hidden parts of nature, it is necessary that a more perfect use and application of the human mind and intellect be introduced.

For my own part at least, in obedience to the everlasting love of truth, I have committed myself to the uncertainties and difficulties and solitudes of the ways and, relying on the divine assistance, have upheld my mind both against the shocks and embattled ranks of opinion, and against my own private and inward hesitations and scruples, and against the fogs and clouds of nature, and the phantoms flitting about on every side, in the hope of providing at last for the present and future generations guidance more faithful and secure. Wherein if I have made any progress, the way has been opened to me by no other means than the true and legitimate humiliation of the human spirit. For all those who before me have applied themselves to the invention of arts have but cast a glance or two upon facts and examples and experience, and straightway proceeded, as if invention were nothing more than an exercise of thought, to invoke their own spirits to give them oracles. I, on the contrary, dwelling purely and constantly among the facts of nature, withdraw my intellect from them no further than may suffice to let the images and rays of natural objects meet in a point, as they do in the sense of vision; whence it follows that the strength and excellency of the wit has but little to do in the matter.

And the same humility which I use in inventing I employ likewise in teaching. For I do not endeavor either by triumphs of confutation, or pleadings of antiquity, or assumption of authority, or even by the veil of obscurity, to invest these inventions of mine with any majesty, which might easily be done by one who sought to give luster to his own name rather than light to other men's minds. I have not sought (I say) nor do I seek either to force or ensnare men's judgments, but I lead them to things themselves and the concordances of things, that they may see for themselves what they have, what they can dispute, what they can add and contribute to the common stock. And for myself, if in anything I have been either too credulous or too little awake and attentive, or if I have fallen off by the way and left the inquiry incomplete, nevertheless I so present these things naked and open, that my errors can be marked and set aside before the mass of knowledge be further infected by them, and it will be easy also for others to continue and carry on my labors. And by these means I suppose that I have established forever a true and lawful marriage between the empirical and rational faculty, the unkind and ill-starred divorce and separation of which has thrown into confusion all the affairs of the human family.

Wherefore, seeing that these things do not depend upon myself, at the outset of the work I most humbly and fervently pray to God the Father, God the Son, and God the Holy Ghost, that remembering the sorrows of mankind and the pilgrimage of this our life wherein we wear out days few and evil, they will vouchsafe through my hand to endow the human family with new mercies. This likewise I humbly pray, that things human may not interfere with things divine, and that from the opening of the ways of sense and the increase of natural light there may arise in our minds no incredulity or darkness with regard to the divine mysteries; but rather that the understanding being thereby purified and purged of fancies and vanity, and yet not the less subject and entirely submissive to the divine oracles, may give to faith that which is faith's. Lastly, that knowledge being now discharged of that venom which the serpent infused into it, and which makes the mind of man to swell, we may not be wise above measure and sobriety, but cultivate truth in charity.

And now having said my prayers I turn to men, to whom I have certain salutary admonitions to offer and certain fair requests to make. My first admonition (which was also my prayer) is that men confine the sense within the limits of duty in respect of things divine, for the sense is like the sun, which reveals the face of earth, but seals and shuts up the face of heaven. My next, that in flying from this evil they fall not into the opposite error, which they will surely do if they think that the inquisition of nature is in any part interdicted or forbidden. For it was not that pure and uncorrupted natural knowledge whereby Adam gave names to the creatures according to their propriety, which gave occasion to the fall. It was the ambitious and proud desire or moral knowledge to judge of good and evil, to the end that man may revolt from God and give laws to himself, which was the form and manner of the temptation. Whereas of the sciences which regard nature, the divine philosopher declares that "it is the glory of God to conceal a thing, but it is the glory of the King to find a thing out." Even as though the divine nature took pleasure in the innocent and kindly sport of children playing at hide and seek, and vouchsafed of his kindness and goodness to admit the human spirit for his playfellow at that game. Lastly, I would address one general admonition to all: that they consider what are the true ends of knowledge, and that they seek it not either for pleasure of the mind, or for contention, or for superiority to others, or for profit, or fame, or power, or any of these inferior things, but for the benefit and use of life, and that they perfect and govern it in charity. For it was from lust of power that the angels fell, from lust of knowledge that man fell, but of charity there can be no excess, neither did angel or man ever come in danger by it.

The requests I have to make are these. Of myself I say nothing, but in behalf of the business which is in hand I entreat men to believe that it is not an opinion to be held but a work to be done, and to be well assured that I am laboring to lay the foundation, not of any sect or doctrine, but of human utility and power. Next, I ask them to deal fairly by their own interests and laying aside all emulations and prejudices in favor of this or that opinion, to join in consultation for the common good, and being now freed and guarded by the securities and helps which I offer from the errors and impediments of the way, to come forward themselves and take part in that which remains to be done. Moreover, to be of good hope, nor to imagine that this Instauration of mine is a thing infinite and beyond the power of man, when it is in fact the true end and termination of infinite error; and seeing also that it is by no means forgetful of the condition of mortality and humanity (for it does not suppose that the work can be altogether completed within one generation, but provides for its being taken up by another); and finally that it seeks for the sciences not arrogantly in the little cells of human wit, but with reverence in the greater world. But it is the empty things that are vast. Things solid are most contracted and lie in little room. And now I have only one favor more to ask (else injustice to me may perhaps imperil the business itself): that men will consider well how far, upon that which I must needs assert (if I am to be consistent with myself), they are entitled to judge and decide upon these doctrines of mine; inasmuch as all that premature human reasoning which anticipates inquiry, and is abstracted from the facts rashly and sooner than is fit, is by me rejected (so far as the inquisition of nature is concerned) as a thing uncertain, confused, and ill built up; and I cannot be fairly asked to abide by the decision of a tribunal which is itself on trial.

The Plan of the Work

THE WORK IS IN SIX PARTS:

1. The Divisions of the Sciences.

2. The New Organon; or Directions concerning the Interpretation of Nature.

3. The Phenomena of the Universe; or a Natural and Experimental History for the Foundation of Philosophy.

4. The Ladder of the Intellect.

5. The Forerunners; or Anticipations of the New Philosophy.

6. The New Philosophy; or Active Science.

The Arguments of the Several Parts

It being part of my design to set everything forth, as far as may be, plainly and perspicuously (for nakedness of the mind is still, as nakedness of the body once was, the companion of innocence and simplicity), let me first explain the order and plan of the work. I distribute it into six parts.

The first part exhibits a summary or general description of the knowledge which the human race at present possesses. For I thought it good to make some pause upon that which is received that thereby the old may be more easily made perfect and the new more easily approached. And I hold the improvement of that which we have to be as much an object as the acquisition of more. Besides which it will make me the better listened to, for "He that is ignorant (says the proverb) receives not the words of knowledge, unless thou first tell him that which is in his own heart." We will therefore make a coasting voyage along the shores of the arts and sciences received; not without importing into them some useful things by the way.

In laying out the divisions of the sciences, however, I take into account not only things already invented and known, but likewise things omitted which ought to be there. For there are found in the intellectual as in the terrestrial globe waste regions as well as cultivated ones. It is no wonder therefore if I am sometimes obliged to depart from the ordinary divisions. For in adding to the total you necessarily alter the parts and sections, and the received divisions of the sciences are fitted only to the received sum of them as it stands now.

With regard to those things which I shall mark as omitted, I intend not merely to set down a simple title or a concise argument of that which is wanted. For as often as I have occasion to report anything as deficient, the nature of which is at all obscure, so that men may not perhaps easily understand what I mean or what the work is which I have in my head, I shall always (provided it be a matter of any worth) take care to subjoin either directions for the execution of such work, or else a portion of the work itself executed by myself as a sample of the whole—thus giving assistance in every case either by work or by counsel. For if it were for the sake of my own reputation only and other men's interests were not concerned in it, I would not have any man think that in such cases merely some light and vague notion has crossed my mind, and that the things which I desire and offer at are no better than wishes, when they are in fact things which men may certainly command if they will and of which I have formed in my own mind a clear and detailed conception. For I do not propose merely to survey these regions in my mind, like an augur taking auspices, but to enter them like a general who means to take possession. So much for the first part of the work.

Having thus coasted past the ancient arts, the next point is to equip the intellect for passing beyond. To the second part, therefore, belongs the doctrine concerning the better and more perfect use of human reason in the inquisition of things, and the true helps of the understanding, that thereby (as far as the condition of mortality and humanity allows) the intellect may be raised and exalted and made capable of overcoming the difficulties and obscurities of nature. The art which I introduce with this view (which I call *Interpretation of Nature*) is a kind of logic, though the differences between it and the ordinary logic is great, indeed, immense. For the ordinary logic professes to contrive and prepare helps and guards for the understanding, as mine does, and in this one point they agree. But mine differs from it in three points especially: namely, in the end aimed at, in the order of demonstration, and in the starting point of the inquiry.

For the end which this science of mine proposes is the invention not of arguments but of arts; not of things in accordance with principles, but of principles themselves; not of probable reasons, but of designations and directions for works. And as the intention is different, so accordingly is the effect; the effect of the one being to overcome an opponent in argument, of the other to command nature in action.

In accordance with this end is also the nature and order of the demonstrations. For in the ordinary logic almost all the work is spent about the syllogism. Of induction the logicians seem hardly to have taken notice, and hasten on to the formulae of disputation. I, on the contrary, reject demonstration by syllogism as acting too confusedly and letting nature slip out of its hands. For although no one can doubt that things which agree in a middle term agree with one another (which is a proposition of mathematical certainty), yet it leaves an opening for deception, which is this: the syllogism consists of propositions; propositions of words; and words are the tokens and signs of notions. Now if the very notions of the mind (which are as the soul of words and the basis of the whole structure) be improperly and overhastily abstracted from facts, vague, not sufficiently definite, faulty in short in many ways, the whole edifice tumbles. I therefore reject the syllogism and that not only as regards principles (for to principles the logicians themselves do not apply it) but also as regards middle propositions, which, though obtainable no doubt by the syllogism, are, when so obtained, barren of works, remote from practice, and altogether unavailable for the active department of the sciences. Although, therefore, I leave to the syllogism and these famous and boasted modes of demonstration their jurisdiction over popular arts and such as are matters of opinion (in which department I leave all as it is), yet in dealing with the nature of things I use induction throughout and that in the minor propositions as well as the major. For I consider induction to be that form of demonstration which upholds the sense, and closes with nature, and comes to the very brink of operation, if it does not actually deal with it.

Hence it follows that the order of demonstration is likewise inverted. For hitherto the proceeding has been to fly at once from the sense and particulars up to the most general propositions, as certain fixed poles for the argument to turn upon, and from these to derive the rest by middle terms—a short way, no doubt, but precipitate, and one which will never lead to nature, though it offers an easy and ready way to disputation. Now my plan is to proceed regularly and gradually from one axiom to another so that the most general are not reached till the last; but then when you do come to them you find them to be not empty notions, but well defined, and such as nature would really recognize as her first principles, and such as lie at the heart and marrow of things.

But the greatest change I introduce is in the form itself of induction and the judgment made thereby. For the induction of which the logicians speak, which proceeds by simple enumeration, is a puerile thing, concludes at hazard, is always liable to be upset by a contradictory instance, takes into account only what is known and ordinary, and leads to no result.

Now what the sciences stand in need of is a form of induction which shall analyze experience and take it to pieces, and by a due process of exclusion and rejection lead to an inevitable conclusion. And if that ordinary mode of judgment practiced by the logicians was so laborious and found exercise for such great wits, how much more labor must we be prepared to bestow upon this other, which is extracted not merely out of the depths of the mind, but out of the very bowels of nature.

Nor is this all. For I also sink the foundations of the sciences deeper and firmer; and I begin the inquiry nearer the source than men have done heretofore, submitting to examination those things which the common logic takes on trust. For first, the logicians borrow the principles of each science from the science itself; secondly, they hold in reverence the first notions of the mind; and lastly, they receive as conclusive the immediate informations of the sense, when well disposed. Now upon the first point, I hold that true logic ought to enter the several provinces of science armed with a higher authority than belongs to the principles of those sciences themselves, and ought to call those putative principles to account until they are fully established. Then with regard to the first notions of the intellect, there is not one of the impressions taken by the intellect when left to go its own way, but I hold it for suspected and no way established until it has submitted to a new trial and a fresh judgment has been thereupon pronounced. And lastly, the information of the sense itself I sift and examine in many ways. For certain it is that the senses deceive; but then at the same time they supply the means of discovering their own errors; only the errors are here, the means of discovery are to seek.

The sense fails in two ways. Sometimes it gives no information, sometimes it gives false information. For first, there are very many things which escape the sense, even when best disposed and no way obstructed, by reason either of the subtlety of the whole body, or the minuteness of the parts, or distance of place, or slowness or else swiftness of motion, or familiarity of the object, or other causes. And again when the sense does apprehend a thing, its apprehension is not much to be relied upon. For the testimony and information of the sense has reference always to man, not to the universe; and it is a great error to assert that the sense is the measure of things.

To meet these difficulties, I have sought on all sides diligently and faithfully to provide helps for the sense—substitutes to supply its failures, rectifications to correct its errors—and this I endeavor to accomplish not so much by instruments as by experiments. For the subtlety of experiments is far greater than that of the sense itself, even when assisted by exquisite instruments; such experiments, I mean, as are skillfully and artificially devised for the express purpose of determining the point in question. To the immediate and proper perception of the sense therefore I do not give much weight; but I contrive that the office of the sense shall be only to judge of the experiment, and that the experiment itself shall judge of the thing. And thus I conceive that I perform the office of a true priest of the sense (from which all knowledge in nature must be sought unless men mean to go mad) and a not unskillful interpreter of its oracles; and that while others only profess to uphold and cultivate the sense, I do so in fact. Such then are the provisions I make for finding the genuine light of nature and kindling and bringing it to bear. And they would be sufficient of themselves, if the human intellect were even, and like a fair sheet of paper with no writing on it. But since the minds of men are strangely possessed and beset, so that there is no true and even surface left to reflect the genuine rays of things, it is necessary to seek a remedy for this also.

Now the idols or phantoms by which the mind is occupied are either adventitious or innate. The adventitious come into the mind from without: namely, either from the doctrines and sects of philosophers or from perverse rules of demonstration. But the innate are inherent in the very nature of the intellect, which is far more prone to error than the sense is. For let men please themselves as they will in admiring and almost adoring the human mind, this is certain: that as an uneven mirror distorts the rays of objects according to its own figure and section, so the mind, when it receives impressions of objects through the sense, cannot be trusted to report them truly, but in forming its notions mixes up its own nature with the nature of things.

And as the first two kinds of idols are hard to eradicate, so idols of this last kind cannot be eradicated at all. All that can be done is to point them out, so that this insidious action of the mind may be marked and reproved (else as fast as old errors are destroyed new ones will spring up out of the ill complexion of the mind itself, and so we shall have but a change of errors and not a clearance), and to lay it down once for all as a fixed and established maxim that the intellect is not qualified to judge except by means of induction, and induction in its legitimate form. This doctrine, then, of the expurgation of the intellect to qualify it for dealing with truth is comprised in three refutations: the refutation of the Philosophies, the refutation of the Demonstrations, and the refutation of the Natural Human Reason. The explanation of which things, and of the true relation between the nature of things and the nature of the mind, is as the strewing and decoration of the bridal chamber of the Mind and the Universe, the Divine Goodness assisting, out of which marriage let us hope (and be this the prayer of the bridal song) there may spring helps to man, and a line and race of inventions that may in some degree subdue and overcome the necessities and miseries of humanity. This is the second part of the work.

But I design not only to indicate and make out the ways but also to enter them. And therefore the third part of the work embraces the Phenomena of the Universe, that is to say, experience of every kind, and such a natural history as may serve for a foundation to build philosophy upon. For a good method of demonstration or form of interpreting nature may keep the mind from going astray or stumbling, but it is not any excellence of method that can supply it with the material of knowledge. Those, however, who aspire not to guess and divine, but to discover and know—who propose not to devise fabulous worlds of their own, but to examine and dissect the nature of this very world itself—must go to facts themselves for everything. Nor can the place of this labor and search and worldwide perambulation be supplied by any genius or meditation or argumentation; no, not if all men's wits could meet in one. This therefore we must have, or the business must be forever abandoned. But up to this day such has been the condition of men in this matter that it is no wonder if nature will not give herself into their hands.

For first, the information of the sense itself, sometimes failing, sometimes false; observation, careless, irregular, and led by chance; tradition, vain and fed on rumor; practice, slavishly bent upon its work; experiment, blind, stupid, vague, and prematurely broken off; lastly, natural history trivial and poor—all these have contributed to supply the understanding with very bad materials for philosophy and the sciences.

Then an attempt is made to mend the matter by a preposterous subtlety and winnowing or argument. But this comes too late, the case being already past remedy; and is far from setting the business right or sifting away the errors. The only hope therefore of any greater increase or progress lies in a reconstruction of the sciences.

Of this reconstruction the foundation must be laid in natural history, and that of a new kind and gathered on a new principle. For it is in vain that you polish the mirror if there are no images to be reflected; and it is as necessary that the intellect should be supplied with fit matter to work upon, as with safeguards to guide its working. But my history differs from that in use (as my logic does) in many things—in end and office, in mass and composition, in subtlety, in selection also and setting forth, with a view to the operations which are to follow.

For first, the object of the natural history which I propose is not so much to delight with variety of matter or to help with present use of experiments, as to give light to the discovery of causes and supply a suckling philosophy with its first food. For though it be true that I am principally in pursuit of works and the active department of the sciences, yet I wait for harvest time, and do not attempt to mow the moss or to reap the green corn. For I well know that axioms once rightly discovered will carry whole troops of works along with them, and produce them, not here and there one, but in clusters. And that unseasonable and puerile hurry to snatch by way of earnest at the first works which come within reach, I utterly condemn and reject, as an Atalanta's apple that hinders the race. Such then is the office of this natural history of mine.

Next, with regard to the mass and composition of it: I mean it to be a history not only of nature free and at large (when she is left to her own course and does her work her own way)—such as that of the heavenly bodies, meteors, earth and sea, minerals, plants, animals—but much more of nature under constraint and vexed; that is to say, when by art and the hand of man she is forced out of her natural state, and squeezed and molded. Therefore I set down at length all experiments of the mechanical arts, of the operative part of the liberal arts, of the many crafts which have not yet grown into arts properly so called, so far as I have been able to examine them and as they conduce to the end in view. Nay (to say the plain truth) I do in fact (low and vulgar as men may think it) count more upon this part both for helps and safeguards than upon the other, seeing that the nature of things betrays itself more readily under the vexations of art than in its natural freedom.

Nor do I confine the history to bodies, but I have thought it my duty besides to make a separate history of such virtues as may be considered cardinal in nature. I mean those original passions or desires of matter which constitute the primary elements of nature; such as dense and rare, hot and cold, solid and fluid, heavy and light, and several others.

Then again, to speak of subtlety: I seek out and get together a kind of experiments much subtler and simpler than those which occur accidentally. For I drag into light many things which no one who was not proceeding by a regular and certain way to the discovery of causes would have thought of inquiring after, being indeed in themselves of no great use, which shows that they were not sought for on their own account, but having just the same relation to things and works which the letters of the alphabet have to speech and words—which, though in themselves useless, are the elements of which all discourse is made up.

Further, in the selection of the relation and experiments, I conceive I have been a more cautious purveyor than those who have hitherto dealt with natural history. For I admit nothing but on the faith of eyes, or at least of careful and severe examination, so that nothing is exaggerated for wonder's sake, but what I state is sound and without mixture of fables or vanity. All received or current falsehoods also (which by strange negligence have been allowed for many ages to prevail and become established) I proscribe and brand by name, that the sciences may be no more troubled with them. For it has been well observed that the fables and superstitions and follies which nurses instill into children do serious injury to their minds, and the same consideration makes me anxious, having the management of the childhood as it were of philosophy in its course of natural history, not to let it accustom itself in the beginning to any vanity. Moreover, whenever I come to a new experiment of any subtlety (though it be in my own opinion certain and approved), I nevertheless subjoin a clear account of the manner in which I made it, that men knowing exactly how each point was made out, may see whether there be any error connected with it, and may arouse themselves to devise proofs more trustworthy and exquisite, if such can be found. And finally, I interpose everywhere admonitions and scruples and cautions, with a religious care to eject, repress, and as it were exorcise every kind of phantasm.

Lastly, knowing how much the sight of man's mind is distracted by experience and history, and how hard it is at the first (especially for minds either tender or preoccupied) to become familiar with nature, I not infrequently subjoin observations of my own, being as the first offers, inclinations, and as it were glances of history towards philosophy; both by way of an assurance to men that they will not be kept forever tossing on the waves of experience, and also that when the time comes for the intellect to begin its work, it may find everything the more ready. By such a natural history then as I have described, I conceive that a safe and convenient approach may be made to nature, and matter supplied of good quality and well prepared for the understanding to work upon.

And now that we have surrounded the intellect with faithful helps and guards, and got together with more careful selection a regular army of divine works, it may seem that we have no more to do but to proceed to philosophy itself. And yet in a matter so difficult and doubtful there are still some things which it seems necessary to premise, partly for convenience of explanation, partly for present use.

Of these the first is to set forth examples of inquiry and invention according to my method, exhibited by anticipation in some particular subjects; choosing such subjects as are at once the most noble in themselves among those under inquiry, and most different one from another, that there may be an example in every kind. I do not speak of those examples which are joined to the several precepts and rules by way of illustration (for of these I have given plenty in the second part of the work), but I mean actual types and models, by which the entire process of the mind and the whole fabric and order of invention from the beginning to the end, in certain subjects, and those various and remarkable, should be set as it were before the eyes. For I remember that in the mathematics it is easy to follow the demonstration when you have a machine beside you, whereas without that help all appears involved and more subtle than it really is. To examples of this kind, being in fact nothing more than an application of the second part in detail and at large, the fourth part of the work is devoted.

The fifth part is for temporary use only, pending the completion of the rest, like interest payable from time to time until the principal be forthcoming. For I do not make so blindly for the end of my journey, as to neglect anything useful that may turn up by the way. And therefore I include in this fifth part such things as I have myself discovered, proved, or added—not however according to the true rules and methods of interpretation, but by the ordinary use of the understanding in inquiring and discovering. For besides that I hope my speculations may in virtue of my continual conversancy with nature have a value beyond the pretensions of my wit, they will serve in the meantime for wayside inns, in which the mind may rest and refresh itself on its journey to more certain conclusions. Nevertheless, I wish it to be understood in the meantime that they are conclusions by which (as not being discovered and proved by the true form of interpretation) I do not at all mean to bind myself. Nor need any one be alarmed at such suspension of judgment, in one who maintains not simply that nothing can be known, but only that nothing can be known except in a certain course and way; and yet establishes provisionally certain degrees of assurance, for use and relief until the mind shall arrive at a knowledge of causes in which it can rest. For even those schools of philosophy which held the absolute impossibility of knowing anything were not inferior to those which took upon them to pronounce. But then they did not provide helps for the sense and understanding, as I have done, but simply took away all their authority, which is quite a different thing— almost the reverse.

The sixth part of my work (to which the rest is subservient and ministrant) discloses and sets forth that philosophy which by the legitimate, chaste, and severe course of inquiry which I have explained and provided is at length developed and established. The completion, however, of this last part is a thing both above my strength and beyond my hopes. I have made a beginning of the work—a beginning, as I hope, not unimportant—the fortune of the human race will give the issue, such an issue, it may be, as in the present condition of things and men's minds cannot easily be conceived or imagined. For the matter in hand is no mere felicity of speculation, but the real business and fortunes of the human race, and all power of operation. For man is but the servant and interpreter of nature: what he does and what he knows is only what he has observed of nature's order in fact or in thought; beyond this he knows nothing and can do nothing. For the chain of causes cannot by any force be loosed or broken, nor can nature be commanded except by being obeyed. And so those twin objects, human knowledge and human power, do really meet in one, and it is from ignorance of causes that operation fails.

And all depends on keeping the eye steadily fixed upon the facts of nature and so receiving their images simply as they are. For God forbid that we should give out a dream of our own imagination for a pattern of the world; rather may he graciously grant to us to write an apocalypse or true vision of the footsteps of the Creator imprinted on his creatures.

Therefore do thou, O Father, who gave the visible light as the first fruits of creation, and did breathe into the face of man the intellectual light as the crown and consummation thereof, guard and protect this work, which coming from thy goodness returneth to thy glory. Thou, when thou turned to look upon the works which thy hands had made, saw that all was very good and did rest from thy labors. But man when he turned to look upon the work which his hands had made, saw that all was vanity and vexation of spirit, and could find no rest therein. Wherefore if we labor in thy works with the sweat of our brows, thou will make us partakers of thy vision and thy Sabbath. Humbly we pray that this mind may be steadfast in us, and that through these our hands, and the hands of others to whom thou shall give the same spirit, thou will vouchsafe to endow the human family with new mercies.

Natural and Experimental History for the Foundation of Philosophy
(The Great Instauration, Part III)

PREFACE

Men are to be admonished, nay urged and entreated as they value their fortunes, to be lowly of mind and search for knowledge in the greater world, and to throw aside all thought of philosophy, or at least to expect but little and poor fruit from it, until an approved and careful Natural and Experimental History be prepared and constructed. For to what purpose are these brain creations and idle displays of power? In ancient times there were philosophical doctrines in plenty—doctrines of Pythagoras, Philolaus, Xenophanes, Heraclitus, Empedocles, Parmenides, Anaxagoras, Leucippus, Democritus, Plato, Aristotle, Zeno, and others. All these invented systems of the universe, each according to his own fancy, like so many arguments of plays; and those their inventions they recited and published; whereof some were more elegant and probable, others harsh and unlikely.

Nor in our age, though by reason of the institutions of schools and colleges wits are more restrained, has the practice entirely ceased—for Patricius, Telesius, Brunus, Severinus the Dane, Gilbert the Englishman, and Campanella have come upon the stage with fresh stories, neither honored by approbation nor elegant in argument. Are we then to wonder at this, as if there would not be innumerable sects and opinions of this kind in all ages? There is not and never will be an end or limit to this. One catches at one thing, another at another. Each has his favorite fancy. Pure and open light there is none. Every one philosophizes out of the cells of his own imagination, as out of Plato's cave, the higher wits with more acuteness, the duller, less happily but with equal pertinacity.

And now of late by the regulation of some learned and (as things now are) excellent men (the former variety and license having I suppose become wearisome), the sciences are confined to certain and prescribed authors, and thus restrained are imposed upon the old and instilled into the young so that now (to use the sarcasm of Cicero concerning Caesar's year), the constellation of Lyra rises by edict, and authority is taken for truth, not truth for authority. Which kind of situation and discipline is excellent for present use, but precludes all prospect of improvement. For we copy the sin of our first parents while we suffer for it. They wished to be like God, but their posterity wish to be even greater. For we create worlds, we direct and domineer over nature, we will have it that all things *are* as in our folly we think they should be, not as seems fittest to the Divine wisdom, or as they are found to be in fact; and I know not whether we more distort the facts of nature or our own wits, but we clearly impress the stamp of our own image on the creatures and works of God, instead of carefully examining and recognizing in them the stamp of the Creator himself. Wherefore our dominion over creatures is a second time forfeited, not undeservedly, and whereas after the fall of man some power over the resistance of creatures was still left to him— the power of subduing and managing them by true and solid arts—yet this too through our insolence, and because we desire to be like God and to follow the dictates of our own reason, we in great part lose.

If, therefore, there be any humility towards the Creator, any reverence for or disposition to magnify His works, any charity for man and anxiety to relieve his sorrows and necessities, any love of truth in nature, any hatred of darkness, any desire for the purification of the understanding, we must entreat men again and again to discard, or at least set apart for a while, these volatile and preposterous philosophies, which have preferred theses to hypotheses, led experience captive, and triumphed over the works of God; and to approach with humility and veneration to unroll the volume of Creation, to linger and meditate therein, and with minds washed clean from opinions, to study it in purity and integrity. For this is that sound and language which went forth into all lands, and did not incur the confusion of Babel; this should men study to be perfect in, and becoming again as little children, condescend to take the alphabet of it into their hands, and spare no pains to search and unravel the interpretation thereof, but pursue it strenuously and persevere even unto death.

Having therefore in my Instauration placed the Natural History—such a Natural History as may serve my purpose—in the third part of the work, I have thought it right to make some anticipation thereof, and to enter upon it at once. For although not a few things, and those among the most important, still remain to be completed in my Organon, yet my design is rather to advance the universal work of Instauration in many things, than to perfect it in a few; ever earnestly desiring, with such a passion as we believe God alone inspires, that this which has been hitherto unattempted may not now be attempted in vain. It has occurred to me likewise, that there are doubtless many wits scattered over Europe, capacious, open, lofty, subtle, solid, and constant. What if one of them were to enter into the plan of my Organon and try to use it? He yet knows not what to do, nor how to prepare and address himself to the work of philosophy. If indeed it were a thing that could be accomplished by reading of philosophical books, or discussion, or meditation, he might be equal to the work, whoever he be, and discharge it well, but if I refer him to natural history and the experiments of arts (as in fact I do), it is out of his line, he has not leisure for it, he cannot afford the expense. Yet I would not ask any one to give up what he has until he can exchange it for something better.

But when a true and copious history of nature and the arts shall have been once collected and digested, and when it shall have been set forth and unfolded before men's eyes, then will there be good hope that those great wits I spoke of before, such as flourished in the old philosophers, and are even still often to be found—wits so vigorous that out of a mere plank or shell (that is out of scanty and trifling experience) they could frame certain barks of philosophy of admirable construction as far as the work is concerned—after they have obtained proper material and provision will raise much more solid structures; and that too though they prefer to walk on in the old path, and not by the way of my Organon, which in my estimation, if not the only, is at least the best course. It comes, therefore, to this: that my Organon, even if it were completed, would not without the Natural History much advance the Instauration of the Sciences, whereas the Natural History without the Organon would advance it not a little. And, therefore, I have thought it better and wiser by all means and above all things, to apply myself to this work. May God, the Founder, Preserver, and Renewer of the universe, in His love and compassion to men, protect and rule this work, both in its ascent to His glory and in its descent to the good of man, through his only Son, God with us.

True Directions Concerning the Interpretation of Nature
(Norum Organum II)

PREFACE

Those who have taken upon them to lay down the law of nature as a thing already searched out and understood, whether they have spoken in simple assurance or professional affectation, have therein done philosophy and the sciences great injury. For as they have been successful in inducing belief, so they have been effective, in quenching and stopping inquiry; and have done more harm by spoiling and putting an end to other men's efforts than good by their own. Those on the other hand who have taken a contrary course, and asserted that absolutely nothing can be known,—whether it were from hatred of the ancient sophists, or from uncertainty and fluctuation of mind, or even from a kind of fulness of learning, that they fell upon this opinion,—have certainly advanced reasons for it that are not to be despised; but yet they have neither started from true principles nor rested in the just conclusion, zeal and affectation having carried them much too far. The more ancient of the Greeks (whose writings are lost) took up with better judgment a position between these two extremes,—between the presumption of pronouncing on everything, and the despair of comprehending anything; and though frequently and bitterly complaining of the difficulty of inquiry and the obscurity of things, and like impatient horses champing the bit, they did not the less follow up their object and engage with Nature; thinking (it seems) that this very question,—viz. whether or no anything can be known,—was to be settled not by arguing, but by trying. And yet they too, trusting entirely to the force of their understanding, applied no rule, but made everything turn upon hard thinking and perpetual working and exercise of the mind.

Now my method, though hard to practise, is easy to explain; and it is this. I propose to establish progressive stages of certainty. The evidence of the sense, helped and guarded by a certain process of correction, I retain. But the mental operation which follows the act of sense I for the most part reject; and instead of it I open and lay out a new and certain path for the mind to proceed in, starting directly from the simple sensuous perception. The necessity of this was felt no doubt by those who attributed so much importance to Logic; showing thereby that they were in search of helps for the understanding, and had no confidence in the native and spontaneous process of the mind. But this remedy comes too late to do any good, when the mind is already, through the daily intercourse and conversation of life, occupied with unsound doctrines and beset on all sides by vain imaginations. And therefore that art of Logic, coming (as I said) too late to the rescue, and no way able to set matters right again, has had the effect of fixing errors rather than disclosing truth. There remains but one course for the recovery of a sound and healthy condition,—namely, that the entire work of the understanding be commenced afresh, and the mind itself be from the very outset not left to take its own course, but guided at every step; and the business be done as if by machinery. Certainly if in things mechanical men had set to work with their naked hands, without help or force of instruments, just as in things intellectual they have set to work with little else than the naked forces of the understanding, very small would the matters have been which, even with their best efforts applied in conjunction, they could have attempted or accomplished. Now (to pause awhile upon this example and look in it as in a glass) let us suppose that some vast obelisk were (for the decoration of a triumph or some such magnificence) to be removed from its place, and that men should set to work upon it with their naked hands; would not any sober spectator think them mad? And if they should then send for more people, thinking that in that way they might manage it, would he not think them all the madder? And if they then proceeded to make a selection, putting away the weaker hands, and using only the strong and vigorous, would he not think them madder than ever? And if lastly, not content with this, they resolved to call in aid the art of athletics, and required all their men to come with hands, arms, and sinews well anointed and medicated according to the rules of art, would he not cry out that they were only taking pains to show a kind of method and discretion in their madness? Yet just so it is that men proceed in matters intellectual,—with just the same kind of mad effort and useless combination of forces,—when they hope great things either from the number and cooperation or from the excellency and acuteness of individual wits; yea, and when they endeavour by Logic (which may be considered as a kind of athletic art) to strengthen the sinews of the understanding; and yet with all this study and endeavour it is apparent to any true judgment that they are but applying the naked intellect all the time; whereas in every great work to be done by the hand of man it is manifestly impossible, without instruments and machinery, either for the strength of each to be exerted or the strength of all to be united.

Upon these premises two things occur to me of which, that they may not be overlooked, I would have men reminded. First it falls out fortunately as I think for the allaying of contradictions and heart-burnings, that the honour and reverence due to the ancients remains untouched and undiminished; while I may carry out my designs and at the same time reap the fruit of my modesty. For if I should profess that I, going the same road as the ancients, have something better to produce, there must needs have been some comparison or rivalry between us (not to be avoided by any art of words) in respect of excellency or ability of wit; and though in this there would be nothing unlawful or new (for if there be anything misapprehended by them, or falsely laid down, why may not I, using a liberty common to all, take exception to it?) yet the contest, however just and allowable, would have been an unequal one perhaps, in respect of the measure of my own powers. As it is however,—my object being to open a new way for the understanding, a way by them untried and unknown,—the case is altered; party zeal and emulation are at an end; and I appear merely as a guide to point out the road; an office of small authority, and depending more upon a kind of luck than upon any ability or excellency. And thus much relates to the persons only. The other point of which I would have men reminded relates to the matter itself.

Be it remembered then that I am far from wishing to interfere with the philosophy which now flourishes, or with any other philosophy more correct and complete than this which has been or may hereafter be propounded. For I do not object to the use of this received philosophy, or others like it, for supplying matter for disputations or ornaments for discourse,—for the professor's lecture and for the business of life. Nay more, I declare openly that for these uses the philosophy which I bring forward will not be much available. It does not lie in the way. It cannot be caught up in passage. It does not flatter the understanding by conformity with preconceived notions. Nor will it come down to the apprehension of the vulgar except by its utility and effects.

Let there be therefore (and may it be for the benefit of both) two streams and two dispensations of knowledge; and in like manner two tribes or kindreds of students in philosophy—tribes not hostile or alien to each other, but bound together by mutual services—let there in short be one method for the cultivation, another for the invention, of knowledge.

And for those who prefer the former, either from hurry or from considerations of business or for want of mental power to take in and embrace the other (which must needs be most men's case), I wish that they may succeed to their desire in what they are about, and obtain what they are pursuing. But if any man there be who, not content to rest in and use the knowledge which has already been discovered, aspires to penetrate further; to overcome, not an adversary in argument, but nature in action; to seek, not pretty and probable conjectures, but certain and demonstrable knowledge—I invite all such to join themselves, as true sons of knowledge, with me, that passing by the outer courts of nature, which numbers have trodden, we may find a way at length into her inner chambers. And to make my meaning clearer and to familiarise the thing by giving it a name, I have chosen to call one of these methods or ways *Anticipation of the Mind*, the other *Interpretation of Nature*.

Moreover I have one request to make. I have on my own part made it my care and study that the things which I shall propound should not only be true, but should also be presented to men's minds, how strangely soever preoccupied and obstructed, in a manner not harsh or unpleasant. It is but reasonable however (especially in so great a restoration of learning and knowledge) that I should claim of men one favour in return; which is this; If any one would form an opinion or judgment either out of his own observation, or out of the crowd of authorities, or out of the forms of demonstration (which have now acquired a sanction like that of judicial laws), concerning these speculations of mine, let him not hope that he can do it in passage or by the by; but let him examine the thing thoroughly; let him make some little trial for himself of the way which I describe and lay out; let him familiarise his thoughts with that subtlety of nature to which experience bears witness; let him correct by seasonable patience and due delay the depraved and deep-rooted habits of his mind; and when all this is done and he has begun to be his own master, let him (if he will) use his own judgment.

Letter to My Treasurer Burghley (1592)

... I confess that I have as vast contemplative ends, as I have moderate civil ends: for I have taken all knowledge to be my province; and if I could purge it of two sorts of rovers, whereof the one with frivolous disputations, confutations, and verbosities, the other with blind experiments and auricular traditions and impostures, hath committed so many spoils, I hope I should bring in industrious observations, grounded conclusions, and profitable inventions and discoveries; the best state of that province. This, whether it be curiosity, or vain glory, or nature, or (if one take it favourably) *philanthropia*, is so fixed in my mind as it cannot be removed. And I do easily see, that place of any reasonable countenance doth bring commandment of more wits than of a man's own; which is the thing I greatly affect. And for your Lordship, perhaps you shall not find more strength and less encounter in any other. And if your Lordship shall find now, or at any time, that I do seek or affect any place whereunto any that is nearer unto your Lordship shall be concurrent, say then that I am a most dishonest man. And if your Lordship will not carry me on, I will not do as Anaxagoras did, who reduced himself with contemplation unto voluntary poverty: but this I will do; I will sell the inheritance that I have, and purchase some lease of quick revenue, or some office of gain that shall be executed by deputy, and so give over all care of service, and become some sorry bookmaker, or a true pioneer in that mine of truth, which (he said) lay so deep. This which I have writ unto your Lordship is rather thoughts than words, being set down without all art, disguising, or reservation. Wherein I have done honour both to your Lordship's wisdom, in judging that that will be best believed of your Lordship which is truest, and to your Lordship's good nature, in retaining nothing from you. And even so I wish your Lordship all happiness, and to myself means and occasion to be added to my faithful desire to do you service. From my lodging at Gray's Inn.

TO
THE RIGHT REVEREND FATHER IN GOD,
Lancelot Andrews,
LORD BISHOP OF WINCHESTER, AND COUNSELLOR OF ESTATE
to his majesty (1687)

My Lord,

Amongst consolations, it is not the least, to represent to a man's self like examples of calamity in others. For examples give a quicker impression than arguments; and besides, they certify us, that which the Scripture also tendereth for satisfaction, *that no new thing is happened unto us.* This they do the better, by how much the examples are liker in circumstances to our own case; and more especially if they fall upon persons that are greater and worthier than ourselves. For as it savoureth of vanity, to match ourselves highly in our own conceit; so on the other side it is a good sound conclusion, that if our betters have sustained the like events, we have the less cause to be grieved.

In this kind of consolation I have not been wanting to myself; though as a Christian I have tasted (through God's great goodness) of higher remedies. Having therefore, through the variety of my reading, set before me many examples both of ancient and later times, my thoughts (I confess) have chiefly stayed upon three particulars, as the most eminent and the most resembling. All three, persons that had held chief place of authority in their countries; all three ruined, not by war, or by any other disaster, but by justice and sentence, as delinquents and criminals; all three famous writers, insomuch as the remembrance of their calamity is now as to posterity but as a little picture of night-work, remaining amongst the fair and excellent tables of their acts and works; and all three (if that were any thing to the matter) fit examples to quench any man's ambition of rising again; for that they were everyone of them restored with great glory, but to their further ruin and destruction, ending in a violent death. The men were, Demosthenes, Cicero, and Seneca; persons that I durst not claim affinity with, except the similitude of our fortunes had contracted it. When I had cast mine eyes upon these examples, I was carried on further to observe how they did bear their fortunes, and principally how they did employ their times, being banished and disabled for public business: to the end that I might learn by them; and that they might be as well my counsellors as my comforters.

These examples confirmed me much in a resolution (whereunto I was otherwise inclined) to spend my time wholly in writing; and to put forth that poor talent, or half talent, or what it is, that God hath given me, not as heretofore to particular exchanges, but to banks or mounts of perpetuity, which will not break. Therefore having not long since set forth a part of my Instauration; which is the work, that in mine own judgment (*si nunquam fallit imago*) I do most esteem; I think to proceed in some new parts thereof. And although I have received from many parts beyond the seas, testimonies touching that work, such as beyond which I could not expect at the first in so abtruse an argument; yet nevertheless I have just cause to doubt, that it flies too high over men's heads: I have a purpose therefore (though I break the order of time) to draw it down to the sense, by some patterns of a Natural Story and Inquisition. And again, for that my book of Advancement of Learning may be some preparative, or key, for the better opening of the Instauration; because it exhibits a mixture of new conceits and old; whereas the Instauration gives the new unmixed, otherwise than with some little aspersion of the old for taste's sake; I have thought good to procure a translation of that book into the general language, not without great and ample additions and enrichment thereof, especially in the second book, which handleth the Partition of Sciences; in such sort, as I hold it may serve in lieu of the first part of the Instauration, and acquit my promise in that part. Again, because I cannot altogether desert the civil person that I have borne; which if I should forget, enough would remember; I have also entered into a work touching Laws, propounding a character of Justice, in a middle term, between the speculative and reverend discourses of philosophers, and the writings of lawyers which are tied and obnoxious to their particular laws. And although it be true, that I had a purpose to make a particular digest or recompilement of the laws of mine own nation; yet because it is a work of assistance, and that that I cannot master by mine own forces and pen, I have laid it aside. Now having in the work of my Instauration had in contemplation the general good of men in their very being, and the dowries of nature: and in my work of Laws, the general good of men likewise in society, and the dowries of government; I thought in duty I owed somewhat unto mine own country, which I ever loved; insomuch as although my place hath been far above my desert, yet my thoughts and cares concerning the good thereof were beyond and over and above my place: so now being (as I am) no more able to do my country service, it remained unto me to do it honour: which I have endeavoured to do in my work of The reign of King Henry the Seventh. As for my Essays, and some other particulars of that nature, I count them but as the recreations of my other studies, and in that sort purpose to continue them; though I am not ignorant that those kind of writings would with loss pains and embracement (perhaps) yield more lustre and reputation to my name than those other which I have in hand. But I account the use that a man should seek of the publishing of his own writings before his death, to be but an untimely anticipation of that which is proper to follow a man and not to go along with him.

But revolving with myself my writings, as well those which I have published, as those which I had in hand, methought they went all into the city, and none into the temple, where because I have found so great consolation, I desire likewise to make some poor oblation. Therefore I have chosen an argument mixt of religious and civil considerations; and likewise mixt between contemplative and active. For who can tell whether there may not be an *Exoriere aliquis*. Great matters (especially if they be religious) have (many times) small beginnings: and the platform may draw on the building. This work, because I was ever an enemy to flattering dedications, I have dedicated to your Lordship, in respect of our ancient and private acquaintance; and because amongst the men of our times I hold you in special reverence.

Your Lordship's loving friend,
Fr. St. Alban.

8

RENÉ DESCARTES
Moving Toward Clarity

René Descartes (1596–1650) was educated at the Jesuit school of La Flèche. After studying law at Poitiers, he volunteered in the Dutch and Bavarian armies. Recognizing that a military life would not suit him, he turned his gifts and attention to mathematics, physics, and optics. He unified algebra and geometry; he gave a rough formulation of the law of inertia; and he proposed to reduce secondary sensory qualities to the primary—and quantifiable—properties of extension: shape, size, and motion. Arguing that scientific demonstration should not appeal to authority, tradition, canonical texts or literary allusions, he modeled the theoretical natural sciences—physics and optics, for example—on deductive geometry. Descartes established the criteria for what became the canonical method of proof in the theoretical sciences, deriving increasingly complex theorems from premises and definitions by the application of the law of noncontradiction.

Descartes also experimented with different philosophic genres, each with a distinctive model and method suited to different audiences. His reconstructed idealized intellectual autobiography *Discourse on the Method of Rightly Conducting One's Reason and Seeking the Truth in the Sciences* (1637) was published as the preface to a collection of scientific essays (*Optics, Meteorology*, and *Geometry*). In his dedication to Faculty of Theology at the Sorbonne, Descartes announced that the *Meditations on First Philosophy* (1641) was designed to provide a rational demonstration of the existence of God and the immortality of the soul. Cast in the form of a traditional spiritual exercise, it retained some Scholastic aims and premises. Descartes asked Mersenne to solicit objections to the claims of the *Meditations*. These objections, along with his detailed replies were appended to the work. The *Principles of Philosophy* (1644) and *Rules for the Direction of the Mind* provide guiding rules and principles for logical analysis and demonstration. His *Treatise on the Passions of the Soul* (1649) is a reply to objections and questions about the psychology of the emotions that had been raised by Princess Elizabeth of Bohemia. Descartes also carried on a vast correspondence with the major scientific and philosophic figures of his time, including Hobbes, Huygens, Gassendi, Mersenne, and Harvey.

Discourse on the Method of Rightly Conducting One's Reason and Seeking the Truth in the Sciences

If this discourse seems too long to be read at a sitting you may divide it into six parts. In the first you will find various considerations regarding the sciences; in the second, the principal rules of the method which the author has sought; in the third, some of the moral rules he has derived from this method; in the fourth, the arguments by which he proves the existence of God and the human soul, which are the foundations of his metaphysics; in the fifth, the order of the questions in physics that he has investigated, particularly the explanation of the movement of the heart and of some other difficulties pertaining to medicine, and also the difference between our soul and that of the beasts; and in the last, the things he believes necessary in order to make further progress in the investigation of nature than he has made, and the reasons which made him write this discourse.

PART ONE

Good sense is the best distributed thing in the world: for everyone thinks himself so well endowed with it that even those who are the hardest to please in everything else do not usually desire more of it than they possess. In this it is unlikely that everyone is mistaken. It indicates rather that the power of judging well and of distinguishing the true from the false—which is what we properly call 'good sense' or 'reason'—is naturally equal in all men, and consequently that the diversity of our opinions does not arise because some of us are more reasonable than others but solely because we direct our thoughts along different paths and do not attend to the same things. For it is not enough to have a good mind; the main thing is to apply it well. The greatest souls are capable of the greatest vices as well as the greatest virtues; and those who proceed but very slowly can make much greater progress, if they always follow the right path, than those who hurry and stray from it.

For my part, I have never presumed my mind to be in any way more perfect than that of the ordinary man; indeed, I have often wished to have as quick a wit, or as sharp and distinct an imagination, or as ample or prompt a memory as some others. And apart from these, I know of no other qualities which serve to perfect the mind; for, as regards reason or sense, since it is the only thing that makes us men and distinguishes us from the beasts, I am inclined to believe that it exists whole and complete in each of us. Here I follow the common opinion of the philosophers, who say there are differences of degree only between the *accidents*, and not between the *forms* (or natures) of *individuals* of the same *species*.

But I say without hesitation that I consider myself very fortunate to have happened upon certain paths in my youth which led me to considerations and maxims from which I formed a method whereby, it seems to me, I can increase my knowledge gradually and raise it little by little to the highest point allowed by the mediocrity of my mind and the short duration of my life. Now I always try to lean towards diffidence rather than presumption in the judgements I make about myself; and when I cast a philosophical eye upon the various activities and undertakings of mankind, there are almost none which I do not consider vain and useless. Nevertheless I have already reaped such fruits from this method that I cannot but feel extremely satisfied with the progress I think I have already made in the search for truth, and I cannot but entertain such hopes for the future as to venture the opinion that if any purely human occupation has solid worth and importance, it is the one I have chosen.

Yet I may be wrong: perhaps what I take for gold and diamonds is nothing but a bit of copper and glass. I know how much we are liable to err in matters that concern us, and also how much the judgements of our friends should be distrusted when they are in our favour. I shall be glad, nevertheless, to reveal in this discourse what paths I have followed, and to represent my life in it as if in a picture, so that everyone may judge it for himself; and thus, learning from public response the opinions held of it, I shall add a new means of self-instruction to those I am accustomed to using.

My present aim, then, is not to teach the method which everyone must follow in order to direct his reason correctly, but only to reveal how I have tried to direct my own. One who presumes to give precepts must think himself more skillful than those to whom he gives them; and if he makes the slightest mistake, he may be blamed. But I am presenting this work only as a history or, if you prefer, a fable in which, among certain examples worthy of imitation, you will perhaps also find many others that it would be right not to follow; and so I hope it will be useful for some without being harmful to any, and that everyone will be grateful to me for my frankness.

From my childhood I have been nourished upon letters, and because I was persuaded that by their means one could acquire a clear and certain knowledge of all that is useful in life, I was extremely eager to learn them. But as soon as I had completed the course of study at the end of which one is normally admitted to the ranks of the learned, I completely changed my opinion. For I found myself beset by so many doubts and errors that I came to think I had gained nothing from my attempts to become educated but increasing recognition of my ignorance. And yet I was at one of the most famous schools in Europe, where I thought there must be learned men if they existed anywhere on earth. There I had learned everything that the others were learning; moreover, not content with the subjects they taught us, I had gone through all the books that fell into my hands concerning the subjects that are considered most abstruse and unusual. At the same time, I knew how the others judged me, and I saw that they did not regard me as inferior to my fellow students, even though several among them were already destined to take the place of our teachers. And finally, the age in which we live seemed to me to be as flourishing, and as rich in good minds, as any before it. This made me feel free to judge all others by reference to myself and think there was no knowledge in the world such as I had previously been led to hope for.

I did not, however, cease to value the exercises done in the Schools. I knew that the languages learned there are necessary for understanding the works of the ancients; that the charm of fables awakens the mind, while the memorable deeds told in histories uplift it and help to shape one's judgement if they are read with discretion; that reading good books is like having a conversation with the most distinguished men of past ages—indeed, a rehearsed conversation in which these authors reveal to us only the best of their thoughts; that oratory has incomparable powers and beauties; that poetry has quite ravishing delicacy and sweetness; that mathematics contains some very subtle devices which serve as much to satisfy the curious as to further all the arts and lessen man's labours; that writings on morals contain many very useful teachings and exhortations to virtue; that theology instructs us how to reach heaven; that philosophy gives us the means of speaking plausibly about any subject and of winning the admiration of the less learned; that jurisprudence, medicine, and other sciences bring honours and riches to those who cultivate them; and, finally, that it is good to have examined all these subjects, even those full of superstition and falsehood, in order to know their true value and guard against being deceived by them.

But I thought I had already given enough time to languages and likewise to reading the works of the ancients, both their histories and their fables. For con-

versing with those of past centuries is much the same as travelling. It is good to
know something of the customs of various peoples, so that we may judge our
own more soundly and not think that everything contrary to our own ways is
ridiculous and irrational, as those who have seen nothing of the world ordinarily
do. But one who spends too much time travelling eventually becomes a stranger
in his own country; and one who is too curious about the practices of past ages
usually remains quite ignorant about those of the present. Moreover, fables make
us imagine many events as possible when they are not. And even the most accurate histories, while not altering or exaggerating the importance of matters to
make them more worthy of being read, at any rate almost always omit the baser
and less notable events; as a result, the other events appear in a false light, and
those who regulate their conduct by examples drawn from these works are liable
to fall into the excesses of the knights-errant in our tales of chivalry, and conceive
plans beyond their powers.

I valued oratory and was fond of poetry; but I thought both were gifts of the
mind rather than fruits of study. Those with the strongest reasoning and the most
skill at ordering their thoughts so as to make them clear and intelligible are
always the most persuasive, even if they speak only low Breton and have never
learned rhetoric. And those with the most pleasing conceits and the ability to
express them with the most embellishment and sweetness would still be the best
poets, even if they knew nothing of the theory of poetry.

Above all I delighted in mathematics, because of the certainty and self-
evidence of its reasonings. But I did not yet notice its real use; and since I thought
it was of service only in the mechanical arts, I was surprised that nothing more
exalted had been built upon such firm and solid foundations. On the other hand,
I compared the moral writings of the ancient pagans to very proud and magnificent palaces built only on sand and mud. They extol the virtues, and make them
appear more estimable than anything else in the world; but they do not adequately explain how to recognize a virtue, and often what they call by this fine
name is nothing but a case of callousness, or vanity, or desperation, or parricide.

I revered our theology, and aspired as much as anyone else to reach heaven.
But having learned as an established fact that the way to heaven is open no less
to the most ignorant than to the most learned, and that the revealed truths which
guide us there are beyond our understanding, I would not have dared submit
them to my weak reasonings; and I thought that to undertake an examination of
them and succeed, I would need to have some extraordinary aid from heaven
and to be more than a mere man.

Regarding philosophy, I shall say only this: seeing that it has been cultivated
for many centuries by the most excellent minds and yet there is still no point in
it which is not disputed and hence doubtful, I was not so presumptuous as to
hope to achieve any more in it than others had done. And, considering how many
diverse opinions learned men may maintain on a single question—even though
it is impossible for more than one to be true—I held as well-nigh false everything
that was merely probable.

As for the other sciences, in so far as they borrow their principles from philosophy I decided that nothing solid could have been built upon such shaky
foundations. Neither the honour nor the riches they offered was enough to induce
me to learn them. For my circumstances did not, thanks to God, oblige me to
augment my fortune by making science my profession; and although I did not
profess to scorn glory, like a Cynic, yet I thought very little of the glory which I

could hope to acquire only through false pretences. Finally, as for the false sciences, I thought that I already knew their worth well enough not to be liable to be deceived by the promises of an alchemist or the predictions of an astrologer, the tricks of a magician or the frauds and boasts of those who profess to know more than they do.

That is why, as soon as I was old enough to emerge from the control of my teachers, I entirely abandoned the study of letters. Resolving to seek no knowledge other than that which could be found in myself or else in the great book of the world, I spent the rest of my youth travelling, visiting courts and armies, mixing with people of diverse temperaments and ranks, gathering various experiences, testing myself in the situations which fortune offered me, and at all times reflecting upon whatever came my way so as to derive some profit from it. For it seemed to me that much more truth could be found in the reasonings which a man makes concerning matters that concern him than in those which some scholar makes in his study about speculative matters. For the consequences of the former will soon punish the man if he judges wrongly, whereas the latter have no practical consequences and no importance for the scholar except that perhaps the further they are from common sense the more pride he will take in them, since he will have had to use so much more skill and ingenuity in trying to render them plausible. And it was always my most earnest desire to learn to distinguish the true from the false in order to see clearly into my own actions and proceed with confidence in this life.

It is true that, so long as I merely considered the customs of other men, I found hardly any reason for confidence, for I observed in them almost as much diversity as I had found previously among the opinions of philosophers. In fact the greatest benefit I derived from these observations was that they showed me many things which, although seeming very extravagant and ridiculous to us, are nevertheless commonly accepted and approved in other great nations; and so I learned not to believe too firmly anything of which I had been persuaded only by example and custom. Thus I gradually freed myself from many errors which may obscure our natural light and make us less capable of heeding reason. But after I had spent some years pursuing these studies in the book of the world and trying to gain some experience, I resolved one day to undertake studies within myself too and to use all the powers of my mind in choosing the paths I should follow. In this I have had much more success, I think, than I would have had if I had never left my country or my books.

PART TWO

At that time I was in Germany, where I had been called by the wars that are not yet ended there. While I was returning to the army from the coronation of the Emperor, the onset of winter detained me in quarters where, finding no conversation to divert me and fortunately having no cares or passions to trouble me, I stayed all day shut up alone in a stove-heated room, where I was completely free to converse with myself about my own thoughts. Among the first that occurred to me was the thought that there is not usually so much perfection in works composed of several parts and produced by various different craftsmen as in the works of one man. Thus we see that buildings undertaken and completed by a single architect are usually more attractive and better planned than those which several have tried to patch up by adapting old walls built for different purposes. Again, ancient cities which have gradually grown from mere villages into large towns are usually ill-proportioned, compared with those orderly towns which planners lay out as they fancy on level ground. Looking at the buildings of the former individually, you will often find as much art in them, if not more, than in those of the latter; but in view of their arrangement—a tall one here, a small one there—and the way they make the streets crooked and irregular, you would say it is chance, rather than the will of men using reason, that placed them so. And when you consider that there have always been certain officials whose job is to see that private buildings embellish public places, you will understand how difficult it is to make something perfect by working only on what others have produced. Again, I thought, peoples who have grown gradually from a half-savage to a civilized state, and have made their laws only in so far as they were forced to by the inconvenience of crimes and quarrels, could not be so well governed as those who from the beginning of their society have observed the basic laws laid down by some wise law-giver. Similarly, it is quite certain that the constitution of the true religion, whose articles have been made by God alone, must be incomparably better ordered than all the others. And to speak of human affairs, I believe that if Sparta was at one time very flourishing, this was not because each of its laws in particular was good (seeing that some were very strange and even contrary to good morals), but because they were devised by a single man and hence all tended to the same end. And so I thought that since the sciences contained in books—at least those based upon merely probable, not demonstrative, reasoning—is compounded and amassed little by little from the opinions of many different persons, it never comes so close to the truth as the simple reasoning which a man of good sense naturally makes concerning what-ever he comes across. So, too, I reflected that we were all children before being men and had to be governed for some time by our appetites and our teachers, which were often opposed to each other and neither of which, perhaps, always gave us the best advice; hence I thought it virtually impossible that our judge-ments should be as unclouded and firm as they would have been if we had had the full use of our reason from the moment of our birth, and if we had always been guided by it alone.

Admittedly, we never see people pulling down all the houses of a city for the sole purpose of rebuilding them in a different style to make the streets more attractive; but we do see many individuals having their houses pulled down in order to rebuild them, some even being forced to do so when the houses are in danger of falling down and their foundations are insecure. This example con-vinced me that it would be unreasonable for an individual to plan to reform a state by changing it from the foundations up and overturning it in order to set it up again; or again for him to plan to reform the body of the sciences or the established order of teaching them in the schools. But regarding the opinions to which I had hitherto given credence, I thought that I could not do better than undertake to get rid of them, all at one go, in order to replace them afterwards with better ones, or with the same ones once I had squared them with the stan-dards of reason. I firmly believed that in this way I would succeed in conducting my life much better than if I built only upon old foundations and relied only upon principles that I had accepted in my youth without ever examining whether they were true. For although I noted various difficulties in this undertaking, they were not insurmountable. Nor could they be compared with those encountered in the reform of even minor matters affecting public institutions. These large bodies are too difficult to raise up once overthrown, or even to hold up once they begin to totter, and their fall cannot but be a hard one. Moreover, any imperfections they may possess—and their very diversity suffices to ensure that many do possess them—have doubtless been much smoothed over by custom; and custom has even prevented or imperceptibly corrected many imperfections that prudence could not so well provide against. Finally, it is almost always easier to put up with their imperfections than to change them, just as it is much better to follow the main roads that wind through mountains, which have gradually become smooth and convenient through frequent use, than to try to take a more direct route by clambering over rocks and descending to the foot of precipices.

That is why I cannot by any means approve of those meddlesome and restless characters who, called neither by birth nor by fortune to the management of public affairs, are yet forever thinking up some new reform. And if I thought this book contained the slightest ground for suspecting me of such folly, I would be very reluctant to permit its publication. My plan has never gone beyond trying to reform my own thoughts and construct them upon a foundation which is all my own. If I am sufficiently pleased with my work to present you with this sample of it, this does not mean that I would advise anyone to imitate it. Those on whom God has bestowed more of his favours will perhaps have higher aims; but I fear that even my aim may be too bold for many people. The simple resolution to abandon all the opinions one has hitherto accepted is not an example that everyone ought to follow. The world is largely composed of two types of minds for whom it is quite unsuitable. First, there are those who, believing themselves cleverer than they are, cannot avoid precipitate judgements and never have the patience to direct all their thoughts in an orderly manner; consequently, if they once took the liberty of doubting the principles they accepted and of straying from the common path, they could never stick to the track that must be taken as a short-cut, and they would remain lost all their lives. Second, there are those who have enough reason or modesty to recognize that they are less capable of distinguishing the true from the false than certain others by whom they can be taught; such people should be content to follow the opinions of these others rather than seek better opinions themselves.

For myself, I would undoubtedly have been counted among the latter if I had had only one teacher or if I had never known the differences that have always existed among the opinions of the most learned. But in my college days I discovered that nothing can be imagined which is too strange or incredible to have been said by some philosopher; and since then I have recognized through my travels that those with views quite contrary to ours are not on that account barbarians or savages, but that many of them make use of reason as much or more than we do. I thought, too, how the same man, with the same mind, if brought up from infancy among the French or Germans, develops otherwise than he would if he had always lived among the Chinese or cannibals; and how, even in our fashions of dress, the very thing that pleased us ten years ago, and will perhaps please us again ten years hence, now strikes us as extravagant and ridiculous. Thus it is custom and example that persuade us, rather than any certain knowledge. And yet a majority vote is worthless as a proof of truths that are at all difficult to discover; for a single man is much more likely to hit upon them than a group of people. I was, then, unable to choose anyone whose opinions struck me as preferable to those of all others, and I found myself as it were forced to become my own guide.

But, like a man who walks alone in the dark, I resolved to proceed so slowly, and to use such circumspection in all things, that even if I made but little progress I should at least be sure not to fall. Nor would I begin rejecting completely any of the opinions which may have slipped into my mind without having been introduced there by reason, until I had first spent enough time in planning the work I was undertaking and in seeking the true method of attaining the knowledge of everything within my mental capabilities.

When I was younger, my philosophical studies had included some logic, and my mathematical studies some geometrical analysis and algebra. These three arts or sciences, it seemed, ought to contribute something to my plan. But on further examination I observed with regard to logic that syllogisms and most of its other techniques are of less use for learning things than for explaining to others the things one already knows or even, as in the art of Lully, for speaking without judgement about matters of which one is ignorant. And although logic does contain many excellent and true precepts, these are mixed up with so many others which are harmful or superfluous that it is almost as difficult to distinguish them as it is to carve a Diana or a Minerva from an unhewn block of marble. As to the analysis of the ancients and the algebra of the moderns, they cover only highly abstract matters, which seem to have no use. Moreover the former is so closely tied to the examination of figures that it cannot exercise the intellect without greatly tiring the imagination; and the latter is so confined to certain rules and symbols that the end result is a confused and obscure art which encumbers the mind, rather than a science which cultivates it. For this reason I thought I had to seek some other method comprising the advantages of these three subjects but free from their defects. Now a multiplicity of laws often provides an excuse for vices, so that a state is much better governed when it has but few laws which are strictly observed; in the same way, I thought, in place of the large number of rules that make up logic, I would find the following four to be sufficient, provided that I made a strong and unswerving resolution never to fail to observe them.

The first was never to accept anything as true if I did not have evident knowledge of its truth: that is, carefully to avoid precipitate conclusions and preconceptions, and to include nothing more in my judgements than what presented itself to my mind so clearly and so distinctly that I had no occasion to doubt it.

The second, to divide each of the difficulties I examined into as many parts as possible and as may be required in order to resolve them better.

The third, to direct my thoughts in an orderly manner, by beginning with the simplest and most easily known objects in order to ascend little by little, step by step, to knowledge of the most complex, and by supposing some order even among objects that have no natural order of precedence.

And the last, throughout to make enumerations so complete, and reviews so comprehensive, that I could be sure of leaving nothing out.

Those long chains composed of very simple and easy reasonings, which geometers customarily use to arrive at their most difficult demonstrations, had given me occasion to suppose that all the things which can fall under human knowledge are interconnected in the same way. And I thought that, provided we refrain from accepting anything as true which is not, and always keep to the order required for deducing one thing from another, there can be nothing too remote to be reached in the end or too well hidden to be discovered. I had no great difficulty in deciding which things to begin with, for I knew already that it must be with the simplest and most easily known. Reflecting, too, that of all those who have hitherto sought after truth in the sciences, mathematicians alone have been able to find any demonstrations—that is to say, certain and evident reasonings—I had no doubt that I should begin with the very things that they studied. From this, however, the only advantage I hoped to gain was to accustom my mind to nourish itself on truths and not to be satisfied with bad reasoning. Nor did I have any intention of trying to learn all the special sciences commonly called 'mathematics'. For I saw that, despite the diversity of their objects, they agree in considering nothing but the various relations or proportions that hold between these objects. And so I thought it best to examine only such proportions in general, supposing them to hold only between such items as would help me to know them more easily. At the same time I would not restrict them to these items, so that I could apply them the better afterwards to whatever others they might fit. Next I observed that in order to know these proportions I would need sometimes to consider them separately, and sometimes merely to keep them in mind or understand many together. And I thought that in order the better to consider them separately I should suppose them to hold between lines, because I did not find anything simpler, nor anything that I could represent more distinctly to my imagination and senses. But in order to keep them in mind or understand several together, I thought it necessary to designate them by the briefest possible symbols. In this way I would take over all that is best in geometrical analysis and in algebra, using the one to correct all the defects of the other.

In fact, I venture to say that by strictly observing the few rules I had chosen. I became very adept at unravelling all the questions which fall under these two sciences. So much so, in fact, that in the two or three months I spent in examining them—beginning with the simplest and most general and using each truth I found as a rule for finding further truths—not only did I solve many problems which I had previously thought very difficult, but also it seemed to me towards the end that even in those cases where I was still in the dark I could determine by what means and to what extent it was possible to find a solution. This claim will not appear too arrogant if you consider that since there is only one truth concerning any matter, whoever discovers this truth knows as much about it as can be known. For example, if a child who has been taught arithmetic does a sum following the rules, he can be sure of having found everything the human mind can discover regarding the sum he was considering. In short, the method which instructs us to follow the correct order, and to enumerate exactly all the relevant factors, contains everything that gives certainty to the rules of arithmetic.

But what pleased me most about this method was that by following it I was sure in every case to use my reason, if not perfectly, at least as well as was in my power. Moreover, as I practised the method I felt my mind gradually become accustomed to conceiving its objects more clearly and distinctly; and since I did not restrict the method to any particular subject-matter, I hoped to apply it as usefully to the problems of the other sciences as I had to those of algebra. Not that I would have dared to try at the outset to examine every problem that might arise, for that would itself have been contrary to the order which the method prescribes. But observing that the principles of these sciences must all be derived from philosophy, in which I had not yet discovered any certain ones, I thought that first of all I had to try to establish some certain principles in philosophy. And since this is the most important task of all, and the one in which precipitate conclusions and preconceptions are most to be feared, I thought that I ought not try accomplish it until I had reached a more mature age than twenty-three, as I then was, and until I had first spent a long time in preparing myself for it. I had to uproot from my mind all the wrong opinions I had previously accepted, amass a variety of experiences to serve as the subject-matter of my reasonings, and practise constantly my self-prescribed method in order to strengthen myself more and more in its use.

PART THREE

Now, before starting to rebuild your house, it is not enough simply to pull it down, to make provision for materials and architects (or else train yourself in architecture), and to have carefully drawn up the plans; you must also provide yourself with some other place where you can live comfortably while building is in progress. Likewise, lest I should remain indecisive in my actions while reason obliged me to be so in my judgements, and in order to live as happily as I could during this time, I formed for myself a provisional moral code consisting of just three or four maxims, which I should like to tell you about.

The first was to obey the laws and customs of my country, holding constantly to the religion in which by God's grace I had been instructed from my childhood, and governing myself in all other matters according to the most moderate and least extreme opinions—the opinions commonly accepted in practice by the most sensible of those with whom I should have to live. For I had begun at this time to count my own opinions as worthless, because I wished to submit them all to examination, and so I was sure I could do no better than follow those of the most sensible men. And although there may be men as sensible among the Persians or Chinese as among ourselves, I thought it would be most useful for me to be guided by those with whom I should have to live. I thought too that in order to discover what opinions they really held I had to attend to what they did rather than what they said. For with our declining standards of behaviour, few people are willing to say everything that they believe; and besides, many people do not know what they believe, since believing something and knowing that one believes it are different acts of thinking, and the one often occurs without the other. Where many opinions were equally well accepted, I chose only the most moderate, both because these are always the easiest to act upon and probably the best (excess being usually bad), and also so that if I made a mistake, I should depart less from the right path than I would if I chose one extreme when I ought to have pursued the other. In particular, I counted as excessive all promises by which we give up some of our freedom. It was not that I disapproved of laws which remedy the inconstancy of weak minds by allowing us to make vows or contracts that oblige perseverance in some worthy project (or even, for the security of commerce, in some indifferent one). But I saw nothing in the world which remained always in the same state, and for my part I was determined to make my judgements more and more perfect, rather than worse. For these reasons I thought I would be sinning against good sense if I were to take my previous approval of something as obliging me to regard it as good later on, when it had perhaps ceased to be good or I no longer regarded it as such.

My second maxim was to be as firm and decisive in my actions as I could, and to follow even the most doubtful opinions, once I had adopted them, with no less constancy than if they had been quite certain. In this respect I would be imitating a traveller who, upon finding himself lost in a forest, should not wander about turning this way and that, and still less stay in one place, but should keep walking as straight as he can in one direction, never changing it for slight reasons even if mere chance made him choose it in the first place: for in this way, even if he does not go exactly where he wishes, he will at least end up in a place where he is likely to be better off than in the middle of a forest. Similarly, since in everyday life we must often act without delay, it is a most certain truth that when it is not in our power to discern the truest opinions, we must follow the most probable. Even when no opinions appear more probable than any others, we must still adopt some; and having done so we must then regard them not as doubtful, from a practical point of view, but as most true and certain, on the grounds that the reason which made us adopt them is itself true and certain. By following this maxim I could free myself from all the regrets and remorse which usually trouble the consciences of those weak and faltering spirits who allow themselves to set out on some supposedly good course of action which later, in their inconstancy, they judge to be bad.

My third maxim was to try always to master myself rather than fortune, and change my desires rather than the order of the world. In general I would become accustomed to believing that nothing lies entirely within our power except our thoughts, so that after doing our best in dealing with matters external to us, whatever we fail to achieve is absolutely impossible so far as we are concerned. This alone, I thought, would be sufficient to prevent me from desiring in future something I could not get, and so to make me content. For our will naturally tends to desire only what our intellect represents to it as somehow possible; and so it is certain that if we consider all external goods as equally beyond our power, we shall not regret the absence of goods which seem to be our birthright when we are deprived of them through no fault of our own, any more than we regret not possessing the kingdom of China or of Mexico. Making a virtue of necessity, as they say, we shall not desire to be healthy when ill or free when imprisoned, any more than we now desire to have bodies of a material as indestructible as diamond or wings to fly like the birds. But I admit that it takes long practice and repeated meditation to become accustomed to seeing everything in this light. In this, I believe, lay the secret of those philosophers who in earlier times were able to escape from the dominion of fortune and, despite suffering and poverty, rival their gods in happiness. Through constant reflection upon the limits prescribed for them by nature, they became perfectly convinced that nothing was in their power but their thoughts, and this alone was sufficient to prevent them from being attracted to other things. Their mastery over their thoughts was so absolute that they had reason to count themselves richer, more powerful, freer and happier than other men who, because they lack this philosophy, never achieve such mastery over all their desires, however favoured by nature and fortune they may be.

Finally, to conclude this moral code, I decided to review the various occupations which men have in this life, in order to try to choose the best. Without wishing to say anything about the occupations of others, I thought I could do no better than to continue with the very one I was engaged in, and devote my whole life to cultivating my reason and advancing as far as I could in the knowledge of the truth, following the method I had prescribed for myself. Since beginning to use this method I had felt such extreme contentment that I did not think one could enjoy any sweeter or purer one in this life. Every day I discovered by its means truths which, it seemed to me, were quite important and were generally unknown by other men; and the satisfaction they gave me so filled my mind that nothing else mattered to me. Besides, the sole basis of the foregoing three maxims was the plan I had to continue my self-instruction. For since God has given each of us a light to distinguish truth from falsehood, I should not have thought myself obliged to rest content with the opinions of others for a single moment if I had not intended in due course to examine them using my own judgement; and I could not have avoided having scruples about following these opinions, if I had not hoped to lose no opportunity to discover better ones, in case there were any. Lastly, I could not have limited my desires, or been happy, had I not been following a path by which I thought I was sure to acquire all the knowledge of which I was capable, and in this way all the true goods within my reach. For since our will tends to pursue or avoid only what our intellect represents as good or bad, we need only to judge well in order to act well, and to judge as well as we can in order to do our best—that is to say, in order to acquire all the virtues and in general all the other goods we can acquire. And when we are certain of this, we cannot fail to be happy.

Once I had established these maxims and set them on one side together with the truths of faith, which have always been foremost among my beliefs, I judged that I could freely undertake to rid myself of all the rest of my opinions. As I expected to be able to achieve this more readily by talking with other men than by staying shut up in the stove-heated room where I had had all these thoughts, I set out on my travels again before the end of winter. Throughout the following nine years I did nothing but roam about in the world, trying to be a spectator rather than an actor in all the comedies that are played out there. Reflecting especially upon the points in every subject which might make it suspect and give occasion for us to make mistakes, I kept uprooting from my mind any errors that might previously have slipped into it. In doing this I was not copying the sceptics, who doubt only for the sake of doubting and pretend to be always undecided; on the contrary, my whole aim was to reach certainty—to cast aside the loose earth and sand so as to come upon rock or clay. In this I think I was quite successful. For I tried to expose the falsity or uncertainty of the propositions I was examining by clear and certain arguments, not by weak conjectures; and I never encountered any proposition so doubtful that I could not draw from it some quite certain conclusion, if only the conclusion that it contained nothing certain. And, just as in pulling down an old house we usually keep the remnants for use in building a new one, so in destroying all those opinions of mine that I judged ill-founded I made various observations and acquired many experiences which I have since used in establishing more certain opinions. Moreover, I continued practising the method I had prescribed for myself. Besides taking care in general to conduct all my thoughts according to its rules, I set aside some hours now and again to apply it more particularly to mathematical problems. I also applied it to certain other problems which I could put into something like mathematical form by detaching them from all the principles of the other sciences, which I did not find sufficiently secure (as you will see I have done in many problems discussed later in this book). Thus, while appearing to live like those concerned only to lead an agreeable and blameless life, who take care to keep their pleasures free from vices, and who engage in every honest pastime in order to enjoy their leisure without boredom, I never stopped pursuing my project, and I made perhaps more progress in the knowledge of the truth than I would have if I had done nothing but read books or mix with men of letters.

Those nine years passed by, however, without my taking any side regarding the questions which are commonly debated among the learned, or beginning to search for the foundations of any philosophy more certain than the commonly accepted one. The example of many fine intellects who had previously had this project, but had not, I thought, met with success, made me imagine the difficulties to be so great that I would not have dared to embark upon it so soon if I had not noticed that some people were spreading the rumour that I had already completed it. I cannot say what basis they had for this opinion. If I contributed anything to it by my conversation, it must have been because I confessed my ignorance more ingenuously than is customary for those with a little learning, and perhaps also because I displayed the reasons I had for doubting many things which others regard as certain, rather than because I boasted of some learning. But as I was honest enough not to wish to be taken for what I was not, I thought I had to try by every means to become worthy of the reputation that was given me. Exactly eight years ago this desire made me resolve to move away from any place where I might have acquaintances and retire to this country, where the long duration of the war has led to the establishment of such order that the armies maintained here seem to serve only to make the enjoyment of the fruits of peace all the more secure. Living here, amidst this great mass of busy people who are more concerned with their own affairs than curious about those of others, I have been able to lead a life as solitary and withdrawn as if I were in the most remote desert, while lacking none of the comforts found in the most populous cities.

Descartes' Dreams
(Adrien Baillet, *La Vie de Monsieur Descartes*)

Baillet purports to transcribe Descartes' notes on some dreams of November 1969, when he announced "I was filled with enthusiasm when I discovered the foundations of a marvelous science." (Olympiques, 1619–20)

Descartes tell us that, on the 10th of November, 1619, having gone to bed full of enthusiasm, and wholly filled with the thought of having found that day the foundations of the admirable science, he had three consecutive dreams in one night, which he believed could only have come from above. After falling asleep, his imagination was struck by the appearance before him of ghosts, who terrified him so that, believing he was walking in the street, he had to lean to his left to get where he was going, because he felt very weak on his right side, which he couldn't hold up. Ashamed to be walking like this, he made an effort to stand straight; but he felt a strong whirlwind which made him rotate three or four times on his left foot. That was not yet what terrified him. It was so hard for him to hobble like this that at every step he was sure he would fall down, until he saw an open school on his way, and went inside to rest and find a remedy to his problem. He was able to get to the school's church, where his first thought was to say his prayers; but noticing that he had passed an acquaintance of his without greeting him, he tried to turn around to go say hello, and was pushed back violently by the wind that was blowing against the church. At the same time he saw someone else in the middle of the school's courtyard, who called him by his name in polite and obliging terms, and told him that, were he to go find Mr. N., the latter had something to give him. M. Descartes imagined that it was probably a melon that had been brought back from a foreign country. But what surprised him more was to see that these people were upright and steady on their feet, whereas he was still hobbling and withering. [Meanwhile] the wind had considerably diminished. He woke up at that point, and felt right then an actual pain, which led him to fear that an evil genius was trying to trick him. At once he turned over onto his right side; for it was on his left side that he had fallen asleep and had the dream. He said a prayer to God, asking to be protected from the ill effects of his dream, and to be preserved from all the misfortunes that might befall him as punishment for his sins, which he thought might draw divine anger, even though he had lived until then a rather blameless life by human standards.

He [then] fell asleep again, after almost two hours of various thoughts on the goods and evils of this world. Another dream came to him right away, in which he believed he heard a high-pitched, crashing noise, which he took for thunder. He was so frightened that he woke up instantly; and, having opened his eyes, he noticed many sparks of fire all around the room. This had already happened often enough, and it was by no means unusual, whenever he woke up in the middle of the night, for his eyes to be bright enough for him to catch a glimpse of the objects closest to him. But this time, he chose to appeal to philosophical rationality; and after having observed, by alternately opening and closing his eyes, the nature of the objects presented to him, his fright dissipated and he fell back asleep quite calmly.

Soon after, he had a third dream, which contained nothing as horrible as the first two. In this last dream, he found a book on his table, and didn't know who had put it there. He opened it and, seeing that it was a dictionary, was gladdened with the hope that it could be useful to him. At the same time, he found another book which was just as new to him, since he didn't know where it came from either. He found that it was a collection of various authors' Poetry, entitled Corpus poetarum, etc. . . . He was curious to read some of it and, upon opening the book, came upon the line.

Quod vitae sectabor iter? etc. . . .

At the same moment, he saw a man he didn't know, but who presented to him a verse piece, starting with Est et Non, which he praised as excellent. M. Descartes told him he knew the piece and that it was part of the "Idylles d'Ausone," which were included in the anthology of the poets which lay on his table. He wanted to show it to the man himself, and started to finger through the book, which he was proud of knowing the order and organization of perfectly. While he looked for the piece, the man asked him where he had gotten the book, and M. Descartes answered that he could not say how he had gotten it; but that a moment beforehand he had handled another one, which had just disappeared, knowing neither who had brought it nor who had taken it back. He hadn't finished talking when he saw the book re-appear on the other end of the table. But he found that this Dictionary was not complete, as it had been the first time. In the meantime, he had found the Poems of Ausone in the *Anthology of the Poets*; and, unable to locate the piece that started with Est et Non, he told the man that he knew an even more beautiful one by the same Poet, which began with the words Quod vitae sectabor iter? The man asked to be shown, and M. Descartes started to look for it, when he came upon numerous little engraved portraits, which led him to remark that this book was quite beautiful, but that it wasn't the same as the one he knew. At that point, both the book and the man disappeared and erased themselves from his imagination, yet without waking him up. What is strange is that, unsure whether what he had just seen was a dream or a vision, he not only determined while sleeping that it was a dream, but he also interpreted it before waking up. He found that the dictionary represented nothing other than the sum of all the Sciences and that the Anthology of Poems, Corpus poetarum, represented in particular and more distinctly Philosophy and Wisdom joined together. For he did not find it surprising at all that the poets, even the sillier ones, produced graver, deeper, and better expressed sentences than those found in the works of the philosophers. He attributed this marvel to the divinity of enthusiasm, and to the strength of imagination, which helps the seeds of wisdom (which exist in the spirit of each man, like sparks of fire in each stone) grow much more easily, and with much more brilliance, than the Philosophers' Reason ever could. M. Descartes, still interpreting the dream in his sleep, found that the verse piece about the uncertainty of which type of life one should choose, starting with Quod vitae sectabor iter, represented the advice of a wise person, or even Moral Theology.

Thereupon, uncertain of whether he was dreaming or meditating, he woke up without emotion and continued, with his eyes open, the interpretation of his dream with the same idea. He understood the poets gathered in the anthology as signifying revelation and enthusiasm, with which he hoped to to be blessed. The verse piece "Est et Non," which is Pythagoras' "Yes and No," was truth and falsehood in human knowledge and the profane sciences. Since applying all these things worked so well, he strongly persuaded himself that it was the Spirit of Truth who, with this dream, had wanted to open for him the treasures of all the sciences. And since all he had left to explain were the little engraved portraits that he had seen in the second book, he no longer looked for an explanation . . .

This last dream, which contained nothing but very sweet and pleasurable things, marked the future according to him, and concerned only what was to happen to him in the rest of his life. But he took the two first ones to be menacing warnings about his life which until then, had not been as innocent before God as it had before men. And he believed that explained the terror and fright which accompanied those two dreams. The melon which was to be offered as a present in the first dream represented, to him, the charms of solitude. . . . The wind that pushed him toward the school's church, while his right side was aching, was nothing else than the Evil Genius who was trying to throw him by force into a place he wanted to go to willingly.

This is why God did not allow him to advance any further and get carried away, even to a sacred place, by a Spirit that he had not sent: although he was quite convinced that it was the Spirit of God that had led him to make his first steps toward the Church. As he understood it, the fright that struck him in the second dream represented the remorse of his conscience for the sins he might have committed during his life until then. The lightning whose crash he heard was the Spirit of Truth descending on him to possess him.

This last imagination certainly had something to do with enthusiasm, and might easily lead us to believe that M. Descartes drank before going to bed. Indeed, it was the eve of Saint Martin's day, when the custom was to have a spree. But he assures us that he had spent the evening and all of the day perfectly sober, and that he hadn't had any wine in three whole months. He adds that the Spirit that excited the enthusiasm that had been heating his brain for the past few days had predicted these dreams to him before he had gone to bed, and that his own spirits had nothing to do with it.

Be that as it may, the impression remaining from these agitations led him the next day to various reflections on which course to take. Because of the difficulties he was having deciding, he prayed God to make his will known, to enlighten him and to guide him in the search for the Truth. Next he appealed to the Holy Virgin to recommend to her a matter which he judged to be the most important of his life. And to catch the interest of this blessed Mother of God even more urgently, he took advantage of a trip he was planning to Italy in a few days to formulate a wish for a pilgrimage to Notre-Dame-de-Lorette. His zeal went even further and led him to promise that, as soon as he reached Venice, he would make the pilgrimage from there to Lorette by foot: that if he could not sustain the effort, he would take on the most devoted and humble outwardly attitude, in order to make up for it. He wanted to undertake this trip by the end of November. But it seems that God disposed him differently. The fulfillment of his wish had to be put off to another time, for he had to postpone his trip to Italy for reasons which were not revealed to us, and undertook it only approximately four years after this resolution.

His enthusiasm left him a few days later, and although his spirit had regained its usual composure and its initial serenity, he didn't become any more decisive about the choices he had to make. Winter passed slowly in the solitude of his room and, to make it less boring, he started writing a treaty, which he hoped to finish before Easter of 1620. As early as February, he was looking for publishers to negotiate getting the book printed. But there is much evidence that this treaty was interrupted around that time and that it has remained incomplete ever since. What is contained in this treaty which perhaps never had a name has been ignored until now. It is certain that the *Olympiques* were written during the end of 1619 and the beginning of 1620, and that they have in common with the treaty the fact that they are unfinished. But there is so little order and connection in the manuscripts that make up the Olympiques that it is easy to infer that M. Descartes never intended to make it into a standard, orderly treaty, and much less to make it public.

To Princess Elizabeth, 6 October 1645

I have sometimes asked myself the following question: Is it better to be cheerful and content, imagining the goods one possesses to be greater and more valuable than they are, and not knowing or caring to consider those one lacks; or is it better to have more consideration and knowledge, so as to know the just value of both, and thus grow sad? If I thought joy the supreme good, I should not doubt that one ought to try to make oneself joyful at any price, and I should approve the brutishness of those who drown their sorrows in wine, or dull them with tobacco. But I make a distinction between the supreme good—which consists in the exercise of virtue, or, what comes to the same, the possession of all those goods whose acquisition depends upon our free will—and the satisfaction of mind which results from that acquisition. Consequently, seeing that it is a greater perfection to know the truth than to be ignorant of it, even when it is to our disadvantage, I must conclude that it is better to be less cheerful and possess more knowledge. So it is not always the most cheerful person who has the most satisfied mind; on the contrary, great joys are commonly sober and serious, and only slight and passing joys are accompanied by laughter. So I cannot approve of trying to deceive oneself by feeding on false imaginations; for the resulting pleasure can touch only the surface of the soul, leaving it to feel inner bitterness when it perceives their falsehood. It could indeed happen that the soul was so continually diverted that it never perceived this; but that would not amount to the enjoyment of the happiness we are discussing, since the latter must depend on our conduct, whereas the former could come only from fortune.

But the case is different when we can turn our minds to different considerations which are equally true, some leading to contentment and others preventing it. In such a case it seems to me that prudence demands that we dwell primarily on those which give us satisfaction. Indeed, since almost everything in the world can be looked at from one point of view which makes it appear good, and from another which brings out its defects, I think that the primary way in which we should display skill is in looking at things from the point of view which makes them seem most to our advantage, provided this does not involve self-deception.

So, when Your Highness considers the circumstances which have given her more leisure to cultivate her reason than many others of her age, if she will please also consider how much more she has profited from them than others, I am sure that she will have reason to be contented. And I do not see why she should prefer to compare herself to other women in a matter which gives her cause for regret than in a matter which could give her satisfaction. Our nature is so constituted that our mind needs much relaxation if it is to be able to spend usefully a few moments in the search for truth. Too great application to study does not refine the mind, but wears it down. Consequently, we should not reckon the time which we could have spent on instructing ourselves by comparison with the number of hours we have had at our disposition but rather, I think, by comparison with what we see commonly happens to others, as an indication of the normal scope of the human mind.

I think also that there is nothing to repent of when we have done what we judged best at the time when we had to decide to act, even though later, thinking it over at our leisure, we judge that we made a mistake. There would be more ground for repentance if we had acted against our conscience, even though we realized afterwards that we had done better than we thought. For we are responsible only for our thoughts, and it does not belong to human nature to be omniscient, or always to judge as well on the spur of the moment as when there is plenty of time to deliberate.

Besides, the vanity which makes a man think better of himself than he deserves is a vice which only weak and base souls display; but this does not mean that the strongest and most noble souls have a duty to despise themselves. We must do ourselves justice, and recognize our perfections as well as our faults. Propriety forbids us to boast of our good qualities, but it does not forbid us to be aware of them.

Finally, it is true that we lack the infinite knowledge which would be necessary for a perfect acquaintance with all the goods between which we have to choose in the various situations of our lives. We must, I think, be contented with a modest knowledge of the most necessary truths such as those I listed in my last letter.

In that letter I have already given my opinion on Your Highness's question whether it is more correct to see everything in relation to oneself or to put oneself to great anxiety for others. If we thought only of ourselves, we could enjoy only the goods which are peculiar to ourselves; whereas, if we consider ourselves as parts of some other body, we share also in the goods which are common to its members, without losing any of those which belong only to ourselves. With evils, the case is not the same, because philosophy teaches that evil is nothing real, but only a privation. When we are sad on account of some evil which has happened to our friends, we do not share in the defect in which this evil consists; and whatever sadness or distress we feel on such occasions cannot be as great as the inner satisfaction which always accompanies good actions, and especially actions which proceed from a pure affection for others which has no reference to oneself, that is, from the Christian virtue called charity. In this way it is possible, even while weeping and deeply distressed, to have more pleasure than while laughing and at one's ease.

It is easy to show that the pleasure of the soul which constitutes happiness is not inseparable from cheerfulness and bodily comfort. This is proved by tragedies, which please us more the sadder they make us, and by bodily exercises like hunting and tennis which are pleasant in spite of being arduous—indeed we see that often the fatigue and exertion involved increase the pleasure. The soul derives contentment from such exercise because in the process it is made aware of the strength, or skill, or some other perfection of the body to which it is joined; but the contentment which it finds in weeping at some pitiable and tragic episode in the theatre arises chiefly from its impression that it is performing a virtuous action in having compassion for the afflicted. Indeed in general the soul is pleased to feel passions arise in itself no matter what they are, provided it remains in control of them.

But I must examine these passions in more detail so as to be able to define them. It will be easier for me to do so in this letter than if I were writing to anyone else, because Your Highness has taken the trouble to read the treatise which I once drafted on the nature of animal. You know already how I think various impressions are formed in their brain: some by the external objects which act upon the senses, and others by the internal dispositions of the body, either by the traces of previous impressions left in the memory, or by the agitation of the spirits which come from the heart. In man the brain is also acted on by the soul, which has some power to change cerebral impressions, just as these impressions in their turn have the power to arouse thoughts in the soul which do not depend on the will. Consequently, the term 'passion' can be applied in general to all the thoughts which are thus aroused in the soul by cerebral impressions alone, without the concurrence of its will, and therefore without any action of the soul itself; for whatever is not an action is a passion. Commonly, however, the term is restricted to thoughts which are caused by some special agitation of the spirits. For thoughts that come from external objects, or from internal dispositions of the body—such as the perception of colours, sounds, smells, hunger, thirst, pain, and the like—are called external or internal sensations. Those that depend solely on the traces left by previous impressions in the memory and the ordinary movement of the spirits are dreams, whether they are real dreams in sleep or daydreams in waking life when the soul does not determine itself to anything of its own accord, but idly follows the impressions that happen to be in the brain. But when the soul uses the will to determine itself to some thought which is not just intelligible but also imaginable, this thought makes a new impression in the brain; this is not a passion within the soul, but an action—and this is what is properly called imagination. Finally, when the normal flow of the spirits is such that it commonly arouses sad or cheerful thoughts or the like, this is not attributed to passion, but to the nature or humour of the person in whom they are aroused; and so we say that one person has a sad nature, another is of a cheerful humour, and so on. So there remain only the thoughts that come from some special agitation of the spirits, whose effects are felt as in the soul itself. It is these that are passions properly so called.

Of course almost all our thoughts depend on more than one of the causes I have just listed; but each thought is called after its chief cause or the cause with which we are chiefly concerned. This makes many people confuse the sensation of pain with the passion of sadness, and pleasurable sensation with the passion of joy, which they also call enjoyment or delight. People also confuse the sensations of thirst and hunger with the desires to drink and eat, which are passions. This is because the causes that give rise to pain commonly also agitate the spirits in such a way as to arouse sadness, and those that produce a pleasurable sensation agitate them in such a way as to arouse joy, and likewise in other cases.

Sometimes also people confuse the inclinations or habits which dispose to a certain passion with the passion itself, though the two are easy to distinguish. For instance, when it is announced in a town that enemies are coming to besiege it, the inhabitants at once make a judgement about the evil which may result to them: this judgement is an action of their soul and not a passion. And though this judgement is to be found in many alike, they are not all equally affected by it; some are more affected than others in proportion to the greater or less habit or inclination they have towards fear. Their souls can receive the emotion that constitutes the passion only after they have made the judgement, or else at least conceived the danger without making a judgement, and then imprinted an image of it in the brain, by another action, namely imagining. When a soul does this it acts upon the spirits which travel from the brain through the nerves into the muscles, and makes them enter the muscles whose function is to close the openings of the heart. This retards the circulation of the blood so that the whole body becomes pale, cold and trembling, and the fresh spirits returning from the heart to the brain are agitated in such a way that they are useless for forming any images except those which excite in the soul the passion of fear. All these things happen so quickly one after the other that the whole thing seems like a single operation. Similarly, in all the other passions there occurs some special agitation in the spirits leaving the heart.

That is what I was going to write to Your Highness a week ago, and I was planning to add a detailed explanation of all the passions. But I found it difficult to list them, and so I had to let the postman leave without my letter. Having in the meantime received the one Your Highness was kind enough to write me, I now have more points to answer, and so I must postpone the examination of the passions.

I must say at once that all the reasons that prove that God exists and is the first and immutable cause of all effects that do not depend on human free will prove similarly, I think, that he is also the cause of all effects that do so depend. For the only way to prove that he exists is to consider him as a supremely perfect being; and he would not be supremely perfect if anything could happen in the world without coming entirely from him. It is true that faith alone tells us about the nature of the grace by which God raises us to a supernatural bliss; but philosophy by itself is able to discover that the slightest thought could not enter into a person's mind without God's willing, and having willed from all eternity, that it should so enter. The scholastic distinction between universal and particular causes is out of place here. The sun, although the universal cause of all flowers, is not the cause of the difference between tulips and roses; but that is because their production depends also on some other particular causes which are not subordinated to the sun. But God is the universal cause of everything in such a way as to be also the total cause of everything; and so nothing can happen without his will.

It is true also that knowledge of the immortality of the soul, and of the felicity of which it will be capable after this life, might give occasion to those who are tired of this life to leave it, if they were certain that they would afterwards enjoy all that felicity. But no reason guarantees this, and there is nothing to show that the present life is bad except the false philosophy of Hegesias (whose book was banned by Ptolemy because many of its readers killed themselves). True philosophy, on the contrary, teaches that even amid the saddest disasters and most bitter pains we can always be content, provided that we know how to use our reason.

As for the extent of the universe, I do not see how the consideration of it tempts one to separate particular providence from the idea we have of God. God is quite different from finite powers. They can be used up; so when we see that they are employed in many great effects, we have reason to judge it unlikely that they also extend to lesser ones. But the greater we deem the works of God to be, the better we observe the infinity of his power; and the better known this infinity is to us, the more certain we are that it extends even to the most particular actions of human beings.

When Your Highness speaks of the particular providence of God as being the foundation of theology, I do not think that you have in mind some change in God's decrees occasioned by actions that depend on our free will. No such change is theologically tenable; and when we are told to pray to God, that is not so that we should inform him of our needs, or that we should try to get him to change anything in the order established from all eternity by his providence—either of these aims would be blameworthy—but simply to obtain whatever he has, from all eternity, willed to be obtained by our prayers. I believe that all theologians agree on this, including the Arminians, who seem the most jealous of the rights of free will.

I agree that it is difficult to determine exactly how far reason ordains that we should devote ourselves to the community. However, it is not a matter on which it is necessary to be very precise; it is enough to satisfy one's conscience, and in doing so one can leave a lot of room for one's inclination. For God has so established the order of things, and has joined men together in so close a community, that even if everyone were to relate everything to himself and had no charity for others, he would still commonly work for them as much as was in his power, provided he exercised prudence, and especially if he lived in an age in which morals were not corrupted. Moreover, as it is a nobler and more glorious thing to do good to others than to oneself, it is the noblest souls who have the greatest inclination thereto and who make least account of the goods they possess. Only weak and base souls value themselves more than they ought, and are like small vessels that a few drops of water can fill. I know that Your Highness is not at all like that. Base souls cannot be persuaded to take trouble for others unless you can show them that they will reap some profit for themselves; but in order to persuade Your Highness to look after her health, it is necessary to point out to her that she cannot long be useful to those she loves if she neglects herself.

To Princess Elizabeth, 3 November 1645

So seldom do good arguments come my way, not only in the conversations I have in this isolated place but also in the books I consult, that I cannot read those which occur in Your Highness's letters without feeling an extraordinary joy. What is more, I find your arguments so strong that I would rather confess I am overwhelmed by them than attempt to rebut them. For, although the comparison which Your Highness refuses to make to her advantage could be adequately confirmed by experience, yet the virtue of judging others favourably is so praiseworthy, and it fits so well with the generosity that prevents you from wishing to measure the scope of the human mind by the example of the average person, that I am bound to hold both these virtues of yours in very high esteem.

Nor would I venture to contradict what Your Highness writes about repentance. For this is a Christian virtue which serves to make us correct our faults—not only those committed voluntarily, but also those done through ignorance, when some passion has prevented us from knowing the truth.

I agree that the sadness of tragedies would not please as it does if we feared that it might become so excessive as to make us uncomfortable. But when I said that there are passions which are the more useful the more they tend to excess, I only meant to speak of those which are altogether good; as I indicated when I added that they should be subject to reason. There are, indeed, two kinds of excess. There is one which changes the nature of a thing, and turns it from good to bad, and prevents it from remaining subject to reason; and there is another which only increases its quantity, and turns it from good to better. Thus excess of courage is recklessness only when the courage passes the limits of reason; but while remaining within those limits, it can have another kind of excess, which consists in the absence of irresolution and fear.

These last few days I have been thinking about the number and order of all the passions, in order to examine their nature in detail. But I have not yet sufficiently digested my opinions on this topic to dare to tell them to Your Highness. I shall not fail to do so as soon as I can.

As for free will, I agree that if we think only of ourselves we cannot help regarding ourselves as independent; but when we think of the infinite power of God, we cannot help believing that all things depend on him, and hence that our free will is not exempt from this dependence. For it involves a contradiction to say that God has created human beings of such a nature that the actions of their will do not depend on his. It is the same as saying that his power is both finite and infinite: finite, since there is something which does not depend on it; infinite, since he was able to create that independent thing. But just as the knowledge of the existence of God should not take away our certainty of the free will which we experience and feel in ourselves, so also the knowledge of our free will should not make us doubt the existence of God. The independence which we experience and feel in ourselves, and which suffices to make our actions praiseworthy or blameworthy, is not incompatible with a dependence of quite another kind, whereby all things are subject to God.

As for the state of the soul after this life: Leaving aside what faith tells us, I agree that by natural reason alone we can make many favorable conjectures and have fine hopes, but we cannot have any certainty. The same natural reason teaches us also that we have always more good than evil in this life, and that we should never leave what is certain for what is uncertain. Consequently, in my opinion, it teaches that though we should not seriously fear death, we should equally never seek it.

I do not need to reply to the objection which theologians may make about the vast extent which I have attributed to the universe, since Your Highness has already replied on my behalf. I will add only that if such a vast extent could make the mysteries of our Faith less credible, the same is true of the vast extent that the astronomers have always attributed to the heavens. They have always thought them so large as to make the earth, by comparison, only a point; yet the objection is never made against them.

If prudence were mistress of events, I do not doubt that Your Highness would succeed in everything she undertakes; but all men would have to be perfectly wise before one could infer from what they ought to do what they will in fact do. At least it would be necessary to know in detail the humour of all those with whom one was to have any dealings. Even that would not be enough, because they have in addition their own free will, whose movements are known only to God. Our judgements about the actions of others are normally based on what we would wish to do ourselves if we were in their place. And so it often happens that ordinary and mediocre minds, being similar to those which they have to deal with, see into their purposes with greater penetration and enable them to succeed in their undertakings more easily than more refined minds do; for the latter, dealing only with those who are inferior in knowledge and prudence, make judgements about matters in an utterly different way. Your Highness should be consoled by this fact when fortune is opposed to your plans.

9

BLAISE PASCAL
The Limits of Thought

Blaise Pascal (1623–1662) was a brilliant mathematician and physicist whose early work in projective geometry and infinitesimal analysis influenced Leibniz. Although he was not a Jansenist, he published an anonymous defense of their Augustinian views on free will against the Jesuits (*Letttres Provinciales*, 1656–1657). His most influential work is a set of balanced aphorisms whose interpretation has remained in dispute (*Pensées*, 1670). Some scholars see him as an antirationalist skeptic who held that both theology and scientific knowledge rest on unjustifiable premises. Others see Pascal's skeptical position as a step toward a pragmatic, calculative fideism that presents a rational argument for betting on both the truth of Christianity and the reliability of scientific knowledge. Yet other scholars interpret the conclusion of the wager argument as an indication of the limits of reason, its inability to produce belief, and its reliance on faith to supply its fundamental principles.

The Frailty of Human Thought
(The Provincial Letters)

The last thing one settles in writing a book is what one should put in first.

Order.—Why should I undertake to divide my virtues into four rather than into six? Why should I rather establish virtue in four, in two, in one? Why into *Abstine et sustine* rather than into "Follow Nature," or, "Conduct your private affairs without injustice," as Plato, or anything else? But there, you will say, everything is contained in one world. Yes, but it is useless without explanation, and when we come to explain it, as soon as we unfold this maxim which contains all the rest, they emerge in that first confusion which you desired to avoid. So, when they are all included in one, they are hidden and useless, as in a chest, and never appear save in their natural confusion. Nature has established them all without including one in the other.

Nature has made all her truths independent of one another. Our art makes one dependent on the other. But this is not natural. Each keeps its own place.

Let no one say that I have said nothing new; the arrangement of the subject is new. When we play tennis, we both play with the same ball, but one of us places it better.

I had as soon it said that I used words employed before. And in the same way if the same thoughts in a different arrangement do not form a different discourse, no more do the same words in their different arrangement form different thoughts!

People of education are not called poets or mathematicians, etc.; but they are all these, and judges of all these. No one guesses what they are. When they come into society, they talk on matters about which the rest are talking. We do not observe in them one quality rather than another, save when they have to make use of it. But then we remember it, for it is characteristic of such persons that we do not say of them that they are fine speakers, when it is not a question of oratory, and that we say of them that they are fine speakers, when it is such a question.

It is therefore false praise to give a man when we say of him, on his entry, that he is a very clever poet; and it is a bad sign when a man is not asked to give his judgment on some verses.

Man is full of wants: he loves only those who can satisfy them all. "This one is a good mathematician," one will say. But I have nothing to do with mathematics; he would take me for a proposition. "That one is a good soldier." He would take me for a besieged town. I need, then, an upright man who can accommodate himself generally to all my wants.

Order.—I might well have taken this discourse in an order like this: to show the vanity of all conditions of men, to show the vanity of ordinary lives, and then the vanity of philosophic lives, sceptics, stoics; but the order would not have been kept. I know a little what it is, and how few people understand it. No human science can keep it. Saint Thomas did not keep it. Mathematics keep it, but they are useless on account of their depth.

One must know oneself. If this does not serve to discover truth, it at least serves as a rule of life, and there is nothing better.

Let man consider what he is in comparison with all existence; let him regard himself as lost in this remote corner of nature; and from the little cell in which he finds himself lodged, I mean the universe, let him estimate at their true value the earth, kingdoms, cities, and himself. What is a man in the Infinite?

But to show him another prodigy equally astonishing, let him examine the most delicate things he knows. Let a mite be given him, with its minute body and parts incomparably more minute, limbs with their joints, veins in the limbs, blood in the veins, humours in the blood, drops in the humours, vapours in the drops. Dividing these last things again, let him exhaust his powers of conception, and let the last object at which he can arrive be now that of our discourse. Perhaps he will think that here is the smallest point in nature. I will let him see therein a new abyss. I will paint for him not only the visible universe, but all that he can conceive of nature's immensity in the womb of this abridged atom. Let him see therein an infinity of universes, each of which has its firmament, its planets, its earth, in the same proportion as in the visible world; in each earth animals, and in the last mites, in which he will find again all that the first had, finding still in these others the same thing without end and without cessation. Let him lose himself in wonders as amazing in their littleness as the others in their vastness. For who will not be astounded at the fact that our body, which a little while ago was imperceptible in the universe, itself imperceptible in the bosom of the whole, is now a colossus, a world, or rather a whole, in respect of the nothingness which we cannot reach? He who regards himself in this light will be afraid of himself, and observing himself sustained in the body given him by nature between those two abysses of the Infinite and Nothing, will tremble at the sight of these marvels; and I think that, as his curiosity changes into admiration, he will be more disposed to contemplate them in silence than to examine them with presumption.

For in fact what is man in nature? A Nothing in comparison with the Infinite, an All in comparison with the Nothing, a mean between nothing and everything. Since he is infinitely removed from comprehending the extremes, the end of things and their beginning are hopelessly hidden from him in an impenetrable secret; he is equally incapable of seeing the Nothing from which he was made, and the Infinite in which he is swallowed up.

If man made himself the first object of study, he would see how incapable he is of going further. How can a part know the whole? But he may perhaps aspire to know at least the parts to which he bears some proportion. But the parts of the world are all so related and linked to one another, that I believe it impossible to know one without the other and without the whole.

Man, for instance, is related to all he knows. He needs a place wherein to abide, time through which to live, motion in order to live, elements to compose him, warmth and food to nourish him, air to breathe. He sees light; he feels bodies; in short, he is in a dependent alliance with everything. To know man, then, it is necessary to know how it happens that he needs air to live, and, to know the air, we must know how it is thus related to the life of man, etc. Flame cannot exist without air; therefore to understand the one, we must understand the other.

Since everything then is cause and effect, dependent and supporting, mediate and immediate, and all is held together by a natural though imperceptible chain, which binds together things most distant and most different, I hold it equally impossible to know the parts without knowing the whole, and to know the whole without knowing the parts in detail.

And what completes our incapability of knowing things, is the fact that they are simple, and that we are composed of two opposite natures, different in kind, soul and body. For it is impossible that our rational part should be other than spiritual; and if any one maintain that we are simply corporeal, this would far more exclude us from the knowledge of things, there being nothing so inconceivable as to say that matter knows itself. It is impossible to imagine how it should know itself.

So if we are simply material, we can know nothing at all; and if we are composed of mind and matter, we cannot know perfectly things which are simple, whether spiritual or corporeal. Hence it comes that almost all philosophers have confused ideas of things, and speak of material things in spiritual terms, and of spiritual things in material terms. For they say boldly that bodies have a tendency to fall, that they seek after their centre, that they fly from destruction, that they fear the void, that they have inclinations, sympathies, antipathies, all of which attributes pertain only to mind. And in speaking of minds, they consider them as in a place, and attribute to them movement from one place to another; and these are qualities which belong only to bodies.

Instead of receiving the ideas of these things in their purity, we colour them with our own qualities, and stamp with our composite being all the simple things which we contemplate.

Men seek rest in a struggle against difficulties; and when they have conquered these, rest becomes insufferable. For we think either of the misfortunes we have or of those which threaten us. And even if we should see ourselves sufficiently sheltered on all sides, weariness of its own accord would not fail to arise from the depths of the heart wherein it has its natural roots, and to fill the mind with its poison.

Thus so wretched is man that he would weary even without any cause for weariness from the peculiar state of his disposition; and so frivolous is he, that, though full of a thousand reasons for weariness, the least thing, such as playing billiards or hitting a ball, is sufficient to amuse him.

Man is obviously made to think. It is his whole dignity and his whole merit; and his whole duty is to think as he ought. Now, the order of thought is to begin with self, and with its Author and its end.

Now, of what does the world think? Never of this, but of dancing, playing the lute, singing, making verses, running at the ring, etc., fighting, making oneself king, without thinking what it is to be a king and what to be a man.

We do not content ourselves with the life we have in ourselves and in our own being; we desire to live an imaginary life in the mind of others, and for this purpose we endeavour to shine. We labour unceasingly to adorn and preserve this imaginary existence, and neglect the real. And if we possess calmness, or generosity, or truthfulness, we are eager to make it known, so as to attach these virtues to that imaginary existence. We would rather separate them from ourselves to join them to it; and we would willingly be cowards in order to acquire the reputation of being brave. A great proof of the nothingness of our being, not to be satisfied with the one without the other, and to renounce the one for the other! For he would be infamous who would not die to preserve his honour.

A man in a dungeon, ignorant whether his sentence be pronounced, and having only one hour to learn it, but this hour enough, if he knew that it is pronounced, to obtain its repeal, would act unnaturally in spending that hour, not in ascertaining his sentence, but in playing piquet. So it is against nature that man, etc. It is making heavy the hand of God.

Thus not only the zeal of those who seek Him proves God, but also the blindness of those who seek Him not.

When I consider the short duration of my life, swallowed up in the eternity before and after, the little space which I fill, and even can see, engulfed in the infinite immensity of spaces of which I am ignorant, and which know me not, I am frightened, and am astonished at being here rather than there; for there is no reason why here rather than there, why now rather than then. Who has put me here? By whose order and direction have this place and time been allotted to me? *Memoria hospitis unius diei prætereuntis.*

The eternal silence of these infinite spaces frightens me.

We are fools to depend upon the society of our fellow-men. Wretched as we are, powerless as we are, they will not aid us; we shall die alone. We should therefore act as if we were alone, and in that case should we build fine houses, etc. We should seek the truth without hesitation; and, if we refuse it, we show that we value the esteem of men more than the search for truth.

Instability.—It is a horrible thing to feel all that we possess slipping away.

Between us and heaven or hell there is only life, which is the frailest thing in the world.

Injustice.—That presumption should be joined to meanness is extreme injustice.

This is what I see and what troubles me. I look on all sides, and I see only darkness everywhere. Nature presents to me nothing which is not matter of doubt and concern. If I saw nothing there which revealed a Divinity, I would come to a negative conclusion; if I saw everywhere the signs of a Creator, I would remain peacefully in faith. But, seeing too much to deny and too little to be sure, I am in a state to be pitied; wherefore I have a hundred times wished that if a God maintains nature, she should testify to Him unequivocally, and that, if the signs she gives are deceptive, she should suppress them altogether; that she should say everything or nothing, that I might see which cause I ought to follow. Whereas in my present state, ignorant of what I am or of what I ought to do, I know neither my condition nor my duty. My heart inclines wholly to know where is the true good, in order to follow it; nothing would be too dear to me for eternity.

I envy those whom I see living in the faith with such carelessness, and who make such a bad use of a gift of which it seems to me I would make such a different use.

It is incomprehensible that God should exist, and it is incomprehensible that He should not exist; that the soul should be joined to the body, and that we should have no soul; that the world should be created, and that it should not be created, etc.; that original sin should be, and that it should not be.

If we must not act save on a certainty, we ought not to act on religion, for it is not certain. But how many things we do on an uncertainty, sea voyages, battles! I say then we must do nothing at all, for nothing is certain, and that there is more certainty in religion than there is as to whether we may see to-morrow; for it is not certain that we may see tomorrow, and it is certainly possible that we may not see it. We cannot say as much about religion. It is not certain that it is; but who will venture to say that it is certainly possible that it is not? Now when we work for to-morrow, and so on an uncertainty, we act reasonably; for we ought to work for an uncertainty according to the doctrine of chance which was demonstrated above.

Saint Augustine has seen that we work for an uncertainty, on sea, in battle, etc. But he has not seen the doctrine of chance which proves that we should do so. Montaigne has seen that we are shocked at a fool, and that habit is all-powerful; but he has not seen the reason of this effect.

All these persons have seen the effects, but they have not seen the causes. They are, in comparison with those who have discovered the causes, as those who have only eyes are in comparison with those who have intellect. For the effects are perceptible by sense, and the causes are visible only to the intellect. And although these effects are seen by the mind, this mind is, in comparison with the mind which sees the causes, as the bodily senses are in comparison with the intellect.

Thought constitutes the greatness of man.

Man is but a reed, the most feeble thing in nature; but he is a thinking reed. The entire universe need not arm itself to crush him. A vapour, a drop of water suffices to kill him. But, if the universe were to crush him, man would still be more noble than that which killed him, because he knows that he dies and the advantage which the universe has over him; the universe knows nothing of this.

All our dignity consists, then, in thought. By it we must elevate ourselves, and not by space and time which we cannot fill. Let us endeavour, then, to think well; this is the principle of morality.

A thinking reed.—It is not from space that I must seek my dignity, but from the government of my thought. I shall have no more if I possess worlds. By space the universe encompasses and swallows me up like an atom; by thought I comprehend the world.

Thought.—All the dignity of man consists in thought. Thought is therefore by its nature a wonderful and incomparable thing. It must have strange defects to be contemptible. But it has such, so that nothing is more ridiculous. How great it is in its nature! How vile it is in its defects!

But what is this thought? How foolish it is!

In writing down my thought, it sometimes escapes me; but this makes me remember my weakness, that I constantly forget. This is as instructive to me as my forgotten thought; for I strive only to know my nothingness.

Scepticism.—I shall here write my thoughts without order, and not perhaps in unintentional confusion; that is true order, which will always indicate my object by its very disorder. I should do too much honour to my subject, if I treated it with order, since I want to show that it is incapable of it.

What astonishes me most is to see that all the world is not astonished at its own weakness. Men act seriously, and each follows his own mode of life, not because it is in fact good to follow since it is the custom, but as if each man knew certainly where reason and justice are. They find themselves continually deceived, and by a comical humility think it is their own fault, and not that of the art which they claim always to possess. But it is well there are so many such people in the world, who are not sceptics for the glory of septicism, in order to show that man is quite capable of the most extravagant opinions, since he is capable of believing that he is not in a state of natural and inevitable weakness, but, on the contrary, of natural wisdom.

Nothing fortifies scepticism more than that there are some who are not sceptics; if all were so, they would be wrong.

Scepticism.—Excess, like defect of intellect, is accused of madness. Nothing is good but mediocrity. The majority has settled that, and finds fault with him who escapes it at whichever end. I will not oppose it. I quite consent to put myself there, and refuse to be at the lower end, not because it is low, but because it is an end; for I would likewise refuse to be placed at the top. To leave the mean is to abandon humanity. The greatness of the human soul consists in knowing how to preserve the mean. So far from greatness consisting in leaving it, it consists in not leaving it.

It is not good to have too much liberty. It is not good to have all one wants.

All good maxims are in the world. We only need to apply them. For instance, we do not doubt that we ought to risk our lives in defence of the public good; but for religion, no.

It is true there must be inequality among men; but if this be conceded, the door is opened not only to the highest power, but to the highest tyranny.

We must relax our minds a little; but this opens the door to the greatest debauchery. Let us mark the limits. There are no limits in things. Laws would put them there, and the mind cannot suffer it.

There is internal war in man between reason and the passions.

If he had only reason without passions . . .

If he had only passions without reason . . .

But having both, he cannot be without strife, being unable to be at peace with the one without being at war with the other. Thus he is always divided against, and opposed to himself.

10

THOMAS HOBBES
"Justice I Teach, and Reverence Justice"
John Aubrey, "The Life of Hobbes"

Thomas Hobbes (1588–1679) was an accomplished classicist and mathematician as well as an immensely influential systematic philosopher. His first published work was a translation of Thucydides' *The Peloponnesian War*; and among his last were translations of *The Iliad* and *The Odyssey*. Tutor to the Earl of Devonshire and to Charles II, friend of Abbé Mersenne, he lived in exile in France during the civil wars. Although his *De Cive* (1642) and *The Elements of Law* (1650) had been used as a text by royalists, Hobbes nevertheless became sufficiently reconciled with Oliver Cromwell so that he returned to England in 1651. Always political agile, Hobbes received the privilege of a royal pension from Charles II after the Restoration.

Much impressed by the new sciences of Keppler, Galileo and Bacon, Hobbes developed a materialist metaphysics that provided the premises of a mechanistic psychology, and as he hoped, the basis of a contractarian political theory (*Leviathan*, 1651). His thought experiment posited a natural condition of scarcity that set men at odds with one another to secure a marginal advantage for survival. Prompted by fear and an instinct for self-preservation, foresighted calculative reason led to the contractual establishment of a sovereignty endowed with absolute power. Materialist contractarian that he was, Hobbes nevertheless held that his political views were consonant with Scripture. Indeed he feared that discrediting religion could readily lead to sedition and civil strife. When Parliament passed a bill for the suppression of atheism, a committee was nevertheless appointed to investigate the orthodoxy of the *Leviathan*. Although the matter was dropped, Hobbes was forbidden to publish his views. He submitted his *Behemoth* for approval to Charles II, who recommended against its publication. It was eventually published posthumously.

Recent commentators follow his contemporaries in disagreeing about whether Hobbes' accommodation of religion was astutely self-protective or a recommendation to sovereigns about the strategy of ensuring security and peace.

The Elements of Law

TO THE RIGHT HONOURABLE
William, Earl of Newcastle,
GOVERNOR TO THE PRINCE HIS HIGHNESS,
ONE OF HIS MAJESTY'S MOST HONOURABLE PRIVY COUNCIL.

THE EPISTLE DEDICATORY.

My most honoured Lord,

From the two principal parts of our nature, Reason and Passion, have proceeded two kinds of learning, mathematical and dogmatical. The former is free from controversies and dispute, because it consisteth in comparing figures and motion only; in which things truth and the interest of men oppose not each other. But in the later there is nothing not disputable, because it compareth men, and meddleth with their right and profit; in which, as oft as reason is against a man, so oft will a man be against reason. And from hence it cometh, that they that have written of justice and policy in general, do all invade each other, and themselves, with contradiction. To reduce this doctrine to the rules and infallibility of reason, there is no way, but first to put such principles down for a foundation, as passion not mistrusting, may not seek to displace; and afterward to build thereon the truth of cases in the law of nature (which hitherto have been built in the air) by degrees, till the whole be inexpugnable. Now (my Lord) the principles fit for such a foundation, are those which I have heretofore acquainted your Lordship withal in private discourse, and which by your command I have here put into method. To examine cases thereby between sovereign and sovereign, or between sovereign and subject, I leave to them that shall find leisure and encouragement thereto. For my part, I present this to your Lordship for the true and only foundation of such science. For the style, it is therefore the worse, because I was forced to consult when I was writing, more with logic than with rhetoric. But for the doctrine, it is not slightly proved; and the conclusions thereof are of such nature, as, for want of them, government and peace have been nothing else to this day, but mutual fear. And it would be an incomparable benefit to commonwealth, if every man held the opinions concerning law and policy here delivered. The ambition therefore of this book, in seeking by your Lordship's countenance to insinuate itself with those whom the matter it containeth most nearly concerneth, is to be excused. For myself, I desire no greater honour than I enjoy already in your Lordship's known favour; unless it be that you would be pleased, in continuance thereof, to give me more exercise in your commands; which, as I am bound by your many great favours, I shall obey, being,

My most honoured Lord,
Your Lordship's most humble and obliged Servant,
Thomas Hobbes

May 9, 1640

De Cive or The Citizen

TO THE RIGHT HONOURABLE,
William, Earl of Devonshire,
MY MOST HONOURED LORD,

May it please your Lordship,

Wisdom properly so called is nothing else but this, the perfect knowledge of the truth in all matters whatsoever. Which being derived from the registers and records of things, and that as it were through the conduit of certain definite appellations, cannot possibly be the work of a sudden acuteness, but of a well-balanced reason, which by the compendium of a word, we call philosophy. For by this it is, that a way is opened to us, in which we travel from the contemplation of particular things to the inference or result of universal actions. Now look how many sorts of things there are which properly fall within the cognizance of human reason, into so many branches does the tree of philosophy divide itself. And from the diversity of the matter about which they are conversant, there hath been given to those branches a diversity of names too. For treating of figures, it is called geometry; of motion, physic; of natural right, morals; put all together, and they make up philosophy. Just as the British, the Atlantic, and the Indian seas, being diversely christened from the diversity of their shores, do notwithstanding all together make up the ocean. And truly the geometricians have very admirably performed their part. For whatsoever assistance doth accrue to the life of man, whether from the observation of the heavens, or from the description of the earth, from the notation of times, or from the remotest experiments of navigation; finally, whatsoever things they are in which this present age doth differ from the rude simpleness of antiquity, we must acknowledge to be a debt which we owe merely to geometry. If the moral philosophers had as happily discharged their duty, I know not what could have been added by human industry to the completion of that happiness, which is consistent with human life. For were the nature of human actions as distinctly known, as the nature of quantity in geometrical figures, the strength of avarice and ambition, which is sustained by the erroneous opinions of the vulgar, as touching the nature of right and wrong, would presently faint and languish; and mankind should enjoy such an immortal peace, that (unless it were for habitation, on supposition that the earth should grow too narrow for her inhabitants) there would hardly be left any pretence for war. But now on the contrary, that neither the sword nor the pen should be allowed any cessation; that the knowledge of the law of nature should lose its growth, not advancing a whit beyond its ancient stature; that there should still be such siding with the several factions of philosophers, that the very same action should be decried by some, and as much elevated by others; that the very same man should at several times embrace his several opinions, and esteem his own actions far otherwise in himself than he does in others; these I say are so many signs, so many manifest arguments, that what hath hitherto been written by moral philosophers, hath not made any progress in the knowledge of the truth; but yet hath took with the world, not so much by giving any light to the understanding, as entertainment to the affections, whilst by the successful rhetorications of their speech they have confirmed them in their rashly received opinions. So that this part of philosophy hath suffered the same destiny with the public ways, which lie open to all passengers to traverse up and down, or the same lot with highways and open streets; some for divertisement, and some for business; so that what with the impertinences of some, and the altercations of others, those ways have never a seeds-time, and therefore yield never a harvest. The only reason of which unluckiness should seem to be this; that amongst all the writers of that part of philosophy, there is not one that hath used an idoneous principle of tractation. For we may not, as in a circle, begin the handling of a science from what point we please. There is a certain clue of reason, whose beginning is in the dark, but by the benefit of whose conduct, we are led as it were by the hand into the clearest light, so that the principle of tractation is to be taken from that darkness, and then the light to be carried thither for irradiating its doubts. As often therefore as any writer, doth either weakly forsake that clue, or wilfully cut it asunder, he describes the footsteps, not of his progress in science, but of his wanderings from it. And upon this it was, that when I applied my thoughts to the investigation of natural justice, I was presently advertised from the very word justice, (which signifies a steady will of giving every one his own) that my first enquiry was to be, from whence it proceeded, that any man should call anything rather his own, than another man's. And when I found that this proceeded not from nature, but consent, (for what nature at first laid forth in common, men did afterwards distribute into several impropriations), I was conducted from thence to another inquiry, namely to what end, and upon what impulsives, when all was equally every man's in common, men did rather think it fitting, that every man should have his inclosure. And I found the reason was, that from a community of goods, there must needs arise contention whose enjoyment should be greatest, and from that contention all kind of calamities must unavoidably ensue, which by the instinct of nature, every man is taught to shun. Having therefore thus arrived at two maxims of human nature, the one arising from the concupiscible part, which desires to appropriate to itself the use of those things in which all others have a joint interest, the other proceeding from the rational, which teaches every man to fly a contra-natural dissolution, as the greatest mischief that can arrive to nature; which principles being laid down, I seem from them to have demonstrated by a most evident connexion, in this little work of mine, first the absolute necessity of leagues and contracts, and thence the rudiments both of moral and of civil prudence. That appendage which is added concerning the regiment of God, hath been done with this intent, that the dictates of God Almighty in the law of nature, might not seem repugnant to the written law, revealed to us in his word. I have also been very wary in the whole tenour of my discourse, not to meddle with the civil laws of any particular nation whatsoever, that is to say, I have avoided coming ashore, which those times have so infested both with shelves and tempests. At what expense of time and industry I have been in this scrutiny after truth, I am not ignorant; but to what purpose, I know not. For being partial judges of ourselves, we lay a partial estimate upon our own productions. I therefore offer up this book to your Lordship's, not favour, but censure first; as having found by many experiments, that it is not the credit of the author, nor the newness of the work, nor yet the ornament of the style, but only the weight of reason, which recommends any opinion to your Lordship's favour and approbation. If it fortune to please, that is to say, if it be sound, if it be useful, if it be not vulgar; I humbly offer it to your Lordship as both my glory and my protection; but if in anything I have erred, your Lordship will yet accept it as a testimony of my gratitude, for that the means of study which I enjoyed by your Lordship's goodness, I have employed to the procurement of your Lordship's favour. The God of heaven crown your Lordship with length of days in this earthly station, and in the heavenly Jerusalem, with a crown of glory.

Your Honour's most humble,
and most devoted Servant,
Thomas Hobbes.

The Author's Preface to the Reader

Reader, I promise thee here such things, which ordinarily promised, do seem to challenge the greatest attention, and I lay them here before thine eyes, whether thou regard the dignity or profit of the matter treated of, or the right method of handling it, or the honest motive, and good advice to undertake it, or lastly the moderation of the author. In this book thou shalt find briefly described the duties of men, first as men; then as subjects, lastly, as Christians; under which duties are contained not only the elements of the laws of nature, and of nations, together with the true original and power of justice, but also the very essence of Christian religion itself, so far forth as the measure of this my purpose could well bear it.

Concerning my method, I thought it not sufficient to use a plain and evident style in what I have to deliver, except I took my beginning from the very matter of civil government, and thence proceeded to its generation, and form, and the first beginning of justice; for everything is best understood by its constitutive causes. For as in a watch, or some such small engine, the matter, figure, and motion of the wheels cannot well be known, except it be taken in sunder, and viewed in parts; so to make a more curious search into the rights of states, and duties of subjects, it is necessary, (I say not to take them in sunder, but yet that) they be so considered, as if they were dissolved, that is, that we rightly understand what the quality of human nature is, in what matters it is, in what not, fit to make up a civil government, and how men must be agreed amongst themselves, that intend to grow up into a well-grounded state. Having therefore followed this kind of method, in the first place I set down for a principle by experience known to all men, and denied by none, to wit, that the dispositions of men are naturally such, that except they be restrained through fear of some coercive power, every man will distrust and dread each other, and as by natural right he may, so by necessity he will be forced to make use of the strength he hath, toward the preservation of himself. You will object perhaps, that there are some who deny this; truly so it happens, that very many do deny it. But shall I therefore seem to fight against myself because I affirm that the same men confess, and deny the same thing? In truth I do not, but they do, whose actions disavow what their discourses approve of. We see all countries, though they be at peace with their neighbours, yet guarding their frontiers with armed men, their towns with walls and ports, and keeping constant watches. To what purpose is all this, if there be no fear of the neighbouring power? We see even in well-governed states, where there are laws and punishments appointed for offenders, yet particular men travel not without their sword by their sides, for their defences, neither sleep they without shutting not only their doors against their fellow subjects, but also their trunks and coffers for fear of domestics. Can men give a clearer testimony of the distrust they have each of other, and all, of all? How since they do thus, and even countries as well as men, they publicly profess their mutual fear and diffidence? But in disputing they deny it, that is as much as to say, that out of a desire they have to contradict others, they gainsay themselves. Some object that this principle being admitted, it would needs follow, not only that all men were wicked (which perhaps though it seem hard, yet we must yield to, since it is so clearly declared by holy writ) but also wicked by nature (which cannot be granted without impiety). But this, that men are evil by nature, follows not from this principle; for though the wicked were fewer than the righteous, yet because we cannot distinguish them, there is a necessity of suspecting, heeding, anticipating, subjugating, self-defending, ever incident to the most honest and fairest conditioned: much less does it follow that those who are wicked are so by nature, for though from nature, that is from their first birth, as they are merely sensible creatures, they have this disposition, that immediately as much as in them lies, they desire and do whatsoever is best pleasing to them, and that either through fear they fly from, or through hardness repel those dangers which approach them, yet are they not for this reason to be accounted wicked. For the affections of the mind which arise only from the lower parts of the soul are not wicked themselves, but the actions thence proceeding may be so sometimes, as when they are either offensive, or against duty. Unless you give children all they ask for, they are peevish, and cry, aye and strike their parents sometimes, and all this they have from nature, yet are they free from guilt, neither may we properly call them wicked; first, because they cannot hurt; next, because wanting the free use of reason they are exempted from all duty. These when they come to riper years, having acquired power whereby they may do hurt, if they shall continue to do the same things, then truly they both begin to be, and are properly accounted wicked; in so much as a wicked man is almost the same thing with a child grown strong and sturdy, or a man of a childish disposition; and malice the same with a defect of reason in that age, when nature ought to be better governed through good education and experience. Unless therefore we will say that men are naturally evil, because they receive not their education and use of reason from nature, we must needs acknowledge that men may derive desire, fear, anger, and other passions from nature, and yet not impute the evil effects of those unto nature. The foundation therefore which I have laid standing firm, I demonstrate in the first place, that the state of men without civil society (which state we may properly call the state of nature) is nothing else but a mere war of all against all; and in that war all men have equal right unto all things; next, that all men as soon as they arrive to understanding of this hateful condition, do desire (even nature itself compelling them) to be freed from this misery. But that this cannot be done except by compact, they all quit that right they have to all things. Furthermore I declare, and confirm what the nature of compact is; how and by what means the right of one might be transferred unto another to make their compacts valid; also what rights, and to whom they must necessarily be granted for the establishing of peace, I mean what those dictates of reason are, which may properly be termed the laws of nature; and all these are contained in that part of this book which I entitle Liberty.

These grounds thus laid, I show further what civil government, and the supreme power in it, and the divers kinds of it are; by what means it becomes so, and what rights particular men, who intend to constitute this civil government, must so necessarily transfer from themselves on the supreme power, whether it be one man or an assembly of men, that except they do so it will evidently appear to be no civil government, but the rights which all men have to all things, that is the rights of war will still remain. Next, I distinguish the divers kinds of it, to wit, monarchy, aristocracy, democracy, and paternal dominion, and that of masters over their servants. I declare how they are constituted, and I compare their several conveniences and inconveniences each with other. Furthermore, I unfold what those things are which destroy it, and what his or their duty is who rule in chief. Last of all, I explicate the natures of law, and of sin, and I distinguish law from counsel, from compact, from that which I call right; all which I comprehend under the title of Dominion.

In the last part of it, which is entitled Religion, lest that right which by strong reason I had confirmed the sovereign powers in the preceding discourse have over their subjects, might seem to be repugnant to the sacred Scriptures, I show in the first place how it repugns not the divine right, for as much as God overrules all rulers by nature, that is, by the dictates of natural reason. In the second, for as much as God himself had a peculiar dominion over the Jews by virtue of that ancient covenant of circumcision. In the third, because God doth now rule over us Christians by virtue of our covenant of baptism; and therefore the authority of rulers in chief, or of civil government, is not at all, we see, contrary to religion.

In the last place I declare what duties are necessarily required from us, to enter into the kingdom of heaven; and of those I plainly demonstrate, and conclude out of evident testimonies of holy writ, according to the interpretation made by all, that the obedience which I have affirmed to be due from particular Christian subjects unto their Christian princes cannot possibly in the least sort be repugnant unto Christian religion.

I have not yet made this book out of a desire of praise (although if I had, I might have defended myself with this fair excuse, that very few do things laudably, who are not affected with commendation) but for your sakes, readers, who I persuaded myself, when you should rightly apprehend and thoroughly understand this doctrine I here present you with, would rather choose to brook with patience some inconveniences under government (because human affairs cannot possibly be without some) than self-opiniatedly disturb the quiet of the public; that, weighing the justice of those things you are about, not by the persuasion and advice of private men, but by the laws of the realm, you will no longer suffer ambitious men through the streams of your blood to wade to their own power; that you will esteem it better to enjoy yourselves in the present state, though perhaps not the best, than by waging war, endeavour to procure a reformation for other men in another age, yourselves in the meanwhile either killed, or consumed with age. Furthermore, for those who will not acknowledge themselves subject to the civil magistrate, and will be exempt from all public burthens, and yet will live under his jurisdiction, and look for protection from the violence and injuries of others, that you would not look on them as fellow-subjects, but esteem them for enemies, and spies, and that ye rashly admit not for God's word all which either openly or privately they shall pretend to be so. I say more plainly, if any preacher, confessor, or casuist, shall but say that this doctrine is agreeable with God's word, namely, that the chief ruler, nay any private man may lawfully be put to death without the chief's command, or that subjects may resist, conspire, or covenant against the supreme power; that ye by no means believe them, but instantly declare their names. He who approves of these reasons, will also like my intentions in writing this book.

Last of all, I have propounded to myself this rule through this whole discourse; first, not to define aught which concerns the justice of single actions, but leave them to be determined by the laws. Next, not to dispute the laws of any government in special, that is, not to point which are the laws of any country, but to declare what the laws of all countries are. Thirdly, not to seem of opinion, that there is a less proportion of obedience due to an aristocracy or democracy, than a monarchy; for though I have endeavoured by arguments in my tenth chapter to gain a belief in men, that monarchy is the most commodious government (which one thing alone I confess in this whole book not to be demonstrated, but only probably stated) yet every where I expressly say, that in all kind of government whatsoever, there ought to be a supreme and equal power. Fourthly, not in anywise to dispute the positions of divines, except those which strip subjects of their obedience, and shake the foundations of civil government. Lastly, lest I might imprudently set forth somewhat of which there would be no need, what I had thus written, I would not presently expose to public interest, wherefore I got some few copies privately dispersed among some of my friends, that discrying the opinions of others, if any things appeared erroneous, hard, or obscure, I might correct, soften, and explain them.

These things I found most bitterly excepted against: that I had made the civil powers too large, but this by ecclesiastical persons; that I had utterly taken away liberty of conscience, but this by sectaries; that I had set princes above the civil laws, but this by lawyers. Wherefore I was not much moved by these men's reprehensions, (as who in doing this did but do their own business) except it were to tie those knots somewhat faster.

But for their sakes who have a little been staggered at the principles themselves, to wit the nature of men, the authority or right of nature, the nature of compacts and contracts, and the original of civil government, because in finding fault they have not so much followed their passions, as their common-sense, I have therefore in some places added some annotations whereby I presumed I might give some satisfaction to their differing thoughts; lastly I have endeavoured to offend none beside those whose principles these contradict, and whose tender minds are lightly offended by every difference of opinions.

Wherefore if ye shall meet with some things which have more of sharpness, and less of certainty than they ought to have, since they are not so much spoken for the maintenance of parties, as the establishment of peace, and by one whose just grief for the present calamities of his country, may very charitably be allowed some liberty, it is his only request to ye, readers, ye will deign to receive them with an equal mind.

Leviathan

TO MY MOST HONOR'D FRIEND
Mr. Francis Godolphin,
of Godolphin

Honor'd Sir,

Your most worthy brother, Mr. *Sidney Godolphin*, when he lived, was pleased to think my studies something, and otherwise to oblige me, as you know, with real testimonies of his good opinion, great in themselves, and the greater for the worthiness of his person. For there is not any virtue that disposeth a man, either to the service of God or to the service of his country, to civil society or private friendship, that did not manifestly appear in his conversation; not as acquired by necessity or affected upon occasion, but inherent, and shining in a generous constitution of his nature. Therefore, in honour and gratitude to him, and with devotion to yourself, I humbly dedicate unto you this my discourse of Commonwealth.

I know not how the world will receive it, nor how it may reflect on those that shall seem to favour it. For in a way beset with those that contend, on one side for too great liberty, and on the other side for too much authority, 'tis hard to pass between the points of both unwounded. But yet, methinks, the endeavour to advance the civil power, should not be by the civil power condemned; nor private men, by reprehending it, declare they think that power too great. Besides, I speak not of the men, but (in the abstract) of the seat of power (like to those simple and unpartial creatures in the Roman Capitol, that with their noise defended those within it, not because they were they, but there), offending none, I think, but those without, or such within (if there be any such) as favour them.

That which perhaps may most offend are certain texts of Holy Scripture, alleged by me to other purpose than ordinarily they use to be by others. But I have done it with due submission, and also (in order to my subject) necessarily; for they are the outworks of the enemy, from whence they impugn the civil power. If notwithstanding this, you find my labour generally decried, you may be pleased to excuse yourself, and say, I am a man that love my own opinions, and think all true I say, that I honoured your brother, and honour you, and have presumed on that, to assume the title (without your knowledge) of being, as I am,

Sir,
Your most humble, and most obedient Servant,
Thomas Hobbes.

Paris, April 15/25, 1651.

The Introduction

[1] Nature (the art whereby God hath made and governs the world) is by the *art* of man, as in many other things, so in this also imitated, that it can make an artificial animal. For seeing life is but a motion of limbs, the beginning whereof is in some principal part within, why may we not say that all *automata* (engines that move themselves by springs and wheels as doth a watch) have an artificial life? For what is the *heart*, but a *spring;* and the *nerves*, but so many *strings;* and the *joints*, but so many *wheels*, giving motion to the whole body, such as was intended by the artificer? *Art* goes yet further, imitating that rational and most excellent work of nature, *man*. For by art is created that great *Leviathan* called a *Commonwealth*, or *State* (in Latin *Civitas*), which is but an artificial man, though of greater stature and strength than the natural, for whose protection and defence it was intended; and in which the *sovereignty* is an artificial soul, as giving life and motion to the whole body; the *magistrates* and other *officers* of judicature and execution, artificial *joints; reward* and *punishment* (by which fastened to the seat of the sovereignty every joint and member is moved to perform his duty) are the *nerves*, that do the same in the body natural; the *wealth* and *riches* of all the particular members are the *strength; salus populi* (the people's safety) its *business; counsellors*, by whom all things needful for it to know are suggested unto it, are the *memory; equity* and *laws*, an artificial *reason* and *will; concord, health; sedition, sickness;* and *civil war, death.* Lastly, the *pacts* and *covenants* by which the parts of this body politic were at first made, set together, and united, resemble that *fiat*, or the *let us make man*, pronounced by God in the creation.

[2] To describe the nature of this artificial man, I will consider

> First, the *matter* thereof, and the *artificer*, both which is *man*.
> Secondly, *how* and by what *covenants* it is made;
> what are the *rights* and *just power* or *authority* of a *sovereign;*
> and what it is that *preserveth* and *dissolveth* it.
> Thirdly, what is a *Christian commonwealth.*
> Lastly, what is the *kingdom of darkness.*

[3] Concerning the first, there is a saying much usurped of late, that *wisdom* is acquired, not by reading of *books*, but of *men*. Consequently whereunto, those persons that for the most part can give no other proof of being wise take great delight to show what they think they have read in men, by uncharitable censures of one another behind their backs. But there is another saying not of late understood, by which they might learn truly to read one another, if they would take the pains; and that is, *nosce teipsum, read thy self*, which was not meant, as it is now used, to countenance either the barbarous state of men in power towards their inferiors, or to encourage men of low degree to a saucy behaviour towards

their betters, but to teach us that for the similitude of the thoughts and passions of one man to the thoughts and passions of another, whosoever looketh into himself and considereth what he doth, when he does *think, opine, reason, hope, fear*, &c, and upon what grounds, he shall thereby read and know, what are the thoughts and passions of all other men upon the like occasions. I say the similitude of *passions*, which are the same in all men, *desire, fear, hope*, &c, not the similitude of the *objects* of the passions, which are the things *desired, feared, hoped*, &c; for these the constitution individual and particular education do so vary, and they are so easy to be kept from our knowledge, that the characters of man's heart, blotted and confounded as they are with dissembling, lying, counterfeiting, and erroneous doctrines, are legible only to him that searcheth hearts. And though by men's actions we do discover their design sometimes, yet to do it without comparing them with our own, and distinguishing all circumstances by which the case may come to be altered, is to decipher without a key, and be for the most part deceived, by too much trust, or by too much diffidence, as he that reads is himself a good or evil man.

[4] But let one man read another by his actions never so perfectly, it serves him only with his acquaintance, which are but few. He that is to govern a whole nation must read in himself, not this or that particular man, but mankind, which though it be hard to do, harder than to learn any language or science, yet when I shall have set down my own reading orderly and perspicuously, the pains left another will be only to consider if he also find not the same in himself. For this kind of doctrine admitteth no other demonstration.

My Life

In Fifteen Hundred Eighty Eight, Old Style,
When that armada did invade our isle,
Called the invincible, whose freight was then,
Nothing but murd'ring steel, and murd'ring men,
Most of which navy was disperst, or lost,
And had the fate to perish on our coast,
April the fifth (though now with age outworn)
I'th'early spring, I, a poor worm, was born.
In Malmesbury baptiz'd, and named there
By my own father, then a minister.
Many things worth relating had this town;
And first, a monastery of renown,
And castle, or two rather it may seem,
On a hill seated, with a double stream
Almost environ'd, from whence still are sent
Two burgesses to sit in Parliament.
Here lie the Bones of Noble Athelstane,
Whose stone effigies do there remain;
Who for reward gave them the neighboring plains,
Which he had moist'ned with the blood of Danes.
Here was the Roman muse by Adelm brought,
Here also the first Latin school was taught.
My native place I'm not ashamed to own;
Th'ill times, and ills born with me, I bemoan.
For fame had rumour'd that a fleet at sea,

Would cause our nation's catastrophe.
And hereupon it was my mother dear
Did bring forth twins at once, both me and fear.
For this, my countries foes I e'r did hate,
With calm peace and my muse associate.
Did learn to speak four languages, to write
And read them too, which was my sole delight.
Six years i'th'Greek and Latin tongue I spent,
And at fourteen I was to Oxford sent;
And there of Magd'len-Hall admitted, I
Myself to logic first did then apply,
And sedulously I my tutor heard,
Who gravely read, althou'he had no beard.
Barbara, Celarent, Darii, Ferio, Baralypton,
Cesare, Camestres, Festino, Baroco, Darapti,
This hath of modes the same variety.
Felapton, Disamis, Datisi, Bocardo, Ferison,
These just so many modes are look'd upon.
Which I, tho' slowly Learn, and then dispense
With them, and prove things after my own sense.
Then physics read, and my tutor display'd,
How all things were of form and matter made.
The aery particles which makes forms we see,
Both visible and audible; to be
Th'effects of sympathy, antipathy.
And many things above my reach taught me.
Therefore, more pleasant studies I then sought,
Which I was formerly, tho' not well, taught.
My fancy and my mind divert I do,
With maps celestial and terrestrial too.
Rejoice t'accompany Sol cloath'd with rays,
Know by what art he measures all our days;
How Drake and Cavendish a girdle made
Quite round the world, what climates they survey'd;
And strive to find the smaller cells of men.
And painted monsters in their unknown den
Nay, there's a fullness in geography;
For Nature e'r abhor'd vacuity.
Thus in due time took I my first degree
Of Bachelor i'th'University.
Then Oxford left, serv'd Ca'ndish, known to be
A noble and conspicuous family.
Our college rector did me recommend,
Where I most pleasantly my days did spend.
Thus youth tutor'd a youth, for he was still
Under command, and at his father's will:
Serv'd him full twenty years, who prov'd to be,
Not a lord only, but a friend to me.
That my life's sweetest comfort was, and made
My slumbers pleasant in night's darkest shade.
Thus I at ease did live, of books, whilst he
Did with all sorts supply my library.

Then I our own historians did peruse,
Greek, Latin, and convers'd too with my muse.
Homer and Virgil, Horace, Sophocles,
Plautus, Euripides, Aristophones,
I understood, nay more; but of all these,
There's none that pleas'd me like Thucydides.
He says Democracy's foolish thing,
Than a republic wiser is one king,
This author I taught English, that even he
A guide to rhetoricians might be.
To foreign countries at that time did I
Travel, saw France, Italy, Germany.
This debonair lord, th'Earl of Devonshire,
I serv'd complete the space of twenty year.
His life by sickness conquer'd, fled away,
T'exchange it for a better the last day.
But yet provided ere he di'd for me,
Who liv'd with little most contentedly.
I left my pleasant mansion, went away
To Paris, and there eighteen months did stay,
Thence to be tutor I'm cal'd back again,
To my Lord's son, the Earl of Devon then.
This noble lord I did instruct when young,
Both how to speak and write the Roman tongue;
And by what arts the rhetor deceives those
That are illiterate; taught him verse and prose;
The mathematics precepts too, with all
The windings in the globe terrestrial;
The whole design of law, and how he must
Judge between that which equal is and just.
Seven years to him these arts I did explain:
He quickly learnt, and firmly did retain.
We spent not all this time in books alone,
Unless you'd take the world for to be one;
Travel'd through't Italy and France, did view
The sweet retirements of Savoy too.
Whether on horse, in coach or ship, still I
Was most intent on my philosophy.
One only thing i'th'world seem'd true to me,
Tho'several ways that falsified be.
One only true thing, the basis of all
Those things whereby we any thing do call.
How sleep does fly away, and what things still
By optics I can multiply at will.
Fancy's internal, th'issue of our brain,
Th'internal parts only motion contain:
And he that studies physics first must know
What motion is, and what motion can do.
To matter, motion, I myself apply,
And thus I spend my time in Italy.
I scribbled nothing o'er, nor then e'r wrought;
I ever had a mistress that me taught.

Then leaving Italy, return we do
To Paris, and its stately fabrics view.
Here with Mersennus I acquainted grew,
Shew'd him of motion what I ever knew.
He both prais'd and approv'd it, and so, Sir,
I was reputed a philosopher.
Eight months elaps'd, I return'd, and thought good
For to connect what e'r I understood.
That principles at second hand more clear,
By their concatenation might appear.
To various matter various motion brings
Me, and the different Species of Things.
Man's Inward Motions and his Thoughts to know,
The good of Government, and Justice too,
These were my Studies then, and in these three
Consists the whole Course of Philosophy.
Man, Body, Citizen, for these I do
Heap Matter up, designing three Books too.
I'th'interim breaks forth a horrid War,
Injurious to my Study, and a Bar.
In the year sixteen hundred forty, then
Brake out a Sickness, whereof many Men
Of Learning, languishing, gave up their breath
At last, and yielded to impartial death.
Wherewith, when seized, he reputed was
The Man that knew Divine and Humane Laws,
The War's now hot, I dread to see it so,
Therefore to Paris well-belov'd, I go.
Two years elaps'd, I published in Print
My Book De Cive; the new Matter in't
Gratified Learned Men, which was the Cause,
It was Translated, and with great Applause
By Several Nations, and great Scholars read,
So that my name was Famous, and far spread.
England in her sad Pangs of War, and those
Commend it too, whom I do most oppose.
But what's disadvantageous now, who wou'd,
Though it be Just, ever esteem it Good?
Then I four years spent to contrive which way
To Pen my Book de Corpore, Night and Day;
Compare together each Corporeal Thing,
Think whence the known changes of forms do spring.
Inquire how I compel this Proteus may,
His Cheats and Artifices to Display.
About this time Mersennus was (by Name)
A Friar Minorite, yet of Great Fame,
Learned, Wise, Good, whose single Cell might be
Prefer'd before an University.
To him all Persons brought what e'r they found
By Learning, if new Principle, or Ground,
In clear and proper Phrase, without the Dress
of Gawdy Rhetoric, Pride, Deceitfulness.

Which he impart to th'Learned, who might there
Discuss them, or at leisure, anywhere.
Publish'd some Rare Inventions, to the Fame
Of their own Author, with each Authors Name.
About Mersenne, like an Axis, here
Each Star wheel'd round, as in its Orb or Sphere.
England, Scotland, Ireland was the Stage
Of Civil War, and with its four years Rage,
Harras'd and wasted was; Perfidious Fate
Exil'd the Good, and Help'd the Profligate.
Nay, Charles, the Kingdom's Heir, attended then,
By a Retinue of Brave, Noble Men,
To Paris came, in hope Times might amend,
And Popular Fury once be at an end.
My Book de Corpore then I designed
To write, all things being ready to my Mind.
But must desist: such Crimes and Sufferings I
Will not impute unto the Deity.
First I resolv'd Divine Laws to fulfil;
This by Degrees, and carefully I will.
My Prince's studies I then waited on,
But could not constantly attend my own.
Then for six Months was sick; but yet at length,
Though very weak, I did recover strength,
And finished it in my own Mother-Tongue,
To be read for the good of old and young.
The Book at London printed was, and thence,
Hath visited the Neighboring Nations since,
Was read by many a great and learned Man,
Known by its dreadful name, Leviathan,
This book contended with all kings, and they
By any title, who bear royal sway.
In the mean time the King's sold by the Scot,
Murder'd by th'English, an eternal blot.
King Charles at Paris who did then reside,
Had right to England's Scepter undenied.
A rebel rout the kingdom kept in awe,
And ruled the giddy rabble without law,
Who boldly Parliament themselves did call,
Though but a poor handful of men in all.
Blood-thirsty leeches, hating all that's good,
Glutted with innocent and noble blood.
Down go the miters, neither do we see
That they establish the Presbytery.
Th'ambition of the stateliest clergymen,
Did not at all prevail in England then.
Hence many scholars to the King did go,
Expelled, Sad, indigent, burthensome too.
As yet my studies undisturbed were,
And my grand climacteric past one year.
When that book was perused by knowing men,
The gates of Janus temple opened them;

And they accused me to the King, that I
Seemed to approve Cromwell's impiety,
And countenance the worst of wickedness:
This was believed, and I appeared no less
Than a grand enemy, so that I was for't
Banished both the King's presence and his court.
Then I began on this to ruminate
On Dorislaus, and on Ascham's fate,
And stood amazed, like a poor exile,
Encompassed with terror all the while.
Nor could I blame the young King for his Assent
To those intrusted with his government.
Then home I came, not sure of safety there,
Though I could not be safer anywhere.
The wind, frost, snow, sharp, with age grown gray,
A plunging beast, and most unpleasant way.
At London, lest I should appear a spy,
Unto the state myself I did apply;
That done, I quietly retired to
Follow my study, as I used to do.
A Parliament so called did govern here;
There was no prelate then, nor presbyter.
Nothing but arms and soldiers, one alone
Designed top rule, and Cromwell was that one.
What royalist can there, or man alive,
Blame my defense o'th'King's prerogative?
All men did scribble what they would, content
And yielding to the present government.
My book de Corpore through this liberty.
I wore, which proved through this liberty
I wrote, which proved a constant war to me.
The clergy at Leviathan repines,
And both of them opposed were by divines.
For whilst I did inveigh 'gainst papal pride,
These, though prohibited, were not denied
T'appear in print: gainst my Leviathan
They rail, which made it read by many a man,
And did confirm 't the more; tis hoped by me,
That it will last to all eternity.
Twill be the rule of justice and severe
Reproof of those men that ambitious are.
The King's defence and guard, the people's good,
And satisfaction, read, and understood.
I, two years after, print a book to show
How every reader may himself well know.
Where I teach ethics, the phantoms of the sense,
How th'wife with spectres, fearless may dispense.
Published my book de corpore withal,
Whose matter's wholly geometrical.
With great applause the algebrists then read
Wallis his algebra now published.
A hundred years that geometric pest

Ago began, which did that age infest.
The art of finding out the numbers sought
Which Diophantus once, and Gheber taught:
And then Vieta tells you that by this,
Each geometric problem solved is.
Savil the Oxford reader did supply
Wallis with principles noble and high,
That infinite had end, and finite should
Have parts, but yet those without end allowed.
Both which opinions did enrage and scare
All those who geometricasters were.
This was enough to set me writing, who
Was then in years no less than seventy-two,
And in six dialogues I do inveigh
Against that new and geometric way,
But to no purpose, great men it doth please,
And thus the med'cine yields to the disease.
I printed then two treatises that stung
The Bishop Bramhall in our mother-tongue.
The question at that time was, and is still,
Whether at God's, or our own choice, we will.
And this was the result proceeding thence,
He the schools followed, I made use of sense.
Six problems, not long after, published I,
A tract but small, yet pure philosophy.
Wherein I teach how nature does cast down
All weighty bodies, and huge massy stone:
How vapors are exhaled by the Sun;
How winds engender cold, when that is done;
The reason of their Levity, and how
The barren Clouds do hang on Heaven's brow;
How move, and then that they are pregnant grown
With moisture, do in violent showers pour down.
By what cement hard matter is conjoined,
And how hard things grow soft, the cause do find:
Whence lightning, snow and ice do proceed, and Thunder,
Breaking through wat'ry clouds, even to wonder:
How loadstones Iron attract: how and which way
They th'Arctic and Antarctic poles obey.
Why from the sea unequal waves do glide,
I'th'year, or month, eaoh day a double tide;
And why a ship doth sail against the wind,
In that small treatise all these things you find,
Which may in time tread with applause the stage,
As yet unblamed in such a carping age.
The nature of the air I do descry
In a small volume, and most pithily,
Composed on purpose for to obviate
An inanic machine formed of late.
Then leaving Physics, I return again
To my beloved mathematics strain:
For now the barb'rous bloody enemy

Had left the place, where my estate did lie.
The truth I could not teach; for none but fools
May hope t'instruct in their declaiming schools.
Another book of principles I print,
Nothing could be more clear than what was in't.
Whereby the nature of proportion is
Explained so fully, none can say amiss.
Upon this subject most agreed that I
Of every one had gained the victory;
Others seem in it to find error's store,
But they are crazy grown, and I the more
Press upon them; then do ascend the high
And lofty summit of Geometry.
The circle's quadrature I publish then;
The Pythian God's Porisma teach all men.
By a new method I thought to o'ercome,
Though not by the same reasons, neither, some
O'th'former demonstrations, but in vain.
Mathematicians half-witted complain,
Who blush for to subscribe, but I'll not lose
My labor any longer, thinking those
Indocile brutes will ever master sense,
Or with good literature ever dispense.
Then my Rosetum was put forth, which I
Stored with rare flowers of geometry.
Wallis opposes, and I lost the day,
As both divines and Algebrists do say.
The army then discamped, and gone, thereby
Wallis of nothing thinks, but victory;
Who having chosen an unpleasant field,
Which thick and troublesome deep roots did yield,
Liking the combat, I turn, scatter quite
All in a moment, numbers infinite.
These were my wars; what more have I to say?
How rich I am, that is, how wise, I pray?
No matter for my money or my land;
If any ask that, let him understand,
A small parcel of ground I had to show,
My own inheritance, and let him know,
That this I on my brother did bestow:
Of small extent, but a most fertile ground,
Which did with store of bladed wheat abound
Fit for a prince; and had not every thing
Run cross, I had been counted a great king.
When I the civil War approaching find,
And people led by every breath of wind,
I sought than this a more commodious place
To live and study in, and that Paris was.
Stocked with five hundred pounds of coin before
I did desert, or leave my native shore;
To these two hundred added, but withal
A weighty lasting grief did me befall.

(Thou'rt dead, Godolphin, who lov'dst reason, true
Justice and peace, soldier belov'd, adieu)
Twice forty pounds, a yearly pension, then
I from my own country received; and when
King Charles restored was, a hundred more
Was allowed me out of his private store.
A noble gift: I slight reproaches, when
I know I'm good, from other black-mouth'd men.
Content with this, desire no more pelf,
Who but a madman lives beneath himself?
Let my estate by yours computed be,
And greater seem; if not, it's enough for me.
My sums are small, and yet live happy so,
Richer than Croesus far, and Crassus too.
Verdusius, thou know'st my temper well,
And those who read my works, and with thee dwell,
My life and writings speak one congruous sense;
Justice I teach, and justice reverence.
None but the covetous we wicked call,
For avarice can do no good at all.
I've now completed my eighty-fourth year,
And death approaching, prompts me not to fear.

[John Aubrey records an additional verse, written not long before Hobbes died.]

Tho' I am now past ninety, and too old
T'expect preferment in the court of Cupid,
And many winters made me ev'n so cold
I am become almost all over stupid,
Yet I can love and have a mistress too,
As fair as can be and as wise as fair;
And yet not proud, nor anything will do
To make me of her favor to despair.
To tell you who she is were very bold;
But if i'th' character yourself you find
Think not the man a fool, though he be old,
Who loves in body fair a fairer mind. [I, 364–5]

John Aubrey, *Life of Hobbes*

Thomas Hobbes, then, whose life I write, was second son of Mr. Thomas Hobbes, vicar of Westport, near Malmesbury . . . also vicar of Charlton (a mile hence). They are annexed and are both worth 60 or 80 pounds per annum. Thomas, the father, was one of the ignorant 'Sir Johns' of Queen Elizabeth's time, could only read the prayers of the Church and the homilies, and disesteemed learning (his son Edmund told me so), as not knowing the sweetness of it . . . He had an elder brother whose name was Francis, a wealthy man, and had been alderman of the borough. [I, 347–4]

When he was a boy, he was playsome enough, but withall he had even then a contemplative melancholiness. He would get him into a corner, and learn his lesson by heart presently. His hair was black, and his schoolfellows were wont to call him "crow." [I, 329] When young he loved music, and practised on the lute . . . he was unhealthy, and of an ill complection (yellowish). [I, 347]

Mr. Robert Latimer [was] a young man of about 19 or 20, newly come from the University, who then kept a private school in Westport . . . a bachelor, and delighted in his scholar, T. H.'s company, and used to instruct him, and two or three ingenious youths more, in the evening till 9 a clock. Here T. H. so well profited in his learning, that at fourteen years of age, he went away a good school-scholar to Magdalen Hall, in Oxford. It is not to be forgotten, he had turned Euripedes' *Medea* out of Greek into Latin iambics, which he presented to his master. [I, 328–9]

The old vicar Hobbes was a good fellow and had been at cards all night, and at church in his sleep he cries out "Trafells [clubs] is trumps" . . . He was a choleric man, and a parson (which I think succeeded him at Westport) provoked him (a purpose) at the church door, so Hobbes struck him, and was forced to fly for it and[lived] in obscurity beyond London. [I, 387]

Having no child, [Francis Hobbes] contributed much to, or rather altogether maintained, his nephew Thomas at Magdalen Hall . . . and when he died, gave him a mowing ground . . . worth 16 or 18 pounds a year. [I, 324]

After he had taken his bachelor of arts degree, the then principal of Magdalen Hall recommended him to his young lord when he left Oxford, who had a conceit that he should profit more in his learning if he had a scholar of his own age to wait on him than if he had the information of a grave doctor. He was his lordship's page, and rode a hunting and hawking with him, and kept his privy purse. By this way of life he had almost forgot his Latin. He therefore bought him books of an Amsterdam print that he might carry in his pocket (particularly Caesar's *Commentary*) which he did read in the lobby, or ante-chamber, whilst his lord was making his visits. [330–1] His lord, who was a waster, sent him up and down to borrow money, and to get gentlemen to be bound for him, being ashamed to speak himself. He took colds, being wet in his feet (then were no hackney coaches to stand in the streets), and trod both his shoes aside the same way. Notwithstanding he was well-beloved. They loved his company for his pleasant facetiousness and good nature. [I, 347]

The Lord Chancellor Bacon loved to converse with him. He assisted his lordship in translating several of his essays into Latin . . . His lordship was a very contemplative person, and was wont to contemplate in his delicious walks at Gorambery, and dictate to . . . [the] gentlemen, that attended him with ink and paper ready to set down presently his thoughts. His lordship would often say that he better liked Mr. Hobbes' taking his thoughts, than any of the other, because he understood what he wrote, which the others not understanding, my Lord would many times have a hard task to make sense of what they writ. It is to be remembered that about these times Mr. T. H. was much addicted to music and practised on the bass-viol. [331]

He was 40 years old before he looked on geometry, which happened accidentally. Being in a gentleman's library, Euclid's *Elements* lay open, and 'twas the 47th Prop. of Book I. He read the proposition. "By G——," said he (he would now and then swear, by way of emphasis), "this is impossible!" So he reads the demonstration of it, which referred him back to such a proposition; which proposition he read. That referred him back to another, which he also read. And so on, until at least he was demonstratively convinced of that truth. This made him in love with geometry. I have heard Sir Jonas Moore (and others) say that 'twas a great pity he had not begun the study of mathematics sooner, for such a working head [energetic mind] would have made great advancement in it. So had he done, he would not have lain so open to his learned mathematical antagonists. [I, 332–3]

When the Parliament sat that began in April 1640 and was dissolved in May following, and in which many points of the regal power, which were necessary for the peace of the kingdom and safety of his majesty's person, were disputed and denied, Mr. Hobbes wrote a little treatise in English, wherein he did set forth and demonstrate that the said power and rights were inseparably annexed to the sovereignty, which sovereignty they did not then deny to be in the king; but it seems understood not, or would not understand, that inseparability. Of this treatise, though not printed, many gentlemen had copies, which occasioned much talk of the author; and had not his majesty dissolved the parliament, it had brought him in danger of his life . . . He told me that Bishop Manwaring preached his doctrine, for which, among others, he was sent prisoner to the Tower. Then thought Mr. Hobbes, 'tis now time for me to shift for myself, and so withdrew into France, and resided at Paris. [I, 333–4]

Descartes and he were acquainted and mutually respected one another. He would say that had he kept himself to geometry, he had been the best geometer in the world, but that his head did not lie for philosophy . . . he could not pardon him for his writing in defence of transubstantiation, which he knew was absolutely against his opinion and done merely to put a compliment on the Jesuits. [I, 367]

For his being branded with atheism, his writings and virtuous life testify against it. No man hath written better of [God?], perhaps not so well. To prevent such false and malicious reports, I thought fit to insert and affirm as above said. And that he was a Christian 'tis clear, for he received the sacrament of Dr. Pierson, and in his confession to Dr. John Cosins . . . on his (as he thought) deathbed, declared that he liked the religion of the Church of England best of all other. [I, 353]

[From] Elizabeth, viscountess Purbec. When Mr. T. Hobbes was sick in France, the divines came to him, and tormented him (both Roman Catholic, Church of England, and Geneva). Said he to them "Let me alone, or else I will detect all your cheats from Aaron to yourselves." I think I have heard him speak something to this purpose. [I, 357–8]

It happened, about two or three days after his majesty's happy return, that, as he was passing in his coach through the Strand, Mr. Hobbes was standing at Little Salisbury-house gate (where his lord then lived). The King espied him, put off his hat very kindly to him, and asked him how he did. About a week after, he had oral conference with his majesty at Mr. S. Cowper's, where, as he sat for his picture, he was diverted by Mr. Hobbes' pleasant discourse. Here his majesty's favors were redintegrated to him, and order was given that he should have free access to his majesty, who was always much delighted in his wit and smart repartees. The wits at court were wont to bait him. But he feared none of them, and would make his part good. The King would call him "the bear"—"Here comes the bear to be baited." [I, 340]

There was a report (and surely true) that in parliament, not long after the King was settled, some of the bishops made a motion to have the good old gentleman burned for a heretic. Which he hearing, feared that his papers might be searched by their order, and he told me that he had burned part of them. [I, 339]

When Spinoza's *Tractatus theologico-politicus* first came out, Mr. Edmund Waller sent it to my lord of Devonshire and desired him to send him word what Mr. Hobbes said of it. Mr. H. told his lordship: "Judge not that ye be not judged." [Matthew 7:1] He told me he had out thrown him a bar's length, for he durst not write so boldly. [I, 357]

He was very charitable (to the best of his ability) to those that were true objects of his bounty. One time, I remember, going in the Strand, a poor and infirm old man craved his alms. He, beholding him with eyes of pity and compassion, put his hand in his pocket, and gave him 6 pence. Said a divine (Dr. Jaspar Mayne) that stood by: "Would you have done this, if it had not been Christ's command?" "Yea," said he. "Why?" quoth the other. "Because," said he, "I was in pain to consider the miserable condition of the old man; and now my alms, giving him some relief, doth also ease me." [I, 352]

From forty or better, he grew healthier, and then he had a fresh ruddy complection . . . In his old age he used to sing prick-song [written vocal music] every night, when all were gone and sure nobody could hear him, for his health, which he did believe would make him live two or three years longer. [I, 347] He had a good eye, and that of a hazel color, which was full of life and spirit, even to the last. When he was earnest in discourse, there shone, as it were, a bright live-coal within it. He had two kind of looks: when he laughed, was witty, and in a merry humor, one could scarce see his eyes; by and by, when he was serious and positive, he opened his eyes round . . . He was six foot high, and something better, and went indifferently erect, or rather, considering his great age, very erect . . . He had read much, if one considers his long life, but his contemplation was much more than his reading. He was wont to say that if he had read as much as other men, he should have known no more than other men. [I, 348–9] 'Tis not consistent with an harmonical soul to be a woman-hater, neither had he an abhorrescence to good wine, but . . . this only between us. He was, even in his youth, generally temperate, both as to wine and women . . . "I am a man, and think nothing human alien to myself." For his last 30+ years, his diet, etc., was very moderate and regular. After 60 he drank no wine, his stomach grew weak, and he did eat most fish, especially whiting, for he said he digested fish better than flesh. He rose about seven, had his breakfast of bread and butter, and took his walk, meditating till ten; then he did put down the minutes of his thoughts, which he penned in the afternoon . . . Besides his daily walking, he did twice or thrice a year play at tennis (at about 75 he did it); then went to bed there and was well rubbed. This he did believe would make him live two or three years the longer. [I, 350–1] He had the shaking palsy in his hands, which began in France before the year 1650, and has grown on him by degrees, ever since, so that he has not been able to write very legibly since 1665 or 1666. [I, 352]

11

BARUCH SPINOZA
Wisdom and the Improvement of the Understanding

Born in Amsterdam to a Jewish family of Portuguese origin, Baruch Spinoza (1632–1677) received his first education in scriptural and Talmudic studies. Influenced by his reading of Maimonides, he turned to philosophy and immersed himself in Cartesian studies. As his views on the divine nature became increasingly unorthodox, he ceased being a practicing Jew and was excommunicated by the Jewish community in 1656. In 1663, he recast and revised Descartes' *Principles of Philosophy* in a deductive form. The *Theological-Political Treatise*—which argued for the freedom of thought and speech as a support for civic peace and harmony—appeared anonymously in 1670. Deeply affected by the political turbulence marked by the murder of the DeWitt brothers, Spinoza determined to avoid being entangled in political and religious controversies. He declined a professorship in philosophy at the University of Heidelberg in 1673 on the grounds that he wanted to philosophize "in accordance with his own mind." Earning his living as a lens grinder, he contributed to the optics of the times. Along with his unfinished *Political Treatise* and the *Treatise on the Improvement of the Understanding*, Spinoza's major work, *Ethics Demonstrated in Geometrical Order*, was published posthumously, in 1677. Cast on the deductive model of Euclid's *Elements of Geometry*—with definitions, postulates, and axioms—the book begins with a theological treatise on divine substance; it then turns to an argument for nonreductive mind-body identity, moves to an attack on the distinction between the will and the understanding, and to a psychological study of the correction of the passions. The book culminates with an argument that freedom and salvation are achieved through the intellectual love of God.

Treatise on the Emendation of the Intellect and on the way by which it is best directed toward the true knowledge of things

After experience had taught me that all the things which regularly occur in ordinary life are empty and futile, and I saw that all the things which were the cause or object of my fear had nothing of good or bad in themselves, except insofar as [my] mind was moved by them, I resolved at last to try to find out whether there was anything which would be the true good, capable of communicating itself, and which alone would affect the mind, all others being rejected—whether there was something which, once found and acquired, would continuously give me the greatest joy, to eternity.

I say that *I resolved at last*—for at first glance it seemed ill-advised to be willing to lose something certain for something then uncertain. I saw, of course, the advantages that honor and wealth bring, and that I would be forced to abstain from seeking them, if I wished to devote myself seriously to something new and different; and if by chance the greatest happiness lay in them, I saw that I should have to do without it. But if it did not lie in them, and I devoted my energies only to acquiring them, then I would equally go without it.

So I wondered whether perhaps it would be possible to reach my new goal—or at least the certainty of attaining it—without changing the conduct and plan of life which I shared with other men. Often I tried this, but in vain. For most things which present themselves in life, and which, to judge from their actions, men think to be the highest good, may be reduced to these three: wealth, honor, and sensual pleasure. The mind is so distracted by these three that it cannot give the slightest thought to any other good.

For as far as sensual pleasure is concerned, the mind is so caught up in it, as if a peace in a [true] good, that it is quite prevented from thinking of anything else. But after the enjoyment of sensual pleasure is past, the greatest sadness follows. If this does not completely engross, still it thoroughly confuses and dulls the mind.

The mind is also distracted not a little by the pursuit of honors and wealth, particularly when the latter is sought only for its own sake, because it is assumed to be the highest good. [5] But the mind is far more distracted by honor. For this is always assumed to be good through itself and the ultimate end toward which everything is directed.

Nor do honor and wealth have, as sensual pleasure does, repentance as a natural consequence. The more each of these is possessed, the more joy is increased, and hence the more we are spurred on to increase them. But if our hopes should chance to be frustrated, we experience the greatest sadness. And finally, honor has this great disadvantage: to pursue it, we must direct our lives according to other men's powers of understanding—fleeing what they commonly flee and seeking what they commonly seek.

Since I saw that all of these things stood in the way of my working toward this new goal, indeed were so opposed to it that one or the other must be given up, I was forced to ask what would be more useful to me. For as I say, I seemed to be willing to lose the certain good for the uncertain one. But after I had considered the matter a little, I first found that, if I devoted myself to this new plan of life, and gave up the old, I would be giving up a good by its nature uncertain (as we can clearly infer from what has been said) for one uncertain not by its nature (for I was seeking a permanent good) but only in respect to its attainment.

By persistent meditation, however, I came to the conclusion that, if only I could resolve, wholeheartedly, [to change my plan of life], I would be giving up certain evils for a certain good. For I saw that I was in the greatest danger, and that I was forced to seek a remedy with all my strength, however uncertain it might be—like a man suffering from a fatal illness, who, foreseeing certain death unless he employs a remedy, is forced to seek it, however uncertain, with all his strength. For all his hope lies there. But all those things men ordinarily strive for, not only provide no remedy to preserve our being, but in fact hinder that preservation, often cause the destruction of those who posses them, and always cause the destruction of those who are possessed by them.

There are a great many examples of people who have suffered persecution to the death on account of their wealth, or have exposed themselves to so many dangers to acquire wealth that they have at last paid the penalty for their folly with their life. Nor are there fewer examples of people who, to attain or defend honor, have suffered most miserably. And there are innumerable examples of people who have hastened their death through too much sensual pleasure.

Furthermore, these evils seemed to have arisen from the fact that all happiness or unhappiness was placed in the quality of the object to which we cling with love. For strife will never arise on account of what is not loved, nor will there be sadness if it perishes, nor envy if it is possessed by another, nor fear, nor hatred—in a word, no disturbances of the mind. Indeed, all these happen only in the love of those things that can perish, as all the things we have just spoken of can do.

But love toward the eternal and infinite thing feeds the mind with a joy entirely exempt from sadness. This is greatly to be desired, and to be sought with all our strength.

But not without reason did I use these words *if only I could resolve in earnest*. For though I perceived these things [NS: this evil] so clearly in my mind, I still could not, on that account, put aside all greed, desire for sensual pleasure and love of esteem.

I saw this, however: that so long as the mind was turned toward these thoughts, it was turned away from those things, and was thinking seriously about the new goal. That was a great comfort to me. For I saw that those evils would not refuse to yield to remedies. And although in the beginning these intervals were rare, and lasted a very short time, nevertheless, after the true good became more and more known to me, the intervals became more frequent and longer— especially after I saw that the acquisition of money, sensual pleasure, and esteem are only obstacles so long as they are sought for their own sakes, and not as means to other things. But if they are sought as means, then they will have a limit, and will not be obstacles at all. On the contrary, they will be of great use in attaining the end on account of which they are sought, as we shall show in its place.

Here I shall only say briefly what I understand by the true good, and at the same time, what the highest good is. To understand this properly, it must be noted that good and bad are said of things only in a certain respect, so that one and the same thing can be called both good and bad according to different respects. The same applies to perfect and imperfect. For nothing, considered in its own nature, will be called perfect or imperfect, especially after we have recognized that everything that happens happens according to the eternal order, and according to certain laws of Nature.

But since human weakness does not grasp that order by its own thought, and meanwhile man conceives a human nature much stronger and more enduring than his own, and at the same time sees that nothing prevents his acquiring such a nature, he is spurred to seek means that will lead him to such a perfection. Whatever can be a means to his attaining it is called a true good; but the highest good is to arrive—together with other individuals if possible—at the enjoyment of such a nature. What that nature is we shall show in its proper place: that it is the knowledge of the union that the mind has with the whole of Nature.

This, then, is the end I aim at: to acquire such a nature, and to strive that many acquire it with me. That is, it is part of my happiness to take pains that, many others may understand as I understand, so that their intellect and desire agree entirely with my intellect and desire. To do this it is necessary, *first* to understand as much of Nature as suffices for acquiring such a nature; *next*, to form a society of the kind that is desirable, so that as many as possible may attain it as easily and surely as possible.

Third, attention must be paid to Moral Philosophy and to Instruction concerning the Education of children. Because Health is no small means to achieving this end, *fourthly*, the whole of Medicine must be worked out. And because many difficult things are rendered easy by ingenuity, and we can gain much time and convenience in this life, *fifthly*, Mechanics is in no way to be despised.

But before anything else we must devise a way of healing the intellect, and purifying it, as much as we can in the beginning, so that it understands things successfully, without error and as well as possible. Everyone will now be able to see that I wish to direct all the sciences toward one end and goal, viz. that we should achieve, as we have said, the highest human perfection. So anything in the sciences which does nothing to advance us toward our goal must be rejected as useless—in a word, all our activities and thoughts are to be directed to this end.

But while we pursue this end, and devote ourselves to bringing the intellect back to the right path, it is necessary to live. So we are forced, before we do anything else, to assume certain rules of living as good:

1. To speak according to the power of understanding of ordinary people, and do whatever does not interfere with our attaining our purpose. For we can gain a considerable advantage, if we yield as much to their understanding as we can. In this way, they will give a favorable hearing to the truth.

2. To enjoy pleasures just so far as suffices for safeguarding our health.

3. Finally, to seek money, or anything else, just so far as suffices for sustaining life and health, and conforming to those customs of the community that do not conflict with our aim.

Having laid down these rules, I come now to what must be done first, before all else: emending the intellect and rendering it capable of understanding things in the way the attainment of our end requires. To do this, the order we naturally have requires me to survey here all the modes of perceiving which I have had up to now for affirming or denying something without doubt, so that I may choose the best of all, and at the same time begin to know my powers and the nature that I desire to perfect.

If I consider them accurately, I can reduce them all to four main kinds:

1. There is the Perception we have from report or from some conventional sign.

2. There is the Perception we have from random experience, that is, from experience that is not determined by the intellect. But it has this name only because it comes to us by chance, and we have no other experiment that opposes it. So it remains with us unshaken.

3. There is the Perception that we have when the essence of a thing is inferred from another thing, but not adequately. This happens, either when we infer the cause from some effect, or when something is inferred from some universal, which some property always accompanies.

4. Finally, there is the Perception we have when a thing is perceived through its essence alone, or through knowledge of its proximate cause. . . . Only [this mode of perception] is without danger of error.

To the learned and sagacious William de Blyenbergh (1665)

The original, which is lost, was written in Dutch. The Latin is a translation from the Dutch, perhaps by Spinoza.

My unknown friend,

I gather from your letter and its philosophical questions that you are deeply devoted to truth, which you make the sole aim of all your endeavours. Since I have exactly the same objective, this has determined me not only to grant without stint your request to answer to the best of my ability the questions which you are now sending me and will send me in the future, but also to do everything in my power conducive to further acquaintance and sincere friendship. For my part, of all things that are not under my control, what I most value is to enter into a bond of friendship with sincere lovers of truth. For I believe that such a loving relationship affords us a serenity surpassing any other boon in the whole wide world. The love that such men bear to one another, grounded as it is in the love that each has for knowledge of truth, is as unshakable as is the acceptance of truth once it has been perceived. It is, moreover, the highest source of happiness to be found in things not under our command, for truth more than anything else has the power to effect a close union between different sentiments and disposi-tions. I say nothing of the considerable advantages that derive therefrom, not wishing to detain you any longer on a matter on which you need no instruction. This much I have said so that you may better understand how pleased I am, and shall continue to be, to have the opportunity of serving you.

To avail myself of the present opportunity, I shall now go on to answer your question. This seems to hinge on the following point, that it seems clearly to follow, both from God's providence, which is identical with his will, and from God's concurrence and the continuous creation of things, either that there is no such thing as sin or evil, or that God brings about that sin and that evil. But you do not explain what you mean by evil, and as far as one can gather from the example of Adam's determinate will, by evil you seem to mean the will itself in so far as it is conceived as determined in a particular way, or in so far as it is in opposition to God's command. So you say it is quite absurd (and I would agree, if the case were as you say) to maintain either of the following alternatives, that God himself brings to pass what is contrary to his will, or else that what is opposed to God's will can nevertheless be good. For my own part, I cannot con-cede that sin and evil are anything positive, much less than anything can be or come to pass against God's will. On the contrary, I not only assert that sin is not anything positive; I maintain that it is only by speaking improperly or in merely human fashion that we say that we sin against God, as in the expression that men make God angry.

To the noble and learned Henry Oldenburg (1665)

. . . I rejoice that your philosophers are alive, and are mindful of themselves and their republic. I shall expect news of what they have recently done, when the warriors are sated with blood and are resting so as to renew their strength somewhat. If [Democritus] were alive today, he would surely be dying of laughter. For my part, these troubles move me neither to laughter nor again to tears, but rather to philosophising, and to a closer observation of human nature. For I do not think it right to laugh at nature, and far less to grieve over it, reflecting that men, like all else, are only a part of nature, and that I do not know how each part of nature harmonises with the whole, and how it coheres with other parts. And I realise that it is merely through such lack of understanding that certain features of nature—which I thus perceived only partly and in a fragmentary way, and which are not in keeping with out philosophical attitude of mind—once seemed to me vain, disordered and absurd. But now I let everyone go his own way. Those who wish can by all means die for their own good, as long as I am allowed to live for truth.

I am now writing a treatise [*Tractatus Theologico-Politicus*] on my views regarding Scripture. The reasons that move me to do so are these:

1. The prejudices of theologians. For I know that these are the main obstacles which prevent men from giving their minds to philosophy. So I apply myself to exposing such prejudices and removing them from the minds of sensible people.

2. The opinion of me held by the common people, who constantly accuse me of atheism. I am driven to avert this accusation, too, as far as I can.

3. The freedom to philosophise and to say what we think. This I want to vindicate completely, for here it is in every way suppressed by the excessive authority and egotism of preachers.

To the learned and accomplished Jacob Ostens (1671)

Most learned Sir,

You are doubtless surprised that I have kept you waiting so long, but I can hardly bring myself to answer that man's letter, which you kindly sent me. Nor do I do so now for any other reason than to keep my promise. But to satisfy myself, too, as far as that can be, I shall discharge my debt in as few words as possible, and briefly show how perversely he has misinterpreted my meaning—whether from malice or ignorance, I cannot say. But to the matter in hand.

First, he says 'it is of no importance to know of what nationality I am, or what manner of life I pursue'. But surely if he had known this, he would not have been so readily convinced that I teach atheism. For atheists are usually inordinately fond of honours and riches, which I have always despised, as is known to all who are acquainted with me. Then, to pave the way to the end he has in view, he says that I am not unintelligent, doubtless so that he may more easily establish that I have argued cleverly, cunningly, and with evil intent on behalf of the evil cause of the Deists. This is a clear indication that he has not understood my line of reasoning. For who can be so clever and so astute as to pretend to present so many powerful arguments in support of something he deems false? Whom, I say, will he hereafter believe to have written in all sincerity, if he thinks that the fictitious can be proved as soundly as the true? But this does not now surprise me, [for it] is what often happens to all good men.

He then continues, 'to avoid the accusation of superstition, I think he has renounced all religion'. What he understands by religion and what by superstition, I do not know. Does that man, pray, renounce all religion, who declares that God must be acknowledged as the highest good, and that he must be loved as such in a free spirit? And that in this alone does our supreme happiness and our highest freedom consist? And further, that the reward of virtue is virtue itself, while the punishment of folly and weakness is folly itself? And lastly, that everyone is in duty bound to love his neighbour and obey the commands of the sovereign power? I not only said this explicitly, but also proved it with the strongest arguments. But I think I see in what mire this man is stuck. He finds nothing to please him in virtue itself and in intellect, and would choose to live under the impulsion of his passions but for one obstacle, his fear of punishment. So he abstains from evil deeds and obeys the divine commandments like a slave, reluctantly and waveringly, and in return for this servitude he expects to reap rewards from God far sweeter to him than the divine love itself, and the more so as he dislikes the good that he does, and does it unwillingly. Consequently, he believes that all who are not restrained by this fear lead unbridled lives and renounce all religion. But I let this pass, and turn to his conclusion, where he seeks to prove that I teach atheism by clandestine and disguised arguments.

The basis of his reasoning is this, that he thinks that I do away with God's freedom and subject him to fate. This is completely false. For I have asserted that everything follows by an inevitable necessity from God's nature in just the same way that all assert that it follows from God's nature that he understands himself. Surely no one denies that this necessarily follows from the divine nature, and yet no one conceives that God, in understanding himself, is under the compulsion of some fate; it is conceived that he does so altogether freely, although necessarily. Here I find nothing that is beyond anyone's perception. And if he still believes that these assertions are made with evil intent, what does he think of his own Descartes, who declared that nothing is done by us that is not preordained by God; nay, that we are at every single moment created by God anew, as it were, and that nevertheless we act from freedom of our own will. This is surely something, as Descartes himself admits, that no one can understand.

Furthermore, this inevitable necessity of things does not do away with either divine or human laws. For moral precepts, whether or not they receive the form of law from God himself, are still divine and salutary. And whether the good that follows from virtue and love of God is bestowed on us by God as judge, or whether it emanates from the necessity of the divine nature, it will not on that account be more or less desirable, just as on the other hand the evils that follow from evil deeds are not less to be feared because they necessarily follow from them. And finally, whether we do what we do necessarily or freely, we are still led by hope or by fear. Therefore he is wrong in saying that 'I assert that no room is left for precepts and commandments', or, as he goes on to say, 'there is no expectation of reward or punishment when all is attributed to fate, or when it is asserted that all things emanate from God by an inevitable necessity'.

I do not here inquire why it is the same, or not very different, to assert that all things emanate necessarily from God's nature and that the universe is God, but I should like you to note that which he adds in no less malignant vein, 'that I hold that a man ought to devote himself to virtue not because of God's commandment and law, nor through hope of reward or fear of punishment, but . . . etc.' This you will certainly find nowhere in my Treatise; on the contrary, in chapter 4 I expressly said that the substance of the divine law (which is divinely inscribed in our minds, as I said in chapter 12) and its supreme commandment is to love God as the highest good; that is, not from fear of some punishment (for love cannot spring from fear) nor from love of something else from which we hope to derive pleasure—for then we should be loving the object of our desire rather than God himself. And in the same chapter I showed that God has revealed this very law to his prophets, and whether I maintain that this law of God received its authoritative form from God himself or whether I conceive it to be like the rest of God's decrees which involve eternal necessity and truth, it will nevertheless remain God's decree and a teaching for salvation. And whether I love God freely or through the necessity of God's decree, I shall still love God, and I shall be saved. Therefore I can now say that this man is to be classed with those of whom I said at the end of my Preface that I would prefer them to leave my book entirely alone rather than make themselves a nuisance by misinterpreting it, as is their wont in all cases, and hinder others without any benefit to themselves.

Although I think that this suffices to show what I intended, I consider it worthwhile to add some brief observations. He is wrong in thinking that I am referring to that axiom of the theologians who make a distinction between the words of a prophet when he is proclaiming dogma and his words when he is merely narrating something.

Furthermore, I do not see why he says that I think that all those will agree with me who deny that reason and philosophy are the interpreters of Scripture. For I have refused the views both of these and of Maimonides.

It would take too long to review all his remarks which indicate that it is in no equable spirit that he has passed judgment on me. So I move on to his conclusion where he says that 'I have left myself with no argument to prove that Mahomet was not a true prophet', which he tries to prove from the views I have expressed. Yet from these it clearly follows that Mahomet was an impostor, since he completely abolishes the freedom which is granted by that universal religion revealed by the natural and prophetic light, and which I have shown ought to be fully granted. And even if this were not so, am I bound, pray, to show that some prophet is false? On the contrary, the prophets were bound to show that they were true prophets. And if he replies that Mahomet, too, taught the divine law and gave sure signs of his mission as did the other prophets, there is certainly no reason for him to deny that Mahomet was a true prophet.

As for the Turks and the other Gentiles, if they worship God by the exercise of justice and by love of their neighbour, I believe that they possess the spirit of Christ and are saved, whatever convictions they may hold in their ignorance regarding Mahomet and the oracles.

So you see, my friend, that this man has strayed far from the truth. Yet I grant that he does me no injury, but much to himself, when he is not ashamed to proclaim that I teach atheism with clandestine and disguised arguments.

In general, I do not think that you will here find any expression which you might consider over-harsh against this man. However, if you come across anything of that sort, please either delete it or amend it as you think fit. It is not my intention to provoke him, whoever he may be, and to get for myself enemies of my own making. It is because this is often the result of disputes of this kind that I could scarcely prevail on myself to reply, and I would not have done so had I not promised.

To the most honourable and noble Mr. J. Louis Fabritius, Professor in the University of Heidelberg and Councillor to the Elector Palatine, (1673)

Most honourable Sir,

If I had ever had any desire to undertake a professorship in any faculty, I could have wished for none other than that which is offered me through you by His Serene Highness the Elector Palatine, especially on account of the freedom to philosophise which this most gracious Prince is pleased to grant, not to mention my long-felt wish to live under the rule of a Prince whose wisdom is universally admired. But since I have never intended to engage in public teaching, I cannot induce myself to embrace this excellent opportunity, although I have given long consideration to the matter. For, first, I reflect that if I am to find time to instruct young students, I must give up my further progress in philosophy. Secondly, I do not know within what limits the freedom to philosophise must be confined if I am to avoid appearing to disturb the publicly established religion. For divisions arise not so much from an ardent devotion to religion as from the different dispositions of men, or through their love of contradiction which leads them to distort or to condemn all things, even those that are stated aright. Now since I have already experienced this while leading a private and solitary life, it would be much more to be feared after I have risen to this position of eminence. So you see, most Honourable Sir, that my reluctance is not due to the hope of some better fortune, but to my love of peace, which I believe I can enjoy in some measure if I refrain from lecturing in public. Therefore I most earnestly beg you to pray His Serene Highness the Elector to grant me more time to deliberate on this matter. And please continue to commend to the favour of the most gracious Prince his most devoted admirer, whereby you will oblige even more.

12

JOHN LOCKE
The Origins of Philosophical Ideas

After a traditional classical education at Westminister and Oxford, John Locke (1632–1704) developed an interest in the experimental sciences. Remaining at Oxford after his degree, he became acquainted with Robert Boyle and the physician Thomas Sydenham. Although he did not officially receive a medical degree, he was trained as a physician. Offered a position as secretary to the Earl of Sandwich, then ambassador to Spain, he preferred to continue his studies at Oxford. But his friendship with the Earl of Shaftesbury—whom he also served as a personal physician—kept him at the center of political life. He helped write the Constitution of the Carolina colony, and was secretary of the Council of Trade and Plantations until 1700.

Locke went to France in 1675, initially for reasons of health. Once there, he found an agreeable intellectual circle around Gassendi, who introduced him to other critics of Cartesian philosophy. After returning to England in 1679, he became a political advisor to the Whig opponents of the royalist party. When the Earl of Shaftesbury fled to the Netherlands, Locke—who had been kept under surveillance for his political views—followed him in 1683. During his stay in Holland he wrote the *First Letter Concerning Toleration* which was published anonymously in 1689. He was active in advancing the accession of William of Orange, and returned to England in 1689 as the official escort of Princess Mary. Locke's *Two Treatises of Government* (1690) defended a liberal, contractarian political theory, resting on the premise that the proper function of government is the protection of citizens' lives, liberty and property. Locke also wrote tracts on public policy: a report on the condition of paupers in England and *Some Thoughts Concerning Education* (1693).

Even while he was actively involved in politics, Locke continued to work on epistemology. Although he thought that moral and mathematical ideas are innate, he developed a thorough-going empiricist psychology and epistemology. The *Essay Concerning Human Understanding*, begun in 1671 and published in 1689/90, traces the sources of ideas of physical objects, causation, personal identity and the operations of the mind. He spent his later years in the household of Sir Francis and Lady Masham, where he was visited by such scientists as Newton and Clarke.

An Essay Concerning Human Understanding

THE EPISTLE TO THE READER

Reader,

I have put into thy hands what has been the diversion of some of my idle and heavy hours. If it has the good luck to prove so of any of thine, and thou hast but half so much pleasure in reading as I had in writing it, thou wilt as little think thy money, as I do my pains, ill bestowed. Mistake not this for a commendation of my work; nor conclude, because I was pleased with the doing of it, that therefore I am fondly taken with it now it is done. He that hawks at larks and sparrows has no less sport, though a much less considerable quarry, than he that flies at nobler game: and he is little acquainted with the subject of this treatise— the *understanding*—who does not know that, as it is the most elevated faculty of the soul, so it is employed with a greater and more constant delight than any of the other. Its searches after truth are a sort of hawking and hunting, wherein the very pursuit makes a great part of the pleasure. Every step the mind takes in its progress towards Knowledge makes some discovery, which is not only new, but the best too, for the time at least.

For the understanding, like the eye, judging of objects only by its own sight, cannot but be pleased with what it discovers, having less regret for what has escaped it, because it is unknown. Thus he who has raised himself above the alms-basket, and, not content to live lazily on scraps of begged opinions, sets his own thoughts on work, to find and follow truth, will (whatever he lights on) not miss the hunter's satisfaction; every moment of his pursuit will reward his pains with some delight; and he will have reason to think his time not ill spent, even when he cannot much boast of any great acquisition.

This, Reader, is the entertainment of those who let loose their own thoughts, and follow them in writing; which thou oughtest not to envy them, since they afford thee an opportunity of the like diversion, if thou wilt make use of thy own thoughts in reading. It is to them, if they are thy own, that I refer myself: but if they are taken upon trust from others, it is no great matter what they are; they are not following truth, but some meaner consideration; and it is not worth while to be concerned what he says or thinks, who says or thinks only as he is directed by another. If thou judgest for thyself I know thou wilt judge candidly, and then I shall not be harmed or offended, whatever be thy censure. For though it be certain that there is nothing in this Treatise of the truth whereof I am not fully persuaded, yet I consider myself as liable to mistakes as I can think thee, and know that this book must stand or fall with thee, not by any opinion I have of it, but thy own. If thou findest little in it new or instructive to thee, thou art not to blame me for it. It was not meant for those that had already mastered this subject, and made a thorough acquaintance with their own understandings; but for my own information, and the satisfaction of a few friends, who acknowledged themselves not to have sufficiently considered it.

Were it fit to trouble thee with the history of this *Essay*, I should tell thee, that five or six friends meeting at my chamber, and discoursing on a subject very remote from this, found themselves quickly at a stand, by the difficulties that rose on every side. After we had awhile puzzled ourselves, without coming any nearer a resolution of those doubts which perplexed us, it came into my thoughts that we took a wrong course; and that before we set ourselves upon inquiries of that nature, it was necessary to examine our own abilities, and see what objects our understandings were, or were not, fitted to deal with. This I proposed to the company, who all readily assented; and thereupon it was agreed that this should be our first inquiry. Some hasty and undigested thoughts, on a subject I had never before considered, which I set down against our next meeting, gave the first entrance into this Discourse; which having been thus begun by chance, was continued by intreaty; written by incoherent parcels; and after long intervals of neglect, resumed again, as my humour or occasions permitted; and at last, in a retirement where an attendance on my health gave me leisure, it was brought into that order thou now seest it.

This discontinued way of writing may have occasioned, besides others, two contrary faults, viz., that too little and too much may be said in it. If thou findest anything wanting, I shall be glad that what I have written gives thee any desire that I should have gone further. If it seems too much to thee, thou must blame the subject; for when I put pen to paper, I thought all I should have to say on this matter would have been contained in one sheet of paper; but the further I went the larger prospect I had; new discoveries led me still on, and so it grew insensibly to the bulk it now appears in. I will not deny, but possibly it might be reduced to a narrower compass than it is, and that some parts of it might be contracted, the way it has been writ in, by catches, and many long intervals of interruption, being apt to cause some repetitions. But to confess the truth, I am now too lazy, or too busy, to make it shorter.

I am not ignorant how little I herein consult my own reputation, when I knowingly let it go with a fault, so apt to disgust the most judicious, who are always the nicest readers. But they who know sloth is apt to content itself with any excuse, will pardon me if mine has prevailed on me, where I think I have a very good one. I will not therefore allege in my defence, that the same notion, having different respects, may be convenient or necessary to prove or illustrate several parts of the same discourse, and that so it has happened in many parts of this: but waiving that, I shall frankly avow that I have sometimes dwelt long upon the same argument, and expressed it different ways, with a quite different design. I pretend not to publish this *Essay* for the information of men of large thoughts and quick apprehensions; to such masters of knowledge I profess myself a scholar, and therefore warn them beforehand not to expect anything here, but what, being spun out of my own coarse thoughts, is fitted to men of my own size, to whom, perhaps, it will not be unacceptable that I have taken some pains to make plain and familiar to their thoughts some truths which established prejudice, or the abstractedness of the ideas themselves, might render difficult. Some objects had need be turned on every side; and when the notion is new, as I confess some of these are to me; or out of the ordinary road, as I suspect they will appear to others, it is not one simple view of it that will gain it admittance into every understanding, or fix it there with a clear and lasting impression. There are few, I believe, who have not observed in themselves or others, that what in one way of proposing was very obscure, another way of expressing it has made very clear and intelligible; though afterwards the mind found little difference in the phrases, and wondered why one failed to be understood more than the other. But everything does not hit alike upon every man's imagination. We have our understandings no less different than our palates; and he that thinks the same truth shall be equally relished by every one in the same dress, may as well hope to feast every one with the same sort of cookery: the meat may be the same, and the nourishment good, yet every one not be able to receive it with that seasoning; and it must be dressed another way, if you will have it go down with some, even of strong constitutions. The truth is, those who advised me to publish it, advised me, for this reason, to publish it as it is: and since I have been brought to let it go abroad, I desire it should be understood by whoever gives himself the pains to read it. I have so little affection to be in print, that if I were not flattered this *Essay* might be of some use to others, as I think it has been to me, I should have confined it to the view of some friends, who gave the first occasion to it. My appearing therefore in print being on purpose to be as useful as I may, I think it necessary to make what I have to say as easy and intelligible to all sorts of readers as I can. And I had much rather the speculative and quick-sighted should complain of my being in some parts tedious, than that any one, not accustomed to abstract speculations, or prepossessed with different notions, should mistake or not comprehend my meaning.

It will possibly be censured as a great piece of vanity or insolence in me, to pretend to instruct this our knowing age; it amounting to little less, when I own, that I publish this *Essay* with hopes it may be useful to others. But, if it may be permitted to speak freely of those who with a feigned modesty condemn as useless what they themselves write, methinks it savours much more of vanity or insolence to publish a book for any other end; and he fails very much of that respect he owes the public, who prints, and consequently expects men should read, that wherein he intends not they should meet with anything of use to themselves or others: and should nothing else be found allowable in this Treatise, yet my design will not cease to be so; and the goodness of my intention ought to be some excuse for the worthlessness of my present. It is that chiefly which secures me from the fear of censure, which I expect not to escape more than better writers. Men's principles, notions, and relishes are so different, that it is hard to find a book which pleases or displeases all men. I acknowledge the age we live in is not the least knowing, and therefore not the most easy to be satisfied. If I have not the good luck to please, yet nobody ought to be offended with me. I plainly tell all my readers, except half a dozen, this Treatise was not at first intended for them; and therefore they need not be at the trouble to be of that number. But yet if any one thinks fit to be angry and rail at it, he may do it securely, for I shall find some better way of spending my time than in such kind of conversation. I shall always have the satisfaction to have aimed sincerely at truth and usefulness, though in one of the meanest ways. The commonwealth of learning is not at this time without master-builders, whose mighty designs, in advancing the sciences, will leave lasting monuments to the admiration of posterity: ambition enough to be employed as an under-labourer in clearing the ground a little, and removing some of the rubbish that lies in the way to knowledge;—which certainly had been very much more advanced in the world, if the endeavours of ingenious and industrious men had not been much cumbered with the learned but frivolous use of uncouth, affected, or unintelligible terms, introduced into the sciences, and there made an art of, to that degree that Philosophy, which is nothing but the true knowledge of things, was thought unfit or incapable to be brought into well-bred company and polite conversation. Vague and insignificant forms of speech, and abuse of language, have so long passed for mysteries of science; and hard and misapplied words, with little or no meaning, have, by prescription, such a right to be mistaken for deep learning and height of speculation, that it will not be easy to persuade either those who speak or those who hear them, that they are but the covers of ignorance, and hindrance of true knowledge. To break in upon the sanctuary of vanity and ignorance will be, I suppose, some service to human understanding; though so few are apt to think they deceive or are deceived in the use of words; or that the language of the sect they are of has any faults in it which ought to be examined or corrected; that I hope I shall be pardoned if I have in the Third Book dwelt long on this subject, and endeavoured to make it so plain, that neither the inveterateness of the mischief, nor the prevalency of the fashion, shall be any excuse for those who will not take care about the meaning of their own words, and will not suffer the significancy of their expressions to be inquired into.

I have been told that a short Epitome of this Treatise, which was printed in 1688, was by some condemned without reading, because *innate ideas* were denied in it; they too hastily concluding, that if innate ideas were not supposed, there would be little left either of the notion or proof of spirits. If any one take the like offence at the entrance of this Treatise, I shall desire him to read it through; and then I hope he will be convinced, that the taking away false foundations is not to the prejudice but advantage of truth, which is never injured or endangered so much as when mixed with, or built on, falsehood.

Reflections on How to Live
(Henry Fox Bourne, *The Life of John Locke*)

"Thus, I think;—It is a man's proper business to seek happiness and avoid misery. Happiness consists in what delights and contents the mind; misery in what disturbs, discomposes, or torments it. I will therefore make it my business to seek satisfaction and delight, and avoid uneasiness and disquiet; to have as much of the one, and as little of the other, as may be. But here I must have a care I mistake not, for if I prefer a short pleasure to a lasting one, it is plain I cross my own happiness.

"Let me then see wherein consist the most lasting pleasures of this life; and that, as far as I can observe, is in these things:—1st. Health,—without which no sensual pleasure can have any relish. 2nd. Reputation,—for that I find everybody is pleased with, and the want of it is a constant torment. 3rd. Knowledge,—for the little knowledge I have, I find I would not sell at any rate, nor part with for any other pleasure. 4th. Doing good,—for I find the well-cooked meat I eat to-day does now no more delight me, nay, I am diseased after a full meal: the perfumes I smelt yesterday now no more affect me with any pleasure; but the good turn I did yesterday, a year, seven years since, continues still to please and delight me as often as I reflect on it. 5th. The expectation of eternal and incomprehensible happiness in another world is that also which carries a constant pleasure with it.

"If then I will faithfully pursue that happiness I propose to myself, whatever pleasure offers itself to me, I must carefully look that it cross not any of those five great and constant pleasures above mentioned. For example, the fruit I see tempts me with the taste of it that I love, but if it endanger my health, I part with a constant and lasting for a very short and transient pleasure, and so foolishly make myself unhappy, and am not true to my own interest. Hunting, plays, and other innocent diversions delight me: if I make use of them to refresh myself after study and business, they preserve my health, restore the vigour of my mind, and increase my pleasure; but if I spend all, or the greatest part of my time in them, they hinder my improvement in knowledge and useful arts, they blast my credit, and give me up to the uneasy state of shame, ignorance, and contempt, in which I cannot but be very unhappy. Drinking, gaming, and vicious delights will do me this mischief, not only by wasting my time, but by a positive efficacy endanger my health, impair my parts, imprint ill habits, lessen my esteem, and leave a constant lasting torment on my conscience.

"Therefore all vicious and unlawful pleasures I will always avoid, because such a mastery of my passions will afford me a constant pleasure greater than any such enjoyments; and also deliver me from the certain evil of several kinds, that by indulging myself in a present temptation I shall certainly afterwards suffer. All innocent diversions and delights, as far as they will contribute to my health, and consist with my improvement, condition, and my other more solid pleasures of knowledge and reputation, I will enjoy, but no further, and this I will carefully watch and examine, that I may not be deceived by the flattery of a present pleasure to lose a greater."

"The extent of knowledge, or things knowable," then, "is so vast, our duration here so short, and the entrance by which the knowledge of things gets into our understanding so narrow, that the whole time of our life is not enough to acquaint us with all those things, I will not say which we are capable of knowing, but which it would be not only convenient but very advantageous to know. It therefore much behoves us to improve the best we can our time and talent in this respect, and, since we have a long journey to go, and the days are but short, to take the straightest and most direct road we can."

"I am sure the principal end why we are to get knowledge here is to make use of it for the benefit of ourselves and others in this world, but, if by gaining it we destroy our health, we labour for a thing that will be useless in our hands. He that sinks his vessel by overloading it, though it be with gold and silver and precious stones, will give his owner but an ill account of his voyage."

"[For this task, we must studiously avoid] First: All that maze of words and phrases which have been invented and employed only to instruct and amuse people in the art of disputing; and with this kind of stuff the logics, physics, ethics, metaphysics, and divinity of the schools are thought by some to be too much filled. Empty sounds will no more improve our understandings and strengthen our reason than the noise of a jack will fill our bellies or strengthen our bodies, and the art to fence with those which are called subtleties is of no more use than it would be to be dexterous in tying and untying knots in cobwebs." "Second: An aim and desire to know what have been other men's opinions. If a traveller gets a knowledge of the right way, it is no matter whether he knows the infinite windings, bye-ways, and turnings where others have been misled: the knowledge of the right secures him from the wrong, and that is his great business. I do not say this to undervalue the light we receive from others, or to think there are not those who assist us mightily in our endeavours after knowledge; but I think it is an idle and useless thing to make it one's business to study what have been other men's sentiments in things where reason is only to be judge, on purpose to be furnished with them, and to be able to cite them on all occasions." "Third: Purity of language, a polished style, and exact criticism in foreign languages. To spend much time in these may perhaps serve to set one off in the world and give one the reputation of a scholar; but, if that be all, methinks it is labouring for an outside. It is at best but a handsome dress of truth or falsehood that one busies one's self about, and makes most of those who lay out their time this way rather fashionable gentlemen than wise or useful men." "Fourth: Antiquity and history, as far as they are designed only to furnish us with story and talk. I do not deny but history is very useful and very instructive of human life; but, if it be studied only for the reputation of being an historian, it is a very empty thing, and he that can tell all the particulars of Herodotus and Plutarch, Curtius and Livy, without making any other use of them, may be an ignorant man with a good memory." "Fifth: Nice questions and remote useless speculations; as, where the earthly paradise was, or what fruit it was that was forbidden, where Lazarus's soul was whilst his body lay dead, and what kind of bodies we shall have at the resurrection."

"In questions where there are arguments on both sides, one positive proof is to preponderate to a great many negatives, because a positive proof is always founded upon some real existence which we know and apprehend, whereas the negative arguments terminate generally in nothing, in our not being able to conceive, and so may be nothing but conclusions from our ignorance or incapacity, and not from the truth of things which may, and we have experience do, really exist, though they exceed our comprehension. This, amongst the things we know and lie obvious to our senses, is very evident; for, though we are very well acquainted with matter, motion and distance, yet there are many things in them which we by no means comprehend. Even in the things most obvious and familiar to us, our understanding is nonplussed and presently discovers its weakness; whenever it enters upon the consideration of anything that is unlimited, or would penetrate into the modes or manner of being or operation, it presently meets with unconquerable difficulties. Matter and figure and motion, and the degrees of both, we have clear notions of; but, when we begin to think of the extension or divisibility of the one or the beginning of either, our understanding sticks and boggles and knows not which way to turn. We also have no other notion of operation but of matter by motion—at least I must confess I have not, and should be glad to have any one explain to me intelligibly any other—and yet we shall find it hard to make out any phenomenon by those causes. We know very well that we think, and at pleasure move ourselves, and yet, if we will think a negative argument sufficient to build on, we shall have reason to doubt whether we can do one or other; it being to me inconceivable how matter should think, and as incomprehensible how an immaterial thinking thing should be able to move material or be affected by it. We having, therefore, positive experience of our thinking and motion, the negative arguments against them and the impossibility of understanding them never shake our assent to these truths; which, perhaps, will prove a considerable rule to determine us in very material questions."

"The subject being chosen, the body and mind being both in a temper fit for study, what remains but that a man betake himself to it? These certainly are good preparatories; yet, if there be still something else done, perhaps we shall not make all the profit we might. It is a duty we owe to God, as the fountain and author of all truth, who is truth itself—and it is a duty also we owe to our own selves, if we will deal candidly and sincerely with our own souls—to have our minds constantly disposed to entertain and receive truth wheresoever we meet with it, and under whatsoever appearance of plain or ordinary, strange, new or perhaps displeasing, it may come in our way. Truth is the proper object, the proper riches and furniture of the mind, and according as his stock of this is, so is the difference and value of one man above another. He that fills his head with vain notions and false opinions may have his mind perhaps puffed up and seemingly much enlarged; but in truth it is narrow and empty; for all that it comprehends, all that it contains, amounts to nothing, or less than nothing; for falsehood is below ignorance, and a lie worse than nothing. Our first and great duty then is to bring to our studies and to our inquiries after knowledge a mind covetous of truth, that seeks after nothing else, and after that impartially, and embraces it, how poor, how contemptible, how unfashionable soever it may seem." "It is of great use in the pursuit of knowledge, not to be too confident nor too distrustful of our own judgment, not to believe we can comprehend all things nor nothing. He that distrusts his own judgment in everything, and thinks his understanding not to be relied on in the search of truth, cuts off his own legs that he may be carried up and down by others, and makes himself a ridiculous dependant upon the knowledge of others, which can possibly be of no use to him; for I can no more know anything by another man's understanding than I can see by another man's eyes. So much I know, so much truth I have got, so far I am in the right, as I do really know myself. Whatever other men have, it is in their possession, it belongs not to me, nor can be communicated to me but by making me alike knowing; it is a treasure that cannot be lent or made over. On the other side, he that thinks his understanding capable of all things, mounts upon wings of his own fancy, though indeed nature never meant him any, and so, venturing upon the vast expanse of incomprehensible verities, only makes good the fable of Icarus and loses himself in the abyss. We are here in the state of mediocrity; finite creatures, furnished with powers and faculties very well fitted to some purposes, but very disproportionate to the west and unlimited extent of things."

Locke's Own Epitaph

Stay, wayfarer,

Near here lies John Locke. If you ask what sort of man he was, his answer is that he lived content with his modest lot. Educated in letters, he accomplished as much as satisfied the demands solely of truth. This you may learn from his writings; which will also tell you whatever else there is to be said of him, more truly than the doubtful praises of an epitaph. Any virtues he had were more slight than should encourage you, in praise of him, to follow his example; may his faults be interred with him. If a model of conduct you seek, you have it in the Gospels; if only of vices, look for it in no place; if of mortality (of what benefit it may be) assuredly you have it here and everywhere.

> That he was born in the year of Our Lord 1632 August 29th,
> Died in the year of Our Lord 1704 October 28th,
> This tablet, that may itself soon perish, is a record.

13

GOTTFRIED WILHELM LEIBNIZ
God, Mind, and Logic

Gottfried Wilhelm Leibniz (1646–1716) was the polymath's polymath. Trained in jurisprudence, he codified Roman laws; independently of Newton, he invented the infinitesimal calculus; he undertook engineering projects; he began work on a universal grammar; serving as an advisor to the Elector of Mainz, he was sent as an ambassador to the court of Louis XIV; he urged the conquest of Egypt and the construction of a canal in the Isthmus of Suez. Himself descended from a Lutheran family, he proposed an ecumenical council to reconcile Protestants and Catholics; from 1676 until his death, he served the House of Hanover as an engineer, historian, librarian, statesman. He traveled to Holland, Austria, and Italy, and he met with Peter the Great to discuss educational programs and the formation of a Russian Academy of Science. And of course he was a logician, metaphysician, epistemologist, theologian. He waited to publish his attack of Locke's theory of ideas (*New Essays on Human Understanding*) until Locke died in 1704. As a metaphysician, he argued for the identity of indiscernibles; as a theologian, he used the principle of sufficient reason to reconcile determinism with the doctrine of free will (*Theodicy*, 1710); as a physicist, he defended the relativity of space, time, and motion in the *Monadology* (1714). His correspondence with Samuel Clark, Malebranche, Spinoza, Arnauld, and Huygens was largely polemical.

Preface to a Universal Characteristic (1678–79)

There is an old saying that God made everything in accordance with weight, measure, and number. But there are things which cannot be weighed, namely, those that lack force and power [*vis ac potentia*], and there are also things that lack parts and thus cannot be measured. But there is nothing that cannot be numbered. And so number is, as it were, metaphysical shape, and arithmetic is, in a certain sense, the Statics of the Universe, that by which the powers of things are investigated.

As far as I know, no mortal until now has seen the true principle by which each thing can be assigned its own characteristic number. Indeed, the most learned persons have admitted that they did not understand what I was talking about when I casually mentioned something of this sort in their presence. Not long ago, some distinguished persons devised a certain language or Universal Characteristic in which all notions and things are nicely ordered, a language with whose help different nations can communicate their thoughts, and each, in its own language, read what the other wrote. But no one has put forward a language or characteristic which embodies, at the same time, both the art of discovery and the art of judgment, that is, a language whose marks or characters perform the same task as arithmetic marks do for numbers and algebraic marks do for magnitudes considered abstractly. And yet, when God bestowed these two sciences on the human race, it seems that he wanted to suggest to us that a much greater secret lies hidden in our intellect, a secret of which these two sciences are but shadows.

However, by some chance it happened that I fell upon such thoughts when still a boy, and as usually happens with such first inclinations, these thoughts, deeply imprinted, attached themselves to my mind ever after. Two things marvelously benefited me in this (things otherwise problematic, however, and often harmful to many): first, that I was nearly self-taught and, second, that I sought out what was new in each and every branch of knowledge, as soon as I came into contact with it, even though I often had not yet sufficiently grasped things commonly known. But these two things gave me an advantage; the first prevented me from filling my mind with trifles, things that ought to be forgotten, things that are accepted on the authority of teachers rather than because of arguments, and the second prevented me from resting before I probed all the way to the depths of each subject and arrived at its very principles, from which everything I extracted could be discovered by my own efforts.

Therefore, when I was led from reading histories (which wonderfully delighted me from my youth on) and from the concern with style (which I exercised in prose and the like with such ease that my teachers feared that I would be held back by its charms) to logic and philosophy, then as soon as I began to understand something of these matters, what a blessed multitude of these fantasies that arose in my brain did I scribble down on paper and show immediately to my amazed teachers. Among other things, I sometimes posed an objection concerning the predicaments. For, I said, just as there are predicaments or classes of simple notions, so ought there to be a new genus of predicaments in which propositions themselves or complex terms might also be set out in a natural order; indeed, at that time I didn't even dream of including demonstrations, and I didn't know that geometers, who arrange propositions in accordance with which one is demonstrated from others, do what it is I sought to do. And so my objection was, indeed, empty. But since my teachers could not answer it, pursuing these thoughts on account of their novelty, I worked on constructing such predicaments for complex terms or propositions. When, through my eagerness for this project, I applied myself more intently, I inevitably stumbled onto this wonderful observation, namely, that one can devise a certain alphabet of human thoughts and that, through the combination of the letters of this alphabet and through the analysis of words produced from them, all things can both be discovered and judged. Having grasped this, I was quite overjoyed, indeed, with childlike delight, for at that time I hadn't sufficiently grasped the magnitude of the project. But afterwards, the more progress I made in understanding these matters, the more confirmed I was in my plan to follow out such a project. As it happened, when I was older, by now twenty years old, I was working on an academic exercise. And so I wrote a dissertation, *On the Art of Combinations*, published in the form of a little book in 1666, in which I presented this marvelous discovery to the public. It is, indeed, the sort of dissertation that a young man, freshly out of school, could have written, a young man not yet steeped in the real sciences, for mathematics was not cultivated in those parts, and, if I had spent my youth in Paris, as Pascal did, then perhaps I would have contributed to those sciences sooner. However, I am not sorry to have written this dissertation, for two reasons, first because it greatly pleased many very ingenious gentlemen and also because in it I already gave the world some hint of my discovery, so that now it won't seem as if I have just invented it for the first time.

Indeed, I often wondered why, as far as the recorded history of mankind extends, no mortal had approached such a project, for meditations of this kind ought to be among the first to occur to those reasoning in proper order, just as they occurred to me. I came to this discovery while still a youth, working on logic, before I had touched on morals or mathematics or physics, for the sole reason that I always searched for first principles. The real reason why people have missed the doorway [into this discovery] is, I think, because principles are, for the most part, dry and insufficiently agreeable to people, and so, barely tasted, they are dismissed. However, there are three men I am especially surprised did not approach the matter, Aristotle, Joachim Jungius, and René Descartes. For when Aristotle wrote his *Organon* and his *Metaphysics*, he examined the inner depth of notions with great skill. And while Joachim Jungius of Lübeck is a man little known even in Germany itself, he was clearly of such judiciousness and such capacity of mind that I know of no other mortal, including even Descartes himself, from whom we could better have expected a great restoration of the sciences, had Jungius been either known or assisted. Moreover, he was already of a mature age when Descartes began to flourish, so it is quite regrettable that they did not know one another. As far as Descartes goes, this is certainly not the place to praise a man who, due to the magnitude of his genius, is almost beyond praise. Certainly, he prepared the path through these ideas, a path that is true and straight, a path that leads up to this very point. But since his own path was directed too much toward applause, he seems to have broken off the thread of his investigation and, overly eager, gave us his *Metaphysical Meditations* and a piece of his geometry, by which he captured people's attention. As for other subjects, he decided to investigate the nature of matter for the sake of medicine, and rightly so, had he but completed the task of ordering the ideas he had in mind, for then he would have shed more light by his experiments than anyone could believe. And so, the reason why he didn't apply his mind to this task can only be the fact that he had not sufficiently grasped the reason for pursuing such a program and its import. For if he had seen a way of establishing a rational philosophy as clear and unshakable as arithmetic, one can hardly believe that he would have used any other way for creating a sect, something he dearly wanted. For by the very nature of things, a sect using this sort of reasoning would immediately arise as soon as it exercised control over reason, as in geometry, and would not perish or weaken until the human race lost knowledge altogether through the invasion of some new barbarian horde.

Though distracted in so many other ways, I was absorbed in these meditations for the sole reason that I saw their great importance and saw a wonderfully easy way of attaining the goal. And indeed, by rigorous meditation I finally discovered the very thing I sought. And so now, nothing more is needed to construct the characteristic I am working on to the point where it is sufficient both to provide a grammar of such a wonderful language and a dictionary for most of the more frequent items, that is, to the point of having characteristic numbers for all ideas; I say, nothing more is needed than for the philosophical and mathematical curriculum [*cursus*], as it is called, to be set up in accordance with a certain new method that I could set out. So conceived, the curriculum would contain nothing in itself either more difficult than other curricula or very far from what is ordinarily used and understood, or very foreign to common habits of writing. Nor does it require much more work than we see already expended on several curricula or encyclopedias, as they are called. I think that a few chosen persons could complete the task in five years; in two years they could set forth those doctrines most often used in daily life, that is, morals and metaphysics in an unshakable calculus.

Once the characteristic numbers of most notions are determined, the human race will have a new kind of tool, a tool that will increase the power of the mind much more than optical lenses helped our eyes, a tool that will be as far superior to microscopes or telescopes as reason is to vision. The compass never provided navigators with anything more useful than what this North Star would give us for swimming the sea of experiments. What other consequences will follow from this tool are in the hands of the fates, but they can only be great and good. For although people can be made worse off by all other gifts, correct reasoning alone can only be for the good. Moreover, who could doubt that reasoning will finally be correct, when it is everywhere as clear and certain as arithmetic has been up until now. And so that troublesome objection by which one antagonist now commonly harasses the other would be eliminated, an objection that turns many away from wanting to reason. What I have in mind is that, when someone offers a proof, his opponent doesn't examine the argument as much as he responds in general terms, how do you know that your reason is more correct than mine? What criterion of truth do you have? And even if the one antagonist appeals to his arguments, listeners lack the patience to examine them. For it is usually the case that many things must thoroughly be examined, a task taking several weeks, if we were carefully to follow the laws of reasoning accepted up until now. And so, after great agitation, emotions rather than reasons win most often, and we end the dispute by cutting the Gordian knot rather than untying it. This happens especially in deliberations pertaining to life, where something must be decided; here only a few people can weigh (as on a balance) the favorable and unfavorable factors, both of which are often numerous. And so, the better someone has learned to represent to himself more forcefully, here one, there another circumstance, following the various inclinations of his soul, or to ornament and paint them for others more eloquently and effectively, the more he will stir himself up and capture for himself the minds of men, especially if he is astute in using their emotions. There is scarcely anyone who can take account of both sides of the complete table of credits and debits, that is, who not only can enumerate the favorable and unfavorable factors, but can also weigh them correctly. And so two people who argue look to me almost like two merchants who owe money to one another from numerous transactions, but who never want to reckon up the accounts, while meanwhile each in different ways exaggerates what he himself is owed by the other and exaggerates the validity and size of certain particular claims. Thus, the controversy will never end. We should not be surprised that this happens in a large proportion of the controversies where the matter is unclear, that is, where the dispute cannot be reduced to numerical terms. But now our characteristic will reduce them all to numerical terms, so that even reasons can be weighed, just as if we had a special kind of balance. For even probabilities are subject to calculation and demonstration, since one can always judge what is more likely [*probabilius*] to happen on the basis of given circumstances. And, finally, anyone who has been persuaded of the certain truth of religion and, what follows from this, anyone who embraces others with such love that he hopes for the conversion of the human race will certainly admit, as soon as he understands these things, that nothing is more effective for the propagation of faith than this invention, except for miracles and the holiness of an Apostolic man or the victories of a great monarch. For wherever missionaries can once introduce this language, the true religion, the religion entirely in agreement with reason will be established and in the future apostasy will be feared no more than we fear that people will condemn arithmetic or geometry, once they have learned it.

And so I repeat what I have often said, that a person who is neither prophet nor prince could undertake nothing better adapted to the good of the human race or to the glory of God. But we must go beyond words. Since, due to the wonderful interconnection of things, it is extremely difficult to produce the characteristic numbers of just a few things, considered apart from the others, I have contrived a device, quite elegant, if I am not mistaken, by which I can show that it is possible to corroborate reasoning through numbers. And so, I imagine that those so very wonderful characteristic numbers are already given, and, having observed a certain general property that characteristic numbers have, I meanwhile assume that these numbers I imagine, whatever they might be, have that property. By using these numbers I can immediately demonstrate through numbers, and in an amazing way, all of the logical rules and show how one can know whether certain arguments are in proper form. When we have the true characteristic numbers of things, then at last, without any mental effort or danger of error, we will be able to judge whether arguments are indeed materially sound and draw the right conclusions.

Letter to Countess Elizabeth(?), On God and Formal Logic (1678?)

If Your Highness had not ordered me to explain more distinctly what said in passing about Descartes and his proof for the existence of God, it would have been presumptuous of me to try. For Your Highness's extraordinary intelligence (which I recognized far better when I had the honor of hearing you speak for a moment, than by reading what so many great men had published about you) anticipates everything one can tell you with respect to a subject which, no doubt, has long been the object of your most profound thoughts. Therefore, I undertake this discourse, not because I intend to propose something new to you, but in order to learn your judgment, which I do not aspire to solicit.

Your Highness knows that there is nothing more trite today than demonstrations of God's existence; I observe that it is almost like proofs for squaring the circle and perpetual motion. The greenest student of mathematics and of mechanics lays claim to these sublime problems, and there is not a distiller, even the most ignorant, who does not promise himself the philosopher's stone. Similarly, all those who have learned a little metaphysics begin first with the demonstration of God's existence and the immortality of our souls, which, in my opinion, are the fruits of all our studies, since they constitute the foundation of our greatest hopes. I admit that Your Highness would have no reason to have a better opinion of me unless I told her that I came to these matters after having prepared my mind by extremely precise investigations in the rigorous sciences, which are the touchstone of our thoughts. Everywhere else people flatter themselves and find flatterers, but there are very few mathematicians who have spread errors, and there are none who could get others to approve their mistakes. In my early years I was well enough versed in the subtleties of the Thomists and Scotists, and when I left school, I threw myself into the arms of jurisprudence, which required history as well. But my travels allowed me to know some great persons who gave me a taste for mathematics. I applied myself to it with an almost disproportionate passion during the four years I resided in Paris, which resulted in greater success and public praise than a novice and stranger could have expected.

As for myself, I cherished mathematics only because I found in it the traces of the art *of invention in general*; and it seems to me that I discovered, in the end, that Descartes himself had not yet penetrated the mystery of this great science. I recall that he said somewhere that the excellence of his method, which only appears probable from his physics, is demonstrated by his geometry. But I must admit that I mainly recognized the imperfection of his method in his geometry itself. For, we should not be surprised if there is much to criticize in his physics, since Descartes did not have enough experiments at his disposal. But geometry depends only on ourselves; it does not need external help.

I do not wish to discuss physics here, even though I have demonstrated rules of motion that are quite different from those of Descartes. I come, then, to metaphysics, and I can state that it is for the love of metaphysics that I have passed through all these stages. For I have recognized that metaphysics is scarcely different from the true logic, that is, from the art of invention in general; for, in fact, metaphysics is natural theology, and the same God who is the source of all goods is also the principle of all knowledge. This is because the idea of God contains within it absolute being, that is, what is simple in our thoughts, from which everything that we think draws its origin. Descartes did not go about it in this way. He gave two ways of proving the existence of God. The *first* is that there is an idea of God in us since, no doubt, we think about God, and we cannot think of something without having its idea. Now, if we have an idea of God, and if it is true [*véritable*], that is, if it is the idea of an infinite being, and if it represents it faithfully, it could not be caused by something lesser, and consequently, God himself must be its cause. Therefore, he must exist. The *other* reasoning is even shorter. It is that God is a being who possesses all perfections, and consequently, he possesses existence, which is to be counted as one of the perfections. Therefore, he exists. It must be said that these reasonings are somewhat suspect, because they go too fast, and because they force themselves upon us without enlightening us. Real demonstrations, on the other hand, generally fill the mind with some solid nourishment. However, the crux of the matter is difficult to find, and I see that many able people who have formulated objections to Descartes were led astray.

Some have believed that there is no idea of God because he is not subject to imagination, assuming that idea and image are the same thing. I am not of their opinion, and I know perfectly well that there are ideas of thought, existence, and similar things, of which there are no images. For we think of something and when we notice in there what it is that allows us to recognize it, this is what constitutes the idea of the thing, insofar as it is in our soul. This is why there is also an idea of what is not material or imaginable.

Others agree that there is an idea of God, and that this idea contains all perfections, but they cannot understand how existence follows from it, either because they do not agree that existence is to be counted among the perfections, or because they do not see how a simple idea or thought can imply an existence outside us. As for me, I genuinely believe that anyone who has recognized this idea of God, and who sees that existence is a perfection, must admit that existence belongs to God. In fact, I do not question the idea of God any more than I do his existence; on the contrary, I claim to have a demonstration of it. But I do not want us to flatter ourselves and persuade ourselves that we can arrive at such a great thing with such little cost. Paralogisms are dangerous in this matter; when they occur, they reflect on us, and they strengthen the opposite side. I therefore say that we must prove with the greatest imaginable exactness that there is an idea of a completely perfect being, that is, an idea of God. It is true that the objections of those who believed that they could prove the contrary because there is no image of God are worthless, as I have just shown. But we also have to admit that the proof Descartes gives to establish the idea of God is imperfect. How, he would say, can one speak of God without thinking of him, and how can one think of him without having an idea of him? Yes, no doubt we sometimes think about impossible things and we even construct demonstrations from them. For example, Descartes holds that squaring the circle is impossible, and yet we still think about it and draw consequences about what would happen if it were given. The motion having the greatest speed is impossible in any body whatsoever, because, for example, if we assumed it in a circle, then another circle concentric to the former circle, surrounding it and firmly attached to it, would move with a speed still greater than the former, which, consequently, would not be of the greatest degree, in contradiction to what we had assumed. In spite of all that, we think about this greatest speed, something that has no idea since it is impossible. Similarly, the greatest circle of all is an impossible thing, and the number of all possible units is no less so; we have a demonstration of this. And nevertheless, we think about all this. That is why there are surely grounds for wondering whether we should be careful about the idea of the greatest of all beings, and whether it might not contain a contradiction.

For I fully understand, for example, the nature of motion and speed and what it is to be greatest, but, for all that, I do not understand whether all those notions are compatible, and whether there is a way of joining them and making them into an idea of the greatest speed of which motion is capable. Similarly, although I know what being is, and what it is to be the greatest and most perfect, nevertheless I do not yet know, for all that, whether there isn't a hidden contradiction in joining all that together, as there is, in fact, in the previously stated examples. In brief, I do not yet know, for all that, whether such a being is possible, for if it were not possible, there would be no idea of it. However, I must admit that God has a great advantage, in this respect, over all other things. For to prove that he exists, it would be sufficient to prove that he is possible, something we find nowhere else, as far as I know. Moreover, I infer from that that there is a presumption that God exists. For there is always a presumption on the side of possibility, that is, everything is held to be possible unless it is proven to be impossible. There is, therefore, a presumption that God is possible, that is, that he exists, since in him existence follows from possibility. This is sufficient for practical matters in life, but it is not sufficient for a demonstration. I have strongly disputed this matter with several Cartesians, but I finally succeeded in this with some of the most able of them who have frankly admitted, after having understood the force of my reasons, that this possibility is still to be demonstrated. There are even some who, after having been called away from me, have undertaken this demonstration, but they have not yet succeeded.

Since Your Highness is intelligent, you see what the state of things is and you see we can do nothing unless we prove this possibility. When I consider all this, I take pity on man's weakness, and I take care not to exclude myself from it. Descartes, who was no doubt one of the greatest men of this century, erred in so visible a manner, and many illustrious people erred with him. Nevertheless, we do not question their intelligence or their care. All of this could give some people a bad opinion of the certainty of our knowledge in general. For, one can say, with so many able men unable to avoid a trap, what can I hope for, I, who am nothing compared to them? Nevertheless, we must not lose our courage. There is a way of avoiding error, which these able men have not condescended to use; it would have been contrary to the greatness of their minds, at least in appearance, and with respect to the common people. All those who wish to appear to be great figures and who set themselves up as leaders of sects have a bit of the acrobat in them. A tightrope walker does not allow himself to be braced in order to avoid falling; if he did so, he would be sure of his act, but he would no longer appear a skillful man. I will be asked, what then is this wonderful way that can prevent us from falling? I am almost afraid to say it—it appears to be too lowly. But I am speaking to Your Highness who does not judge things by their appearance. In brief, it is to construct arguments only in proper form [*in forma*]. I seem to see only people who cry out against me and who send me back to school. But I beg them to be a little patient, for perhaps they do not understand me.

Any rigorous demonstration that does not omit anything necessary for the force of reasoning is of this kind, and I dare say that the account of an accountant and a calculation of analysis are arguments in proper form, since there is nothing missing in them and since the form or arrangement of the whole reasoning is the cause of their being evident. It is only the form that distinguishes an account book made according to the practice we commonly call Italian (of which Stevin has written a whole treatise) from the confused journal of someone ignorant of business. That is why I maintain that, in order to reason with evidence in all subjects, we must hold some consistent formalism [*formalité constante*]. There would be less eloquence, but more certainty. But in order to determine the formalism that would do no less in metaphysics, physics, and morals, than calculation does in mathematics, that would even give us degrees of probability when we can only reason probabilistically, I would have to relate here the thoughts I have on a new characteristic [*charactéristique*], something that would take too long. Nevertheless, I will say, in brief, that this characteristic would represent our thoughts truly and distinctly, and that when a thought is composed of other simpler ones, its character would also be similarly composed. I dare not say what would follow from this for the perfection of the sciences—it would appear incredible. And yet, there is a demonstration of this. The only thing I will say here is that since that which we know is from reasoning or experience, it is certain that henceforth all reasoning in demonstrative or probable matters will demand no more skill than a calculation in algebra does; that is, one would derive from given experiments everything that can be derived, just as in algebra. But for now it is sufficient for me to note that the foundation of my characteristic is also the foundation of the demonstration of God's existence. For simple thoughts are the elements of the characteristic and simple forms are the source of things. I maintain that all simple forms are compatible among themselves. That is a proposition whose demonstration I cannot give without having to explain the fundamentals of the characteristic at length. But if that is granted, it follows that God's nature, which contains all simple forms taken absolutely, is possible. Now, we have proven above that God exists, as long as he is possible. Therefore, he exists. And that is what needed to be demonstrated.

A New System of the Nature and Communication of Substances, and of the Union of the Soul and Body (1695)

A few years have already passed since I conceived this system and communicated with some learned men about it, especially with one of the greatest theologians and philosophers of our time, who had learned about some of my opinions through a person of the highest nobility, and had found them extremely paradoxical. But having received my explanations, he changed his attitude in the most generous and edifying way possible; and, having approved some of my propositions, he withdrew his censure regarding the others, with which he still disagreed. Since that time I have continued my meditations, as circumstances allow, so as to give the public only well-examined opinions; I have also tried to satisfy objections raised against my essays on dynamics, which are connected with this system. Finally, since some important persons have desired to see my opinions further clarified, I have risked publishing these meditations, even though they are not at all popular, nor can they be appreciated by all sorts of minds. I have decided upon this mainly to profit from the judgments of persons enlightened in these matters, since it would be too troublesome to seek out and call individually upon all those who would be disposed to give me instruction—which I shall always be glad to receive, provided that it contains the love of truth, rather than a passion for preconceived opinions.

Although I am someone who has done much work on mathematics, I have continued to meditate on philosophy since my youth, for it always seemed to me that one can establish something solid there through clear demonstrations. I had penetrated far into the territory of the Scholastics, when mathematics and the modern authors made me withdraw from it, while I was still young. I was charmed by their beautiful ways of explaining nature mechanically, and I rightly despised the method of those who use only forms or faculties, from which one can learn nothing. But since then, having attempted to examine the very principles of mechanics in order to explain the laws of nature we learn from experience, I perceived that considering *extended mass* alone was not sufficient, and that it was necessary, in addition, to make use of the notion of *force*, which is very intelligible, despite the fact that it belongs in the domain of metaphysics. It also seemed to me that although the opinion of those who transform or degrade animals into pure machines may be possible, it is improbable, and even contrary to the order of things.

In the beginning, when I had freed myself from the yoke of Aristotle, I accepted the void and atoms, for they best satisfy the imagination. But on recovering from that, after much reflection, I perceived that it is impossible to find *the principles of a true unity* in matter alone, or in what is only passive, since everything in it is only a collection or aggregation of parts to infinity. Now, a multitude can derive its reality only from *true unities*, which have some other origin and are considerably different from [[mathematical]] points [[which are only the extremities and modifications of extension,]] which all agree cannot make up the *continuum*. Therefore, in order to find these *real entities* I was forced to have recourse to a formal atom, since a material thing cannot be both material and, at the same time, perfectly indivisible, that is, endowed with a true unity. Hence, it was necessary to restore, and, as it were, to rehabilitate the *substantial forms* which are in such disrepute today, but in a way that would render them intelligible, and separate the use one should make of them from the abuse that has been made of them. I found then that their nature consists in force, and that from this there follows something analogous to sensation and appetite, so that we must conceive of them on the model of the notion we have of *souls*. But just as soul must not be used to explain the particular details of the economy of the animal's body, I judged that we must not use these forms to explain the particular problems of nature, even though they are necessary to establish the true general principles. Aristotle calls them *first entelechies*; I call them, perhaps more intelligibly, *primitive forces*, which contain not only *act* or the completion of possibility, but also an original *activity*.

I saw that these forms and souls must be indivisible, as our mind is; I remembered that this was Saint Thomas's view on the souls of animals. But this truth revived the great difficulties about the origin and duration of souls and forms. For, since every [[*simple*]] *substance* which has a true unity can begin and end only by miracle, it follows that they can begin only by creation and end only by annihilation. Thus I was forced to recognize that, except for the souls that God wishes to create expressly, the forms constitutive of substances must have been created together with the world, and must always subsist. Moreover, certain Scholastics, like Albertus Magnus and John Bacon, glimpsed a part of the truth about the origin of these forms. This should not appear extraordinary, since we ascribe to forms only duration, which the Gassendists grant their atoms.

I judged, however, that we must not indiscriminately confuse *minds* or rational souls [[with other forms or souls]], for they are of a higher order, and have incomparably greater perfection than the forms thrust into matter [[(which, in my view, are found everywhere)]], minds being like little gods in comparison with them, made in the image of God, and having in them some ray of the light of divinity. That is why God governs minds like a prince governs his subjects, and even like a father cares for his children, whereas he disposes of other substances like an engineer handles his machines. Thus minds have particular laws, which place them above the upheavals [*revolutions*] in matter, [[through the very order which God has put in them]]; and we can say that everything else is made only for them, and that these tumultuous motions themselves are adjusted for the happiness of the good and the punishment of the wicked.

This made me judge that there is only one reasonable view to take—namely, the conservation not only of the soul, but also of the animal itself and its organic machine, even though the destruction of its larger parts reduces it to a smallness which escapes our senses, just as it was before its birth. Moreover, no one can specify the true time of death, which for a long time may pass for a simple suspension of noticeable actions, and is basically never anything else in simple animals—witness the *resuscitations* of drowned flies buried under pulverized chalk, and several other similar examples which are sufficient to show that there would be many other resuscitations, and greater ones, if men were in a position to restore the machine. This may be similar to something the great Democritus discussed, complete atomist that he was, though Pliny made fun of him. It is therefore natural that an animal, having always been alive and organized (as some persons of great insight are beginning to recognize), always remains so. And since there is no first birth or entirely new generation of an animal, it follows that there will not be any final extinction or complete death, in a strict metaphysical sense. Consequently, instead of the *transmigration* of souls, there is only a *transformation* of the same animal, according to whether its organs are differently enfolded and more or less developed.

However, rational souls follow much higher laws, and are exempt from anything that might make them lose the quality of being citizens of the society of minds; God has provided so well that no changes of matter can make them lose the moral qualities of their personhood. And we can say that everything tends not only toward the perfection of the universe in general, but also toward the perfection of these creatures in particular, creatures who are destined for such a degree of happiness that the universe finds itself benefited by virtue of the divine goodness that is communicated to each, to the extent that supreme wisdom can allow.

With respect to ordinary animal bodies and other corporeal substances, whose complete extinction has been accepted until now, and whose changes depend on mechanical rules rather than moral laws, I noted with pleasure that the ancient author of the book *De diaeta*, attributed to Hippocrates, had glimpsed something of the truth when he stated explicitly that animals are not born and do not die, and that things we believe to begin and perish merely appear and disappear. This was also the opinion of Parmenides and Melissus, according to Aristotle. For these ancients were much more solid than people believe.

I am the most readily disposed person to do justice to the moderns, yet I find that they have carried reform too far, among other things, by confusing natural things with artificial things, because they have lacked sufficiently grand ideas of the majesty of nature. They think that the difference between natural machines and ours is only the difference between great and small. I believe that this conception does not give us a sufficiently just or worthy idea of nature, and that my system alone allows us to understand the true and immense distance between the least productions and mechanisms of divine wisdom and the greatest masterpieces that derive from the craft of a limited mind; this difference is not simply a difference of degree, but a difference of kind. We must then know that the machines of nature have a truly infinite number of organs, and are so well supplied and so resistant to all accidents that it is not possible to destroy them. A natural machine still remains a machine in its least parts, and moreover, it always remains the same machine that it has been, being merely transformed through the different enfolding it undergoes, sometimes extended, sometimes compressed and concentrated, as it were, when it is thought to have perished.

In addition, by means of the soul or form there is a true unity corresponding to what is called *the self* [*moy*] in us. Such a unity could not occur in the machines made by a craftsman or in a simple mass of matter, however organized it may be; such a mass can only be considered as an army or a herd, or a pond full of fish, or like a watch composed of springs and wheels. Yet if there were no true *substantial unities*, there would be nothing substantial or real in the collection. That was what forced Cordemoy to abandon Descartes and to embrace the Democritean doctrine of atoms in order to find a true unity. But *atoms of matter* are contrary to reason. Furthermore, they are still composed of parts, since the invincible attachment of one part to another (if we can reasonably conceive or assume this) does not eliminate diversity of those parts. There are only *atoms of substance*, that is, real unities absolutely destitute of parts, which are the source of actions, the first absolute principles of the composition of things, and, as it were, the final elements in the analysis of substantial things. We could call them *metaphysical points*: they have *something vital*, a kind of *perception*, and *mathematical points* are the *points of view* from which they express the universe. But when corporeal substances are contracted, all their organs together constitute only a *physical point* relative to us. Thus physical points are indivisible only in appearance; mathematical points are exact, but they are merely modalities. Only metaphysical points or points of substance (constituted by forms or souls) are exact and real, and without them there would be nothing real, since without true unities there would be no multitude.

Preface to the New Essays (1703–05)

Since the *Essays on the Understanding*, published by [John Locke] an illustrious Englishman, is one of the finest and most esteemed works of our age, I resolved to comment on it, insofar as I had given sufficient thought for some time to the same subject and to most of the matters touched upon there; I thought that this would be a good opportunity to publish something entitled *New Essays on the Understanding* and to procure a more favorable reception for my thoughts by putting them in such good company. I further thought that I might profit from someone else's work, not only to make my task easier (since, in fact, it is easier to follow the thread of a good author than to work out everything anew), but also to add something to what he has given us, which is always easier than starting from the beginning. It is true that I often hold an opinion different from his, but far from denying on that account the merit of this famous writer, I bear witness to it by showing in what and why, I differ from his view, when I deem it necessary to prevent his authority from prevailing against reason on some important points.

In fact, although the author of the *Essay* says a thousand fine things of which I approve, our systems are very different. His bears more relation to Aristotle's and mine to Plato's, although we both differ in many ways from the doctrines of these two ancients. He is more popular while I am forced at times to be a little more esoteric and abstract, which is not an advantage to me, especially when writing in a living language. However, I believe that by making two characters speak, one of whom presents the views of the author of the *Essay*, while the other adds my observations, the parallel will be more to the liking of the reader than some dry remarks, whose reading would have to be interrupted at every moment by the necessity of having to return to the author's book in order to understand mine. Nevertheless, it would be good to compare our writings from time to time, and to judge his views by his work alone, even though I have usually retained his expressions. It is true that the constraint of having to follow the thread of someone else's discourse in making my remarks has meant that I could not think of capturing the charm of which the dialogue is capable, but I hope that the content will make up for the defect in style.

Our differences are about subjects of some importance. There is the question about whether the soul in itself is completely empty like tablets upon which nothing has been written (*tabula rasa*), as Aristotle and the author of the *Essay* maintain, and whether everything inscribed on it comes solely from the senses and from experience, or whether the soul contains from the beginning the source [*principe*] of several notions and doctrines, which external objects awaken only on certain occasions, as I believe with Plato and even with the Schoolmen, and with all those who find this meaning in the passage of St. Paul (Romans 2:15) where he states that the law of God is written in our hearts. The Stoics call these principles *Prolepses*, that is, fundamental assumptions, or what is taken as agreed in advance. Mathematicians call them *common notions*, (*koinai ennoiai*). Modern philosophers give them other fine names, and Julius Scaliger in particular called them the seeds of eternity, and also *zopyra*, meaning living fires, or flashes of light hidden inside us but made to appear through the contact of the senses, like sparks that can be struck from a steel. And it is not unreasonable to believe that these flashes reveal something divine and eternal, something that especially appears in necessary truths. This raises another question, namely, whether all truths depend upon experience, that is, upon induction and instances, or whether some of them also have another foundation. For if some occurrences can be foreseen before they have been tested, it is obvious that we contribute something of our own here. Although the senses are necessary for all our actual knowledge, they are not sufficient to give us all of it, since the senses never give us anything but instances, that is, particular or individual truths. Now all the instances confirming a general truth, however numerous they may be, are not sufficient to establish the universal necessity of that same truth, for it does not follow that what has happened before will always happen in the same way. For example, the Greeks, Romans, and all other people of the earth have always observed that before the passage of twenty-four hours, day changes into night and night into day. But they would have been mistaken if they had believed that the same rule is observed everywhere, since the contrary was observed during a visit to Nova Zembla. And anyone who believed that this is a necessary and eternal truth, at least in our climate, would also be mistaken, since we must recognize that the earth and even the sun do not exist necessarily, and that there may be a time when this beautiful star will no longer exist, at least in its present form, and neither will its whole system. As a result it appears that necessary truths, such as we find in pure mathematics and particularly in arithmetic and geometry, must have principles whose proof does not depend on instances nor, consequently, on the testimony of the senses, although without the senses it would never occur to us to think of them. This is a distinction that should be noted carefully, and it is one Euclid understood so well that he proves by reason things that are sufficiently evident through experience and sensible images. Logic, together with metaphysics and morals, of which the one shapes natural theology and the other natural jurisprudence, are full of such truths, and consequently, their proof can only arise from internal principles, which are called innate. It is true that we must not imagine that we can read these eternal laws of reason in the soul from an open book, as the edict of the praetor can be read from his tablet without effort and scrutiny. But it is enough that they can be discovered in us by dint of attention; the senses furnish occasions for this, and the success of experiments also serves to confirm reason, a bit like empirical trials help us avoid errors of calculation in arithmetic when the reasoning is long. Also, it is in this respect that human knowledge differs from that of beasts. Beasts are purely empirical and are guided solely by instances, for, as far as we are able to judge, they never manage to form necessary propositions, whereas man is capable of demonstrative knowledge [*sciences démonstratives*]. In this, the faculty beasts have for drawing consequences is inferior to the reason humans have. The consequences beasts draw are just like those of simple empirics who claim that what has happened will happen again in a case where what strikes them is similar, without being able to determine whether the same reasons are at work. This is what makes it so easy for men to capture beasts and so easy for simple empirics to make mistakes. Not even people made skillful by age and experience are exempt from this when they rely too much on their past experiences. This has happened to several people in civil and military affairs, since they do not take sufficiently into consideration the fact that the world changes and that men have become more skillful in finding thousands of new tricks, unlike the stags and hares of today, who have not become any more clever than those of yesterday. The consequences beasts draw are only a shadow of reasoning, that is, they are only connections of imagination, transitions from one image to another; for, when a new situation appears similar to the preceding one, they expect to find again what was previously joined to it, as though things were linked in fact, just because their images are linked in the memory. It is, indeed, true that reason ordinarily counsels us to expect that we will find in the future that which conforms to our long experience of the past; but this is not, on that account, a necessary and infallible truth, and it can fail us when we least expect it, when the reasons which have maintained it change. This is why the wisest people do not rely on it to such an extent that they do not try to probe into the reason for what happens (if that is possible), so as to judge when exceptions must be made. For only reason is capable of establishing sure rules and of providing what uncertain rules lack by formulating exceptions to them, and lastly, capable of finding connections that are certain in the compulsiveness [*force*] of necessary consequences. This often provides a way of foreseeing an occurrence without having to experience the sensible links between images, which the beasts are reduced to doing. Thus what justifies the internal principles of necessary truths also distinguishes humans from beasts.

Letter to Thomas Hobbes

Mainz, July 13/22, 1670

Most esteemed Sir,

To my great delight I recently learned from the letters of a friend visiting in England that you are still alive and in full health at so great an age. Hence I could not refrain from writing. If my doing so is inopportune, you can punish it by silence; for me it will still suffice to have given witness of my feeling. I believe I have read almost all your works, in part separately and in part in the collected edition, and I freely admit that I have profited from them as much as from few others in our century. I am not given to flattery, but everyone who has had the privilege of following your writings on the theory of the state will acknowledge, as I do, that nothing can be added in such brevity to its admirable clearness. There is nothing more polished and better adapted to the public good than your definitions. Among the theorems which you deduce from them there are many which will remain established. There are some who have abused them, but I believe that in most cases this occurred because the right principles of application were ignored. If one were to apply the general principles of motion—such, for example, as that nothing begins to move unless it is moved by another body, that a body at rest, however large, can be impelled by the slightest motion of a moving body, however small, and others—if one were to apply these by an ill-timed leap to sensible things, he would be derided by the common man unless he had demonstrated in advance, and to minds prepared for it, that for the most part bodies which seem to be at rest are insensibly in motion. Similarly, if one were to apply what you have demonstrated about the state and republic to all groups which are commonly called by that name, and what you attribute to the supreme power to all who claim for themselves the name of king, prince, monarch, or majesty, and your views about complete freedom in the state of nature to all cases in which citizens of different states transact certain affairs among themselves; then, if I am not mistaken, he too would be very much in error about your opinion. For you acknowledge that there are many communities on earth which are not one state but a confederation of many and that there are many titular monarchs to whom others have never transferred their will. Nor will you deny that, assuming a ruler of the world, there can be no purely natural state of man which would place him beyond the pale of any community, since God is the common monarch of all; and that certain men are therefore wrong in ascribing license and impiety to your hypotheses.

As I have said, I have always understood your works in this way, and I acknowledge that I have received great light from them in carrying out a work on rational jurisprudence on which I am collaborating with a friend. For I observed the unbelievable subtlety and soundness of expression with which the Roman jurisconsults gathered their answers which are preserved in the Pandects—qualities in which your own writings strongly resemble theirs. I realized that a large part of them were arrived at almost entirely by demonstration from the law of nature alone and that the rest were deduced with the same degree of certainty from a few principles which were arbitrary, it is true, but drawn from the practice of the Republic. When I first set my feet in the paths of jurisprudence, therefore, I began four years ago to work out a plan for compiling in the fewest words possible the elements of the law contained in the Roman Corpus (in the manner of the old Perpetual Edict), so that one could, so to speak, finally demonstrate from them its universal laws. There are many laws which will prove refractory to this method, especially in the Imperial Rescripts, because they do not belong to natural law. However, these are clearly discernible among the rest and will be counterbalanced by the multitude of the others—especially since I venture to assert that half of the Roman law is mere natural law. And it is well known that almost all of Europe uses this law wherever it has not been distinctly invalidated by local custom.

But I must confess that I sometimes vary these long and tedious concerns with other more pleasant ones, for I also have the habit of sometimes meditating upon the nature of things, though this is like being carried into a foreign world. I have been thinking about the abstract principles of motion, where the foundations which you have laid seem to me remarkably justified. I agree absolutely with you that one body is not moved by another unless the latter touches it and is in motion and that, once begun, every motion continues unless impeded by something. Yet I confess that there are certain matters about which I have hesitated, especially about this: I have not found that you account clearly for the cause of consistency, or, what is the same thing, of cohesion in things.

Letter to Nicolas Remond

Vienna, January 10, 1714

... I find it natural that you have enjoyed some of my thoughts after having penetrated into Plato's, an author who has meant much to me and who deserves to be systematized. I believe that I can carry out the demonstration of truths which he has merely advanced. Having followed his steps and those of certain other great men, I flatter myself to have profited by them and to have penetrated, at least to a point, the bright temples of wisdom:

Edita doctrina, sapientum templa serena.

This relates to general truths which do not depend upon facts but which are nonetheless, in my opinion, the key to the knowledge which judges facts.

I should venture to add that if I had been less distracted, or if I were younger or had talented young men to help me, I should still hope to create a kind of *universal symbolistic* [*spécieuse générale*] in which all truths of reason would be reduced to a kind of calculus. At the same time this could be a kind of universal language or writing, though infinitely different from all such languages which have thus far been proposed, for the characters and the words themselves would give directions to reason, and the errors—except those of fact—would be only mistakes in calculation. It would be very difficult to form or invent this language or characteristic but very easy to learn it without any dictionaries. When we lack sufficient data to arrive at certainty in our truths, it would also serve to estimate degrees of probability and to see what is needed to provide this certainty. Such an estimate would be most important for the problems of life and for practical considerations, where our errors in estimating probabilities often amount to more than a half. . . .

. . . Besides always taking care to direct my study toward edification, I have tried to uncover and unite the truth buried and scattered under the opinions of all the different philosophical sects, and I believe I have added something of my own which takes a few steps forward. The circumstances under which my studies proceeded from my earliest youth have given me some facility in this. I discovered Aristotle as a lad, and even the Scholastics did not repel me; even now I do not regret this. But then Plato too, and Plotinus, gave me some satisfaction, not to mention other ancient thinkers whom I consulted later. After having finished the schools, I fell upon the moderns, and I recall walking in a grove on the outskirts of Leipzig called the Rosental, at the age of fifteen, and deliberating whether to preserve substantial forms or not. Mechanism finally prevailed and led me to apply myself to mathematics.

It is true that I did not penetrate into its depths until after some conversations with Mr. Huygens in Paris. But when I looked for the ultimate reasons for mechanism, and even for the laws of motion, I was greatly surprised to see that they could not be found in mathematics but that I should have to return to metaphysics. This led me back to entelechies, and from the material to the formal, and at last brought me to understand, after many corrections and forward steps in my thinking, that monads or simple substances are the only true substances and that material things are only phenomena, though well founded and well connected. Of this, Plato, and even the later Academics and the skeptics too, had caught some glimpses, but these successors of Plato did not make as good use of it as did he himself.

I have found that most of the sects are right in a good part of what they propose, but not so much in what they deny. The formalists, Platonists and Aristotelians, for example, are right in seeking the source of things in final and formal causes. But they are wrong in neglecting efficient and material causes and in inferring from this, as did Henry More in England and certain other Platonists, that there are phenomena which cannot be explained mechanically. The materialists, on the other hand, or those who accept only a mechanical philosophy, are wrong in rejecting metaphysical considerations and trying to explain everything in terms of sense experience.

I flatter myself to have penetrated into the harmony of these different realms and to have seen that both sides are right provided that they do not clash with each other; that everything in nature happens mechanically and at the same time metaphysically but that the source of mechanics is in metaphysics. It was not easy to uncover this mystery, because there are few men who take the pains to combine both types of study.

Descartes did it, but not thoroughly enough. He went too fast in setting up most of his doctrines; one may say that his philosophy is the entrance hall to the truth. What held him back most was that he did not know the true laws of mechanics or of motion; these could have put him back on the track. Mr. Huygens was the first to see them, though imperfectly, but he had no taste for metaphysics, any more than did other capable men who have followed him in investigating this subject. I have observed in my book that, if Descartes had seen that nature conserves not only the same force but also the same total direction in the laws of motion, he would not have held that the soul can change the direction of the body more easily than its force, and he would have gone straightway to the system of *pre-established harmony*, which is a necessary conclusion from the conservation of both force and direction. . . .

Letter to Simon Foucher (1675)

I agree with you that it is important once and for all to examine all our presuppositions in order to establish something sound. For I hold that it is only when we can prove everything we assert that we understand perfectly the thing being considered. I know that such studies are not very popular, but I also know that to take the pains to understand matters to their roots is not very popular. As I see it, your purpose is to examine those truths which affirm that there is something outside of us. You seem to be most fair in this, for thus you will grant us all hypothetical truths which affirm, not that something does exist outside of us, but only what would happen if anything existed there. So we at once save arithmetic, geometry, and a large number of propositions in metaphysics, physics, and morals, whose convenient expression depends on arbitrarily chosen definitions, and whose truth depends on those axioms which I am wont to call identical; such for example, as that two contradictories cannot exist and that at any given time a thing is as it is; that it is, for example, equal to itself, as great as itself, similar to itself, etc.

But, although you do not enter explicitly into an examination of hypothetical propositions, I am still of the opinion that this should be done and that we should admit none without having entirely demonstrated and resolved it into identities.

It is the truths which deal with what is in fact outside of us which are the primary subject of your investigations. Now in the first place, we cannot deny that the very truth of hypothetical propositions themselves is something outside of us and independent of us. For all hypothetical propositions assert what would be or would not be, if something or its contrary were posited; consequently, they assume two things at the same time which agree with each other, or the possibility or impossibility, necessity or indifference, of something. But this possibility, impossibility, or necessity (for the necessity of one thing is the impossibility of its contrary) is not a chimera which we create, since all that we do consists in recognizing them, in spite of ourselves and in a constant manner. So, of all the things which actually are, the possibility or impossibility of being is itself the first. But this possibility and this necessity form or compose what are called the essences or natures and the truths which are usually called eternal. And we are right in calling them this, for there is nothing so eternal as what is necessary. Thus the nature of the circle with its properties is something which exists and is eternal, that is, there is some constant cause outside of us which makes everyone who thinks carefully about a circle discover the same thing, not merely in the sense that their thoughts agree with each other, for this could be attributed solely to the nature of the human mind, but also in the sense that phenomena or experiences confirm them when some appearance of a circle strikes our senses. These phenomena necessarily have some cause outside of us.

But, although the existence of necessities comes before all others in itself and in the order of nature, I nevertheless agree that it is not first in the order of our knowledge. For you see that, in order to prove its existence, I have taken for granted that we think and that we have sensations. So there are two absolute general truths; truths, that is, which tell of the actual existence of things. One is that we think; the other, that there is a great variety in our thoughts. From the former it follows that we are; from the latter, that there is something other than us, that is to say, something other than that which thinks, which is the cause of the variety of our experiences. Now one of these truths is just as incontestable and as independent as the other, and, having stressed only the former in the order of his meditations, Descartes failed to attain the perfection to which he had aspired.

But not even the greatest genius can force things; we must of necessity enter through the openings which nature has made in order to avoid being lost. What is more, one man alone cannot do everything all at once, and for myself, when I think of all that Descartes has said that is excellent and original, I am more amazed at what he has done than at some things which he failed to do. I admit that I have not yet been able to read his writings with all the care that I had intended to give them, and, as my friends know, it happened that I read most of the other modern philosophers before I read him. Bacon and Gassendi were the first to fall into my hands. Their familiar and easy style was better adapted to a man who wanted to read everything. It is true that I have often glanced through Galileo and Descartes, but since I have only recently become a geometrician, I was soon repelled by their style of writing, which requires deep meditation. Personally, though I have always loved to think by myself, I have always found it hard to read books which one cannot understand without much meditation, for in following one's own thoughts one follows a certain natural inclination and so gains profit with pleasure. One is violently disturbed, in contrast, when compelled to follow the thoughts of someone else. I always liked books which contained some good thoughts, but which I could run through without stopping, for they aroused ideas in me which I could follow up in my own fancy and pursue as far as I pleased. This also prevented me from reading the books on geometry carefully; I freely admit that I have not yet been able to make myself read Euclid in any other way than one usually reads history. I have learned from experience that this method is good in general, yet I have recognized nevertheless that there are authors for whom one must make an exception, such as Plato and Aristotle among ancient philosophers, and Galileo and Descartes among our own. Yet what I know of the metaphysical and physical meditations of Descartes has come almost entirely from the reading of a number of books written in a more popular style which report his opinions. And perhaps I have not as yet understood him well. To the extent that I have read him over myself, however, it seems to me that I have at least been able to discover what he has not done or tried to do, and, among other things, this is to analyze all our assumptions. This is why I am inclined to applaud all who examine even the smallest truth to the end, for I know that it is much to understand something perfectly, no matter how small or easy it may seem. One can go very far in this way and, finally, establish the art of discovery, which depends on knowledge of the simplest things, but on a distinct and perfect knowledge of them.

But I return to these truths which are primary with respect to ourselves, and first to those which assert that there is something outside of us; namely, that we think and that there is a great variety in our thoughts. This variety cannot come from that which thinks, since one thing by itself cannot be the cause of the changes occurring in it. For everything remains in the state in which it is, unless there is something which changes it. And since it has not been determined by itself to undergo certain changes rather than others, we cannot begin to attribute any variety to it without saying something which admittedly has no reason, which is absurd. Even if we tried to say that our thoughts have no beginning, we should be obliged to assert that each of us has existed from all eternity; yet we should not escape the difficulty, for we should always have to admit that there is no reason for this variety which would have existed from all eternity in our thoughts, since there is nothing in us which determines us to one variety rather than another. Thus there is some cause outside of us for the variety of our thoughts. And since we agree that there are some subordinate causes of this variety which themselves still need a cause, we have established particular beings or substances to whom we ascribe some action, that is, from whose change we think that some change follows in us. So we make great strides toward fabricating what we call matter and body.

But at this point you are right in stopping us for a while and renewing the criticisms of the ancient Academy. For at bottom all our experiences assure us of only two things: first, that there is a connection among our appearances which provides the means to predict future appearances successfully; and, second, that this connection must have a constant cause. But it does not follow strictly from this that matter or bodies exist but only that there is something which gives us appearances in a good sequence. For if some invisible power were to take pleasure in giving us dreams that are well tied into our preceding life and in conformity with each other, could we distinguish them from reality before we had awakened? Now, what prevents the course of our life from being one long well-ordered dream, about which we could be undeceived in a moment? Nor do I see that such a power would be imperfect just on this ground, as Descartes asserts, to say nothing of the fact that its imperfection is not involved in the present question. For it might be a kind of subordinate power, or a demon who for some unknown reason could interfere with our affairs and who would have at least as much power over us as that caliph had over the man whom he caused to be carried, drunk, into his palace, and let taste of the paradise of Mohammed after he was awakened; after which he was once more made drunk and returned in that condition to the place where he had been found. When this man came to himself, he naturally interpreted this experience, which seemed inconsistent with the course of his life, as a vision, and spread among the people maxims and revelations which he believed he had learned in his pretended paradise; this was precisely what the caliph wished. Since reality has thus passed for a vision, what is to prevent a vision from passing for reality? The more consistency we see in what happens to us, it is true, the more our belief is confirmed that what appears to us is reality. But it is also true that, the more closely we examine our appearances, the better ordered we find them, as microscopes and other means of observation have shown. This permanent consistency gives us great assurance, but, after all, it will be only moral until somebody discovers a priori the origin of the world which we see and pursues the question of why things are as they appear back to its foundations in essence. For when this is done, he will have demonstrated that what appears to us is reality and that it is impossible for us ever to be deceived in it. But I believe that this would very nearly approach the beatific vision and that it is difficult to aspire to this in our present state. Yet we do learn therefrom how confused the knowledge which we commonly have of the body and matter must be, since we believe we are certain that they exist, but eventually find that we could be mistaken. This confirms Mr. Descartes's excellent thought concerning the proof of the difference between body and soul, since one can doubt the one without being able to question the other. For even if there were only appearances or dreams, we should be nonetheless certain of the existence of that which thinks, as Descartes has very well said. I may add that one could still demonstrate the existence of God by ways different from those of Descartes but, I believe, leading farther. For we have no need to assume a being who guarantees us against being deceived, since it lies in our power to undeceive ourselves about many things, at least about the most important ones.

I wish, Sir, that your meditations on this matter may have all the success you desire; but, to accomplish this, it is well to proceed in order and to establish your propositions. This is the way to gain ground and make sure progress. I believe you would oblige the public also by conveying to it, from time to time, selections from the Academy and especially from Plato, for I know that there are things in them more beautiful and substantial than is usually thought.

Letter to Gabriel Wagner on the Value of Logic (1696)

For my part, I confess that in my early youth I was inclined to reject much of what had been introduced into the learned world. But with growing years and deeper insight I discovered the value of many things which I had before considered trivial, and I learned *not to condemn anything too easily*, a rule which I consider better and safer than that taught by certain Stoic lovers of wisdom and after them by Horace—*not to wonder at anything.* I have made this clear to the so-called Cartesians in France and elsewhere and have warned them that, by attacking the schools, they are helping neither themselves nor scholarship but are merely making learned men more bitter toward new ideas, however good. I have never been able to approve of efforts to rule out, first, the critical study of Greek and Roman antiquities, then the reading of the rabbinical and Arabic literature, then the industry of the astronomers, and then something else, for, after all, these things all have their value, and it is good that there are people working at them, who must therefore be encouraged through praise further to pursue their great work, which they often carry on without reward, instead of being frightened away from it through contempt. I have no doubt that you are for the most part in agreement with this, since you have expressed yourself ably on oriental languages, astronomy, and other fields.

However, since you have in the main tended, if I understand you, to reject the art of reasoning or logic entirely and to ban it and its close relative, the universal science or metaphysics, and since you have explicitly included me (upon whom you bestow too much praise) among those who despise logic, I consider it all the more important to explain my position to you. I have no doubt that you have written as you have because of a sincere zeal for the true and useful sciences, so that men need not be delayed and led to lose valuable time through fruitless grubbing; and I do not doubt that you have honored me by calling upon me as witness to such a worthy aim. But as my opinion on the matter is in a certain measure different from yours, I should like to see if we can understand and compare each other's positions. I believe that you are right in your intentions but that your expressions say more than you mean. By logic or the art of reasoning I understand the art of using the understanding not only to judge proposed truth but also to discover hidden truth. If such an art is possible, in other words, if there are marked advantages to be found in such processes, it follows that it ought by all means to be sought and valued highly, indeed, to be considered as the key to all the arts and sciences. You seem to admit that there are excellent advantages to be gained by thought and investigation; if you are merely unwilling to admit that this procedure should be named logic, our controversy concerns only a word. But, since I do not think that this is your purpose, I can take your position to mean only that you are rejecting, not the true logic, but what we have heretofore honored by that name.

If this is your opinion, I must indeed confess that all our logics until now are but a shadow of what I should wish and what I see from afar; but I must also confess, to stick to the truth and give everyone his due, that I also find much that is good and useful in the logic of the past. Gratitude as well compels me to say this, for I think I can truthfully say that even the logic taught me in school has been most fruitful for me. Before I entered a class in which it was taught, I was steeped in the historians and poets, for I had begun to read history as soon as I could read at all, and I found great pleasure and value in verse. But as soon as I began to learn logic, I was greatly stirred by the classification and order which I perceived in its principles. I came at once to notice that there must be something great in it, as far as a lad of thirteen years could notice such a thing. My greatest pleasure lay in the categories, which seemed to me to be a standard roll of every-thing in the world, and I examined many logics to see where the best and most exhaustive lists could be found. I often asked myself and my companions into which category and subdivision of it this or that concept might belong, although I was not at all pleased to find that so many things were entirely excluded, and I found, too, that some of the categories, especially the last two or perhaps four, dropped away completely for me because they were included in the earlier ones or because I could find no actual use for them. I soon made the amusing discovery of a method of guessing or of recalling to mind, by means of the categories, something forgotten when one has a picture of it but cannot get at it in his brain. One needs only to ask one's self or others about certain categories and their subdivisions (of which I had compiled an extensive table out of various logics) and examine the answers, and one can readily exclude all irrelevant matters and narrow the problem down until the missing thing can be discovered. Nebuchad-nezzar could perhaps have reconstructed his forgotten dream in this way. In such tabulations of knowledge I attained practice in division and subdivision as a basis of order and a bond of thoughts. Whenever I found a list of things belonging together, and especially whenever I found a genus or universal under which a number of particular species was subsumed, as, for example, the number of the emotions or of the virtues and vices, I had to put them into a table and to see if the species fell into a successive order. I always found that the enumeration was incomplete and that more species could be added. I took great pleasure in such matters and wrote out all kinds of stuff, but then forgot it and let it be lost. Many years later, however, I found some of it and discovered that it did not entirely displease me. Later on I found the value of these exercises when I came to work out certain problems. I recall that once, when I had set up a construction of some kind, a learned friend asked me how I could think of everything that I had put in, even when its applicability was not at once apparent. I replied—what was true—that I did it by division and subdivision, using these as a net or snare to capture the elusive game. I found too that such division served to make for accurate descriptions of things, not to mention other advantages. Fortunately I was well advanced in the so-called humanities before this occurred to me, or I could hardly have prevailed upon myself to return again from the things to the words. . . .

[But] at that time I did not know that mathematical demonstrations were what I was seeking. I also observed that the topics or loci of the methods of explanation and demonstration were of great use in recalling for us, at the proper time, things already in our head but not in our thoughts, so that we might not merely prate about things but investigate them better. I observed that such loci or principles are to be used as sources, not merely for the methods of providing a represented truth, but also for the methods of explaining an object directly presented, and that we may thus speak of them not merely as principles of proof (*argumentabilia*) but also as principles of description (*predicabilia*).

14

GEORGE BERKELEY
Philosophy Does Not Need Abstract Ideas

Born in Ireland, George Berkeley (1685–1753) studied theology at Trinity College Dublin, where he remained until 1713, writing most of his philsophic work during his tenure as a Fellow of the College. (1707–1713). The *Essay Towards a New Theory of Vision* (1709) was critical of both neo-Cartesian and Lockeian theories of vision. Against Descartes, Berkeley argued that judging distance is learned from experience rather than calculated. Against Locke, he argued that tactile and visual ideas are distinct because their sensory origins are different. The *Principles of Human Knowledge* (1710) develops the view that we learn about physical objects from perception, and that the abstract ideas of absolute space, time and motion are empty notions. Berkeley took his perceptual idealism ("to be is to be perceived") to be a philosophical articulation and amplification of common sense. The continuity of (what we think of as) physical objects is assured in the mind of God. Berkeley's philosophical psychology led him to theology, to writing *Three Dialogues Between Hylas and Philonous* (1713) and *Alciphron* (1732). He argued that far from being skeptical, his version of idealism is consistent with Scripture and Christian doctrine.

Having developed a strong interest in education, Berkeley attempted to raise funds to establish a college in Bermuda. While vainly waiting for Crown funds, he lived in Rhode Island during 1728–1732. After he was made the Anglican Bishop of Cloyne in 1734. He wrote numerous pamphlets on the poverty and plight of Ireland. In his old age, Berkeley speculated on a variety of medical therapies, analyzing the benefits of tar-water.

Principles of Human Knowledge

INTRODUCTION (DRAFT)

Philosophy being nothing else but the study of wisdom and truth, it may seem strange that they who have spent much time and pains in it, do usually find themselves embarrass'd with more doubts and difficulties than they were before they came to that study. There is nothing these men can touch with their hands or behold with their eyes but has its inaccessible and dark sides. Something they imagine to be in every drop of water, every grain of sand which can puzzle [and confound the most clear and elevated understanding, and are often by their principles led into a necessity of admitting the most irreconcilable opinions for true, or (which is worse) of sitting down in a forlorn scepticism.

The cause of this is thought to be the obscurity of things, together with the natural weakness and imperfection of our understanding. It is said the senses we have are few, and these design'd by nature only for the support of life, and not to penetrate into the constitution and inward essence of things. Besides, the mind of man being finite when it treats of things which partake of infinity, it is not to be wonder'd at if it run into absurdities and contradictions, out of which it is absolutely impossible it should ever extricate itself, it being of the nature of Infinite not to be comprehended by that which is finite.

But I cannot think our faculties are so weak and inadequate in respect of things, as these men would make us believe. I cannot be brought to suppose that right deductions from true principles should ever end in consequences which cannot be maintain'd or made consistent. We should believe that God has dealt more bountifully with the sons of men than to give them a strong desire for that which he had placed quite out of their reach, and so made it impossible for them to obtain. Surely our wise and good Creatour would never have made us so eager in the search of truth meerly to baulk and perplex us, to make us blame our faculties, and bewail our inevitable ignorance. This were not agreeable to the wonted indulgent methods of Providence, which, whatever appetites it may have implanted in the creatures, doth usually furnish them with such means as, if rightly made use of, will not fail to satisfy them. Upon the whole my opinion is, that the far greatest part, if not all, of those difficultys which have hitherto amus'd philosophers, and block'd up the way to knowledge, are entirely owing to themselves. That they have first rais'd a dust, and then complain they cannot see.

My purpose therefore is, to try if I can discover and point out what those principles are which have introduc'd all that doubtfulness and uncertainty, those absurditys and contradictions into the several sects of philosophy, insomuch that the wisest men have thought our ignorance incurable, conceiving it to arise from the natural dulness and limitation of our faculties. And at the same time to establish such principles in their stead, as shall be free from the like consequences, and lead the mind into a clear view of truth. And surely it is a work well deserving of our pains, to try to extend the limits of our knowledge, and do right to human understanding, by making it to appear that those lets and difficultys which stay and embarrass the mind in its enquirys after truth do not spring from any darkness and intricacy in the objects, or natural defect in the intellectual powers, so much as from false principles which have been insisted on, and might have been avoided.

How difficult and discouraging soever this attempt may seem, when I consider what a number of men of very great and extraordinary abilitys have gone before me, and miscarry'd in the like designs, yet I am not without some hopes, upon the consideration that the largest views are not always the clearest, and that he who is shortsighted will be apt to draw the object nearer, and by a close and narrow survey may perhaps discern that which had escaped far better eyes.

In my entrance upon this work I think it necessary to take notice of that wch seems to have been the source of a great many errours, and to have made the way to knowledge very intricate and perplex'd, that wch seems to have had a chiefe part in rendering speculation intricate and perplex'd, and to have been the source of innumerable errours and difficulties in almost all parts of knowledge—and that is the opinion that there are Abstract Ideas or General Conceptions of Things. He who is not a perfect stranger to the writings and notions of philosophers must needs acknowledge that no small part of them are spent about Abstract Ideas. These are, in a more special manner, thought to be the objects of those sciences that go by the name of logic and metaphysics, and of all that which passes under the notion of the most abstracted and sublime philosophy. In all which speculative sciences you shall scarce find any question handled by the philosophers in such a manner as does not suppose their existence in the mind, and that it is very well acquainted with them; so that these parts of learning must of necessity be overrun with very much useless wrangling and jargon, innumerable absurdities and contradictions opinions, if so be that Abstract General Ideas are perfectly inconceivable, as I am well assur'd they never were—cannot be conceived by me, nor do I think it possible they should be conceiv'd by any one else.

I intreat the reader to reflect with himself, and see if it does not oft happen, either in hearing, or reading a discourse, that the passions of delight, love, hatred, admiration, disdain, &c. do not arise immediately in his mind upon the perception of certain words without any ideas coming between. At first, indeed, the words might have occasion'd ideas that may be apt to produce those emotions of mind. But if I mistake not, it will be found that when language is once grown familiar, to a man the hearing of the sound or light of the characters is oft immediately attended with those passions which at first were wont to be produc'd by the intervention of ideas that are now quite omitted.

Further, the communicating of ideas marked by words is not the chief and only end of language, as is commonly suppos'd. There are other ends, as the raising of some passion, the exciting to or deterring from an action. To which the former is in many cases barely subservient, and sometimes entirely omitted when these can be obtain'd without it, as I think does not infrequently happen in the familiar use of language.

I ask any man whether every time he tells another that such an action is honourable and vertuous, with an intention to excite him to the performance of it, he has at that instant ideas of honour and virtue in his thoug view, and whether in reality his intention be to raise that idea, together with their agreement to the particular idea of that particular action, in the understanding of him he speaks to or rather whether this be not his full purpose, namely, that those words should excite in the mind of the hearer an esteem of that particular action, and stir him up to the performance of it.

It is plain therefore that a man may understand what is said to him without having a clear and determinate idea annexed to and marked by every particular word in the discourse he hears. Nay, he may perfectly understand it. For what is it, I pray, to understand perfectly, but only to understand all that is meant by the person that speaks? which very oft is nothing more than barely to excite in his mind certain emotions without any thought of those ideas so much talk'd of and so little understood. For the truth whereof I appeal to every man's one's experience.

I know not how this doctrine will go down with those philosophers who may be apt to give the titles of gibberish and jargon to all discourse whatsoever so far forth as the words contained in it are not made the signs of clear and determinate ideas, who think it nonsense for a man to assent to any proposition each term whereof doth not bring into his mind a clear and distinct idea, and tell us over and over that every pertinent word hath an idea annexed unto which never fails to accompany it where 'tis rightly understood. Which opinion of theirs, how plausibly soever it might have been maintain'd by some, seems to me to have introduced a great deal of difficulty and nonsense into the reasonings of men. Certainly nothing could be fitter to bring forth and cherish the doctrine of abstract ideas. For when men were indubitably conscious to themselves that many words they used did not denote any particular ideas, lest they should be thought altogether insignificant, they were of necessity driven into the opinion that they stood for general ones.

But more effectually to shew the absurdity of an opinion that carrys with it so great an appearance of clearness and strength of reason, but is in fact most dangerous and destructive both to reason and religion, I shall, if I mistake not, in the progress of this work demonstrate there be names well known and familiar to men, which tho' they mark and stand and signify things, cannot be suppos'd to signifie ideas of any sort, either general or particular, without the greatest nonsense and contradiction; it being absolutely impossible, and a direct repugnancy, that any intellect, how exalted and comprehensive soever, should frame ideas of these things.

We have, I think, shewn the impossibility of abstract ideas. We have consider'd what has been said in behalf of them by their ablest patrons, and endeavour'd to demonstrate they are of no use for those ends to which they are thought necessary. And, lastly, we have traced them to the source from whence they flow, which appears evidently to be language.

Since therefore words have been discover'd to be so very apt to impose on the understandings of men, I am resolv'd in my inquiries to make as little use of them as possibly I can. Whatever ideas I consider, I shall endeavour to take them bare and naked into my view, keeping out of my thoughts, so far as I am able, those names which long and constant use hath so strictly united to them.

Let us conceive a solitary man, one born and bred in such a place of the world, and in such circumstances, as he shall never have had occasion to make use of universal signs for his ideas. That man shall have a constant train of particular ideas passing in his mind. Whatever he sees, hears, imagines, or anywise conceives, is on all hands, even by the patrons of abstract ideas, granted to be particular. Let us withall suppose him under no necessity of labouring to secure himself from hunger and cold, but at full ease, naturally of good facultys, and contemplative. Such a one I should take to be nearer the discovery of certain great and excellent truths yet unknown, than he that has had the education of schools, has been instructed in the ancient and modern philosophy, and by much reading and conversation has furnish'd his head attain'd to the knowledge of those arts and sciences that make so great a noise in the learned world. It is true, the knowledge of our solitary philosopher is not like to be so very wide and extended, it being confin'd to those few particulars that come within his own observation. But then, if he is like to have less knowledge, he is withall like to have fewer mistakes than other men.

It cannot be deny'd that words are of excellent use, in that by their means all that stock of knowledge, which has been purchas'd by the joynt labours of inquisitive men in all ages and nations, may be drawn into the view, and made the possession of one particular single person. But there are some parts of learning which contain the knowledge of things the most noble and important of any within the reach of human reason, that have had the ill fate to be so signally perplex'd and darken'd by the abuse of words and general ways of speech wherein they are deliver'd, that in the study of them a man cannot be too much upon his guard, whether in his private meditations, or in reading the writings or hearing the discourses of other men, to prevent his being cheated by the glibness and familiarity of speech into a belief that those words stand for ideas which, in truth, stand for none at all: which grand mistake it is almost incredible what a mist and darkness it has cast over the understandings of men, otherwise the most rational and clear-sighted.

I shall therefore endeavour, so far as I am able, to put myself in the posture of the solitary philosopher. I will confine my thoughts and enquiries to the naked scene of my own particular ideas, from which I may expect to derive the following advantages.

First. I shall be sure to get clear of all verbal controversies purely verbal. The springing up of which weeds in almost all the sciences has been the a most fatal obstruction to the growth of true and sound knowledge: and accordingly is at this day esteem'd as such, and made the great and just complaint of the wisest men.

Secondly. 'Tis reasonable to expect that by this the trouble of sounding, or examining, or comprehending any notion may be very much abridg'd. For it oft happens that a notion, when it is cloathed with words, seems tedious and operose, and hard to be conceiv'd, which yet being stript of that garniture, the ideas shrink into a narrow compass, and are view'd almost by one glance of thought.

Thirdly. I shall have fewer objects to consider than other men seem to have had. Because I find myself to want several of those supposed ideas, in contemplating of which the philosophers do usually spend much pains and study, nay, even of those (which without doubt will appear very surprising) that pass for simple, particular ideas. It is inconceivable what cannot be believ'd what a wonderful emptyness and scarcity of ideas that man shall desery who will lay aside all use of words in his meditations.

Fourthly. Having remov'd the veil of words, I may expect to have a clearer prospect of the ideas that remain in my understanding. To behold the deformity of errour we need only undress it.

Fifthly. This seemeth to be a sure way to extricate myself out of that fine and subtile net of abstract ideas; which has so miserably perplex'd and entangled the minds of men, and that with this peculiar circumstance, that by how much the finer and the more curious was the wit of any man, by so much the deeper was he like to be ensnar'd and faster held therein.

Sixthly. So long as I confine my thoughts to my own ideas divested of words, I do not see how I can easily be mistaken. The objects I consider I clearly and adequately know. I cannot be deceiv'd in thinking I have an idea which I have not. Nor, on the other hand, can I be ignorant of any idea that I have. It is not possible for me to think any of my own ideas are alike or unlike which are not truly so. To discern the agreements and disagreements there are between my ideas, to see what simple ideas are included in any compound idea, and what not, there is nothing requisite but an attentive perception of what passes in my own understanding.

But the attainment of all these advantages does presuppose an entire deliverance from the deception of words, which I dare scarce promise myself. So difficult a thing it is to dissolve a union so early begun, and confirm'd by so long a habit, as that betwixt words and ideas.

A man may deliver himself from the imposture of words. He that knows he hath no other than particular ideas, will not puzzle himself in vain to find out and conceive the abstract idea annexed to any name. And he that knows names when made use of in the propriety of language do not always stand for ideas, will spare himself the labour of looking for ideas where there are none to be had.

Those obstacles being now remov'd, I earnestly desire that every one would use his utmost endeavour to attain a clear and naked view of the ideas he would consider [by separating] from them all that varnish and mist of words, which so fatally blinds the judgment and dissipates the attention of men.

This is, I am confident, the shortest way to knowledge, and cannot cost too much pains in coming at. In vain do we extend our view into the heavens, and rake into the entrails of the earth. In vain do we consult the writings and discourses of learned men, and trace the dark footsteps of antiquity. We need only draw the curtain of words, to behold the fairest tree of knowledge, whose fruit is excellent and within the reach of our hand.

Unless we take care to clear the first principles of knowledge from the incumbrance and delusion of words, the consequences we draw from them we may make infinite reasonings upon them to no purpose. We may deduce consequences from consequences, and be never the wiser. The farther we go, we shall only lose ourselves the more irrecoverably, and be the deeper entangled in difficulties and mistakes.

I do therefore intreat whoever designs to read the following sheets, that he would make my words the occasion of his own thinking, and endeavour to attain the same train of thoughts in reading that I had in writing them. By this means it will be easy for him to discover the truth or falsity of what I say. He will be out of all danger of being deceiv'd by my words. And I do not see what inducement he can have to err in considering his own naked, undisguised ideas.

That I may contribute, so far as in me lies, to expose my thoughts to the fairly to the understanding of the reader, I shall throughout endeavour to express myself in the clearest, plainest, and most familiar manner, abstaining from all flourish and pomp of words, all hard and unusual terms which are commonly pretended by those that use them to cover a sense intricate and abstracted and sublime.

I pretend not to treat of anything but what is obvious and accommodated to the understanding of every reasonable man.

Three Dialogues between Hylas and Philonous

Though it seems the general opinion of the world, no less than the design of nature and providence, that the end of speculation be practice, or the improvement and regulation of our lives and actions; yet those, who are most addicted to speculative studies, seem as generally of another mind. And, indeed, if we consider the pains that have been taken, to perplex the plainest things, that distrust of the senses, those doubts and scruples, those abstractions and refinements that occur in the very entrance of the sciences; it will not seem strange, that men of leisure and curiosity should lay themselves out in fruitless disquisitions, without descending to the practical parts of life, or informing themselves in the more necessary and important parts of knowledge.

Upon the common principles of philosophers, we are not assured of the existence of things from their being perceived. And we are taught to distinguish their real nature from that which falls under our senses. Hence arise *scepticism* and *paradoxes*. It is not enough, that we see and feel, that we taste and smell a thing. Its true nature, its absolute external entity, is still concealed. For, though it be the fiction of our own brain, we have made it inaccessible to all our faculties.

Sense is fallacious, reason defective. We spend our lives in doubting of those things which other men evidently know, and believing those things which they laugh at, and despise.

In order, therefore, to divert the busy mind of man from vain researches, it seemed necessary to inquire into the source of its perplexities; and, if possible, to lay down such principles, as, by an easy solution of them, together with their own native evidence, may, at once, recommend themselves for genuine to the mind, and rescue it from those endless pursuits it is engaged in. Which, with a plain demonstration of the immediate providence of an all-seeing God, and the natural immortality of the soul, should seem the readiest preparation, as well as the strongest motive, to the study and practice of virtue.

It has been my aim to introduce the notions I advance, into the mind, in the most easy and familiar manner; especially, because they carry with them a great opposition to the prejudices of philosophers, which have so far prevailed against the common sense and natural notions of mankind.

If the principles, which I here endeavor to propagate, are admitted for true; the consequences which, I think, evidently flow from thence, are, that *atheism* and *scepticism* will be utterly destroyed, many intricate points made plain, great difficulties solved, several useless parts of science retrenched, speculation referred to practice, and men reduced from paradoxes to common sense.

And although it may, perhaps, seem an uneasy reflection to some, that when they have taken a circuit through so many refined and unvulgar notions, they should at last come to think like other men: yet, methinks, this return to the simple dictates of nature, after having wandered through the wild mazes of philosophy, is not unpleasant. It is like coming home from a long voyage: a man reflects with pleasure on the many difficulties and perplexities he has passed through, sets his heart at ease, and enjoys himself with more satisfaction for the future.

As it was my intention to convince *sceptics* and *infidels* by reason, so it has been my endeavor strictly to observe the most rigid laws of reasoning. And, to an impartial reader, I hope, it will be manifest, that the sublime notion of a God, and the comfortable expectation of immortality, do naturally arise from a close and methodical application of thought: whatever may be the result of that loose, rambling way, not altogether improperly termed *free-thinking*, by certain libertines in thought, who can no more endure the restraints of *logic*, than those of *religion*, or *government*.

It will, perhaps, be objected to my design, that so far as it tends to ease the mind of difficult and useless inquiries, it can affect only a few speculative persons; but, if by their speculations rightly placed, the study of morality and the law of nature were brought more into fashion among men of parts and genius, the discouragements that draw to *scepticism* removed, the measures of right and wrong accurately defined, and the principles of natural religion reduced into regular systems, as artfully disposed and clearly connected as those of some other sciences: there are grounds to think, these effects would not only have a gradual influence in repairing the too much defaced sense of virtue in the world; but also, by showing, that such parts of revelation, as lie within the reach of human inquiry, are most agreeable to right reason, would dispose all prudent, unprejudiced persons, to a modest and wary treatment of those sacred mysteries, which are above the comprehension of our faculties.

It remains, that I desire the reader to withhold his censure of these Dialogues, till he has read them through. Otherwise, he may lay them aside in a mistake of their design, or on account of difficulties or objections which he would find answered in the sequel. A treatise of this nature would require to be once read over coherently, in order to comprehend its design, the proofs, solution of difficulties, and the connection and disposition of its parts. If it be thought to deserve a second reading; this, I imagine, will make the entire scheme very plain: especially, if recourse be had to an Essay I wrote, some years since, upon *Vision*, and the Treatise concerning the *Principles of Human Knowledge*. Wherein divers notions advanced in these *Dialogues*, are farther pursued, or placed in different lights, and other points handled, which naturally tend to confirm and illustrate them.

Philosophical Commentaries

My end is not to deliver Metaphysiques altogether in a General Scholastique way but in some measure to accommodate them to the Sciences, & shew how they may be useful in Optiques, Geometry &c.

I abstain from all flourish & pomp of words & figures using a great plainness & simplicity of stile having oft found it difficult to understand those that use the Lofty & Platonic or Subtil & Scholastique strain.

There are men who say there are insensible extensions, there are others who say the Wall is not white, the fire is not hot &c We Irish men cannot attain to these truths.

The Mathematicians think there are insensible lines, about these they harangue, these cut in a point, at all angles these are divisible and infinitum. We Irish men can conceive no such lines.

How could I venture thoughts into the world, before I knew the[y] would be of use to the world? and how could I know that till I had try'd how the suited other men's ideas.

I Publish not this so much for anything else as to know whether other men have the same Ideas as we Irishmen. this is my end and not to be inform'd as to my own Particular.

I am young, I am an upstart, I am a pretender, I am vain, very well. I shall Endeavour patiently to bear up under the most lessening, vilifying appellations the pride & rage of man can devise. But one thing, I know, I am not guilty of. I do not pin my faith on the sleeve of any great man. I act not out of prejudice & prepossession. I do not adhere to any opinion because it is an old one, a receiv'd one, a fashionable one, or one that I have spent much time in the study and cultivation of.

Mem: most carefully to inculcate & set forth how that the Endeavouring to Express abstract philosophic Thoughts by words unavoidably runs a man into Difficulties.

Mem: upon all occasions to use the Utmost Modesty. to Confute the Mathematicians wth the utmost civility & respect. not to stile them Nihilarians etc:

N.B. to rein in y^r Satyrical nature.

Blame me not if I use my words sometimes in some latitude. 'tis w^t cannot be helpt. Tis the fault of Language that you cannot always apprehend the clear & determinate meaning of my words.

The chief thing I do or pretend to do is onely to remove the mist or veil of Words. This has occasion'd Ignorance & confusion. This has ruin'd the Scholemen & Mathematicians, Lawyers & Divines.

I must acknowlege my self beholding to the Philosophers have gone before me. They have given good rules tho perhaps they do not always observe them. Similitude of Adventurers who tho they them selves attained not the desir'd Port, they by their wrecks have made known the Rocks & sands, whereby the Passage of aftercomers is made more secure & easy.

I must not pretend to promise much of Demonstration, I must cancell all passages that look like that sort of Pride, that raising of Expectation in my Readers.

15

DAVID HUME
My Life

Before going to the University of Edinburgh to study law, David Hume (1711–1776) had read Cicero, the Latin and French poets and essayists, mathematics and natural philosophy, history and moral philosophy. Finding that he had no taste for law, he turned to writing philosophy. Having worked himself ill on what became *A Treatise of Human Nature*, Hume went to France to recuperate. While there he may have had some discussions with scholars at the nearby Jesuit College of La Flèche. When the *Treatise* was published anonymously in 1739–40, it fell, as he said, "stillborn from the press." Stoically weathering his disappointment, he turned to writing *Essays Moral, Political and Literary* (1741–1752). His application for a chairs in philosophy at the University of Edinburgh (1745) and at Glasgow (1752) were refused on the grounds that he was too skeptical, perhaps even irreligious. He received a consolation appointment as Librarian for the Faculty of Advocates in Edinburgh, where he served from 1752–1757. During that time, wrote his *History of England*, published between 1754 and 1762. Much admired for his statecraft, Hume served as a diplomatic secretary in the British embassies of France and Italy from 1746 to 1749 and again from 1763 to 1766.

Hume reworked and re-presented some of the arguments of the *Treatise* in *An Enquiry concerning Human Understanding* (1748) and *An Enquiry concerning the Principles of Morals* (1751). *The Natural History of Religion* appeared in 1757. A close friend of Adam Smith, he also wrote some essays on economic and monetary theory. His brief, characteristically modest autobiography, *My Own Life* (1777), and his *Dialogues on Natural Religion* were published posthumously.

Despite the clarity and directness of his style, Hume is seen as an early proponent of radically different philosophic traditions: he has been characterized as a late skeptic and an early phenomenalist. Some commentators see him as a nominalist; others have considered him a phenomenalist or a precursor of logical positivism. Still others—impressed by his account of the role of the imagination in constructing ideas of causality and personal identity—have classified him as an idealist or even a social constructivist.

The Perils of Philosophy
(A Treatise of Human Nature)

Before I launch out into those immense depths of philosophy, which lie before me, I find myself inclin'd to stop a moment in my present station, and to ponder that voyage, which I have undertaken, and which undoubtedly requires the utmost art and industry to be brought to a happy conclusion. Methinks I am like a man, who having struck on many shoals, and having narrowly escap'd shipwreck in passing a small frith, has yet the temerity to put out to sea in the same leaky weather-beaten vessel, and even carries his ambition so far as to think of compassing the globe under these disadvantageous circumstances. My memory of past errors and perplexities, makes me diffident for the future. The wretched condition, weakness, and disorder of the faculties, I must employ in my enquiries, encrease my apprehensions. And the impossibility of amending or correcting these faculties, reduces me almost to despair, and makes me resolve to perish on the barren rock, on which I am at present, rather than venture myself upon that boundless ocean, which runs out into immensity. This sudden view of my danger strikes me with melancholy; and as 'tis usual for that passion, above all others, to indulge itself; I cannot forbear feeding my despair, with all those desponding reflections, which the present subject furnishes me with in such abundance.

I am first affrighted and confounded with that forelorn solitude, in which I am plac'd in my philosophy, and fancy myself some strange uncouth monster, who not being able to mingle and unite in society, has been expell'd all human commerce, and left utterly abandon'd and disconsolate. Fain wou'd I run into the crowd for shelter and warmth; but cannot prevail with myself to mix with such deformity. I call upon others to join me, in order to make a company apart; but no one will hearken to me. Every one keeps at a distance, and dreads that storm, which beats upon me from every side. I have expos'd myself to the enmity of all metaphysicians, logicians, mathematicians, and even theologians; and can I wonder at the insults I must suffer? I have declar'd my dis-approbation of their systems; and can I be surpriz'd, if they shou'd express a hatred of mine and of my person? When I look abroad, I foresee on every side, dispute, contradiction, anger, calumny and detraction. When I turn my eye inward, I find nothing but doubt and ignorance. All the world conspires to oppose and contradict me; tho' such is my weakness, that I feel all my opinions loosen and fall of themselves, when unsupported by the approbation of others. Every step I take is with hesitation, and every new reflection makes me dread an error and absurdity in my reasoning.

For with what confidence can I venture upon such bold enterprizes, when beside those numberless infirmities peculiar to myself, I find so many which are common to human nature? Can I be sure, that in leaving all establish'd opinions I am following truth; and by what criterion shall I distinguish her, even if fortune shou'd at last guide me on her foot-steps? After the most accurate and exact of my reasonings, I can give no reason why I shou'd assent to it; and feel nothing but a *strong* propensity to consider objects *strongly* in that view, under which they appear to me. Experience is a principle, which instructs me in the several conjunctions of objects for the past. Habit is another principle, which determines me to expect the same for the future; and both of them conspiring to operate upon the imagination, make me form certain ideas in a more intense and lively manner, than others, which are not attended with the same advantages. Without this quality, by which the mind enlivens some ideas beyond others (which seemingly is so trivial, and so little founded on reason) we cou'd never assent to any argument, nor carry our view beyond those few objects, which are present to our senses. Nay, even to these objects we cou'd never attribute any existence, but what was dependent on the senses; and must comprehend them entirely in that succession of perceptions, which constitutes our self or person. Nay farther, even with relation to that succession, we cou'd only admit of those perceptions, which are immediately present to our consciousness, nor cou'd those lively images, with which the memory presents us, be ever receiv'd as true pictures of past perceptions. The memory, senses, and understanding are, therefore, all of them founded on the imagination, or the vivacity of our ideas.

No wonder a principle so inconstant and fallacious shou'd lead us into errors, when implicitely follow'd (as it must be) in all its variations. 'Tis this principle, which makes us reason from causes and effects; and 'tis the same principle, which convinces us of the continu'd existence of external objects, when absent from the senses. But tho' these two operations be equally natural and necessary in the human mind, yet in some circumstances they are directly contrary, nor is it possible for us to reason justly and regularly from causes and effects, and at the same time believe the continu'd existence of matter. How then shall we adjust those principles together? Which of them shall we prefer? Or in case we prefer neither of them, but successively assent to both, as is usual among philosophers, with what confidence can we afterwards usurp that glorious title, when we thus knowingly embrace a manifest contradiction?

This contradiction wou'd be more excusable, were it compensated by any degree of solidity and satisfaction in the other parts of our reasoning. But the case is quite contrary. When we trace up the human understanding to its first principles, we find it to lead us into such sentiments, as seem to turn into ridicule all our past pains and industry, and to discourage us from future enquiries. Nothing is more curiously enquir'd after by the mind of man, than the causes of every phaenomenon; nor are we content with knowing the immediate causes, but push on our enquiries, till we arrive at the original and ultimate principle. We wou'd not willingly stop before we are acquainted with that energy in the cause, by which it operates on its effect; that tie, which connects them together; and that efficacious quality, on which the tie depends. This is our aim in all our studies and reflections: And how must we be disappointed, when we learn, that this connexion, tie, or energy lies merely in ourselves, and is nothing but that determination of the mind, which is acquir'd by custom, and causes us to make a transition from an object to its usual attendant, and from the impression of one to the lively idea of the other? Such a discovery not only cuts off all hope of ever attaining satisfaction, but even prevents our very wishes; since it appears, that when we say we desire to know the ultimate and operating principle, as something, which resides in the external object, we either contradict ourselves, or talk without a meaning.

This deficiency in our ideas is not indeed, perceiv'd in common life, nor are we sensible, that in the most usual conjunctions of cause and effect we are as ignorant of the ultimate principle, which binds them together, as in the most unusual and extraordinary. But this proceeds merely from an illusion of the imagination; and the question is, how far we ought to yield to these illusions. This question is very difficult, and reduces us to a very dangerous dilemma, whichever way we answer it. For if we assent to every trivial suggestion of the fancy; beside that these suggestions are often contrary to each other; they lead us into such errors, absurdities, and obscurities, that we must at last become asham'd of our credulity. Nothing is more dangerous to reason than the flights of the imagination, and nothing has been the occasion of more mistakes among philosophers. Men of bright fancies may in this respect be compar'd to those angels, whom the scripture represents as covering their eyes with their wings. This has already appear'd in so many instances, that we may spare ourselves the trouble of enlarging upon it any farther.

But on the other hand, if the consideration of these instances makes us take a resolution to reject all the trivial suggestions of the fancy, and adhere to the understanding, that is, to the general and more establish'd properties of the imagination; even this resolution, if steadily executed, wou'd be dangerous, and attended with the most fatal consequences. For I have already shewn, that the understanding, when it acts alone, and according to its most general principles, entirely subverts itself, and leaves not the lowest degree of evidence in any proposition, either in philosophy of common life. We save ourselves from this total scepticism only by means of that singular and seemingly trivial property of the fancy, by which we enter with difficulty into remote views of things, and are not able to accompany them with so sensible an impression, as we do those, which are more easy and natural. Shall we, then, establish it for a general maxim, that no refin'd or elaborate reasoning is ever to be receiv'd? Consider well the consequences of such a principle. By this means you cut off entirely all science and philosophy: You proceed upon one singular quality of the imagination, and by a parity of reason must embrace all of them: And you expressly contradict yourself; since this maxim must be built on the preceding reasoning, which will be allow'd to be sufficiently refin'd and metaphysical. What party, then, shall we choose among these difficulties? If we embrace this principle, and condemn all refin'd reasoning, we run into the most manifest absurdities. If we reject it in favour of these reasonings, we subvert entirely the human understanding. We have, therefore, no choice left but betwixt a false reason and none at all. For my part, I know not what ought to be done in the present case. I can only observe what is commonly done; which is, that this difficulty is seldom or never thought of; and even where it has once been present to the mind, is quickly forgot, and leaves but a small impression behind it. Very refin'd reflections have little or no influence upon us; and yet we do not, and cannot establish it for a rule, that they ought not to have any influence; which implies a manifest contradiction.

But what have I here said, that reflections very refin'd and metaphysical have little or no influence upon us? This opinion I can scarce forbear retracting, and condemning from my present feeling and experience. The *intense* view of these manifold contradictions and imperfections in human reason has so wrought upon me, and heated my brain, that I am ready to reject all belief and reasoning, and can look upon no opinion even as more probable or likely than another. Where am I, or what? From what causes do I derive my existence, and to what condition shall I return? Whose favour shall I court, and whose anger must I dread? What beings surround me? and on whom have I any influence, or who have any influence on me? I am confounded with all these questions, and begin to fancy myself in the most deplorable condition imaginable, inviron'd with the deepest darkness, and utterly depriv'd of the use of every member and faculty.

Most fortunately it happens, that since reason is incapable of dispelling these clouds, nature herself suffices to that purpose, and cures me of this philosophical melancholy and delirium, either by relaxing this bent of mind, or by some avocation, and lively impression of my senses, which obliterate all these chimeras. I dine, I play a game of back-gammon, I converse, and am merry with my friends; and when after three or four hours' amusement, I wou'd return to these speculations, they appear so cold, and strain'd, and ridiculous, that I cannot find in my heart to enter into them any farther.

Here then I find myself absolutely and necessarily determin'd to live, and talk, and act like other people in the common affairs of life. But notwithstanding that my natural propensity, and the course of my animal spirits and passions reduce me to this indolent belief in the general maxims of the world, I still feel such remains of my former disposition, that I am ready to throw all my books and papers into the fire, and resolve never more to renounce the pleasures of life for

the sake of reasoning and philosophy. For those are my sentiments in that sple-
netic humour, which governs me at present. I may, nay I must yield to the current
of nature, in submitting to my senses and understanding; and in this blind submission I shew most perfectly my sceptical disposition and principles. But does
it follow, that I must strive against the current of nature, which leads me to
indolence and pleasure; that I must seclude myself, in some measure, from the
commerce and society of men, which is so agreeable; and that I must torture my
brain with subtilities and sophistries, at the very time that I cannot satisfy myself
concerning the reasonableness of so painful an application, nor have any tolerable prospect of arriving by its means at truth and certainty. Under what obligation do I lie of making such an abuse of time? And to what end can it serve
either for the service of mankind, or for my own private interest? No: If I must
be a fool, as all those who reason or believe any thing *certainly* are, my follies
shall at least be natural and agreeable. Where I strive against my inclination, I
shall have a good reason for my resistance; and will no more be led a wandering
into such dreary solitudes, and rough passages, as I have hitherto met with.

These are the sentiments of my spleen and indolence; and indeed I must confess, that philosophy has nothing to oppose to them, and expects a victory more
from the returns of a serious good-humour'd disposition, than from the force of
reason and conviction. In all the incidents of life we ought still to preserve our
scepticism. If we believe, that fire warms, or water refreshes, 'tis only because it
costs us too much pains to think otherwise. Nay if we are philosophers, it ought
only to be upon sceptical principles, and from an inclination, which we feel to
the employing ourselves after that manner. Where reason is lively, and mixes
itself with some propensity, it ought to be assented to. Where it does not, it never
can have any title to operate upon us.

At the time, therefore, that I am tir'd with amusement and company, and have
indulg'd a *reverie* in my chamber, or in a solitary walk by a river-side, I feel my
mind all collected within itself, and am naturally *inclin'd* to carry my view into
all those subjects, about which I have met with so many disputes in the course
of my reading and conversation. I cannot forbear having a curiosity to be acquainted with the principles of moral good and evil, the nature and foundation
of government, and the cause of those several passions and inclinations, which
actuate and govern me. I am uneasy to think I approve of one object, and dis-
approve of another; call one thing beautiful, and another deform'd; decide concerning truth and falshood, reason and folly, without knowing upon what principles I proceed. I am concern'd for the condition of the learned world, which
lies under such a deplorable ignorance in all these particulars. I *feel* an ambition
to arise in me of contributing to the instruction of mankind, and of acquiring a
name by my inventions and discoveries. These sentiments spring up naturally
in my present disposition; and shou'd I endeavour to banish them, by attaching
myself to any other business or diversion, I *feel* I shou'd be a loser in point of
pleasure; and this is the origin of my philosophy.

But even suppose this curiosity and ambition shou'd not transport me into
speculations without the sphere of common life, it wou'd necessarily happen,
that from my very weakness I must be led into such enquiries. 'Tis certain, that
superstition is much more bold in its systems and hypotheses than philosophy;
and while the latter contents itself with assigning new causes and principles to
the phænomena, which appear in the visible world, the former opens a world of
its own, and presents us with scenes, and beings, and objects, which are alto-

gether new. Since therefore 'tis almost impossible for the mind of man to rest, like those of beasts, in that narrow circle of objects, which are the subject of daily conversation and action, we ought only to deliberate concerning the choice of our guide, and ought to prefer that which is safest and most agreeable. And in this respect I make bold to recommend philosophy, and shall not scruple to give it the preference to superstition of every kind or denomination. For as superstition arises naturally and easily from the popular opinions of mankind, it seizes more strongly on the mind, and is often able to disturb us in the conduct of our lives and actions. Philosophy on the contrary, if just, can present us only with mild and moderate sentiments; and if false and extravagant, its opinions are merely the objects of a cold and general speculation, and seldom go so far as to interrupt the course of our natural propensities. The *Cynics* are an extraordinary instance of philosophers, who from reasonings purely philosophical ran into as great extravagancies of conduct as any *Monk* or *Dervise* that ever was in the world. Generally speaking, the errors in religion are dangerous; those in philosophy only ridiculous.

I am sensible, that these two cases of the strength and weakness of the mind will not comprehend all mankind, and that there are in *England*, in particular, many honest gentlemen, who being always employ'd in their domestic affairs, or amusing themselves in common recreations, have carried their thoughts very little beyond those objects, which are every day expos'd to their senses. And indeed, of such as these I pretend not to make philosophers, nor do I expect them either to be associates in these researches or auditors of these discoveries. They do well to keep themselves in their present situation; and instead of refining them into philosophers, I wish we cou'd communicate to our founders of systems, a share of this gross earthy mixture, as an ingredient, which they commonly stand much in need of, and which wou'd serve to temper those fiery particles, of which they are compos'd. While a warm imagination is allow'd to enter into philosophy, and hypotheses embrac'd merely for being specious and agreeable, we can never have any steady principles, nor any sentiments, which will suit with common practice and experience. But were these hypotheses once remov'd, we might hope to establish a system or set of opinions, which if not true (for that, perhaps, is too much to be hop'd for) might at least be satisfactory to the human mind, and might stand the test of the most critical examination. Nor shou'd we despair of attaining this end, because of the many chimerical systems, which have successively arisen and decay'd away among men, wou'd we consider the shortness of that period, wherein these questions have been the subjects of enquiry and reasoning. Two thousand years with such long interruptions, and under such mighty discouragements are a small space of time to give any tolerable perfection to the sciences; and perhaps we are still in too early an age of the world to discover any principles, which will bear the examination of the latest posterity. For my part, my only hope is, that I may contribute a little to the advancement of knowledge, by giving in some particulars a different turn to the speculations of philosophers, and pointing out to them more distinctly those subjects, where alone they can expect assurance and conviction. Human Nature is the only science of man; and yet has been hitherto the most neglected. 'Twill be sufficient for me, if I can bring it a little more into fashion; and the hope of this serves to compose my temper from that spleen, and invigorate it from that indolence, which sometimes prevail upon me. If the reader finds himself in the same easy disposition, let him follow me in my future speculations. If not, let him follow his inclination, and wait the returns of application and good humour. The conduct of a man, who studies philosophy in this careless manner, is more truly sceptical than that of one, who feeling in himself an inclination to it, is yet so over-whelm'd with doubts and scruples, as totally to reject it. A true sceptic will be diffident of his philosophical doubts, as well as of his philosophical conviction; and will never refuse any innocent satisfaction, which offers itself, upon account of either of them.

Nor is it only proper we shou'd in general indulge our inclination in the most elaborate philosophical researches, notwithstanding our sceptical principles, but also that we shou'd yield to that propensity, which inclines us to be positive and certain in *particular points*, according to the light, in which we survey them in any *particular instant*. 'Tis easier to forbear all examination and enquiry, than to check ourselves in so natural a propensity, and guard against that assurance, which always arises from an exact and full survey of an object. On such an occasion we are apt not only to forget our scepticism, but even our modesty too; and make use of such terms as these, *'tis evident, 'tis certain, 'tis undeniable;* which a due deference to the public ought, perhaps, to prevent. I may have fallen into this fault after the example of others; but I here enter a *caveat* against any objections, which may be offer'd on that head; and declare that such expressions were extorted from me by the present view of the object, and imply no dogmatical spirit, nor conceited idea of my own judgment, which are sentiments that I am sensible can become no body, and a sceptic still less than any other.

LETTER TO THE COMTESSE DE BOUFFLERS

Compiègne, 14 July, 1764.

I shall venture to say, dear Madam, that no letter, which even you have ever wrote, conveyed more satisfaction than did that with which you favoured me. What pleasure to receive testimonies and assurances of good-will from a person whom we highly value, and whose sentiments are of such importance to us! You could not possibly have done an action more charitable, than to speak to me in so friendly a manner. You have thereby supplied me for a long time with matter for the most agreeable musing; and I shall henceforth, I hope, bid defiance to all returns of diffidence and jealousy. I confess with shame, that I am but too subject to this sentiment, even in friendship. I never doubt of my friend's probity or honour; but often of his attachment to me, and sometimes, as I have afterwards found, without reason. If such was my disposition even in youth, you may judge that, having arrived at a time of life when I can less expect to please, I must be more subject to inroads of suspicion. Common sense requires that I should keep at a distance from all attachments that can imply passion. But it must surely be the height of folly, to lay myself at the mercy of a person whose situation seems calculated to inspire doubt, and who, being so little at her own disposal, could not be able, even if willing, to seek such remedies as might appease that tormenting sentiment.

Should I meet with one, in any future time, (for to be sure I know of none such at present) who was endowed with graces and charms beyond all expression, whose character and understanding were equally an object of esteem, as her person was of tenderness; I ought to fly her company, to avoid all connexion with her, even such as might bear the name of friendship; and to endeavour to forget her as soon as possible. I know not if it would be prudent even to bid her adieu: surely, it would be highly imprudent to receive from her any testimonies of friendship and regard. But who, in that situation, could have resolution to reject them? Who would not drink up the poison with joy and satisfaction?

But let us return, dear Madam, from imaginary suppositions to our real selves. I am much pleased that your leisure allows you to betake yourself to your old occupation of reading; and that your relish for it still remains entire. I have frequently, in the course of my life, met with interruptions, from business and dissipation; yet always returned to my closet with pleasure. I have no other prospect for easing the burthen of old age than in these enjoyments; and if I sometimes join the chimerical project of relaxing the severities of study, by the society of a person dear to me, and who could have indulgence for me, I consider it a pleasing dream, in which I can repose no confidence. My only comfort is, that I am myself a person free as the air we breathe, and that, wherever such a blessing might present itself, I could there fix my habitation.

LETTER TO THE REV. HUGH BLAIR

Dear Doctor.

I had askd M. Rousseau the Question you propose to me: He answer'd, that the Story of his Heloise had some general and distant Resemblance to Reality; such as was sufficient to warm his Imagination and assist his Invention: But that all the chief Circumstances were fictitious. I have heard in France, that he had been employ'd to teach Music to a young Lady, a Boarder in a Convent at Lyons; and that the Master & Scholar fell mutually in love with each other, but the Affair was not attended with any Consequences. I think this Work his Master-piece; tho' he himself told me, that he valu'd most his *Contrat sociale;* which is as preposterous a Judgement as that of Milton, who preferd the Paradise regaind to all his other Performances.

This Man, the most singular of all human Beings, has at last left me; and I have very little hopes of ever being able for the future to enjoy much of his Company; tho' he says, that, if I settle either in London or Edinburgh, he will take a Journey on foot every Year to visit me. Mr Davenport, a Gentleman of 5 or 6000 pounds in the North of England, and a Man of great Humanity and of a good Understanding, has taken the Charge of him. He has a House, called Wooton, in the Peake of Derby, situated amidst Mountains and Rocks and Streams and Forrests, which pleases the wild Imagination and solitary Humour of Rousseau; and as the Master seldom inhabited it, and only kept there a plain Table for some Servants, he offer'd me to give it up to my Friend: I accepted, on condition that he wou'd take from him 30 pounds a Year of Board, for himself and his Gouvernante, which he was so good natur'd as to agree to. Rousseau has about 80 pounds a Year, which he has acquird by Contracts with his Booksellers, and by a Liferent Annuity of 25 pounds a Year, which he accepted from Lord Mareschal. This is the only Man who has yet been able to make him accept of Money.

He was desperately resolv'd to rush into this Solitude, notwithstanding all my Remonstrances; and I forsee, that he will be unhappy in that Situation, as he has indeed been always, in all Situations. He will be entirely without Occupation, without Company, and almost without Amusement of any kind. He has read very little during the Course of his Life, and has now totally renounc'd all Reading: He has seen very little, and has no manner of Curiosity to see or remark: He has reflected, properly speaking, and study'd very little; and has not indeed much Knowledge: He has only felt, during the whole Course of his Life; and in this Respect, his Sensibility rises to a Pitch beyond what I have seen any Example of: But it still gives him a more acute Feeling of Pain than of Pleasure. He is like a Man who were stript not only of his Cloaths but of his Skin, and turn'd out in that Situation to combat with the rude and boisterous Elements, such as perpetually disturb this lower World. I shall give you a remarkable Instance of his turn of Character in this respect. It passd in my Room, the Evening before his Departure.

He had resolv'd to set out with his Gouvernante in a Post chaise; but Davenport, willing to cheat him and save him some Money, told him, that he had found a Retour Chaise for the Place, which he might have for a Trifle, and that luckily, it set out the very day in which Rousseau intended to depart: His Purpose was to hire a Chaise, and make him believe this Story.

He succeeded at first; but Rousseau, afterwards ruminating on the Circumstances, began to entertain a Suspicion of the Trick. He communicated his Doubts to me, complaining that he was treated like a Child, that tho' he was poor he chose rather to conform himself to his Circumstances than live like a Beggar, on alms, and that he was very unhappy in not speaking the Language familiarly, so as to guard himself against these Impositions. I told him, that I was ignorant of the Matter, and knew nothing more of it than I was told by Mr Davenport; but if he pleas'd I shou'd make Enquiry about it. *Never tell me that*, reply'd he, *if this be really a Contrivance of Davenports, you are acquainted with it, and consenting to it; and you cou'd not possibly have done me a greater Displeasure.* Upon which he sate down very sullen and silent; and all my Attempts were in vain to revive the Conversation and to turn it on other Subjects: He still answerd me very dryly & coldly. At last, after passing near an Hour in this ill-humour, he rose up and took a Turn about the Room: But Judge of my Surprize, when he sat down suddenly on my Knee, threw his hands about my Neck, kiss'd me with the greatest Warmth, and bedewing all my Face with Tears, exclaim'd, *Is it possible you can ever forgive me, my Dear Friend: After all the Testimonies of Affection I have receivd from you, I reward you at last with this Folly & ill Behaviour: But I have notwithstanding a Heart worthy of your Friendship: I love you, I esteem you; and not an Instance of your Kindness is thrown away upon me.* I hope you have not so bad an Opinion of me as to think I was not melted on this Occasion: I assure you I kissd him and embrac'd him twenty times, with a plentiful Effusion of Tears. I think no Scene of my Life was ever more affecting.

I now understand perfectly his Aversion to company, which appears so surprizing in a Man well qualify'd for the Entertainment of Company, and which the greatest Part of the World takes for Affectation. He has frequent and long Fits of the Spleen, from the State of his Mind or Body, call it which you please, and from his extreme Sensibility of Temper. During that Disposition, Company is a Torment to him. When his Spirits and Health & good Humour return, his Fancy affords him so much & such agreeable Occupation that to call him off from it gives him Uneasyness; and even the writing of Books, he tells me, as it limits and restrains his Fancy to one Subject, is not an agreeable Entertainment. He never will write any more; and never shou'd have wrote at all, could he have slept a nights. But he lies awake commonly, and to keep himself from tiring he usually compos'd something which he wrote down when he arose. He assures me, that he composes very slowly and with great Labour and Difficulty.

He is naturally very modest, and even ignorant of his own Superiority: His Fire, which frequently rises in Conversation, is gentle and temperate; he is never, in the least, arrogant & domineering, and is indeed one of the best bred Men I ever knew. I shall give you such an Instance of his Modesty as must necessarily be sincere. When we were on the Road I recommended to him the learning of English, without which, I told him, he wou'd never enjoy entire Liberty, nor be fully independant, and at his own Disposal. He was sensible I was in the right; and said, that he heard there were two English Translations of his *Emile* or *Treatise of Education:* He would get them, as soon as he arriv'd in London; and as he knew the Subject, he would have no other Trouble than to learn or guess the Words: This woud save him some Pains in consulting the Dictionary; and as he improvd, it would amuse him to compare the Translations, and judge which was the best. Accordingly, soon after our Arrival, I procurd him the Books; but he returnd them in a few days, saying that they coud be of no Use to him. *What is the Matter*, reply'd I. *I cannot endure them*, said he, *they are my own Work; and ever since I deliverd my Books to the Press, I never coud open them or read a Page of them without Disgust. That is Strange*, said I, *I wonder the good Reception they have met with from the World has not put you more in conceit with them. Why!* said he, *if I were to count Suffrages, there are perhaps more against them than for them. But*, rejoind I, *it is impossible but the Style & Eloquence and Ornaments must please you. To tell the Truth*, said he, *I am not displeasd with myself in that particular: But I still dread, that my Writings are good for nothing at the bottom, and that all my Theories are full of Extragance.* Je craigne toujours que je peche par le fond, et que touts mes systemes ne sont que des extravagances. You see, that this is judging himself with the utmost Severity, and censuring his Writings on the Side where they are most expos'd to Criticism. No feign'd Modesty is ever capable of this Courage. I never heard Robertson reproach himself with the godly Strain of his History: No body ever heard you express any Remorse for having put Ossian on the same footing with Homer.

Have I tir'd you, or will you have any more Anecdotes of this singular Personage? I think I hear you desire me to go on. He attempted once to justify to me the Moral of his new Heloisa, which, he knew, was blam'd, as instructing young People in the Art of gratifying their Passions, under the Cover of Virtue and noble refind Sentiments. *You may observe*, said he, *that my Julia is faithful to her Husband's Bed, tho she is seduc'd from her Duty during her single State. But this last Circumstance can be of no Consequence in France, where all the young Ladies are shut up in Convents & have it not in their power to transgress: It might indeed have a bad Effect in a protestant Country.* But notwithstanding this Reflection, he told me, that he has wrote a Continuation of his Emilius, which may soon be published: He there attempts to show the Effect of his Plan of Education, by representing Emilius in all the most trying Situations, and still extricating himself with Courage & Virtue. Among the rest, he discovers that Sophia, the amiable, the virtuous, the estimable Sophia is unfaithful to his Bed, which fatal Accident he bears with a manly, superior Spirit. *In this Work*, added he, *I have endeavourd to represent Sophia in such a light that she will appear equally amiable, equally virtuous, & equally estimable, as if she had no such Frailty. You take a Pleasure, I see*, said I, *to combat with Difficulties in all your Works. Yes,* said he, *I hate marvellous & supernatural Events in Novels. The only thing that can give pleasure in such Performances is to place the Personages in Situations difficult and singular.* Thus you see, that nothing remains for him but to write a Book for the Instruction of Widows; unless perhaps he imagines that they can learn their Lesson without Instruction.

Adieu, Dear Doctor: You say that you sometimes read my Letters to our common Friends; but you must read this only to the initiated. Yours, usque ad aras

David Hume

Lisle Street, Leicester Fields
25 of March 1766
To The Reverend Dr Hugh Blair at Edinburgh

LETTER TO JEAN-JACQUES ROUSSEAU

My dear Sir

We have had very bad Weather for some time past, which has made me uneasy with regard to you. I hope you was able to get thro' the Mountains of Derbyshire without any bad Accident.

The Artist has brought me a Model of your Bust, and told me, that you intended it for a Friend. Pray tell me to whom I shall deliver it.

Mr Malthus was with me to day, who desires his Compliments to you.

Yours sincerely
David Hume

27 of March 1766

LETTER TO THE COMTESSE DE BOUFFLERS

Lisle Street, Leicester Fields, April 3, 1766.

It is impossible for me, dear Madam, to express the difficulty which I have to bear your absence, and the continual want which I feel of your society. I had accustomed myself, of a long time, to think of you as a friend from whom I was never to be separated during any considerable time; and I had flattered myself that we were peculiarly fitted to pass our lives in intimacy and cordiality with each other. Age and a natural equability of temper were in danger of reducing my heart to too great indifference about every thing: it was enlivened by the charms of your conversation, and the vivacity of your character. Your mind, more agitated both by unhappy circumstances in your situation and by your natural disposition, could repose itself in the more calm sympathy which you found with me. But behold! three months are elapsed since I left you; and it is impossible for me to assign a time when I can hope to join you.

Oh, my dear friend, how I dread that it may still be long ere you reach a state of tranquility, in a distress which so little admits of any remedy, and which the natural elevation of your character, instead of putting you above it, makes you feel with greater sensibility. I could only wish to administer the temporary consolation, which the presence of a friend never fails to afford.

The chief circumstance which hinders me from repenting of my journey, is the use I have been to poor Rousseau, the most singular, and often the most amiable man in the world.

I have now settled him in a manner entirely to my satisfaction, and to his own. . . .

I must however confess, that I have not the consolation to think he will long be happy there. Never was man, who so well deserves happiness, so little calculated by nature to attain it. The extreme sensibility of his character is one great cause; but still more, the frequent and violent fits of spleen and discontent and impatience, to which, either from the constitution of his mind or body, he is so subject. These disqualify him for society, and are the chief reason why he so much affects solitude. When his health and good-humour return, his lively imagination gives him so much entertainment, that company, by disturbing his musing and meditation, is rather troublesome to him; so that, in either case, he is not framed for society. He is commonly however the best company in the world, when he will submit to live with men. Every one who saw him here, admires the simplicity of his manners, his natural unaffected politeness, the gaiety and finesse of his conversation. For my part, I never saw a man, and very few women, of a more agreeable commerce.

I shall tell you a very singular story of him, which proves his extreme sensibility and good heart. Mr Davenport had thought of a contrivance to save him part of the expenses of his journey. He hired a chaise, and told him that it was a retour chaise, which would only cost a trifle. He succeeded at first; but M. Rousseau, the evening before his departure, began to entertain suspicions from some circumstances which had escaped Mr Davenport's attention. He complained to me grievously of the trick, and said that, though he was poor, he chose rather to conform himself to his circumstances, than live like a beggar upon alms; and such pretended favours were real injuries. I replied, that I was ignorant of the matter, but should inform myself of Mr Davenport. No, cried he, no; if this be a contrivance, you are not ignorant of it: it has not been executed without your connivance and consent; but nothing could possibly be more disagreeable to me. Upon which he sate down in a very sullen humour; and all attempts which I could make, to revive the conversation and turn it on other subjects, were in vain. After near an hour, he rose up, and walked a little about the room. Judge of my surprise when, all of a sudden, he sat down upon my knee, threw his arms about my neck, kissed me with the greatest ardour, and bedewed all my face with tears! Ah, my dear friend, exclaimed he, is it possible you can ever forgive my folly? This ill humour is the return I make you for all the instances of your kindness towards me. But notwithstanding all my faults and follies, I have a heart worthy of your friendship, because it knows both to love and to esteem you.

I hope, dear Madam, that you have not so bad an opinion of me as not to think I was extremely affected with this scene. I confess that my tears flowed as plentifully as his; and that I embraced him with no less cordiality.

My Own Life

It is difficult for a man to speak long of himself without vanity; therefore, I shall be short. It may be thought an instance of vanity that I pretend at all to write my life; but this Narrative shall contain little more than the History of my Writings; as, indeed, almost all my life has been spent in literary pursuits and occupations. The first success of most of my writings was not such as to be an object of vanity.

I was born the 26th of April 1711, old style, at Edinburgh. I was of a good family, both by father and mother: my father's family is a branch of the Earl of Home's, or Hume's; and my ancestors had been proprietors of the estate, which my brother possesses, for several generations. My mother was daughter of Sir

David Falconer, President of the College of Justice: the title of Lord Halkerton came by succession to her brother.

My family, however, was not rich, and being myself a younger brother, my patrimony, according to the mode of my country, was of course very slender. My father, who passed for a man of parts, died when I was an infant, leaving me, with an elder brother and a sister, under the care of our mother, a woman of singular merit, who, though young and handsome, devoted herself entirely to the rearing and educating of her children. I passed through the ordinary course of education with success, and was seized very early with a passion for literature, which has been the ruling passion of my life, and the great source of my enjoyments. My studious disposition, my sobriety, and my industry, gave my family a notion that the law was a proper profession for me; but I found an unsurmountable aversion to every thing but the pursuits of philosophy and general learning; and while they fancied I was poring upon Voet and Vinnius, Cicero and Virgil were the authors which I was secretly devouring.

My very slender fortune, however, being unsuitable to this plan of life, and my health being a little broken by my ardent application, I was tempted, or rather forced, to make a very feeble trial for entering into a more active scene of life. In 1734, I went to Bristol, with some recommendations to eminent merchants, but in a few months found that scene totally unsuitable to me. I went over to France, with a view of prosecuting my studies in a country retreat; and I there laid that plan of life, which I have steadily and successfully pursued. I resolved to make a very rigid frugality supply my deficiency of fortune, to maintain unimpaired my independency, and to regard every object as contemptible, except the improvement of my talents in literature.

During my retreat in France, first at Reims, but chiefly at La Fleche, in Anjou, I composed my *Treatise of Human Nature*. After passing three years very agreeably in that country, I came over to London in 1737. In the end of 1738, I published my Treatise, and immediately went down to my mother and my brother, who lived at his country-house, and was employing himself very judiciously and successfully in the improvement of his fortune.

Never literary attempt was more unfortunate than my Treatise of Human Nature. It fell *dead-born from the press*, without reaching such distinction, as even to excite a murmur among the zealots. But being naturally of a cheerful and sanguine temper, I very soon recovered the blow, and prosecuted with great ardour my studies in the country. In 1742, I printed at Edinburgh the first part of my Essays: the work was favourably received, and soon made me entirely forget my former disappointment. I continued with my mother and brother in the country, and in that time recovered the knowledge of the Greek language, which I had too much neglected in my early youth.

In 1745, I received a letter from the Marquis of Annandale, inviting me to come and live with him in England; I found also, that the friends and family of that young nobleman were desirous of putting him under my care and direction, for the state of his mind and health required it.—I lived with him a twelvemonth. My appointments during that time made a considerable accession to my small fortune. I then received an invitation from General St. Clair to attend him as a secretary to his expedition, which was at first meant against Canada, but ended in an incursion on the coast of France. Next year, to wit, 1747, I received an invitation from the General to attend him in the same station in his military embassy to the courts of Vienna and Turin. I then wore the uniform of an officer, and was introduced at these courts as aid-de-camp to the general, along with Sir Harry Erskine and Captain Grant, now General Grant. These two years were almost the only interruptions which my studies have received during the course of my life: I passed them agreeably, and in good company; and my appointments, with my frugality, had made me reach a fortune, which I called independent, though most of my friends were inclined to smile when I said so; in short, I was now master of near a thousand pounds.

I had always entertained a notion, that my want of success in publishing the *Treatise of Human Nature*, had proceeded more from the manner than the matter, and that I had been guilty of a very usual indiscretion, in going to the press too early. I, therefore, cast the first part of that work anew in the *Enquiry concerning Human Understanding*, which was published while I was at Turin. But this piece was at first little more successful than the *Treatise of Human Nature*. On my return from Italy, I had the mortification to find all England in a ferment, on account of Dr. Middleton's *Free Enquiry*, while my performance was entirely overlooked and neglected. A new edition, which had been published at London of my *Essays, moral and political*, met not with a much better reception.

Such is the force of natural temper, that these disappointments made little or no impression on me. I went down in 1749, and lived two years with my brother at his country-house, for my mother was now dead. I there composed the second part of my Essays, which I called *Political Discourses*, and also my *Enquiry concerning the Principles of Morals*, which is another part of my treatise that I cast anew. Meanwhile, my bookseller, A. Millar, informed me, that my former publications (all but the unfortunate Treatise) were beginning to be the subject of conversation; that the sale of them was gradually increasing, and that new editions were demanded. Answers by Reverends, and Right Reverends, came out two or three in a year; and I found, by Dr. Warburton's railing, that the books were beginning to be esteemed in good company. However, I had fixed a resolution, which I inflexibly maintained, never to reply to any body; and not being very irascible in my temper, I have easily kept myself clear of all literary squabbles. These symptoms of a rising reputation gave me encouragement, as I was ever more disposed to see the favourable than unfavourable side of things; a turn of mind which it is more happy to possess, than to be born to an estate of ten thousand a year.

In 1751, I removed from the country to the town, the true scene for a man of letters. In 1752, were published at Edinburgh, where I then lived, my *Political Discourses*, the only work of mine that was successful on the first publication. It was well received abroad and at home. In the same year was published at London, my *Enquiry concerning the Principles of Morals*; which, in my own opinion (who ought not to judge on that subject), is of all my writings, historical, philosophical, or literary, incomparably the best. It came unnoticed and unobserved into the world.

In 1752, the Faculty of Advocates chose me their Librarian, an office from which I received little or no emolument, but which gave me the command of a large library. I then formed the plan of writing the *History of England*; but being frightened with the notion of continuing a narrative through a period of 1700 years, I commenced with the accession of the House of Stuart, an epoch when, I thought, the misrepresentations of faction began chiefly to take place. I was, I own, sanguine in my expectations of the success of this work. I thought that I was the only historian, that had at once neglected present power, interest, and authority, and the cry of popular prejudices; and as the subject was suited to every capacity, I expected proportional applause. But miserable was my disappointment: I was assailed by one cry of reproach, disapprobation, and even detestation; English, Scotch, and Irish, Whig and Tory, churchman and sectary, freethinker and religionist, patriot and courtier, united in their rage against the man, who had presumed to shed a generous tear for the fate of Charles I. and the Earl of Strafford; and after the first ebullitions of their fury were over, what was still more mortifying, the book seemed to sink into oblivion. Mr. Millar told me, that in a twelvemonth he sold only forty-five copies of it. I scarcely, indeed, heard of one man in the three kingdoms, considerable for rank or letters, that could endure the book. I must only except the primate of England, Dr. Herring, and the primate of Ireland, Dr. Stone, which seem two odd exceptions. These dignified prelates separately sent me messages not to be discouraged.

I was, however, I confess, discouraged; and had not the war been at that time breaking out between France and England, I had certainly retired to some provincial town of the former kingdom, have changed my name, and never more have returned to my native country. But as this scheme was not now practicable, and the subsequent volume was considerably advanced, I resolved to pick up courage and to persevere.

In this interval, I published at London my *Natural History of Religion*, along with some other small pieces: its public entry was rather obscure, except only that Dr. Hurd wrote a pamphlet against it, with all the illiberal petulance, arrogance, and scurrility, which distinguish the Warburtonian school. This pamphlet gave me some consolation for the otherwise indifferent reception of my performance.

In 1756, two years after the fall of the first volume, was published the second volume of my History, containing the period from the death of Charles I. till the Revolution. This performance happened to give less displeasure to the Whigs, and was better received. It not only rose itself, but helped to buoy up its unfortunate brother.

But though I had been taught by experience, that the Whig party were in possession of bestowing all places, both in the state and in literature, I was so little inclined to yield to their senseless clamour, that in above a hundred alterations, which farther study, reading, or reflection engaged me to make in the reigns of the two first Stuarts, I have made all of them invariably to the Tory side. It is ridiculous to consider the English constitution before that period as a regular plan of liberty.

In 1759, I published my *History of the House of Tudor*. The clamour against this performance was almost equal to that against the History of the two first Stuarts. The reign of Elizabeth was particularly obnoxious. But I was now callous against the impressions of public folly, and continued very peaceably and contentedly in my retreat at Edinburgh, to finish, in two volumes, the more early part of the English History, which I gave to the public in 1761, with tolerable, and but tolerable success.

But, notwithstanding this variety of winds and seasons, to which my writings had been exposed, they had still been making such advances, that the copy-money given me by the booksellers, much exceeded any thing formerly known in England; I was become not only independent, but opulent. I retired to my native country of Scotland, determined never more to set my foot out of it; and retaining the satisfaction of never having preferred a request to one great man, or even making advances of friendship to any of them. As I was now turned of fifty, I thought of passing all the rest of my life in this philosophical manner, when I received, in 1763, an invitation from the Earl of Hertford, with whom I was not in the least acquainted, to attend him on his embassy to Paris, with a near prospect of being appointed secretary to the embassy; and, in the meanwhile, of performing the functions of that office. This offer, however inviting, I at first declined, both because I was reluctant to begin connexions with the great, and because I was afraid that the civilities and gay company of Paris, would prove disagreeable to a person of my age and humour: but on his lordship's repeating the invitation, I accepted of it. I have every reason, both of pleasure and interest, to think myself happy in my connexions with that nobleman, as well as afterwards with his brother, General Conway.

Those who have not seen the strange effects of modes, will never imagine the reception I met with at Paris, from men and women of all ranks and stations. The more I resiled from their excessive civilities, the more I was loaded with them. There is, however, a real satisfaction in living at Paris, from the great number of sensible, knowing, and polite company with which that city abounds above all places in the universe. I thought once of settling there for life.

I was appointed secretary to the embassy; and, in summer 1765, Lord Hertford left me, being appointed Lord Lieutenant of Ireland. I was *chargé d'affaires* till the arrival of the Duke of Richmond, towards the end of the year. In the beginning of 1766, I left Paris, and next summer went to Edinburgh, with the same view as formerly, of burying myself in a philosophical retreat. I returned to that place, not richer, but with much more money, and a much larger income, by means of Lord Hertford's friendship, than I left it; and I was desirous of trying what superfluity could produce, as I had formerly made an experiment of a competency. But, in 1767, I received from Mr. Conway an invitation to be Under-secretary; and this invitation, both the character of the person, and my connexions with Lord Hertford, prevented me from declining. I returned to Edinburgh in 1769, very opulent (for I possessed a revenue of 1000*l.* a year), healthy, and though somewhat stricken in years, with the prospect of enjoying long my ease, and of seeing the increase of my reputation.

In spring 1775, I was struck with a disorder in my bowels, which at first gave me no alarm, but has since, as I apprehend it, become mortal and incurable. I now reckon upon a speedy dissolution. I have suffered very little pain from my disorder; and what is more strange, have, notwithstanding the great decline of my person, never suffered a moment's abatement of my spirits; insomuch, that were I to name the period of my life, which I should most choose to pass over again, I might be tempted to point to this later period. I possess the same ardour as ever in study, and the same gaiety in company. I consider, besides, that a man of sixty-five, by dying, cuts off only a few years of infirmities; and though I see many symptoms of my literary reputation's breaking out at last with additional lustre, I knew that I could have but few years to enjoy it. It is difficult to be more detached from life than I am at present.

To conclude historically with my own character. I am, or rather was (for that is the style I must now use in speaking of myself, which emboldens me the more to speak my sentiments); I was, I say, a man of mild dispositions, of command of temper, of an open, social, and cheerful humour, capable of attachment, but little susceptible of enmity, and of great moderation in all my passions. Even my love of literary fame, my ruling passion, never soured my temper, notwithstanding my frequent disappointments. My company was not unacceptable to the young and careless, as well as to the studious and literary; and as I took a particular pleasure in the company of modest women, I had no reason to be displeased with the reception I met with from them. In a word, though most men any wise eminent, have found reason to complain of calumny, I never was touched, or even attacked by her baleful tooth: and though I wantonly exposed myself to the rage of both civil and religious factions, they seemed to be disarmed in my behalf of their wonted fury. My friends never had occasion to vindicate any one circumstance of my character and conduct: not but that the zealots, we may well suppose, would have been glad to invent and propagate any story to my disadvantage, but they could never find any which they thought would wear the face of probability. I cannot say there is no vanity in making this funeral oration of myself, but I hope it is not a misplaced one; and this is a matter of fact which is easily cleared and ascertained.

April 18, 1776.

Letter from Adam Smith, LL.D.
to William Strahan, Esq.

Kirkaldy, Fifeshire, Nov. 9, 1776.

Dear Sir,

It is with a real, though a very melancholy pleasure, that I sit down to give you some account of the behaviour of our late excellent friend, Mr. Hume, during his last illness.

Though, in his own judgment, his disease was mortal and incurable, yet he allowed himself to be prevailed upon, by the entreaty of his friends, to try what might be the effects of a long journey. A few days before he set out, he wrote that account of his own life, which, together with his other papers, he has left to your care. My account, therefore, shall begin where his ends.

He set out for London towards the end of April, and at Morpeth met with Mr. John Home and myself, who had both come down from London on purpose to see him, expecting to have found him at Edinburgh. Mr. Home returned with him, and attended him during the whole of his stay in England, with that care and attention which might be expected from a temper so perfectly friendly and affectionate. As I had written to my mother that she might expect me in Scotland, I was under the necessity of continuing my journey. His disease seemed to yield to exercise and change of air, and when he arrived in London, he was apparently in much better health than when he left Edinburgh. He was advised to go to Bath to drink the waters, which appeared for some time to have so good an effect upon him, that even he himself began to entertain, what he was not apt to do, a better opinion of his own health. His symptoms, however, soon returned with their usual violence, and from that moment he gave up all thoughts of recovery, but submitted with the utmost cheerfulness, and the most perfect complacency and resignation. Upon his return to Edinburgh, though he found himself much weaker, yet his cheerfulness never abated, and he continued to divert himself, as usual, with correcting his own works for a new edition, with reading books of amusement, with the conversation of his friends; and, sometimes in the evening, with a party at his favourite game of whist. His cheerfulness was so great, and his conversation and amusements run so much in their usual strain, that, notwithstanding all bad symptoms, many people could not believe he was dying. "I shall tell your friend, Colonel Edmondstone," said Doctor Dundas to him one day, "that I left you much better, and in a fair way of recovery." "Doctor," said he, "as I believe you would not chuse to tell any thing but the truth, you had better tell him, that I am dying as fast as my enemies, if I have any, could wish, and as easily and cheerfully as my best friends could desire." Colonel Edmondstone soon afterwards came to see him, and take leave of him; and on his way home, he could not forbear writing him a letter bidding him once more an eternal adieu, and applying to him, as to a dying man, the beautiful French verses in which the Abbé Chaulieu, in expectation of his own death, laments his approaching separation from his friend, the Marquis de la Fare. Mr. Hume's magnanimity and firmness were such, that his most affectionate friends knew, that they hazarded nothing in talking or writing to him as to a dying man, and that so far from being hurt by this frankness, he was rather pleased and flattered by it. I happened to come into his room while he was reading this letter, which he had just received, and which he immediately showed me. I told him, that though I was sensible how very much he was weakened, and that appearances were in many respects very bad, yet his cheerfulness was still so great, the spirit of life seemed still to be so very strong in him, that I could not help entertaining some faint hopes. He answered, "Your hopes are groundless. An habitual diarrhoea of more than a year's standing, would be a very bad disease at any age: at my age it is a mortal one. When I lie down in the evening, I feel myself weaker than when I rose in the morning; and when I rise in the morning, weaker than when I lay down in the evening. I am sensible, besides, that some of my vital parts are affected, so that I must soon die." "Well," said I, "if it must be so, you have at least the satisfaction of leaving all your friends, your brother's family in particular, in great prosperity." He said that he felt that satisfaction so sensibly, that when he was reading a few days before, Lucian's *Dialogues of the Dead*, among all the excuses which are alleged to Charon for not entering readily into his boat, he could not find one that fitted him; he had no house to finish, he had no daughter to provide for, he had no enemies upon whom he wished to revenge himself. "I could not well imagine," said he, "what excuse I could make to Charon in order to obtain a little delay. I have done every thing of consequence which I ever meant to do, and I could at no time expect to leave my relations and friends in a better situation than that in which I am now likely to leave them; I, therefore, have all reason to die contented." He then diverted himself with inventing several jocular excuses, which he supposed he might make to Charon, and with imagining the very surly answers which it might suit the character of Charon to return to them. "Upon further consideration," said he, "I thought I might say to him, Good Charon, I have been correcting my works for a new edition. Allow me a little time, that I may see how the Public receives the alterations." But Charon would answer, "When you have seen the effect of these, you will be for making other alterations. There will be no end of such excuses; so, honest friend, please step into the boat." But I might still urge, "Have a little patience, good Charon, I have been endeavouring to open the eyes of the Public. If I live a few years longer, I may have the satisfaction of seeing the downfall of some of the prevailing systems of superstition." But Charon would then lose all temper and decency. "You loitering rogue, that will not happen these many hundred years. Do you fancy I will grant you a lease for so long a term? Get into the boat this instant, you lazy loitering rogue."

But, though Mr. Hume always talked of his approaching dissolution with great cheerfulness, he never affected to make any parade of his magnanimity. He never mentioned the subject but when the conversation naturally led to it, and never dwelt longer upon it than the course of the conversation happened to require: it was a subject indeed which occurred pretty frequently, in consequence of the inquiries which his friends, who came to see him, naturally made concerning the state of his health. The conversation which I mentioned above, and which passed on Thursday the 8th of August, was the last, except one, that I ever had with him. He had now become so very weak, that the company of his most intimate friends fatigued him; for his cheerfulness was still so great, his complaisance and social disposition were still so entire, that when any friend was with him, he could not help talking more, and with greater exertion, than suited the weakness of his body. At his own desire, therefore, I agreed to leave Edinburgh, where I was staying partly upon his account, and returned to my mother's house here, at Kirkaldy, upon condition that he would send for me whenever he wished to see me; the physician who saw him most frequently, Doctor Black, undertaking, in the mean time, to write me occasionally an account of the state of his health.

On the 22d of August, the Doctor wrote me the following letter:

"Since my last, Mr. Hume has passed his time pretty easily, but is much weaker. He sits up, goes down stairs once a day, and amuses himself with reading, but seldom sees any body. He finds that even the conversation of his most intimate friends fatigues and oppresses him; and it is happy that he does not need it, for he is quite free from anxiety, impatience, or low spirits, and passes his time very well with the assistance of amusing books."

I received the day after a letter from Mr. Hume himself, of which the following is an extract.

Edinburgh, 23d August, 1776.
"My dearest friend, I am obliged to make use of my nephew's hand in writing to you, as I do not rise to-day. . . .

"I go very fast to decline, and last night had a small fever, which I hoped might put a quicker period to this tedious illness, but unluckily it has, in a great measure, gone off. I cannot submit to your coming over here on my account, as it is possible for me to see you so small a part of the day, but Doctor Black can better inform you concerning the degree of strength which may from time to time remain with me. Adieu, &c."

Three days after I received the following letter from Doctor Black.

Edinburgh, Monday, 26th August, 1776.
"Dear Sir, Yesterday about four o'clock afternoon, Mr. Hume expired. The near approach of his death became evident in the night between Thursday and Friday, when his disease became excessive, and soon weakened him so much, that he could no longer rise out of his bed. He continued to the last perfectly sensible, and free from much pain or feelings of distress. He never dropped the smallest expression of impatience; but when he had occasion to speak to the people about him, always did it with affection and tenderness. I thought it improper to write to bring you over, especially as I heard that he had dictated

a letter to you desiring you not to come. When he became very weak, it cost him an effort to speak, and he died in such a happy composure of mind, that nothing could exceed it."

Thus died our most excellent, and never to be forgotten friend; concerning whose philosophical opinions men will, no doubt, judge variously, every one approving, or condemning them, according as they happen to coincide or disagree with his own; but concerning whose character and conduct there can scarce be a difference of opinion. His temper, indeed, seemed to be more happily balanced, if I may be allowed such an expression, than that perhaps of any other man I have ever known. Even in the lowest state of his fortune, his great and necessary frugality never hindered him from exercising, upon proper occasions, acts both of charity and generosity. It was a frugality founded, not upon avarice, but upon the love of independency. The extreme gentleness of his nature never weakened either the firmness of his mind, or the steadiness of his resolutions. His constant pleasantry was the genuine effusion of good-nature and good-humour, tempered with delicacy and modesty, and without even the slightest tincture of malignity, so frequently the disagreeable source of what is called wit in other men. It never was the meaning of his raillery to mortify; and therefore, far from offending, it seldom failed to please and delight, even those who were the objects of it. To his friends, who were frequently the objects of it, there was not perhaps any one of all his great and amiable qualities, which contributed more to endear his conversation. And that gaiety of temper, so agreeable in society, but which is so often accompanied with frivolous and superficial qualities, was in him certainly attended with the most severe application, the most extensive learning, the greatest depth of thought, and a capacity in every respect the most comprehensive. Upon the whole, I have always considered him, both in his lifetime and since his death, as approaching as nearly to the idea of a perfectly wise and virtuous man, as perhaps the nature of human frailty will permit.

I ever am, dear Sir,
Most affectionately your's,
Adam Smith.

iii

FROM VICO TO
SCHOPENHAUER

16

GIAMBATTISTA VICO
Imagination, Language, and the Inventions of Philosophy

Born in Naples, Giambattista Vico (1668–1744) attended a Jesuit school but was primarily self-taught, reading widely in philosophy and Roman history. Appointed professor of rhetoric at the University of Naples, he offered a set of lectures on the history of pedagogy, "On the Method of Studies in Our Time" (1709). His ambitious work *On Universal Law* (1720–1721) was not well received. Although he was denied a prestigious chair of law in 1723, Charles of Bourbon nevertheless appointed him as royal historiographer in 1735. Revised in 1725 and again in 1730, *La Scienza Nuova* was posthumously published in its final form in 1744. Written partly in the third person, Vico's *Autobiography* (1728–1731) combines strong partisanship with cool distance.

Vico's "new science" was based on the premise that men can only truly understand what they have invented or constructed: mathematics, history, civic institutions. He outlined the stages of human development from bestiality to primitive superstition to heroism and finally to "the age of humanity." Vico thought that these transformations in mentality are expressed in distinctive modes of reasoning and motivation as well as in social and economic organization. Despite its apparent developmental force, history is not straightforwardly progressive: internal disorders in each historical period typically trigger cyclical regressions.

Vico's influence extended broadly. His emphasis on the originating power of the imagination—myth, *fantasia*, poetry—strongly inspired the Romanticist rejection of reductive materialist science. Michelet, Croce, and Isaiah Berlin admired his philosophy of history; James Joyce and Coleridge appropriated his theory of the imagination; Edmund Leach tried to bring his anthropology to the attention of Anglo-American scholars.

Vico Speaks of His Life
From the *Autobiography*

He applied himself seriously to the ethics of the ancient Greeks, beginning with that of Aristotle, to which, as he had observed in his reading, the authorities on the various principles of the civil institutes frequently referred. And in this study he noticed that Roman jurisprudence was an art of equity conveyed by innumerable specific precepts of natural law which the jurists had extracted from the reasons of the laws and the intentions of the legislators. But the science of justice taught by moral philosophers proceeded from a few eternal truths dictated in metaphysics by an ideal justice, which in the work of cities plays the rôle of architect and commands the two particular justices, the commutative and the distributive, as it were two divine artisans, to measure utilities by two eternal measures, namely the two proportions demonstrated in mathematics, the arithmetical and the geometrical. Thus he began to realize how the legal discipline is less than half learned by the method of study which is commonly observed. Hence he was again brought round to the study of metaphysics, but since in this connection that of Aristotle, which he had learned from Suarez, was of no help to him, nor could he see the reason why, he proceeded to study that of Plato, guided only by his fame as the prince of divine philosophers. Only after he had made considerable progress did he understand why the metaphysics of Aristotle had been of no avail to him in the study of moral philosophy, as indeed it had not availed Averroes, whose *Commentary* left the Arabs no more humane or civilized than they had been before. For the metaphysics of Aristotle leads to a physical principle, which is matter, from which the particular forms are drawn; and indeed makes God a potter who works at things outside himself. But the metaphysics of Plato leads to a metaphysical principle, which is the eternal idea, drawing out and creating matter from itself, like a seminal spirit that forms its own egg. In conformity with this metaphysic he founds a moral philosophy on an ideal or architectonic virtue or justice. Consequently he devoted himself to meditating an ideal commonwealth, to which he gave, in his laws, an equally ideal justice. So that from the time that Vico felt himself dissatisfied with the metaphysic of Aristotle as an aid to the understanding of moral philosophy, and found himself instructed by that of Plato, there began to dawn on him, without his being aware of it, the thought of meditating an ideal eternal law that should be observed in a universal city after the idea or design of providence, upon which idea have since been founded all the commonwealths of all times and all nations. This was the ideal republic that Plato should have contemplated as a consequence of his metaphysic; but he was shut off from it by ignorance of the fall of the first man.

At the same time the philosophical writings of Cicero, Aristotle and Plato, all worked out with a view to the good ordering of mankind in civil society, caused him to take little or no pleasure in the moral philosophies of the Stoics and Epicureans. For they are each a moral philosophy of solitaries: the Epicurean, of idlers inclosed in their own little gardens; the Stoic, of contemplatives who endeavor to feel no emotion. And the leap which he had made at the start from logic to metaphysics caused Vico thereafter to esteem lightly the physics of Aristotle and Epicurus and finally of René Descartes; whence he found himself disposed to look with favor on the physics of Timaeus adopted by Plato, which holds the world to be made of numbers. Nor could he bring himself to despise the physics of the Stoics, which holds the world to consist of points, for between this and the Timaean there is no substantial difference; later indeed he tried to reestablish it in his book *On the Most Ancient Wisdom of the Italians.* And finally he could not accept either seriously or playfully the mechanical physics of Epicurus or Descartes, for both start from a false position.

When Vico saw how both Plato and Aristotle often employ mathematical proofs to demonstrate what they discuss in philosophy, he realized that he fell short of being able to understand them well, so he decided to apply himself to geometry and to penetrate as far as the fifth proposition of Euclid. And reflecting that its demonstration turned on a congruence of triangles, the sides and angles of one triangle being shown one by one to be equal to the corresponding sides and angles of the other, he found in himself that it was an easier matter to grasp all those minute truths together, as in a metaphysical genus, than to understand those particular geometrical quantities. And to his cost he learned that that study proper to minute wits is not easy for minds already made universal by metaphysics. So he gave up this study as one which chained and confined his mind, now accustomed through long study of metaphysics to move freely in the infinite of genera; and in the constant reading of orators, historians and poets his intellect took increasing delight in observing between the remotest matters ties that bound them together in some common relation. It is these ties that are the beautiful ornaments of eloquence which make subtleties delightful.

When he had discovered that the whole secret of the geometric method comes to this: first to define the terms one has to reason with; then to set up certain common maxims agreed to by one's companion in argument; finally, at need, to ask discretely for such concessions as the nature of things permits, in order to supply a basis for arguments, which without some such assumption could not reach their conclusions; and with these principles to proceed step by step in one's demonstrations from simpler to more complex truths, and never to affirm the complex truths without first examining singly their component parts,—he thought the only advantage of having learned how geometricians proceed in their reasoning was that if he ever had occasion to reason in that manner he would know how.

By reading Lucretius he learned that Epicurus, because he denied any generic difference of substance between mind and body and so for want of a sound metaphysic remained of limited mind, had to take as the starting point for his philosophy matter already formed and divided into multiform ultimate parts composed of other parts which he imagined to be inseparable because there was no void between them. This is a philosophy to satisfy the circumscribed minds of children and the weak ones of silly women. And though Epicurus had no knowledge even of geometry, yet, by a well-ordered deduction, he built on his mechanical physics a metaphysics entirely sensualistic just like that of John Locke, and a hedonistic morality suitable for men who are to live in solitude, as indeed he enjoined upon all his disciples. And, to give him his due, Vico followed his explanation of the forms of corporeal nature with as much delight as he felt ridicule or pity on seeing him under the hard necessity of going off into a thousand inanities and absurdities to explain the operations of the human mind. This reading therefore served only to confirm him still further in the doctrines of Plato, who from the very form of our human mind, without any hypothesis, establishes the eternal idea as the principle of all things on the basis of the knowledge and consciousness [*scienza e coscienza*] that we have of ourselves. For in our mind there are certain eternal truths that we cannot mistake or deny, and which are therefore not of our making. But for the rest we feel a liberty by thinking them to make all the things that are dependent on the body, and therefore we make them in time, that is when we choose to turn our attention to them, and we make them all by thinking them and contain them all within ourselves. For example, we make images by imagination, recollections by memory, passions by appetite; smells, tastes, colors, sounds and touches by the senses; and all these things we contain within us. But for the eternal truths which are not of our making and have no dependence on our bodies, we must conceive as principle of all things an eternal idea altogether separate from body, which, in its consciousness, when it wills, creates all things in time and contains them within itself, and by containing them sustains them. By this principle of philosophy Plato establishes, in metaphysics, abstract substances as having more reality than corporeal ones. From it he derives a morality well adapted throughout for civil life, so that the school of Socrates, both in itself and through its successors, furnished the greatest lights of Greece in the arts both of peace and of war.

Up to this time Vico had admired two only above all other learned men: Plato and Tacitus; for with an incomparable metaphysical mind Tacitus contemplates man as he is, Plato as he should be. And as Plato with his universal knowledge explores the parts of nobility which constitute the man of intellectual wisdom, so Tacitus descends into all the counsels of utility whereby, among the infinite irregular chances of malice and fortune, the man of practical wisdom brings things to good issue. Now Vico's admiration of these two great authors from this point of view was a foreshadowing of that plan on which he later worked out an ideal eternal history to be traversed by the universal history of all times, carrying out on it, by certain eternal properties of civil affairs, the development, acme and decay of all nations. From this it follows that the wise man should be formed both of esoteric wisdom such as Plato's and of common wisdom such as that of Tacitus. And now at length Vico's attention was drawn to Francis Bacon, Lord Verulam, a man of incomparable wisdom both common and esoteric, at one and the same time a universal man in theory and in practice, a rare philosopher and a great English minister of state. Leaving aside his other works, on whose subjects there were perhaps writers as good or better, from his *De augmentis scientiarum* Vico concluded that, as Plato is the prince of Greek wisdom, and the Greeks have no Tacitus, so Romans and Greeks alike have no Bacon. He marveled that one sole man could see in the world of letters what studies remained to be discovered and developed, and how many and what kinds of defects must be corrected in those it already contained; and that without professional or sectarian bias, save for a few things which offend the Catholic religion, he did justice to all the sciences, and always with the design that each should make its special contribution to that *summa* which the universal republic of letters constitutes. Vico now proposed to have these three unique authors ever before him in meditation and writing, and so he went on elaborating his works of discovery, which culminated in *The One Principle of Universal Law*.

Accordingly he was wont, in his orations delivered in successive years at the annual opening of studies in the Royal University, to propose universal arguments brought down from metaphysics and given social application. From this point of view he treated of the ends of the various studies, as in the first six orations, or of the method of study, as in the latter part of the sixth and in the entire seventh. The first three treat principally of the ends suitable to human nature, the next two principally of the political ends, the sixth of the Christian end.

The first, delivered the 18th of October 1699, proposes that we cultivate the force of our divine mind in all its faculties. Its thesis is: "That the knowledge of oneself is for each of us the greatest incentive to the compendious study of every branch of learning." It proves that the human mind is by analogy the god of man, just as God is the mind of the whole [of things]. It shows severally how the marvelous faculties of the mind, whether senses or imagination or memory or invention or reason, perform with divine powers of quickness, facility and efficiency the most numerous and varied tasks at one and the same time.

The second oration, delivered in 1700, urges that we inform the spirit with the virtues by following the truths of the mind. Its argument is: "That there is no enmity more dire and dangerous than that of the fool against himself." It represents this universe as a great city in which God by an eternal law condemns the foolish to wage against themselves a war thus conceived: "Its law has as many chapters, written out by an omnipotent hand, as there are natures of all things. Let us recite the chapter on man. 'Let man be of mortal body and eternal soul. Let him be born for two things, truth and goodness, that is to say for Me alone. Let his mind distinguish the true from the false. Let not his senses impose upon his mind. Let reason be the principle, guide and lord of his life. Let his desire submit to his reason. . . . Let him win praise for himself by the good arts of his spirit. By virtue and constancy let him attain to human felicity. If anyone foolishly breaks these laws, whether through malice or luxury or sloth or mere imprudence, he is guilty of treason: let him wage war against himself.' " And it proceeds to a tragic description of the war.

The third oration, delivered in the year 1701, is a kind of practical appendix to the two preceding ones. Its argument is: "That the society of letters must be rid of every deceit, if you would study to be adorned with true not feigned, solid not empty, erudition."

The fourth oration, delivered in the year 1704, has this for its argument: "He who would reap from the study of letters the greatest advantages, combined always with honor, let him be educated for the glory and good of the community." It is directed against the false scholars who study for advantage alone and therefore take more pains to seem learned than to be so.

In the fifth oration, delivered in the year 1705, it is proposed "That commonwealths have been most renowned for military glory and most powerful politically when letters have most flourished in them."

In the sixth oration, delivered in the year 1707, he treats of this argument, which is partly on the ends of the various studies and partly on the order of studying them. "The knowledge of the corrupt nature of man invites us to study the complete cycle of the liberal arts and sciences, and propounds and expounds the true, easy and unvarying order in which they are to be acquired." In it he leads his hearers to meditate on themselves, how man under pain of sin is divided from man by tongue, mind and heart. By the tongue, which often fails and often betrays the ideas through which man would but cannot unite himself to man. By the mind, through the variety of opinions springing from diversity of sensuous tastes, in which men do not agree. And finally by the heart, whose corruption prevents even the conciliation of man with man by uniformity of vice. Whence Vico proves that the pain of our corruption must be healed by virtue, knowledge and eloquence; for through these three things only does one man feel the same as another. This brings Vico to the end of the various studies, and fixes the point of view from which he considers the order of study. He shows that as languages were the most powerful means for setting up human society, so the studies should begin with them, since they depend altogether on memory which in childhood is marvelously strong. The age of childhood, weak in reason, is regulated only by examples, which to be effective must be grasped with vividness of imagination, for which childhood is marvelous. Hence children should be occupied with the reading of history, both fabulous and true. The age of childhood is reasonable but it has no material on which to reason; let children then be prepared for the art of good reasoning through a study of the quantitative sciences, which call for memory and imagination and at the same time check the tendency to corpulence of the imaginative faculty, which when swollen is the mother of all our errors and woes. In early youth the senses prevail and draw the pure mind in their train; let youths then apply themselves to physics, which leads to the contemplation of the corporeal universe and has need of mathematics for the science of the cosmic system. Thus by the vast and corpulent physical ideas and by the delicate ideas of lines and numbers let them be prepared to grasp the abstract metaphysical infinite by the science of being and the one. And when they have come to know their mind in this science let them be prepared to contemplate their spirit and in consequence of eternal truths to perceive that it is corrupt, so that they may be disposed to amend it naturally by morality at an age when they have had some experience of the evil guidance of the passions, which are most violent in childhood. And when they have learned that by its nature pagan morality is insufficient to tame and subdue philauty or self-love, and when by experience in metaphysics they understand that the infinite is more certain than the finite, mind than body, God than man (who cannot tell how he himself moves, feels or knows), then with humbled intellect let them make ready to receive revealed theology, from which let them descend to Christian ethics, and thus purged let them finally pass to Christian jurisprudence.

Vico found himself obliged to read Hugo Grotius *On the Law of War and Peace*. And here he found a fourth author to add to the three he had set before himself. For Plato adorns rather than confirms his esoteric wisdom with the common wisdom of Homer. Tacitus intersperses his metaphysics, ethics and politics with the facts, as they have come down to him from the times, scattered and confused and without system. Bacon sees that the sum of human and divine knowledge of his time needs supplementing and emending, but as far as laws are concerned he does not succeed with his canons in compassing the universe of cities and the course of all times, or the extent of all nations. Grotius, however, embraces in a system of universal law the whole of philosophy and philology, including both parts of the latter, the history on the one hand of facts and events, both fabulous and real, and on the other of the three languages, Hebrew, Greek and Latin; that is to say, the three learned languages of antiquity that have been handed down to us by the Christian religion.

Vico finally came to perceive that there was not yet in the world of letters a system so devised as to bring the best philosophy, that of Plato made subordinate to the Christian faith, into harmony with a philology exhibiting scientific necessity in both its branches, that is in the two histories, that of languages and that of things; to give certainty to the history of languages by reference to the history of things; and to bring into accord the maxims of the academic sages and the practices of the political sages.

At the solemn public opening of studies in 1719 he therefore proposed this argument: "All divine and human learning has three elements: knowledge, will and power, whose single principle is the mind, with reason for its eye, to which God brings the light of eternal truth." And he divided the argument thus: "Now as to these three elements, which we know to exist and to belong to us as certainly as we know that we ourselves live, let us explain them by that one thing of which we cannot by any means doubt, that is of course by thought. That we may the more easily do this, I divide this entire discourse into three parts. In the first of these let us demonstrate that all the principles of the sciences are from God. In the second, that the divine light or eternal truth, by the three elements above set forth, permeates all the sciences, disposes them all in an order in which they are linked by the closest ties one with another, and relates them all to God as their source. In the third, that whatever has been written or said concerning the foundations of divine and human learning, if it agrees with these principles, is true, if it disagrees is false. Three further matters concerning the knowledge of divine and human things I shall also treat: its origin, circularity, and consistency; and I shall show that the origins of all things proceed from God, that all return to God by a circle, that all have their consistency in God, and that apart from God they are all darkness and error." And he discoursed on this argument for an hour and more.

Hence he divides these principles [of the first origins of science in the beginning of sacred history] into two parts: one of ideas, the other of languages. In the part devoted to ideas he discovers new historical principles of geography and chronology, the two eyes of history, and thence the principles of universal history hitherto lacking. He discovers new historical principles of philosophy, and first of all a metaphysics of the human race. That is to say, a natural theology of all nations by which each people naturally created by itself its own gods through a certain natural instinct that man has for divinity. Fear of these gods led the first founders of nations to unite themselves with certain women in a lifelong companionship. This was the first human form of marriage. Thus he discovers the identity of the grand principle of gentile theology with that of the poetry of the theological poets, who were the world's first poets as well as the first poets of all gentile humanity. From this metaphysics he derives a morality and thence a politics common to all the nations, and on this he bases a jurisprudence of the human race, varying with certain sects of the times, as the nations unfold the ideas of their nature, with consequent developmental changes in their governments. The final form of the latter he shows to be monarchy, in which the nations by nature come at last to rest.

In the teaching of his subject Vico was always most interested in the progress of the young men, and to open their eyes and prevent them from being deceived by false doctors he was willing to incur the hostility of pedants. He never discussed matters pertaining to eloquence apart from wisdom, but would say that eloquence is nothing but wisdom speaking; that his chair was the one that should give direction to minds and make them universal; that others were concerned with the various parts of knowledge, but his should teach it as an integral whole in which each part accords with every other and gets its meaning from the whole. No matter what the subject, he showed in his lectures how by eloquence it was animated as it were by a single spirit drawing life from all the sciences that had any bearing upon it. This was the meaning of what he had written in his book *On the Method of the Studies*: that a Plato (to take a conspicuous example) among the ancients was the equivalent of an entire university of studies of our day, all harmonized in one system. Thus Vico lectured every day with as much elegance and profundity in various branches of scholarship as if famous men of letters had come from abroad to attend his classes and to hear him.

Vico was choleric to a fault. Though he guarded himself from it as best he could in his writing, he publicly confessed this failing. He would inveigh too violently against the errors of thought or scholarship or against the misconduct of those men of letters who were his rivals, which as a charitable Christian or a true philosopher he should rather have overlooked or pitied. But if he was bitter toward those who belittled him and his works, he was correspondingly grateful to those who formed a just opinion of both; and the latter were always the best and the most learned men of the city. Among the caitiff semi-learned or pseudo-learned, the more shameless called him a fool, or in somewhat more courteous terms they said that he was obscure or eccentric and had odd ideas. The more malicious damned him with such compliments as these: some said he was a good teacher for young men when they had completed their course of study, that is when their studies had made them quite satisfied with their own knowledge (as if Quintilian had not wished that the children of the great might like Alexander be entrusted from boyhood to men like Aristotle); others went so far as to pay him the compliment, as dangerous as it was flattering, that he would make an excellent instructor of teachers themselves. He however blessed all these adversities as so many occasions for withdrawing to his desk, as to his high impregnable citadel, to meditate and to write further works which he was wont to call "so many noble acts of vengeance against his detractors." These finally led him to the discovery of his *New Science*. And when he had written this work, enjoying life, liberty and honor, he held himself more fortunate than Socrates, on whom Phaedrus has these fine lines:

> I would not shun his death to win his fame;
> I'd yield to odium, if absolved when dust.

17

VOLTAIRE
Good Sense and Nonsense

Putting aside his early Jesuit education, François-Marie Arouet de Voltaire (1694–1778) set himself to writing satirical anti-clerical essays that led to his being exiled to Holland in 1713 and imprisoned in the Bastille in 1717. Released in 1718, he turned to writing plays that won him considerable literary fame; but a quarrel with the powerful Chevalier de Rohan nevertheless mandated another exile in 1726, this time to England. There he learned English, read widely in philosophy, law and science and came to admire the British empiricism of Bacon and Locke and the rigor of Newtonian science. Returning to France in 1729, he published a set of reflections on liberalism and empiricism that were, in essence, a critique of l'ancien régime. Lettres Philosophiques (1743) forced another retreat from Paris. In Lorraine, under the protection of Mme du Châtelet, he studied physics, metaphysics and history. Through the influence of Mme de Pompadour, he was named historiagrapher of France and elected to the French Academy in 1746. In 1750, he was invited to the court of Frederick the Great to serve for three years as an intellectual in residence. After quarreling with Frederick, he spent some years in Geneva and returned to France in 1759. A shrewd investor, he became wealthy, acquired an estate and settled to write essays, plays, a philosophical dictionary, treatises, poems, novels, letters. Addressing serious topics in ethics, law, theology and the philosophy of history, he retained a witty, mocking tone even when he was most indignant and outraged. Of metaphysics, he said "Metaphysics, in my opinion, is made up of two things, what all men of good sense know, the second what they will never know."

Although he called himself a militant theist, Voltaire criticized what he saw as the anti-rationalistic obscurantism of Pascal. But he found Leibniz' theodicy—its attempt to reconcile the existence of evil with divine benvolence—equally repellent. His attack on Leibnizean optimism was most pointedly expressed in Zadig (1748), Poème sur le désastre de Lisbonne and Candide (1759). A humanist, a legal and social reformer (Traité sur la Tolérance (1763)), Voltaire also wrote an astonishing range of less well-known but brilliant historical works (Charles XII (1731), Siècle de Louis XIV (1751), a history of the Russian Empire under Peter the Great (1759), as well as the more philosophical Philosophie de l'histoire (1765) and Essai sur les moeurs de l'ésprit des nations (1769)). His last work, written just before his death, Prix de la Justice et de l'Humanité, advances a set of judicial reforms that influenced the authors of the Declaration of the Rights of Man.

Letters to Frederick the Great

17th April, 1737.

Monseigneur,

I do not think there is any demonstration properly so called of the existence of the Supreme Being independent of matter. I remember that in England I did not fail to embarrass the famous Dr. Clarke when I said to him: We cannot call that a demonstration which is only a chain of ideas leaving many difficulties. To say that the square on the hypotenuse of a right-angled triangle is equal to the sum of the squares on the other two sides is a demonstration which, however complicated it may be, leaves no difficulty; but the existence of a Creative Being leaves difficulties insurmountable to the human mind. Therefore this truth cannot be placed among demonstrations properly so called. It is a truth I believe; but I believe it as being the most probable; 'tis a light which strikes me amid a thousand shadows.

Many things might be said on this topic, but it is carrying gold to Peru to fatigue your Royal Highness with philosophical reflections.

All metaphysics, in my opinion, contain two things: The first all that men of good sense know; the second what they will never know.

For example we know what constitutes a simple and a composite idea; we shall never know what the being is which has these ideas. We measure bodies; we shall never know what matter is. We can only judge of this by analogy; 'tis a staff nature has given to the blind and with it we walk and also fall.

Analogy teaches me that animals, being made as I am, having sentiments like me, ideas like me, may well be what I am. When I try to go beyond I find an abyss and I halt on the edge of the precipice. All I know is, whether matter be eternal (which is quite incomprehensible), whether it was created in time (which is subject to great difficulties), whether our soul perishes with us, or enjoys immortality—in these uncertainties you cannot choose a wiser course or one more worthy of yourself than that you take, which is to give your soul, whether it be perishable or not, all the virtues, all the pleasures, all the instruction of which it is capable, to live as a prince, as a man, as a sage, to be happy and to render others happy. I look upon you as a present sent from Heaven to earth. I am amazed that at your age you are not carried away with a taste for pleasure and I congratulate you infinitely that philosophy leaves you the taste for pleasure. We are not born solely to read Plato and Leibnitz, to measure curves and to arrange facts in our heads; we are born with hearts which must be filled, with passions which must be satisfied without our being dominated by them. Monseigneur, I am charmed with your system of morals! My heart feels it was born only to be a subject of yours.

One of the greatest benefits you can confer upon mankind is to trample under foot superstition and fanaticism; not to allow a man in a gown to persecute others who do not think as he does. It is quite certain that philosophers never trouble States. Why then trouble philosophers? What did it matter to Holland that Bayle was right? Why must it be that a fanatical minister like Jurieu had the interest to tear Bayle from his little fortune? Philosophers ask for nothing but tranquility; they only wish to live in peace under the established government, and there is not a theologian who does not wish to be master of the State. Is it possible that men who have no knowledge save the gift of speaking without understanding themselves or being understood, should have dominated and still do dominate almost everywhere?

The northern countries have this advantage over the south of Europe, that these tyrants of souls have there less power than elsewhere. The princes of the north, therefore, are generally less superstitious and less malevolent than elsewhere. An Italian prince will deal in poison and then go to confession. Protestant Germany does not produce such fools and such monsters; and in general I should have no difficulty in proving that the least superstitious kings have always been the best princes.

You see, worthy heir of the spirit of Marcus Aurelius, with what liberty I dare to speak to you. You are almost the only person in the world who deserves to be spoken to thus.

Cirey, 27th May, 1737.

Monseigneur,

In the little paradise of Cirey we await impatiently two things which are very rare in France—the portrait of a prince such as you, and M. de Keyserlingk, whom your Royal Highness honors with the name of your intimate friend.

Louis XIV said one day to a man who had rendered important services to Charles II, King of Spain, and who had been one of his familiars; "Then the King of Spain loved you?" "Ah! Sire," replied the poor courtier, "Do kings love anything?"

You, Monseigneur, would have all the virtues which are so uselessly desired in kings and for which they have always been praised so inopportunely; it is not enough to be superior to men in mind as well as in rank, you are so in the heart. You, prince and friend! There are two great titles joined together which hitherto have been thought incompatible.

Yet I have always dared to think that princes could feel pure friendship, for usually private men who pretend to be friends are rivals. We have always something to quarrel about: Fame, position, women, and above all the favors of you masters of the earth, which we struggle for even more than for those of women, who nevertheless are quite as valuable as you are. But it seems to me that a prince, especially a prince like you, has nothing to quarrel over, has no rival to fear, and can feel friendship without embarrassment and at his ease. Happy is he, Monseigneur, who can share the bounties of a heart like yours! Doubtless M. de Keyserlingk has nothing to desire. My only surprise is that he should travel.

Cirey, Monseigneur, is also a little temple dedicated to Friendship. Madame du Châtelet, who I assure you possesses all the virtues of a great man with the graces of her sex, is not unworthy of his visit and will receive him as the Friend of Prince Frederick.

I reproach myself for having said nothing in my letters to your Royal Highness of French literature, in which you deign to take an interest; but I live in a profound solitude near the most estimable lady of this age and the books of the last; in my solitude I have received no novelties which deserve to be sent to Mount Remus.

Our belles-lettres begin to degenerate considerably, either because they lack encouragement or because the French, having found the good in the age of Louis XIV, are always so unfortunate as to seek the best; or because in all countries nature reposes after great efforts, like the fields after an abundant harvest.

That part of philosophy which is the most useful to men—that which treats of the soul—will never be of any value among us so long as we cannot think freely. A certain number of superstitious people here do great damage to every truth. Only the Jesuits are permitted to say anything; and if your Royal Highness has read what they say, I doubt whether you will do them the same honor you have done M. Rollin. History can only be well written in a free country; but most of the French refugees in Holland and in England have corrupted the purity of their language.

Cirey, October 1737

Monseigneur,

You command me, Monseigneur, to give you some account of my metaphysical doubts; I am taking the liberty of sending you an extract from a chapter On Liberty. Your Royal Highness will at least find good faith in it though you may find ignorance. Would to God all who are ignorant were at least sincere!

Perhaps humanity, the principal of all my thoughts, has seduced me in this work; perhaps my idea that there would be neither vice nor virtue, that neither reward nor punishment would be needed, that society especially among philosophers would be an exchange of malignancy and hypocrisy, if man did not possess full and absolute liberty—perhaps, I say, this opinion carries me too far. But if you find errors in my thoughts, forgive them for the sake of the principle which produced them.

As far as I can I always bring back my metaphysics to morality. I have inquired sincerely and with all the attention of which I am capable whether I can attain any notions of the human soul, and I have seen that the fruit of all my searching is ignorance. I find that this thinking, free, active agent is nearly in the same position as God; my reason tells me that God exists, but this very same reason also tells me that I cannot know what He is. Indeed, how can we know what our soul is, we who can form no conception of light when we have the misfortune to be born blind? Therefore I perceive with anguish that everything which has been written about the soul cannot teach us the least truth.

After groping about this soul to guess its kind, my principal object is to try at least to regulate it; 'tis the works of our clock. All Descartes's fine ideas about elasticity do not tell me the nature of these works; I do not know what is the cause of elasticity; yet I wind up my clock and somehow or other it goes.

I examine man. Whatever materials he may be composed of, we must see whether vice and virtue do in fact exist. This is the important point concerning man, I do not mean concerning a given society living under given laws, but the human race. For you, Monseigneur, who are to reign, for the woodcutter in your forest, for the Chinese doctor, and for the American savage. Locke, the wisest metaphysician I know, seems, by combating (with reason) innate ideas, to think that there is no universal principle of morality. On this point I dare to combat or rather to elucidate that great man's ideas. I agree with him that there is not really any innate idea; it follows obviously that there is no moral proposition innate in our souls; but because we are not born with beards, does it follow that we inhabitants of this Continent are not born to be bearded at a certain age? We are not born with the strength to walk; but whosoever is born with two feet will one day walk. Thus nobody is born with the idea that he must be just; but God has so arranged men's organs that all at a certain age agree upon this truth.

It seems to me obvious that God meant us to live in society, even as He gave bees the instinct and instruments proper to make honey. Since our society could not exist without the ideas of justice and injustice, He gave us the means of acquiring them. Our different customs, it is true, will never allow us to attach the same idea of justice to the same notions. What is a crime in Europe will be a virtue in Asia, just as certain German stews will never please the epicures of France; but God has so constructed Germans and Frenchmen that they all enjoy good cheer. All societies therefore will not have the same laws, but no society will be without laws. Here then the good of society is established by all men from Pekin to Ireland as the immutable rule of virtue; what is useful to society is therefore good in all countries. This single idea at once conciliates all the contradictions which appear in the morality of men. Theft was permitted in Sparta; but why? Because property was there held in common and because to steal from a miser who kept for himself alone what the law gave the public was serving society.

It is said there are savages who eat men and think they do right. I reply that these savages have the same idea of justice and injustice as we have. They make war as we do from madness and passion; we see the same crimes committed everywhere, and eating one's enemies is but an additional ceremony. The wrong is not putting them on the spit but killing them, and I dare to assert that no savage thinks he acts well when he murders his friend. I saw four savages from Louisiana who were brought to France in 1723. Among them was a woman of a very gentle character. I asked through the interpreter if she had ever eaten the flesh of her enemies and if she liked it; she answered: Yes; I then asked if she would willingly have killed or have caused to be killed any of her compatriots in order to eat them; she replied with a shudder and with a visible horror for this crime. I defy the most determined liar among travelers to dare to assert that there is a tribe, a family, where it is permitted to break one's word. I am justified in believing that since God created certain animals to feed in common, others to see each other only in pairs very seldom, spiders to make webs, every species possesses the instruments necessary for the work it has to do. Man has been given everything needed to live in society; just as he has been given a stomach to digest, eyes to see, a soul to judge.

Place two men on the earth; they will only call that good, virtuous, and just which is good for both of them. Place four, and there will be nothing virtuous except what is suitable to all four; and if one of the four eats another's supper, or beats or kills him, he will assuredly arouse the others. What I say of these four men must be said of the whole universe. That, Monseigneur, is roughly the plan on which I have written this moral metaphysics; but should I speak of virtue in your presence?

Cirey, 18th October, 1738.

I observe with a satisfaction approaching pride, Monseigneur, that the little oppositions I endure in my own country arouse indignation in your Royal Highness's great heart. You cannot doubt but that your approval amply rewards me for all these annoyances; they are common to all who have cultivated the sciences and those men of letters who have most loved the truth have always been the most persecuted.

Calumny attempted the death of Descartes and Bayle; Racine and Boileau would have died of grief had they not found a protector in Louis XIV. We still possess verses made against Virgil. I am far indeed from being able to compare myself with those great men; but I am more fortunate than they; I enjoy repose, I have a fortune sufficient for a private man and greater than a philosopher needs, I live in a delicious solitude beside a most estimable woman whose society ever provides me with new lessons. And then, Monseigneur, you are graciously pleased to love me; the most virtuous, the most amiable prince in Europe deigns to open his heart to me, to confide to me his works and his thoughts and to correct mine. What more do I need? Health alone fails me; but there is not a sick man in the world happier than I.

Les Délices, August 30, 1755.

I have received, sir, your new book against the human species, and I thank you for it. You will please people by your manner of telling them the truth about themselves, but you will not alter them. The horrors of that human society—from which in our feebleness and ignorance we expect so many consolations—have never been painted in more striking colors: no one has ever been so witty as you are in trying to turn us into brutes: to read your book makes one long to go on all fours. Since, however, it is now some sixty years since I gave up the practice, I feel that it is unfortunately impossible for me to resume it: I leave this natural habit to those more fit for it than are you and I. Nor can I set sail to discover the aborigines of Canada, in the first place because my ill-health ties me to the side of the greatest doctor in Europe, and I should not find the same professional assistance among the Missouris: and secondly because war is going on in that country, and the example of the civilized nations has made the barbarians almost as wicked as we are ourselves. I must confine myself to being a peaceful savage in the retreat I have chosen—close to your country, where you yourself should be.

18

JEAN-JACQUES ROUSSEAU
Meditations on My Troubled Heart

Born in Geneva, raised by an aunt after the death of his mother, Jean-Jacques Rousseau (1712–1778) was, he tells us, largely educated by his solitary reading of Cicero and Romantic French novels. When he left Geneva in 1728, he became associated with Mme Warens, who influenced his (temporary) conversion from Calvinism to Catholicism. In 1748, he went to Paris, intending to make his fame as a musician. His opera, *Le Devin du Village* (1752), was not a great success, but he became a visible intellectual figure, and Diderot invited him to contribute to the *Encyclopédie*. Against the background of a theory of human nature, both *The Discourse on the Arts and Sciences* (1750) and *The Discourse on the Origins of Inequality* (1755) present severely critical descriptions of social luxury and political corruption. The *Lettre à d'Alembert* (1758) charges opera and the theater with debasing public morality. As he saw it, social corruption arises from a ramified and entrenched division of labor that engenders dependency, passivity, and resentment. Rousseau's major works present therapeutic programs for these ills. *La Nouvelle Heloise* (1761) is a psychological novel of domesticity and romance; *Émile* (1762) presents an educational regimen that is intended to preserve autonomy; *The Social Contract or Principles of Right* (1762) and *Considerations on the Government of Poland* (1770) present a political solution, sketching a contractarian theory of political legitimation and organization. The three therapeutic modes are interdependent: all are intended to preserve the autonomy of man in the "state of nature"; all substitute rationally based civic sentiments for the opposition of passion and calculative rationality; all introduce a benign patriarchal guiding figure; all attempt to reconcile the requirements of equality with those of autonomy.

In a different mode, Rousseau's autobiographical works are artful attempts at artless self-expression. Commentators see the *Confessions* (1781), *Rousseau Judge of Jean Jacques* (1772–1776) and *Reveries of a Solitary Walker* (1782) as psychologically acute, yet self-deceptively self-justifying. Impulsive and tempestuous, he made and broke the supportive friendships of Diderot, Voltaire, and Hume. Because commentators have tended to concentrate on one or another of his works without seeing their tensed and balanced interconnections, there is considerable disagreement about how best to interpret him. He has variously been seen as an early Romantic, a totalitarian, a democratic theorist, and a precursor of Montessori and Dewey.

Letter to M. Jacob Vernes, Feb. 18, 1758

I do not at all like to have anyone's conscience subjected to formulas in the matter of faith. I have a religious faith, my friend, and it is a good thing for me. I do not believe that any man in the world has as much need of it as I. I have passed my life among unbelievers without allowing myself to be shaken. I loved them, esteemed them very much, and yet I could not stand their doctrine. I have always told them that I did not know how to combat them, but that I would not believe them.

Philosophy, which has neither bottom nor shore in these matters and lacks the primary ideas and elementary principles, is nothing but a sea of uncertainty and doubt, whence the metaphysician never extricates himself. So I have abandoned reason to its fate, and consulted nature, that is to say, the internal sentiment which directs my belief independently of my reason. I have left them arranging their 'chances,' their 'lots,' their 'necessary motions,' and whilst they were constructing their universe from a throw of dice I was looking at that unity of purpose which showed me that in spite of them there was a single original author.

It was just as if they had told me the *Iliad* had been composed merely by a chance throw of letters, whereas I said to them very resolutely: Such things are possible, but they are not true; and I have no other reason for not believing them except the fact that I do not believe. That's prejudice, they say. Very well. But what can reason do, rude though it be, against a prejudice which is more persuasive than itself. Another endless argument against that distinction of the two substances from each other [matter and spirit]; another conviction on my part that there is nothing common to a tree and my thought; and it has amused me in all this to see them driven by their own sophisms to the point of preferring to endow stones with consciousness rather than concede a soul to man.

My friend, I believe in God, and God would not be just if my soul were not immortal. There, it seems to me, you have all that is essential and useful in religion. Let us leave the rest to the arguers. In regard to the eternity of punishment, that could not be harmonized with the fact of man's weakness or with the justice of God, and so I reject it. It is true there are some souls so black that I cannot conceive how they ever could enjoy that eternal beatitude, the sweetest feeling of which, it seems to me, must be one's contentment with oneself. That makes me wonder whether it might not well be the case that the souls of the wicked are annihilated at death, and whether existence and consciousness are not themselves the reward of a good life. However that may be, what does it matter about the future of the wicked. It is enough for me that I do not see the end of my hopes but await a happier existence after having suffered so much in this world. Even if I should be mistaken in this hope, it is a good in itself that will have enabled me to bear all my misfortunes more easily. I await in peace the revelation of these great truths now concealed from me, thoroughly convinced, regardless of any metaphysical solution, that if virtue does not always make man happy, he cannot possibly be happy without it, and that the afflictions of the just are not without some compensation, and that even the tears of innocence are more grateful to the heart than is the prosperity of the wicked.

Letter to M. Moultou, Minister of the Gospel, Geneva
Montmorency, Jan. 29, 1760

If I am remiss with you, Sir, I do not have the fault, at any rate, of not realizing that fact and reproaching myself for it. My silence is very much more a reflection on myself than on you, for how am I to reply to a letter that honours me so much, and where I recognize so little of myself? I will pass by the part of your letter that does not fit me; I shall return none of the compliments you have paid me; I am supposing that you would not care to hear them, and I will try in the future to deserve to have you think the same of me.

Besides, you are the first, so far as I know, to show that the pretended charity of the rich is only another luxury for him: he feeds the poor like dogs and horses. The worst of it is that dogs and horses serve his pleasure, whereas in the end the poor become tiresome, and it is the vogue to let them die, just as it was one at first to aid them.

I fear that in showing the incompatibility of luxury with equality you have only done the opposite of what you intended. You cannot be ignorant of the fact that the partisans of luxury are hostile to equality, and when you show them how the latter is destroyed you simply make them love luxury the more. One must make them see on the contrary, that when public opinion favours wealth and luxury it abolishes the inequalities of station, and that every accession of credit to the wealthy is just so much lost to the magistrates. It seems to me that there might be another sermon to deliver on that theme, very much more useful, more profound, even more significant politically, and one in which while saying pleasant things to them you could tell very important truths which would strike the attention of all the world.

You speak to me of that man, Voltaire! Why does the name of that buffoon sully your letters? The miserable fellow has ruined my country; I would hate him more if I despised him less. I only see in his great gifts something additionally shameful, which dishonour him by the unworthy use he makes of them. His gifts only serve, like his riches, to nourish the depravity of his heart. Oh citizens of Geneva, he makes you pay well for the refuge you have given him! He knew not where else to go to do evil: you will be his last victims. I do not believe that many other men will be tempted to have such a guest after your experience.

Let us have no more illusions, Sir—I was mistaken in my *Letter to D'Alembert*. I did not believe things had gone so far with us or that our morals were so 'advanced.' Our ills are henceforth without remedy; we need only palliatives now, and Comedy is one of them. Honest man, do not waste your burning eloquence preaching equality to us, for you will not be heard. We are but slaves: still teach us, if possible, not to be wicked. *Non ad vetera instituta, quae jam pridem, corruptis moribus, ludibrio sunt, revocans*, [Not by recalling us to the ancient institutions which are long since a mockery, thanks to the corrupt morals] but by slowing up the progress of evil from reasons of interest, which alone can affect the hearts of corrupt men. Goodbye, Sir, I embrace you.

Reveries of the Solitary Walker

FIRST WALK

I am now alone on earth, no longer having any brother, neighbor, friend, or society other than myself. The most sociable and the most loving of humans has been proscribed from society by a unanimous agreement. In the refinements of their hatred, they have sought the torment which would be cruelest to my sensitive soul and have violently broken all the ties which attached me to them. I would have loved men in spite of themselves. Only by ceasing to be humane, have they been able to slip away from my affection. They are now strangers, unknowns, in short, nonentities to me—because that is what they wanted. But I, detached from them and from everything, what am I? That is what remains for me to seek. Unfortunately, that inquiry must be preceded by a glance at my position. This is an idea I must necessarily follow out in order to get from them to me.

Although I have been in this curious position for fifteen years and more, it still seems like a dream to me. I still imagine that I am being tormented by indigestion, that I am sleeping badly, and that I am going to wake up fully relieved of my pain and find myself once again with my friends. No doubt about it, I must have unwittingly made a jump from wakefulness to sleep or rather from life to death. Dragged, I know not how, out of the order of things, I have seen myself cast into an incomprehensible chaos where I distinguish nothing at all; and the more I think about my present situation the less I can understand where I am.

And how could I have foreseen the destiny which awaited me? How can I conceive of it even today when I am given up to it? Could I in my good sense have supposed that one day I, the same man that I was, the same that I still am, would—without the slightest doubt—pass for and be taken as a monster, a poisoner, an assassin; that I would become the horror of the human race, the plaything of the rabble; that the only greeting passerby would give me would be to spit on me; that an entire generation would, by a unanimous agreement, find delight in burying me alive? When this strange revolution occurred, taken unprepared, I was at first overwhelmed by it. My agitation, my indignation, plunged me into a delirium which has taken no less than ten years to be calmed; and having stumbled in the interval from one error to another, from one mistake to another, from one foolish act to another, my imprudent actions furnished the masters of my fate all the tools they have skillfully utilized to make it irreversible.

I struggled for a long time as violently as I did in vain. Without cleverness, without craft, without dissimulation, without prudence, candid, open, impatient, carried away, I only entangled myself more by struggling and incessantly gave them new holds they have been careful not to neglect. Finally, feeling that all my efforts were useless and that I was tormenting myself to no avail, I took the only course which remained—that of submitting to my fate without railing against necessity any longer. I have found compensation for all my hurts in this resignation through the tranquility it provides me, tranquility which could not be united with the continual toil of a resistance as painful as it was fruitless.

Another thing has contributed to this tranquility. Among all the refinements of their hatred, my persecutors omitted one which their animosity made them forget: that was to increase its effects so gradually that they could incessantly sustain and renew my sufferings by forever hurting me in a new way. If they had been clever enough to leave me some glimmer of hope, they would still have that hold on me. They would still be able to make me their plaything by means of some false lure and then break my heart by a continually new torment that would frustrate my expectations. But they exhausted all their resources in advance; in leaving me nothing, they deprived themselves of everything. The defamation, depression, derision, and disgrace with which they have covered me are no more susceptible of being increased than mollified; they are as incapable of aggravating them as I am of escaping them. They were in such a hurry to bring the toll of my misery to its peak that all human power aided by all the tricks of Hell could add nothing more to it. Physical suffering itself, instead of increasing my torments, would bring diversion from them. By forcing screams from me, it would perhaps spare me groans; and the rending of my body would stay the rending of my heart.

What do I still have to fear from them, since everything is over? No longer able to make my condition worse, they can no longer alarm me. Worry and fright are evils they have delivered me from forever: that's always a comfort. Real evils have little hold on me; I resign myself easily to those I experience, but not to those I dread. My alarmed imagination brings them together, turns them over and over, draws them out, and increases them. Anticipating them torments me a hundred times more than being in their presence, and the threat of them terrifies me more than their actual arrival. As soon as they occur, the event—removing whatever imaginary power they had—reduces them to their correct value. Then I find them greatly inferior to what I had imagined; and even in the midst of my suffering I do not fail to feel relieved. In this state, freed from any new fear and delivered from the turmoil induced by hope, habit alone will suffice to make more bearable for me day by day a situation which nothing can make worse; and to the extent that feeling becomes blunted with the lapse of time, they have no other way to stir it up again. That is the good my persecutors have done me by prodigally using up all the shafts of their animosity. They have deprived themselves of all mastery over me, and henceforth I can laugh at them.

Not quite two months ago, complete calm was reestablished in my heart. For a long time I no longer feared anything, but I still hoped; and this hope, deluded one moment and frustrated another, was a hold by which a thousand diverse passions incessantly perturbed me. An event as sad as it was unforeseen has finally just erased this weak ray of hope from my heart and has made me see my fate forever and irreversibly fastened here-below. Since then I have become unreservedly resigned, and I have found peace again.

As soon as I began to catch a glimpse of the whole extent of the plot, I gave up forever the idea of winning the public back over to my side during my lifetime; and, for that matter, now that this winning them back can no longer be reciprocal, it would henceforth be quite useless to me. In vain would men return to me; they would no longer find me. Because of the disdain they have inspired in me, dealing with them would be insipid to me and even burdensome; and I am a hundred times happier in my solitude than I could ever be living among them. They have torn all the charms of society from my heart. At my age, those charms cannot sprout anew; it is too late. Henceforth, whether men do good or evil to me, nothing concerning them makes any difference to me; and no matter what they do, my contemporaries will never mean anything to me.

But I still counted on the future; and I hoped that a better generation, examining more fairly both the judgments made about me by this one and its conduct toward me, would easily unravel the cunning of those who direct it and would finally see me as I am. This is the hope which made me write my *Dialogues* and prompted me to a thousand foolish attempts to pass them on to posterity. This hope, though remote, held my soul in the same agitation as when I was still looking for a just heart in this century; and the hope that I cast in vain into the future also rendered me the plaything of the men of today. I stated in my *Dialogues* what I founded this expectation on. I was mistaken. Fortunately, I sensed it early enough to find an interlude of complete calm and absolute rest before my last hour. This interlude began in the period of which I am speaking, and I have reason to believe it will not be interrupted again.

Very few days pass without new reflections confirming how greatly mistaken

I was to count on winning back the public even in another age, since with respect to me it is led by guides who are continually renewed in the groups that have taken a dislike to me. Individuals die, but not collective groups. The same passions are perpetuated in them, and their ardent hatred—as immortal as the Demon which inspires it—is as active as always. When all of my individual enemies are dead, doctors and Oratorians will still live; and even if I had only those two groups as persecutors, I could be sure that they would not leave my memory in greater peace after my death than they leave me in during my lifetime. In time, perhaps, the doctors—whom I really offended—can be appeased. But the Oratorians—whom I loved, whom I esteemed, in whom I had complete trust, and whom I never offended—the Oratorians, church people and half monks, will be forever implacable. Their own iniquity constitutes the crime for which their self-love will never forgive me. And the public, whose animosity they will take care to nourish and stir up continually, will be no more appeased than they.

Everything is finished for me on earth. People can no longer do good or evil to me here. I have nothing more to hope for or to fear in this world; and here I am, tranquil at the bottom of the abyss, a poor unfortunate mortal, but unperturbed, like God Himself.

Everything external is henceforth foreign to me. I no longer have neighbors, fellow creatures, or brothers in this world. I am on earth as though on a foreign planet onto which I have fallen from the one I inhabited. If I recognize anything around me, it is only objects which distress me and tear my heart asunder; and I cannot cast my eyes on what touches and surrounds me without forever finding some disdainful object which makes me indignant or a painful one which distresses me. So let me remove from my mind all the troublesome objects I would bother myself with as painfully as I would uselessly. Alone for the rest of my life—since I find consolation, hope, and peace only in myself—I no longer ought nor want to concern myself with anything but me. It is in this state that I again take up the sequel to the severe and sincere examination I formerly called my *Confessions*. I consecrate my last days to studying myself and to preparing in advance the account I will give of myself before long. Let me give myself up entirely to the sweetness of conversing with my soul, since that is the only thing men cannot take away from me. If by dint of reflecting upon my inner dispositions I succeed in putting them in better order and in correcting the evil which may remain in them, my meditations will not be entirely useless; and even though I am no longer good for anything on earth, I will not have completely wasted my last days. The leisurely moments of my daily walks have often been filled with charming periods of contemplation which I regret having forgotten. I will set down in writing those which still come to me and each time I reread them I will enjoy them anew. I will forget my misfortunes, my persecutors, my disgrace, while dreaming of the prize my heart deserved.

These pages will, properly speaking, be only a shapeless diary of my reveries. There will be much concerning me in them, because a solitary person who reflects is necessarily greatly preoccupied with himself. Moreover, all the foreign ideas which pass through my head while I am walking will also find their place in them. I will say what I have thought just as it came to me and with as little connection as the ideas of the day before ordinarily have with those of the following day. But a new understanding of my natural temperament and disposition will come from that all the same by means of a new understanding of the feelings and thoughts which constitute the daily fodder of my mind in the strange state I am in. These pages can be considered, then, as an appendix to my *Confessions*; but I no longer give them that title, no longer feeling anything to say which merits it. My heart has been purified in the forge of adversity and, in carefully sounding it, I hardly find any reprehensible inclinations remaining. What would I still have to confess now that all earthly affections have been torn from it? I have no more reason to praise than to blame myself: I am henceforth nothing among men, and that is all I can be, no longer having any real relations or true society with them. No longer able to do any good which does not turn to evil, no longer able to act without harming another or myself, to abstain has become my sole duty and I fulfill it as much as it is in me to do so. But despite this desuetude of my body, my soul is still active; it still produces feelings and thoughts; and its internal and moral life seems to have grown even more with the death of every earthly and temporal interest. My body is no longer anything to me but an encumbrance, an obstacle, and I disengage myself from it beforehand as much as I can.

Such a unique situation surely deserves to be examined and described, and to this examination I consecrate my last moments of leisure. To do so successfully, it would be necessary to proceed with order and method; but I am incapable of such work, and it would even take me away from my goal, which is to make myself aware of the modifications of my soul and of their sequence. I will perform on myself, to a certain extent, the measurements natural scientists perform on the air in order to know its daily condition. I will apply the barometer to my soul, and these measurements, carefully executed and repeated over a long period of time, may furnish me results as certain as theirs. But I do not extend my enterprise that far. I will be content to keep a record of the measurements without seeking to reduce them to a system. My enterprise is the same as Montaigne's, but my goal is the complete opposite of his: he wrote his *Essays* only for others, and I write my reveries only for myself. If in my later days as the moment of departure approaches, I continue—as I hope—to have the same disposition as I now have, reading them will recall the delight I enjoy in writing them and causing the past to be born again for me will, so to speak, double my existence. In spite of mankind, I will still be able to enjoy the charm of society; and decrepit, I will live with myself in another age as if I were living with a younger friend.

I wrote my first *Confessions* and my *Dialogues* in constant anxiety about ways to keep them from the rapacious hands of my persecutors in order to transmit them, if it were possible, to other generations. With this work, the same worry no longer torments me; I know it would be useless. And now that the desire to be better understood by men has been extinguished in my heart, only profound indifference remains about the fate of my true writings and of the testimonies to my innocence—which have perhaps already all been forever reduced to nothing. Let them spy out what I am doing, let them worry about these pages, let them seize them, suppress them, falsify them; henceforth none of that bothers me. I neither hide nor show them. If they take them away from me while I am living, they will not take away from me the pleasure of having written them, nor the memory of their content, nor the solitary meditations whose fruit they are and whose source can be extinguished only when my soul is. If from the time of my first calamities I had known not to rail against my fate and to take the course I take today, all the efforts of men, all of their dreadful contrivances, would have had no effect on me, and they would no more have disturbed my rest by all their plots than they can henceforth disturb it by all the successful results of those plots. Let them enjoy my disgrace at will; they will not prevent me from enjoying my innocence and from finishing my days in peace in spite of them.

EIGHTH WALK

In meditating upon the dispositions of my soul during all the situations of my life, I am quite struck to see so little proportion between the different phases of my fate and the habitual feelings of well-being or uneasiness by which they affected me. My various, brief intervals of prosperity have left me almost no pleasant memory of the intimate and permanent manner in which they affected me. Conversely, during all the miserable moments of my life, I constantly felt myself filled with tender, touching, delightful sentiments which, pouring a salutary balm over the wounds of my broken heart, seemed to transform its suffering into pleasure. And separated from the memory of the evils I felt at the same time, only the gentle memory of those sentiments comes back to me. It seems to me that I have savored the sweetness of existence more, that I have really lived more, when my sentiments—drawn back around my heart, so to speak, by my fate— were not being wasted on all the objects of men's esteem which are of so little merit in themselves, but which are the sole concern of the people we believe to be happy.

When all was in order around me, when I was content with all that surrounded me and with the sphere in which I was to live, I filled it with my affectionate feelings. My expansive soul extended itself to other objects and, continually drawn outside myself by a thousand different kinds of fancies, by gentle attachments which continually busied my heart, I somehow forgot even myself. I was entirely devoted to what was alien to me; and in the continual agitation of my heart, I experienced all the vicissitudes of human things. This stormy life left me neither peace within nor rest without. Happy in appearance, I had not one sentiment which could withstand the test of reflection and truly please me. I was never perfectly satisfied with others or myself. The tumult of the world made my head swim; solitude bored me; I needed to move around constantly; and I was comfortable nowhere. I was, however, entertained, welcomed, well received, and treated with affection everywhere. I had not one enemy, no one ill-disposed toward me, no one envious of me. Since people sought only to do me favors, I often had the pleasure of doing favors for many people myself. And, without wealth, without employment, without a protector, without great talents that were either well developed or well known, I enjoyed the advantages which went along with all that. And I saw nobody in any station whose lot appeared preferable to mine. What was I lacking, then, to be happy? I don't know, but I do know that I was not happy.

What am I lacking today to be the most unfortunate of mortals? Nothing of anything men have been able to do to make me so. And yet in this deplorable condition, I still would not change being or destiny with the most fortunate among them, and I still prefer to be myself in all my misery than to be any of those people in all their prosperity. Left only to myself, I feed, it is true, on my own substance; but it is not depleted. And I am sufficient unto myself, even though I ruminate on an empty stomach, so to speak, and though my withered imagination and my burned-out ideas furnish no more nourishment for my heart. My soul—clouded and obstructed by my organs—sinks down day by day and, [beneath the] weight of these heavy masses, no longer has enough vigor to thrust itself out of its old wrapping as it used to do.

Adversity forces us to this turning in on ourselves; and that is perhaps what renders it most unbearable for the greater part of men. As for me, who finds only faults for which to reproach myself, I blame them on my weakness and console myself, for premeditated evil never approached my heart.

However, unless I am stupid, how can I contemplate my situation for a moment without seeing that it is as horrible as they have made it and without perishing from sorrow and despair? Far from that, I, the most sensitive of beings, contemplate it and am not disturbed by it; and without struggling or exerting myself, I see myself almost with indifference in a condition whose sight perhaps no other man could bear without horror.

How have I come to that? For I was quite far from this peaceful disposition when I first suspected the conspiracy in which I had long been entangled without having noticed it at all. This new discovery overwhelmed me. Infamy and betrayal caught me unawares. What honest soul is prepared for such suffering? It would be necessary that one deserve it in order to foresee it. I fell into all the snares they placed along my path; indignation, fury, delirium, took possession of me. I was completely disoriented. My mind was overwhelmed. And in the horrible darkness in which they did not cease to keep me immersed, I no longer perceived a glimmer of light to guide me or a support or stay to steady myself by and resist the despair which carried me away.

How could I live happily and serenely in this dreadful condition? I am, however, still in it and deeper so than ever. In it, I have again found calm and peace. In it, I live happily and serenely. In it, I laugh at the incredible torments my persecutors constantly give themselves in vain while I remain at peace, busied with flowers, stamens, and childish things and do not even think of them.

How was this transition made? Naturally, imperceptibly, and without toil. The first surprise was frightful. I, who felt myself worthy of love and esteem; I, who believed myself honored, cherished, as I deserved to be; I saw myself suddenly misrepresented as a dreadful monster the likes of which has never existed. I saw a whole generation rush headlong into this strange opinion, without explanation, without doubt, without shame, and without my ever being able at the very least to get to know the cause of this strange revolution. I struggled violently and only entangled myself more. I wanted to force my persecutors to explain themselves to me; they took care not to. After having unsuccessfully tormented myself for a long time, it was quite necessary to catch my breath. However, I always hoped. I said to myself: so stupid a blindness, so absurd a prepossession, will never be able to win over the whole human race. There are sensible men who do not share this delirium; there are just souls who detest knavery and traitors. Let me seek, I will perhaps eventually find a man; if I find him, they are confounded. I sought in vain; I have not found him. The league is universal, without exception, past all hope; and I am sure I will finish my days in this dreadful rejection without ever penetrating the mystery of it.

It is in this deplorable condition that, after lengthy anguish instead of the despair which seemed bound to be my share in the end, I again found serenity, tranquility, peace, even happiness, since each day of my life reminds me with pleasure of the previous day and since I desire no other for the morrow.

What gives rise to this difference? A single thing: I have learned to bear the yoke of necessity without murmur. I was still forcing myself to hold on to a thousand things, but now that they have all slipped away from me one after the other and I am left only to myself, I have finally regained my composure. Pressed on all sides, I dwell in equilibrium because, no longer attached to anything else, I depend only on myself.

When I rose up against opinion with so much ardor, I was still bearing its yoke without having noticed it. We want to be esteemed by the people we esteem; and as long as I could judge men, or at least some men, favorably, the judgments they held about me could not be uninteresting to me. I saw that the judgments of the public are often equitable. But I did not see that this very equity was the effect of chance, that the rules on which they base their opinions are drawn only from their passions or their prejudices, which are the work of their passions, and that even when they judge well, these good judgments still frequently arise from a bad principle—as when they feign to honor a man's merit because of some success, not from a spirit of justice, but to seem impartial, while slandering the same man on other points with no qualms whatever.

But after long and vain research, I still saw them all, without exception, participating in the most iniquitous and absurd system an infernal mind could invent. I saw that with respect to me reason was banished from every head and equity from every heart. I saw a frenetic generation completely cede to the blind fury of its leaders against an unfortunate man who never did, willed, or rendered evil to anybody. After having sought ten years for a man in vain, I finally had to extinguish my lantern and cry out: "There are no more!" Then I began to see myself alone on earth and I understood that in relation to me my contemporaries were nothing more than automatons who acted only on impulse and whose action I could calculate only from the laws of motion. Whatever intention, whatever passion, I might have supposed in their souls would never have explained their conduct with respect to me in a way I could have understood. Thus their interior dispositions ceased to be of any importance to me. I no longer saw in them anything but randomly moved masses, destitute of all morality with respect to me.

In all the evils which befall us, we look more to the intention than to the effect. A shingle falling off a roof can injure us more, but does not grieve us as much as a stone thrown on purpose by a malevolent hand. The blow sometimes goes astray, but the intention never misses its mark. Material suffering is what we feel least in the blows of fortune; and when the unfortunate do not know whom to blame for their misfortunes, they blame fate which they personify and to which they ascribe eyes and an intelligence to torment them intentionally. Thus it is that a gambler, vexed by his losses, becomes furious at he knows not whom. He imagines a fate which relentlessly and intentionally torments him and, finding fuel for his anger, he becomes irritated and inflamed against the enemy he has created for himself. The wise man, who sees only the blows of blind necessity, in all the misfortunes which befall him, does not have this insane agitation. He cries out in his suffering, but without being carried away, without anger. He feels only the material blow of the evil to which he is prey, and the beatings he receives injure his body in vain—not one reaches his heart.

It is a lot to have reached this point, but it is not all. If we stop here, we have indeed cut out the evil, but we have left the root. For this root is not in the beings who are alien to us, but in ourselves; and that is where we must exert ourselves to extract it completely. That is what I felt perfectly from the moment I began to turn back to myself. My reason showing me only absurdities in all the explanations I sought to give to what befalls me, I understood that the causes, the instruments, and the means of all that, unknown and inexplicable to me, ought not to matter to me. I understood that I ought to regard all the details of my fate as so many acts of pure fatality to which I ought not ascribe direction, intention, or moral cause. I understood that I had to submit to it without reasoning and without struggling, because that would be useless. I understood that since all I had yet to do on earth was to regard myself on it as a purely passive being, I ought not to use up, in futilely resisting my fate, the strength I had left to endure it. That is what I told myself; my reason and my heart acquiesced in it; and yet I still felt this heart of mine grumble. What gave rise to this grumbling? I sought for it and found it: it came from self-love which, after having become indignant about men, also rebelled against reason.

This discovery was not as easy to make as one might believe, for an innocent persecuted man considers his petty self-pride as pure love of justice for a long time. Still, once the true source is known, it can easily be dried up or at least diverted. Self-esteem is the greatest motive force of proud souls. Self-love, fertile in illusions, disguises itself and passes itself off as this esteem. But when the fraud is finally discovered and self-love can no longer hide itself, from then on it is no more to be feared; and even though we stifle it with difficulty, we at least easily overcome it.

I never had much of a bent for self-love, but this factitious passion had become magnified in me when I was in the world, especially when I was an author. I had perhaps even less of it than others, but I had it prodigiously. The terrible lessons I received soon confined it to its former limits. It began by revolting against injustice, but finished by disdaining it. By withdrawing into my soul and severing the external relations which make it demanding, by renouncing comparisons and preferences, it was satisfied with my being good in my own eyes. Then, again becoming love of myself, it returned to the natural order and delivered me from the yoke of opinion.

From that moment, I again found peace of soul and almost felicity. In whatever situation we find ourselves, it is only because of self-love that we are constantly unhappy. When self-love is quiet and reason speaks, reason eventually consoles us for all the bad things we have not been able to avoid. Reason annihilates them insofar as they do not immediately affect us; for by ceasing to be preoccupied with them, we are sure of avoiding their most poignant blows. They are nothing for the person who does not think about them. Offenses, acts of revenge, slights, insults, injustices are nothing for the person who, in the bad things he endures, sees only the bad itself and not any intention, for the person whose rank in his own esteem does not depend on the one others are willing to accord him. However men may wish to view me, they cannot change my being; and, regardless of their power and all their underhanded intrigues, I will continue to be what I am, whatever they might do and in spite of them. It is true that the way they are disposed to me influences my actual situation; the barrier they have placed between them and me deprives me of every source of subsistence and assistance in my old age and time of need. This barrier even makes money useless to me, because it cannot procure me the necessary services. There is no longer mutual exchange and assistance, no longer any correspondence between them and me. Alone in the midst of them, I have only myself as a source, and this source is very feeble at my age and in my present condition. These evils are great, but they have lost all their force for me since I have learned how to bear them without becoming irritated. The times in which true need makes itself felt are always rare. Foresight and imagination increase them, and as these feelings continue we worry and make ourselves unhappy. As for me, it matters little that I know I will suffer tomorrow; to be at peace, it is sufficient that I not suffer today. I am not affected by the evil I foresee, but only by the one I feel and that limits it considerably. Alone, sick and forsaken in my bed, I can [suffer] there from indigence, cold, and hunger without anybody caring. But what does it matter, if not even I care and if I become as little affected as the others about my destiny, whatever it may be? Is it nothing, especially at my age, to have learned to view life and death, sickness and health, wealth and misery, glory and infamy with the same indifference? All other old men are worried about everything; I am worried about nothing. Whatever may happen, I am completely indifferent to it; and this indifference is not the work of my wisdom; it is that of my enemies. Let me learn, therefore, to accept these advantages as compensation for the evils they do to me. In making me insensitive to adversity, they have done me more good than if they had spared me its blows. In not experiencing it, I might have always feared it; instead, by overcoming it, I no longer fear it.

In the midst of the things that hinder my life, this disposition delivers me up to my natural carefreeness almost as fully as if I were living in the most complete prosperity. Apart from the brief moments when I am recalled to the most distressing worries by the presence of objects, all the rest of the time, given up by my inclinations to the affections which attract me, my heart is still nourished by the sentiments for which it was born and I enjoy them with the imaginary beings who produce and share them, as though these beings really existed. They exist for me who has created them, and I am not afraid they will betray or abandon me. They will last as long as my misfortunes themselves and will suffice to make me forget them.

Everything brings me back to the happy and sweet life for which I was born. I pass three-fourths of my life occupied with instructive and even agreeable objects in which I indulge my mind and my senses with delight, or with the children of my fancy whom I have created according to my heart and whose company sustains its sentiments, or with myself alone, satisfied with myself and already full of the happiness I feel to be due me. In all this, love of myself does all the work; self-love has nothing to do with it. This is not the case during the sorrowful moments I still pass in the midst of men—a plaything of their treacherous flattery, bombastic and derisive compliments, and honeyed malignity. No matter what I might try to do, self-love then comes into play. The hatred and animosity I discern through the coarse wrapping of their hearts tear my own heart apart with sorrow; and the idea of being taken for a dupe in this foolish way adds a very childish spite to this sorrow—the result of a foolish self-love whose complete folly I sense, but which I cannot overcome. The efforts I have made to become inured to these rude and mocking looks are unbelievable. A hundred times I have passed along the public walks and through the most frequented spots with the sole intention of inuring myself to those cruel taunts. Not only have I not been able to succeed, I have not made any progress; and all my painful, but vain, efforts have left me as easy to disturb, to grieve, and to render indignant as before.

Dominated by my senses whatever I may do, I have never been able to resist their impulses; and as long as an object acts upon them, my heart does not fail to be affected. But these passing affections last only as long as the sensation which causes them. The presence of a hateful man violently affects me. But as soon as he disappears, the impression ceases. The instant I no longer see him, I no longer think about him. It matters little that I know he is going to pay attention to me; I cannot pay any attention to him. The evil I do not feel at this moment affects me in no way; the persecutor I do not see is nothing for me. I am aware of the advantage this position gives to those who dispense my fate. Let them dispense it, then, with no qualms whatever. I still prefer to have them torment me without resisting than to have to think about them so as to protect myself from their attacks.

The way my senses thus work upon my heart constitutes the sole torment of my life. The days I see no one I no longer think about my fate, I no longer feel it, I no longer suffer; I am happy and satisfied without distraction, without obstacle. But I can rarely escape any perceptible slight; and when I am least thinking about it, a gesture, a sinister look I perceive, a venomous word I hear, an ill-disposed person I meet, is enough to overwhelm me. All I am capable of in such a case is very quickly forgetting and fleeing. The disturbance in my heart disappears with the object which has caused it, and I return to calm as soon as I am alone. Or if something does worry me, it is the fear of encountering some new cause of sorrow along my way. That is my only torment, but it suffices to alter my happiness. I reside in the middle of Paris. When I leave my home, I long for the countryside and solitude. But it is necessary to go so far to seek it that before I can breathe easily, I find a thousand objects along my path which constrict my heart, and half the day is passed in anguish before I have reached the refuge I am seeking. At least I am happy when they let me reach my destination. The moment I slip away from the retinue of the wicked is delightful; and as soon as I find myself under the trees and in the midst of greenery, I believe I am in an earthly paradise and I savor an inner pleasure as intense as if I were the happiest of mortals.

I remember perfectly that during my brief moment of prosperity these same solitary walks which are so delightful for me today were insipid and boring. When I was at someone's house in the country, the need to get some exercise and to breathe fresh air often made me go out alone; and sneaking away like a thief, I would go walk about the park or the countryside. But far from finding the happy calm I savor there today, I took along the disturbance of the vain ideas which had preoccupied me in the drawing room. Memory of the company I had left followed me into solitude. The fumes of self-love and the tumult of the world made the freshness of the groves seem dull and troubled the peace of the retreat. I fled deep into the woods in vain; an importunate crowd followed me everywhere and veiled all of nature to me. It is only after having detached myself from social passions and their sad retinue that I have again found nature with all its charms.

Convinced of the impossibility of containing these first involuntary motions, I gave up all my efforts to do so. Now, at each blow I let my blood boil. I let anger and indignation take possession of my senses. I yield this first explosion, that all my strength could neither stop nor delay, to nature. I try only to stop its consequences before it produces any effect. Flashing eyes, an inflamed face, trembling limbs, a throbbing heart—that is all purely physical, and reasoning can do nothing about it. But after having let our natural temperament have its first explosion, we can become our own master again as we regain our senses bit by bit. That is what I unsuccessfully tried to do for a long time, but with more luck at last. And ceasing to use up my strength by vainly resisting, I wait for the moment when I can conquer by letting my reason act; for it speaks to me only when it can make itself heard. Alas! What am I saying, my reason! I would be very wrong to honor it with this triumph, for it hardly plays a role in any of this. Everything comes out the same when a changeable temperament is irritated by an impetuous wind, but becomes calm again the instant the wind stops blowing. My ardent natural temperament irritates me; my indolent natural temperament pacifies me. I yield to all present impulses; every conflict sets off an intense and short motion in me. As soon as the conflict subsides, the motion ceases. Nothing imparted from outside can prolong itself in me. All the accidents of fortune, all the contrivances of men have little hold on a man thus constituted. To affect me with lasting sorrows, the impulse would have to be renewed each instant. For the intervals, however brief they may be, are enough for me to come back to myself. I am what men please, as long as they can act on my senses. But in the first instant of respite, I again become what nature wanted. Whatever they may do, this is my most constant condition and the one through which, in spite of my fate, I savor a happiness for which I feel myself constituted. I have described this condition in one of my reveries. It suits me so well that I desire nothing other than its duration and fear only to see it troubled. The evil that men have done me in no way bothers me. Only the fear of the evil they can still do to me is capable of disturbing me. But certain that they have no other new hold by which they can affect me with a permanent feeling, I laugh at all their intrigues and enjoy myself in spite of them.

19

DENIS DIDEROT
Clarity Against Dogmatic Superstition

Denis Diderot (1713–1784) was the driving spirit behind the Enlightenment project of the *Encyclopédie des arts et sciences* (1751–65, 1780). With D'Alembert, he defined the topics and selected the authors of that immensely influential work. The underlying thesis of the *Encyclopédie* was practice oriented. The technology of the crafts and trades was treated as the sound beginning of scientific understanding. A polymath, Diderot also wrote literary and art criticism (*Discourse on Dramatic Poetry*, 1758); *Essais sur la Peinture* and *Salons* (1739–1781) as well as essays in the natural sciences (*Elements of Physiology*, 1774–80) and *On the Interpretation of Nature* (1745). He was briefly imprisoned for his attack on Christianity (*The Skeptics' Walk*, 1747) and for the materialism of his Lucretian essay, *Letter on the Blind* (1749). Although early commentators treated Diderot's ironic dialogues, *Rameau's Nephew* (1767) and *Jacques the Fatalist* (1765–1784), as brilliant examples of Romanticist psychology, recent literary critics have interpreted them as deconstructivist satire.

The Encyclopedia of Arts and Sciences

FOREWORD TO VOLUME VIII (1765)

When we first became preoccupied with this undertaking, perhaps the most comprehensive that has ever been conceived in literature, we expected only those difficulties that would arise from the extent and variety of our aims; but it was a passing illusion, and we did not have to wait long to see a multitude of physical obstacles that we had anticipated increase with an infinite number of moral obstacles for which we had not at all been prepared. No matter how old the world grows, it does not change. It is possible that the individual improves, but the mass of the species becomes neither better nor worse. The sum of maleficent passions remains the same, and the enemies of all good and useful things are as innumerable today as in the past.

Of all the persecutions that have been endured in all times and among all peoples by those who have devoted themselves to the seductive and dangerous rivalry of inscribing their names on the list of benefactors of the human race, there are practically none that have not been used against us. Whatever history has transmitted to us in base deeds of envy, ignorance, and fanaticism, we have already experienced. In the space of twenty consecutive years we are hardly able to count a few moments of peace. After days consumed in ungrateful and incessant work, how many nights have we spent waiting for the abuses that malice sought to bring upon us! How many times have we not been roused from our sleep undecided about our course of action: if we were to yield to the cries of calumny, would we not tear ourselves away from our relatives, our friends, and our fellow countrymen in order to go under a foreign sky in search of the calm necessary for our work and the protection that was offered us there! But our country was dear to us and we have always waited for prejudice to give place to justice. This is, moreover, the nature of a man who intends to do good and who proves this to himself. As his courage becomes inflamed with the obstacles that are set before him, his innocence hides or makes him scorn the dangers that threaten. The just man is capable of an enthusiasm which the malicious person does not experience.

We have also encountered in other people those honest and generous feelings that have sustained us. All of our colleagues have hastened to make our work fruitful. When our enemies were pleased to have overwhelmed us, we saw men of letters and society, who until that time had been happy to encourage and pity us, come to our assistance and associate themselves with our efforts. May we be permitted to single out for public recognition all these courageous and talented collaborators! . . .

The public has judged the first seven volumes. We only ask the same indulgence for these following ones. If people do not wish to regard this dictionary as a fine and noble work, then they will be in agreement with us, provided they do not begrudge us even the privilege of having prepared all of the material. From the point from where we began to the point arrived at, the distance was immense; and in order to reach the goal that we had the daring or the temerity to set for ourselves, it was perhaps only necessary to have found the project in its present state and been forced to begin where we now finish. Thanks to our work, those who will come after us will be able to go further. Without mentioning what they will still have to do, we pass on to them at least the most beautiful compilation of tools and machines that has existed, with those plates regarding the mechanical arts, the most complete description that has ever been given of them, and an infinite amount of valuable pieces on all the sciences. O fellow countrymen and contemporaries, however severe you are in judging this work, remember that it was undertaken, continued, and finished by a small number of isolated men who were thwarted in their intentions, flaunted in the most odious way, slandered and insulted in the most atrocious manner, and who had no other incentive than a love of what is good, no other support than the sanction of a few voices, no other assistance than that found in the confidence of three or four businessmen.

Our principal object was to gather together all the discoveries of the preceding centuries. Without having neglected this first perspective, we do not exaggerate by estimating our contribution to the storehouse of ancient knowledge at several volumes in folio of new wealth. Let us suppose that a revolution, whose seed were to grow perhaps in some unknown region of the earth or to germinate secretly in the very center of civilized states, should burst forth in the future, overthrow cities, once again disperse the nations, and bring back ignorance and darkness. If a single complete edition of this work were to be conserved, all would not be lost.

I believe that at least one will not be able to contest that our work has been on a level with our century, and that is already something. The most educated of men will find in the text some ideas and facts that were unknown to him. May the general education take such rapid strides that in twenty years there will hardly be a single line in twenty of our pages that is not common knowledge! It is up to the masters of the world to hasten this happy revolution, for they have the power to spread or to restrict the sphere of enlightenment. Happy will be the time when they have all understood that security consists in governing educated men! The great attempts to assassinate rulers have been made only by blind fanatics.

Would we venture to grumble about our difficulties and to regret our years of work, if we were able to flatter ourselves about having weakened those feelings of confusion and bewilderment that are so contrary to the peace of societies? Would we complain if we had in fact induced our fellow men to love and tolerate each other as well as to recognize that universal morality is superior to all the particular moralities which inspire hatred and dissension and break or loosen the general and common ties of society?

This has been our goal at all times. Our enemies will have earned quite a rare and grand honor for the obstacles they created for us. The undertaking which they have opposed with such tenacity is reaching completion. If there is anything good in it, they will certainly not be praised for their role, and perhaps they will be blamed for the shortcomings of our project. However that may be, we invite them to glance through these final volumes. If they exhaust all the severity of their criticism on them and pour all the bitterness of their gall upon us, we are ready to pardon a hundred insulting remarks for one good observation. If they acknowledge that they have seen us constantly prostrated before the two things that create the good fortune and happiness of societies and are the only things truly deserving of homage, Virtue and Truth, they will find us indifferent to all their imputations.

As for our colleagues, we beg them to consider that the materials of these final volumes were gathered together in haste and arranged in a state of agitation, that the printing was done with unprecedented speed, that it was impossible for any man, whoever he might be, to keep his head in the revision and proof-reading of an infinite number of diverse and for the most part rather abstract subjects, if mistakes should arise and mar their articles, they should be neither offended nor surprised. So that the high reputation they enjoy and consider most precious be not compromised, we shall be content if all the flaws of this edition are imputed to us without reservation. After such an unrestricted yet precise statement, if some of our colleagues have forgotten that we have been forced to work in se-clusion without their advice, this could only be the result of our dissatisfaction, which we had no intention of showing them nor could we possibly have avoided it. Had we anything better to do than to call for the assistance of all those whose friendships and enlightenment had served us so well? Have we not been warned a hundred times of our deficiencies? Have we refused to recognize this? Is there a single one of our colleagues to whom we have not given in happier times all the possible tokens of respect? Will people accuse us of not knowing how much their collaboration was essential for the perfection of our work? If we are so accused, then this is the last moment of distress that has been reserved for us and to which we must still resign ourselves.

If one were to add to the years of our life which had elapsed when we planned this work those which we gave to its execution, it can easily be con-ceived that we have lived more than there remains for us to live. But we shall have obtained the reward that we desire of our contemporaries and grandchil-dren if we have given them cause to say one day that we have not lived a com-pletely useless life.

"The Encyclopedia" in *The Encyclopedia*

(FIRST PUBLISHED IN 1755.)

Encyclopedia, noun, feminine gender. (*Philosophy.*) This word signifies *unity of knowledge;* it is made up of the Greek prefix EN, *in*, and the nouns KYKLOS, *circle*, and PAIDEIA, *instruction, science, knowledge*. In truth, the aim of an *encyclopedia* is to collect all the knowledge that now lies scattered over the face of the earth, to make known its general structure to the men among whom we live, and to transmit it to those who will come after us, in order that the labors of past ages may be useful to the ages to come, that our grandsons, as they become better educated, may at the same time become more virtuous and more happy, and that we may not die without having deserved well of the human race.

It would have been difficult to set for oneself a more enormous task than this of dealing with everything that relates to man's curiosity, his duties, his needs and his pleasures. Accordingly, some people, accustomed as they are to judging the feasibility of an enterprise by the poverty of their own resources, have asserted that we would never finish our task. Our only answer to them will be the following passage from the writings of Chancellor Bacon, which seems to be addressed especially to them: "Those works are possible, which may be accomplished by some person, though not by every one; which may be done by many, though not by one; which may be completed in the succession of ages, though not within the hour-glass of one man's life; and which may be reached by public effort, though not by private endeavor." (*The Advancement of Learning*, Book II, Chapter I)

When one comes to reflect upon the vast subject matter of an encyclopedia, the one thing that can be perceived distinctly is that it cannot be the work of a single man. For how could one man, in the short space of his lifetime, hope to know and describe the universal system of nature and of art, seeing that the numerous and erudite society of academicians of *La Crusca* has taken forty years to compose its dictionary, and that the members of our French Academy worked sixty years on their *Dictionary* before publishing its first edition? Yet what is a linguistic dictionary, what is a compilation of the words of a language, assuming that it is executed as perfectly as possible? It is a very exact résumé of the articles to be included in a systematic encyclopedic dictionary.

But a single man, it may be said, can master all existing knowledge and can make such use as he desires of all the riches that other men have piled up. I cannot agree with this assumption. I am unable to believe that it is within the power of a single man to know all that can be known; to make use of all the knowledge that exists; to see all that is to be seen; to understand all that is comprehensible. Even if a systematic dictionary of the sciences and of the arts were to be nothing but a methodical collection of elementary principles, I should still want to know who is capable of discerning what is fundamental, and I should still ask who is the proper person to compose the elementary explanations; whether the description of the fundamental principles of a science or art should be a pupil's first attempt or the mature work of a master. . . .

We shall have to conclude, then, that a good dictionary can never be brought to completion without the co-operation of a large number of men endowed with special talents, because definitions of words are in no way different from definitions of things, and because a thing cannot be well defined or described except by those who have made a long study of it. But if this is admitted, how much more would be required for the execution of a work which, far from being limited to the definition of words, aims at describing in detail all that pertains to things!

A systematic universal dictionary of the arts and sciences cannot, therefore, be the work of one man alone. I will go further and say that I do not believe it can be done by any of the learned or literary societies that now exist, taken singly or together. . . .

This is a work that cannot be completed except by a society of men of letters and skilled workmen, each working separately on his own part, but all bound together solely by their zeal for the best interests of the human race and a feeling of mutual good will.

I say, *a society of men of letters and of skilled workmen,* for it is necessary to assemble all sorts of abilities. I wish the members of this society to work separately because there is no existing society from which one could obtain all the knowledge one needs, and because if one wanted the work to be perpetually in the making, but never finished, the best way to secure that result would be to form a permanent society. For every society has its meetings: there are intervals between meetings; each meeting lasts for only a few hours; part of this time is wasted in disputes; and so the simplest problems consume entire months. . . .

I add: *men bound together by zeal for the best interests of the human race and by a feeling of mutual good will,* because these motives are the most worthy that can animate the souls of upright people and they are also the most lasting. One has an inward sense of self-approval for all that one does; one becomes enthusiastic, and one undertakes, out of regard for one's friends and colleagues, many a task that one would not attempt for any other consideration. I can certainly testify from my own experience that the success of such attempts is all the more assured. The *Encyclopedia* has brought together its materials in a very short time. It is no sordid self-interest that has assembled and spurred on the authors; rather they have seen their efforts seconded by the majority of the men of letters from whom they expected assistance, and the only annoyance they have suffered in the course of their work has been caused by persons who had not the talent necessary to contribute one single good page.

If the government were to meddle with a work of this sort it would never be finished. All that the authorities ought to do is encourage its completion. A monarch may, by a single word, cause a palace to rise up out of the grass; but a society of men of letters is not the same thing as a gang of laborers. An encyclopedia cannot be produced on order. It is a task that needs rather to be pursued with perseverance than to be begun with ardor. . . .

But the circumstance that will give a superannuated appearance to the work and bring it the public's scorn will be above all the revolution that will occur in the minds of men and in the national character. Today, when philosophy is advancing with gigantic strides, when it is bringing under its sway all the matters that are its proper concern, when its tone is the dominant one, and when we are beginning to shake off the yoke of authority and tradition in order to hold fast to the laws of reason, there is scarcely a single elementary or dogmatic book which satisfies us entirely. We find that these works are put together out of the productions of a few men and are not founded upon the truths of nature. We dare to raise doubts about the infallibility of Aristotle and Plato, and the time has come when the works that still enjoy the highest reputation will begin to lose some of their great prestige or even fall into complete oblivion. Certain literary forms—for want of the vital realities and actual custom that once served them as models—will no longer possess an unchanging or even a reasonable poetic meaning and will be abandoned; while others that remain, and whose intrinsic value sustains them will take on an entirely new meaning. Such are the consequences of the progress of reason, an advance that will overthrow so many old idols and perhaps restore to their pedestals some statues that have been cast down. The latter will be those of the rare geniuses who were ahead of their own times.

In a systematic, universal dictionary, as in any work intended for the general education of mankind, you must begin by contemplating your subject in its most general aspects; you must know the state of mind of your nation, foresee the direction of its future development, hasten to anticipate its progress so that the march of events will not leave your book behind but will rather overtake it along the road; you must be prepared to work solely for the good of future generations because the moment of your own existence quickly passes away, and a great enterprise is not likely to be finished before the present generation ceases to exist. But if you would have your work remain fresh and useful for a long time to come—by virtue of its being far in advance of the national spirit, which marches steadily forward—you must shorten your labors by multiplying the number of your helpers, an expedient that is not, indeed, without its disadvantages, as I shall try to make plain hereafter.

Nevertheless, knowledge is not infinite, and cannot be universally diffused beyond a certain point. To be sure, no one knows just where this limit may be. Still less does anyone know to what heights the human race might have attained nor of what it might be capable, if it were in no way hampered in its progress. Revolutions are necessary; there have always been revolutions, and there always will be; the maximum interval between one revolution and another is a fixed quantity, and this is the only limit to what we can attain by our labors. For there is in every science a point beyond which it is virtually impossible to go. Whenever this point is reached, there will be created landmarks which will remain almost forever to astonish all mankind.

But if humanity is subject to certain limitations which set bounds to its strivings, how much narrower are the limits that circumscribe the efforts of individuals! The individual has but a certain quantity of energy both physical and intellectual. He enjoys but a short span of existence, he is constrained to alternate labor with repose; he has both instincts and bodily needs to satisfy, and he is prey to an infinite number of distractions. Whenever the negative elements in this equation add up to the smallest possible sum, or the positive elements add up to the largest possible sum, a man working alone in some branch of human knowledge will be able to carry it forward as far as it is capable of being carried by the efforts of one man. Add to the labors of this extraordinary individual those of another like him, and of still others, until you have filled up the whole interval of time between one scientific revolution and the revolution most remote from it in time, and you will be able to form some notion of the greatest perfection attainable by the whole human race—especially if you take for granted a certain number of accidental circumstances favorable to its labors, or which might have diminished its success had they been adverse.

But the general mass of men are not so made that they can either promote or understand this forward march of the human spirit. The highest level of enlightenment that this mass can achieve is strictly limited; hence it follows that there will always be literary achievements which will be above the capacities of the generality of men; there will be others which by degrees will fall short of that level; and there will be still others which will share both these fates.

No matter to what state of perfection an encyclopedia may be brought, it is clear from the very nature of such a work that it will necessarily be found among this third class of books. There are many things that are in daily use among the common people, things from which they draw their livelihood, and they are incessantly busy gaining a practical knowledge of these things. As many treatises as you like may be written about these matters and still there will always come a time when the practical man will know more about them than the writer of the book. There are other subjects about which the ordinary man will remain almost totally ignorant because the daily accretions to his fund of knowledge are too feeble and too slow ever to form any considerable sum of enlightenment, even if you suppose them to be uninterrupted.

Hence both the man of the people and the learned man will always have equally good reasons for desiring an encyclopedia and for seeking to learn from it.

The most glorious moment for a work of this sort would be that which might come immediately in the wake of some catastrophe so great as to suspend the progress of science, interrupt the labors of craftsmen, and plunge a portion of our hemisphere into darkness once again. What gratitude would not be lavished by the generation that came after this time of troubles upon those men who had discerned the approach of disaster from afar, who had taken measures to ward off its worst ravages by collecting in a safe place the knowledge of all past ages! In such a contingency, men would speak, in the same breath in which they named this great work, of the monarch in whose reign it was undertaken, of the minister to whom it was dedicated, of the eminent men who promoted its execution, of the authors who devoted themselves to it, and all of the men of letters who lent their aid. The same voice that recalled these services would not fail to speak also of the sufferings that the authors were obliged to undergo, of the indignities that were heaped upon them; and the monument raised to their fame would have several faces where one would see in turn the honors accorded to their memory and the signs of posterity's reprobation for the names of their enemies . . .

Both the real universe and the world of ideas have an infinite number of aspects by which they may be made comprehensible, and the number of possible "systems of human knowledge" is as large as the number of these points of view. The only system that would be free from all arbitrariness is, as I have said in our "Prospectus," the one that must have existed from all eternity in the mind of God. Hence the plan according to which one would begin with this eternal Being and then descend from Him to all the lesser beings that have emanated from His bosom in the course of time. This plan would resemble the astronomical hypothesis in which the scientist transports himself in imagination to the center of the heavenly bodies that surround him. It is a scheme that has both simplicity and grandeur, but one may discern in it a defect that would be serious in a work composed by men of science and addressed to all men in all ages to come. This is the fault of being too closely tied to our prevailing theology—a sublime science and one that is undoubtedly useful by reason of the knowledge that the Christian receives from it, but even more useful by reason of the sacrifices it demands and the rewards it promises.

As for a general system from which all that is arbitrary would be excluded—something we mortals can never hope to possess—it might not, perhaps, be so great an advantage to possess it. For what would be the difference between reading a book in which all the hidden springs of the universe were laid bare, and direct study of the universe itself? Virtually none: we shall never be capable of understanding more than a certain portion of this great book. To the extent that our impatience and our curiosity—which overmaster us and so often break up the course of our observations—disturb the orderly conduct of our reading, to that extent is our knowledge liable to become disjointed, as it now is. Losing the chain of inductive logic, and ceasing to perceive the connections between one step and those before and after, we would speedily come upon the same lacks and the same uncertainties. We are now busy trying to fill up the voids by means of the study of nature; we would still be busy trying to fill them up if we possessed and could meditate upon that huge book of which I have spoken; but the book would seem no more perfect to our eyes than would the universe itself, and the book would therefore be no less exposed to our presumptuous doubts and objections.

Since an absolutely perfect general plan would in no way supply the deficiencies arising from the weakness of our understanding, let us instead take hold of those things that are bound up with our human condition, being content to make our way upward from them toward some more general notions. The more elevated the point of view from which we approach our subject, the more territory it will reveal to us, the grander and more instructive will be the prospect we shall survey. It follows that the order must be simple, for there is rarely any grandeur without simplicity; it must be clear and easy to grasp, not a tortuous maze in which one goes astray and never sees anything beyond the point where one stands. No, it must rather be a vast, broad avenue extending far into the distance, intersected by other highways laid out with equal care, each leading by the easiest and shortest path to a remote but single goal.

Another consideration must be kept in view. I mean that if one banishes from the face of the earth the thinking and contemplating entity, man, then the sublime and moving spectacle of nature will be but a sad and silent scene; the universe will be hushed; darkness and silence will regain their sway. All will be changed into a vast solitude where unobserved phenomena take their course unseen and unheard. It is only the presence of men that makes the existence of other beings significant. What better plan, then, in writing the history of these beings, than to subordinate oneself to this consideration? Why should we not introduce man into our *Encyclopedia*, giving him the same place that he occupies in the universe? Why should we not make him the center of all that is? Is there, in all infinite space, any point of origin from which we could more advantageously draw the extended lines which we plan to produce to all the other points? With man at the center, how lively and pleasing will be the ensuing relations between man and other beings, between other beings and man!

For this reason we have decided to seek in man's principal faculties the main divisions within which our work will fall. Another method might be equally satisfactory, provided it did not put a cold, insensitive, silent being in the place of man. For man is the unique starting point, and the end to which everything must finally be related if one wishes to please, to instruct, to move to sympathy, even in the most arid matters and in the driest details. Take away my own existence and that of my fellow men and what does the rest of nature signify?

We have had occasion to learn in the course of our editorial labors that our *Encyclopedia* is a work that could only be attempted in a philosophical century; that this age has indeed dawned; and that posterity, while raising to immortality the names of those who will bring man's knowledge to perfection in the future, will perhaps not disdain to remember our own names. We have felt ourselves spurred on by the ever so agreeable and consoling idea that men may speak to one another about us, too, when we shall have ceased to exist; we have been encouraged by hearing from the mouths of a few of our contemporaries a certain seductive murmur that gives us some hint of what may be said of us by those happy and enlightened men in whose interests we have sacrificed ourselves, whom we esteem and whom we love, even though they have not yet been born. We have sensed within ourselves a growing spirit of emulation which has moved us to sacrifice the better part of ourselves and which has ravished away into the void the few hours of our lives of which we are genuinely proud. Indeed, man reveals himself to his contemporaries and is seen by them for what he is: an odd mixture of sublime talents and shameful weakness. But our failings follow our mortal remains into the tomb and disappear with them forever; the same earth covers them both, and there remains only the eternally lasting evidence of our talents enshrined in the monuments we raise to ourselves, or in the memorials that we owe to public gratitude and respect—honors which a proper awareness of our own deserts enables us to enjoy in anticipation, an enjoyment that is as pure, as great, and as substantial as any other pleasure, and in which there is nothing imaginary except, perhaps, the title deeds on which we base our pretensions. Our own claims are consigned to posterity in the pages of this work, and in the future they will be judged.

I have said that it could only belong to a philosophical age to attempt an *Encyclopedia*; and I say so because a work such as this demands more intellectual courage than is commonly to be found in ages of pusillanimous taste. All things must be examined, all must be winnowed and sifted without exception and without sparing anyone's sensibilities. One must dare to see, as we are beginning to do, that the history of literary forms is much the same as that of the first codification of law or the earliest foundation of cities—all owe their origin to some accident, to some odd circumstance, sometimes to a flight of human genius; and those who come after the first inventors are for the most part no more than their slaves. Achievements that ought to have been regarded only as first steps came blindly to be taken for the highest possible degree of development, and so, instead of advancing a branch of art toward perfection, these first triumphs only served to retard its growth by reducing all other artists to the condition of servile imitators. As soon as a name was given to some composition of a particular kind everyone was obliged to model all his productions rigorously after that model, which was perhaps only a sketch. If, from time to time, there appeared men of bold and original genius who, weary under the prevailing yoke, dared to shake it off, to strike out in a new direction away from the beaten path, and to give birth to some work of art to which the conventional labels and the prescribed rules were not exactly applicable, they fell into oblivion and remained for a long time forgotten.

Now, in our own age, we must trample mercilessly upon all these ancient puerilities, overturn the barriers that reason never erected, give back to the arts and sciences the liberty that is so precious to them. ... The world has long awaited a reasoning age, an age when the rules would be sought no longer in the classical authors but in nature, when men would come to sense the false and the true that are mingled in so many of the arbitrary philosophies of art, whatever field one works in. (I take the term *philosophy of art* in its most general meaning, that of a system of accepted rules to which it is claimed that one must conform in order to succeed.)

But the world has waited so long for this age to dawn that I have often thought how fortunate a nation would be if it never produced a man of exceptional ability under whose aegis an art still in its infancy makes its first too-rapid and too-ambitious steps forward, thereby interrupting its natural, imperceptible rhythm of development. The works of such a man must necessarily be a monstrous composite for the reason that genius and good taste are two different things. Nature bestows the first in an instant; the second is the product of centuries. These monsters come to be models for a whole nation; they determine standards of taste for a whole people. Men of talent who come later find that a preference in favor of the earlier genius has taken so firm a hold that they dare not affront it. The idea of what is beautiful will then grow dim, just as the idea of what is good would grow dim among savages who fell into an attitude of excessive veneration for some chieftain of dubious character who might have earned their gratitude by his preeminent services or by his fortunate vices. In morality, only God should serve men as a model, and in the arts, only nature. When the arts and sciences advance by imperceptible degrees, one man will not differ enough from another man to inspire the latter with awe, to lay the foundations of a new style or to form the national taste. Consequently, nature and reason are safeguarded in all their rights. Should these have been lost, they are on the point of being recovered: we shall go on to show how important it is to be able to recognize and to seize upon such a moment. . . .

Because it is at least as important to make men better as it is to make them less ignorant, I should not be at all displeased if someone were to make a collection of all the most striking instances of virtuous behavior. These would have to be carefully verified and then they could be arranged under various headings which they would illuminate and make vivid. Why should we be so concerned to preserve the history of men's thoughts to the neglect of the history of their good deeds? Is not the latter history the more useful? Is it not the latter that does the most honor to the human race? I have no wish to see evil deeds preserved; it would be better if they had never taken place. Men have no need of bad examples, nor has human nature any need of being further cried down. It should not be necessary to make any mention of discreditable actions except when these have been followed—not by the loss of the evildoer's life and worldly goods, which is all too often the sad consequence of virtuous behavior—but by a more fitting punishment of the wicked man: I want him to be wretched and despised as he contemplates the splendid rewards he has gained by his crimes. . . .

It is not the same with the origin and progress of an art or trade as it is with the origin and progress of a science. Learned men discuss things with each other, they write, they call attention to their discoveries, they contradict one another and are contradicted. These disputes make the facts plain and establish dates. Craftsmen, by contrast, live isolated, obscure, unknown lives; everything they do is done to serve their own interests; they almost never do anything just for the sake of glory. There have been inventions that have stayed for whole centuries in the closely guarded custody of single families; they are handed down from father to son; they undergo improvement or they degenerate without anyone's knowing to whom or to what time their discovery is to be assigned. The imperceptible steps by which an art develops necessarily makes dates meaningless. One man harvests hemp, another thinks of soaking it in water, a third combs it; at first it is a clumsy rope, then a thread, finally a fabric, but a whole age goes by in the interval between each of these steps and the one to follow. A man who first carried out the production of something from its natural state to its most perfect finished form would with difficulty remain unknown. How could it happen that a nation would find itself all of a sudden clothed in some new fabric and would fail to ask who was responsible for its creation? But such events never happen or, if they do, it is only at rare intervals.

Generally chance prompts the first experiments; either these are unfruitful and remain unknown, or someone else takes them up and obtains some successful results, but not enough to attract much attention. A third follows in the footsteps of the second, a fourth in the footsteps of the third, and so on until at last someone gets excellent results—this final product is the first to create a sensation. Or again, it may happen that an idea has scarcely made its appearance in one man's workshop before it bursts forth and spreads far and wide. People work at the same thing in several places, each one performs the same manipulations on his own initiative; and the same invention results. It is claimed by several people at the same time; it really belongs to no one; and it is attributed to the man who first makes a fortune out of it. If the invention is taken over from a foreign country, national jealousy suppresses the name of the inventor and his name remains unknown. . . .

There are trades where the craftsmen are so secretive that the shortest way of gaining the necessary information would be to bind oneself out to some master as an apprentice or to have this done by some trustworthy person. There would be few secrets that one would fail to ferret out by this method; all would have to be divulged without any exception.

I know that this desire for an end to secrecy is not shared by everyone. There are narrow minds, ill-formed souls, who are indifferent to the fate of the human race, and who are so completely absorbed in their own little group that they can see nothing beyond the boundaries of its special interests. These men insist that they deserve the title of good citizens, and I will allow it to them provided they will permit me to call them *bad men*. To listen to them talk, one would say that a well-executed encyclopedia, a general history of the industrial arts, should only take the form of a huge manuscript that would be carefully locked up in the King's library, hidden away from all other eyes but his, a state document and not a popular book. What is the good of divulging the knowledge a nation possesses, its private affairs, its inventions, its industrial processes, its resources, its trade secrets, its enlightenment, its arts, and all its wisdom! Is it not to these things that it partly owes its superiority over the rival nations that surround it? This is what they say; but this is what one might add: would it not be a fine thing if, instead of enlightening the foreigner, we could spread darkness over him or even plunge all the rest of the world into barbarism? People who argue thus do not realize that they occupy only a single point on our globe and that they will endure only an instant. To this point and to this instant they would sacrifice the happiness of future ages and that of the whole human race.

They know as well as anyone that the average duration of empires is less than two thousand years, and that in a briefer period of time, perhaps, the name *Frenchman*—a name that will endure forever in history—will be sought after in vain on the surface of the earth. Such considerations do not appreciably broaden the views of such persons; it seems that the word *humanity* is for them a word without meaning. Even so, they should be consistent! Yet in the very next breath they deliver tirades against the impenetrability of the Egyptian sanctuaries; they deplore the loss of the knowledge of the ancients; they are full of blame for the silence or negligence of ancient authors who have omitted something essential, or who speak so cryptically of many important subjects; and these critics do not see that they are demanding of the writers of earlier ages something they call a crime when a present-day writer does it, that they are blaming others for doing what they think it honorable to do. These "good citizens" are the most dangerous enemies that we have had in our capacity as editors.

In general we have tried to profit from criticism without ever replying in our own defense when the criticism was sound; we have ignored all attacks that were without foundation. It is not a sufficiently pleasant prospect for those who have been zealously blackening paper with attacks on us that if ten years hence the *Encyclopedia* has retained the reputation it enjoys today, there will no longer be anyone to read their scribblings—and that if the *Encyclopedia* is then forgotten, their diatribes will be even more completely so! I have heard it said that M. de Fontenelle's rooms were not large enough to hold all the writings that were published against him. Who today knows the title of a single one of them? Montesquieu's *Esprit des Lois* and Buffon's *Histoire Naturelle* have only just appeared, and the writings that attacked them are entirely forgotten.

We have already remarked that among those who have set themselves up as self-appointed censors of the *Encyclopedia* there is hardly a single one who had enough talent to enrich it by even one good article. I do not think I would be exaggerating if I should add that it is a work the greater part of which is about matters that these people have yet to study. It is written in a philosophical spirit, and in this respect the majority of those who pass adverse judgment on it are far from being up to the level of their own century. I call their works in evidence. It is for this reason that they will not endure; and for this same reason we may expect that our *Encyclopedia* will be more widely read and more highly appreciated in a few years' time than it is today. It would not be difficult to cite other authors who have had, and will have, a similar fate. Some (as we have already said) were once praised to the skies because they wrote for the multitude, they submitted to the yoke of prevailing ideas, and they kept within the ordinary reader's capacity for understanding; but these authors have lost their reputations in proportion as the human mind has made advances, and they have finally been forgotten altogether. Others, by contrast, too daring for the time during which their books appeared, have been little read, have been understood by only a few, have been little appreciated, and have long remained in obscurity, up to the day when the age they had outstripped had run its course, and another century, whose true children they were before it had even dawned, finally caught up with them and gave them in the end the justice their merits deserved.

20

IMMANUEL KANT
The Tasks of Philosophy

Born in a pietistic family of Scots origin, Immanuel Kant (1724–1804) studied theology, natural science, and philosophy at the University of Koenigsberg. Influenced by students of Leibniz and Christian Wolff, he was also impressed by his reading of Hume and Rousseau. After spending nine years as a private tutor, Kant was appointed as lecturer and eventually as a professor at the University of Koenigsberg.

His early work, published in the 1760s, consisted largely of criticisms and modifications of Wolff, Leibniz, and Descartes. From 1781–1790, he wrote his major—and monumental—critical works: *The Critique of Pure Reason* (1781), *Prolegomena to Any Future Metaphysics* (1783), *Groundwork of the Metaphysics of Morals* (1785), *Critique of Practical Reason* (1788), and *Critique of Judgment* (1790). The *Metaphysics of Morals* (1797) extended and applied his earlier ethical theory. Because *Religion Within the Limits of Reason Alone* (1794) raised the suspicion of the Prussian censor, Kant was forbidden to publish on religious subjects. That prohibition lapsed with the death of Frederick William III. Kant's later more popular essays—*On Perpetual Peace* (1795), *The Idea of a Universal History from a Cosmopolitan Point of View* (1784), and *What Is Enlightenment?* (1784)—were widely circulated and widely read.

Kant's critical, transcendental method transformed philosophy. He rephrased metaphysical questions to ask: What must be the case, if science provides a truthful account of experience? What must be the case if the commands of morality are universally obligatory? The condition that makes morality possible is that the will is both rational and autonomous—capable of freely legislating universally binding moral principles. The conditions that legitimate science are: (1) the forms of perceptual "intuitions" are a priori, that is, they are spatially and temporally structured by every rational mind; (2) judgments of experience are necessarily and universally structured by a system of a priori categories; and (3) both science and morality form unified, self-contained, rational systems.

Kant's work is the magnetic starting point for virtually all subsequent philosophy. Even his critics—Kierkegaard, Nietzsche, Marx—react to what they see as Kant's worldview. His influence on Hegel, Fichte, Schopenhauer, and such disparate contemporary philosophers as Rawls and Chomsky is manifest throughout their work.

Prolegomena to Any Future Metaphysics

INTRODUCTION

These *Prolegomena* are for the use, not of mere learners, but of future teachers, and even the latter should not expect that they will be serviceable for the systematic exposition of a ready-made science, but merely for the discovery of the science itself.

There are scholarly men to whom the history of philosophy (both ancient and modern) is philosophy itself; for these the present *Prolegomena* are not written. They must wait till those who endeavor to draw from the fountain of reason itself have completed their work; it will then be the turn of these scholars to inform the world of what has been done. Unfortunately, nothing can be said which, in their opinion, has not been said before, and truly the same prophecy applies to all future time; for since the human reason has for many centuries speculated upon innumerable objects in various ways, it is hardly to be expected that we should not be able to discover analogies for every new idea among the old sayings of past ages.

My purpose is to persuade all those who think metaphysics worth studying that it is absolutely necessary to pause a moment and, regarding all that has been done as though undone, to propose first the preliminary question, "Whether such a thing as metaphysics be even possible at all?"

If it be science, how is it that it cannot, like other sciences, obtain universal and lasting recognition? If not, how can it maintain its pretensions and keep the human mind in suspense with hopes never ceasing, yet never fulfilled? Whether then we demonstrate our knowledge or our ignorance in this field, we must come once for all to a definite conclusion respecting the nature of this so-called science, which cannot possibly remain on its present footing. It seems almost ridiculous, while every other science is continually advancing, that in this, which pretends to be wisdom incarnate, for whose oracle everyone inquires, we should constantly move round the same spot, without gaining a single step. And so its votaries having melted away, we do not find men confident of their ability to shine in other sciences venturing their reputation here, where everybody, however ignorant in other matters, presumes to deliver a final verdict, because in this domain there is actually as yet no standard weight and measure to distinguish sound knowledge from shallow talk.

After all it is nothing extraordinary in the elaboration of a science that, when men begin to wonder how far it has advanced, the question should at last occur whether and how such a science is possible at all. Human reason so delights building that it has several times built up a tower and then razed it to see how the foundation was laid. It is never too late to become reasonable and wise; but if the knowledge comes late, there is always more difficulty in starting a reform.

The question whether a science be possible presupposes a doubt as to its actuality. But such a doubt offends the men whose whole fortune consists of this supposed jewel; hence he who raises the doubt must expect opposition from all sides. Some, in the proud consciousness of their possessions, which are ancient and therefore considered legitimate, will take their metaphysical compendia in their hands and look down on him with contempt; others, who never see anything except it be identical with what they have elsewhere seen before, will not understand him, and everything will remain for a time as if nothing had happened to excite the concern or the hope for an impending change.

Nevertheless, I venture to predict that the independent reader of these *Prolegomena* will not only doubt his previous science, but ultimately be fully persuaded that it cannot exist unless the demands here stated on which its possibility depends be satisfied; and, as this has never been done, that there is, as yet, no such thing as metaphysics. But as it can never cease to be in demand—since the interest of common sense are so intimately interwoven with it—he must confess that a radical reform, or rather a new birth of the science, after a new plan, is unavoidable, however men may struggle against it for a while.

Since the *Essays* of Locke and Leibniz, or rather since the origin of metaphysics so far as we know its history, nothing has ever happened which could have been more decisive to its fate than the attack made upon it by David Hume. He threw no light on this species of knowledge, but he certainly struck a spark by which light might have been kindled had it caught some inflammable substance and had its smouldering fire been carefully nursed and developed.

Hume started chiefly from a single but important concept in metaphysics, namely, that of the connection of cause and effect (including its derivatives force and action, and so on). He challenged reason, which pretends to have given birth to this concept of herself, to answer him by what right she thinks anything could be so constituted that if that thing be posited, something else also must necessarily be posited; for this is the meaning of the concept of cause. He demonstrated irrefutably that it was perfectly impossible for reason to think *a priori* and by means of concepts such a combination, for it implies necessity. We cannot at all see why, in consequence of the existence of one thing, another must necessarily exist or how the concept of such a combination can arise *a priori*. Hence he inferred that reason was altogether deluded with reference to this concept, which she erroneously considered as one of her own children, whereas in reality it was nothing but a bastard of imagination, impregnated by experience, which subsumed certain representations under the law of association and mistook a subjective necessity (habit) for an objective necessity arising from insight. Hence he inferred that reason had no power to think such combinations, even in general, because her concepts would then be purely fictitious and all her pretended *a priori* cognitions nothing but common experiences marked with a false stamp. In plain language, this means that there is not and cannot be any such thing as metaphysics at all.

However hasty and mistaken Hume's inference may appear, it was at least founded upon investigation, and this investigation deserved the concentrated attention of the brighter spirits of his day as well as determined efforts on their part to discover, if possible, a happier solution of the problem in the sense proposed by him, all of which would have speedily resulted in a complete reform of the science.

But Hume suffered the usual misfortune of metaphysicians, of not being understood. It is positively painful to see how utterly his opponents missed the point of the problem; for while they were ever taking for granted that which he doubted, and demonstrating with zeal and often with impudence that which he never thought of doubting, they so misconstrued his valuable suggestion that everything remained in its old condition, as if nothing had happened. The question was not whether the concept of cause was right, useful, and even indispensable for our knowledge of nature, for this Hume had never doubted; but whether that concept could be thought by reason *a priori*, and consequently whether it possessed an inner truth, independent of all experience, implying a perhaps more extended use not restricted merely to objects of experience. This was Hume's problem. It was solely a question concerning the *origin*, not concerning the *indispensable* need of using the concept. Were the former decided, the conditions of the use and the sphere of its valid application would have been determined as a matter of course.

But to satisfy the conditions of the problem, the opponents of the great thinker should have penetrated very deeply into the nature of reason, so far as it is concerned with pure thinking—a task which did not suit them. They found a more convenient method of being defiant without any insight, namely, the appeal to *common sense*: It is indeed a great gift of? God to possess right or (as they now call it) plain common sense. But this common sense must be shown in action by well-considered and reasonable thoughts and words, not by appealing to it as an oracle when no rational justification for one's position can be advanced. To appeal to common sense when insight and science fail, and no sooner—this is one of the subtle discoveries of modern times, by means of which the most superficial ranter can safely enter the lists with the most thorough thinker and hold his own. But as long as a particle of insight remains, no one would think of having recourse to this subterfuge. Seen clearly, it is but an appeal to the opinion of the multitude, of whose applause the philosopher is ashamed, while the popular charlatan glories and boasts in it. Critical reason keeps common sense in check and prevents it from speculating, or, if speculations are under discussion, restrains the desire to decide because it cannot satisfy itself concerning its own premises. By this means alone can common sense remain sound. Chisels and hammers may suffice to work a piece of wood, but for etching we require an etcher's needle. Thus common sense and speculative understanding are each serviceable, but each in its own way: the former in judgments which apply immediately to experience; the latter when we judge universally from mere concepts, as in metaphysics, where that which calls itself, in spite of the inappropriateness of the name, sound common sense, has no right to judge at all.

I openly confess my recollection of David Hume was the very thing which many years ago first interrupted my dogmatic slumber and gave my investigations in the field of speculative philosophy a quite new direction. I was far from following him in the conclusions at which he arrived by regarding, not the whole of his problem, but a part, which by itself can give us no information. If we start from a well-founded, but undeveloped, thought which another has bequeathed to us, we may well hope by continued reflection to advance farther than the acute man to whom we owe the first spark of light.

I therefore first tried whether Hume's objection could not be put into a general form, and soon found that the concept of the connection of cause and effect was by no means the only concept by which the understanding thinks the connection of things *a priori*, but rather that metaphysics consists altogether of such concepts. I sought to ascertain their number; and when I had satisfactorily succeeded in this by starting from a single principle, I proceeded to the deduction of these concepts, which I was now certain were not derived from experience, as Hume had attempted to derive them, but sprang from the pure understanding. This deduction (which seemed impossible to my acute predecessor, which had never even occurred to anyone else, though no one had hesitated to use the concepts without investigating the basis of their objective validity) was the most difficult task which ever could have been undertaken in the service of metaphysics; and the worst was that metaphysics, such as it is, could not assist me in the least because this deduction alone can render metaphysics possible. But as soon as I had succeeded in solving Hume's problem, not merely in a particular case, but with respect to the whole faculty of pure reason, I could proceed safely, though slowly, to determine the whole sphere of pure reason completely and from universal principles, in its boundaries as well as in its contents. This was required for metaphysics in order to construct its system according to a safe plan.

But I fear that the execution of Hume's problem in its widest extent (namely, my *Critique of Pure Reason*) will fare as the problem itself fared when first proposed. It will be misjudged because it is misunderstood, and misunderstood because men choose to skim through the book and not to think through it—a disagreeable task, because the work is dry, obscure, opposed to all ordinary notions, and moreover long-winded. I confess, however, I did not expect to hear from philosophers complaints of want of popularity, entertainment, and facility when the existence of highly prized and indispensable knowledge is at stake, which cannot be established otherwise than by the strictest rules of a scholastic precision. Popularity may follow, but is inadmissible at the beginning. Yet as regards a certain obscurity, arising partly from the diffuseness of the plan, owing to which the principal points of the investigation are easily lost sight of, the complaint is just, and I intend to remove it by the present *Prolegomena*.

If in a new science which is wholly isolated and unique in its kind, we started with the prejudice that we can judge of things by means of alleged knowledge previously acquired—though this is precisely what has first to be called in question—we should only fancy we saw everywhere what we had already known, because the expressions have a similar sound. But everything would appear utterly metamorphosed, senseless, and unintelligible, because we should have as a foundation our own thoughts, made by long habit a second nature, instead of the author's. But the long-windedness of the work, so far as it depends on the subject and not on the exposition, its consequent unavoidable dryness and its scholastic precision, are qualities which can only benefit the science, though they may discredit the book.

Making plans is often the occupation of an opulent and boastful mind, which thus obtains the reputation of a creative genius by demanding what it cannot itself supply, by censuring what it cannot improve, and by proposing what it knows not where to find. And yet something more should belong to a sound plan of a general critique of pure reason than mere conjectures if this plan is to be other than the usual declamations of pious aspirations. But pure reason is a sphere so separate and self-contained that we cannot touch a part without affecting all the rest. We can do nothing without first determining the position of each part and its relation to the rest; for, as our judgment within this sphere cannot be corrected by anything without, the validity and use of every part depends upon the relation in which it stands to all the rest within the domain of reason. As in the structure of an organized body, the end of each member can only be deduced from the full conception of the whole. It may, then, be said of such a critique that it is never trustworthy except it be perfectly complete, down to the most minute elements of pure reason. In the sphere of this faculty you can determine and define either everything or nothing.

But although a mere sketch preceding the *Critique of Pure Reason* would be unintelligible, unreliable, and useless, it is all the more useful as a sequel. It enables us to grasp the whole, to examine in detail the chief points of importance in the science, and to improve in many respects our exposition, as compared with the first execution of the work.

With that work complete, I offer here a sketch based on an *analytical* method, while the *Critique* itself had to be executed in the *synthetical* style, in order that the science may present all its articulations, as the structure of a peculiar cognitive faculty, in their natural combination. But should any reader find this sketch, which I publish as the *Prolegomena to Any Future Metaphysics*, still obscure, let him consider that not everyone is bound to study metaphysics; that many minds will succeed very well in the exact and even in deep sciences more closely allied to the empirical, while they cannot succeed in investigations dealing exclusively with abstract concepts. In such cases men should apply their talents to other subjects. But he who undertakes to judge or, still more, to construct a system of metaphysics must satisfy the demands here made, either by adopting my solution or by thoroughly refuting it and substituting another. To evade it is impossible.

In conclusion, let it be remembered that this much abused obscurity (frequently serving as a mere pretext under which people hide their own indolence or dullness) has its uses, since all who in other sciences observe a judicious silence speak authoritatively in metaphysics and make bold decisions, because their ignorance is not here contrasted with the knowledge of others. Yet it does contrast with sound critical principles, which we may therefore commend in the words of Virgil:

"They defend the hives against drones, those indolent creatures."

All metaphysicians are therefore solemnly and legally suspended from their occupations till they shall have adequately answered the question, "How are synthetic cognitions *a priori* possible?" For the answer contains the only credentials which they must show when they have anything to offer us in the name of pure reason. But if they do not possess these credentials, they can expect nothing else of reasonable people, who have been deceived so often, than to be dismissed without further inquiry.

If they, on the other hand, desire to carry on their business, not as a science, but as an art of wholesome persuasion suitable to the common sense of man, this calling cannot in justice be denied them. They will then speak the modest language of a rational belief; they will grant that they are not allowed even to conjecture, far less to know, anything which lies beyond the bounds of all possible experience, but only to assume (not for speculative use, which they must abandon, but for practical use only) the existence of something possible and even indispensable for the guidance of the understanding and of the will in life. In this manner alone can they be called useful and wise men, and the more so as they renounce the title of metaphysicians. For the latter profess to be speculative philosophers; and since, when judgments *a priori* are under discussion, poor probabilities cannot be admitted (for what is declared to be known *a priori* is thereby announced as necessary), such men cannot be permitted to play with conjectures, but their assertion must be either science or nothing at all.

It may be said that the entire transcendental philosophy, which necessarily precedes all metaphysics, is nothing but the complete solution of the problem here propounded, in systematic order and completeness, and hence we have hitherto never had any transcendental philosophy. For what goes by its name is properly a part of metaphysics, whereas the former science is intended only to constitute the possibility of the latter and must therefore precede all metaphysics. And it is not surprising that when a whole science, deprived of all help from other sciences and consequently in itself quite new, is required to answer a single question satisfactorily, we should find the answer troublesome and difficult, nay, even shrouded in obscurity.

As we now proceed to this solution according to the analytical method, in which we assume that such cognitions from pure reason actually exist, we can only appeal to two sciences of theoretical knowledge (which alone is under consideration here), namely, pure mathematics and pure natural science. For these alone can exhibit to us objects in intuition, and consequently (if there should occur in them a cognition *a priori* can show the truth or conformity of the cognition to the object *in concreto*, that is, its actuality, from which we could proceed to the ground of its possibility by the analytical method. This facilitates our work greatly for here universal considerations are not only applied to facts, but even start from them, while in a synthetic procedure they must strictly be derived *in abstracto* from concepts.

But in order to rise from these actual and, at the same time, well-grounded pure cognitions *a priori* to a possible knowledge of the kind as we are seeking, namely, to metaphysics as a science, we must comprehend that which occasions it—I mean the mere natural, though in spite of its truth still suspect, cognition *a priori* which lies at the basis of that science, the elaboration of which without any critical investigation of its possibility is commonly called metaphysics. In a word, we must comprehend the natural conditions of such a science as a part of our inquiry, and thus the transcendental problem will be gradually answered by a division into four questions:

1. How is pure mathematics possible?

2. How is pure natural science possible?

3. How is metaphysics in general possible?

4. How is metaphysics as a science possible?

It may be seen that the solution of these problems, though chiefly designed to exhibit the essential matter of the *Critique*, has yet something peculiar, which for itself alone deserves attention. This is the search for the sources of given sciences in reason itself, so that its faculty of knowing something *a priori* may by its own deeds be investigated and measured. By this procedure these sciences gain, if not with regard to their contents, yet as to their proper use; and while they throw light on the higher question concerning their common origin, they give, at the same time, an occasion better to explain their own nature.

The Critique of Pure Reason

On the Canon of Pure Reason
  Second Section
On the ideal of the highest good,
  as a determining ground
of the ultimate end of pure reason.

In its speculative use reason led us through the field of experiences, and, since it could never find complete satisfaction for itself there, it led us on from there to speculative ideas, which in the end, however, led us back again to experience, and thus fulfilled its aim in a way that is quite useful but not quite in accord with our expectation. Now yet another experiment remains open to us: namely, whether pure reason is also to be found in practical use, whether in that use it leads us to the ideas that attain the highest ends of pure reason which we have just adduced, and thus whether from the point of view of its practical interest reason may not be able to guarantee that which in regard to its speculative interest it entirely refuses to us.

All interest of my reason (the speculative as well as the practical) is united in the following three questions:

1. What can I know?

2. What should I do?

3. What may I hope?

The first question is merely speculative. We have (as I flatter myself) already exhausted all possible replies to it, and finally found that with which reason must certainly satisfy itself and with which, if it does not look to the practical, it also has cause to be content; but from the two great ends to which this entire effort of pure reason was really directed we remain just as distant as if, out of a concern for comfort, we had declined this labor at the outset. If, therefore, the issue is knowledge, then this much at least is certain and settled, that we can never partake of knowledge with respect to those two problems.

The second question is merely practical. As such, to be sure, it can belong to pure reason, but in that case it is not transcendental, but moral, and thus it cannot be in itself a subject for our critique.

The third question, namely, "If I do what I should, what may I then hope?" is simultaneously practical and theoretical, so that the practical leads like a clue to a reply to the theoretical question and, in its highest form, the speculative question. For all hope concerns happiness, and with respect to the practical and the moral law it is the very same as what knowledge and the natural law is with regard to theoretical cognition of things. The former finally comes down to the inference that something is (which determines the ultimate final end) because something ought to happen; the latter, that something is (which acts as the supreme cause) because something does happen.

The Critique of Practical Reason

CONCLUSION

Two things fill the mind with ever new and increasing admiration and awe, the oftener and the more steadily we reflect on them: *the starry heavens above and the moral law within.* I have not to search for them and conjecture them as though they were veiled in darkness or were in the transcendent region beyond my horizon; I see them before me and connect them directly with the consciousness of my existence. The former begins from the place I occupy in the external world of sense, and enlarges my connexion therein to an unbounded extent with worlds upon worlds and systems of systems, and moreover into limitless times of their periodic motion, its beginning and continuance. The second begins from my invisible self, my personality, and exhibits me in a world which has true infinity, but which is traceable only by the understanding, and with which I discern that I am not in a merely contingent but in a universal and necessary connexion, as I am also thereby with all those visible worlds. The former view of a countless multitude of worlds annihilates, as it were, my importance as an *animal creature*, which after it has been for a short time provided with vital power, one knows not how, must again give back the matter of which it was formed to the planet it inhabits (a mere speck in the universe). The second, on the contrary, infinitely elevates my worth as an *intelligence* by my personality, in which the moral law reveals to me a life independent on animality and even on the whole sensible world—at least so far as may be inferred from the destination assigned to my existence by this law, a destination not restricted to conditions and limits of this life, but reaching into the infinite.

But though admiration and respect may excite to inquiry, they cannot supply the want of it. What, then, is to be done in order to enter on this in a useful manner and one adapted to the loftiness of the subject? Examples may serve in this as a warning, and also for imitation. The contemplation of the world began from the noblest spectacle that the human senses present to us, and that our understanding can bear to follow in their vast reach; and it ended—in astrology. Morality began with the noblest attribute of human nature, the development and cultivation of which give a prospect of infinite utility; and ended—in fanaticism or superstition. So it is with all crude attempts where the principal part of the business depends on the use of reason, a use which does not come of itself, like the use of the feet, by frequent exercise, especially when attributes are in question which cannot be directly exhibited in common experience. But after the maxim had come into vogue, though late, to examine carefully beforehand all the steps that reason purposes to take, and not to let it proceed otherwise than in the track of a previously well-considered method, then the study of the structure of the universe took quite a different direction, and thereby attained an incomparably happier result. The fall of a stone, the motion of a sling, resolved into their elements and the forces that are manifested in them, and treated mathematically, produced at last that clear and henceforward unchangeable insight into the system of the world, which as observation is continued may hope always to extend itself, but need never fear to be compelled to retreat.

This example may suggest to us to enter on the same path in treating of the moral capacities of our nature, and may give us hope of a like good result. We have at hand the instances of the moral judgment of reason. By analysing these into their elementary conceptions, and in default of *mathematics* adopting a process similar to that of *chemistry*, the *separation* of the empirical from the rational elements that may be found in them, by repeated experiments on common sense, we may exhibit both *pure*, and learn with certainty what each part can accomplish of itself, so as to prevent on the one hand the errors of a still *crude* untrained judgment, and on the other hand (what is far more necessary) the *extravagances of genius*, by which, as by the adepts of the philosopher's stone, without any methodical study or knowledge of nature, visionary treasures are promised and the true are thrown away. In one word, science (critically undertaken and methodically directed) is the narrow gate that leads to the true *doctrine of practical wisdom*, if we understand by this not merely what one ought to do, but what ought to serve *teachers* as a guide to construct well and clearly the road to wisdom which everyone should travel, and to secure others from going astray. Philosophy must always continue to be the guardian of this science; and although the public does not take any interest in its subtle investigations, it must take an interest in the resulting *doctrines*, which such an examination first puts in a clear light.

From *Fragments*

I am myself by inclination a seeker after truth. I feel a consuming thirst for knowledge and a restless passion to advance in it, as well as satisfaction in every forward step. There was a time when I thought that this alone could constitute the honor of mankind, and I despised the common man who knows nothing. Rousseau set me right. This blind prejudice vanished; I learned to respect human nature, and I should consider myself far more useless than the ordinary working-man if I did not believe that this view could give worth to all others to establish the rights of man.

LETTER TO JOHANN HEINRICH LAMBERT

December 31, 1765

Dear Sir:

For a number of years I have carried on my philosophical reflections on every earthly subject, and after many capsizings, on which occasions I always looked for the source of my error or tried to get some insight into the nature of my blunder, I have finally reached the point where I feel secure about the method that has to be followed if one wants to escape the cognitive fantasy that has us constantly expecting to reach a conclusion, yet just as constantly makes us retrace our steps, a fantasy from which the devastating disunity among supposed philosophers also arises; for we lack a common standard with which to procure agreement from them. Now, whatever the nature of the investigation before me, I always look to see what it is I have to know in order to solve a particular problem, and what degree of knowledge is possible for a given question, so that the judgment I make is often more limited but also more definite and secure than is customary in philosophy. All of my endeavors are directed mainly at the proper method of metaphysics and thereby also the proper method for philosophy as a whole.

You complain with reason, dear sir, of the eternal trifling of punsters and the wearying chatter of today's reputed writers, with whom the only evidence of taste is that they talk about taste. I think, though, that this is the *euthanasia* of erroneous philosophy, that it is perishing amid these foolish pranks, and it would be far worse to have it carried to the grave ceremoniously, with serious but dishonest hairsplitting. Before true philosophy can come to life, the old one must destroy itself; and just as putrefaction signifies the total dissolution that always precedes the start of a new creation, so the current crisis in learning magnifies my hopes that the great, long-awaited revolution in the sciences is not too far off. For there is no shortage of good minds.

LETTER TO MOSES MENDELSSOHN

April 8, 1766

Dear Sir,

For your kind efforts in forwarding the writings I sent you, I again send my sincerest thanks and my readiness to reciprocate in any way that I might be of service.

The unfavorable impression you express concerning the tone of my little book proves to me that you have formed a good opinion of the sincerity of my character, and your very reluctance to see that character ambiguously expressed is both precious and pleasing to me. In fact, you shall never have cause to change this opinion. For though there may be flaws that even the most steadfast determination cannot eradicate completely, I shall certainly never become a fickle or fraudulent person, after having devoted the largest part of my life of studying how to despise those things that tend to corrupt one's character. Losing the self-respect that stems from a sense of honesty would therefore be the greatest evil that could, but most certainly shall not, befall me. Although I am absolutely convinced of many things that I shall never have the courage to say, I shall never say anything I do not believe.

I wonder whether, in reading this rather untidily completed book, you noticed certain indications of my reluctance to write it. For since I had made some inquiries after learning of Swedenborg's visions first from people who knew him personally, then from some letters, and finally from his published works, I knew that I would never be at peace from the incessant questions of people who thought I knew something about this subject until I had disposed of all these anecdotes.

It was in fact difficult for me to devise the right style with which to clothe my thoughts, so as not to expose myself to derision. It seemed to me wisest to forestall other people's mockery by first of all mocking myself; and this procedure was actually quite honest, since my mind is really in a state of conflict on this matter. As regards the spirit reports, I cannot help but be charmed by stories of this kind, and I cannot rid myself of the suspicion that there is some truth to their validity, regardless of the absurdities in these stories and the fancies and unintelligible notions that infect their rational foundations and undermine their value.

As to my expressed opinion of the value of metaphysics in general, perhaps here and again my words were not sufficiently careful and qualified. But I cannot conceal my repugnance, and even a certain hatred, toward the inflated arrogance of whole volumes full of what are passed off nowadays as insights; for I am fully convinced that the path that has been selected is completely wrong, that the methods now in vogue must infinitely increase the amount of folly and error in the world, and that even the total extermination of all these chimerical insights would be less harmful than the dream science itself, with its confounded contagion.

I am far from regarding metaphysics itself, objectively considered, to be trivial or dispensable; in fact I have been convinced for some time now that I understand its nature and its proper place among the disciplines of human knowledge and that the true and lasting welfare of the human race depends on metaphysics— an appraisal that would seem fantastic and audacious to anyone but you. It befits brilliant men such as you to create a new epoch in this science, to begin completely afresh, to draw up the plans for this heretofore haphazardly constructed discipline with a master's hand. As for the stock of knowledge currently available, which is now publicly up for sale, I think it best to pull off its dogmatic dress and treat its pretended insights skeptically. My feeling is not the result of frivolous inconstancy but of an extensive investigation. Admittedly, my suggested treatment will serve a merely negative purpose, the avoidance of stupidity, but it will prepare the way for a positive one. Although the innocence of a healthy but uninstructed understanding requires only an *organon* in order to arrive at insight, a *katharticon* [cathartic] is needed to get rid of the pseudo-insight of a spoiled head. If I may be permitted to mention something of my own efforts, I think I have reached some important insights in this discipline since I last published anything on questions of this sort, insights that will establish the proper procedure for metaphysics. My notions are not merely general ones but provide a specific criterion. To the extent that my other distractions permit, I am gradually preparing to submit these ideas to public scrutiny, but principally to yours; for I flatter myself that if you could be persuaded to collaborate with me (and I include in this your noticing my errors) the development of science might be significantly advanced.

In my opinion, everything depends on our seeking out data for the problem, *how is the soul present in the world, both in material and in non-material things.* In other words, we need to investigate the nature of that power of external agency in a substance of this kind, and the nature of that *receptivity* or capacity of being affected, of which the union of a soul with a human body is only a special case. Since we have no experience through which we can get to know such a subject in its various relationships (and experience is the only thing that can disclose the subject's external power or capacity), and since the harmony of the soul with the body discloses only the reciprocal relationship of the *inner* condition (thinking or willing) of the soul to the *outer* condition of the material body (not a relation of one *external* activity to another *external* activity) and consequently is not at all capable of solving the problem, the upshot of all this is that one is led to ask whether it is really possible to settle questions about these powers of spiritual substances by means of a priori rational judgments. This investigation resolves itself into another, namely, whether one can by means of rational inferences discover a *primitive* power, that is, the primary, fundamental relationship of cause to effect. And since I am certain that this is impossible, it follows that, if these powers are not given in experience, they can only be the product of poetic invention. But this invention (an heuristic fiction or hypothesis) can never even be proved to be possible, and it is a mere delusion to argue from the fact of its conceivability (which has its plausibility only because no impossibility can be derived from the concept either). Such delusions are Swedenborg's daydreams, though I myself tried to defend them against someone who would argue that they are impossible; and my analogy between a real moral influx by spiritual beings and the force of universal gravitation is not intended seriously; it is only an example of how far one can go in philosophical fabrications, completely unhindered, when there are no *data*, and it illustrates how important it is, in such exercises, first to decide what is required for a solution of the problem and whether the necessary data for a solution are really available. If, for the time being, we put aside arguments based on fitingness or on divine purposes and ask whether it is ever possible to attain such knowledge of the nature of the soul from our experience—a knowledge sufficient to inform us of the manner in which the soul is present in the universe, how it is linked both to matter and to beings of its own sort—we shall then see whether *birth* (in the metaphysical sense), *life*, and *death* are matters we can ever hope to understand by means of reason. Here we must decide whether there really are not boundaries imposed upon us by the limitations of our reason, or rather, the limitations of experience that contains the *data* for our reason.

Your most devoted servant,
I. Kant

Königsberg

LETTER TO JOHANN GOTTFRIED HERDER

May 9, 1768

Reverend, esteemed Sir,

   As for my own work, since I am committed to nothing and with total indifference to my own and others' opinions, often turn my whole system upside down and observe it from a variety of perspectives in order finally perhaps to discover one which I can hope to point me in the direction of the truth, I have, since we parted, exchanged many of my views for other insights. My principal aim is to know the actual nature and limits of human capacities and inclinations, and I think I have finally more or less succeeded as far as ethics is concerned. I am now working on a Metaphysics of Ethics in which I fancy I shall be able to present the evident and fruitful principles of conduct and the method that must be employed if the so prevalent but for the most part sterile efforts in this area of knowledge are ever to produce useful results. I hope to be finished with this work this year, unless my fragile health prevents it.

your most devoted friend and servant,

I. Kant

Königsberg
the 9th of May
1767

LETTER TO MARCUS HERZ

toward the end of 1773

Noble Sir,
Esteemed friend,

   I doubt that many have tried to formulate and carry out to completion an entirely new conceptual science. You can hardly imagine how much time and effort this project requires, considering the method, the divisions, the search for exactly appropriate terms. Nevertheless, it inspires me with a hope that, without fear of being suspected of the greatest vanity, I reveal to no one but you: the hope that by means of this work philosophy will be given durable form, a different and—for religion and morality—more favorable turn, but at the same time that philosophy will be given an appearance that will make her attractive to shy mathematicians, so that they may regard her pursuit as both possible and respectable.

   I am eager to see your investigation of moral philosophy appear. I wish, however, that you did not want to apply the concept of reality to moral philosophy, a concept that is so important in the highest abstractions of speculative reason and so empty when applied to the practical. For this concept is transcendental, whereas the highest practical elements are pleasure and displeasure, which are empirical, and their object may thus be anything at all. Now, a mere pure concept of the understanding cannot state the laws or prescriptions for the objects of pleasure and displeasure, since the pure concept is entirely undetermined in regard to objects of sense experience. The highest ground of morality must not simply be inferred from the pleasant; it must itself be pleasing in the highest degree. For it is no mere speculative idea; it must have the power to move. Therefore, though the highest ground of morality is intellectual, it must nevertheless have a direct relation to the primary springs of the will. I shall be glad when I have finished my transcendental philosophy, which is actually a critique of pure reason, as then I can turn to metaphysics: it has only two parts, the metaphysics of nature and the metaphysics of morals. I shall bring out the latter of these first and I really look forward to it.

This winter I am giving, for the second time, a lecture course on *Anthropologie*, a subject that I now intend to make into a proper academic discipline. But my plan is quite unique. I intend to use it to disclose the sources of all the [practical] sciences, the science of morality, of skill, of human intercourse, of the way to educate and govern human beings, and thus of everything that pertains to the practical. I shall seek to discuss phenomena and their laws rather than the foundations of the possibility of human thinking in general. Hence the subtle and, to my view, eternally futile inquiries as to the manner in which bodily organs are connected with thought I omit entirely. I include so many observations of ordinary life that my auditors have constant occasion to compare their ordinary experience with my remarks and thus, from beginning to end, find the lectures entertaining and never dry. In my spare time, I am trying to prepare a preliminary study for the students out of this very pleasant empirical study, an analysis of the nature of skill (prudence) and even wisdom that, along with physical geography and distinct from all other learning, can be called knowledge of the world.

I saw my portrait on the front of the [issue of the *Allgemeine deutsche*] *Bibliothek*. It is an honor that disturbs me a little, for, as you know, I earnestly avoid all appearance of surreptitiously seeking eulogies or ostentatiously creating a stir. The portrait is well struck though not striking. But it pleases me to see that this sort of gesture stems from the amiable partisanship of my former students.

I am, with most sincere affection and regard,

Your devoted servant and friend,
I. Kant

LETTER TO MOSES MENDELSSOHN

August 16, 1783

Esteemed Sir,

That you feel yourself dead to metaphysics does not offend me, since virtually the entire learned world seems to be dead to her, and of course, there is the matter of your nervous indisposition (of which, by the way, there is not the slightest sign in your book, *Jerusalem*). I do regret that your penetrating mind, alienated from metaphysics, cannot be drawn to the *Critique*, which is concerned with investigating the foundations of that structure. However, though I regret this, and regret that the *Critique* repels you, I am not offended by this. For although the book is the product of nearly twelve years of reflection. I completed it hastily, in perhaps four or five months, with the greatest attentiveness to its content but less care about its style and ease of comprehension. Even now I think my decision was correct, for otherwise, if I had delayed further in order to make the book more popular, it would probably have remained unfinished. As it is, the weaknesses can be remedied little by little, once the work is there in rough form. For I am now too old to devote uninterrupted effort both to completing a work and also to the rounding, smoothing, and lubricating of each of its parts. I certainly would have been able to clarify every difficult point; but I was constantly worried that a more detailed presentation would detract both from the clarity and continuity of the work. Therefore I abstained, intending to take care of this in a later discussion, after my statements, as I hoped, would gradually have become understood. For an author who has projected himself into a system and become comfortable with its concepts cannot always guess what might be obscure or indefinite or inadequately demonstrated to the reader. Few men are so fortunate as to be able to think for themselves and at the same time be able to put themselves into someone else's position and adjust their style exactly to his requirements. There is only one Mendelssohn.

LETTER TO CARL FRIEDRICH STÄUDLIN

May 4, 1793

. . . The plan I prescribed for myself a long time ago calls for an examination of the field of pure philosophy with a view to solving three problems: (1) What can I know? (metaphysics). (2) What ought I to do? (moral philosophy). (3) What may I hope? (philosophy of religion). A fourth question ought to follow, finally: What is man? (anthropology, a subject on which I have lectured for over twenty years). With the enclosed work, *Religion within the Limits [of Reason Alone]*, I have tried to complete the third part of my plan. In this book I have proceeded conscientiously and with genuine respect for the Christian religion but also with a befitting candor, concealing nothing but rather presenting openly the way in which I believe that a possible union of Christianity with the purest practical reason is possible.

The biblical theologian can oppose reason only with another reason or with force, and if he intends to avoid the criticism that attends the latter move (which is much to be feared in the current crisis, when freedom of public expression is universally restricted), he must show our rational grounds to be weak, if he thinks ours are wrong, by offering other rational grounds. He must not attack us with anathemas launched from out of the clouds over officialdom. The complete education of a biblical theologian should unite into one system the products of his own powers and whatever contrary lessons he can learn from philosophy. By assessing his doctrines from the point of view of rational grounds, he shall be armed against any future attack.

Declaration concerning Fichte's *Wissenschaftslehre* (1799)

Public Declarations, No. 6; *Werke*, Ak. 12: 370–1.

I hereby declare that I regard *Fichte's Wissenschaftslehre* as a totally indefensible system. For pure theory of science is nothing more or less than mere *logic*, and the principles of logic cannot lead to any material knowledge, since logic, that is to say, *pure logic*, abstracts from the content of knowledge; the attempt to cull a real object out of logic is a vain effort and therefore something that no one has ever achieved. If the transcendental philosophy is correct, such a task requires a passing over into metaphysics. But I am so opposed to metaphysics, as defined according to *Fichtean* principles, that I have advised him, in a letter, to turn his fine literary gifts to the problem of applying the *Critique of Pure Reason* rather than squander them in cultivating fruitless sophistries. He, however, has replied politely by explaining that "he would not make light of scholasticism after all." Thus the question whether *I* take the spirit of Fichtean philosophy to be a genuinely critical philosophy is already answered by Fichte himself, and it is unnecessary for me to express my opinion of its value or lack of value. For the issue here does not concern an object that is being appraised but concerns rather the appraising subject, and so it is enough that I renounce any connection with that philosophy.

I must remark here that the assumption that I have intended to publish only a *propaedeutic* to transcendental philosophy and not the actual system of this philosophy is incomprehensible to me. Such an intention could never have occurred to me, since I took the completeness of pure philosophy within the *Critique of Pure Reason* to be the best indication of the truth of my work.

Since some reviewers maintain that the *Critique* is not to be taken literally in what it says about sensibility and that anyone who wants to understand the *Critique* must first master the requisite "standpoint" because Kant's precise words, like Aristotle's, destroy the spirit. I therefore declare again that the *Critique* is to be understood by considering exactly what it says and that it requires only the common standpoint that any mind sufficiently cultivated in such abstract investigations will bring to it.

There is an Italian proverb: May God protect us from our friends, for we shall watch out for our enemies ourselves. There are friends who mean well by us but who are doltish in choosing the means for promoting our ends. But there are also treacherous friends, deceitful, bent on our destruction while speaking the language of good will (*aliud lingua promptum, aliud pectore inclusum genere*, "who think one thing and say another"), and one cannot be too cautious about such men and the snares they have set. Nevertheless the critical philosophy must remain confident of its irresistible propensity to satisfy the theoretical as well as the moral, practical purposes of reason, confident that no change of opinions, no touching up or reconstruction into some other form, is in store for it; the system of the *Critique* rests on a fully secured foundation, established forever; it will be indispensable too for the noblest ends of mankind in all future ages.

Immanuel Kant

21

JOHANN GOTTFRIED HERDER
Culture and the Stages
of the Imagination

Born in Prussia, Johann Gottfried Herder (1744–1803) received a classical education before studying theology at Koenigsberg. After traveling widely, he was
ordained as a Lutheran minister. Goethe's influence assured his appointment as
head of the Lutheran clergy in Weimar in 1776. An eclectic thinker with a wide
scope of interests, he wrote on the philosophy of language (*Essay on the Origin
of Language*, 1772), the philosophy of history (*Ideas for the Philosophy of the
History of Mankind*, 1784–1791), and philosophical psychology (*Of the Cognition
and Sensation of the Human Soul*, 1778). A member of the Berlin Academy, he
took an active part in discussions about the relative merits of nationalism and
cosmopolitanism. A friend of Hamann, he speculated on the dynamic relation
between language and culture; a friend of Goethe, he developed theories about
the sources of thought in natural, organic processes. His influence extended
beyond Hegel and Schelling to the vitalism of Schopenhauer and Bergson, and
to Heidegger's nationalistic period.

Journal of My Voyage in the Year 1769

1. AUTOBIOGRAPHICAL REFLECTIONS

Every farewell is bewildering. One thinks and feels far less than one anticipated.
The intensity with which the mind focuses on the future blurs the sensibilities
towards what is left behind. If, in addition, the farewell is too drawn out, it also
tends to become wearisome. Only after departing does one begin to reflect on the
past and to regret lost opportunities. Thus I found myself confessing that I made
far from the best use of the library. It would have been of obvious advantage to
me had I drawn up a systematic plan of study in the subjects for which I was
responsible and made the history of their respective domains my chief concern.
O God, how infinitely fruitful, had I studied mathematics in its diverse aspects
and surveyed from this base the other sciences—physics and natural history—in
the most thorough fashion and with the aid of all the relevant data! Likewise,
my studies could only have gained in illumination had I made fuller use of the
books that were illustrated by engravings. Above all, I should have concentrated
far more on the French language. That would have been making use of my position [as librarian] and proving worthy of it. It would have enriched my education in the most agreeable manner, and prevented it from being neglected or
becoming wearisome. If only I had included in my studies mathematical drawing,
historical exposition, practice in speaking French! God, how much one loses in
those years through violent passions, through levity and through allowing oneself
to be carried away into the paths of chance, years that can never be regained.

I deplore the loss of those years of my mortal life; yet was it not entirely up to me to make better and more rewarding use of them? Had not Fate itself offered me ample dispositions towards this end? Had I chosen the studies mentioned, had I made French, history, natural science, mathematics, drawing, social intercourse and the aptitude for lively discussion my principal objects, into what society could they not have brought me? How much they could have facilitated the enjoyment of subsequent years! Then, thank God, I would not have become an author, and how much time I would have saved by this! How often I would have been spared from losing myself in audacious ventures and vain preoccupations! How much false honour, ambition, irritability and false love of learning; how many hours of mental confusion, how much folly in my reading, writing and thinking I would have avoided! Then too I would probably not have become a preacher, or at least not yet, and to be sure I would have lost many opportunities in just that sphere where I think I have made the best impression; but there too what an awkward situation I would have escaped! I would have learned to enjoy my life, to acquire thorough, practical knowledge, and to apply all that I learned. I would not have become an inkpot, a purveyor of pedantic scribblings, a dictionary of arts and sciences that I have not seen and do not understand; I would not have become a bookcase full of papers and books, whose only place is in the study. I would have avoided situations which confined my spirit and thus restricted it to a false, *intensive* knowledge of human nature, whereas it should rather have learned to know the world, men, societies, women and pleasure *extensively*—with the noble, fiery curiosity of a youth, who enters the world and runs quickly and tirelessly from one experience to another. How different a dwelling for how different a soul! Tender, resourceful, rich in experience rather than in booklearning, cheerful, lively and youthful, maturing into a happy manhood and a happy old age! Oh, what irreparable damage it does, the desire—the compulsion—to affect fruits when one should bear only blossoms! The fruits are artificial and premature; they not only fall off, but bear witness to the corruption of the tree! 'But then I would not have become what I am!' Well, and what would I have lost by that? How much I would have gained!

O God, who knoweth the elements of human souls and hath fitted them to their bodily vessels, was it necessary only for the design as a whole, or also for the happiness of the individual, that there should be souls which, having as it were entered this world in timid confusion, never know what they are doing or what they are about to do, never arrive where they wish to go and thought they were going, who never really *are* where they happen to be, and only rush from one mental state into another in a haze of feverish activity, astonished by their own whereabouts? When, o God, Thou Father of souls, will these find rest and philosophical poise? In this world? At least in their old age? Or are they destined to end their lives prematurely through just such a feverish, nightmarish activity, without ever really having achieved anything or enjoyed anything properly, snatching at everything in haste like hurried, frightened vagrants, only to embark in death on a new pilgrimage not unlike that of their lives? Father of men, wilt Thou vouchsafe to instruct me?

Thus one thinks when one moves from one situation into another; and what a wide scope for thought a ship, suspended between sky and sea, provides! Everything here adds wings to one's thoughts, gives them motion and an ample sphere! The fluttering sail, the ever-rolling ship, the rippling waves, the flying clouds, the broad, infinite atmosphere! On land one is chained to a fixed point and restricted to the narrow limits of a situation. Often this point is a student's chair in a musty study, a place at a monotonous boarding-house table, a pulpit, a lecture-desk. And the situation is often a small town, where one is the idol of an audience of three, to whom alone one pays attention, and a monotony of occupation in which one is jostled alike by conventionality and presumption. How petty and restricted do life, honour, esteem, desires, fears, hate, aversion, love, friendship, delight in learning, professional duties and inclinations become in such circumstances; how narrow and cramped the whole spirit in the end! But let a man suddenly retire from this scene—or rather be thrown out, without books, writing occupation, or homogenous society—what a different prospect! Where is the solid land on which I stood so solidly, and the little pulpit, and the armchair, and the lecture desk at which I used to give myself airs? Where are the people of whom I stood in awe, and whom I loved? O soul, how will it be with you when you leave this little world? The narrow, firm, restricted center of your sphere of activity is no more; you flutter in the wind or float on a sea—the world is vanishing from you—has vanished beneath you! What a changed perspective! But such a new mode of looking at things costs tears, remorse, the extrication of one's heart from old attachments, self-condemnation! I was no longer satisfied with myself even as regards my virtue; I saw it as nothing but a weakness, an abstract name which everyone learns from his youth onward to transform into a reality. Whether it was the sea air, the effect of the food on board, restless sleep, or whatever else, I had hours in which I could not comprehend any virtue, even the virtue of a wife, which I had always thought the highest and truest. Even as regards man's improvement—individual cases apart—I found only weakening of character, self-torture, or the old faults in new disguise. Oh, why is man deluded by language into thinking that abstract shadow images represent solid bodies, existing realities? When will I reach the stage at which I can destroy in myself everything I have learned so far and rediscover, in my own convictions alone, what I have really learned, what I really think and believe? Companions of my youth, how much I will have to tell you when I see you again, when I can enlighten you about the darkness which at this time still hung over me! Nothing is virtue but human life and happiness; action is the only thing that matters; everything else is a shadow, is sophistry. Too much chastity, when it weakens a man, is just as much vice as too much unchastity; every renunciation should be negation only: to make it into privation for its own sake, and then to make this into a positive element of one's chief virtue—where will this lead us? . . .

Our first conversations are naturally family conversations, in which we learn to know characters that we did not know before; in this way I came to know a tormentor, a spoiled boy, etc. Then, one readily throws oneself back on ideas to which one has been accustomed, and in this way I became a philosopher on the boat—but a philosopher who had as yet learned imperfectly how to philosophize from nature without books and instruments. Had I this ability, what a vantage point I would have had, sitting at the foot of a mast on the wide ocean, from which to philosophize on the sky, the sun, the stars, the moon, the air, the wind, the sea, the rain, the currents, the fish and the ocean floor, and to discover the physical laws governing all these from within, as it were. Philosopher of nature— that should be your position with the youth whom you are teaching! Place yourself with your pupil on the wide sea and show him facts and the real properties of things; and do not explain them to him in words, but let him explain everything for himself. And I myself, I too will place myself at the foot of the mast, where I once sat, and will trace the course of the electric spark from the impulse of the initial wave to the thunderstorm, link water pressure to atmospheric pressure, follow the motion of the ship, embraced by the waters, in relation to the form and motion of the stars, and not stop until I know everything from immediate personal conviction, as now I know nothing. . . .

2. ARRIVAL IN FRANCE

A first work, a first book, a first system, a first visit, a first thought, a first design or plan, a first conception—these always assume in my mind gothic dimensions, and much in my plans, designs, works, conceptions, has either not yet passed from this gigantic style into one of finer proportions, or else has vanished at the first stage. A feeling for the sublime, then, is the bent of my soul; it determines my love, my hate, my admiration, my dreams of happiness and unhappiness, my resolution to live in society, my expression, my style, my deportment, my physiognomy, my conversation, my occupation—everything. When I am in love, for example, my emotions border on the sublime, to the point of tears. How powerfully separation affects me, whereas to the Angolas only the present moment matters! How a single misfortune of my loved one, a single tear in her eye, can move me! What attached me to her more closely than this? What has ever moved me more than separation from her?—From this same source comes also my taste for speculation and for the sombre in philosophy, poetry, stories and ideas! From this comes my fascination for bygone ages and the shades of antiquity, my liking for the Hebrews, considered as a nation, for the Greeks, Egyptians, Celts, Scots, etc.! From this also resulted my early dedication to holy orders. Beyond a doubt, local prejudices of my boyhood played a large part in this; but so, with equal certainty, did my impressions of church and altar, of pulpit and sacred eloquence, of the church service and religious reverence. From this came my first series of undertakings, my youthful dreams of a water-world, my favourite pursuits in the garden, my solitary walks, the shudder which accompanied my psychological discoveries, with their revelation of new thoughts in the human soul, my half-comprehensible, half-sombre style, my perspective of *Fragments, Groves, Torsos, Archives of the Human Race*—everything! My life is a passage through gothic arches or an avenue full of green shadows. The prospect is always awe-inspiring and sublime; the entrance into it a sort of shudder, the exit full of perplexities and confusion—then the avenue suddenly leads into wide open country. It is then that I have to put my ideas to the best use I can; to tread thoughtfully but also to notice the sun breaking through the leaves and painting shadows that are all the lovelier for the rays being broken by the leaves; to see the meadows with their bustle of activity; and yet, all the time, to keep to the path . . .

What have I done in the past that I should be fated always to see shadows instead of experiencing real things? I enjoy little, or rather, I enjoy too much, to excess, and therefore without relish. The sense of touch and the world of sensuous pleasures—these I have not enjoyed. I see and feel *at a distance* and put obstacles in the way of my own enjoyment through over-eager anticipation and through weakness and foolishness in the moment of experience itself. In my friendships and my contact with society I feel in advance a premature anxiety or a strange, excessive expectation; the first makes it difficult for me to enter into a relationship, while the second always deceives and makes a fool of me. So in every situation my imagination, swelling up in advance and turning away from the realities of the situation, kills my enjoyment, makes it jaded and dull, and only afterwards allows me to see that I have not enjoyed my experience, that it has in fact been jaded and dull. So I am even in love, which I feel platonically, in absence more than in the present moment, in fear and hope more than in enjoyment; in abstractions, intellectual conceptions, more than in realities. So I am in my reading: how I burn with eagerness to read a book, to possess it, and how my spirits sink when I do read it, when I do possess it! How many even of the best authors have I read through—purely for the sake of factual information, absorbed in the illusion of their systems, carried away by the work as a whole, interested only in the surface content—without pausing to fully savour the spirit of the work! Thus do I read, plan, work, travel, write; thus I am in all things!

Feelings of this kind led me to the notion of thinking out a work *on the youth and aging of the human soul*, in which—partly from my own sad experience, partly from the example of other souls that I have had the opportunity of knowing—I would teach men how to avert such premature old age, to rejoice in their youth and to enjoy it as they should. This plan had already taken shape in Riga, in gloomy days when the whole organization of my mind was, as it were, paralysed, when the driving wheel of external experience was motionless, and my mind, penned in its own wretched ego, had lost the happy longing to gather in fresh ideas and pleasures and notions of perfection. I went around stupid, unthinking, apathetic and idle, talked nonsense, etc., took up a hundred books only to throw them away again and still to know nothing. Then I suddenly thought of the noble Swift, who shrugged his shoulders at the old, wretched, gray-haired man he saw in his mirror and in contrast portrayed—for himself and for me—the young, happy world of Plato and Socrates, in which, amid jests and play, men exercised and trained their minds and bodies and made them slender, strong and firm, like beautiful olive trees at the rim of a spring. I thought of the old and ever-young Montaigne, who always knew how to rejuvenate himself in his old age, and I stood there perplexed, bewildered and old in my youth.

The human mind has its ages like the body. Its youth is curiosity, and therefore childish belief, an insatiable desire to see things, especially wonderful things; it is the gift of learning languages—provided that they are taught only on the basis of firm conceptions and real things; it is youthful flexibility and vigour, etc. An old person who has this sort of curiosity is always contemptible and childish.

The child cannot take much real interest in all the things he learns through his curiosity: he merely sees, wonders and admires. Hence his reverence for old people who seem to him really worthy of veneration. Hence the depth of his impressions, which are as it were driven into him by wonder and admiration. But the more our minds and bodies grow, the more the sap increases and wells up in both, the closer we approach the objects of our experience or the more strongly we attract them towards ourselves. We colour them with the fire of our blood—and this is *imagination*, the dominant trait of youth. Love in all its aspects becomes the enchanted world in which it roams. In solitude it evokes the poet in us and the craving for poetry, for stories of the distant past, for romances. It kindles our first enthusiasms, as those of friendship, and paints them in didactic or poetic colours. It fashions our world of pleasures, our sympathies and tender feelings. Even the world of learning assumes in the youthful imagination the form of images, of sensations, of upsurging delight. All this is natural to youth. In an old greybeard such ardent, fiery feelings are as foolish as they are trifling.

The youth becomes a man and a member of society—but primarily the latter—and thus, as our world demands, the strong sallies of his imagination are stifled:

he learns to adapt himself to the ways of others, and at the same time to distinguish himself from them; that is to say, he develops wit and discrimination. He becomes a part of the social world and learns all the refinements of social polish, refinements to which he is encouraged by love, by the desire to please his fair one and cut a worthy figure in her eyes; by friendship, which is mostly a social matter with us; by pleasures, which are never so universal unless they are social—in short, by everything . . . Through becoming part of society at large the youth develops into manhood, the latter being the really important stage, to which the former merely constitutes the preliminary process: a process that is indispensable, yet not to be lingered over. In the man, *bon sens* and wisdom in affairs predominate. He has traversed the paths of curiosity and has found that there is much in life that is empty, that deserves a first glance and nothing more; he has lived through the age of the passions and feels that they are good insofar as they teach him about life and the world, but he must beware lest they come to dominate the rest of his life for then everything is lost. Hence he must acquire calmness, genuine kindness, friendship, wisdom, usefulness, in short, *bon sens*. This is the most crucial age in a man's social life, the period when his mental and physical activities are at their peak. It is during manhood that man can be a true philosopher of action, of wisdom and experience.

The old man is a prater and a philosopher in words. He recites his experiences in the form of dull, long-winded lessons, completely devoid of focus and exactitude, mere commonplaces. He has a great store of these because he thinks himself rich in experience, and pontificates about the laxity of present-day youth from which he is too far removed to be able to join in. This is the age of rest. The mind is scarcely open to new impressions any more and little disposed to new experiences. As it closes its gates, so to speak, it also becomes more timid, more rigid, incapable of benefiting from instruction, satiated, as it were, with lessons and precepts.

Every man must pass through these stages, for they develop out of each other; and *one can never enjoy any given stage if he has not enjoyed the preceding one*: the first always contains the data necessary for the second, and the whole series proceeds in geometric, not arithmetic, progression. Only in the totality of its sequences can one enjoy life and only by reviewing it as one continuous whole can one also enjoy a tranquil old age. *One can never wholly annul what has gone before (even by way of improvement) without sacrificing the present.*

But, on the other hand, if a man 1) fails to do justice to the stage of life in which he finds himself, 2) goes on too soon to the next, 3) tries to live them all at once, or 4) returns to a stage he has already lived through, then the order of nature is upset: then we have prematurely aged souls, young greybeards, greybeard youths. And the prejudices of our society afford many chances for such monsters to develop. These prejudices assume some stages of life prematurely, encourage regression in others and thus subvert the whole nature of man. Our education, our instruction, our whole way of life is like this. A single voice raised for truth and humanity would be a blessing here; it could ensure the enjoyment of the whole of a human lifetime—it would be invaluable.

All this suggests one master rule: *Make the images of your imagination so enduring that you do not lose them, yet, at the same time, refrain from recalling them at inappropriate moments!* This may serve as a rule for preserving the eternal youth of the mind. He whose earliest images are so weak that he cannot express them strongly—with exactly the degree of strength in which he received them—that man is feeble and old. This is what happens to all widely read men and to men who read too much, who either never have the chance to recall in a strong and lively manner what they have read, or who do not have sufficient vivacity to read as though they themselves saw, felt, experienced and applied what they were reading; or, finally, who sacrifice their own individuality through excessive, sporadic, scattered reading!

The ship is the archetype of a very special and severe form of government. Since it is a small state which sees enemies everywhere around it—sky, storm, wind, sea, currents, cliffs, darkness, other ships, the shore—it requires a government which comes close to the despotism of the early hostile ages. Here is a monarch with his prime minister, the helmsman; everyone below him has his appointed place and duties, and any neglect of these—especially any rebellion against them—is very severely punished. There are two reasons, then, why Russia does not as yet have a good navy. First, there is no discipline on their ships— just where it should be strictest unless the whole ship is to be lost. Anecdotes from Peter's life show that even he had to submit to this state of affairs and allow himself to be thrust, sword in hand, into his cabin, because he commanded unjustly. Secondly, instead of everyone having his assigned place, anyone is used for anything. The decrepit old soldier who no longer has the desire or the ability to learn anything new becomes a sailor, and soon thinks himself a real seaman when he can hardly clamber up the rigging. In bygone days, when navigation as an art was scarcely known, when ships consisted of oars and hands, men and soldiers, and nothing more, this state of affairs might have been feasible. But nowadays there is no art more complex than navigation. Everything may depend on a single oversight, a single case of ignorance. The Russians, therefore, would have to become accustomed to the sea from their youth and learn from other nations before they practice . . . No nation is more eager to imitate, to adopt the ways of others than they; but then, when they think they know everything, they never investigate further and so always remain bunglers in everything they undertake. It is not only as seafarers that they try to copy others. They show the same facile tendency when they pretend to assume French manners and the French language. The same is true of their handicrafts, their manufactures and their arts. But in all these spheres they stop short of really becoming *proficient* imitators. They never get beyond a certain point. All the same, I see in this desire to imitate, in this childlike passion for innovation, nothing but the healthy disposition of a developing nation—a tendency in the right direction. Let it learn, imitate and compile from all sides; let it even remain for a time less than fully developed. But let there also come a time, a monarch, a century which will lead the nation to the stage of fruition. What a great intellectual undertaking we have here for a statesman—to consider how the energies of a youthful, half-savage people can be brought to maturity so that it becomes a genuinely great and original nation. Peter the Great will always remain the creator who brought about the dawn of a new day; but the noontide is yet to come, and the great work of 'civilizing a nation to perfection' is yet to be accomplished . . .

One imagines that as one glides past countries and continents at sea one will think a great deal about them; but actually one does not see them. They are only mists lying in the distance, and so, for the most part, are the ideas which ordinary minds form of them. In this respect the navigation of the ancients was different: it showed the sailor coasts and races of men. In their battles we hear characters, real men speaking. Today everything is a science—battles, war, navigation, everything. I wanted to enlist the aid of travel-books so that I could form an opinion about the countries whose coasts we were passing, as if I had seen the countries themselves; but this too was in vain. I found nothing on the ship but lists of landfalls and saw nothing but distant coasts.

Livonia, thou province of barbarism and luxury, of ignorance and pretended taste, of freedom and slavery, how much would there be to do in thee! How much to do to destroy barbarism, to root out ignorance, to spread culture and freedom, to be a second Zwingli, Calvin or Luther to this province! Can I do this? Do I have the disposition, the opportunity, the talents? What must I do to attain this end? What must I destroy in myself?—Do I need to ask? I must give up writing useless criticisms and pursuing dead researches; raise myself above disputations and literary fame; dedicate myself to the benefit and the education of the living world; win the confidence of the administration, the imperial government and the court; travel through France, England and Italy with this in mind and acquire the French language and *savoir-faire*, the English sense of reality and freedom, the Italian taste for subtle invention, the German thoroughness and knowledge, and lastly, where it is necessary, Dutch erudition; arouse others to a high opinion of me and myself to great plans; conform to the age in which I live and acquire the spirit of commerce and polity; dare to examine everything from the point of view of politics, the state and finances; not expose myself to any further ridicule and try to make good as quickly as possible my previous mistakes in this respect; concentrate night and day on becoming this guiding genius of Livonia, on getting to know the country from A to Z, on thinking and acting practically in all things, on accustoming myself to talk persuasively to society, the nobility and the common men and win them over to my side.

But is all this really dormant within you, noble-minded youth? Is it just a matter of neglect, a case of having failed so far to translate it into reality? The narrowness of your education, the slavery of your native land, the petty, trifling spirit of your century, the uncertain state of your career, have all combined to limit you, to debase you so that you scarcely recognize yourself. You are wasting the fire of your youth, the finest heat of your genius, the strongest part of your ambitious passion in useless, coarse, wretched critical groves. You have a soul as sluggish and slack as all the fibres and nerves of your body. Wretched man, what manner of things do you busy yourself with? How do they compare with the things which you should, and—since the occasion, the opportunity and the obligation are there—*could* be doing? O that a Fury would appear in my groves to frighten me, to chase me out of them forever and banish me to the useful activity of the great world! Livonia is a province given over to foreigners! And many foreigners have enjoyed it in the past, but only in their merchants' way, in order to get rich from it; to me, also a foreigner, it is given for a higher purpose, that I may develop it! . . . Let my first prospect be the study of the human soul, in itself and in its manifestations on this earth; its strains and stresses, its hopes and satisfactions, its influence on a man's character and on his conception of his duties; in short, let me discover the springs of human happiness. Everything else is to be set aside whilst I am engaged in gathering materials for this task and in learning to know, arouse, control and use every motive force in the human heart, from fear and wonder to quiet meditation and gentle day-dreaming. For this purpose I will collect data from the history of all ages; each shall yield to me the picture of its own customs, usages, virtues, and vices, and of its own conception of happiness; and I will trace them all down to the present and so learn to use it rightly. In every age—though in each in a different way—the human race has had happiness as its objective; we in our own times are misled if like Rousseau, we extol ages which no longer exist and never did exist, if we make ourselves miserable by painting romantic pictures of these ages to the disparagement of our own, instead of finding enjoyment in the present. Seek then even in biblical times only that religion and virtue, those examples, those forms of happiness, which are appropriate to us: become a preacher of the virtue *of your own age!* Oh, how much I have to do to achieve this! . . .

I. In what does true culture consist? Not merely in providing laws but in cultivating morals and customs, especially if the laws are derived from imported foreign principles. And in framing legislation for Russia, should 'honour' be of high priority? What image does Russia project as a nation? Its laziness is not as bad as it is made out to be; up to a point it is also perfectly natural: every nation went through such a sleepy stage before its true awakening. Its cunning, its passion for imitation, its frivolity: do these not also contain seeds of good? How are these seeds to be nurtured into germination? What are the obstacles one might meet? Which path leads to freedom gradually, since sudden freedom might prove harmful? What form should the institutions take? Could not the sudden acquisition of colonies present a real danger? Would it not prove equally hazardous to be too quick in adopting other countries, such as Germany, as models? The excellence of good institutions counts for more than the best of laws and certainly as much as any example set by the court, especially in such spheres as agriculture, family life and housekeeping. I would comment on the dependence of the subjects, their taxes and their general way of life, and make some proposals for a new economic order of society more in keeping with the spirit of the Russian economy. No other country—not even Sweden—can always serve here as a model. Concerning luxury, I would argue that mere decrees are of no avail whatsoever; mention of the evil consequences of such decrees in Riga should drive this point home. The example of the court [in this respect] is only valid at the court, though even there its prestigious advantages are not without disadvantages. Many individual examples taken from the diverse provinces or, better still, from individual households should prove more relevant and effective. I would show also that as a result of a number of Russian gentlemen lining their pockets in Petersburg, the state of Petersburg is degenerating into tasteless splendour—though the Empress is working against this. In France conditions are somewhat different because of the constant visits of foreigners and the different nature of the institutions; but even there the country is faced with exhaustion largely as a result of the bad example set by provincial governors and by the supervisors on farms and in the factories.

II. Next I would point out that neither English, nor French, nor German legal minds can legislate for Russia; and that neither Greece nor Rome can be taken as models. It is not obvious enough, how mistaken Russia was to imitate Sweden? There are peoples in the East from whom Russia can learn far more: Persians, Assyrians, Egyptians, Chinese and Japanese. The principles underlying legislation must, moreover, pay heed to the character of Russia's nations, their multiplicity and their various levels of culture: there are regions which are highly developed, but there are also those which are still very primitive or underdeveloped. The laws which the latter need for their development are the basic laws of mankind generally—the laws of crude primitive times. Russia can make excellent use of her underdeveloped peoples. The semi-developed regions require laws that will in the first place do no more than turn them into governable provinces. The differences between the spirit and culture in the provinces and in the capitals must also be kept in mind. Clearly, the capitals and commercial cities need laws of their own. In all this Montesquieu could serve me as a guide. I would first describe the primitive peoples on the borders; then the semi-developed areas of the interior; and finally the developed regions along the sea-coast. The Ukraine would command my particular attention: here I would mention my former plans.

III. The material content of the laws and the contribution made by each to the development and education of the people would form the third part of my study. I would treat everything according to Montesquieu's method, briefly and with examples, but without his system. The errors of Russian legislation will be freely criticized, and its good points freely praised. Plenty of examples, reports and facts will be adduced. It should be a great work! And if it achieved its purpose: what a calling to be a legislator for princes and kings! This is the moment to act in Russia: the age, the century, the spirit, the very taste demand it.

22

JOHANN GOTTLIEB FICHTE
Idealism and Self-Reflection

Johann Gottlieb Fichte (1762–1814) studied philosophy and theology at the Universities of Jena and Leipzig, both Kantian strongholds. Although he was also influenced by Jacobi and Solomon ben Maimon, he set himself the task of (what he saw as) completing Kant's project of uniting theoretical and practical reason. They are, he thought, fused within the essentially moral activity of the self-conscious, self-defining ego. Fichte undertook to apply the antirealist, transcendental idealist position that he had developed in *The Concept of the Wissenschaftslehre* (1794) to political theory. In *The Foundations of Natural Right* (1796–1797) he developed the view that the subjectivity which pervades all conscious experience is coordinate with—and limited by—the realization of the freedom of others. A conception of justice is, he maintained, implicit in the activities of self-awareness.

In *On the Basis of Our Belief in a Divine Governance of the World* (1798) Fichte argued that a universal and necessary morality follows from the rational reflection of a free self-positing agent rather than from the commands of a divine lawgiver. Charged with atheism and nihilism, forced to resign his professorial chair at Jena, he wrote *The Vocation of Man* (1800). After moving to Berlin, Fichte turned his attention to political questions and wrote *Addresses to the German Nation* (1808), proposing a culturally nationalistic system of education.

Much to Fichte's grief, Kant denounced Fichte's claim to provide definitive interpretations of his work. While Hegel and Schelling criticized (what they regarded as) his extreme subjectivism, they acknowledged their indebtedness to him, as did such Romantics as Schlegel and Novalis.

Concerning the Concept of the *Wissenschaftslehre* or, of So-called Philosophy

Reading the modern skeptics has convinced the author of this treatise of something which already appeared to be most probable, namely, that despite the recent efforts of the most perspicacious men, philosophy has not yet been raised to the level of a clearly evident science. The author believes that he has found the reason for this, and believes that he has discovered a simple way to satisfy completely all those very well-grounded demands which the skeptics make upon the Critical Philosophy, and in a manner which at the same time provides a way to unite the conflicting claims of the dogmatic and critical systems, just as the Critical Philosophy unifies the conflicting claims of the various dogmatic systems. The author is not in the habit of speaking about things that he has not accomplished, and, in the present case, would either have carried out his intentions or kept forever silent on the subject, were it not for the fact the present occasion seems to demand that he render an account, both of how he has employed his leisure until now and of the work to which he intends to dedicate himself in the future.

The investigation which follows pretends to no more than hypothetical validity, though from this it by no means follows that the author is able to base his assertions only upon unprovable hypotheses, nor that they are not the results of a more profound and sound system. Admittedly, it will be years before I can promise to be able to lay this system before the public in a worthy form. Nevertheless, I still expect that people will be fair enough to postpone disputation until they have examined the whole system.

The primary object of this work is to permit students at the university to which I have been called to decide whether to entrust themselves to my guidance along that path which leads to the supreme science, and to allow them to judge whether they can entertain the hope that I can shed enough light on this path to enable them to follow it without stumbling dangerously. Its second object is to solicit the judgment of my path and friends regarding my undertaking.

The remarks which follow are intended for those readers who belong to neither of the above classes.

The author remains convinced that no human understanding can advance further than that boundary on which Kant, especially in the *Critique of Judgment*, stood, and which he declared to be the final boundary of finite knowing—but without ever telling us specifically where it lies. I realize that I will never be able to say anything which has not already—directly or indirectly and with more or less clarity—been indicated by Kant. I leave to future ages the task of fathoming the genius of this man who, often as if inspired from on high, drove philosophical judgment so decisively from the standpoint at which he found it toward its final goal.

One can philosophize about metaphysics itself (which does not have to be a theory of the so-called things in themselves, but may be a genetic deduction of what we find in our consciousness). One can embark on investigations into the possibility, the real meaning, and the rules governing such a science. And this is very advantageous for the cultivation of the science of metaphysics itself. The philosophical name for a system of this sort of inquiry is "critique." This, anyway, is all that ought to be called by that name. Critique itself is not metaphysics, but lies beyond metaphysics. It is related to metaphysics in exactly the same way that metaphysics is related to the ordinary point of view of natural understanding. Metaphysics explains the ordinary point of view, and metaphysics is itself explained by critique. The object of genuine critique is philosophical thinking. If philosophy itself is also to be called "critical," this can only mean that it criticizes natural thinking. A pure critique is intermixed with no metaphysical investigations. The Kantian critique for example, which presents itself as a *critique*, is by no means pure, but is itself largely metaphysics. Sometimes it criticizes philosophical thinking, and sometimes it criticizes natural thinking—which, taken by itself, would be no cause for reproach, if only the distinction between the two kinds of critique had been clearly indicated, as well as the kind to which each individual investigation belonged. A pure metaphysics, as such, includes no additional critique beyond that critique with which one is supposed to have come to terms in advance. Accordingly, none of the previous versions of the *Wissenschaftslehre*, which present themselves as metaphysics, are pure metaphysics—nor could they have been, since this unaccustomed way of thinking could not have been expected to gain a hearing without the critical pointers which accompanied it.

Some Lectures Concerning the Scholar's Vocation

PREFACE

These lectures were delivered this past summer semester before a considerable number of our students. They provide entry into a whole which the author wishes to complete and to lay before the public at the proper time. External circumstances, which can contribute nothing to the correct evaluation or understanding of these pages, have induced me to have these first five lectures printed separately and, moreover, to have them printed exactly in the form in which they were first delivered, without altering one single word. This may excuse several careless expressions. Owing to my other work, I was from the beginning unable to polish them in the way I would have liked. Declamation can be used to assist an oral delivery, but revising them for publication would have conflicted with my secondary aim in publishing them.

Several expressions found in these lectures will not please every reader, but for this the author should not be blamed. In pursuing my inquiries I did not ask whether something would meet with approval or not, but rather, whether it might be true; and what, according to the best of my knowledge, I considered to be true I expressed as well as I could.

In addition, however, to those readers who have their own reasons to be displeased by what is said here, there may be others for whom what is said here will seem to be useless, because it is something which cannot be achieved and which fails to correspond to anything in the real world as it now exists. Indeed, I am afraid that the majority of otherwise upright, respectable, and sober persons will judge these lectures in this way. For although the number of persons capable of lifting themselves to the level of ideas has always been a minority in every age, this number (for reasons which I can certainly leave unmentioned) has never been smaller than it is right now. It may be true that, within that area to which ordinary experience assigns us, people have never thought for themselves more widely or judged more correctly than they do now; however, just as soon as they are supposed to go any distance beyond this familiar area, most persons are completely lost and blind. If it is not possible to rekindle the higher genius in such persons once it has been extinguished, then we must permit them to remain peacefully within the circle of ordinary experience. And insofar as they are useful and indispensible within this circle, we must grant them their undiminished value in and for this area. They are, however, guilty of a great injustice if they try to pull down to their own level everything which they cannot themselves reach: if, for example, they demand that everything which is published should be as easy to use as a cookbook or an arithmetic book or a book of rules and regulations, and if they decry everything which cannot be employed in such a manner.

That ideals cannot be depicted within the real world is something that we others know just as well as such persons do—perhaps we know this better than they. All we maintain is that reality must be judged in accordance with ideals and must be modified by those who feel themselves able to do so. Supposing that such persons cannot be convinced that this is true, still, since they are what they are, they lose very little by not being convinced, and mankind loses nothing. It merely becomes clear from this that they cannot be counted on to contribute anything to the project of improving mankind. Mankind will undoubtedly continue on its way. May a kindly nature reign over such persons, may it bestow upon them rain and sunshine at the proper time, wholesome food and undisturbed circulation, and in addition—intelligent thoughts!

Jena, Michaelmas 1794

First Lecture

CONCERNING THE VOCATION OF MAN AS SUCH

I would like to answer—or rather, I would like to prompt you to answer—the following questions: What is the scholar's vocation? What is his relationship to mankind as a whole, as well as to the individual classes of men? What are his surest means of fulfilling his lofty vocation?

The scholar is a scholar only insofar as he is distinguished from other men who are not scholars. The concept of the scholar arises by comparison and by reference to society (by which is understood here not merely the state, but any aggregate whatsoever of rational men, living alongside each other and thus joined in mutual relations).

It follows that the scholar's vocation is conceivable only within society. The answer to the question What is the scholar's vocation? thus presupposes an answer to another question: What is the vocation of man within society?

The answer to this latter question presupposes, in turn, an answer to yet another, higher one: What is the vocation of man as such? That is to say, what is the vocation of man considered simply qua man, merely according to the concept of man as such—man isolated and considered apart from all the associations which are not necessarily included in the concept of man?

If I may assert something without proof, something which has undoubtably already been demonstrated to many of you for a long time and something which others among you feel obscurely, but no less strongly on that account: All philosophy, all human thinking and teaching, all of your studies, and, in particular, everything which I will ever be able to present to you can have no purpose other than answering the questions just raised, and especially the last and highest question: What is the vocation of man as such, and what are his surest means for fulfilling it?

For a clear, distinct, and complete insight into this vocation (though not, of course, for a feeling of it), philosophy in its entirety—and moreover a well-grounded and exhaustive philosophy—is presupposed. Yet the vocation of man as such is the subject of my lecture for today. You can see that, unless I intend to treat philosophy in its entirety within this hour, I will be unable to deduce what I have to say on this topic completely and from its foundations. What I can do is to build upon your feelings. At the same time you can see that the *last* task of all philosophical inquiry is to answer that question which I wish to answer in these public lectures: What is the vocation of the scholar? or (which amounts to the same thing, as will become evident later), What is the vocation of the highest and truest man? And you can see as well that the *first* task of all philosophical inquiry is to answer the question What is the vocation of man as such?

Letter to Kant, September 20, 1793

Most esteemed patron, it was with sincere pleasure that I received your letter—the proof that even from a distance you find me worthy of your benevolence.

The destination of my journey was Zurich, where even during my previous stay, a young and very worthy lady considered me worthy of her special friendship. Even prior to my trip to Konigsberg, she desired for me to return to Zurich and cement: the bond between us. Since I had accomplished nothing at that point, I did not consider it permissible to do what I now can: for I at least seem to have the promise of doing something in the future. Though it has been postponed until now by certain unforeseen difficulties that the laws of Zurich pose for foreigners, the marriage will take place in a few weeks. This marriage would give me the opportunity to dedicate myself to study in independent leisure—were it not that the character of the Zurichers makes me wish for a change of domicile. In itself this character is kind, but it is most incompatible with my own.

I have read your *Religion within the Limits etc.* with pleasure, and expect a similar pleasure from the publication of your *Metaphysics of Morals*. My project concerning natural law, civil law, and political theory is progressing, and I could easily devote half a lifetime to the accomplishment of this project. Thus I will always have the happy prospect of being able to make use of your work for this purpose. Until then, if I should encounter unexpected difficulties in forming my ideas, would you permit me to solicit your good advice? Perhaps even while they are struggling to develop I will lay my ideas in various forms before the public for judgment—though of course I would do so anonymously. I confess that I have already published something of this sort, though at present I do not wish to be known as its author, because in it I have denounced many injustices with utter candor and zeal. For the moment I have done so without making any proposals concerning the means for remedying these injustices without disorder, since I have not yet advanced to that point I have seen *one* piece of enthusiastic praise for this book, but have not yet seen any thorough evaluation of it. If you will permit me this—what should I say? this confidence or familiarity?—I will send a copy for your judgment just as soon as I have received the sequel from the printer. You, esteemed sir, are the only person whose judgment and strict discretion I trust completely. In the present extraordinary confusion almost everyone—first-rate thinkers included—has unfortunately chosen sides when it comes to political matters: they have become either timid adherents of anything that is old or else ardent enemies of the same and in both cases merely *because* it is old. Should you be so kind as to permit me to send you this book (without your permission I would not even think of doing so). I believe that Court Chaplin Schulz will be able to see that any letters will reach me.

No, great man, you who are of such importance for the human race, your work will not perish! It will bear rich fruits. It will give mankind a fresh impetus; it will bring about a total rebirth of man's first principles, opinions, and ways of thinking. Believe me, there is nothing which will be unaffected by the consequences of your work, and your discoveries have joyous prospects. I have communicated to Court Chaplin Schulz a few remarks on this subject, which I wrote during my journey, and I have asked him to share these with you.

Oh great and good man, what must it be like toward the end of one's earthly life to be able to have such feelings as you can have! I confess that the thought of your example will always be my guide and will impel me not to retire from the stage before I have been of some use to mankind, to the extent that it lies within my power to be of such use.

I commend myself to your continued benevolence, and I am, with the greatest respect and esteem,

Faithfully yours,
Fichte

Letter to Reinhold, July 2, 1795

Nothing makes such an impression upon my heart as frankness. You, dearest friend, have conquered my heart with the frankness of your last letter, through your open comparison of our individual characters. I, for my part, acknowledge your description and find it completely true. You have made me love you warmly. Your individual character makes this the necessary way for you to seal a friendship. I have always taken and wanted to take the opposite path: from respect to love. I see from your last letter that you do not deny me the former (not on account of my philosophical talent, which cannot be at issue here, but because of my character), and I am firmly convinced that you will in the end love me as I love you.

You are quite right that the difference in our temperaments must have greatly influenced the manner in which we philosophize. You obviously always aim not so much to secure your fondest expectations for yourself and others as to protect these expectations (because they spring from a different source) against all attacks of that degenerate reason which has become merely speculative. Your interest in philosophy is practical; this practical interest is the reason you philosophize, and it is the force which governs your writings. I, since my earliest youth, have looked speculation confidently and coolly in the eye. I could do so thanks to a freer upbringing in my earliest childhood, followed by the pressures—which I soon cast off—of the Pforta school, and because of my lighthearted nature and rather good health, which facilitated a firm sense of self-confidence (the injurious excesses of which I will try to avoid). It is, of course, of no small benefit for me to have mastered a philosophy which places my head and heart in agreement. Nevertheless, I would not hesitate for a moment to give up this philosophy if I were shown that it is incorrect and to accept in its place a teaching which completely destroyed this harmony, if that teaching were correct. In that case, too, I would believe I had done my duty. The essay "On Stimulating and Increasing the Pure Interest in Truth" in the January issue of the *Horen* shows more or less what I think about this and also how I believe I act. I believe I philosophize solely in the interests of philosophy. I eagerly await the appearance of your *Socrates* Like you, I am firmly convinced that intellectual honesty is the sole condition for correct philosophizing, despite the fact that I attribute no great value at all to that good-naturedness which is also often called "good-heartedness," and therefore I attribute little value to it in philosophy either. But there is certainly no argument between us on this point, for surely you place as little value on this as I.

Allow me to give you another clue why you and most others find the *Wissenschaftslehre* incomprehensible, while, on the other hand, some others find it more easily comprehensible than almost any other philosophical book. I believe it is for the same reason that the study of Kant's writing was so difficult for you, whereas for me, for instance, it was very easy. You should not assign to my expressions the same sort of worth which, for example, yours certainly possess. It has been noted, and I believe rightly, that it is almost impossible to express those thoughts peculiar to your philosophy in any way other than in the specific way in which you have expressed them. Such is not the case with my thoughts, nor, I believe, is it the case with Kant's. They can be expressed in an infinite variety of ways, and it is not to be expected (of me, in any case) that the first mode of presentation selected is also the most perfect one. The body in which you clothe the spirit fits it very closely. The body in which I clothe it is looser and is easily cast aside. What I am trying to communicate is something which can be neither *said* nor *grasped conceptually*; it can only be *intuited*. My words are only supposed to guide the reader in such a way that the desired intuition is formed within him. I advise anyone who wishes to study my writings to let words be words and simply try to enter into my series of intuitions at one point or another. I advise him to go on reading even if he has not completely understood what went before, until at some point a spark of light is finally struck. This spark of light, if it is whole and not half, will suddenly place him in that position in the series of my intuitions from which the whole must be viewed. For example, the heart of my system is the proposition "The I simply posits itself." These words have no meaning or value unless the I has an inner intuition of itself. In conversation I have very often been able to elicit this intuition in people who could not understand me at all, who then suddenly understood me completely. It is said that absolutely all operations of the mind presuppose that there is an I as well as something opposed to it, that is, a not-I. Only through the I and the not-I are any mental operations possible. There is no reason why the I is I and the thing is not-I; this opposition occurs absolutely. (We do not learn from experience what we should include and *not* include as part of ourselves. Nor is there any a priori first principle according to which this can be determined. Instead, the distinction is absolute, and only in consequence of this distinction are all a priori first principles and all experience possible.) The unification of the I and not-I by means of *quantity*, mutual restriction, determination, limitation, or whatever you wish to call it, also occurs absolutely. No philosophy can go beyond these propositions, but *from them all of philosophy*, that is, the entire operation of the human mind, *must be developed*.

Letter to Reinhold, April 22, 1799

My dear friend,

. . . The reason that I have had such bad luck as an author is that I am so little capable of placing myself in the frame of mind of the reading public; I always assume that many things are self-evident which hardly anyone else finds to be self-evident. I have discussed the relationship between the philosophical and the everyday points of view with all the clarity I could muster in my *Wissenschaftslehre*, in the "Introductions" to the *Wissenschaftslehre* which appeared in the *Philosophisches Journal*, in the introduction to my *Natural Right*, in the first part of my *Ethical Theory*, and goodness knows where else. The only thing that I forgot to do was to attack directly that prejudice which encourages people to confuse philosophy with practical wisdom—a prejudice which is deeply rooted in all previous philosophy.

It was during the present quarrel over my theory of God that this misunderstanding became obvious and began to have serious consequences.

You have always nurtured the hope of using philosophy to *improve* mankind, and you still nurture this hope. You hope to use philosophy to *convert* men and to *instruct* them concerning their duties in this life and their hopes for the next one. You are beginning to realize that scientific idealism is just as poorly suited for this purpose as was your previous system; indeed, idealism threatens to carry the confusion and scandal to an even higher pitch. This, it seems to me, is the reason why you are looking for some middle standpoint [between Jacobi's and my own].

I, on the other hand, believe that one of the distinctive advantages of scientific idealism is that it knows itself very well and humbly renounces the exalted goal of improving and instructing mankind. Life can be improved only by those things which themselves proceed from life. Idealism, however, is the true opposite of life. The proper goal of idealism is knowledge for its own sake. It is of practical benefit only *indirectly*—that is, its utility is *pedagogic*, in the broadest sense of the term.

I think it is absolutely meaningless to associate philosophy with any particular attitudes and ways of thinking. Is *philosophy* as such atheistic or not? This is a question which I cannot understand. For me this is like asking whether a triangle is red or green, sweet or bitter. The only sense that I can make of the accusation of atheism against some *actual philosophical* system (among which I count my own) is the following: *The system in question provides the foundation for an allegedly atheistic pedagogics* (theory of God); that is, *it is conducive of an atheistic way of thinking.* Now at the moment there are very few people indeed who are in any position to declare that such is the case with my system. That people— and totally unphilosophical people at that—should try at this early date to judge my philosophy in this respect is a blunder, one which, God willing, will seem amusing a few years from now. That this issue is being discussed at this point is something which is completely contrary to my desires and plans. But undoubtedly this fate—and I do believe it is *fate*—will have its salutary consequences.

There are two very different standpoints for the activity of thinking. The natural and common way of thinking is to *think directly of objects*. Or, one can consciously and intentionally think of one's own *thinking* itself. People generally prefer to call this latter way of thinking artificial. The former way of thinking is that of ordinary life and of *science* (*materialiter sic dicta*); the latter is the standpoint of transcendental philosophy, which, precisely for this reason, I have called *Wissenschaftslehre* or the "Theory of Scientific Knowledge," that is, the theory and science of all knowledge (though by no means is such a theory itself an instance of real, objective knowledge).

For the most part the pre-Kantian philosophical systems lacked any correct awareness of their own standpoint and simply wavered back and forth between the two ways of thinking described above. The system of Wolff and Baumgarten, which was the one which prevailed immediately before Kant's, consciously adopted the standpoint of ordinary thinking and proposed to do nothing less than expand the sphere of ordinary thinking and, through the power of its syllogisms, create new objects for such thinking.

Our system is directly opposed to this one. For our system completely rejects the possibility of using pure thinking to produce any object which could be of any concern to life and the (material) sciences. Our system recognizes nothing to be real *which is not based upon some inner or outer perception*. Thus, insofar as metaphysics is taken to be a system of real knowledge which is produced merely by thinking, then Kant and I both entirely reject the possibility of metaphysics. Kant prides himself on having totally eradicated this sort of meta-physics, and, since no one has yet had a single intelligent or intelligible word to say in its defense, this is surely where the matter will rest forever.

In rejecting the attempts of others to expand the realm of ordinary thinking, it would never occur to us in turn to try to employ our system to expand the sphere of ordinary thinking (which is the only kind of thinking which deals with reality). Instead, all that our system aims to do is to comprehend and present this ordinary way of thinking in an exhaustive manner.

Our philosophical *thinking* has no meaning [by itself] and has not the least content. All meaning and content is to be found only in that thinking which is *thought of* in our philosophical thinking. Our philosophical thinking is no more than the instrument we use to assemble our work. Once the work is finished then the instrument can be discarded as of no further use.

I have lost my position—or should I say that I have resigned it? It would take me too long to describe to you here the incomprehensible way in which people have behaved in this affair. The story will shortly become known to the entire public. I am sorry that I am unable to say that I am entirely in the right and that the others are entirely wrong. Of course I am not in the wrong vis-à-vis them, but I am not entirely in the right vis-à-vis myself. I should not have engaged them on their own ground, and thus I entirely deserved to be outwitted by them.

You may, however, set your mind at ease about one thing: it is not *as an atheist* that I am being turned out.

I have to collect and arrange documents and put my domestic affairs in order. I will also have to seek some place of refuge where I can for a while enjoy a bit of leisure *in complete anonymity*, where I will be safe from the literary and political news which fills me with an unconquerable and deadly disgust, and where I will be protected from the anathemas of the priests and the stones of the faithful. Such leisure will not be useless in terms of my own self-education.

Nevertheless, I will most probably *have to* hold out here long enough to re-ceive another letter from you and to reply to it. (Holding out here will be a hard *necessity*. You can scarcely believe the way people are behaving toward me.) There is no need for you to worry about the vacation time; from now on I am on permanent vacation.

Introductions to the Wissenschaftslehre
[First]

1.

Attend to yourself; turn your gaze from everything surrounding you and look within yourself: this is the first demand philosophy makes upon anyone who studies it. Here you will not be concerned with anything that lies outside of you, but only with yourself.

Even on the most cursory self-observation, everyone will perceive a remark-able difference between the various ways in which his consciousness is imme-diately determined, and one could call these immediate determinations of con-sciousness "representations." Some of these determinations appear to us to depend entirely upon our own freedom, and it is impossible for us to believe that anything outside of us, i.e., something that exists independently of our own efforts, corresponds to representations of this sort. Our imagination and our will appear to us to be free. We also possess representations of another sort. We refer representations of this second type to a truth that is supposed to be firmly established independently of us and is supposed to serve as the model for these representations. When a representation of ours is supposed to correspond to this truth, we discover that we are constrained in determining this representation. In the case of cognition, we do not consider ourselves to be free with respect to the content of our cognitions. In short, we could say that some of our representations are accompanied by a feeling of freedom and others are accompanied by a feeling of necessity.

We cannot reasonably ask why the representations that depend upon our freedom are determined in just the way they are determined and not in some other way. For when we posit them to be dependent upon freedom, we deny that the concept of a "basis" (or "foundation" or "reason" or "ground") has any applicability in this case. These representations are what they are for the simple reason that I have determined them to be like this. If I had determined them differently, then they would be different.

But what is the basis of the system of those representations accompanied by a feeling of necessity, and what is the basis of this feeling of necessity itself? This is a question well worth pondering. It is the task of philosophy to answer this question; indeed, to my mind, nothing is philosophy except that science that discharges this task. Another name for the system of representations accompanied by a feeling of necessity is "experience"—whether inner or outer. We thus could express the task of philosophy in different words as follows: Philosophy has to display the basis or foundation of all experience.

Only three objections can be raised against this conception of philosophy's task. On the one hand, one might deny that consciousness contains any representations that are accompanied by a feeling of necessity and that refer to a truth determined without any help from us. A person who denies this would either do so against his own better knowledge, or else he would have to be constituted differently than other human beings. If so, then in this case nothing would exist for him which he could deny, and thus there would be no denial. Consequently, we could dismiss his objection without any further ado. Or else, someone might contend that the question we have raised is completely unanswerable and that we are and must remain in a state of invincible ignorance on this point. It is superfluous to engage in reasoned debate with someone who makes this objection. The best way to refute him is by actually answering the question, in which case there will be nothing left for him to do but to examine our effort and to indicate where and why it seems to him to be insufficient. Finally, someone might lay a rival claim to the name "philosophy" and maintain that philosophy is something completely different or something more than what we have claimed. It would be easy to prove to anyone who raises this objection that this is precisely what all of the experts have at all times considered philosophy to be, that all the other things he might like to pass off as philosophy already possess other names of their own, and therefore, that if the word "philosophy" is to have any definite meaning at all, it has to designate precisely the science we have indicated.

We have no desire, however, to engage in a fruitless dispute over a word; and this is why we have long ceased to lay any claim to the name "philosophy" and have given the name *Wissenschaftslehre*, or "Theory of Scientific Knowledge," to the science that actually has to carry out the task indicated.

2.

One can ask for a basis or foundation only in the case of something one judges to be contingent, i.e., only if one presupposes that the thing in question could also have been different from the way it is, even though it is not something determined by freedom. Indeed, something becomes contingent for someone precisely insofar as he inquires concerning its basis. To seek a basis or reason for something contingent, one has to look toward something else, something determinate, whose determinacy explains why what is based upon it is determined in precisely the way it is and not in any of the many other ways in which it could have been determined. It follows from the mere thought of a basis or reason that it must lie outside of what it grounds or explains. The basis of an explanation and what is explained thereby thus become posited—as such—in opposition to one another, and are related to one another in such a way that the former explains the latter.

Philosophy has to display the basis or foundation of all experience. Consequently, philosophy's object must necessarily lie *outside of all experience*. This is a principle that is supposed to be true of all philosophy, and it really has applied to all philosophy produced right up to the era of the Kantians, with their "facts of consciousness" and hence of "inner experience."

No objection whatsoever can be made to the principle just advanced, for the premise of our argument is derived simply from an analysis of the previously stipulated concept of philosophy, and our conclusion is merely inferred from this premise. Naturally, we cannot prevent anyone who wishes to do so from maintaining that the concept of a basis or foundation has to be explicated in some other way, nor can we prevent him from employing this term to designate whatever he wishes. We, however, are fully entitled to declare that we do not wish the preceding description of "philosophy" to be understood to include anything except what *we* have stated. Accordingly, if one does not wish to accept this definition of philosophy, then one has to deny the very possibility of philosophy in the sense we have indicated, and we have already taken this objection into account.

3

A finite rational being possesses nothing whatsoever beyond experience. The entire contents of his thinking are comprised within experience. These same conditions necessarily apply to the philosopher, and thus it appears incomprehensible how he could ever succeed in elevating himself above experience.

The philosopher, however, is able to engage in abstraction. That is to say, by means of a free act of thinking he is able to separate things that are connected with each other within experience. The *thing*, i.e., a determinate something that exists independently of our freedom and to which our cognition is supposed to be directed, and the *intellect*, i.e., the subject that is supposed to be engaged in this activity of cognizing, are inseparably connected with each other within experience. The philosopher is able to abstract from either one of these, and when he does so he has abstracted from experience and has thereby succeeded in elevating himself above experience. If he abstracts from the thing, then he is left with an intellect in itself as the explanatory ground of experience; that is to say, he is left with the intellect in abstraction from its relationship to experience. If he abstracts from the intellect, then he is left with a thing in itself (that is, in abstraction from the fact that it occurs within experience) as the explanatory ground of experience. The first way of proceeding is called *idealism;* the second is called *dogmatism.*

As one will surely become convinced by the present account, these two philosophical systems are the only ones possible. According to the former system, the representations accompanied by a feeling of necessity are products of the intellect, which is what this system presupposes in order to explain experience. According to the latter, dogmatic system, such representations are a product of the thing in itself, which is what this system presupposes.

Anyone who wishes to dispute the claim that these two systems are the only ones possible either must prove that there is some other way to elevate oneself above experience except by means of abstraction, or else he must prove that consciousness of experience contains some additional component beyond the two already mentioned.

Regarding the first system, it will indeed become clear later on that what is called "the intellect" is actually present within consciousness, albeit under another designation, and is not, therefore, something produced purely by means of abstraction. We will also see, however, that our consciousness of the latter is conditioned by an act of abstraction, albeit one quite natural to human beings.

This is by no means to deny that it might very well be possible to construct a whole by fusing together fragments from each of these two very different systems. Nor would we deny that people have, in fact, very often engaged in just such an inconsistent enterprise. We do, however, deny that any system other than these two is possible so long as one proceeds consistently.

If a philosopher is to be considered a philosopher at all, he must necessarily occupy a certain standpoint, a standpoint that will sooner or later be attained in the course of human thinking, even if this occurs without any conscious effort on one's own part. When a philosopher considers things from this standpoint, all he discovers is that *he must entertain representations* both of himself as free and of determinate things external to himself. It is impossible for a person simply to remain at this level of thinking. The thought of a mere representation is only half a thought, a broken fragment of a thought. We must also think of something else as well, namely, of something that corresponds to this representation and exists independently of the act of representing. In other words, a representation cannot subsist simply for itself and purely on its own. It is something only in conjunction with something else; by itself, it is nothing. It is precisely the necessity of thinking in this way that drives us from our initial standpoint and makes us ask: What is the basis of representations? Or, what amounts to exactly the same question: What corresponds to representations?

The representation of the self-sufficiency of the I can certainly co-exist with a representation of the self-sufficiency of the thing, though the self-sufficiency of the I itself cannot co-exist with that of the thing. Only one of these two can come first; only one can be the starting point; only one can be independent. The one that comes second, just because it comes second, necessarily becomes dependent upon the one that comes first, with which it is supposed to be connected.

Which of these two should come first? This is not a question that can be decided simply by consulting reason alone. For what we are concerned with here is not how some member is to be connected to a series (which is the only sort of question that can be decided on the basis of rational grounds), but rather, with the act of beginning the entire series; and since this act is absolutely primary, it can depend upon nothing but the freedom of thinking. Consequently, the decision between these two systems is one that is determined by free choice; and thus, since even a free decision is supposed to have some basis, it is a decision determined by *inclination* and *interest*. What ultimately distinguishes the idealist from the dogmatist is, accordingly, a difference of interest.

One's supreme interest and the foundation of all one's other interests is one's *interest in oneself*. This is just as true of a philosopher as it is of anyone else. The interest that invisibly guides all of his thinking is this: to avoid losing himself in argumentation, and instead to preserve and to affirm himself therein. But there are two different levels of human development, and, so long as everyone has not yet reached the highest level in the course of the progress of our species, there are two main sub-species of human beings. Some people—namely, those who have not yet attained a full feeling of their own freedom and absolute self-sufficiency—discover themselves only in the act of representing things. Their self-consciousness is dispersed and attached to objects and must be gleaned from the manifold of the latter. They glimpse their own image only insofar as it is reflected through things, as in a mirror. If they were to be deprived of these things, then they would lose themselves at the same time. Thus, for the sake of their own selves, they cannot renounce their belief in the self-sufficiency of things; for they themselves continue to exist only in conjunction with these things. It is really through the external world that they have become everything they are, and a person who is in fact nothing but a product of things will never be able to view himself in any other way. He will, furthermore, be correct—so long as he speaks only of himself and of those who are like him in this respect. The dogmatist's principle is belief in things for the sake of himself. Thus he possesses only an indirect or mediated belief in his own dispersed self, which is conveyed to him only by objects.

Anyone, however, who is conscious of his own self-sufficiency and independence from everything outside of himself—a consciousness that can be obtained only by making something of oneself on one's own and independently of everything else—will not require things in order to support his self, nor can he employ them for this purpose, for they abolish his self-sufficiency and transform it into a mere illusion. The I that he possesses and that interests him cancels this type of belief in things. His belief in his own self-sufficiency is based upon inclination, and it is with passion that he shoulders his own self-sufficiency. His belief in himself is immediate.

This interest also permits us to understand why the defense of a philosophical system is customarily accompanied by a certain amount of passion. When the dogmatist's system is attacked he is in real danger of losing his own self. Yet he is not well prepared to defend himself against such attacks, for there is something within his own inner self which agrees with his assailant. This is why he defends himself with so much vehemence and bitterness. The idealist, in contrast, is quite unable to prevent himself from looking down upon the dogmatist with a certain amount of disrespect, since the dogmatist cannot say anything to him which he himself has not long since known and already rejected as erroneous. For one becomes an idealist only by passing through a disposition toward dogmatism—if not by passing through dogmatism itself. Confounded, the dogmatist grows angry and, if it were only in his power to do so, would prosecute; while the idealist remains cool and is in danger of ridiculing the dogmatist.

The kind of philosophy one chooses thus depends upon the kind of person one is. For a philosophical system is not a lifeless household item one can put aside or pick up as one wishes; instead, it is animated by the very soul of the person who adopts it. Someone whose character is naturally slack or who has been enervated and twisted by spiritual servitude, scholarly self-indulgence, and vanity will never be able to raise himself to the level of idealism.

As we will show in a moment, one can point out to the dogmatist the inadequacy and inconsistency of his system; one can confuse and worry him on every side; but one cannot convince him, for he is incapable of calmly and coolly listening to and evaluating a theory that he finds to be simply unendurable. If idealism should prove to be the only true philosophy, then from this it would follow that in order to philosophize one must be born a philosopher, must be reared as a philosopher, and must educate oneself as a philosopher. But no application of human art or skill can make one into a philosopher. This science, therefore, does not expect to make many converts among people who are *already firmly set in their ways*. If it may entertain any hopes at all in this regard, these are pinned on the young, whose innate energy has not yet been ruined by the slackness of the present age.

"My theory is—if, out of tolerance, one wishes to spare me from the hateful term *atheism*—at the very least a form of *pantheism*. According to me [. . .], *the moral world order itself is God, and we require no other God*. Indeed, *they* and *I* and *all of us* are the members who constitute this moral world, and *our relationship to one another* (for the moment, anyway, it may remain undecided whether this relationship is present without our having to do anything, or whether it has to be produced through our morality) is the *order* of this world. We ourselves, therefore, either *are* or daily *make* God, and nothing similar to a God remains anywhere—nothing except we ourselves."—Once instructed in this way, it also became easier for me to read approximately the same thing asserted in the previously mentioned, confused rubbish, and since then I have no longer been in the least surprised to read, not only in the most insignificant philosophical reviews and occasional writings, but also in the writings of men who have indisputably penetrated the innermost speculative depths, that I deny the existence of a *living, powerful*, and *active* God (this, despite the fact that my own words [. . .] expressly state that "this *living* and *acting* moral order is God") and that my God is *nothing but a concept*, etc.

The situation with this misunderstanding is as follows: These writers take as the most proximate objects of their own philosophizing nothing but *concepts*, concepts that are present in finished form and are, taken by themselves, dead. They then hear the word "order," a term they understand very well. It designates something *already made*, an already completed, determinate *being*-alongside-one-another and *being*-one-after-another of a manifold—just as, for example, the household items in your room are arranged in a certain order (*ordo ordinatus*). It never occurs to them that this same word might also have another, higher meaning, for they entirely lack the organ required for grasping this higher meaning. When they hear it said that "God is the moral world order" they reason in the manner just indicated; and *for them* such reasoning is correct, unavoidable, and irrefutable. Starting with their own premises, they are *unable* to infer in any other way than this.

In contrast, something stable, at rest, and dead can by no means enter the domain of what *I* call philosophy, within which all is act, movement, and life. This philosophy discovers nothing; instead, it allows everything to arise before its eyes. One of the implications of this is that I completely deny the name "philosophy" to trafficking in dead concepts. In my view, the latter is nothing but reasoning for the purposes of *actual life*, the business of which is precisely the opposite of speculation. In actual life, one proceeds by way of concepts simply in order to shorten one's path and to arrive more quickly at one's destination, which, to be sure, must once again be some type of acting—if, that is, all of our thinking is not to have been an empty game. Accordingly, if I employ the expression "order" in a speech or in a text that I describe as *philosophical*, then it is and should be clear, without any further ado, that by the term "order" [*Ordnung*] I understand nothing but an *active ordering* (*ordo ordinans*). I am so wedded to this way of speaking that I cannot construe any word ending in "—*ung*" in any other way. Thus, for example, I always understand the word "effect" [*Wirkung*] to mean the very act of effecting [*Wirken*] and never the mere result or "effect" [*Effect*] thereof (though other philosophers may well understand this word in this way); instead, I render the latter as "what is effected" [*das Bewirkte*]. I am so wedded to this way of speaking that when I begin to philosophize in the manner that is natural to me no other meaning comes into my thoughts at all; thus one might have continued for a decade to shout at me "You are an atheist," and I still would not have realized on my own that the basis for this misunderstanding might very well lie precisely here.

Do I then have a right to demand that one be acquainted with the way I use language? I undoubtedly do have this right, because I have loudly and sufficiently indicated—even in the very journal in which "On the Basis of Our Belief" appeared[9]—that one of the distinctive features of my philosophy is the fact that it deals only with what is living and by no means with what is dead. From this, reasonable readers will undoubtedly draw the small inference that, since this is the case with all of my philosophical theses, it also applies to my assertions concerning the moral world order. Nevertheless, there are those who read, evaluate, pass judgment on, and write about a single essay written by a systematic philosopher without having read a single line by this philosopher beyond what is contained in this one essay, and who even pride themselves in this fact!

But why do I not confine myself to ordinary linguistic usage? My friend, I wish that you would find the occasion to tell those who ask this question that I consider such a remark to be one of the "formal absurdities" of our age, an absurdity that, it is to be hoped, is merely passed on from one person to another, purely on the authority of the last person who said it, without anyone ever stopping to consider what he is actually saying. To bid a thinker who actually intends to introduce something new to confine himself to ordinary usage is—overlooking the hyperbole—exactly the same as if one were to bid the the native inhabitants of Tierra del Fuego to produce European arts, sciences, and mores, and yet to do so in the words of their previous language and without changing the definitions of these words. If I generate within myself a new concept, then it surely follows that the sign I employ to signify this concept *for you* (since, for myself, no sign at all is required) is, for you, something new; and the word that I employ for this purpose thus obtains a new meaning, since you did not previously possess what is signified thereby. If someone says, "Until now you have had no correct philosophy; I will construct one for you," then he also asserts at the same time, "You also have had no correct philosophical usage of language; I must also construct this for you as well." Should you seek to quarrel with him, then, in a well-meaning manner, I would advise you simply to attack his philosophy directly, and not his use of language. If you succeed in defeating his philosophy, then, without any further ado, his linguistic usage will perish along with his philosophy. If, on the other hand, you cannot raise objections to his philosophy, then you will have to learn the language of this philosophy simply in order to be able to penetrate this very philosophy.—To claim that one should stick with ordinary linguistic usage is, at bottom, to say that one should stick with the ordinary *manner of thinking* and should introduce no innovations. It is certainly possible that some people who make such a claim actually do understand it in just this way, but if this is the case, then they could express their true opinion in a much more direct manner.

I said that *I had the right to demand* that no one pass judgment on me without being acquainted with my way of using language. However, once one has acquired such an acquaintance—and this is far and away the main point—one should then be able to gather from the context what I mean by the concept of a moral world order. You, my friend, have the opportunity to meet with some of my opponents. I would ask that you acquaint them with this context and that you present them with an overview of my argument in the notorious essay in question, and, with this goal in mind, I will now do the same for you.

GEORG WILHELM FRIEDRICH HEGEL
The New Science of Philosophy

G.W.F. Hegel (1770–1831) studied theology and classics at the University of Tü-
bingen. His first university post was at Jena, where he met Fichte, Schelling, and
the Schlegels. His academic trajectory carried him to Heidelberg in 1816 and to
Berlin in 1818. Having first focused on current issues in moral theory and the
philosophy of religion, Hegel turned to a critical development of Kantian philosophy. At Jena, he began—and quickly finished—his vast, ambitious *Phenomenology of Spirit* (which, as popular legend has it, was completed when Napoleon's troops invaded Jena on October 12, 1807). The *Phenomenology* presents
a rational reconstruction of stages in the development of consciousness, starting
from sense awareness, through perception and understanding, to the social
world and fully articulated self-consciousness. This "movement" charts isomor-
phic phases in the maturation of individual psychology, the development of
social relations, and the growth of self-consciousness in world history. Hegel
attempted to break down—to unite, to show the interdependence—of an array
of familiar philosophical oppositions: duty and inclination, objectivity and subjectivity, action and reaction, form and matter, mind and body, freedom and
determinism, the individual and the state, the particular and the universal, morality and science, language and reality, truth and fiction, imagination and reason,
invention and discovery, empiricism and idealism, experience and the experienced, casual and logical relations. Each of these philosophic terms represents
a partial perspective on Reality, which is, when properly understood, realized
to be a unified, systematically interconnected system. Hegel thought of Absolute Spirit as the pervasive, immanent spirit that actively unfolds itself in a
process that moves dialectically toward greater articulation and determinacy,
revealing the rational interconnectedness of all the "parts" or "aspects" of
Reality.

There are strong echoes of Spinoza in Hegel's thought, and echoes of Hegel
in Wordsworth. While Marx claimed to have "stood Hegel on his head," he
incorporated many Hegelian premises and argumentative strategies. The Frankfurt School of neo-Marxists and—through the influence of Kojève—French phenomenologists bear the imprint of Hegel's influence. In the United States, Dewey
and other communitarians domesticated and democratized Hegel's politically
conservative views.

What Is Philosophy?

Philosophy misses an advantage enjoyed by the other sciences. It cannot like
them rest the existence of its objects on the natural admissions of consciousness,
nor can it assume that its method of cognition, either for starting or for contin-

uing, is one already accepted. The objects of philosophy, it is true, are upon the whole the same as those of religion. In both the object is Truth, in that supreme sense in which God and God only is the Truth. Both in like manner go on to treat of the finite worlds of Nature and the human Mind, with their relation to each other and to their truth in God. Some *acquaintance* with its objects, therefore, philosophy may and even must presume, that and a certain interest in them to boot, were it for no other reason than this: that in point of time the mind makes general *images* of objects, long before it makes *notions* of them, and that it is only through these mental images, and by recourse to them, that the thinking mind rises to know and comprehend *thinkingly*.

But with the rise of this thinking study of things, it soon becomes evident that thought will be satisfied with nothing short of showing the *necessity* of its facts, of demonstrating the existence of its objects, as well as their nature and qualities. Our original acquaintance with them is thus discovered to be inadequate. We can assume nothing, and assert nothing dogmatically; nor can we accept the assertions and assumptions of others. And yet we must make a beginning: and a beginning, as primary and underived, makes an assumption, or rather is an assumption. It seems as if it were impossible to make a beginning at all.

This *thinking study of things* may serve, in a general way, as a description of philosophy. But the description is too wide. If it be correct to say, that thought makes the distinction between man and the lower animals, then everything human is human, for the sole and simple reason that it is due to the operation of thought. Philosophy, on the other hand, is a peculiar mode of thinking—a mode in which thinking becomes knowledge, and knowledge through notions. However great therefore may be the identity and essential unity of the two modes of thought, the philosophic mode gets to be different from the more general thought which acts in all that is human, in all that gives humanity its distinctive character. And this difference connects itself with the fact that the strictly human and thought-induced phenomena of consciousness do not originally appear in the form of a thought, but as a feeling, a perception, or mental image—all of which aspects must be distinguished from the form of thought proper.

According to an old preconceived idea, which has passed into a trivial proposition, it is thought which marks the man off from the animals. Yet trivial as this old belief may seem, it must, strangely enough, be recalled to mind in presence of certain preconceived ideas of the present day. These ideas would put feeling and thought so far apart as to make them opposites, and would represent them as so antagonistic, that feeling, particularly religious feeling, is supposed to be contaminated, perverted, and even annihilated by thought. They also emphatically hold that religion and piety grow out of, and rest upon something else, and not on thought. But those who make this separation forget meanwhile that only man has the capacity for religion, and that animals no more have religion than they have law and morality.

Those who insist on this separation of religion from thinking usually have before their minds the sort of thought that may be styled *after-thought*. They mean "reflective" thinking, which has to deal with thoughts as thoughts, and brings them into consciousness. Slackness to perceive and keep in view this distinction which philosophy definitely draws in respect of thinking is the source of the crudest objections and reproaches against philosophy. Man—and that just because it is his nature to think—is the only being that possesses law, religion, and morality. In these spheres of human life, therefore, thinking, under the guise of feeling, faith, or generalised image, has not been inactive: its action and its productions are there present and therein contained. But it is one thing to have such feelings and generalised images that have been moulded and permeated by thought, and another thing to have thoughts about them. The thoughts, to which after-thought upon those modes of consciousness gives rise, are what is comprised under reflection, general reasoning, and the like, as well as under philosophy itself.

The neglect of this distinction between thought in general and the reflective thought of philosophy has also led to another and more frequent misunderstanding. Reflection of this kind has been often maintained to be the condition, or even the only way, of attaining a consciousness and certitude of the Eternal and True. The (now somewhat antiquated) metaphysical proofs of God's existence, for example, have been treated, as if a knowledge of them and a conviction of their truth were the only and essential means of producing a belief and conviction that there is a God. Such a doctrine would find its parallel, if we said that eating was impossible before we had acquired a knowledge of the chemical, botanical, and zoological characters of our food; and that we must delay digestion till we had finished the study of anatomy and physiology. Were it so, these sciences in their field, like philosophy in its, would gain greatly in point of utility; in fact, their utility would rise to the height of absolute and universal indispensableness. Or rather, instead of being indispensable, they would not exist at all.

Attitudes of Thought to Objectivity

The term "Objective Thoughts" indicates the *truth*—the truth which is to be the absolute *object* of philosophy, and not merely the goal at which it aims. But the very expression cannot fail to suggest an opposition, to characterise and appreciate which is the main motive of the philosophical attitude of the present time, and which forms the real problem of the question about truth and our means of ascertaining it. If the thought-forms are vitiated by a fixed antithesis, *i.e.*, if they are only of a finite character, they are unsuitable for the self-centred universe of truth, and truth can find no adequate receptacle in thought. Such thought, which can produce only limited and partial categories and proceed by their means, is what in the stricter sense of the word is termed Understanding. The finitude, further, of these categories lies in two points. Firstly, they are only subjective, and the antithesis of an objective permanently clings to them. Secondly, they are always of restricted content, and so persist in antithesis to one another and still more to the Absolute. In order more fully to explain the position and import here attributed to logic, the attitudes in which thought is supposed to stand to objectivity will next be examined by way of further introduction.

In my *Phenomenology of the Spirit*, which on that account was at its publication described as the first part of the "System of Philosophy," the method adopted was to begin with the first and simplest phase of mind, immediate consciousness, and to show how that stage gradually of necessity worked onward to the philosophical point of view, the necessity of that view being proved by the process. But in these circumstances it was impossible to restrict the quest to the mere form of consciousness. For the stage of philosophical knowledge is the richest in material and organisation, and therefore, as it came before us in the shape of a result, it pre-supposed the existence of the concrete formations of consciousness, such as individual and social morality, art, and religion. In the development of consciousness, which at first sight appears limited to the point of form merely, there is thus at the same time included the development of the matter or of the objects discussed in the special branches of philosophy. But the latter process must, so to speak, go on behind consciousness, since those facts are the essential nucleus which is raised into consciousness. The exposition accordingly is rendered more intricate, because so much that properly belongs to the concrete branches is prematurely dragged into the introduction. The survey which follows in the present work has even more the inconvenience of being only historical and inferential in its method. But it tries especially to show how the questions men have proposed, outside the school, on the nature of Knowledge, Faith, and the like—questions which they imagine to have no connexion with abstract thoughts—are really reducible to the simple categories, which first get cleared up in Logic.

FIRST ATTITUDE OF THOUGHT TO OBJECTIVITY

The first of these attitudes of thought is seen in the method which has no doubts and no sense of the contradiction in thought, or of the hostility of thought against itself. It entertains an unquestioning belief that reflection is the means of ascertaining the truth, and of bringing the objects before the mind as they really are. And in this belief it advances straight upon its objects, takes the materials furnished by sense and perception, and reproduces them from itself as facts of thought; and then, believing this result to be the truth, the method is content. Philosophy in its earliest stages, all the sciences, and even the daily action and movement of consciousness live in this faith.

This method of thought has never become aware of the antithesis of subjective and objective; and to that extent there is nothing to prevent its statements from possessing a genuinely philosophical and speculative character, though it is just as possible that they may never get beyond finite categories, or the stage where the antithesis is still unresolved. In the present introduction the main question for us is to observe this attitude of thought in its extreme form; and we shall accordingly first of all examine its second and inferior aspect as a philosophic system. One of the clearest instances of it, and one lying nearest to ourselves, may be found in the Metaphysic of the Past as it subsisted among us previous to the philosophy of Kant. It is however only in reference to the history of philosophy that this Metaphysic can be said to belong to the past: the thing is always and at all places to be found, as the view which the abstract understanding takes of the objects of reason. And it is in this point that the real and immediate good lies of a closer examination of its main scope and its *modus operandi*.

This metaphysical system took the laws and forms of thought to be the fundamental laws and forms of things.

The difficulty of the philosophical cognition of mind consists in the fact that in this we are no longer dealing with the comparatively abstract, simple logical Idea, but with the most concrete, most developed form achieved by the Idea in its self-actualization. Even finite or subjective mind, not only absolute mind, must be grasped as an actualization of the Idea. The treatment of mind is only truly philosophical when it cognizes the Notion of mind in its living development and actualization, which simply means, when it comprehends mind as a type of the absolute Idea. But it belongs to the nature of mind to cognize its

Notion. Consequently, the summons to the Greeks of the Delphic Apollo, *Know thyself*, does not have the meaning of a law externally imposed on the human mind by an alien power; on the contrary, the god who impels to self-knowledge is none other than the absolute law of mind itself. Mind is, therefore, in its every act only apprehending itself, and the aim of all genuine science is just this, that mind shall recognize itself in everything in heaven and on earth. An out-and-out Other simply does not exist for mind. Even the Oriental does not wholly lose himself in the object of his worship; but the Greeks were the first to grasp expressly as mind what they opposed to themselves as the Divine, although even they did not attain, either in philosophy or in religion, to a knowledge of the absolute infinitude of mind; therefore with the Greeks the relation of the human mind to the Divine is still not one of absolute freedom. It was Christianity, by its doctrine of the Incarnation and of the presence of the Holy Spirit in the community of believers, that first gave to human consciousness a perfectly free relationship to the infinite and thereby made possible the comprehensive knowledge of mind in its absolute infinitude.

Henceforth, such a knowledge alone merits the name of a philosophical treatment. Self-knowledge in the usual trivial meaning of an inquiry into the foibles and faults of the single self has interest and importance only for the individual, not for philosophy; but even in relation to the individual, the more the focus of interest is shifted from the general intellectual and moral nature of man, and the more the inquiry, disregarding duties and the genuine content of the will, degenerates into a self-complacent absorption of the individual in the idiosyncrasies so dear to him, the less is the value of that self-knowledge. The same is true of the so-called knowledge of *human nature*, which likewise is directed to the peculiarities of individual minds. This knowledge is, of course, useful and necessary in the conduct of life, especially in bad political conditions where right and morality have given place to the self-will, whims and caprice of individuals, in the field of intrigues where characters do not rely on the nature of the matter in hand but hold their own by cunningly exploiting the peculiarities of others and seeking by this means to attain their arbitrary ends. For philosophy, however, this knowledge of human nature is devoid of interest in so far as it is incapable of rising above the consideration of contingent particularities to the understanding of the characters of great men, by which alone the true nature of man in its serene purity is brought to view. But this knowledge of human nature can even be harmful for philosophy if, as happens in the so-called pragmatic treatment of history, through failure to appreciate the substantial character of world-historical individuals and to see that great deeds can only be carried out by great characters, the supposedly clever attempt is made to trace back the greatest events in history to the accidental idiosyncrasies of those heroes, to their presumed petty aims, propensities, and passions. In such a procedure history, which is ruled by divine Providence, is reduced to a play of meaningless activity and contingent happenings.

Philosophy is the unity of Art and Religion. Whereas the vision-method of Art, external in point of form, is but subjective production and shivers the substantial content into many separate shapes, and whereas Religion, with its separation into parts, opens it out in mental picture, and mediates what is thus opened out; Philosophy not merely keeps them together to make a totality, but even unifies them into the simple spiritual vision, and then in that raises them to self-conscious thought. Such consciousness is thus the intelligible unity (cognized by thought) of art and religion, in which the diverse elements in the content are cognized as necessary, and this necessary as free.

Philosophy thus characterizes itself as a cognition of the necessity in the content of the absolute picture-idea, as also of the necessity in the two forms—on one hand, immediate vision and its poetry, and the objective and external revelation presupposed by representation—on the other hand, first the subjective retreat inwards, then the subjective movement of faith and its final identification with the presupposed object. This cognition is thus the *recognition* of this content and its form; it is the liberation from the one-sidedness of the forms, elevation of them into the absolute form, which determines itself to content, remains identical with it, and is in that the cognition of that essential and actual necessity. This movement, which philosophy is, finds itself already accomplished, when at the close it seizes its own notion—i.e., only *looks back* on its knowledge.

Here might seem to be the place to treat in a definite exposition of the reciprocal relations of philosophy and religion. The whole question turns entirely on the difference of the forms of speculative thought from the forms of mental representation and "reflecting" intellect. But it is the whole cycle of philosophy, and of logic in particular, which has not merely taught and made known this difference, but also criticized it, or rather has let its nature develop and judge itself by these very categories. It is only by an insight into the value of these forms that the true and needful conviction can be gained, that the content of religion and philosophy is the same—leaving out, of course, the further details of external nature and finite mind which fall outside the range of religion. But religion is the truth *for all men:* faith rests on the witness of the spirit, which as witnessing is the spirit in man. This witness—the underlying essence in all humanity—takes, when driven to expound itself, its first definite form under those acquired habits of thought which his secular consciousness and intellect otherwise employs. In this way the truth becomes liable to the terms and conditions of finitude in general. This does not prevent the spirit, even in employing sensuous ideas and finite categories of thought, from retaining its content (which as religion is essentially speculative) with a tenacity which does violence to them, and acts *inconsistently* towards them. By this inconsistency it corrects their defects. Nothing easier therefore for the "Rationalist" than to point out contradictions in the exposition of the faith, and then to prepare triumphs for its principle of formal identity. If the spirit yields to this finite reflection, which has usurped the title of reason and philosophy—("Rationalism")—it strips religious truth of its infinity and makes it in reality nought. Religion in that case is completely in the right in guarding herself against such reason and philosophy and treating them as enemies. But it is another thing when religion sets herself against comprehending reason, and against philosophy in general, and specially against a philosophy of which the doctrine is speculative, and so religious. Such an opposition proceeds from failure to appreciate the difference indicated and the value of spiritual form in general, and particularly of the logical form; or, to be more precise still, from failure to note the distinction of the content—which may be in both the same—from these forms. It is on the ground of form that philosophy has been reproached and accused by the religious party; just as conversely its speculative content has brought the same changes upon it from a self-styled philosophy—and from a pithless orthodoxy. It had too little of God in it for the former; too much for the latter.

The Phenomenology of Spirit

PREFACE: ON SCIENTIFIC COGNITION

It is customary to preface a work with an explanation of the author's aim, why he wrote the book, and the relationship in which he believes it to stand to other earlier or contemporary treatises on the same subject. In the case of a philosophical work, however, such an explanation seems not only superfluous but, in view of the nature of the subject-matter, even inappropriate and misleading. For whatever might appropriately be said about philosophy in a preface—say a historical *statement* of the main drift and the point of view, the general content and results, a string of random assertions and assurances about truth—none of this can be accepted as the way in which to expound philosophical truth. Also, since philosophy moves essentially in the element of universality, which includes within itself the particular, it might seem that here more than in any of the other sciences the subject-matter itself, and even in its complete nature, were expressed in the aim and the final results, the execution being by contrast really the unessential factor. On the other hand, in the ordinary view of anatomy, for instance (say, the knowledge of the parts of the body regarded as inanimate), we are quite sure that we do not as yet possess the subject-matter itself, the content of this science, but must in addition exert ourselves to know the particulars. Further, in the case of such an aggregate of information, which has no right to bear the name of Science, an opening talk about aim and other such generalities is usually conducted in the same historical and uncomprehending way in which the content itself (these nerves, muscles, etc.) is spoken of. In the case of philosophy, on the other hand, this would give rise to the incongruity that along with the employment of such a method its inability to grasp the truth would also be demonstrated.

Furthermore, the very attempt to define how a philosophical work is supposed to be connected with other efforts to deal with the same subject-matter drags in an extraneous concern, and what is really important for the cognition of the truth is obscured. The more conventional opinion gets fixated on the antithesis of truth and falsity, the more it tends to expect a given philosophical system to be either accepted or contradicted; and hence it finds only acceptance or rejection. It does not comprehend the diversity of philosophical systems as the progressive unfolding of truth, but rather sees in it simple disagreements. The bud disappears in the bursting-forth of the blossom, and one might say that the former is refuted by the latter; similarly, when the fruit appears, the blossom is shown up in its turn as a false manifestation of the plant, and the fruit now emerges as the truth of it instead. These forms are not just distinguished from one another, they also supplant one another as mutually incompatible. Yet at the same time their fluid nature makes them moments of an organic unity in which they not only do not conflict, but in which each is as necessary as the other; and this mutual necessity alone constitutes the life of the whole. But he who rejects a philosophical system [i.e the new philosopher] does not usually comprehend what he is doing in this way; and he who grasps the contradiction between them [i.e. the historian of philosophy] does not, as a general rule, know how to free it from its one-sidedness, or maintain it in its freedom by recognizing the reciprocally necessary moments that take shape as a conflict and seeming incompatibility.

Culture and its laborious emergence from the immediacy of substantial life must always begin by getting acquainted with *general* principles and points of view, so as at first to work up to a *general conception* [*Gedanke*] of the real issue, as well as learning to support and refute the general conception with reasons; then to apprehend the rich and concrete abundance [of life] by differential classification; and finally to give accurate instruction and pass serious judgement upon it. From its very beginning, culture must leave room for the earnestness of life in its concrete richness; this leads the way to an experience of the real issue. And even when the real issue has been penetrated to its depths by serious speculative effort, this kind of knowing and judging will still retain its appropriate place in ordinary conversation.

The true shape in which truth exists can only be the scientific system of such truth. To help bring philosophy closer to the form of Science, to the goal where it can lay aside the title '*love* of knowing' and be *actual* knowing—that is what I have set myself to do. The inner necessity that knowing should be Science lies in its nature, and only the systematic exposition of philosophy itself provides it. But the *external* necessity, so far as it is grasped in a general way, setting aside accidental matters of person and motivation, is the same as the inner, or in other words it lies in the shape in which time sets forth the sequential existence of its moments. To show that now is the time for philosophy to be raised to the status of a Science would therefore be the only true justification of any effort that has this aim, for to do so would demonstrate the necessity of the aim, would indeed at the same time be the accomplishing of it.

Whoever seeks mere edification, and whoever wants to shroud in a mist the manifold variety of his earthly existence and of thought, in order to pursue the indeterminate enjoyment of this indeterminate divinity, may look where he likes to find all this. He will find ample opportunity to dream up something for himself. But philosophy must beware of the wish to be edifying.

Still less must this complacency which abjures Science claim that such rapturous haziness is superior to Science. This prophetic talk supposes that it is staying right in the centre and in the depths, looks disdainfully at determinateness (*Horos*), and deliberately holds aloof from Notion and Necessity as products of that reflection which is at home only in the finite. But just as there is an empty breadth, so too there is an empty depth; and just as there is an extension of substance that pours forth as a finite multiplicity without the force to hold the multiplicity together, so there is an intensity without content, one that holds itself in as a sheer force without spread, and this is in no way distinguishable from superficiality. The power of Spirit is only as great as its expression, its depth only as deep as it dares to spread out and lose itself in its exposition. Moreover, when this non-conceptual, substantial knowledge professes to have sunk the idiosyncrasy of the self in essential being, and to philosophize in a true and holy manner, it hides the truth from itself: by spurning measure and definition, instead of being devoted to God, it merely gives free rein both to the contingency of the content within it, and to its own caprice. Such minds, when they give themselves up to the uncontrolled ferment of [the divine] substance, imagine that, by drawing a veil over self-consciousness and surrendering understanding they become the beloved of God to whom He gives wisdom in sleep; and hence what they in fact receive, and bring to birth in their sleep, is nothing but dreams.

Besides, it is not difficult to see that ours is a birth-time and a period of transition to a new era. Spirit has broken with the world it has hitherto inhabited and imagined, and is of a mind to submerge it in the past, and in the labour of its own transformation. Spirit is indeed never at rest but always engaged in moving forward. But just as the first breath drawn by a child after its long, quiet nourishment breaks the gradualness of merely quantitative growth—there is a qualitative leap, and the child is born—so likewise the Spirit in its formation matures slowly and quietly into its new shape, dissolving bit by bit the structure of its previous world, whose tottering state is only hinted at by isolated symptoms. The frivolity and boredom which unsettle the established order, the vague foreboding of something unknown, these are the heralds of approaching change. The gradual crumbling that left unaltered the face of the whole is cut short by a sunburst which, in one flash, illuminates the features of the new world.

But this new world is no more a complete actuality than is a new-born child; it is essential to bear this in mind. It comes on the scene for the first time in its immediacy. Just as little as a building is finished when its foundation has been laid, so little is the achieved Notion of the whole the whole itself. When we wish to see an oak with its massive trunk and spreading branches and foliage, we are not content to be shown an acorn instead. So too, Science, the crown of a world of Spirit, is not complete in its beginnings. The onset of the new spirit is the product of a widespread upheaval in various forms of culture, the prize at the end of a complicated, tortuous path and of just as variegated and strenuous an effort. It is the whole which, having traversed its content in time and space, has returned into itself, and is the resultant *simple Notion* of the whole. But the actuality of this simple whole consists in those various shapes and forms which have become its moments, and which will now develop and take shape afresh, this time in their new element, in their newly acquired meaning.

While the initial appearance of the new world is, to begin with, only the whole veiled in its *simplicity*, or the general foundation of the whole, the wealth of previous existence is still present to consciousness in memory. Consciousness misses in the newly emerging shape its former range and specificity of content, and even more the articulation of form whereby distinctions are securely defined, and stand arrayed in their fixed relations. Without such articulation, Science lacks universal intelligibility, and gives the appearance of being the esoteric possession of a few individuals: an esoteric possession, since it is as yet present only in its Notion or in its inwardness; of a few individuals, since its undiffused manifestation makes its existence something singular. Only what is completely determined is at once exoteric, comprehensible, and capable of being learned and appropriated by all. The intelligible form of Science is the way open and equally accessible to everyone, and consciousness as it approaches Science justly demands that it be able to attain to rational knowledge by way of the ordinary understanding; for the understanding is thought, the pure 'I' as such; and what is intelligible is what is already familiar and common to Science and the unscientific consciousness alike, the latter through its having afforded direct access to the former.

Reason is *purposive activity*. The exaltation of a supposed Nature over a misconceived thinking, and especially the rejection of external teleology, has brought the form of purpose in general into discredit. Still, in the sense in which Aristotle, too, defines Nature as purposive activity, purpose is what is immediate and *at rest*, the unmoved which is also *self-moving*, and as such is Subject. Its power to move, taken abstractly, is *being-for-self* or pure negativity. The result is the same as the beginning, only because the *beginning* is the *purpose*; in other words, the actual is the same as its Notion only because the immediate, as purpose, contains the self or pure actuality, is movement and unfolded becoming; but it is just this unrest that is the self; and the self is like that immediacy and simplicity of the beginning because it is the result, that which has returned into itself, the latter being similarly just the self. And the self is the sameness and simplicity that relates itself to itself.

That the True is actual only as system, or that Substance is essentially Subject, is expressed in the representation of the Absolute as *Spirit*—the most sublime Notion and the one which belongs to the modern age and its religion. The spiritual alone is the *actual*; it is essence, or that which has *being in itself*; it is that which *relates itself to itself* and is *determinate*, it is *other-being* and *being-for-self*, and in this determinateness, or in its self-externality, abides within itself; in other words, it is *in and for itself.*—But this being-in-and-for-itself is at first only for us, or *in itself*, it is spiritual *Substance*. It must also be this *for itself*, it must be the knowledge of the spiritual, and the knowledge of itself as Spirit, i.e. it must be an *object* to itself, but just as immediately a sublated object, reflected into itself. It is *for itself* only for *us*, in so far as its spiritual content is generated by itself. But in so far as it is also for itself for its own self, this self-generation, the pure Notion, is for it the objective element in which it has its existence, and it is in this way, in its existence for itself, an object reflected into itself. The Spirit that, so developed, knows itself as Spirit, is *Science*; Science is its actuality and the realm which it builds for itself in its own element.

'True' and 'false' belong among those determinate notions which are held to be inert and wholly separate essences, one here and one there, each standing fixed and isolated from the other, with which it has nothing in common. Against this view it must be maintained that truth is not a minted coin that can be given and pocketed ready-made. Nor *is* there such a thing as the false, any more than there *is* something evil. The evil and the false, to be sure, are not as bad as the devil, for in the devil they are even made into a particular *subjective agent*; as the false and the evil, they are mere *universals*, though each has its own essence as against the other.

The false (for here it is only of this that we speak) would be the other, the negative of the substance, which as the content of knowledge is the True. But the substance is itself essentially the negative, partly as a distinction and determination of the content, and partly as a *simple* distinguishing, i.e. as self and knowledge in general. One can, of course, know something falsely. To know something falsely means that there is a disparity between knowledge and its Substance. But this very disparity is the process of distinguishing in general, which is an essential moment [in knowing]. Out of this distinguishing, of course, comes their identity, and this resultant identity is the truth. But it is not truth as if the disparity had been thrown away, like dross from pure metal, not even like the tool which remains separate from the finished vessel; disparity, rather, as the negative, the self, is itself still directly present in the True as such. Yet we cannot therefore say that the false is a moment of the True, let alone a component part of it. To say that in every falsehood there is a grain of truth is to treat the two like oil and water, which cannot be mixed and are only externally combined. It is precisely on account of the importance of designating the moment of *complete otherness* that the terms 'true' and 'false' must no longer be used where such otherness has been annulled. Just as to talk of the *unity* of subject and object, of finite and infinite, of being and thought, etc. is inept, since object and subject, etc. signify what they are *outside* of their unity, and since in their unity they are not meant to be what their expression says they are, just so the false is no longer *qua* false, a moment of truth.

Dogmatism as a way of thinking, whether in ordinary knowing or in the study of philosophy, is nothing else but the opinion that the True consists in a proposition which is a fixed result, or which is immediately known. To such questions as, When was Caesar born?, or How many feet were there in a stadium?, etc. a clear-cut answer ought to be given, just as it is definitely true that the square on the hypotenuse is equal to the sum of the squares on the other two sides of a right-angled triangle. But the nature of a so-called truth of that kind is different from the nature of philosophical truths.

The study of philosophy is as much hindered by the conceit that will not argue, as it is by the argumentative approach. This conceit relies on truths which are taken for granted and which it sees no need to re-examine; it just lays them down, and believes it is entitled to assert them, as well as to judge and pass sentence by appealing to them. In view of this, it is especially necessary that philosophizing should again be made a serious business. In the case of all other sciences, arts, skills, and crafts, everyone is convinced that a complex and laborious programme of learning and practice is necessary for competence. Yet when it comes to philosophy, there seems to be a currently prevailing prejudice to the effect that, although not everyone who has eyes and fingers, and is given leather and last, is at once in a position to make shoes, everyone nevertheless immediately understands how to philosophize, and how to evaluate philosophy, since he possesses the criterion for doing so in his natural reason—as if he did not likewise possess the measure for a shoe in his own foot. It seems that philosophical competence consists precisely in an absence of information and study, as though philosophy left off where they began. Philosophy is frequently taken to be a purely formal kind of knowledge, void of content, and the insight is sadly lacking that, whatever truth there may be in the content of any discipline or science, it can only deserve the name if such truth has been engendered by philosophy. Let the other sciences try to argue as much as they like without philosophy—without it they can have in them neither life, Spirit, nor truth.

In place of the long process of culture towards genuine philosophy, a movement as rich as it is profound, through which Spirit achieves knowledge, we are offered as quite equivalent either direct revelations from heaven, or the sound common sense that has never laboured over, or informed itself regarding, other knowledge or genuine philosophy; and we are assured that these are quite as good substitutes as some claim chicory is for coffee. It is not a pleasant experience to see ignorance, and a crudity without form or taste, which cannot focus its thought on a single abstract proposition, still less on a connected chain of them, claiming at one moment to be freedom of thought and toleration, and at the next to be even genius. Genius, we all know, was once all the rage in poetry, as it now is in philosophy; but when its productions made sense at all, such genius begat only trite prose instead of poetry, or, getting beyond that, only crazy rhetoric. So, nowadays, philosophizing by the light of nature, which regards itself as too good for the Notion, and as being an intuitive and poetic thinking in virtue of this deficiency, brings to market the arbitrary combinations of an imagination that has only been disorganized by its thoughts, an imagery that is neither fish nor flesh, neither poetry nor philosophy.

On the other hand, when philosophizing by the light of nature flows along the more even course of sound common sense, it offers at its very best only a rhetoric of trivial truths. And, if reproached with the insignificance of these truths, it assures us in reply that their meaning and fulfilment reside in its heart, and must surely be present in the hearts of others too, since it reckons to have said the last word once the innocence of the heart, the purity of conscience, and such like have been mentioned. These are ultimate truths to which no exception can be taken, and beyond which nothing more can be demanded. It is just the point, however, that the best should not remain in the recesses of what is inner, but should be brought out of these depths into the light of day. But it would be better by far to spare oneself the effort of bringing forth ultimate truths of that kind; for they have long since been available in catechisms or in popular sayings, etc.—It is not difficult to grasp such vague and misleading truths, or even to show that the mind in believing them is also aware of their very opposite. When it labours to extricate itself from the bewilderment this sets up, it falls into fresh contradictions, and may very well burst out with the assertion that the question is settled, that so and so is the truth, and that the other views are sophistries. For 'sophistry' is a slogan used by ordinary common sense against educated reason, just as the expression 'visionary dreaming' sums up, once and for all, what philosophy means to those who are ignorant of it.—Since the man of common sense makes his appeal to feeling, to an oracle within his breast, he is finished and done with anyone who does not agree; he only has to explain that he has nothing more to say to anyone who does not find and feel the same in himself. In other words, he tramples underfoot the roots of humanity. For it is the nature of humanity to press onward to agreement with others; human nature only really exists in an achieved community of minds. The anti-human, the merely animal, consists in staying within the sphere of feeling, and being able to communicate only at that level.

Should anyone ask for a royal road to Science, there is no more easy-going way than to rely on sound common sense; and for the rest, in order to keep up with the times, and with advances in philosophy, to read reviews of philosophical works, perhaps even to read their prefaces and first paragraphs. For these preliminary pages give the general principles on which everything turns, and the reviews, as well as providing historical accounts, also provide the critical appraisal which, being a judgment, stands high above the work judged. This common road can be taken in casual dress; but the high sense for the Eternal, the Holy, the Infinite strides along in the robes of a high priest, on a road that is from the first no road, but has immediate being as its centre, the genius of profound original ideas and lofty flashes of inspiration. But just as profundity of this kind still does not reveal the source of essential being, so, too, these sky-rockets of inspiration are not yet the empyrean. True thoughts and scientific insight are only to be won through the labour of the Notion. Only the Notion can produce the universality of knowledge which is neither common vagueness nor the inadequacy of ordinary common sense, but a fully developed, perfected cognition; not the uncommon universality of a reason whose talents have been ruined by indolence and the conceit of genius, but a truth ripened to its properly matured form so as to be capable of being the property of all self-conscious Reason.

Since I hold that Science exists solely in the self-movement of the Notion, and since my view differs from, and is in fact wholly opposed to, current ideas regarding the nature and form of truth, both those referred to above and other peripheral aspects of them, it seems that any attempt to expound the system of Science from this point of view is unlikely to be favourably received. In the meantime, I can bear in mind that if at times the excellence of Plato's philosophy has been held to lie in his scientifically valueless myths, there have also been times, even called times of ecstatic dreaming, when Aristotle's philosophy was esteemed for its speculative depth, and Plato's *Parmenides* (surely the greatest artistic achievement of the ancient dialectic) was regarded as the true disclosure and positive expression of the divine life, and times when, despite the obscurity generated by ecstasy, this misunderstood ecstasy was in fact supposed to be nothing else than the pure Notion. Furthermore, what really is excellent in the philosophy of our time takes its value to lie in its scientific quality, and even though others take a different view, it is in fact only in virtue of its scientific character that it exerts any influence. Hence, I may hope, too, that this attempt to vindicate Science for the Notion, and to expound it in this its proper element, will succeed in winning acceptance through the inner truth of the subject-matter. We must hold to the conviction that it is the nature of truth to prevail when its time has come, and that it appears only when this time has come, and therefore never appears prematurely, nor finds a public not ripe to receive it; also we must accept that the individual needs that this should be so in order to verify what is as yet a matter for himself alone, and to experience the conviction, which in the first place belongs only to a particular individual, as something universally held. But in this connection the public must often be distinguished from those who pose as its representatives and spokesmen. In many respects the attitude of the public is quite different from, even contrary to, that of these spokesmen. Whereas the public is inclined good-naturedly to blame itself when a philosophical work makes no appeal to it, these others, certain of their own competence, put all the blame on the author. The effect of such a work on the public is more noiseless than the action of these dead men when they bury their dead. The general level of insight now is altogether more educated, its curiosity more awake, and its judgment more swiftly reached, so that the feet of those who will carry you out are already at the door. But from this we must often distinguish the more gradual effect which corrects the attention extorted by imposing assurances and corrects, too, contemptuous censure, and gives some writers an audience only after a time, while others after a time have no audience left.

For the rest, at a time when the universality of Spirit has gathered such strength, and the singular detail, as is fitting, has become correspondingly less important, when, too, that universal aspect claims and holds on to the whole range of the wealth it has developed, the share in the total work of Spirit which falls to the individual can only be very small. Because of this, the individual must all the more forget himself, as the nature of Science implies and requires. Of course, he must make of himself and achieve what he can; but less must be demanded of him, just as he in turn can expect less of himself, and may demand less for himself.

Letter from Hegel to His Fiancée

[Nuremberg, Summer 1811]

. . . I have hurt you by a few things I said. This causes me pain. I have hurt you by seeming to censure moral views I can only repudiate, as if they were principles of your own thought and action. About this I now say to you only that I reject these views in part inasmuch as they abolish the difference between what the heart likes—i.e., what pleases it—and duty; or rather inasmuch as they completely eliminate duty and destroy morality. But likewise—and this is the most important matter between us—please believe me when I tell you that I do not attribute these views, insofar as they have this consequence, to *you*, to your self; that I view them as lying merely within your reflection; that you do not think, know, or gain an overview of them in their [*Ihrer*] logical connection; that they serve you as a way of excusing others. To justify is something else, for what one may excuse in others is not therefore considered permissible in oneself. Yet what one can justify is right for everyone, and thus for ourselves as well.

With regard to myself and my manner of explanation, do not forget that if I condemn maxims, I too easily lose consciousness of the way in which they are actual in determinate individuals—in you, for instance. Nor should you forget that such maxims appear before my eyes too earnestly in their universality, in their logical consequences, extended results, and applications. Far from taking these things to be entailed for you, you give them no thought. At the same time you yourself know that, even though character and the maxims governing insight are different, what maxims govern insight and judgment is not unimportant. Yet I know just as well that maxims, when they contradict character, are still less important in the case of women than men.

Lastly, you know that there are evil men who torture their wives merely so that their behavior, along with their patience and love, may be constantly tested. I do not believe I am that evil. Yet although no harm ought ever be done to such a dear human being as you, I could almost be free of regret for having hurt you. For through the deeper insight into your being that I have thus gained I feel the intimacy and depth of my love for you have increased. So be consoled that what may have been unkind and harsh in my replies will all vanish through the fact that I feel and recognize ever more deeply how thoroughly lovable, loving, and full of love you are.

I have to go lecture. Farewell, dearest, dearest, most lovely Marie. Your Wilhelm.

24

ARTHUR SCHOPENHAUER
Vitality and the Tasks of Life

Arthur Schopenhauer (1788–1860) came from a wealthy and well-connected family in Danzig. After private education and travel, he studied medicine at the University of Göttingen and philosophy in Berlin and Jena. In his early work, *On the Fourfold Root of the Principle of Sufficient Reason* (1813), he developed the view that the logical principle of sufficient reason entails metaphysical determinism: every event, every object, every moment of consciousness is necessarily determined by—and determines—others. In his major work, *The World as Will and Representation* (1818), Schopenhauer argues that Kant's thing-in-itself is not a postulate: it can be directly experienced as an activity of Willing. Equally critical of Hegel, he argued that Hegel's dictum "the Real is the Rational" must be abandoned; the agonistic striving of the Will cannot be rationally reconstructed. Influenced by his study of the Upanishads, Schopenhauer saw human suffering as a manifestation of the Will's expression of—and struggles against— the conflict and suffering brought about by the psychological dominance of unsatisfiable desires. Because artistic creation is also an expression of the Will, aesthetic experience can nevertheless present us with another—more serene— avenue to reality.

Although Nietzsche eventually became critical of (what he saw as) Schopenhauer's simplistic, unremitting pessimism, his theories of the Will to Power and of Eternal Recurrence are indebted to his predecessor. More recently, commentators have found Schopenhauerian traces in Wittgenstein and Heidegger.

The World as Will and Representation
Preface to the First Edition

I propose to state here how this book is to be read in order that it may be thoroughly understood. What is to be imparted by it is a single thought.

According as we consider under different aspects this one thought that is to be imparted, it appears as what has been called metaphysics, what has been called ethics, and what has been called aesthetics; and naturally it was bound to be all these, if it is what I have already acknowledged it to be.

A *system of thought* must always have an architectonic connexion or coherence, that is to say, a connexion in which one part always supports the other, though not the latter the former; in which the foundation-stone carries all the parts without being carried by them; and in which the pinnacle is upheld without upholding. On the other hand, *a single thought*, however comprehensive, must preserve the most perfect unity. If, all the same, it can be split up into parts for the purpose of being communicated, then the connexion of these parts must once more be organic, i.e., of such a kind that every part supports the whole just as much as it is supported by the whole; a connexion in which no part is first and no part last, in which the whole gains in clearness from every part, and even the

smallest part cannot be fully understood until the whole has been first understood. But a book must have a first and a last line, and to this extent will always
remain very unlike an organism, however like one its contents may be. Consequently, form and matter will here be in contradiction.

The World as Will and Representation
Preface to the Second Edition

Not to my contemporaries or my compatriots, but to mankind I consign my now
complete work, confident that it will not be without value to humanity, even if
this value should be recognized only tardily, as is the inevitable fate of the good
in whatever form. It can have been only for mankind, and not for the quickly
passing generation engrossed with its delusion of the moment, that my mind,
almost against my will, has pursued its work without interruption throughout a
long life. As time has passed, not even lack of sympathy has been able to shake
my belief in its value. I constantly saw the false and the bad, and finally the
absurd and the senseless, [in Hegelian philosophy] standing in universal admiration and honour, and I thought to myself that, if those who are capable of
recognizing the genuine and right were not so rare that we can spend some
twenty years looking about for them in vain, those who are capable of producing
it might not be so few that their works afterwards form an exception to the tran-
sitoriness of earthly things. In this way, the comforting prospect of posterity,
which everyone who sets himself a high aim needs to fortify him, would then
be lost. Whoever takes up and seriously pursues a matter that does not lead to
material advantage, ought not to count on the sympathy of his contemporaries.
But for the most part he will see that in the meantime the superficial aspect of
such matter becomes current in the world and enjoys its day; and this is as it
should be. For the matter itself also must be pursued for its own sake, otherwise
there can be no success, since every purpose or intention is always dangerous to
insight. Accordingly, as the history of literature testifies throughout, everything
of value needs a long time to gain authority, especially if it is of the instructive
and not of the entertaining sort; and meanwhile the false flourishes. For to unite
the matter with the superficial aspect of the matter is difficult, if not impossible.
Indeed, this is just the curse of this world of want and need, that everything must
serve and slave for these. Therefore it is not so constituted that any noble and
sublime endeavour, like that after light and truth, can thrive in it unhindered,
and exist for its own sake. But even when such an endeavour has once been able
to 'assert itself, and the idea of it is thus introduced, material interests and personal aims will at once take possession of it to make it their tool or their mask.
Accordingly, after Kant had brought philosophy once more into repute, it was
bound to become very soon the tool of political aims from above, and of personal
aims from below: though, to be accurate, not philosophy, but its double that
passes for it. This should not even surprise us, for the incredibly great majority
of men are by their nature absolutely incapable of any but material aims; they
cannot even comprehend any others. Accordingly, the pursuit of truth alone is a
pursuit far too lofty and eccentric for us to expect that all or many, or indeed
even a mere few, will sincerely take part in it. But if we see, as we do for instance
in Germany at the moment, a remarkable activity, a general bustling, writing, and
talking on matters of philosophy, then it may be confidently assumed that, in
spite of all the solemn looks and assurances, only real, not ideal, aims are the

actual *primum mobile*, the concealed motive, of such a movement; that is, that it is personal, official, ecclesiastical, political, in short material interests which are here kept in view, and that in consequence mere party ends set in such vigorous motion the many pens of pretended philosophers. Thus intentions, not intelligence, are the guiding star of these disturbers; and truth is certainly the last thing thought of in this connexion. It finds no partisans; on the contrary, it can pursue its way as silently and unheeded through such philosophical contention and tumult as through the winter night of the darkest century, involved in the most rigid faith of the Church, where it was communicated only as esoteric doctrine to a few adepts, or even entrusted only to parchment. In fact, I might say that no time can be more unfavourable to philosophy than that in which it is shamefully misused as a political means on the one hand, and a means of livelihood on the other. Or are we to believe that, with such effort and turmoil, the truth, by no means their aim, will also come to light? Truth is no harlot who throws her arms round the neck of him who does not desire her; on the contrary, she is so coy a beauty that even the man who sacrifices everything to her can still not be certain of her favours.

Now, if governments make philosophy the means to their political ends, then scholars see in professorships of philosophy a trade that nourishes the outer man just as does any other. They therefore crowd after them in the assurance of their good way of thinking, in other words, of the purpose or intention to serve those ends. And they keep their word; not truth, not clarity, not Plato or Aristotle, but the aims and ends they were appointed to serve are their guiding star; and these at once become the criterion both of what is true, valuable, and worthy of consideration, and of its opposite. Therefore whatever does not comply with these aims, be it even the most important and extraordinary thing in their department, is either condemned, or, where this seems precarious, suppressed by being unanimously ignored. Look only at their concerted indignation at pantheism; will any simpleton believe that this proceeds from conviction? How could philosophy, degraded to become a means of earning one's bread, generally fail to degenerate into sophistry? Just because this is bound to happen, and the rule "I sing the song of him whose bread I eat" has held good at all times, the making of money by philosophy was among the ancients the characteristic of the sophist. We have still to add that, since everywhere in this world nothing is to be expected, nothing can be demanded, and nothing is to be had for money except mediocrity, we have to put up with this here also. Accordingly, in all the German universities we see the cherished mediocrity straining to bring about from its own resources, and indeed in accordance with a prescribed standard and aim, the philosophy that still does not exist at all; a spectacle at which it would be almost cruel to mock.

While philosophy has long been obliged to serve to such an extent generally as a means to public ends on the one hand, and to private ends on the other, I have followed my course of thought, undisturbed by this fact, for more than thirty years. This I have done simply because I was obliged to, and could not do otherwise, from an instinctive impulse which, however, was supported by the confidence that anything true that a man conceives, and anything obscure that he elucidates, will at some time or other be grasped by another thinking mind, and impress, delight, and console it. To such a man we speak, just as those like us have spoken to us, and have thus become our consolation in this wilderness of life. Meanwhile, the matter is pursued on its own account and for its own sake.

Now it is a strange thing as regards philosophical meditations that only that which a man has thought out and investigated for himself is afterwards of benefit to others, and not that which was originally destined for those others. The former is conspicuously nearest in character to perfect honesty, for we do not try to deceive ourselves, or offer ourselves empty husks. In this way, all sophistication and all idle display of words are then omitted, and as a result every sentence that is written at once repays the trouble of reading. Accordingly, my writings bear the stamp of honesty and openness so distinctly on their face, that they are thus in glaring contrast to those of the three notorious sophists of the post-Kantian period. I am always to be found at the standpoint of *reflection*, in other words, of rational deliberation and honest information, never at that of *inspiration*, called intellectual intuition or even absolute thought; its correct names would be humbug and charlatanism. Therefore, working in this spirit, and meanwhile constantly seeing the false and the bad held in general acceptance, indeed humbug and charlatanism in the highest admiration, I long ago renounced the approbation of my contemporaries. It is impossible that an age which for twenty years has extolled a Hegel, that intellectual Caliban, as the greatest of philosophers so loudly that the echo was heard throughout Europe, could make the man who looked at this eager for its approbation. No longer has it any crowns of honour to bestow; its applause is prostituted, its censure signifies nothing. I mean what I say here, as is obvious from the fact that, if I had in any way aspired to the approbation of my contemporaries, I should have had to strike out twenty passages that wholly contradict all their views, and indeed must in part be offensive to them. But I should reckon it a crime on my part to sacrifice even a single syllable to that approbation. My guiding star has in all seriousness been truth. Following it, I could first aspire only to my own approval, entirely averted from an age that has sunk low as regards all higher intellectual efforts, and from a national literature demoralized but for the exceptions, a literature in which the art of combining lofty words with low sentiments has reached its zenith. Of course, I can never escape from the errors and weaknesses necessarily inherent in my nature as in that of everyone else, but I shall not increase them by unworthy accommodations.

Kant's teaching produces a fundamental change in every mind that has grasped it. This change is so great that it may be regarded as an intellectual rebirth. It alone is capable of really removing the inborn realism which arises from the original disposition of the intellect. Neither Berkeley nor Malebranche is competent to do this, for these men remain too much in the universal, whereas Kant goes into the particular. And this he does in a way which is unexampled either before or after him, and one which has quite a peculiar, one might say immediate, effect on the mind. In consequence of this, the mind undergoes a fundamental undeceiving, and thereafter looks at all things in another light. But only in this way does a man become susceptible to the more positive explanations that I have to give. On the other hand, the man who has not mastered the Kantian philosophy, whatever else he may have studied, is, so to speak, in a state of innocence; in other words, he has remained in the grasp of that natural and childlike realism in which we are all born, and which qualifies one for every possible thing except philosophy. Consequently, such a man is related to the other as a person under age is to an adult. That nowadays this truth sounds paradoxical, as it certainly would not have done in the first thirty years after the appearance of the *Critique of Reason*, is due to the fact that there has since grown up a generation that does not really know Kant. It has never done more than peruse him hastily and impatiently, or listen to an account at second-hand; and this again is due to its having, in consequence of bad guidance, wasted its time on the philosophemes of ordinary, and hence officious and intrusive, heads, or even of bombastic sophists, which have been irresponsibly commended to it. Hence the confusion in the first conceptions, and generally the unspeakable crudity and clumsiness that appear from under the cloak of affectation and pretentiousness in the philosophical attempts of the generation thus brought up. But the man who imagines he can become acquainted with Kant's philosophy from the descriptions of others, labours under a terrible mistake. On the contrary, I must utter a serious warning against accounts of this kind, especially those of recent times. In fact in the most recent years in the writings of the Hegelians I have come across descriptions of the Kantian philosophy which really reach the incredible. How could minds strained and ruined in the freshness of youth by the nonsense of Hegelism still be capable of following Kant's profound investigations? They are early accustomed to regard the hollowest of verbiage as philosophical thoughts, the most miserable sophisms as sagacity, and silly craziness as dialectic; and by accepting frantic word-combinations in which the mind torments and exhausts itself in vain to conceive something, their heads are disorganized. They do not require any *Critique of Reason* or any philosophy; they need a *medicina mentis*, first as a sort of purgative, *un petit cours de senscommunologie*, and after that one must see whether there can still be any talk of philosophy with them. Thus the Kantian doctrine will be sought in vain elsewhere than in Kant's own works; but these are instructive throughout, even where he errs, even where he fails. In consequence of his originality, it is true of him in the highest degree, as indeed of all genuine philosophers, that only from their own works does one come to know them, not from the accounts of others. For the thoughts of those extraordinary minds cannot stand filtration through an ordinary head. Born behind the broad, high, finely arched brows from under which beaming eyes shine forth, they lose all power and life, and no longer appear like themselves, when moved into the narrow lodging and low roofing of the confined, contracted, and thick-walled skulls from which peer out dull glances directed to personal ends. In fact, it can be said that heads of this sort act like uneven mirrors in which everything is twisted and distorted, loses the symmetry of its beauty, and represents a caricature. Only from their creators themselves can we receive philosophical thoughts. Therefore the man who feels himself drawn to philosophy must himself seek out its immortal teachers in the quiet sanctuary of their works. The principal chapters of any one of these genuine philosophers will furnish a hundred times more insight into their doctrines than the cumbersome and distorted accounts of them produced by commonplace minds that are still for the most part deeply entangled in the fashionable philosophy of the time, or in their own pet opinions. But it is astonishing how decidedly the public prefers to grasp at those descriptions at second-hand. In fact, an elective affinity seems to be at work here by virtue of which the common nature is drawn to its like, and accordingly will prefer to hear from one of its kind even what a great mind has said. Perhaps this depends on the same principle as the system of mutual instruction according to which children learn best from other children.

Now one more word for the professors of philosophy. I have always felt compelled to admire not only the sagacity, the correct and fine tact with which, immediately on its appearance, they recognized my philosophy as something quite different from, and indeed dangerous to, their own attempts, or in popular language as something that did not suit their purpose; but also the sure and astute policy by virtue of which they at once found out the only correct procedure towards it, the perfect unanimity with which they applied this, and finally the determination with which they have remained faithful to it. This procedure, which incidentally commended itself also by the ease with which it can be carried out, consists, as is well known, in wholly ignoring and thus in secreting—according to Goethe's malicious expression, which really means suppressing what is of importance and of significance. The effectiveness of this silent method is enhanced by the corybantic shouting with which the birth of the spiritual children of those of the same mind is reciprocally celebrated, shouting which forces the public to look and to notice the important airs with which they greet one another over it. Who could fail to recognize the purpose of this procedure? Is there then nothing to be said against the maxim *primum vivere, deinde philosophari?* The gentlemen want to live, and indeed to live by *philosophy*. To philosophy they are assigned with their wives and children, and in spite of Petrarch's *povera e nuda vai filosofia*, they have taken a chance on it. Now my philosophy is certainly not so ordered that anyone could live by it. It lacks the first indispensable requisite for a well-paid professorial philosophy, namely a speculative theology, which should and must be the principal theme of all philosophy—in spite of the troublesome Kant with his *Critique of Reason;* although such a philosophy thus has the task of for ever talking about that of which it can know absolutely nothing. In fact, my philosophy does not allow of the fiction which has been so cleverly devised by the professors of philosophy and has become indispensable to them, namely the fiction of a reason that knows, perceives, or apprehends immediately and absolutely. One need only impose this fiction on the reader at the very beginning, in order to drive in the most comfortable manner in the world, in a carriage and four so to speak, into that region beyond all possibility of experience, wholly and for ever shut off from our knowledge by Kant. In such a region, then, are to be found, immediately revealed and most beautifully arranged, precisely those fundamental dogmas of modern, Judaizing, optimistic Christianity. My meditative philosophy, deficient in these essential requisites, lacking in consideration and the means of subsistence, has for its pole star truth alone, naked, unrewarded, unbefriended, often persecuted truth, and towards this it steers straight, looking neither to the right nor to the left. Now what in the world has such a philosophy to do with that *alma mater*, the good, substantial university philosophy, which, burdened with a hundred intentions and a thousand considerations, proceeds on its course cautiously tacking, since at all times it has before its eyes the fear of the Lord, the will of the ministry, the dogmas of the established Church, the wishes of the publisher, the encouragement of students, the goodwill of colleagues, the course of current politics, the momentary tendency of the public, and Heaven knows what else? Or what has my silent and serious search for truth in common with the yelling school disputations of the chairs and benches, whose most secret motives are always personal aims? On the contrary, the two kinds of philosophy are fundamentally different. Therefore with me there is no compromise and there is no fellowship, and no one derives any advantage from me, except perhaps the man who is looking for nothing but the truth; none, therefore, of the philosophical parties of the day, for they all pursue their own aims. I, however, have only insight and discernment to offer, which suit none of those aims, because they are simply not modelled on any of them. But if my philosophy itself were to become susceptible to the professor's chair, there would have to be a complete change in the times. It would be a fine thing, then, if such a philosophy, by which no one can live at all, were to gain light and air, not to mention universal regard! Consequently, this had to be guarded against, and all had to oppose it as one man. But a man has not so easy a game with disputing and refuting; moreover, these are precarious and uncertain means, for the very reason that they direct public attention to the matter, and reading my works might ruin the public's taste for the lucubrations of the professors of philosophy. For the man who has tasted the serious will no longer relish the comic, especially when it is of a tedious nature. Therefore the system of silence, so unanimously resorted to, is the only right one, and I can only advise them to stick to it, and go on with it as long as it works—in other words, until ignoring is taken to imply ignorance; then there will still just be time to come round. Meanwhile, everyone is at liberty to pluck a little feather here and there for his own use, for the superfluity of ideas at home is not usually very oppressive. Thus the system of ignoring and of maintaining silence can last for a good while, at any rate for the span of time that I may yet have to live; in this way much is already gained. If in the meantime an indiscreet voice here and there has allowed itself to be heard, it is soon drowned by the loud talking of the professors who, with their airs of importance, know how to entertain the public with quite different things. But I advise a somewhat stricter observance of the unanimity of procedure, and, in particular, supervision of the young men, who at times are terribly indiscreet. For even so, I am unable to guarantee that the commended procedure will last for ever, and I cannot be answerable for the final result. It is a ticklish question, the steering of the public, good and docile as it is on the whole. Although we see the Gorgiases and Hippiases nearly always at the top; although as a rule the absurd culminates, and it seems impossible for the voice of the individual ever to penetrate through the chorus of foolers and the fooled, still there is left to the genuine works of all times a quite peculiar, silent, slow, and powerful influence; and as if by a miracle, we see them rise at last out of the turmoil like a balloon that floats up out of the thick atmosphere of this globe into purer regions. Having once arrived there, it remains at rest, and no one can any longer draw it down again.

Essays and Aphorisms

ON THE SUFFERING OF THE WORLD

1

If the immediate and direct purpose of our life is not suffering then our existence is the most ill-adapted to its purpose in the world: for it is absurd to suppose that the endless affliction of which the world is everywhere full, and which arises out of the need and distress pertaining essentially to life, should be purposeless and purely accidental. Each individual misfortune, to be sure, seems an exceptional occurrence; but misfortune in general is the rule.

2

Just as a stream flows smoothly on as long as it encounters no obstruction, so the nature of man and animal is such that we never really notice or become conscious of what is agreeable to our will; if we are to notice something, our will has to have been thwarted, has to have experienced a shock of some kind. On the other hand, all that opposes, frustrates and resists our will, that is to say all that is unpleasant and painful, impresses itself upon us instantly, directly and with great clarity. Just as we are conscious not of the healthiness of our whole body but only of the little place where the shoe pinches, so we think not of the totality of our successful activities but of some insignificant trifle or other which continues to vex us. On this fact is founded what I have often before drawn attention to: the negativity of well-being and happiness, in antithesis to the positivity of pain.

I therefore know of no greater absurdity than that absurdity which characterizes almost all metaphysical systems: that of explaining evil as something negative. For evil is precisely that which is positive, that which makes itself palpable; and good, on the other hand, i.e. all happiness and all gratification, is that which is negative, the mere abolition of a desire and extinction of a pain.

This is also consistent with the fact that as a rule we find pleasure much less pleasurable, pain much more painful than we expected.

A quick test of the assertion that enjoyment outweighs pain in this world, or that they are at any rate balanced, would be to compare the feelings of an animal engaged in eating another with those of the animal being eaten.

3

Our existence has no foundation on which to rest except the transient present. Thus its form is essentially unceasing *motion*, without any possibility of that repose which we continually strive after. It resembles the course of a man running down a mountain who would fall over if he tried to stop and can stay on his feet only by running on; or a pole balanced on the tip of the finger; or a planet which would fall into its sun if it ever ceased to plunge irresistibly forward. Thus existence is typified by unrest.

In such a world, where no stability of any kind, no enduring state is possible, where everything is involved in restless change and confusion and keeps itself on its tightrope only by continually striding forward—in such a world, happiness is not so much as to be thought of. It cannot dwell where nothing occurs but Plato's 'continual becoming and never being'. In the first place, no man is happy but strives his whole life long after a supposed happiness which he seldom attains, and even if he does it is only to be disappointed with it; as a rule, however, he finally enters harbour shipwrecked and dismasted. In the second place, however, it is all one whether he has been happy or not in a life which has consisted merely of a succession of transient present moments and is now at an end.

5

Life presents itself first and foremost as a task: the task of maintaining itself, *de gagner sa vie*. If this task is accomplished, what has been gained is a burden, and there then appears a second task: that of doing something with it so as to ward off boredom, which hovers over every secure life like a bird of prey. Thus the first task is to gain something and the second to become unconscious of what has been gained, which is otherwise a burden. That human life must be some kind of mistake is sufficiently proved by the simple observation that man is a compound of needs which are hard to satisfy; that their satisfaction achieves nothing but a painless condition in which he is only given over to boredom; and that boredom is a direct proof that existence is in itself valueless, for boredom is nothing other than the sensation of the emptiness of existence. For if life, in the desire for which our essence and existence consists, possessed in itself a positive value and real content, there would be no such thing as boredom: mere existence would fulfill and satisfy us. As things are, we take no pleasure in existence except when we are striving after something—in which case distance and difficulties make our goal look as if it would satisfy us (an illusion which fades when we reach it)—or when engaged in purely intellectual activity, in which case we are really stepping out of life so as to regard it from outside, like spectators at a play. Even sensual pleasure itself consists in a continual striving and ceases as soon as its goal is reached. Whenever we are not involved in one or other of these things but directed back to existence itself we are overtaken by its worthlessness and vanity and this is the sensation called boredom.

6

That the most perfect manifestation of the will to live represented by the human organism, with its incomparably ingenious and complicated machinery, must crumble to dust and its whole essence and all its striving be palpably given over at last to annihilation—this is nature's unambiguous declaration that all the striving of this will is essentially vain. If it were something possessing value in itself, something which ought unconditionally to exist, it would not have non-being as its goal.

Yet what a difference there is between our beginning and our end! We begin in the madness of carnal desire and the transport of voluptuousness, we end in the dissolution of all our parts and the musty stench of corpses. And the road from the one to the other too goes, in regard to our well-being and enjoyment of life, steadily downhill: happily dreaming childhood, exultant youth, toil-filled years of manhood, infirm and often wretched old age, the torment of the last illness and finally the throes of death—does it not look as if existence were an error the consequences of which gradually grow more and more manifest?

We shall do best to think of life as a *desengaño*, as a process of disillusionment: since this is, clearly enough, what everything that happens to us is calculated to produce.

ON PHILOSOPHY AND THE INTELLECT

1

The fundament upon which all our knowledge and learning rests is the inexplicable. It is to this that every explanation, through few or many intermediate stages, leads; as the plummet touches the bottom of the sea now at a greater depth, now at a less, but is bound to reach it somewhere sooner or later. The study of this inexplicable devolves upon metaphysics.

2

For *intellect in the service of will*, that is to say in practical use, there exist only *individual things;* for intellect engaged in art and science, that is to say active for its own sake, there exist only *universals*, entire kinds, species, classes, *ideas* of things. Even the sculptor, in depicting the individual, seeks to depict the idea, the species. The reason for this is that *will* aims directly only at individual things, which are its true objective, for only they possess empirical reality. Concepts, classes, kinds, on the other hand, can become its objective only very indirectly. That is why the ordinary man has no sense for general truths, and why the genius, on the contrary, overlooks and neglects what is individual: to the genius the enforced occupation with the individual as such which constitutes the stuff of practical life is a burdensome drudgery.

3

The two main requirements for philosophizing are: firstly, to have the courage not to keep any question back; and secondly, to attain a clear consciousness of anything that *goes without saying* so as to comprehend it as a problem. Finally, the mind must, if it is really to philosophize, also be truly disengaged: it must prosecute no particular goal or aim, and thus be free from the enticement of will, but devote itself undividedly to the instruction which the perceptible world and its own consciousness imparts to it.

4

The *poet* presents the imagination with images from life and human characters and situations, sets them all in motion and leaves it to the beholder to let these images take his thoughts as far as his mental powers will permit. That is why he is able to engage men of the most differing capabilities, indeed fools and sages together. The *philosopher*, on the other hand, presents not life itself but the finished thoughts which he has abstracted from it and then demands that the reader should think precisely as, and precisely as far as, he himself thinks. That is why his public is so small. The poet can thus be compared with one who presents flowers, the philosopher with one who presents their essence.

5

An odd and unworthy definition of philosophy, which however even Kant gives, is that it is a science *composed only of concepts*. For the entire property of a concept consists of nothing more than what has been begged and borrowed from perceptual knowledge, which is the true and inexhaustible source of all insight. So that a true philosophy cannot be spun out of mere abstract concepts, but has to be founded on observation and experience, inner and outer. Philosophy, just as much as art and poetry, must have its source in perceptual comprehension of the world: nor, however much the head needs to remain on top, ought it to be so cold-blooded a business that the whole man, heart and head, is not finally involved and affected through and through. Philosophy is not algebra: on the contrary, Vauvenargues was right when he said: *Les grandes pensées viennent du coeur.*

6

Mere subtlety may qualify you as a sceptic but not as a philosopher. On the other hand, scepticism is in philosophy what the Opposition is in Parliament; it is just as beneficial, and indeed necessary. It rests everywhere on the fact that philosophy is not capable of producing the kind of evidence mathematics produces.

7

A *dictate of reason* is the name we give to certain propositions which we hold true without investigation and of which we think ourselves so firmly convinced we should be incapable of seriously testing them even if we wanted to, since we should then have to call them provisionally in doubt. We credit these propositions so completely because when we first began to speak and think we continually had them recited to us and they were thus implanted in us; so that the habit of thinking them is as old as the habit of thinking as such and we can no longer separate the two.

8

People never weary of reproaching metaphysics with the very small progress it has made compared with the very great progress of the physical sciences. But what other sciences has been hampered at all times by having an antagonist *ex officio*, a public prosecutor, a king's champion in full armour against it? Metaphysics will never put forth its full powers so long as it is ejected to accommodate itself to dogma. The various religions have taken possession of the metaphysical tendency of mankind, partly by paralysing it through imprinting their dogmas upon the earliest years, partly by forbidding and proscribing all and uninhibited expression of it; so that free investigation of man's most important and interesting concern, of his existence itself, has been in part indirectly hampered, in part made subjectively impossible by the paralysis referred to; and in this way his most sublime tendency has been put in chains.

9

The discovery of truth is prevented most effectively, not by the false appearance things present and which mislead into error, nor directly by weakness of the reasoning powers, but by pre-conceived opinion, by prejudice, which as a pseudo *a priori* stands in the path of truth and is then like a contrary wind driving a ship away from land, so that sail and rudder labour in vain.

10

Every *general* truth is related to specific truths as gold is to silver, inasmuch as it can be converted into a considerable number of specific truths which follow from it in the same way as a gold coin can be converted into small change.

11

From *one* proposition nothing more can follow than what is already contained in it, i.e., than what it itself implies when its meaning is exhausted; but from *two* propositions, if they are joined together as premises of a syllogism, more can follow than is contained in either of them taken individually—just as a body formed by chemical combination exhibits qualities possessed by none of its constituents. That logical conclusions possess value derives from this fact.

12

What light is to the outer physical world intellect is to the inner world of consciousness. For intellect is related to will, and thus also to the organism, which is nothing other than will regarded objectively, in approximately the same way as light is to a combustible body and the oxygen in combination with which it ignites. And as light is the purer the less it is involved with the smoke of the burning body, so also is intellect the purer the more completely it is separated from the will which engendered it. In a bolder metaphor one could even say: Life is known to be a process of combustion; intellect is the light produced by this process.

13

The simplest unprejudiced self-observation, combined with the facts of anatomy, leads to the conclusion that intellect, like its objectivization the brain, is, together with its dependent sense-apparatus, nothing other than a very intense receptivity to influences from without and does not constitute our original and intrinsic being; thus that intellect is not that in us which in a plant is motive power or in a stone weight and chemical forces: it is *will* alone which appears in these forms. Intellect is that in us which in a plant is merely receptivity to external influences, to physical and chemical action and whatever else may help or hinder it to grow and thrive; but in us this receptivity has risen to such a pitch of intensity that by virtue of it the entire objective world, the world as idea, appears; and this, consequently, is how its objectivization originates. It will help to make all this more vivid if you imagine the world without any animal life on it. There will then be nothing on it capable of perceiving it, and therefore it will actually have no objective existence at all. Now imagine a number of plants shooting up out of the ground close beside one another. All kinds of things will begin to operate on them, such as air, wind, the pressure of one plant against another, moisture, cold, light, warmth, electricity, etc. Now imagine the receptivity of these plants to influences of this kind intensified more and more: it will finally become sensation, accompanied by the capacity to refer sensation to its cause, and at last perception: whereupon the world will be there, appearing in space, time and casual connexion—yet it will still be merely the result of external influences on the receptivity of the plants. This pictorial representation brings home very well the merely phenomenal existence of the external world and makes it comprehensible: for no one, surely, would care to assert that a state of affairs which consists of perceptions originating in nothing but relations between external influences and active receptivity represents the truly objective, inner and original constitution of all those natural forces assumed to be acting on the plants; that it represents, that is to say, the world of things in themselves. This picture can thus make it comprehensible to us why the realm of the human intellect should have such narrow boundaries, as Kant demonstrates it has in the *Critique of Pure Reason.*

14

That you should write down valuable ideas that occur to you as soon as possible goes without saying: we sometimes forget even what we have done, so how much more what we have thought. Thoughts, however, come not when *we* but when *they* want. On the other hand, it is better not to copy down what we have received finished and complete from without, what we have merely learned and what can in any case be discovered again in books: for to copy something down is to consign it to forgetfulness. You should deal sternly and despotically with your memory, so that it does not unlearn obedience; if, for example, you cannot call something to mind, a line of poetry or a word perhaps, you should not go and look it up in a book, but periodically plague your memory with it for weeks on end until your memory has done its duty. For the longer you have had to rack your brains for something the more firmly will it stay once you have got it.

15

The *quality* of our thoughts (their formal value) comes from within, their *direction*, and thus their matter, from without; so that what we are thinking at any given moment is the product of two fundamentally different factors. Consequently, the object of thought is to the mind only what the plectrum is to the lyre: which is why the same sight inspires such very different thoughts in differing heads.

16

How very paltry and limited the normal human intellect is, and how little lucidity there is in the human consciousness, may be judged from the fact that, despite the ephemeral brevity of human life, the uncertainty of our existence and the countless enigmas which press upon us from all sides, everyone does not continually and ceaselessly philosophize, but that only the rarest of exceptions do so. The rest live their lives away in this dream not very differently from the animals, from which they are in the end distinguished only by their ability to provide for a few years ahead. If they should ever feel any metaphysical need, it is taken care of from above and in advance by the various religions; and these, whatever they may be like, suffice.

17

One might almost believe that half our thinking takes place unconsciously. Usually we arrive at a conclusion without having clearly thought about the premises which lead to it. This is already evident from the fact that sometimes an occurrence whose consequences we can in no way foresee, still less clearly estimate its possible influence on our own affairs, will nonetheless exercise an unmistakable influence on our whole mood and will change it from cheerful to sad or from sad to cheerful: this can only be the result of unconscious rumination. It is even more obvious in the following: I have familiarized myself with the factual data of a theoretical or practical problem; I do not think about it again, yet often a few days later the answer to any rate the results, the products of this clear thought and vision for the whole species, which is indeed also the intrinsic being of this individual, so that their light may continue to illumine the darkness and stupor of the ordinary human consciousness. It is from this that there arises that instinct which impels genius to labour in solitude to complete its work without regard for reward, applause or sympathy, but neglectful rather even of its own well-being and thinking more of posterity than of the age it lives in, which could only lead it astray. To make its work, as a sacred trust and the true fruit of its existence, the property of mankind, laying it down for a posterity better able to appreciate it: this becomes for genius a goal more important than any other, a goal for which it wears the crown of thorns that shall one day blossom into a laurel-wreath. Its striving to complete and safeguard its work is just as resolute as that of the insect to safeguard its eggs and provide for the brood it will never live to see: it deposits its eggs where it knows they will one day find life and nourishment, and dies contented.

FROM BENTHAM TO RUSSELL

25

JEREMY BENTHAM
Accounting for Rationality

After graduating from Oxford, Jeremy Bentham (1748–1832) studied law at Lincoln's Inn. Although he was admitted to the bar in 1767, he was never in practice. Bentham's monumental work in jurisprudence, *An Introduction to the Principles of Morals and Legislation* (1789), rested on utilitarian principles: legislation should be crafted to promote the greatest happiness for the greatest number. He thought there could be a hedonic calculation of the projectible balance of (physical and psychological) pleasure over pain, taking into account their relative intensity, ramification, and duration, as well as the probability of their occurrence. Bentham applied this principle to the assessment of motives and actions as well as to the evaluation of social policy. Although he is sometimes misrepresented as a radical egoist, his version of hedonism extends to a limited indirect altruism that derives personal pleasure in the well-being of others. While he notoriously claimed that push-pin is as good as poetry, he acknowledged that some intellectual pleasures might be more enduring and ramified than many sensory pleasures. With James and John Stuart Mill, Bentham established University College, London; they also founded and contributed to the politically influential *Westminster Review*. Bentham produced numerous pamphlets on the issues of the day: the selection of juries, laws of libel, debt and usury, rules of evidence, and public education. He took a lively interest in the theory and practice of civic punishment, formulating characteristically elaborate criteria for a deterrent policy. His interest extended to the architecture of prisons, and he sketched a panoptical design that placed guards in the center of a circular tier of cells. He conducted an extensive political correspondence with his brother Samuel, who served in the British legation in Russia, and with Czar Alexander of Russia, whom he tried to persuade to adopt his measures for penal reform. He hoped to interest Catherine the Great in his *Constitutional Code* (1830) but declined her invitation to visit Russia. Bentham was made an honorary citizen of France in 1792.

An Introduction to the Principles of Morals and Legislation (1780)

PREFACE (1789)

The following sheets were, as the title-page expresses, printed so long ago as the year 1780. The design, in pursuance of which they were written, was not so extensive as that announced by the present title. They had at that time no other destination than that of serving as an introduction to a plan of a penal code, *in terminis*, designed to follow them, in the same volume.

The body of the work had received its completion according to the then present extent of the author's views, when, in the investigation of some flaws he had discovered, he found himself unexpectedly entangled in an unsuspected corner of the metaphysical maze. A suspension, at first not apprehended to be more than a temporary one, necessarily ensued: suspension brought on coolness; and coolness, aided by other concurrent causes, ripened into disgust.

Imperfections pervading the whole mass had already been pointed out by the sincerity of severe and discerning friends; and conscience had certified the justness of their censure. The inordinate length of some of the chapters, the apparent inutility of others, and the dry and metaphysical turn of the whole, suggested an apprehension, that, if published in its present form, the work would contend under great disadvantages for any chance, it might on other accounts possess, of being read, and consequently of being of use.

But, though in this manner the idea of completing the present work slid insensibly aside, that was not by any means the case with the considerations which had led him to engage in it. Every opening, which promised to afford the lights he stood in need of, was still pursued: as occasion arose, the several departments connected with that in which he had at first engaged, were successively explored; insomuch that, in one branch or other of the pursuit, his researches have nearly embraced the whole field of legislation.

Several causes have conspired at present to bring to light, under this new title, a work which under its original one had been imperceptibly, but as it had seemed irrevocably, doomed to oblivion. In the course of eight years, materials for various works, corresponding to the different branches of the subject of legislation, had been produced, and some nearly reduced to shape: and, in every one of those works, the principles exhibited in the present publication had been found so necessary, that, either to transcribe them piecemeal, or to exhibit them somewhere, where they could be referred to in the lump, was found unavoidable. The former course would have occasioned repetitions too bulky to be employed without necessity in the execution of a plan unavoidably so voluminous: the latter was therefore indisputably the preferable one.

To publish the materials in the form in which they were already printed, or to work them up into a new one, was therefore the only alternative: the latter had all along been his wish; and, had time and the requisite degree of alacrity been at command, it would as certainly have been realized. Cogent considerations, however, concur with the irksomeness of the task, in placing the accomplishment of it at present at an unfathomable distance.

Another consideration is, that the suppression of the present work, had it been ever so decidedly wished, is no longer altogether in his power. In the course of so long an interval, various incidents have introduced copies into various hands, from some of which they have been transferred, by deaths and other accidents, into others that are unknown to him. Detached, but considerable extracts, have even been published, without any dishonourable views (for the name of the author was very honestly subjoined to them), but without his privity, and in publications undertaken without his knowledge.

It may perhaps be necessary to add, to complete his excuse for offering to the public a work pervaded by blemishes, which have not escaped even the author's partial eye, that the censure, so justly bestowed upon the form, did not extend itself to the matter.

In sending it thus abroad into the world with all its imperfections upon its head, he thinks it may be of assistance to the few readers he can expect, to receive a short intimation of the chief particulars, in respect of which it fails of corresponding with his maturer views. It will thence be observed how in some respects it fails of quadrating with the design announced by its original title, as in others it does with that announced by the one it bears at present.

An introduction to a work which takes for its subject the totality of any science, ought to contain all such matters, and such matters only, as belong in common to every particular branch of that science, or at least to more branches of it than one. Compared with its present title, the present work fails in both ways of being conformable to that rule.

As an introduction to the principles of *morals*, in addition to the analysis it contains of the extensive ideas signified by the terms *pleasure, pain, motive*, and *disposition*, it ought to have given a similar analysis of the not less extensive, though much less determinate, ideas annexed to the terms *emotion, passion, appetite, virtue, vice*, and some others, including the names of the particular *virtues* and *vices*. But as the true, and, if he conceives right, the only true groundwork for the development of the latter set of terms, has been laid by the explanation of the former, the completion of such a dictionary, so to style it, would, in comparison of the commencement, be little more than a mechanical operation.

Again, as an introduction to the principles of *legislation in general*, it ought rather to have included matters belonging exclusively to the *civil* branch, than matters more particularly applicable to the *penal*: the latter being but a means of compassing the ends proposed by the former. In preference, therefore, or at least in priority, to the several chapters which will be found relative to *punishment*, it ought to have exhibited a set of propositions which have since presented themselves to him as affording a standard for the operations performed by government, in the creation and distribution of proprietary and other civil rights. He means certain axioms of what may be termed *mental pathology*, expressive of the connexion betwixt the feelings of the parties concerned, and the several classes of incidents, which either call for, or are produced by, operations of the nature above mentioned.

> [**Bentham's note** For example: *It is worse to lose than simply not to gain. A loss falls the lighter by being divided. The suffering, of a person hurt in gratification of enmity, is greater than the gratification produced by the same cause.* These . . . have the same claim to the appellation of axioms, as those given by mathematicians under that name; since, referring to universal experience as their immediate basis, they are incapable of demonstration, and require only to be developed and illustrated, in order to be recognised as incontestable.]

The consideration of the division of offences, and every thing else that belongs to offences, ought, besides, to have preceded the consideration of punishment: for the idea of *punishment* presupposes the idea of *offence*: punishment, as such, not being inflicted but in consideration of offence.

Lastly, the analytical discussions relative to the classification of offences would, according to his present views, be transferred to a separate treatise, in which the system of legislation is considered solely in respect of its form; in other words, in respect of its *method* and *terminology*.

In these respects, the performance fails of coming up to the author's own ideas of what should have been exhibited in a work, bearing the title he has now given it, viz. that of an *Introduction to the Principles of Morals and Legislation*. He knows however of no other that would be less unsuitable: nor, in particular, would so adequate an intimation of its actual contents have been given, by a title corresponding to the more limited design, with which it was written; viz. that of serving as an *introduction to a penal code*.

Yet more. Dry and tedious as a great part of the discussions it contains must unavoidably be found by the bulk of readers, he knows not how to regret the having written them, nor even the having made them public. Under every head, the practical uses, to which the discussions contained under that head appeared applicable, are indicated: nor is there, he believes, a single proposition that he has not found occasion to build upon in the penning of some article or other of the provisions of detail, of which a body of law, authoritative or unauthoritative, must be composed. He will venture to specify particularly, in this view, the several chapters shortly characterized by the words *Sensibility, Actions, Intentionality, Consciousness, Motives, Disposition, Consequences.* Even in the enormous chapter on the division of offences, which, notwithstanding the forced compression the plan has undergone in several of its parts, in manner there mentioned, occupies no fewer than one hundred and four closely printed quarto pages [in the first edition, 1780—M.P.M.], the ten concluding ones are employed in a statement of the practical advantages that may be reaped from the plan of classification which it exhibits . . . to some readers, as a means of helping them to support the fatigue of wading through an analysis of such enormous length, he would almost recommend the beginning with those ten concluding pages.

One good at least may result from the present publication; viz. that the more he has trespassed on the patience of the reader on this occasion, the less need he will have so to do on future ones: so that this may do to those, the office which is done by books of pure mathematics to books of mixed mathematics and natural philosophy. The narrower the circle of readers is, within which the present work may be condemned to confine itself, the less limited may be the number of those to whom the fruits of his succeeding labours may be found accessible. He may therefore, in this respect, find himself in the condition of those philosophers of antiquity, who are represented as having held two bodies of doctrine, a popular and an occult one: but with this difference, that in his instance the occult and the popular will, he hopes, be found as consistent as in those they were contradictory; and that, in his production, whatever there is of occultness has been the pure result of sad necessity, and in no respect of choice.

There is, or rather there ought to be, a *logic* of the *will*, as well as of the *understanding*: the operations of the former faculty are neither less susceptible, nor less worthy, than those of the latter, of being delineated by rules. Of these two branches of that recondite art, Aristotle saw only the latter: succeeding logicians, treading in the steps of their great founder, have concurred in seeing it with no other eyes. Yet so far as a difference can be assigned between branches so intimately connected, whatever difference there is, in point of importance, is in favour of the logic of the will; since it is only by their capacity of directing this faculty, that the operations of the understanding are of any consequence.

Of this logic of the will, the science of *law*, considered in respect of its *form*, is the most considerable branch,—the most important application. It is, to the art of legislation, what the science of anatomy is to the art of medicine: with this difference, that the subject of it is what the artist has to work *with*, instead of being what he has to operate *upon*. Nor is the body politic less in danger from a want of acquaintance with the one science, than the body natural from ignorance in the other. One example, amongst a thousand that might be adduced in proof of this assertion, may be seen in the note which terminates this volume.

Such, then, were the difficulties: such the preliminaries:—an unexampled work to achieve, and then a new science to create; a new branch to add to one of the most abstruse of sciences.

Yet more: a body of proposed law, how complete soever, would be comparatively useless and uninstructive, unless explained and justified, and that in every tittle, by a continued accompaniment, a perpetual commentary of reasons: [**Bentham's note** To the aggregate of them a common denomination has since been assigned—the *rationale*.] which reasons, that the comparative value of such as point in opposite directions may be estimated, and the conjunct force of such as point in the same direction may be felt, must be marshalled, and put under subordination to such extensive and leading ones as are termed principles. There must be therefore, not one system only, but two parallel and connected systems, running on together; the one of legislative provisions, the other of political reasons; each affording to the other correction and support.

Are enterprises like these achievable? He knows not. This only he knows, that they have been undertaken, proceeded in, and that some progress has been made in all of them. He will venture to add, if at all achievable, never at least by one, to whom the fatigue of attending to discussions, as arid as those which occupy the ensuing pages, would either appear useless, or feel intolerable. He will repeat it boldly (for it has been said before him), truths that form the basis of political and moral science are not to be discovered but by investigations as severe as mathematical ones, and beyond all comparison more intricate and extensive. The familiarity of the terms is a presumption, but it is a most fallacious one, of the facility of the matter. Truths in general have been called stubborn things: the truths just mentioned are so in their own way. They are not to be forced into detached and general propositions, unincumbered with explanations and exceptions. They will not compress themselves into epigrams. They recoil from the tongue and the pen of the declaimer. They flourish not in the same soil with sentiment. They grow among thorns; and are not to be plucked, like daisies, by infants as they run. Labour, the inevitable lot of humanity, is in no track more inevitable than here. In vain would an Alexander bespeak a peculiar road for royal vanity, or a Ptolemy a smoother one for royal indolence. There is no *King's Road*, no *Stadtholder's Gate*, to legislative, any more than to mathematic science.

Mill on Bentham

There are two men, recently deceased, to whom their country is indebted not only for the greater part of the important ideas which have been thrown into circulation among its thinking men in their time, but for a revolution in its general modes of thought and investigation. [The other man was Samuel Taylor Coleridge.] These men, dissimilar in almost all else, agreed in being closet students— secluded in a peculiar degree, by circumstances and character, from the business and intercourse of the world; and both were, through bade mankind compare the two. It was when he had solved the problem himself, or thought he had done so, that he declared all other solutions to be erroneous. Hence, what they produced will not last; it must perish, much of it has already perished, with the errors which it exploded: what he did has its own value, by which it must outlast all errors to which it is opposed. Though we may reject, as we often must, his practical conclusions, yet his premises, the collections of facts and observations from which his conclusions were drawn, remain forever, a part of the materials of philosophy.

A place, therefore, must be assigned to Bentham among the masters of wisdom, the great teachers and permanent intellectual ornaments of the human race. He is among those who have enriched mankind with imperishable gifts; and although these do not transcend all other gifts; nor entitle him to those honors, "above all Greek, above all Roman fame," which, by a natural reaction against the neglect and contempt of the world, many of his admirers were once disposed to accumulate upon him, yet to refuse an admiring recognition of what he was, on account of what he was not, is a much worse error, and one which, pardonable in the vulgar, is no longer permitted to any cultivated and instructed mind.

If we were asked to say, in the fewest possible words, what we conceive to be Bentham's place among these great intellectual benefactors of humanity; what he was, and what he was not; what kind of service he did and did not render to truth—we should say, he was not a great philosopher; but he was a great reformer in philosophy. He brought into philosophy something which it greatly needed, and for want of which it was at a stand. It was not his doctrines which did this: it was his mode of arriving at them. He introduced into morals and politics those habits of thought, and modes of investigation, which are essential to the idea of science, and the absence of which made those departments of inquiry, as physics had been before Bacon, a field of interminable discussion, leading to no result. It was not his opinions, in short, but his method, that constituted the novelty and the value of what he did—a value beyond all price, even though we should reject the whole, as we unquestionably must a large part, of the opinions themselves.

Bentham's method may be shortly described as the method of detail; of treating wholes by separating them into their parts; abstractions, by resolving them into things; classes and generalities, by distinguishing them into the individuals of which they are made up; and breaking every question into pieces before attempting to solve it. Hence his interminable classifications; hence his elaborate demonstrations of the most acknowledged truths. That murder, incendiarism, robbery, are mischievous actions, he will not take for granted, without proof. Let the thing appear ever so self-evident, he will know the why and the how of it with the last degree of precision; he will distinguish all the different mischiefs of a crime.

It is a sound maxim, and one which all close thinkers have felt, but which no one before Bentham ever so consistently applied, that error lurks in generalities; that the human mind is not capable of embracing a complex whole, until it has surveyed and catalogued the parts of which that whole is made up; that abstractions are not realities *per se*, but an abridged mode of expressing facts; and that the only practical mode of dealing with them is to trace them back to the facts (whether of experience or of consciousness) of which they are the expression. Proceeding on this principle, Bentham makes short work with the ordinary modes of moral and political reasoning. These, it appeared to him, when hunted to their source, for the most part terminated in *phrases*. In politics, liberty, social order, constitution, law of nature, social compact, etc., were the catchwords: ethics had its analogous ones. Such were the arguments on which the gravest questions of morality and policy were made to turn; not reasons, but allusions to reasons; sacramental expressions, by which a summary appeal was made to some general sentiment of mankind, or to some maxim in familiar use, which might be true or not, but the limitations of which no one had ever critically examined. And this satisfied other people, but not Bentham. He required something more than opinion as a reason for opinion. Whenever he found a *phrase* used as an argument for or against anything, he insisted upon knowing what it meant; whether it appealed to any standard, or gave intimation of any matter of fact relevant to the question; and, if he could not find that it did either, he treated it as an attempt on the part of the disputant to impose his own individual sentiment on other people, without giving them a reason for it.

Human nature and human life are wide subjects; and whoever would embark in an enterprise requiring a thorough knowledge of them has need both of large stores of his own, and of all aids and appliances from elsewhere. His qualifications for success will be proportional to two things—the degree in which his own nature and circumstances furnish him with a correct and complete picture of man's nature and circumstances, and his capacity of deriving light from other minds.

Bentham failed in deriving light from other minds. His writings contain few traces of the accurate knowledge of any schools of thinking but his own; and many proofs of his entire conviction, that they could teach him nothing worth knowing. For some of the most illustrious of previous thinkers, his contempt was unmeasured.

Bentham's contempt, then, of all other schools of thinkers; his determination to create a philosophy wholly out of the materials furnished by his own mind, and by minds like his own—was his first disqualification as a philosopher. His second was the incompleteness of his own mind as a representative of universal human nature. In many of the most natural and strongest feelings of human nature he had no sympathy; from many of its graver experiences he was altogether cut off; and the faculty by which one mind understands a mind different from itself, and throws itself into the feelings of that other mind, was denied him by his deficiency of imagination.

Bentham's knowledge of human nature is bounded. It is wholly empirical, and the empiricism of one who has had little experience. He had neither internal experience nor external: the quiet, even tenor of his life, and his healthiness of mind, conspired to exclude him from both. He never knew prosperity and adversity, passion nor satiety: he never had even the experiences which sickness gives; he lived from childhood to the age of eighty-five in boyish health. He knew no dejection, no heaviness of heart. He never felt life a sore and a weary burthen. He was a boy to the last. Self-consciousness, that demon of the men of genius of our time, from Wordsworth to Byron, from Goethe to Chateaubriand, and to which this age owes so much both of its cheerful and its mournful wisdom, never was awakened in him. How much of human nature slumbered in him he knew not, neither can we know. He had never been made alive to the unseen influences which were acting on himself, nor, consequently, on his fellow-creatures. Other ages and other nations were a blank to him for purposes of instruction. He measured them but by one standard—their knowledge of facts, and their capability to take correct views of utility, and merge all other objects in it. His own lot was cast in a generation of the leanest and barrenest men whom England had yet produced; and he was an old man when a better race came in with the present century. He saw accordingly, in man, little but what the vulgarest eye can see; recognized no diversities of character but such as he who runs may read. Knowing so little of human feelings, he knew still less of the influences by which those feelings are formed: all the more subtle workings both of the mind upon itself, and of external things upon the mind, escaped him; and no one, probably, who, in a highly instructed age, ever attempted to give a rule to all human conduct, set out with a more limited conception either of the agencies by which human conduct *is*, or of those by which it *should* be, influenced.

This, then, is our idea of Bentham. He was a man both of remarkable endowments for philosophy, and of remarkable deficiencies for it; fitted beyond almost any man for drawing from his premises conclusions not only correct, but sufficiently precise and specific to be practical; but whose general conception of human nature and life furnished him with an unusually slender stock of premises. It is obvious what would be likely to be achieved by such a man; what a thinker, thus gifted and thus disqualified, could do in philosophy. [He could, with close and accurate logic, hunt half-truths to their consequences and practical applications,] on a scale both of greatness and of minuteness not previously exemplified; and this is the character which posterity will probably assign to Bentham.

We express our sincere and well-considered conviction when we say, that there is hardly anything positive in Bentham's philosophy which is not true; that when his practical conclusions are erroneous, which, in our opinion, they are very often, it is not because the considerations which he urges are not rational and valid in themselves, but because some more important principle, which he did not perceive, supersedes those considerations, and turns the scale.

The first question in regard to any man of speculation is, What is his theory of human life? In the minds of many philosophers, whatever theory they have of this sort is latent; and it would be a revelation to themselves to have it pointed out to them in their writings as others can see it, unconsciously molding everything to its own likeness. But Bentham always knew his own premises, and made his reader know them: it was not his custom to leave the theoretic grounds of his practical conclusions to conjecture. Few great thinkers have afforded the means of assigning with so much certainty the exact conception which they had formed of man and of man's life.

Man is conceived by Bentham as a being susceptible of pleasures and pains, and governed in all his conduct partly by the different modifications of self-interest, and the passions commonly classed as selfish, partly by sympathies, or occasionally antipathies, towards other beings. And here Bentham's conception of human nature stops. He does not exclude religion: the prospect of divine rewards and punishments he includes under the head of "self-regarding interest"; and the devotional feeling, under that of sympathy with God. But the whole of the impelling or restraining principles, whether of this or of another world, which he recognizes, are either self-love, or love or hatred towards other sentient beings.

Man is never recognized by him as a being capable of pursuing spiritual perfection as an end; of desiring, for its own, the conformity of his own character to his standard of excellence, without hope of good, or fear of evil, from other source than his own inward consciousness. Even in the more ignited form of conscience, this great fact in human nature escapes him. Nothing is more curious than the absence of recognition, in any of his writings, of the existence of conscience, as a thing distinct from philanthropy, from affection for God or man, and from self-interest in this world or in the next. There is a studied abstinence from any of the phrases, which, in the mouths of others, import the acknowledgment of such a fact. If we find the words "conscience," "principle," "moral rectitude," "moral duty," in his "Table of the Springs of Action," it is among the synonyms of the "love of reputation"; with an intimation as to the two former phrases, that they are also sometimes synonymous with the *religious* motive, or the motive of *sympathy*. The feeling of moral approbation or disapprobation, properly so called, either towards ourselves or our fellow-creatures, he seems unaware of the existence of; and neither the word *self-respect*, nor the idea to which that word is appropriated, occurs even once, so far as our recollection serves us, in his whole writings.

Nor is it only the moral part of man's nature, in the strict sense of the term—the desire of perfection, or the feeling of an approving or of an accusing conscience—that he overlooks: he but faintly recognizes, as a fact in human nature, the pursuit of any other ideal end for its own sake. The sense of *honor* and personal dignity—that feeling of personal exaltation and degradation which acts independently of other people's opinion, or even in defiance of it; the love of *beauty*, the passion of the artist; the love of *order*, of congruity, of consistency in all things, and conformity to their end; the love of *power*, not in the limited form of power over other human beings, but abstract power, the power of making our volitions effectual; the love of *action*, the thirst for movement and activity, a principle scarcely of less influence in human life than its opposite, the love of ease—none of these powerful constituents of human nature are thought worthy of a place among the "Springs of Action."

26

JOHN STUART MILL
Education and Social Progress

J. S. Mill (1806–1873) was the son of James Mill, a leading Benthamite political reformer. The elder Mill oversaw the education of his precocious son, setting him to learn Greek at three and Latin at eight. In 1826, the young Mill went to study in France, where he suffered a severe depression, attributing it to the intensity of his hothouse education. On recovering from his depression, Mill began to read Wordsworth and Coleridge. He became a friend of Carlyle, who encouraged his interest in art. His two-volume *Dissertations and Discussions* (1859)—a collection of occasional pieces written for the *Westminster Review* and the *Fortnightly Review*—includes essays on poetry, and on literary and political subjects. In 1830, he met Mrs. Harriet Taylor, with whom he formed an enduring close friendship. They married in 1851, some two years after the death of her husband. Mill worked as an administrator for the East India Company from 1823 until the company dissolved in 1858; he served as a member of Parliament for a term, 1865–1868. After the death of Harriet Taylor in 1858, he spent a good deal of time in Avignon, until his own death in 1873.

Although he remained a utilitarian, Mill greatly modified Bentham's hedonic calculus by distinguishing qualities, as well as quantities of pleasure and pain. With characteristic modesty, Mill said that his far-reaching revisions of Bentham's views were little more than a revival of Aristotelian eudaimonism. Mill's version of utilitarianism had significant consequences for his views on education: he argued that moral education requires the development of appropriate sentiments as well as the skills of sound empirical and analytic reasoning (*Inaugural Address to the University of St. Andrews*, 1867). Since the political application of utilitarianism requires grounding in the logic of practical reasoning, Mill also wrote a *System of Logic, Deductive and Inductive* (1843) and *Political Economy* (1848). With the aim of providing an empirical basis for the calculation necessary for making sound policy decisions, he developed techniques and methods for inductive reasoning in the social sciences. His applied logic suited his associational philosophical psychology, which traces general ideas back to associations among perceptual experience.

Mill held political views that were considered radical for the times. His influential *On Liberty* (1859) presents an argument that the constraint of individual liberty is only justified when its exercise is likely to limit the liberty of others. The primacy of the liberty of public discussion was, he argued, a condition for the progressive movement toward truth. The principle of unfettered liberty should, he thought, only be applied in societies that have achieved a relatively high level of education. In his movingly reflective *Autobiography* (1867), he attributed his far-reaching views on the status of women to his association with Harriet Taylor. They both advocated women's rights to suffrage and to equal access to education and the occupations. In *The Subjection of Women* (1869), Mill argued that the inequality of women is a bar to progress because it degrades the educational importance of intelligent discussion in the family and provides a harmful model of social life. A utilitarian even in matters of religion, he admired the effective moral force of religious figures and institutions. Recognizing that his views on religion might be thought subversive Mill asked that the publication of his *Three Essays on Religion* (1874) be postponed until after his death.

Early Letters (1812–1848)

LETTER TO THOMAS CARLYLE

India House 11th & 12th April 1833

My dear Carlyle

I write to you again a letter which I could wish were better worth having—*really* an apology for a letter: Your last, which you *called* so, deserved a better name. I would write, if it were only to thank you for having a better opinion of me than I have of myself. It is useless discussing which is right; time will disclose that; though I do not think that my nature is one of the many things into which you see "some ten years farther" than I do. At all events I will not if I can help it give way to gloom and morbid despondency, of which I have had a large share in my short life, and to which I have been indebted for all the most valuable of such insight as I have into the most important matters, neither will this return of it be without similar fruits, as I hope and almost believe; nevertheless I will and must, though it leaves me little enough of energy, master it, or it will surely master me. Whenever it has come to me it has always lasted many months, and has gone off in most cases very gradually.

I have allowed myself to be paralysed more than I should, during the last month or two by these gloomy feelings, though I have had intervals of comparative brightness but they were short. I have therefore a poor account to render of work done.

LETTER TO THOMAS CARLYLE

India House 18th May 1833

My dear Carlyle

... There will be so much to talk over when we meet: and that will be this summer, unless, which is always possible, I should not be in a state of mind in which meeting with *any* one is profitable or delightful to me. I believe I am the least *helpable* of mortals—I have always found that when I am in any difficulty or perplexity of a spiritual kind I must struggle out of it by myself. I believe, if I could, whenever anything is spiritually wrong with me I should shut myself up from the human race, and not see face of man until I had got firm footing again on some solid basis of conviction, and could turn what comes into me from others into wholesome nutriment. I am often in a state almost of scepticism, and have no theory of Human Life at all, or seem to have conflicting theories, or a theory which does not amount to a Belief. This is only a *recent* state, and as I well know, a passing one, and my convictions will be firmer and the result of a larger experience when I emerge from this state, than before: but I have never found any advantage in communion with others while my own mind was unsettled at its foundations, and if I am not much mended when my vacation-time comes round, I will rather postpone a meeting with you until I am. ...

LETTER TO THOMAS CARLYLE

[London,] 5th July 1833

My dear Carlyle

... I shall in future never write on any subject which my mind is not full of when I begin to write; unless the occasion is such that it is better the thing were ill done than not at all, that being the alternative.—I do not think [my paper on Poetry and Art] contains anything erroneous, but I feel that it is far from going to the bottom of the subject, or even very deep into it; I think I see somewhat further into it now, and shall perhaps understand it in time. I think I mentioned to you that I have carried the investigation (rightly or wrongly as it may be) one step farther in a paper (being a review of a new poem) which I wrote for the Examiner: it proved too long for Fonblanque, and it is to appear in Tait, after such additions and alterations as I see it absolutely requires, and which I have not yet found time to give it. You say, you wish that you could help me [to understand Poetry and Art]; you *can*, and *do*, help me in all such matters, not by logical definition, which as I think I have said or written before, I agree with you in thinking not to be your peculiar walk of usefulness; but in *suggesting* deep and pregnant thoughts which might never have occurred to me, but which I am quite able when I have them to subject to all needful logical manipulation. This brings to my mind that I have never explained what I meant when writing once before in this strain I called you a Poet and Artist. I conceive that most of the highest truths, are, to persons endowed by nature in certain ways which I think I could state, intuitive; that is, they need neither explanation nor proof, but if not known before, are assented to as soon as stated. Now it appears to me that the poet or artist is conversant chiefly with *such* truths and that his office in respect to truth is to declare *them*, and to make them *impressive*. This, however, supposes that the reader, hearer, or spectator is a person of the kind to whom those truths *are* intuitive. Such will of course receive them at once, and will lay them to heart in proportion to the impressiveness with which the artist delivers and embodies them. But the other and more numerous kind of people will consider them as nothing but dreaming or madness: and the more so, certainly, the more powerful the artist, *as* an artist: because the means which are good for rendering the truth impressive to those who know it, are not the same and are often absolutely incompatible with those which render it intelligible to those who know it not. Now this last I think is the proper office of the logician or I might say the metaphysician, in truth he must be both. The same person may be poet and logician, but he cannot be both in the same composition: and as heroes have been frustrated of glory *"carent quia vate sacro,"* so I think the *vates* himself has often been misunderstood and successfully cried down for want of a Logician in Ordinary, to supply a logical commentary on his intuitive truths. The artist's is the highest part, for by him alone is real *knowledge* of such truths conveyed: but it is possible to convince him who never could *know* the intuitive truths, that they are not inconsistent with anything he *does* know; that they are even very *probable*, and that he may have faith in them when higher natures than his own affirm that they are truths. He may then build on them and act on them, or at least act nothing contradictory to them. Now this humbler part is, I think, that which is most suitable to my faculties, as a man of speculation. I am not in the least a poet, in any sense; but I can do homage to poetry. I can to a very considerable extent feel it and understand it, and can make others who are my inferiors understand it in proportion to the measure of their capacity. I believe that such a person is more wanted than even the poet himself; that there are more persons living who approximate to the latter character than to the former. I do not think myself at all fit for the one; I do for the other; your walk I conceive to be the higher. Now one thing not useless to do would be to exemplify this difference by enlarging in my logical fashion upon the difference itself: to make those who are not poets, understand that poetry is higher than Logic, and that the union of the two is Philosophy—I shall write out my thoughts more at length somewhere, and some*when*, probably soon. Yours faithfully,

The Value of Ancient Philosophy
(The Inaugural Address to The University of St. Andrews)

Human invention has never produced anything so valuable, in the way both of stimulation and of discipline to the inquiring intellect, as the dialectics of the ancients, of which many of the works of Aristotle illustrate the theory, and those of Plato exhibit the practice. No modern writings come near to these, in teaching, both by precept and example, the way to investigate truth, on those subjects, so vastly important to us, which remain matters of controversy, from the difficulty or impossibility of bringing them to a directly experimental test. To question all things; never to turn away from any difficulty; to accept no doctrine either from ourselves or from other people without a rigid scrutiny by negative criticism, letting no fallacy, or incoherence, or confusion of thought, slip by unperceived; above all, to insist upon having the meaning of a word clearly understood before using it, and the meaning of a proposition before assenting to it; these are the lessons we learn from the ancient dialecticians. With all this vigorous management of the negative element, they inspire no skepticism about the reality of truth, or indifference to its pursuit. The noblest enthusiasm, both for the search after truth and for applying it to its highest uses, pervades these writers, Aristotle no less than Plato, though Plato has incomparably the greater power of imparting those feelings to others. In cultivating, therefore, the ancient languages as our best literary education, we are all the while laying an admirable foundation for ethical and philosophical culture. In purely literary excellence—in perfection of form—the pre-eminence of the ancients is not disputed. In every department which they attempted,—and they attempted almost all,—their composition, like their sculpture, has been to the greatest modern artists an example, to be looked up to with hopeless admiration, but of inappreciable value as a light on high, guiding their own endeavors. In prose and in poetry, in epic, lyric, or dramatic, as in historical, philosophical, and oratorical art, the pinnacle on which they stand is equally eminent. I am now speaking of the form, the artistic perfection of treatment; for, as regards substance, I consider modern poetry to be superior to ancient, in the same manner, though in a less degree, as modern science: it enters deeper into nature. The feelings of the modern mind are more various, more complex and manifold, than those of the ancients ever were. The modern mind is, what the ancient mind was not, brooding and self-conscious; and its meditative self-consciousness has discovered depths in the human soul which the Greeks and Romans did not dream of, and would not have understood. But what they had got to express, they expressed in a manner which few even of the greatest moderns have seriously attempted to rival. It must be remembered that they had more time, and that they wrote chiefly for a select class, possessed of leisure. To us who write in a hurry for people who read in a hurry, the attempt to give an equal degree of finish would be loss of time. But to be familiar with perfect models is not the less important to us because the element in which we work precludes even the effort to equal them. They show us at least what excellence is, and make us desire it, and strive to get as near to it as is within our reach. And this is the value to us of the ancient writers, all the more emphatically, because their excellence does not admit of being copied, or directly imitated. It does not consist in a trick which can be learned, but in the perfect adaptation of means to ends. The secret of the style of the great Greek and Roman authors is, that it is the perfection of good sense. In the first place, they never use a word without a meaning, or a word which adds nothing to the meaning. They always (to begin with) had a meaning; they knew what they wanted to say; and their whole purpose was to say it with the highest degree of exactness and completeness, and bring it home to the mind with the greatest possible clearness and vividness. It never entered into their thoughts to conceive of a piece of writing as beautiful in itself, abstractedly from what it had to express: its beauty must all be subservient to the most perfect expression of the sense.

The most obvious part of the value of scientific instruction—the mere information that it gives—speaks for itself. We are born into a world which we have not made; a world whose phenomena take place according to fixed laws, of which we do not bring any knowledge into the world with us. In such a world we are appointed to live, and in it all our work is to be done. Our whole working power depends on knowing the laws of the world—in other words, the properties of the things which we have to work with, and to work among, and to work upon. We may and do rely, for the greater part of this knowledge, on the few who in each department make its acquisition their main business in life. But unless an elementary knowledge of scientific truths is diffused among the public, they never know what is certain and what is not, or who are entitled to speak with authority and who are not: and they either have no faith at all in the testimony of science, or are the ready dupes of charlatans and impostors. They alternate between ignorant distrust, and blind, often misplaced, confidence. Besides, who is there who would not wish to understand the meaning of the common physical facts that take place under his eye? Who would not wish to know why a pump raises water, why a lever moves heavy weights, why it is hot at the tropics and cold at the poles, why the moon is sometimes dark and sometimes bright, what is the cause of the tides? Do we not feel that he who is totally ignorant of these things, let him be ever so skilled in a special profession, is not an educated man, but an ignoramus? It is surely no small part of education to put us in intelligent possession of the most important and most universally interesting facts of the universe, so that the world which surrounds us may not be a sealed book to us, uninteresting because unintelligible. This, however, is but the simplest and most obvious part of the utility of science, and the part which, if neglected in youth, may be the most easily made up for afterwards. It is more important to understand the value of scientific instruction as a training and disciplining process, to fit the intellect for the proper work of a human being. Facts are the materials of our knowledge, but the mind itself is the instrument; and it is easier to acquire facts, than to judge what they prove, and how, through the facts which we know, to get to those which we want to know.

The most incessant occupation of the human intellect throughout life is the ascertainment of truth. We are always needing to know what is actually true about something or other. It is not given to us all to discover great general truths that are a light to all men and to future generations; though with a better general education the number of those who could do so would be far greater than it is. But we all require the ability to judge between the conflicting opinions which are offered to us as vital truths. And the need we have of knowing how to discriminate truth is not confined to the larger truths. All through life it is our most pressing interest to find out the truth about all the matters we are concerned with. If we are farmers we want to find what will truly improve our soil: if merchants, what will truly influence the markets of our commodities; if judges, or jurymen, or advocates, who it was that truly did an unlawful act, or to whom a disputed right truly belongs. Every time we have to make a new resolution or alter an old one, in any situation in life, we shall go wrong unless we know the truth about the facts on which our resolution depends. Now, however different these searches for truth may look, and however unlike they really are in their subject matter, the methods of getting at truth, and the tests of truth, are in all cases much the same. There are but two roads by which truth can be discovered—observation and reasoning; observation, of course, including experiment. We all observe, and we all reason, and therefore, more or less successfully, we all ascertain truths: but most of us do it very ill, and could not get on at all were we not able to fall back on others who do it better. If we could not do it in any degree, we should be mere instruments in the hands of those who could: they would be able to reduce us to slavery. Then how shall we best learn to do this? By being shown the way in which it has already been successfully done. The processes by which truth is attained, reasoning and observation, have been carried to their greatest known perfection in the physical sciences. As classical literature furnishes the most perfect types of the art of expression, so do the physical sciences those of the art of thinking. Mathematics, and its application to astronomy and natural philosophy, are the most complete example of the discovery of truths by reasoning; experimental science, of their discovery by direct observation. In all these cases we know that we can trust the operation, because the conclusions to which it has led have been found true by subsequent trial. It is by the study of these, then, that we may hope to qualify ourselves for distinguishing truth, in cases where there do not exist the same ready means of verification.

In what consists the principal and most characteristic difference between one human intellect and another? In their ability to judge correctly of evidence. Our direct perceptions of truth are so limited,—we know so few things by immediate intuition, or, as it used to be called, by simple apprehension,—that we depend, for almost all our valuable knowledge, on evidence external to itself; and most of us are very unsafe hands at estimating evidence, where an appeal cannot be made to actual eyesight. The intellectual part of our education has nothing more important to do than to correct or mitigate this almost universal infirmity—this summary and substance of nearly all purely intellectual weakness. To do this with effect needs all the resources which the most perfect system of intellectual training can command. Those resources, as every teacher knows, are but of three kinds: first, models; secondly, rules; thirdly, appropriate practice. The models of the art of estimating evidence are furnished by science; the rules are suggested by science; and the study of science is the most fundamental portion of the practice.

A university exists for the purpose of laying open to each succeeding generation, as far as the conditions of the case admit, the accumulated treasure of the thoughts of mankind. As an indispensable part of this, it has to make known to them what mankind at large, their own country, and the best and wisest individual men, have thought on the great subjects of morals and religion. There should be, and there is in most universities, professorial instruction in moral philosophy; but I could wish that this instruction were of a somewhat different type from what is ordinarily met with. I could wish that it were more expository, less polemical, and above all less dogmatic. The learner should be made acquainted with the principal systems of moral philosophy which have existed and been practically operative among mankind, and should hear what there is to be said for each: the Aristotelian, the Epicurean, the Stoic, the Judaic, the Christian in the various modes of its interpretation, which differ almost as much from one another as the teachings of those earlier schools. He should be made familiar with the different standards of right and wrong which have been taken as the basis of ethics; general utility, natural justice, natural rights, a moral sense, principles of practical reason, and the rest. Among all these, it is not so much the teacher's business to take a side, and fight stoutly for some one against the rest, as it is to direct them all towards the establishment and preservation of the rules of conduct most advantageous to mankind. There is not one of these systems which has not its good side; not one from which there is not something to be learned by the votaries of the others; not one which is not suggested by a keen, though it may not always be a clear, perception of some important truths, which are the prop of the system, and the neglect or undervaluing of which in other systems, is their characteristic infirmity. A system which may be as a whole erroneous, is still valuable, until it has forced upon mankind a sufficient attention to the portion of truth which suggested it. The ethical teacher does his part best when he points out how each system may be strengthened even on its own basis, by taking into more complete account the truths which other systems have realized more fully and made more prominent. I do not mean that he should encourage an essentially skeptical eclecticism. While placing every system in the best aspect it admits of, and endeavoring to draw from all of them the most salutary consequences compatible with their nature, I would by no means debar him from enforcing by his best arguments his own preference for some one of the number. They cannot be all true; though those which are false as theories may contain particular truths, indispensable to the completeness of the true theory. But on this subject, even more than on any of those I have previously mentioned, it is not the teacher's business to impose his own judgment, but to inform and discipline that of his pupil.

There is, besides, a natural affinity between goodness and the cultivation of the Beautiful, when it is real cultivation, and not a mere unguided instinct. He who has learned what beauty is, if he be of a virtuous character, will desire to realize it in his own life—will keep before himself a type of perfect beauty in human character, to light his attempts at self-culture. There is a true meaning in the saying of Goethe, though liable to be misunderstood and perverted, that the Beautiful is greater than the Good; for it includes the Good, and adds something to it: it is the Good made perfect, and fitted with all the collateral perfections which make it a finished and completed thing. Now, this sense of perfection, which would make us demand from every creation of man the very utmost that it ought to give, and render us intolerant of the smallest fault in ourselves or in anything we do, is one of the results of Art cultivation. No other human productions come so near to perfection as works of pure Art. In all other things, we are, and may reasonably be, satisfied if the degree of excellence is as great as the object immediately in view seems to us to be worth: but in Art, the perfection is itself the object. If I were to define Art, I should be inclined to call it, the endeavor after perfection in execution. If we meet with even a piece of mechanical work which bears the marks of being done in this spirit—which is done as if the workman loved it, and tried to make it as good as possible, though something less good would have answered the purpose for which it was ostensibly made—we say that he has worked like an artist. Art, when really cultivated, and not merely practiced empirically, maintains, what it first gave the conception of, an ideal Beauty, to be eternally aimed at, though surpassing what can be actually attained; and by this idea it trains us never to be completely satisfied with imperfection in what we ourselves do and are: to idealize, as much as possible, every work we do, and most of all, our own characters and lives.

Autobiography
[Chapter I]

CHILDHOOD AND EARLY EDUCATION

It seems proper that I should mention the reasons which have made me think it desirable that I should leave behind me such a memorial of so uneventful a life as mine. I do not for a moment imagine that any part of what I have to relate, can be interesting to the public as a narrative, or as being connected with myself. But I have thought that in an age in which education, and its improvement, are the subject of more, if not of profounder study than at any former period of English history, it may be useful that there should be some record of an education which was unusual and remarkable, and which, whatever else it may have done, has proved how much more than is commonly supposed may be taught, and well taught, in those early years which, in the common modes of what is called instruction, are little better than wasted. It has also seemed to me that in an age of transition in opinions, there may be somewhat both of interest and of benefit in noting the successive phases of any mind which was always pressing forward, equally ready to learn and to unlearn either from its own thoughts or from those of others. But a motive which weighs more with me than either of these, is a desire to make acknowledgment of the debts which my intellectual and moral development owes to other persons; some of them of recognised eminence, others less known than they deserve to be, and the one to whom most of all is due, one whom the world had no opportunity of knowing.[1]

How I Wrote "On Liberty"

CHILDHOOD AND EARLY EDUCATION

... It is in this way that all my books have been composed. They were always written at least twice over; a first draft of the entire work was completed to the very end of the subject, then the whole begun again *de novo*; but incorporating, in the second writing, all sentences and parts of sentences of the old draft, which appeared as suitable to my purpose as anything which I could write in lieu of them. I have found great advantages in this system of double redaction. It combines, better than any other mode of composition, the freshness and vigour of the first conception, with the superior precision and completeness resulting from prolonged thought. In my own case, moreover, I have found that the patience necessary for a careful elaboration of the details of composition and expression, costs much less effort after the entire subject has been once gone through, and the substance of all that I find to say has in some manner, however imperfect, been got upon paper. The only thing which I am careful, in the first draft, to make as perfect as I am able, is the arrangement. If that is bad, the whole thread on which the ideas string themselves becomes twisted; thoughts placed in a wrong connexion are not expounded in a manner that suits the right, and a first draft with this original vice is next to useless as a foundation for the final treatment.[1]

During the two years which immediately preceded the cessation of my official life, my wife and I were working together at the "Liberty." I had first planned and written it as a short essay in 1854. It was in [in Rome] mounting the steps of the Capitol, in January, 1855, that the thought first arose of converting it into a volume. None of my writings have been either so carefully composed, or so sedulously corrected as this. After it had been written as usual twice over, we kept it by us, bringing it out from time to time, and going through it *de novo*, reading, weighing, and criticizing every sentence. Its final revision was to have been a work of the winter of 1858–9, the first after my retirement, which we had arranged to pass in the South of Europe. That hope and every other were frustrated by the most unexpected and bitter calamity of her death—at Avignon, [in 1858] on our way to Montpellier, from a sudden attack of pulmonary congestion.

Since then I have sought for such alleviation as my state admitted of, by the mode of life which most enabled me to feel her still near me. I bought a cottage as close as possible to the place where she is buried, and there her daughter (my fellow-sufferer and now my chief comfort) and I, live constantly during a great portion of the year. My objects in life are solely those which were hers; my pursuits and occupations those in which she shared, or sympathized, and which are indissolubly associated with her. Her memory is to me a religion, and her approbation the standard by which, summing up as it does all worthiness, I endeavour to regulate my life.

In resuming my pen some years after closing the preceding narrative, I am influenced by a desire not to have incomplete the record, for the sake of which chiefly this biographical sketch was undertaken, of the obligations I owe to those who have either contributed essentially to my own mental development or had a direct share in my writings and in whatever else of a public nature I have done. In the preceding pages, this record, so far as it relates to my wife, is not so detailed and precise as it ought to be; and since I lost her, I have had other help, not less deserving and requiring acknowledgment.

When two persons have their thoughts and speculations completely in common; when all subjects of intellectual or moral interest are discussed between them in daily life, and probed to much greater depths than are usually or conveniently sounded in writings intended for general readers; when they set out from the same principles, and arrive at their conclusions by processes pursued jointly, it is of little consequence in respect to the question of originality, which of them holds the pen; the one who contributes least to the composition may contribute most to the thought; the writings which result are the joint product of both, and it must often be impossible to disentangle their respective parts, and affirm that this belongs to one and that to the other. In this wide sense, not only during the years of our married life, but during many of the years of confidential friendship which preceded it, all my published writings were as much my wife's work as mine; her share in them constantly increasing as years advanced. But in certain cases, what belongs to her can be distinguished, and specially identified. Over and above the general influence which her mind had over mine, the most valuable ideas and features in these joint productions—those which have been most fruitful of important results, and have contributed most to the success and reputation of the works themselves—originated with her, were emanations from her mind, my part in them being no greater than in any of the thoughts which I found in previous writers, and made my own only by incorporating them with my own system of thought. During the greater part of my literary life I have performed the office in relation to her, which from a rather early period I had considered as the most useful part that I was qualified to take in the domain of thought, that of an interpreter of original thinkers, and mediator between them and the public; for I had always a humble opinion of my own powers as an original thinker, except in abstract science (logic, metaphysics, and the theoretic principles of political economy and politics), but thought myself much superior to most of my contemporaries in willingness and ability to learn from everybody; as I found hardly any one who made such a point of examining what was said in defense of all opinions, however new or however old, in the conviction that even if they were errors there might be a substratum of truth underneath them, and that in any case the discovery of what it was that made them plausible, would be a benefit to truth. I had, in consequence, marked out this as a sphere of usefulness in which I was under a special obligation to make myself active: the more so, as the acquaintance I had formed with the ideas of the Coleridgians, of the German thinkers, and of Carlyle, all of them fiercely opposed to the mode of thought in which I had been brought up, had convinced me that along with much error they possessed much truth, which was veiled from minds otherwise capable of receiving it by the transcendental and mystical phraseology in which they were accustomed to shut it up, and from which they neither cared, nor knew how, to disengage it; and I did not despair of separating the truth from the error, and expressing it in terms which would be intelligible and not repulsive to those on my own side in philosophy. Thus prepared, it will easily be believed that when I came into close intellectual communion with a person of the most eminent faculties, whose genius, as it grew and unfolded itself in thought, continually struck out truths far in advance of me, but in which I could not, as I had done in those others, detect any mixture of error, the greatest part of my mental growth consisted in the assimilation of those truths, and the most valuable part of my intellectual work was in building the bridges and clearing the paths which connected them with my general system of thought.

... What was abstract and purely scientific was generally mine; the properly human element came from her: in all that concerned the application of philosophy to the exigencies of human society and progress, I was her pupil, alike in boldness of speculation and cautiousness of practical judgment. For, on the one hand, she was much more courageous and far-sighted than without her I should have been, in anticipations of an order of things to come, in which many of the limited generalizations now so often confounded with universal principles will cease to be applicable. Those parts of my writings, and especially of the Political Economy, which contemplate possibilities in the future such as, when affirmed by Socialists, have in general been fiercely denied by political economists, would, but for her, either have been absent, or the suggestions would have been made much more timidly and in a more qualified form. But while she thus rendered me bolder in speculation on human affairs, her practical turn of mind, and her almost unerring estimate of practical obstacles, repressed in me all tendencies that were really visionary. Her mind invested all ideas in a concrete shape, and formed to itself a conception of how they would actually work: and her knowledge of the existing feelings and conduct of mankind was so seldom at fault, that the weak point in any unworkable suggestion seldom escaped her.

The "Liberty" was more directly and literally our joint production than anything else which bears my name, for there was not a sentence of it that was not several times gone through by us together, turned over in many ways, and carefully weeded of any faults, either in thought or expression, that we detected in it. It is in consequence of this that, although it never underwent her final revision, it far surpasses, as a mere specimen of composition, anything which has proceeded from me either before or since. With regard to the thoughts, it is difficult to identify any particular part or element as being more hers than all the rest. The whole mode of thinking of which the book was the expression, was emphatically hers. But I also was so thoroughly imbued with it, that the same thoughts naturally occurred to us both. That I was thus penetrated with it, however, I owe in a great degree to her. There was a moment in my mental progress when I might easily have fallen into a tendency towards over-government, both social and political; as there was also a moment when, by reaction from a contrary excess, I might have become a less thorough radical and democrat than I am. In both these points, as in many others, she benefited me as much by keeping me right where I was right, as by leading me to new truths, and ridding me of errors. My great readiness and eagerness to learn from everybody, and to make room in my opinions for every new acquisition by adjusting the old and the new to one another, might, but for her steadying influence, have seduced me into modifying my early opinions too much. She was in nothing more valuable to my mental development than by her just measure of the relative importance of different considerations, which often protected me from allowing to truths I had only recently learnt to see, a more important place in my thoughts than was properly their due.

The "Liberty" is likely to survive longer than anything else that I have written (with the possible exception of the "Logic"), because the conjunction of her mind with mine has rendered it a kind of philosophic text-book of a single truth, which the changes progressively taking place in modern society tend to bring out into ever stronger relief: the importance, to man and society, of a large variety in types of character, and of giving full freedom to human nature to expand itself in innumerable and conflicting directions. Nothing can better show how deep are the foundations of this truth, than the great impression made by the exposition of it at a time which, to superficial observation, did not seem to stand much in need of such a lesson. The fears we expressed, lest the inevitable growth of social equality and of the government of public opinion, should impose on mankind an oppressive yoke of uniformity in opinion and practice, might easily have appeared chimerical to those who looked more at present facts than at tendencies; for the gradual revolution that is taking place in society and institutions has, thus far, been decidedly favourable to the development of new opinions, and has procured for them a much more unprejudiced hearing than they previously met with. But this is a feature belonging to periods of transition, when old notions and feelings have been unsettled, and no new doctrines have yet succeeded to their ascendancy. At such times people of any mental activity, having given up many of their old beliefs, and not feeling quite sure that those they still retain can stand unmodified, listen eagerly to new opinions. But this state of things is necessarily transitory: some particular body of doctrine in time rallies the majority round it, organizes social institutions and modes of action conformably to itself, education impresses this new creed upon the new generations without the mental processes that have led to it, and by degrees it acquires the very same power of compression, so long exercised by the creeds of which it had taken the place. Whether this noxious power will be exercised, depends on whether mankind have by that time become aware that it cannot be exercised without stunting and dwarfing human nature. It is then that the teachings of the "Liberty" will have their greatest value. And it is to be feared that they will retain that value a long time.

As regards originality, it has of course no other than that which every thoughtful mind gives to its own mode of conceiving and expressing truths which are common property. The leading thought of the book is one which thought in many ages confined to insulated thinkers, mankind have probably at no time since the beginning of civilization been entirely without. To speak only of the last few generations, it is distinctly contained in the vein of important thought respecting education and culture, spread through the European mind by the labours and genius of Pestalozzi. The unqualified championship of it by Wilhelm von Humboldt is referred to in the book; but he by no means stood alone in his own country. During the early part of the present century the doctrine of the rights of individuality, and the claim of the moral nature to develop itself in its own way, was pushed by a whole school of German authors even to exaggeration; and the writings of Goethe, the most celebrated of all German authors, though not belonging to that or to any other school, are penetrated throughout by views of morals and of conduct in life, often in my opinion not defensible, but which are incessantly seeking whatever defense they admit of in the theory of the right and duty of self-development. In our own country, before the book "On Liberty" was written, the doctrine of Individuality had been enthusiastically asserted, in a style of vigorous declamation sometimes reminding one of Fichte, by Mr. William Maccall, in a series of writings of which the most elaborate is entitled "Elements of Individualism:" and a remarkable American, Mr. Warren, had framed a System of Society, on the foundation of "the Sovereignty of the Individual," had obtained a number of followers, and had actually commenced the formation of a Village Community (whether it now exists I know not), which, though bearing a superficial resemblance to some of the projects of Socialists, is diametrically opposite to them in principle, since it recognizes no authority whatever in Society over the individual, except to enforce equal freedom of development for all individualities. As the book which bears my name claimed no originality for any of its doctrines, and was not intended to write their history, the only author who had preceded me in their assertion, of whom I thought it appropriate to say anything, was Humboldt. It is hardly necessary here to remark that there are abundant differences in detail, between the conception of the doctrine by any of the predecessors I have mentioned, and that set forth in the book.

NOTES

1. From *The Autobiography of John Stuart Mill* (New York: Columbia University Press, 1924), pp. 155–56, 170–73, 175–80.

[Mill's note] The steps in my mental growth for which I was indebted to her were far from being those which a person wholly uninformed on the subject would probably suspect. It might be supposed, for instance, that my strong convictions on the complete equality in all legal, political, social and domestic relations, which ought to exist between men and women, may have been adopted or learnt from her. This was so far from being the fact, that those convictions were among the earliest results of the application of my mind to political subjects, and the strengths with which I held them was, as I believe, more than anything else, the originating cause of the interest she felt in me. What is true is, that until I knew her, the opinion was in my mind, little more than an abstract principle. I saw no more reason why women should be held in legal subjection to other people, than why men should. I was certain that their interests required fully as much protection as those of men, and were quite as little likely to obtain it without an equal voice in making the laws by which they are to be bound. But that perception of the vast practical bearings of women's disabilities which found expression in the book on the "Subjection of Women" was acquired mainly through her teaching. But for her rare knowledge of human nature and comprehension of moral and social influences, though I should doubtless have held my present opinions, I should have had a very insufficient perception of the mode in which the consequences of the inferior position of women intertwine themselves with all the evils of existing society and with all the difficulties of human improvement. I am indeed painfully conscious how much of her best thoughts on the subject I have failed to reproduce, and how greatly that little treatise falls short of what would have been if she had put on paper her entire mind on this question, or had lived to revise and improve, as she certainly would have done, my imperfect statement of the case.

27

KARL MARX
Philosophy as Political Critique

Karl Marx (1818–1883) studied philosophy at the University of Berlin, where he was influenced by a group of revisionary Hegelians who used Hegel's argumentative strategies to attack religion and the controlling interests of a conservative political regime. After receiving his doctorate in 1842, Marx became an editor of the *Rheinische Zeitung*, a liberal democratic paper. When that paper was suppressed for its increasingly radical views, Marx went to France, where he met Friedrich Engels, who became his lifelong friend and supporter.

Turning from journalism to philosophy, Marx developed a theory that placed activity (*praxis*) rather than philosophical reflection as the fundamental human activity (*Economic and Philosophical Manuscripts of 1844*). Appropriating Feuerbach's critique of alienation, he argued that unjust exploitation—dehumanization—consists in appropriating the results of productive activity. Working together, Marx and Engels collaborated in applying this view to the exploitive power relations in the traditional family (*Holy Family*, 1845) and the ideological subservience of traditional philosophy (*Theses on Feuerbach*, 1845). Delivered at the first meeting of the Communist League in London, *The Communist Manifesto* (1848) presents a historical account of how the dynamic changes in technology and in the modes of production transformed social and political relations of power. It ends with a ringing revolutionary call to the workers of the world to unite to free themselves from their shackles. Unwelcome in Prussia, France and Brussels, Marx moved permanently to London in 1849. He spent the rest of his life writing economic and social-political history and theory. The first volume of *Das Kapital* appeared in 1867; the subsequent volumes, edited by Engels and Kautsky, appeared posthumously. Marx's work prompted the formation of the first International Workingmen's Association. Battle lines were drawn between Communists, Anarchists, and Socialists, between Internationalists and those who argued that communism could only emerge in technologically advanced nations. Lenin and Mao Tse-tung adapted Marxist thought to influence Russian and Chinese communism.

The History of My Opinions

I was taking up law, which discipline, however, I only pursued as a subordinate subject along with philosophy and history. In the year 1842–44, as editor of the *Rheinische Zeitung*, I experienced for the first time the embarrassment of having to take part in discussions on so-called material interests. The proceedings of the Rhenish Landtag on thefts of wood and parcelling of landed property, the official polemic which Herr von Schaper, then *Oberpräsident* of the Rhine Province, opened against the *Rheinische Zeitung* on the conditions of the Moselle peasantry, and finally debates on free trade and protective tariffs provided the first occasions for occupying myself with economic questions. On the other hand, at that time when the good will "to go further" greatly outweighed knowledge of the subject, a philosophically weakly tinged echo of French socialism and communism made itself audible in the *Rheinische Zeitung*. I declared myself against this amateurism, but frankly confessed at the same time in a controversy with the *All-gemeine Augsburger Zeitung* that my previous studies did not permit me even to venture any judgment on the content of the French tendencies. Instead, I eagerly seized on the illusion of the managers of the *Rheinische Zeitung*, who thought that by a weaker attitude on the part of the paper they could secure a remission of the death sentence passed upon it, to withdraw from the public stage into the study.

The first work which I undertook for a solution of the doubts which assailed me was a critical review of the Hegelian philosophy of right. My investigation led to the result that legal relations as well as forms of state are to be grasped neither from themselves nor from the so-called general development of the human mind, but rather have their roots in the material conditions of life, the sum total of which Hegel, following the example of the Englishmen and Frenchmen of the eighteenth century, combines under the name of "civil society," that, however, the anatomy of civil society is to be sought in political economy. The investigation of the latter, which I began in Paris, I continued in Brussels, whither I had emigrated in consequence of an expulsion order of M. Guizot. The general result at which I arrived and which, once won, served as a guiding thread for my studies, can be briefly formulated as follows: In the social production of their life, men enter into definite relations that are indispensable and independent of their will, relations of production which correspond to a definite stage of development of their material productive forces. The sum total of these relations of production constitutes the economic structure of society, the real foundation, on which rises a legal and political superstructure and to which correspond definite forms of social consciousness. The mode of production of material life conditions the social, the political and intellectual life process in general. It is not the consciousness of men that determines their being, but, on the contrary, their social being that determines their consciousness. At a certain stage of their development, the material productive forces of society come in conflict with the existing relations of production, or—what is but a legal expression for the same thing— with the property relations within which they have been at work hitherto. From forms of development of the productive forces these relations turn into their fetters. Then begins an epoch of social revolution. With the change of the economic foundation the entire immense superstructure is more or less rapidly transformed. In considering such transformations a distinction should always be made between the material transformation of the economic conditions of production, which can be determined with the precision of natural science, and the legal, political, religious, aesthetic or philosophic—in short, ideological forms in which men become conscious of this conflict and fight it out. Just as our opinion of an individual is not based on what he thinks of himself, so can we not judge of such a period of transformation by its own consciousness; on the contrary, this consciousness must be explained rather from the contradictions of material life, from the existing conflict between the social productive forces and the relations of production. No social order ever perishes before all the productive forces for which there is room in it have developed; and new, higher relations of production never appear before the material conditions of their existence have matured in the womb of the old society itself. Therefore mankind always sets itself only such tasks as it can solve; since, looking at the matter more closely, it will always be found that the task itself arises only when the material conditions for its solution already exist or are at least in the process of formation. In broad outlines Asiatic, ancient, feudal, and modern bourgeois modes of production can be designated as progressive epochs in the economic formation of society. The bourgeois relations of production are the last antagonistic form of the social process of production—antagonistic not in the sense of individual antagonism, but of one arising from the social conditions of life of the individuals; at the same time the productive forces developing in the womb of bourgeois society create the material conditions for the solution of that antagonism. This social formation brings, therefore, the prehistory of human society to a close.

Frederick Engels, with whom, since the appearance of his brilliant sketch on the criticism of the economic categories (in the *Deutsch-Französische Jahrbücher*), I maintained a constant exchange of ideas by correspondence, had by another road (compare his *The Condition of the Working Class in England in 1844*) arrived at the same result as I, and when in the spring of 1845 he also settled in Brussels, we resolved to work out in common the opposition of our view to the ideological view of German philosophy, in fact, to settle accounts with our erstwhile philosophical conscience. The resolve was carried out in the form of a criticism of post-Hegelian philosophy. The manuscript, two large octavo volumes, had long reached its place of publication in Westphalia when we received the news that altered circumstances did not allow of its being printed. We abandoned the manuscript to the gnawing criticism of the mice all the more willingly as we had achieved our main purpose—self-clarification. Of the scattered works in which we put our views before the public at that time, now from one aspect, now from another, I will mention only the *Manifesto of the Communist Party*, jointly written by Engels and myself, and *Discours sur le libre échange* published by me. The decisive points of our view were first scientifically, although only polemically, indicated in my work published in 1847 and directed against Proudhon: *Misère de la Philosophie*, etc. A dissertation written in German on *Wage Labour*, in which I put together my lectures on this subject delivered in the Brussels German Workers' Society, was interrupted, while being printed, by the February Revolution and my consequent forcible removal from Belgium.

The editing of the *Neue Rheinische Zeitung* in 1848 and 1849, and the subsequent events, interrupted my economic studies which could only be resumed in the year 1850 in London. The enormous material for the history of political economy which is accumulated in the British Museum, the favourable vantage point afforded by London for the observation of bourgeois society, and finally the new stage of development upon which the latter appeared to have entered with the discovery of gold in California and Australia, determined me to begin afresh from the very beginning and to work through the new material critically. These studies led partly of themselves into apparently quite remote subjects on which I had to dwell for a shorter or longer period. Especially, however, was the time at my disposal curtailed by the imperative necessity of earning my living. My contributions, during eight years now, to the first English-American newspaper, the *New York Tribune*, compelled an extraordinary scattering of my studies, since I occupy myself with newspaper correspondence proper only in exceptional cases. However, articles on striking economic events in England and on the Continent constituted so considerable a part of my contributions that I was compelled to make myself familiar with practical details which lie outside the sphere of the actual science of political economy.

This sketch of the course of my studies in the sphere of political economy is intended only to show that my views, however they may be judged and however little they coincide with the interested prejudices of the ruling classes, are the results of conscientious investigation lasting many years. But at the entrance to science, as at the entrance to hell, the demand must be posted:

> Here all mistrust must be abandoned
> And here must perish every craven thought.
>   (Dante, *The Divine Comedy*)

Theses on Feuerbach

I

The chief defect of all hitherto existing materialism is that the thing, reality, sensuousness, is conceived only in the form of the object or of *contemplation*, but not as *human sensuous activity, practice*, not subjectively. Hence it happened that the *active* side, in contradistinction to materialism, was developed by idealism—but only abstractly, since, of course, idealism does not know real, sensuous activity as such. Feuerbach wants sensuous objects, really distinct from the thought objects, but he does not conceive human activity itself as *objective* activity. Hence, in *Das Wesen des Christentums*, he regards the theoretical attitude as the only genuinely human attitude, while practice is conceived and fixed only in its dirty-judaical manifestation. Hence he does not grasp the significance of "revolutionary," of practical-critical, activity.

II

The question whether objective truth can be attributed to human thinking is not a question of theory but is a *practical* question. Man must prove the truth, that is, the reality and power, the this-sidedness of his thinking in practice. The dispute over the reality or non-reality of thinking which is isolated from practice is a purely *scholastic* question.

III

The materialist doctrine that men are products of circumstances and upbringing, and that, therefore, changed men are products of other circumstances and changed upbringing, forgets that it is men who change circumstances and that it is essential to educate the educator himself. Hence, this doctrine necessarily arrives at dividing society into two parts, one of which is superior to society (in Robert Owen, for example).

The coincidence of the changing of circumstances and of human activity can be conceived and rationally understood only as revolutionising practice.

IV

Feuerbach starts out from the fact of religious self-alienation, of the duplication of the world into a religious, imaginary world and a real one. His work consists in resolving the religious world into its secular basis. He overlooks the fact that after completing this work, the chief thing still remains to be done. For the fact that the secular basis detaches itself from itself and establishes itself in the clouds as an independent realm can only be explained by the cleavage and self-contradictions within this secular basis. The latter must itself, therefore, first be understood in its contradiction and then, by the removal of the contradiction, revolutionised in practice. Thus, for instance, after the earthly family is discovered to be the secret of the holy family, the former must then itself be criticised in theory and revolutionised in practice.

V

Feuerbach, not satisfied with *abstract thinking*, appeals to *sensuous contemplation*; but he does not conceive sensuousness as practical, human-sensuous activity.

VI

Feuerbach resolves the religious essence into the human essence. But the human essence is no abstraction inherent in each single individual. In its reality it is the ensemble of the social relations.

Feuerbach, who does not enter upon a criticism of this real essence, is consequently compelled:

(1) To abstract from the historical process and to fix the religious sentiment as something by itself and to presuppose an abstract—*isolated*—human individual.

(2) The human essence, therefore, can with him be comprehended only as "genus," as an internal, dumb generality which merely *naturally* unites the many individuals.

VII

Feuerbach, consequently, does not see that the "religious sentiment" is itself a *social product*, and that the abstract individual whom he analyses belongs in reality to a particular form of society.

VIII

Social life is essentially *practical*. All mysteries which mislead theory into mysticism find their rational solution in human practice and in the comprehension of this practice.

IX

The highest point attained by *contemplative* materialism, that is, materialism which does not comprehend sensuousness as practical activity, is the contemplation of single individuals in "civil society."

X

The standpoint of the old materialism is civil society; the standpoint of the new is human society, or socialised humanity.

XI

The philosophers have only *interpreted* the world, in various ways; the point, however, is to *change* it.

Speech at the Graveside of Karl Marx

FRIEDRICH ENGELS

On the 14th of March, at a quarter to three in the afternoon, the greatest living thinker ceased to think. He had been left alone for scarcely two minutes, and when we came back we found him in his armchair, peacefully gone to sleep—but for ever.

An immeasurable loss has been sustained both by the militant proletariat of Europe and America, and by historical science, in the death of this man. The gap that has been left by the departure of this mighty spirit will soon enough make itself felt.

Just as Darwin discovered the law of development of organic nature, so Marx discovered the law of development of human history: the simple fact, hitherto concealed by an overgrowth of ideology, that mankind must first of all eat, drink, have shelter and clothing, before it can pursue politics, science, art, religion, etc.; that therefore the production of the immediate material means of subsistence and consequently the degree of economic development attained by a given people or during a given epoch form the foundation upon which the state institutions, the legal conceptions, art, and even the ideas on religion, of the people concerned have been evolved, and in the light of which they must, therefore, be explained, instead of *vice versa*, as had hitherto been the case.

But that is not all. Marx also discovered the special law of motion governing the present-day capitalist mode of production and the bourgeois society that this mode of production has created. The discovery of surplus value suddenly threw light on the problem, in trying to solve which all previous investigations, of both bourgeois economists and socialist critics, had been groping in the dark.

Two such discoveries would be enough for one lifetime. Happy the man to whom it is granted to make even one such discovery. But in every single field which Marx investigated—and he investigated very many fields, none of them superficially—in every field, even in that of mathematics, he made independent discoveries.

Such was the man of science. But this was not even half the man. Science was for Marx a historically dynamic, revolutionary force. However great the joy with which he welcomed a new discovery in some theoretical science whose practical application perhaps it was as yet quite impossible to envisage, he experienced quite another kind of joy when the discovery involved immediate revolutionary changes in industry, and in historical development in general. For example, he followed closely the development of the discoveries made in the field of electricity and recently those of Marcel Deprez.

For Marx was before all else a revolutionist. His real mission in life was to contribute, in one way or another, to the overthrow of capitalist society and of the state institutions which it had brought into being, to contribute to the liberation of the modern proletariat, which *he* was the first to make conscious of its own position and its needs, conscious of the conditions of its emancipation. Fighting was his element. And he fought with a passion, a tenacity and a success such as few could rival. Marx was the best hated and most calumniated man of his time. Governments, both absolutist and republican, deported him from their territories. Bourgeois, whether conservative or ultra-democratic, vied with one another in heaping slanders upon him. All this he brushed aside as though it were cobweb, ignoring it, answering only when extreme necessity compelled him. And he died beloved, revered and mourned by millions of revolutionary fellow workers—from the mines of Siberia to California, in all parts of Europe and America—and I make bold to say that though he may have had many opponents he had hardly one personal enemy.

His name will endure through the ages, and so also will his work!

28

SØREN KIERKEGAARD
The Many Faces of an Author

Intending to become a pastor, Søren Kierkegaard (1813–1855) studied theology at the University of Copenhagen. When he became estranged from the established Lutheran Church of Denmark, he abandoned that ambition. After scandalizing Copenhagen society by abruptly breaking his engagement to the daughter of a high-ranking civil servant, he presented himself as an extravagant and dissolute young man about town. As he found himself increasingly absorbed in his philosophic work, he retreated from society and became an eccentric recluse. Many of his books were written in a variety of pseudonyms, each in a distinctive style, suited to represent a particular perspectival point of view. In *Either/Or: A Fragment of Life* (1843) he described three modes of existence: that of an aesthete, a Don Juan of experience, absorbed in the appreciation of the pleasures of the present moment; that of a Kantian moralist, focused on the duties of a consistently unified life; and that of a simple, sincere Christian, an authentic man of faith. In *Concluding Unscientific Postscript* (1846), Kierkegaard contrasts "naturalized or rationalized religion" that connects religion with ethical life and establishes an unproblematic relation to divinity, with "transcendent" religion that finds faith unreachable by reason. *Fear and Trembling* (1843) and *Sickness unto Death* (1844) portray the haunting sense of uncertainty, anxiety and despair of the religious person who no longer believes in a rational account of the relation between God and humankind. *Philosophic Fragments* (1844) develops Kierkegaard's version of Plato's paradox: if we intuitively grasp the truths of religion, we seem not to need revelation or the mediation of Christ the Teacher? If we do not, we cannot understand revealed truth. Unlike Plato, Kierkegaard refuses to resolve the paradox.

Kierkegaard's descriptions of the anxieties of freedom and the haunting sense of guilt, his emphasis on the radical choice of a mode of existence, and his attacks on the rational reconstruction of psychological experience found an echo in Camus and—despite Kierkegaard's longing for faith—in Sartre.

An Author's Point of View

In my career as an author, a point has now been reached where it is permissible to do what I feel a strong impulse to do and so regard as my duty—namely, to explain once for all, as directly and frankly as possible, what is what: what I as an author declare myself to be. The moment (however unpropitious it may be in another sense) is how appropriate; partly because (as I have said) this point has been reached, and partly because I am about to encounter for the second time in the literary field my first production, *Either/Or*, in its second edition, which I was not willing to have published earlier.

There is a time to be silent and a time to speak. So long as I considered the strictest silence my religious duty I strove in every way to preserve it. I have not hesitated to counteract, in a *finite* sense, my own effort by the enigmatic mystery and *double entente* which silence favours. What I have done in that way has been misunderstood, has been explained as pride, arrogance, and God knows what. So long as I considered silence my religious duty I would not do the least thing to obviate such a misunderstanding. But the reason I considered silence my duty was that the authorship was not yet at hand in so complete a form that the understanding of it could be anything but misunderstanding.

The contents of this little book affirm, then, what I truly am as an author, that I am and was a religious author, that the whole of my work as an author is related to Christianity, to the problem 'of becoming a Christian', with a direct or indirect polemic against the monstrous illusion we call Christendom, or against the illusion that in such a land as ours all are Christians of a sort.

I would beg of every one who has the cause of Christianity at heart—and I beg the more urgently the more seriously he takes it to heart—that he make himself acquainted with this little book, not curiously, but devoutly, as one would read a religious work. How far a so-called aesthetic public has found or may find enjoyment in reading, attentively or casually, the productions of an aesthetic character, which are an incognito and a deceit in the service of Christianity, is naturally a matter of indifference to me; for I am a religious writer. Supposing that such a reader understands perfectly and appraises critically the individual aesthetic productions, he will nevertheless totally misunderstand me, inasmuch as he does not understand the religious totality in my whole work as an author. Suppose, then, that another understands my works in the totality of their religious reference, but does not understand a single one of the aesthetic productions contained in them—I would say that this lack of understanding is not an essential lack.

What I write here is for orientation. It is a public attestation; not a defence or an apology. In this respect, truly, if in no other, I believe that I have something in common with Socrates. For when he was accused, and was about to be judged by 'the crowd', his daemon forbade him to *defend* himself. Indeed, if he had done that, how unseemly it would have been, and how self-contradictory! Likewise there is something in me, and in the dialectical position I occupy, which makes it impossible for me, and impossible in itself, to conduct a defence for my work as an author. I have put up with a great deal, and I hope to put up with more without suffering the loss of my self—but who knows? perhaps the future will deal more gently with me than the past. The only thing I cannot put up with—cannot do so without suffering the loss of my self and of the dialectical character of my position (which is just what I cannot put up with)—this only thing is to *defend* myself *qua* author. That would be a falsehood, which, even though it were to help me finitely to gain the whole world, would eternally be my destruction. With humility before God, and also before men, I well know wherein I personally may have offended; but I know also with God that this very work of mine as an author was the prompting of an irresistible inward impulse, a melancholy man's only possibility, the honest effort on the part of a soul deeply humbled and penitent to do something by way of compensation, without shunning any sacrifice or labour in the service of truth. Therefore I know also with God, in whose eyes this undertaking found favour and still finds it, as it rejoices also in His assistance, that with regard to my authorship it is not I that need to defend myself before my contemporaries; for, if in this case I have any part, it is not as counsel for the defence but as prosecutor.

Yet I do not indict my contemporaries, seeing that I have religiously understood it as my duty thus to serve the truth in self-denial, and as my task to do everything to prevent myself becoming esteemed and idolized. Only the man who knows in his own experience what true self-denial is can solve my riddle and perceive that it is self-denial. For the man who in himself has no experience of it must rather call my behavior self-love, pride, eccentricity, madness—for which opinion it would be unreasonable of me to indict him, since I myself in the service of the truth have contributed to form it. There is one thing unconditionally which cannot be understood either by a noisy assembly, or by a 'highly esteemed public', or in half an hour—and that one thing is the character of true Christian self-denial. To understand this requires fear and trembling, silent solitude, and a long interval of time.

That I have understood the truth which I deliver to others, of that I am eternally certain. And I am just as certain that my contemporaries, in so far as they do not understand it, will be compelled, whether by fair means or foul, to understand it some time, in eternity, when they are exempted from many distracting cares and troubles, from which I have been exempted. I have suffered under much misunderstanding; and the fact that I voluntarily exposed myself to it does not indicate that I am insensible to *real* suffering. As well deny the reality of all Christian suffering, for the mark of it is that it is voluntary. Neither does it follow as a matter of course and as a direct inference that 'the others' have no blame, seeing that it is in the service of truth I suffer this. But however much I have suffered from misunderstanding, I cannot but thank God for what is of infinite importance to me, that He has granted me understanding of the truth.

And then only one thing more. It goes without saying that I cannot explain my work as an author wholly, i.e. with the purely personal inwardness in which I possess the explanation of it. And this in part because I cannot make public my God-relationship. It is neither more nor less than the generic human inwardness which every man may have, without regarding it as an official distinction which it were a crime to hide and a duty to proclaim, or which I could appeal to as my legitimation. In part because I cannot wish (and no one can desire that I might) to obtrude upon any one what concerns only my private person—though naturally there is much in this which for me serves to explain my work as an author.

THE DIFFERENCE IN MY PERSONAL MODE OF EXISTENCE CORRESPONDING TO THE ESSENTIAL DIFFERENCE IN THE WORKS

In this age, and indeed for many ages past, people have quite lost sight of the fact that authorship is and ought to be a serious calling implying an appropriate mode of personal existence. They do not realize that the press in general, as an expression of the abstract and impersonal communication of ideas, and the daily press in particular, because of its formal indifference to the question whether what it reports is true or false, contributes enormously to the general demoralization, for the reason that the impersonal, which for the most part is irresponsible and incapable of repentance, is essentially demoralizing. They do not realize that anonymity, as the most absolute expression for the impersonal, the irresponsible, the unrepentant, is a fundamental source of the modern demoralization. On the other hand, they do not reflect that anonymity would be counteracted in the simplest possible way, and that a wholesome corrective would be furnished for the abstractness of printed communication, if people would but turn back again to antiquity and learn what it means to be a single individual man, neither more nor less—which surely even an author is too, neither more nor less. This is perfectly obvious. But in our age, which reckons as wisdom that which is truly the mystery of unrighteousness, viz. that one need not inquire about the communicator, but only about the communication, the objective only—in our age what is an author? An author is often merely an *x*, even when his name is signed, something quite impersonal, which addresses itself abstractly, by the aid of printing, to thousands and thousands, while remaining itself unseen and unknown, living a life as hidden, as anonymous, as it is possible for a life to be, in order, presumably, not to reveal the too obvious and striking contradiction between the prodigious means of communication employed and the fact that the author is only a single individual—perhaps also for fear of the control which in practical life must always be exercised over every one who wishes to teach others, to see whether his personal existence comports with his communication. But all this, which deserves the most serious attention on the part of one who would study the demoralization of the modern state—all this I cannot enter into more particularly here.

THE PERSONAL MODE OF EXISTENCE IN RELATION TO THE AESTHETIC WORKS

I come now to the first period of my authorship and my mode of existence. Here was a religious author, but one who began as an aesthetic author; and this first stage was one of incognito and deceit. Initiated as I was very early and very thoroughly into the secret that *Mundus vult decipi*, I was not in the position of being able to wish to follow such tactics. Quite the contrary. [The world wishes to be deceived.] With me it was a question of deceiving inversely on the greatest possible scale, employing every bit of knowledge I had about men and their weaknesses and their stupidities, not to profit thereby, but to annihilate myself and weaken the impression I made. The secret of the deceit which suits the world which wants to be deceived consists partly in forming a coterie and all that goes with that, in joining one or another of those societies for mutual admiration, whose members support one another with tongue and pen in the pursuit of worldly advantage; and it consists partly in hiding oneself from the human crowd, never being seen, so as to produce a fantastic effect. So I had to do exactly the opposite. I had to exist in absolute isolation and guard my solitude, but at the same time take pains to be seen every hour of the day, living as it were upon the street, in company with Tom, Dick, and Harry, and in the most fortuitous situations. This is truth's way of deceiving, the everlastingly sure way of weakening, in a worldly sense, the impression one makes. It was, moreover, the way followed by men of a very different calibre from mine to make people take notice. Those reputable persons, the deceivers who want the communication to serve them instead of serving the communication, are on the look-out only to win repute for themselves. Those despised persons, the 'witnesses for the truth', who deceive inversely, have ever been wont to suffer themselves to be set at naught in a worldly sense and be counted as nothing—in spite of the fact that they labour day and night, and suffer besides from having no support whatever in the illusion that the work they perform is their career and their 'living'.

So this had to be done, and it was done, not now and then, but every day. I am convinced that one-sixth of *Either/Or*, together with a bit of coterie, and then an author who was never to be seen—especially if this was carried on for a considerable time—must make a much more extraordinary effect. I, however, had made myself sure of being able to work as laboriously as I pleased and as the spirit prompted me, without having to fear that I might get too much renown. For in a certain sense I was working as laboriously in another direction—against myself. Only an author will be able to understand what a task it is to work *qua* author, i.e. with mind and pen, and yet be at the beck and call of everybody. Although this mode of existence enriched me immensely with observations of human life, it is a standard of conduct which would bring most men to despair. For it means the effort to dispel every illusion and to present the idea in all its purity—and verily, it is not truth that rules the world but illusions. Even if a literary achievement were more illustrious than any that has yet been seen—if only the author were to live as is here suggested, he would in a brief time have insured himself against worldly renown and the crowd's brutish adulation. For the crowd possesses no idealism, and hence no power of retaining impressions in spite of contrary appearances. It is always the victim of appearances. To be seen again and again, and to be seen in the most fortuitous situations, is enough to make the crowd forget its first impression of the man and become soon sick and tired of him. And, after all, to keep oneself perpetually in view does not consume a great deal of time, if only one employs one's time shrewdly (i.e. in a worldly sense insanely) and to the best effect, by going back and forth past the same spot, and that the most frequented spot in the city. Every one who husbands his reputation, in a worldly sense, will not return by the same way he went, even if it is the most convenient way. He will avoid being seen twice in so short a time, for fear people might suppose he had nothing to do, whereas if he sat in his room at home three-quarters of the day and was idle, such a thought would never occur to anybody. On the other hand, an hour well spent, in a godly sense, an hour lived for eternity and spent by going back and forth among the common people . . . is not such a small thing after all. And verily it is well pleasing to God that the truth should be served in this way. His Spirit witnesseth mightily with my spirit that it has the full consent of His Divine Majesty. All the witnesses of the truth indicate their approval, recognizing that one is disposed to serve the truth, the idea, and not to betray the truth and profit by the illusion. I experienced a real Christian satisfaction in venturing to perform on Monday a little bit of that which one weeps about on Sunday (when the parson prates about it and weeps too) . . . and on Monday one is ready to laugh about. I had real Christian satisfaction in the thought that, if there were no other, there was definitely one man in Copenhagen whom every poor man could freely accost and converse with on the street; that, if there were no other, there was one man who, whatever the society he more commonly frequented, did not shun contact with the poor, but greeted every maidservant he was acquainted with, every manservant, every common labourer. I felt a real Christian satisfaction in the fact that, if there were no other, there was one man who (several years before existence set the race another lesson to learn) made a practical effort on a small scale to learn the lesson of loving one's neighbor and alas! got at the same time a frightful insight into what an illusion Christendom is, and (a little later, to be sure) an insight also into what a situation the simpler classes suffered themselves to be seduced by paltry newspaper-writers, whose struggle or fight for equality (since it is in the service of a lie) cannot lead to any other result but to prompt the privileged classes in self-defence to stand proudly aloof from the common man, and to make the common man insolent in his forwardness.

The description of my personal existence cannot be carried out here in greater detail; but I am convinced that seldom has any author employed so much cunning, intrigue, and shrewdness to win honour and reputation in the world with a view to deceiving it, as I displayed in order to deceive it inversely in the interest of truth.

I formed the polemical resolution to regard every eulogy as an attack, and every attack as a thing unworthy of notice. Such was my public mode of existence. I almost never made a visit, and at home the rule was strictly observed to receive no one except the poor who came to seek help. For I had no time to receive visitors at home, and any one who entered my home as a visitor might easily get a presentiment of a situation about which he should have no presentiment. Thus I existed. If Copenhagen ever has been of one opinion about anybody, I venture to say that it was of one opinion about me, that I was an idler, a dawdler, a *flâneur*, a frivolous bird, intelligent, perhaps brilliant, witty, &c.—but as for 'seriousness', I lacked it utterly. I represented a worldly irony, *joie de vivre*, the subtlest form of pleasure-seeking—without a trace of 'seriousness and positivity'; on the other hand, I was prodigiously witty and interesting.

When I look back upon that time, I am almost tempted to make some sort of apology to the people of importance and repute in the community. For true enough, I knew perfectly well what I was doing, yet from their standpoint they were right in finding fault with me, because by thus impairing my own prestige I contributed to the movement which was impairing power and renown in general—notwithstanding that I have always been conservative in this respect, and have found joy in paying to the eminent and distinguished the deference, awe, and admiration which are due to them. Yet my conservative disposition did not involve a desire to have this sort of distinction for myself. And just because the eminent and distinguished members of the community have shown me in so many ways not only sympathy but partiality, have sought in so many ways to draw me to their side (which certainly was honest and well-meant on their part)—just for this reason I feel impelled to make them an apology, although naturally I cannot regret what I have done, since I served my idea. People of distinction have always proved more consistent in their treatment of me than the simpler classes, who even from their own standpoint did not behave rightly, since they too (according to the foregoing account) attacked me . . . because I was not superior enough to hold myself aloof—which is very queer and ridiculous of the simpler classes.

This is the first period: by my personal mode of existence I endeavoured to support the pseudonyms, the aesthetic work as a whole. Melancholy, incurably melancholy as I was, suffering prodigious griefs in my inmost soul, having broken in desperation from the world and all that is of the world, strictly brought up from my very childhood in the apprehension that the truth must suffer and be mocked and derided, spending a definite time every day in prayer and devout meditation, and being myself personally a penitent—in short, being what I was, I found (I do not deny it) a certain sort of satisfaction in this life, in this inverse deception, a satisfaction in observing that the deception succeeded so extraordinarily, that the public and I were on the most confidential terms, that I was quite in the fashion as the preacher of a gospel of worldliness, that though I was not in possession of the sort of distinction which can only be earned by an entirely different mode of life, yet in secret (and hence the more heartily loved) I was the darling of the public, regarded by every one as prodigiously interesting and witty. This satisfaction, which was my secret and which sometimes put me into an ecstasy, might have been a dangerous temptation. Not as though the world and such things could tempt me with their flattery and adulation. No, on that side I was safe. If I was to have been capsized, it would have to have been by this thought raised to a higher power, an obsession almost of ecstasy at the thought of how the deception was succeeding. This was an indescribable alleviation to a sense of resentment which smouldered in me from my childhood; because, long before I had seen it with my own eyes, I had been taught that falsehood, pettiness, and injustice ruled the world.—I often had to think of these words in *Either/Or*: 'If ye but knew what it is ye laugh at'—if ye but knew with whom ye have to do, who this *flâneur* is!

THE PERSONAL MODE OF EXISTENCE IN RELATION TO THE RELIGIOUS WORKS

In the month of December 1845 the manuscript of the *Concluding Postscript* was completely finished, and, as my custom was, I had delivered the whole of it at once to Luno [the printer]—which the suspicious do not have to believe on my word, since Luno's account-book is there to prove it. This work constitutes the turning-point in my whole activity as an author, inasmuch as it presents the 'problem', how to become a Christian. With this began the transition to the series of purely religious writings.

I perceived at once that my personal mode of existence must be remodelled to correspond with this change, or that I must try to give my contemporaries a different notion of my personal mode of existence. So I myself had already become aware of what must be done, when there occurred in the most opportune way a little incident in which I perceived a hint of Providence to help me to act decisively in that direction.

It was important for me to alter my personal mode of existence to correspond with the fact that I was making the transition to the statement of religious problems. I must have an existence-form corresponding with this sort of authorship . . .

I had now reckoned out that dialectically the situation would be appropriate for recovering the use of indirect communication. While I was occupied solely with religious productions I could count upon the negative support of daily douches of vulgarity, which would be cooling enough in its effect to ensure that the religious communication would not be too direct, or too directly create for me adherents. The reader could not relate himself directly to me; for now, instead of the incognito of the aesthetical, I had erected the danger of the laughter and grins of irony by which most people are scared away. And he even who was not scared by this would be upset by the next obstacle; by the thought that I had voluntarily exposed myself to all this, giving proof of a sort of lunacy.

I, poor wretch, the Magister of Irony, became the pitiable target for the laughter of a 'highly esteemed public'.

The costume was correct. Every religious author is polemical; for the world is not so good that the religious man can assume that he has triumphed or is in the party of the majority. A victorious religious author who is *in the world* is not a religious author. The essentially religious author is always polemical, and hence he suffers under or suffers from the opposition which corresponds to whatever in his age must be regarded as the specific evil. If it be kings and emperors, popes and bishops . . . and powers that constitute the Evil, the religious author must be recognizable by the fact that he is the object of their attack. If it is the crowd—and prating and the public—and the beastly grin which is the Evil, he must be recognizable by the fact that he is the object of that sort of attack and persecution. When any one asks him on what he bases the claim that he is right and that it is the truth he utters, his answer is: I prove it by the fact that I am persecuted; this is the truth, and I can prove it by the fact that I am derided. That is, he does not substantiate the truth or the righteousness of his cause by appealing to the honour, reputation, &c., which he enjoys, but he does quite the contrary.

THE SHARE DIVINE GOVERNANCE HAD IN MY AUTHORSHIP

What I have written up to this point has in a sense been neither agreeable nor pleasant to write. There is something painful in being obliged to talk so much about oneself. Would to God I might have ventured to hold my peace even longer than I have, yea, even to die in silence about a subject which, like my labour and my literary work, has occupied me day and night. By now, thank God, now I breathe freely, now I actually feel an urge to speak, now I have come to the theme which I find inconceivably pleasant to think about and to talk about. This God-relationship of mine is the 'happy love' in a life which has been in many ways troubled and unhappy. And although the story of this love affair (if I dare call it such) has the essential marks of a true love story, in the fact that only one can completely understand it, and there is no absolute joy but in relating it to one only, namely, the beloved, who in this instance is the Person by whom one is loved,* yet there is a joy also in talking about it to others.

*Perhaps now the reader may be ready to recognize how it is that what has been the misfortune, humanly speaking, of the whole productivity, what has more and more caused it to stand apart as a superfluity, instead of actually coming to grips with the situation, is the fact that it is too religious, or that the author's existence is too religious, that the author *qua* author has been absolutely weak, and therefore has been absolutely in need of God. If the author had been less weak, that is to say, in a human sense stronger (that is, less religious), he would as a matter of course have laid claim to the authorship as his own, he would presumably have acquired a number of confidants and friends, he would have made known beforehand to others what he proposed, would have taken counsel with them and asked their assistance; and they in turn, acting as godfathers, would have enlisted others, so that the authorship would have been interrelated with the instant and effective in the instant—instead of being a superfluity . . . such as God himself is in sooth, more than everything else and everybody else.—Perhaps now the reader may be ready to recognize why I have laboured with so much effort and sacrifice, day in and day out, to prevent falsehood from emerging, a falsehood, it is true, which (as it always does) would have brought me money, honour, reputation, applause, &c., the falsehood that what I had to deliver was 'what the age demands', that it is presented to the indulgent judgement of 'a highly respected public', *item* that it owes its success to the support and acclamation of this same highly respected public. In exact opposition to this, in the fear and love of God, I had to watch sleeplessly to ensure that the truth be expressed: that it was God's aid alone I relied on, that I owed nothing either to the public or to the age, except the wrong it has done me. I had to be on the watch to ensure that the truth might be expressed by the rousing epigram upon this age that at a time when everything was general assemblies and societies and committees, their appointment, continuation, and dissolution, whereas all the while nothing was done, that at this time there was bestowed upon a weakly and solitary man the talent to work on a scale so great that any one might suppose it was more than the labour of a committee. In short, it was my duty to give expression, both in my personal existence and in my author-existence, to the fact that I every day as-

As for the fact that I have needed God's love, and how constantly I have needed it, day after day, year after year—to recall this to my mind and to report it exactly, I do not need the aid of memory or recollection, or of journals or diaries, nor do I need to check the one by the other, so vividly, so feelingly do I live it over again in this very instant. What could not this pen produce if it were a question of hardihood, of enthusiasm, of fervour to the verge of madness! And now that I am to talk about my God-relationship, about what every day is repeated in my prayer of thanksgiving for the indescribable things He has done for me, so infinitely much more than ever I could have expected, about the experience which has taught me to be amazed, amazed at God, at His love and at what a man's impotence is capable of with His aid, about what has taught me to long for eternity and not to fear that I might find it tiresome, since it is exactly the situation I need so as to have nothing else to do but to give thanks. Now that I am to talk about this there awakens in my soul a poetic impatience. More resolutely than that king who cried, 'My kingdom for a horse', and blessedly resolute as he was not, I would give all, and along with that my life, to be able to find what thought has more blessedness in finding than a lover in finding the beloved—to find the 'expression', and then to die with this expression on my lips. And lo! it presents itself—thoughts as enchanting as the fruits in the garden of a fairy-tale, so rich and warm and heartfelt; expressions so soothing to the urge of gratitude within me, so cooling to my hot longing—it seems to me as if, had I a winged pen, yes, ten of them, I still could not follow fast enough to keep pace with the wealth which presents itself. But no sooner have I taken pen in hand, at that very instant I am incapable of moving it, as we say of one that he cannot move hand or foot. In that situation not a line concerning this relationship gets put down on paper. It seems to me as if I heard a voice saying to me: Silly fellow, what does he imagine? Does he not know that obedience is dearer to God than the fat of rams? Then I become perfectly quiet, then there is time enough to write each letter with my slow pen almost painfully. And if that poetic impatience awakes in me again for an instant, it seems as though I heard a voice speaking to me as a teacher speaks to a boy when he says: Now hold the pen right, and form each letter with equal precision. And then I can do it, then I dare not do otherwise, then I write every word, every line, almost without knowing what the next word or the next line is to be. And afterwards when I read it over it satisfies me in quite a different way. For though it may be that one or another glowing expression escapes me, yet the production is quite a different one: it is the outcome, not of the poet's or the thinker's passion, but of godly fear, and for me it is a divine worship.

But what now at this instant I am living over again, or just now have been, is something I have experienced time and again during my whole activity as an author. It is said of the 'poet' that he invokes the muse to supply him with

certained and convinced myself anew that a God exists.—Perhaps now the reader may be ready to recognize why it was I found myself compelled to counteract in a finite sense my own effort, for the sake of ensuring that the responsibility should be all my own. I must in any case be quite alone, absolutely alone, yes, I must even reject assistance, lest my responsibility be too light. Given but one friend and one fellow worker, responsibility becomes a fraction—not to speak of getting a whole generation to come to one's aid. But in the service of truth the point for me was that if I were to go astray, if I were to become presumptuous, if what I said was untrue, Governance might have an absolutely sure hold on me, and that in the possibility of this examination which every instant hung over me I might be kept alert, attentive, obedient.

thoughts. This indeed has never been my case, my individuality prohibits me even from understanding it; but on the contrary I have needed God every day to shield me from too great a wealth of thoughts. Give a person such a productive talent, and along with that such feeble health, and verily he will learn to pray. I have been able at any instant to perform this prodigy, and I can do it still: I could sit down and continue to write for a day and a night, and again for a day and a night; for there was wealth sufficient for it. If I had done it, I should have been broken. Oh, even the least dietetic indiscretion, and I am in mortal danger. When I learn obedience, as I have described above, when I do the work as if it were a sternly prescribed task, hold the pen as I ought, write each letter with pains, then I can do it. And thus, many and many a time, I have had more joy in the relation of obedience to God than in thoughts that I produced. This, it can readily be perceived, is the expression of the fact that I can lay no claim to an immediate relationship with God, that I cannot and dare not say that it is He who immediately inserts the thoughts in me, but that my relationship to God is a reflection-relationship, is inwardness in reflection, as in general the distinguishing trait of my individuality is reflection, so that even in prayer my *forte* is thanksgiving.

Thus it is that in the course of my whole activity as an author I have constantly needed God's aid so as to be able to do the work simply as a prescribed task to which definite hours every day were allotted, outside of which it was not permissible to work. And if only once that rule was transgressed, I had to pay for it dearly. Nothing is less like my procedure than the stormy entrance of genius upon the scene, and then its tumultuous *finale*. Substantially I have lived like a clerk in his *comptoir*. From the very beginning I have been as it were under arrest and every instant have sensed the fact that it was not I that played the part of master, but that another was Master. I have sensed that fact with fear and trembling when He let me feel His omnipotence and my nothingness; have sensed it with indescribable bliss when I turned to Him and did my work in unconditional obedience. The dialectical factor in this is that whatever extraordinary gift may have been entrusted to me, it was entrusted as a precautionary measure with such elasticity that, if I were not to obey, it would strike me dead. It is as if a father were to say to his child: You are allowed to take the whole thing, it is yours; but if you will not be obedient and use it as I wish—very well, I shall not punish you by taking it from you; no, take it as yours . . . it will smash you. Without God I am too strong for myself, and perhaps in the most agonizing of all ways am broken. Since I became an author I have never for a single day had the experience I hear others complain of, namely, a lack of thoughts or their failure to present themselves. If that were to happen to me, it would rather be an occasion for joy, that finally I had obtained a day that was really free. But many a time I have had the experience of being overwhelmed with riches, and every instant I bethought me with horror of the frightful torture of starving in the midst of abundance—if I do not instantly learn obedience, allow God to help me, and produce in the same fashion, as quietly and placidly as one performs a prescribed task.

But in still another sense I have needed God's aid, time and again, day after day, year after year, in the whole course of my activity as a writer. For He has been my one confidant, and only in reliance upon His cognizance have I dared to venture what I have ventured, and to endure what I have endured, and have found bliss in the experience of being literally alone in the whole vast world, alone because wherever I was, whether in the presence of all, or in the presence of a familiar friend, I was always clad in the costume of my deceit, so that I was then as much alone as in the darkness of the night; alone, not in the forests of America with their terrors and their perils, but alone in the company of the most terrible *possibilities*, which transform even the most frightful *actuality* into a refreshment and relief; alone, almost with human speech against me; alone with torments which have taught me more than one new annotation to the text about the thorn in the flesh; alone with decisions in which one had need of the support of friends, the whole race if possible; alone in dialectical tensions which (without God) would drive any man with my imagination to madness; alone in anguish unto death; alone in the face of the meaninglessness of existence, without being able, even if I would, to make myself intelligible to a single soul—but what am I saying, 'to a single soul'?—nay, there were times when it could not be said in the common phrase, '*that* alone was lacking', times when I could not make myself intelligible to myself. When now I reflect that years were passed in this manner, I shudder. When but for a single instant I see amiss, I sink in deep waters. But when I see aright and find repose in the assurance of God's cognizance, blessedness returns again.

29

FRIEDRICH NIETZSCHE
Overcoming My Life

Friedrich Nietzsche (1844–1900) was educated as a classical philologist at Bonn and Leipzig. Until he resigned in 1879 for reasons of ill health, he was a professor of classics at the University of Basel. Strongly influenced by Schopenhauer and Wagner, he wrote a scathing attack on what he saw as the rationalism of Socratic and Platonic philosophy, (*The Birth of Tragedy*, 1872). After celebrating unfettered artistic creativity in *Richard Wagner in Bayreuth* (1876), he turned against (what he came to see as) Wagner's Teutonic-Germanic megalomania, and began writing increasingly antiphilosophic aphorisms and perspectival thought experiments: *Thus Spake Zarathustra* (1883–1885), *Beyond Good and Evil* (1886), *The Genealogy of Morals* (1887), *The Twilight of the Idols* (1889), and *Ecce Homo* (1908). *The Will to Power* was published posthumously.

Like Schopenhauer, Nietzsche held that the will to power is the fundamental organic metaphysical force. His reconstructed genealogical history of morality traces transformations in the expression of that will, substituting the opposition of "good and evil" for the ancient Greek contrast between stellar and defective examples of the species. Archaic Greek heroes are described as joyous, free, and independent, bent on achieving excellence. By contrast, Nietzsche sees the inferior examples of the species are passive and debilitated, further scarred by their animus and resentment. The weak unite to form a resentful herd, moving to self-righteousness as their debased forms of power. Swayed by the poetic magic of prophets and priests, the weak lure the strong and free to the mysteries of religion; in their turn, sovereigns and judges subject them to the restrictions of law; the sanctimonious then bind them to the obligations of morality, and finally, scholars subdue them to the awe of knowledge. The notion of conscience, with its imputation of punishment and guilt (*Schuld*) as payment or reparation, has its origins in a mercantile society, where the infraction of law incurs debt (*Geld*) to society. "Bad conscience" is an illness: the weak turn their corrosive rancor against themselves.

Nietzsche argued that just as each of these moral systems introduces its perspectival categories and language, so too "truth seeking" is a perspectival expression of power. But far from being nihilistic, Nietzsche's cultural diagnosis, "God is dead," is a proclamation of the continuous possibility of the reevaluation of values and of the radical freedom of self-creation.

LETTER TO OVERBECK

Sils Maria, September 14 1884

. . . This is the mistake which I seem to make eternally, that I imagine the sufferings of others as far greater than they really are. Ever since my childhood, the proposition "my greatest dangers lie in pity" has been confirmed again and again. . . .

Nizza, December 22, 1884

. . . I am having translated into German for me (in writing) a longish essay by Emerson, which gives some clarity about his development. If you want it, it is at your disposal and your wife's. I do not know how much I would give if only I could bring it about, *ex post facto*, that such a glorious, great nature, rich in soul and spirit, might have gone through some *strict* discipline, a really *scientific education*. As it is, in Emerson we have *lost a philosopher*. . . .

LETTER TO HIS SISTER

Nizza, March 1885

. . . It seems to me that a human being with the very best of intentions can do immeasurable harm, if he is immodest enough to wish to profit those whose spirit and will are concealed from him. . . .

LETTER TO OVERBECK

Sils Maria, July 2, 1885

. . . I hold up before myself the images of Dante and Spinoza, who were better at accepting the lot of solitude. Of course, their way of thinking, compared to mine, was one which made solitude bearable; and in the end, for all those who some-how still had a "God" for company, what *I* experience as "solitude" really did not yet exist. My life now consists in the wish that it might be otherwise with all things than I comprehend, and that somebody might make *my* "truths" appear incredible to me. . . .

PHILOSOPHY AS WILLFULNESS

Rule? Press my type on others? Dreadful. Is not my happiness precisely the sight of many who are *different?* Problem.

The will to a *system*: in a philosopher, morally speaking, a subtle corruption, a disease of the character; amorally speaking, his will to pose as more stupid than he is—more stupid, that means: stronger, simpler, more commanding, less educated, more masterful, more tyrannical.

Being nationalistic in the sense in which it is now demanded by public opin-ion would, it seems to me, be for us who are more spiritual not mere insipidity but dishonesty, a deliberate deadening of our better will and conscience.

Draft for a Preface
1885

THE WILL TO POWER

A book for *thinking*, nothing else: it belongs to those to whom thinking is a *delight*, nothing else. That it is written in German is untimely, to say the least: I wish I had written it in French so that it might not appear to be a confirmation of the aspirations of the German *Reich*. The Germans of today are not thinkers any more: something else delights and impresses them. The will to power as a principle might be intelligible to them. Among Germans today the least thinking is done. But who knows? In two generations one will no longer require the sacrifice involved in any nationalistic squandering of power, and in hebetation. (Formerly, I wished I had not written my *Zarathustra* in German.)

Ecce Homo

1

Seeing that before long I must confront humanity with the most difficult demand ever made of it, it seems indispensable to me to say *who I am*. Really, one should know it, for I have not left myself "without testimony." But the disproportion between the greatness of my task and the *smallness* of my contemporaries has found expression in the fact that one has neither heard nor even seen me. I live on my own credit; it is perhaps a mere prejudice that I live.

I only need to speak with one of the "educated" who come to the [Alps] for the summer, and I am convinced that I do *not* live.

Under these circumstances I have a duty against which my habits, even more the pride of my instincts, revolt at bottom—namely, to say: *Hear me! For I am such and such a person. Above all, do not mistake me for someone else.*

2

I am, for example, by no means a bogey, or a moralistic monster—I am actually the very opposite of the type of man who so far has been revered as virtuous. Between ourselves, it seems to me that precisely this is part of my pride. I am a disciple of the philosopher Dionysus; I should prefer to be even a satyr to being a saint. But one should really read this essay. Perhaps I have succeeded; perhaps this essay had no other meaning than to give expression to this contrast in a cheerful and philanthropic manner.

The last thing *I* should promise would be to "improve" mankind. No new idols are erected by me; let the old ones learn what feet of clay mean. *Overthrowing idols* (my word for "ideals")—that comes closer to being part of my craft. One has deprived reality of its value, its meaning, its truthfulness, to precisely the extent to which one has mendaciously invented an ideal world.

The "true world" and the "apparent world"—that means: the mendaciously invented world and reality.

The *lie* of the ideal has so far been the curse on reality; on account of it, mankind itself has become mendacious and false down to its most fundamental instincts—to the point of worshipping the *opposite* values of those which alone would guarantee its health, its future, the lofty *right* to its future.

3

Those who can breathe the air of my writings know that it is an air of the heights, a *strong* air. One must be made for it. Otherwise there is no small danger that one may catch cold in it. The ice is near, the solitude tremendous—but how calmly all things lie in the light! How freely one breathes! How much one feels *beneath* oneself!

Philosophy, as I have so far understood and lived it, means living voluntarily among ice and high mountains—seeking out everything strange and questionable in existence, everything so far placed under a ban by morality. Long experience, acquired in the course of such wanderings *in what is forbidden*, taught me to regard the causes that so far have prompted moralizing and idealizing in a very different light from what may seem desirable: the *hidden* history of the philosophers, the psychology of the great names, came to light for me.

How much truth does a spirit *endure*, how much truth does it *dare*? More and more that became for me the real measure of value. Error (faith in the ideal) is not blindness, error is *cowardice*.

Every attainment, every step forward in knowledge, *follows* from courage, from hardness against oneself, from cleanliness in relation to oneself.

I do not refute ideals, I merely put on gloves before them.

Nitimur in vetitum. in this sign my philosophy will triumph one day, for what one has forbidden so far as a matter of principle has always been—truth alone.

4

Among my writings my *Zarathustra* stands to my mind by itself. With that I have given mankind the greatest present that has ever been made to it so far. This book, with a voice bridging centuries, is not only the highest book there is, the book that is truly characterized by the air of the heights—the whole fact of man lies *beneath* it at a tremendous distance—it is also the *deepest*, born out of the innermost wealth of truth, an inexhaustible well to which no pail descends without coming up again filled with gold and goodness. Here no "prophet" is speaking, none of those gruesome hybrids of sickness and will to power whom people call founders of religions. Above all, one must *hear* aright the tone that comes from this mouth, the halcyon tone, lest one should do wretched injustice to the meaning of its wisdom.

"It is the stillest words that bring on the storm. Thoughts that come on doves' feet guide the world."

> The figs are falling from the trees; they are good and sweet; and, as they fall, their red skin bursts. I am a north wind to ripe figs.
> Thus, like figs, these teachings fall to you, my friends: now consume their juice and their sweet meat. It is fall around us, and pure sky and afternoon.

It is no fanatic that speaks here; this is not "preaching"; no *faith* is demanded here: from an infinite abundance of light and depth of happiness falls drop upon drop, word upon word: the tempo of these speeches is a tender adagio.

Why I Am So Wise

1

The good fortune of my existence, its uniqueness perhaps, lies in its fatality: I am, to express it in the form of a riddle, already dead as my father, while as my mother I am still living and becoming old. This dual descent, as it were, both from the highest and the lowest rung on the ladder of life, at the same time a *decadent* and a *beginning*—this, if anything, explains that neutrality, that freedom from all partiality in relation to the total problem of life, that perhaps distinguishes me. I have a subtler sense of smell for the signs of ascent and decline than any other human being before me; I am the teacher *par excellence* for this—I know both, I am both.

My father died at the age of thirty-six: he was delicate, kind, and morbid, as a being that is destined merely to pass by—more a gracious memory of life than life itself. In the same year in which his life went downward, mine, too, went downward: at thirty-six, I reached the lowest point of my vitality—I still lived, but without being able to see three steps ahead. Then—it was 1879—I retired from my professorship at Basel, spent the summer in St. Moritz like a shadow, and the next winter, than which not one in my life has been poorer in sunshine, in Naumburg *as* a shadow. This was my minimum: the *Wanderer and His Shadow* originated at this time. Doubtless, I then knew about shadows.

The following winter, my first one in Genoa, that sweetening and spiritualization which is almost inseparably connected with an extreme poverty of blood and muscle, produced *The Dawn*. The perfect brightness and cheerfulness, even exuberance of the spirit, reflected in this work, is compatible in my case not only with the most profound physiological weakness, but even with an excess of pain. In the midst of the torments that go with an uninterrupted three-day migraine, accompanied by laborious vomiting of phlegm, I possessed a dialectician's clarity *par excellence* and thought through with very cold blood matters for which under healthier circumstances I am not mountain-climber, not subtle, not *cold* enough. My readers know perhaps in what way I consider dialectic as a symptom of decadence; for example in the most famous case, the case of Socrates.

All pathological disturbances of the intellect, even that half-numb state that follows fever, have remained entirely foreign to me to this day; and I had to do research to find out about their nature and frequency. My blood moves slowly. Nobody has ever discovered any fever in me. A physician who treated me for some time as if my nerves were sick finally said: "It's not your nerves, it is rather I that am nervous." There is altogether no sign of any local degeneration; no organically conditioned stomach complaint, however profound the weakness of my gastric system may be as a consequence of over-all exhaustion. My eye trouble, too, though at times dangerously close to blindness, is only a consequence and not a cause: with every increase in vitality my ability to see has also increased again.

A long, all too long, series of years signifies recovery for me; unfortunately it also signifies relapse, decay, the periodicity of a kind of decadence. Need I say after all this that in questions of decadence I am *experienced?* I have spelled them forward and backward. Even that filigree art of grasping and comprehending in general, those fingers for *nuances*, that psychology of "looking around the corner," and whatever else is characteristic of me, was learned only then, is the true present of those days in which everything in me became subtler—observation itself as well as all organs of observation. Looking from the perspective of the sick toward *healthier* concepts and values and, conversely, looking again from the fullness and self-assurance of a *rich* life down into the secret work of the instinct of decadence—in this I have had the longest training, my truest experience; if in anything, I became master in *this*. Now I know how, have the know-how, to *reverse perspectives*: the first reason why a "revaluation of values" is perhaps possible for me alone.

2

Apart from the fact that I am a decadent, I am also the opposite. My proof for this is, among other things, that I have always instinctively chosen the *right* means against wretched states; while the decadent typically chooses means that are disadvantageous for him. I was healthy; as an angle, as a specialty, I was a decadent. The energy to choose absolute solitude and leave the life to which I had become accustomed; the insistence on not allowing myself any longer to be cared for, waited on, and *doctored*—that betrayed an absolute instinctive certainty about *what* was needed above all at that time. I took myself in hand, I made myself healthy again: the condition for this—every physiologist would admit that—is *that one be healthy at bottom*. A typically morbid being cannot become healthy, much less make itself healthy. For a typically healthy person, conversely, being sick can even become an energetic *stimulus* for life, for living *more*. This, in fact, is how that long period of sickness appears to me *now*: as it were, I discovered life anew, including myself; I tasted all good and even little things, as others cannot easily taste them—I turned my will to health, to *life*, into a philosophy.

For it should be noted: it was during the years of my lowest vitality that I *ceased* to be a pessimist; the instinct of self-restoration *forbade* me a philosophy of poverty and discouragement.

What is it, fundamentally, that allows us to recognize *who has turned out well?* That a well-turned-out person pleases our senses, that he is carved from wood that is hard, delicate, and at the same time smells good. He has a taste only for what is good for him; his pleasure, his delight cease where the measure of what is good for him is transgressed. He guesses what remedies avail against what is harmful; he exploits bad accidents to his advantage; what does not kill him makes him stronger. Instinctively, he collects from everything he sees, hears, lives through, *his* sum: he is a principle of selection, he discards much. He is always in his own company, whether he associates with books, human beings, or landscapes: he honors by *choosing*, by *admitting*, by *trusting*. He reacts slowly to all kinds of stimuli, with that slowness which long caution and deliberate pride have bred in him: he examines the stimulus that approaches him, he is far from meeting it halfway. He believes neither in "misfortune" nor in "guilt": he comes to terms with himself, with others; he knows how to *forget*—he is strong enough; hence everything *must* turn out for his best.

Well then, I am the *opposite* of a decadent, for I have just described *myself*.

3

This *dual* series of experiences, this access to apparently separate worlds, is repeated in my nature in every respect: I am a *Doppelgänger,* I have a "second" face in addition to the first. *And* perhaps also a third.

Even by virtue of my descent, I am granted an eye beyond all merely local, merely nationally conditioned perspectives; it is not difficult for me to be a "good European." On the other hand, I am perhaps more German than present-day Germans, mere citizens of the German *Reich*, could possibly be—I, the last *antipolitical* German. And yet my ancestors were Polish noblemen: I have many racial instincts in my body from that source—who knows? In the end perhaps even the *liberum veto.*

When I consider how often I am addressed as a Pole when I travel, even by Poles themselves, and how rarely I am taken for a German, it might seem that I have been merely externally *sprinkled* with what is German. Yet my mother, Franziska Oehler, is at any rate something very German; ditto, my grandmother on my father's side, Erdmuthe Krause. The latter lived all her youth in the middle of good old Weimar, not without some connection with the circle of Goethe. Her brother, the professor of theology Krause in Königsberg, was called to Weimar as general superintendent after Herder's death. It is not impossible that her mother, my great-grandmother, is mentioned in the diary of the young Goethe under the name of "Muthgen." Her second marriage was with the superintendent Nietzsche in Eilenburg; and in the great war year of 1813, on the day that Napoleon entered Eilenburg with his general staff, on the tenth of October, she gave birth. As a Saxon, she was a great admirer of Napoleon; it could be that I still am, too. My father, born in 1813, died in 1849. Before he accepted the pastor's position in the parish of Röcken, not far from Lützen, he lived for a few years in the castle of Altenburg and taught the four princesses there. His pupils are now the Queen of Hanover, the Grand Duchess Constantine, the Grand Duchess of Altenburg, and the Princess Therese of Saxe-Altenburg. He was full of deep reverence for the Prussian king Frederick William IV, from whom he had also received his pastoral position; the events of 1848 grieved him beyond all measure. I myself, born on the birthday of the above named king, on the fifteenth of October, received, as fitting, the Hohenzollern name *Friedrich* Wilhelm. There was at least one advantage to the choice of this day: my birthday was a holiday throughout my childhood.

I consider it a great privilege to have had such a father: it even seems to me that this explains whatever else I have of privileges—*not* including life, the great Yes to life. Above all, that it requires no resolve on my part, but merely biding my time, to enter quite involuntarily into a world of lofty and delicate things: I am at home there, my inmost passion becomes free only there. That I have almost paid with my life for this privilege is certainly no unfair trade.

In order to understand anything at all of my *Zarathustra* one must perhaps be similarly conditioned as I am—with one foot *beyond* life.

4

I have never understood the art of predisposing people against me—this, too, I owe to my incomparable father—even when it seemed highly desirable to me. However un-Christian this may seem, I am not even predisposed against myself. You can turn my life this way and that, you will rarely find traces, and actually only once, that anybody felt ill will toward me—but perhaps rather too many traces of *good* will.

Even my experiences with people with whom everybody has bad experiences bear witness, without exception, in their favor: I tame every bear, I make even buffoons behave themselves. During the seven years that I taught Greek in the senior class in the *Pädagogium* in Basel, I never had occasion to punish anyone; the laziest boys worked hard. I am always equal to accidents; I have to be unprepared to be master of myself. Let the instrument be what it may, let it be as out of tune as only the instrument "man" can be—I should have to be sick if I should not succeed in getting out of it something worth hearing. And how often have I been told by the "instruments" themselves that they had never heard themselves like that.—

If, in spite of that, some small and great misdemeanors have been committed against me, "the will" cannot be blamed for this, least of all any *ill* will: sooner could I complain, as I have already suggested, of the good will that has done no small mischief in my life. My experiences entitle me to be quite generally suspicious of the so-called "selfless" drives, of all "neighbor love" that is ready to give advice and go into action. It always seems a weakness to me, a particular case of being incapable of resisting stimuli: *pity* is considered a virtue only among decadents. I reproach those who are full of pity for easily losing a sense of shame, of respect, of sensitivity for distances; before you know it, pity begins to smell of the mob and becomes scarcely distinguishable from bad manners—and sometimes pitying hands can interfere in a downright destructive manner in a great destiny, in the growing solitude of one wounded, in a privileged right to heavy guilt.

5

At another point as well, I am merely my father once more and, as it were, his continued life after an all-too-early death. Like everyone who has never lived among his equals and who finds the concept of "retaliation" as inaccessible as, say, the concept of "equal rights," I forbid myself all countermeasures, all protective measures, and, as is only fair, also any defense, any "justification," in cases when some small or *very great* folly is perpetrated against me. My kind of retaliation consists in following up the stupidity as fast as possible with some good sense: that way one may actually catch up with it. Metaphorically speaking, I send a box of confections to get rid of a painful story.

One needs only to do me some wrong, I "repay" it—you may be sure of that: soon I find an opportunity for expressing my gratitude to the "evil-doer" (at times even for his evil deed)—or to *ask* him for something, which can be more obliging than giving something.

It also seems to me that the rudest word, the rudest letter are still more benign, more decent than silence. Those who remain silent are almost always lacking in delicacy and courtesy of the heart. Silence is an objection; swallowing things leads of necessity to a bad character—it even upsets the stomach. All who remain silent are dyspeptic.

You see, I don't want rudeness to be underestimated: it is by far the *most humane* form of contradiction and, in the midst of effeminacy, one of our foremost virtues.

If one is rich enough for this, it is even a good fortune to be in the wrong. A god who would come to earth must not *do* anything except wrong: not to take the punishment upon oneself but the *guilt* would be divine.

6

Freedom from *ressentiment*, enlightenment about *ressentiment*—who knows how much I am ultimately indebted, in this respect also, to my protracted sickness! This problem is far from simple: one must have experienced it from strength as well as from weakness. If anything at all must be adduced against being sick and being weak, it is that man's really remedial instinct, his *fighting instinct* wears out. One cannot get rid of anything, one cannot get over anything, one cannot repel anything—everything hurts. Men and things obtrude too closely; experiences strike one too deeply; memory becomes a festering wound. Sickness itself *is* a kind of *ressentiment*.

Against all this the sick person has only one great remedy: I call it *Russian fatalism*, that fatalism without revolt which is exemplified by a Russian soldier who, finding a campaign too strenuous, finally lies down in the snow. No longer to accept anything at all, no longer to take anything, no longer to absorb anything—to cease reacting altogether.

This fatalism is not always merely the courage to die; it can also preserve life under the most perilous conditions by reducing the metabolism, slowing it down, as a kind of will to hibernate. Carrying this logic a few steps further, we arrive at the fakir who sleeps for weeks in a grave.

Because one would use oneself up too quickly if one reacted in *any* way, one does not react at all any more: this is the logic. Nothing burns one up faster than the affects of *ressentiment*. Anger, pathological vulnerability, impotent lust for revenge, thirst for revenge, poison-mixing in any sense—no reaction could be more disadvantageous for the exhausted: such affects involve a rapid consumption of nervous energy, a pathological increase of harmful excretions—for example, of the gall bladder into the stomach. *Ressentiment* is what is forbidden *par excellence* for the sick—it is their specific evil—unfortunately also their most natural inclination.

This was comprehended by that profound physiologist, the Buddha. His "religion" should rather be called a kind of *hygiene*, lest it be confused with such pitiable phenomena as Christianity: its effectiveness was made conditional on the victory over *ressentiment*. To liberate the soul from this is the first step toward recovery. "Not by enmity is enmity ended; by friendliness enmity is ended": these words stand at the beginning of the doctrine of the Buddha. It is *not* morality that speaks thus; thus speaks physiology.

Born of weakness, *ressentiment* is most harmful for the weak themselves. Conversely, given a rich nature, it is a *superfluous* feeling; mastering this feeling is virtually what proves riches. Whoever knows how seriously my philosophy has pursued the fight against vengefulness and rancor, even into the doctrine of "free will"—the fight against Christianity is merely a special case of this—will understand why I am making such a point of my own behavior, my *instinctive sureness* in practice. During periods of decadence I forbade myself such feelings as harmful; as soon as my vitality was rich and proud enough again, I forbade myself such feelings as *beneath* me. I displayed the "Russian fatalism" I mentioned by tenaciously clinging for years to all but intolerable situations, places, apartments, and society, merely because they happened to be given by accident: it was better than changing them, than *feeling* that they could be changed—than rebelling against them.

Any attempt to disturb me in this fatalism, to awaken me by force, used to annoy me mortally—and it actually was mortally dangerous every time.

Accepting oneself as if fated, not wishing oneself "different"—that is in such cases *great reason* itself.

7

War is another matter. I am warlike by nature. Attacking is one of my instincts. Being *able* to be an enemy, *being* an enemy—perhaps that presupposes a strong nature; in any case, it belongs to every strong nature. It needs objects of resistance; hence it *looks for* what resists: the *aggressive* pathos belongs just as necessarily to strength as vengefulness and rancor belong to weakness. Woman, for example, is vengeful: that is due to her weakness, as much as is her susceptibility to the distress of others.

The strength of those who attack can be measured in a way by the opposition they require: every growth is indicated by the search for a mighty opponent—or problem; for a warlike philosopher challenges problems, too, to single combat. The task is *not* simply to master what happens to resist, but what requires us to stake all our strength, suppleness, and fighting skill—opponents that are our *equals*.

Equality before the enemy: the first presupposition of an *honest* duel. Where one feels contempt, one *cannot* wage war; where one commands, where one sees something beneath oneself, one has no business waging war.

My practice of war can be summed up in four propositions. First: I only attack causes that are victorious; I may even wait until they become victorious.

Second: I only attack causes against which I would not find allies, so that I stand alone—so that I compromise myself alone.—I have never taken a step publicly that did not compromise me: that is *my* criterion of doing right.

Third: I never attack persons; I merely avail myself of the person as of a strong magnifying glass that allows one to make visible a general but creeping and elusive calamity. Thus I attacked David Strauss—more precisely, the *success* of a senile book with the "cultured" people in Germany: I caught this culture in the act.

Thus I attacked Wagner—more precisely, the falseness, the half-couth instincts of our "culture" which mistakes the subtle for the rich, and the late for the great.

Fourth: I only attack things when every personal quarrel is excluded, when any background of bad experiences is lacking. On the contrary, attack is in my case a proof of good will, sometimes even of gratitude. I honor, I distinguish by associating my name with that of a cause or a person: pro or con—that makes no difference to me at this point. When I wage war against Christianity I am entitled to this because I have never experienced misfortunes and frustrations from that quarter—the most serious Christians have always been well disposed toward me. I myself, an opponent of Christianity *de rigueur*, am far from blaming individuals for the calamity of millennia.

8

May I still venture to sketch one final trait of my nature that causes me no little difficulties in my contacts with other men? My instinct for cleanliness is characterized by a perfectly uncanny sensitivity so that the proximity or—what am I saying?—the inmost parts, the "entrails" of every soul are physiologically perceived by me—*smelled*.

This sensitivity furnishes me with psychological antennae with which I feel and get a hold of every secret: the abundant *hidden* dirt at the bottom of many a character—perhaps the result of bad blood, but glossed over by education—enters my consciousness almost at the first contact. If my observation has not deceived me, such characters who offend my sense of cleanliness also sense from their side the reserve of my disgust—and this does not make them smell any better.

As has always been my wont—extreme cleanliness in relation to me is the presupposition of my existence; I perish under unclean conditions—I constantly swim and bathe and splash, as it were, in water—in some perfectly transparent and resplendent element. Hence association with people imposes no mean test on my patience: my humanity does *not* consist in feeling with men how they are, but in *enduring* that I feel with them.

My humanity is a constant self-overcoming.

But I need *solitude*—which is to say, recovery, return to myself, the breath of a free, light, playful air.

30

CHARLES SANDERS PEIRCE
Autobiographical Note

Charles Sanders Peirce (1839–1914), the son of the mathematician Benjamin Peirce, was born in Cambridge, Massachusetts, and educated at Harvard, where he took a degree in chemistry. After a few disastrous academic appointments, he worked as a physicist for the U.S. Coast and Geodetic Survey until 1887, when he retired to devote himself to writing philosophy. Living in isolation and poverty, he was supported by his lifelong friend, William James.

Peirce's early papers developed the initial formulation of pragmatism as a theory of meaning. The meaning of a proposition consists in the sum total of all conceivable necessary consequences of its truth. As Peirce saw it, those consequences include not only logical entailments but also projectible experimental observations and conduct. Influenced by his early reading of Hegel, he thought of scientific inquiry—perhaps even philosophical inquiry—as progressively defining-and-discovering reality. Peirce eventually dissociated himself from what he saw as the weaker forms of pragmatism developed by James and Dewey, and insisted on calling his view "pragmaticism."

Peirce's philosophy of language—especially the semiotics that distinguishes the functions of a sign, its referent, and its interpretation—was immensely influential. The further distinctions between "types" and "tokens" and between "icons," "indices," and "symbols" have remained as guideposts in current semantics. His work on the scientific method—especially his introduction of the role of (what he called) "abduction" as a necessary support of induction and deduction—was less influential than his work in quantificational and modal logic. Peirce's philosophical psychology focused largely on an analysis of the relation between belief, doubt, and habits of action. This aspect of his work was developed—and transformed—by James and Dewey.

Most of Peirce's papers remained unpublished until Charles Hartshorne and Paul Weiss edited *The Collected Papers of Charles Sanders Peirce* (1931–1958); the final two volumes of this work were edited by Arthur Burks.

Why I Am a Fallibilist
(Collected Paper)

To erect a philosophical edifice that shall outlast the vicissitudes of time, my care must be, not so much to set each brick with nicest accuracy, as to lay the foundations deep and massive. Aristotle built upon a few deliberately chosen concepts—such as matter and form, act and power—very broad, and in their outlines vague and rough, but solid, unshakable, and not easily undermined; and thence it has come to pass that Aristolelianism is babbled in every nursery, that "English Common Sense," for example, is thoroughly peripatetic, and that ordinary men live so completely within the house of the Stagyrite that whatever they see out of the windows appears to them incomprehensible and metaphysical. Long it has been only too manifest that, fondly habituated though we be to it, the old structure will not do for modern needs; and accordingly, under Descartes, Hobbes, Kant, and others, repairs, alterations, and partial demolitions have been carried on for the last three centuries. One system, also, stands upon its own ground; I mean the new Schelling-Hegel mansion, lately run up in the German taste, but with such oversights in its construction that, although brand new, it is already pronounced uninhabitable. The undertaking which this volume inaugurates is to make a philosophy like that of Aristotle, that is to say, to outline a theory so comprehensive that, for a long time to come, the entire work of human reason, in philosophy of every school and kind, in mathematics, in psychology, in physical science, in history, in sociology, and in whatever other department there may be, shall appear as the filling up of its details. The first step toward this is to find simple concepts applicable to every subject.

But before all else, let me make the acquaintance of my reader, and express my sincere esteem for him and the deep pleasure it is to me to address one so wise and so patient. I know this character pretty well, for both the subject and the style of this book ensure his being one out of millions. He will comprehend that it has not been written for the purpose of confirming him in his preconceived opinions, and he would not take the trouble to read it if it had. He is prepared to meet with propositions that he is inclined at first to dissent from; and he looks to being convinced that some of them are true, after all. He will reflect, too, that the thinking and writing of this book has taken, I won't say how long, quite certainly more than a quarter of an hour, and consequently fundamental objections of so obvious a nature that they must strike everyone instantaneously will have occurred to the author, although the replies to them may not be of that kind whose full force can be instantly apprehended.

The reader has a right to know how the author's opinions were formed. Not, of course, that he is expected to accept any conclusions which are not borne out by argument. But in discussions of extreme difficulty, like these, when good judgment is a factor, and pure ratiocination is not everything, it is prudent to take every element into consideration. From the moment when I could think at all, until now, about forty years, I have been diligently and incessantly occupied with the study of methods [of] inquiry, both those which have been and are pursued and those which ought to be pursued. For ten years before this study began, I had been in training in the chemical laboratory. I was thoroughly grounded not only in all that was then known of physics and chemistry, but also in the way in which those who were successfully advancing knowledge proceeded. I have paid the most attention to the methods of the most exact sciences, have intimately communed with some of the greatest minds of our times in physical science, and have myself made positive contributions—none of them of any very great importance, perhaps—in mathematics, gravitation, optics, chemistry, astronomy, etc. I am saturated, through and through, with the spirit of the physical sciences. I have been a great student of logic, having read everything of any importance on the subject, devoting a great deal of time to medieval thought, without neglecting the works of the Greeks, the English, the Germans, the French, etc., and have produced systems of my own both in deductive and in inductive logic. In metaphysics, my training has been less systematic; yet I have read and deeply pondered upon all the main systems, never being satisfied until I was able to think about them as their own advocates thought.

The first strictly philosophical books that I read were of the classical German schools; and I became so deeply imbued with many of their ways of thinking that I have never been able to disabuse myself of them. Yet my attitude was always that of a dweller in a laboratory, eager only to learn what I did not yet know, and not that of philosophers bred in theological seminaries, whose ruling impulse is to teach what they hold to be infallibly true. I devoted two hours a day to the study of Kant's *Critic of the Pure Reason* for more than three years, until I almost knew the whole book by heart, and had critically examined every section of it. For about two years, I had long and almost daily discussions with Chauncey Wright, one of the most acute of the followers of J. S. Mill.

The effect of these studies was that I came to hold the classical German philosophy to be, upon its argumentative side, of little weight; although I esteem it, perhaps am too partial to it, as a rich mine of philosophical suggestions. The English philosophy, meagre and crude, as it is, in its conceptions, proceeds by surer methods and more accurate logic. The doctrine of the association of ideas is, to my thinking, the finest piece of philosophical work of the prescientific ages. Yet I can but pronounce English sensationalism to be entirely destitute of any solid bottom. From the evolutionary philosophers, I have learned little; although I admit that, however hurriedly their theories have been knocked together, and however antiquated and ignorant Spencer's *First Principles* and general doctrines, yet they are under the guidance of a great and true idea, and are developing it by methods that are in their main features sound and scientific.

The works of Duns Scotus have strongly influenced me. If his logic and metaphysics, not slavishly worshipped, but torn away from its medievalism, be adapted to modern culture, under continual wholesome reminders of nominalistic criticisms, I am convinced that it will go far toward supplying the philosophy which is best to harmonize with physical science. But other conceptions have to be drawn from the history of science and from mathematics.

Thus, in brief, my philosophy may be described as the attempt of a physicist to make such conjecture as to the constitution of the universe as the methods of science may permit, with the aid of all that has been done by previous philosophers. I shall support my propositions by such arguments as I can. Demonstrative proof is not to be thought of. The demonstrations of the metaphysicians are all moonshine. The best that can be done is to supply a hypothesis, not devoid of all likelihood, in the general line of growth of scientific ideas, and capable of being verified or refuted by future observers.

Religious infallibilism, caught in the current of the times, shows symptoms of declaring itself to be only practically speaking infallible; and when it has thus once confessed itself subject to gradations, there will remain over no relic of the good old tenth-century infallibilism, except that of the infallible scientists, under which head I include, not merely the kind of characters that manufacture scientific catechisms and homilies, churches and creeds, and who are indeed "born missionaries," but all those respectable and cultivated persons who, having acquired their notions of science from reading, and not from research, have the idea that "science" means knowledge, while the truth is, it is a misnomer applied to the pursuit of those who are devoured by a desire to find things out. . . .

Though infallibility in scientific matters seems to me irresistibly comical. I should be in a sad way if I could not retain a high respect for those who lay claim to it, for they comprise the greater part of the people who have any conversation at all. When I say they lay claim to it, I mean they assume the functions of it quite naturally and unconsciously. The full meaning of the adage *Humanum est errare*, they have never waked up to. In those sciences of measurement which are the least subject to error—metrology, geodesy, and metrica astronomy—no man of self-respect ever now states his result, without affixing to it its *probable error;* and if this practice is not followed in other sciences it is because in those the probable errors are too vast to be estimated.

I am a man of whom critics have never found anything good to say. When they could see no opportunity to injure me, they have held their peace. The little laudation I have had has come from such sources, that the only satisfaction I have derived from it, has been from such slices of bread and butter as it might waft my way. Only once, as far as I remember, in all my lifetime have I experienced the pleasure of praise—not for what it might bring but in itself. That pleasure was beatific; and the praise that conferred it was meant for blame. It was that a critic said of me that I did not seem to be *absolutely sure of my own conclusions.* Never, if I can help it, shall that critic's eye ever rest on what I am now writing; for I owe a great pleasure to him; and, such was his evident animus, that should he find that out, I fear the fires of hell would be fed with new fuel in his breast.

My book will have no instruction to impart to anybody. Like a mathematical treatise, it will suggest certain ideas and certain reasons for holding them true; but then, if you accept them, it must be because you like my reasons, and the responsibility lies with you. Man is essentially a social animal: but to be social is one thing, to be gregarious is another: I decline to serve as bellwether. My book is meant for people who *want to find out;* and people who want philosophy ladled out to them can go elsewhere. There are philosophical soup shops at every corner, thank God!

The development of my ideas has been the industry of thirty years. I did not know as I ever should get to publish them, their ripening seemed so slow. But the harvest time has come, at last, and to me that harvest seems a wild one, but of course it is not I who have to pass judgment. It is not quite you, either, individual reader; it is experience and history.

For years in the course of this ripening process, I used for myself to collect my ideas under the designation *fallibilism;* and indeed the first step toward *finding out* is to acknowledge you do not satisfactorily know already; so that no blight can so surely arrest all intellectual growth as the blight of cock-sureness; and ninety-nine out of every hundred good heads are reduced to impotence by that malady—of whose inroads they are most strangely unaware!

Indeed, out of a contrite fallibilism, combined with a high faith in the reality of knowledge, and an intense desire to find things out, all my philosophy has always seemed to me to grow. . . .

31

WILLIAM JAMES
Philosophy and Emergent Morality

William James (1842–1910) was the son of Henry James Sr., a somewhat eccentric philosopher with Swedenborgian leanings who gave his five children a cosmopolitan education. Like his father, his brother Henry, and his sister Alice, William was keenly interested in psychology and the phenomenology of introspection. He studied medicine at Harvard and was an active member of the Metaphysical Club, whose members included Peirce, Charles Wendell Holmes Jr., and Chauncey Wright. After suffering a debilitating depression, James began teaching physiology at Harvard, changed his appointment to psychology, and, eventually, in 1879 to philosophy. Besides presenting a critical survey of the field, his *Principles of Psychology* (1890) became the classical spring board for research in psychology. Combining empirical studies with philosophical analysis, James argued for a functionalist account of virtually the entire range of psychological activity: conscious awareness, perception, imagination, cognition, emotion, and decision. *The Will to Believe and Other Essays* (1897) develops a variant of Pascal's wager: instead of suspending belief in the face of the uncertainty, James proposed that it is rational to will to believe what conduces to the best course of continued inquiry and sound activity. From this, it was but a short step to applying pragmatism to religious belief. (*The Varieties of Religious Experience*, 1901–1902). He argued for the soundness—the rational legitimacy—of the claims of religious experience and belief when they "work." James defended himself against his critics in *Pragmatism* (1907) and *A Pluralistic Universe* (1909), claiming that his version of pluralistic pragmatism is compatible with radical empiricism. His many essays, lectures, and letters attack moral and metaphysical dogmatism. He was confident that moral truth, like scientific truth, emerges from experience and experiment.

The Sentiment of Rationality

I

What is the task which philosophers set themselves to perform? And why do they philosophize at all? Almost everyone will immediately reply: They desire to attain a conception of the frame of things which shall on the whole be more rational than the rather fragmentary and chaotic one which everyone by gift of nature carries about with him under his hat. But suppose this rational conception attained by the philosopher, how is he to recognize it for what it is, and not let it slip through ignorance? The only answer can be that he will recognize its rationality as he recognizes everything else, by certain subjective marks with which it affects him. When he gets the marks he may know that he has got the rationality.

What then are the marks? A strong feeling of ease, peace, rest, is one of them. The transition from a state of puzzle and perplexity to rational comprehension is full of lively relief and pleasure.

But this relief seems to be a negative rather than a positive character. Shall we then say that the feeling of rationality is constituted merely by the absence of any feeling of irrationality? I think there are very good grounds for upholding such a view. All feeling whatever, in the light of certain recent psychological speculations, seems to depend for its physical condition not on simple discharge of nerve-currents, but on their discharge under arrest, impediment or resistance. Just as we feel no particular pleasure when we breathe freely, but a very intense feeling of distress when the respiratory motions are prevented; so any unobstructed tendency to action discharges itself without the production of much cogitative accompaniment, and any perfectly fluent course of thought awakens but little feeling. But when the movement is inhibited or when the thought meets with difficulties, we experience a distress which yields to an opposite feeling of pleasure as fast as the obstacle is overcome. It is only when the distress is upon us that we can be said to strive, to crave, or to aspire. When enjoying plenary freedom to energize either in the way of motion or of thought, we are in a sort of an æsthetic state in which we might say with Walt Whitman, if we cared to say anything about ourselves at such times, "I am sufficient as I am." This feeling of the sufficiency of the present moment, of its absoluteness—this absence of all need to explain it, account for it or justify it—is what I call the Sentiment of rationality. As soon, in short, as we are enabled from any cause whatever to think of a thing with perfect fluency, that thing seems to us rational.

Why we should constantly gravitate towards the attainment of such fluency cannot here be said. As this is not an ethical but a psychological essay, it is quite sufficient for our purposes to lay it down as an empirical fact that we strive to formulate rationally a tangled mass of fact by a propensity as natural and invincible as that which makes us exchange a hard high stool for an arm-chair or prefer travelling by railroad to riding in a springless cart:

Whatever modes of conceiving the cosmos facilitate this fluency of our thought, produce the sentiment of rationality. Conceived in such modes Being vouches for itself and needs no further philosophic formulation. But so long as mutually obstructive elements are involved in the conception, the pent-up irritated mind recoiling on its present consciousness will criticize it, worry over it, and never cease in its attempts to discover some new mode of formulation which may give it escape from the irrationality of its actual ideas.

Now mental ease and freedom may be obtained in various ways. Nothing is more familiar than the way in which mere custom makes us at home with ideas or circumstances which, when new, filled the mind with curiosity and the need of explanation. There is no more common sight than that of men's mental worry about things incongruous with personal desire, and their thoughtless incurious acceptance of whatever happens to harmonize with their subjective ends. The existence of evil forms a "mystery"—a "problem": there is no "problem of happiness." But, on the other hand, purely theoretic processes may produce the same mental peace which custom and congruity with our native impulses in other cases give; and we have forthwith to discover how it is that so many processes can produce the same result, and how Philosophy, by emulating or using the means of all, may attain to a conception of the world which shall be rational in the maximum degree, or be warranted in the most composite manner against the inroads of mental unrest or discontent. Discarding for the present both custom and congruity, the present essay will deal with the theoretic way alone.

II

The facts of the world in their sensible diversity are always before us, but the philosophic need craves that they should be conceived in such a way as to satisfy the sentiment of rationality. The philosophic quest then is the quest of a conception. What now is a *conception*? It is a *teleological instrument*. It is a partial aspect of a thing which *for our purpose* we regard as its essential aspect, as the representative of the entire thing. In comparison with this aspect, whatever other properties and qualities the thing may have, are unimportant accidents which we may without blame ignore. But the essence, the ground of conception, varies with the end we have in view. A substance like oil has as many different essences as it has uses to different individuals. One man conceives it as a combustible, another as a lubricator, another as a food; the chemist thinks of it as a hydrocarbon; the furniture-maker as a darkener of wood; the speculator as a commodity whose market price to-day is this and tomorrow that. The soap-boiler, the physicist, the clothes-scourer severally ascribe to it other essences in relation to their needs. The essential quality of a thing is the quality of most *worth*, is strictly true; but the worth is wholly relative to the temporary interests of the conceiver. And, even, when his interest is distinctly defined in his own mind, the discrimination of the quality in the object which has the closest connexion with it, is a thing which no rules can teach. The only à priori advice that can be given to a man embarking on life with a certain purpose is the somewhat barren counsel: Be sure that in the circumstances that meet you, you attend to the *right* ones for your purpose. To pick out the right ones is the measure of the man. The genius is simply he to whom, when he opens his eyes upon the world, the "right" characters are the prominent ones. The fool is he who, with the same purposes as the genius, infallibly gets his attention tangled amid the accidents.

Schopenhauer expresses well this ultimate truth when he says that Intuition (by which in this passage he means the power to distinguish at a glance the essence amid the accidents) "is not only the source of all knowledge: it is knowledge . . . real *insight* . . . *Wisdom*, the true view of life, the right look at things, and the judgment that hits the mark, proceed from the mode in which the man conceives the world which lies before him . . . He who excels in this talent knows the (Platonic) ideas of the world and of life. Every case he looks at stands for countless cases; more and more he goes on to conceive of each thing in accordance with its true nature, and his acts like his judgments bear the stamp of his insight. Gradually his face too acquires the straight and piercing look, the expression of reason, and at last of wisdom. For the direct sight of essences alone can set its mark upon the face. Abstract knowledge about them has no such effect."

The right conception for the philosopher depends then on his interests. Now the interest which he has above other men is that of reducing the manifold in thought to simple form. We can no more say why the philosopher is more peculiarly sensitive to this delight, than we can explain the passion some persons have for matching colours or for arranging cards in a game of solitaire. All these passions resemble each other in one point; they are all illustrations of what may be called the æsthetic Principle of Ease. Our pleasure at finding that a chaos of facts is at bottom the expression of a single underlying fact is like the relief of the musician at resolving a confused mass of sound into melodic or harmonic order. The simplified result is handled with far less mental effort than the original data; and a philosophic conception of nature is thus in no metaphorical sense a labor-saving contrivance. The passion for parsimony, for economy of means in thought, is thus the philosophic passion *par excellence*, and any character or aspect of the world's phenomena which gathers up their diversity into simplicity will gratify that passion, and in the philosopher's mind stand for that essence of things compared with which all their other determinations may by him be overlooked.

More universality or extensiveness is then the one mark the philosopher's conceptions must possess. Unless they appear in an enormous number of cases they will not bring the relief which is his main theoretic need. The knowledge of things by their causes, which is often given as a definition of rational knowledge, is useless to him unless the causes converge to a minimum number whilst still producing the maximum number of effects. The more multiple are the instances he can see to be cases of his fundamental concept, the more flowingly does his mind rove from fact to fact in the world. The phenomenal transitions are no real transitions; each item is the same old friend with a slightly altered dress. This passion for unifying things may gratify itself, as we all know, at truth's expense. Everyone has friends bent on system and everyone has observed how, when their system has once taken definite shape, they become absolutely blind and insensible to the most flagrant facts which cannot be made to fit into it. The ignoring of data is, in fact, the easiest and most popular mode of obtaining unity in one's thought.

But leaving these vulgar excesses let us glance briefly at some more dignified contemporary examples of the hypertrophy of the unifying passion.

The craving for Monism at any cost is the parent of the entire evolutionist movement of our day, so far as it pretends to be more than history. The Philosophy of Evolution tries to show how the world at any given time may be conceived as absolutely identical, except in appearance, with itself at all past times. What it most abhors is the admission of anything which, appearing at a given point, should be judged essentially other than what went before. Notwithstanding the *lacunae* in Mr. Spencer's system; notwithstanding the vagueness of his terms; in spite of the sort of jugglery by which his use of the word "nascent" is made to veil the introduction of new primordial factors like consciousness, as if, like the girl in *Midshipman Easy*, he could excuse the illegitimacy of an infant, by saying it was a very little one—in spite of all this, I say, Mr. Spencer is, and is bound to be, the most popular of all philosophers, because more than any other he seeks to appease our strongest theoretic craving. To undiscriminating minds his system will be a sop; to acute ones a program full of suggestiveness.

The crowning feat of unification at any cost is seen in the Hegelian denial of the Principle of Contradiction. One who is willing to allow that A and not-A are one, can be checked by few farther difficulties in Philosophy. . . .

III

But alongside of the passion for simplification, there exists a sister passion which in some minds—though they perhaps form the minority—is its rival. This is the passion for distinguishing; it is the impulse to be *acquainted* with the parts rather than to comprehend the whole. Loyalty to clearness and integrity of perception, dislike of blurred outlines, of vague identifications, are its characteristics. It loves to recognize particulars in their full completeness, and the more of these it can carry the happier it is. It is the mind of Hume *versus* Spinoza. It prefers any amount of incoherence, abruptness and fragmentariness (so long as the literal details of the separate facts are saved) to a fallacious unity which swamps things rather than explains them.

Clearness *versus* Simplicity is then the theoretic dilemma, and a man's philosophic attitude is determined by the balance in him of these two cravings. When John Mill insists that the ultimate laws of nature cannot possibly be less numerous than the distinguishable qualities of sensation which we possess, he speaks in the name of this æsthetic demand for clearness. When Prof. Bain says:—"There is surely nothing to be dissatisfied with, to complain of, in the circumstance that the elements of our experience are, in the last resort, two, and not one . . . Instead of our being 'unfortunate' in not being able to know the essence of either matter or mind—in not comprehending their union; our misfortune would rather be to have to know anything different from what we do know,"—he is animated by a like motive. All makers of architectonic systems like that of Kant, all multipliers of original principles, all dislikers of vague monotony, whether it bear the character of Eleatic stagnancy or of Heraclitic change, obey this tendency. *Ultimate kinds* of feeling bound together in harmony by laws, which themselves are *ultimate kinds* of relation, form the theoretic resting-place of such philosophers.

The unconditional demand which this need makes of a philosophy is that its fundamental terms should be representable. Phenomena are analyzable into feelings and relations. Causality is a relation between two feelings. To abstract the relation from the feelings, to unify all things by referring them to a first cause, and to leave this latter relation with no term of feeling before it, is to violate the fundamental habits of our thinking, to baffle the imagination, and to exasperate the minds of certain people much as everyone's eye is exasperated by a magic-lantern picture or a microscopic object out of focus. Sharpen it, we say, or for heaven's sake remove it altogether.

The matter is not at all helped when the word Substance is brought forward and the primordial causality said to obtain between this and the phenomena; for Substance *in se* cannot be directly imaged by feeling, and seems in fact but to be a peculiar form of relation between feelings—the relation of organic union between a group of them and time. Such relations, represented as non-phenomenal entities, become thus the *bête noire* and pet aversion of many thinkers. By being posited as existent they challenge our acquaintance but at the same instant defy it by being defined as noumenal. So far is this reaction against the treatment of relational terms as metempirical entities carried, that the reigning British school seems to deny their function even in their legitimate sphere, namely as phenomenal elements or "laws" cementing the mosaic of our feelings into coherent form. Time, likeness, and unlikeness are the only phenomenal relations our English empiricists can tolerate. One of the earliest and perhaps the most famous expression of the dislike to relations considered abstractedly is the well-known passage from Hume: "When we run over libraries, persuaded of these principles, what havoc must we make? If we take in our hand any volume; of divinity or school metaphysics, for instance; let us ask, *Does it contain any abstract reasoning concerning quantity or number?* No. *Does it contain any experimental reasoning concerning matter of fact and existence?* No. Commit it then to the flames: For it can contain nothing but sophistry and illusion."

Many are the variations which succeeding writers have played on this tune. As we spoke of the excesses of the unifying passion, so we may now say of the craving for clear representability that it leads often to an unwillingness to treat any abstractions whatever as if they were intelligible. Even to talk of space, time, feeling, power, &c., oppresses them with a strange sense of uncanniness. Anything to be real for them must be representable in the form of a *lump.* Its other concrete determinations may be abstracted from, but its *tangible* thinghood must remain. Minds of this order, if they can be brought to psychologize at all, abound in such phrases as "tracts" of consciousness, "areas" of emotion, "molecules" of feeling, "agglutinated portions" of thought, "gangs" of ideas &c., &c.

Our first conclusion may then be this: No system of philosophy can hope to be universally accepted among men which grossly violates either of the two great æsthetic needs of our logical nature, the need of unity and the need of clearness, or entirely subordinates the one to the other. Doctrines of mere disintegration like that of Hume and his successors, will be as widely unacceptable on the one hand as doctrines of merely engulphing substantialism like those of Schopenhauer, Hartmann and Spencer on the other. Can we for our own guidance briefly sketch out here some of the conditions of most favorable compromise?

In surveying the connexions between data we are immediately struck by the fact that some are more intimate than others. Propositions which express those we call necessary truths; and with them we contrast the laxer collocations and sequences which are known as empirical, habitual or merely fortuitous. The former seem to have an *inward* reasonableness which the latter are deprived of. The link, whatever it be, which binds the two phenomena together, seems to extend from the heart of one into the heart of the next, and to be an essential reason why the facts should always and indefeasibly be as we now know them. "Within the pale we stand." As Lotze says:—"The intellect is not satisfied with merely associated representations. In its constant critical activity thought seeks to refer each representation to the rational ground which conditions the alliance of what is associated and proves that what is grouped *belongs* together. So it separates from each other those impressions which merely coalesce without inward connexions, and it renews (while corroborating them) the bonds of those which, by the inward kinship of their content, have a right to permanent companionship."

On the other hand many writers seem to deny the existence of any such inward kinship or rational bond between things. Hume says: "All our distinct perceptions are distinct existences, and the mind never perceives any real connexion among distinct existences."

THE MORAL PHILOSOPHER AND THE MORAL LIFE

The main purpose of this paper is to show that there is no such thing possible as an ethical philosophy dogmatically made up in advance. We all help to determine the content of ethical philosophy so far as we contribute to the race's moral life. In other words, there can be no final truth in ethics any more than in physics, until the last man has had his experience and said his say. In the one case as in the other, however, the hypotheses which we now make while waiting, and the acts to which they prompt us, are among the indispensable conditions which determine what that "say" shall be.

First of all, what is the position of him who seeks an ethical philosophy? To begin with, he must be distinguished from all those who are satisfied to be ethical sceptics. He *will* not be a sceptic; therefore so far from ethical scepticism being

one possible fruit of ethical philosophizing, it can only be regarded as that resid-
ual alternative to all philosophy which from the outset menaces every would-be
philosopher who may give up the quest discouraged, and renounce his original
aim. That aim is to find an account of the moral relations that obtain among
things, which will weave them into the unity of a stable system, and make of the
world what one may call a genuine universe from the ethical point of view. So
far as the world resists reduction to the form of unity, so far as ethical propositions seem unstable, so far does the philosopher fail of his ideal. The subject-
matter of his study is the ideals he finds existing in the world; the purpose which
guides him is this ideal of his own, of getting them into a certain form. This ideal
is thus a factor in ethical philosophy whose legitimate presence must never be
overlooked; it is a positive contribution which the philosopher himself necessarily makes to the problem. But it is his only positive contribution. At the outset
of his inquiry he ought to have no other ideals. Were he interested peculiarly in
the triumph of any one kind of good, he would *pro tanto* cease to be a judicial
investigator, and become an advocate for some limited element of the case.

There are three questions in ethics which must be kept apart. Let them be called
respectively the *psychological* question, the *meta-physical* question, and the *casuistic* question. The psychological question asks after the historical *origin* of our
moral ideas and judgments; the metaphysical question asks what the very *meaning* of the words "good," "ill," and "obligation" are; the casuistic question asks
what is the *measure* of the various goods and ills which men recognize, so that
the philosopher may settle the true order of human obligations.

I

The psychological question is for most disputants the only question. When your
ordinary doctor of divinity has proved to his own satisfaction that an altogether
unique faculty called "conscience" must be postulated to tell us what is right
and what is wrong; or when your popular-science enthusiast has proclaimed that
"apriorism" is an exploded superstition, and that our moral judgments have gradually resulted from the teaching of the environment, each of these persons thinks
that ethics is settled and nothing more is to be said. The familiar pair of names,
Intuitionist and *Evolutionist*, so commonly used now to connote all possible differences in ethical opinion, really refer to the psychological question alone. The
discussion of this question hinges so much upon particular details that it is impossible to enter upon it at all within the limits of this paper. I will therefore
only express dogmatically my own belief, which is this—that the Benthams, the
Mills, and the Bains have done a lasting service in taking so many of our human
ideals and showing how they must have arisen from the association with acts of
simple bodily pleasures and reliefs from pain. Association with many remote
pleasures will unquestionably make a thing significant of goodness in our minds;
and the more vaguely the goodness is conceived of, the more mysterious will its
source appear to be. But it is surely impossible to explain all our sentiments and
preferences in this simple way. The more minutely psychology studies human
nature, the more clearly it finds there traces of secondary affections, relating the
impressions of the environment with one another and with our impulses in quite
different ways from those mere associations of coexistence and succession which
are practically all that pure empiricism can admit. Take the love of drunkenness;

take bashfulness, the terror of high places, the tendency to sea-sickness, to faint at the sight of blood, the susceptibility to musical sounds; take the emotion of the comical, the passion for poetry, for mathematics, or for metaphysics—no one of these things can be wholly explained by either association or utility. They *go with* other things that can be so explained, no doubt; and some of them are prophetic of future utilities, since there is nothing in us for which some use may not be found. But their origin is in incidental complications to our cerebral structure, a structure whose original features arose with no reference to the perception of such discords and harmonies as these.

Well, a vast number of our moral perceptions also are certainly of this secondary and brain-born kind. They deal with directly felt fitnesses between things, and often fly in the teeth of all the preposessions of habit and presumptions of utility. The moment you get beyond the coarser and more commonplace moral maxims, the Decalogues and Poor Richard's Almanacs, you fall into schemes and positions which to the eye of common-sense are fantastic and over-strained. The sense for abstract justice which some persons have is as excentric a variation, from the natural-history point of view, as is the passion for music or for the higher philosophical consistencies which consumes the soul of others. The feeling of the inward dignity of certain spiritual attitudes, as peace, serenity, simplicity, veracity; and of the essential vulgarity of others, as querulousness, anxiety, egoistic fussiness, etc.—are quite inexplicable except by an innate preference of the more ideal attitude for its own pure sake. The nobler thing *tastes* better, and that is all that we can say. "Experience" of consequences may truly teach us what things are *wicked*, but what have consequences to do with what is mean and vulgar?

The next [question is] metaphysical: what [do] we mean by the words "obligation," "good," and "ill."

First of all, it appears that such words can have no application or relevancy in a world in which no sentient life exists. Imagine an absolutely material world, containing only physical and chemical facts, and existing from eternity without a God, without even an interested spectator: would there be any sense in saying of that world that one of its states is better than another? Or if there were two such worlds possible, would there be any rhyme or reason in calling one good and the other bad—good or bad positively, I mean, and apart from the fact that one might relate itself better than the other to the philosopher's private interests? But we must leave these private interests out of the account, for the philosopher is a mental fact, and we are asking whether goods and evils and obligations exist in physical facts *per se*. Surely there is no *status* for good and evil to exist in, in a purely insentient world. How can one physical fact, considered simply as a physical fact, be "better" than another? Betterness is not a physical relation. In its mere material capacity, a thing can no more be good or bad than it can be pleasant or painful. Good for what? Good for the production of another physical fact, do you say? But what in a purely physical universe demands the production of that other fact? Physical facts simply *are* or *are not;* and neither when present or absent, can they be supposed to make demands. If they do, they can only do so by having desires; and then they have ceased to be purely physical facts, and have become facts of conscious sensibility. Goodness, badness, and obligation must be *realized* somewhere in order really to exist; and the first step in ethical philosophy is to see that no merely inorganic "nature of things" can realize them.

Neither moral relations nor the moral law can swing *in vacuo*. Their only habitat can be a mind which feels them; and no world composed of merely physical facts can possibly be a world to which ethical propositions apply.

We may now consider that what we distinguished as the metaphysical question in ethical philosophy is sufficiently answered, and that we have learned what the words "good," "bad," and "obligation" severally mean. They mean no absolute natures, independent of personal support. They are objects of feeling and desire, which have no foothold or anchorage in Being, apart from the existence of actually living minds.

Wherever such minds exist, with judgments of good and ill, and demands upon one another, there is an ethical world in its essential features. Were all other things, gods and men and starry heavens, blotted out from this universe, and were there left but one rock with two loving souls upon it, that rock would have as thoroughly moral a constitution as any possible world which the eternities and immensities could harbor. It would be a tragic constitution, because the rock's inhabitants would die. But while they lived, there would be real good things and real bad things in the universe; there would be obligations, claims, and expectations; obediences, refusals, and disappointments; compunctions and longings for harmony to come again, and inward peace of conscience when it was restored; there would, in short, be a moral life, whose active energy would have no limit but the intensity of interest in each other with which the hero and heroine might be endowed.

We, on this terrestrial globe, so far as the visible facts go, are just like the inhabitants of such a rock. Whether a God exist, or whether no God exist, in yon blue heaven above us bent, we form at any rate an ethical republic here below. And the first reflection which this leads to is that ethics have as genuine and real a foothold in a universe where the highest consciousness is human, as in a universe where there is a God as well. "The religion of humanity" affords a basis for ethics as well as theism does. Whether the purely human system can gratify the philosopher's demand as well as the other is a different question, which we ourselves must answer ere we close.

The last fundamental question in Ethics was, it will be remembered, the *casuistic* question. Here we are, in a world where the existence of a divine thinker has been and perhaps always will be doubted by some of the lookers-on, and where, in spite of the presence of a large number of ideals in which human beings agree, there are a mass of others about which no general consensus obtains. It is hardly necessary to present a literary picture of this, for the facts are too well known. The wars of the flesh and the spirit in each man, the concupiscences of different individuals pursuing the same unshareable material or social prizes, the ideals which contrast so according to races, circumstances, temperaments, philosophical beliefs, etc.—all form a maze of apparently inextricable confusion with no obvious Ariadne's thread to lead one out. Yet the philosopher, just because he is a philosopher, adds his own peculiar ideal to the confusion (with which if he were willing to be a sceptic he would be passably content), and insists that over all these individual opinions there is a *system of truth* which he can discover if he only takes sufficient pains.

We stand ourselves at present in the place of that philosopher, and must not fail to realize all the features that the situation comports. In the first place we will not be sceptics; we hold to it that there is a truth to be ascertained. But in the second place we have just gained the insight that that truth cannot be a self-proclaiming set of laws, or an abstract "moral reason," but can only exist in act, or in the shape of an opinion held by some thinker really to be found. There is, however, no visible thinker invested with authority. Shall we then simply proclaim our own ideals as the lawgiving ones? No; for if we are true philosophers we must throw our own spontaneous ideals, even the dearest, impartially in with that total mass of ideals which are fairly to be judged. But how then can we as philosophers ever find a test; how avoid complete moral scepticism on the one hand, and on the other escape bringing a wayward personal standard of our own along with us, on which we simply pin our faith?

The dilemma is a hard one, nor does it grow a bit more easy as we revolve it in our minds. The entire undertaking of the philosopher obliges him to seek an impartial test. That test, however, must be incarnated in the demand of some actually existent person; and how can he pick out the person save by an act in which his own sympathies and prepossessions are implied?

One method indeed presents itself, and has as a matter of history been taken by the more serious ethical schools. If the heap of things demanded proved on inspection less chaotic than at first they seemed, if they furnished their own relative test and measure, then the casuistic problem would be solved. If it were found that all goods *quâ* goods contained a common essence, then the amount of this essence involved in any one good would show its rank in the scale of goodness, and order could be quickly made; for this essence would be *the* good upon which all thinkers were agreed, the relatively objective and universal good that the philosopher seeks. Even his own private ideals would be measured by their share of it, and find their rightful place among the rest.

Various essences of good have thus been found and proposed as bases of the ethical system. Thus, to be a mean between two extremes; to be recognized by a special intuitive faculty; to make the agent happy for the moment; to make others as well as him happy in the long run; to add to his perfection or dignity; to harm no one; to follow from reason or flow from universal law; to be in accordance with the will of God; to promote the survival of the human species on this planet—are so many tests, each of which has been maintained by somebody to constitute the essence of all good things or actions so far as they are good.

No one of the measures that have been actually proposed has, however, given general satisfaction. Some are obviously not universally present in all cases—*e.g.,* the character of harming no one, or that of following a universal law; for the best course is often cruel; and many acts are reckoned good on the sole condition that they be exceptions, and serve not as examples of a universal law. Other characters, such as following the will of God, are unascertainable and vague. Others again, like survival, are quite indeterminate in their consequences, and leave us in the lurch where we most need their help: a philosopher of the Sioux Nation, for example, will be certain to use the survival-criterion in a very different way from ourselves. The best, on the whole, of these marks and measures of goodness seems to be the capacity to bring happiness. But in order not to break down fatally, this test must be taken to cover innumerable acts and impulses that never *aim* at happiness; so that, after all, in seeking for a universal principle we inevitably are carried onward to the *most* universal principle—that *the essence of good is simply to satisfy demand.* The demand may be for anything under the sun. There is really no more ground for supposing that all our demands can be accounted for by one universal underlying kind of motive than there is ground for supposing that all physical phenomena are cases of a single law. The elementary forces in ethics are probably as plural as those of physics are. The various ideals have no common character apart from the fact that they are ideals. No single abstract principle can be so used as to yield to the philosopher anything like a scientifically accurate and genuinely useful casuistic scale.

The actually possible in this world is vastly narrower than all that is demanded; and there is always a *pinch* between the ideal and the actual which can only be got through by leaving part of the ideal behind. There is hardly a good which we can imagine except as competing for the possession of the same bit of space and time with some other imagined good. Every end of desire that presents itself appears exclusive of some other end of desire. Shall a man drink and smoke, *or* keep his nerves in condition?—he cannot do both. Shall he follow his fancy for Amelia, *or* for Henrietta?—both cannot be the choice of his heart. Shall he have the dear old Republican party, *or* a spirit of unsophistication in public affairs?—he cannot have both, etc. So that the ethical philosopher's demand for the right scale of subordination in ideals is the fruit of an altogether practical need. Some part of the ideal must be butchered, and he needs to know which part. It is a tragic situation, and no mere speculative conundrum, with which he has to deal. . . .

A true philosopher must see that there is nothing final in any actually given equilibrium of human ideals, but that, as our present laws and customs have fought and conquered other past ones, so they will in their turn be overthrown by any newly discovered order which will hush up the complaints that they still give rise to, without producing others louder still. "Rules are made for man, not man for rules." And although a man always risks much when he breaks away from established rules and strives to realize a larger ideal whole than they permit, yet the philosopher must allow that it is at all times open to any one to make the experiment, provided he fear not to stake his life and character upon the throw. The pinch is always here. Pent in under every system of moral rules are innumerable persons whom it weighs upon, and goods which it represses; and these are always rumbling and grumbling in the background, and ready for any issue by which they may get free.

. . . No philosophy of ethics is possible in the old-fashioned absolute sense of the term. Everywhere the ethical philosopher must wait on facts. The thinkers who create the ideals come he knows not whence, their sensibilities are evolved he knows not how; and the question as to which of two conflicting ideals will give the best universe then and there, can be answered by him only through the aid of the experience of other men. I said some time ago, in treating of the "first" question, that the intuitional moralists deserve credit for keeping most clearly to the psychological facts. They do much to spoil this merit on the whole, however, by mixing with it that dogmatic temper which, by absolute distinctions and unconditional "thou shalt nots," changes a growing, elastic, and continuous life into a superstitious system of relics and dead bones. In point of fact, there are no absolute evils, and there are no non-moral goods; and the *highest* ethical life— however few may be called to bear its burdens—consists at all times in the breaking of rules which have grown too narrow for the actual case. There is but one unconditional commandment, which is that we should seek incessantly, with fear and trembling, so to vote and to act as to bring about the very largest total universe of good which we can see. Abstract rules indeed can help; but they help the less in proportion as our intuitions are more piercing, and our vocation is the stronger for the moral life. For every real dilemma is in literal strictness a unique situation; and the exact combination of ideals realized and ideals disappointed which each decision creates is always a universe without a precedent, and for which no adequate previous rule exists. The philosopher, then, *quâ* philosopher, is no better able to determine the best universe in the concrete emergency than other men. He sees, indeed, somewhat better than most men what the question always is—not a question of this good or that good simply taken, but of the two total universes with which these goods respectively belong. He knows that he must vote always for the richer universe, for the good which seems most organizable, most fit to enter into complex combinations, most apt to be a member of a more inclusive whole. But which particular universe this is he cannot know for certain in advance; he only knows that if he makes a bad mistake the cries of the wounded will soon inform him of the fact. In all this the philosopher is just like the rest of us non-philosophers, so far as we are just and sympathetic instinctively, and so far as we are open to the voice of complaint. His function is in fact indistinguishable from that of the best kind of statesman at the present day. His books upon ethics, therefore, so far as they truly touch the moral life, must more and more ally themselves with a literature which is confessedly tentative and suggestive rather than dogmatic—I mean with novels and dramas of the deeper sort, with sermons, with books on statecraft and philanthropy and social and economical reform. Treated in this way ethical treatises may be voluminous and luminous as well; but they never can be *final*, except in their abstractest and vaguest features; and they must more and more abandon the old-fashioned, clear-cut, and would-be "scientific" form.

Some Problems in Philosophy (1911)

The progress of society is due to the fact that individuals vary from the human average in all sorts of directions, and that the originality which they show is often so attractive or useful, that they are recognized by their tribe as leaders, and become setters of new ideals and objects of envy or imitation.

Among the variations, every generation of men produces some individuals exceptionally preoccupied with theory. Such men find matter for puzzle and astonishment where no one else does. Their imagination invents explanations and combines them. They store up the learning of their time, utter prophecies and warnings, and are regarded as sages. Philosophy, etymologically meaning the love of wisdom, is the work of this class of minds, regarded with an indulgent relish, if not with admiration, even by those who do not understand them or believe much in the truth which they proclaim.

Philosophy, thus become a race heritage, forms in its totality a monstrously unwieldy mass of learning. So taken, there is no reason why any special science like chemistry, or astronomy, should be excluded from it. By common consent, however, and for reasons presently to be explained, special sciences are to-day excluded, and what remains is manageable enough to be taught under the name of philosophy by one man if his interests be broad enough.

If this were a German text-book I should first give my abstract definition of the topic, thus limited by usage, then proceed to display its *begriff und eintheilung*, and its *aufgabe und methode*. But as such displays are usually unintelligible to beginners, and unnecessary after reading the book, it will conduce to brevity to omit that chapter altogether, useful tho it might possibly be to more advanced readers as a summary of what is to follow.

I will tarry a moment, however, over the matter of definition. Limited by the omission of the special sciences, the name philosophy has come more and more to denote ideas of universal scope exclusively. The principles of explanation that underlie all things without exception, the elements common to gods and men and animals and stones, the first *whence* and the last *whither* of the cosmic procession, the conditions of all knowing, and the most general rules of human action—these furnish the problems generally deemed philosophic *par excellence;* and the 'philosopher' is the man who finds the most to say about them. Philosophy is defined in the usual scholastic text-books as 'the knowledge of things in general by their ultimate causes, so far as natural reason can attain to such knowledge.' This means that explanation of the universe at large, not descriptive of its details, is what philosophy must aim at; and so it happens that a view of anything is termed 'philosophic' just in proportion as it is broad and connected with other views, and as it uses principles not proximate or intermediate, but ultimate and all-embracing, to justify itself. Any very sweeping view of the world is a philosophy, in this sense, even tho it may be a vague one. It is a *weltanschauung*, an intellectualized attitude towards life. Professor Dewey well describes the constitution of all the philosophies that actually exist, when he says that "philosophy expresses a certain attitude, purpose, and temper of conjoined intellect and will rather than a discipline whose boundaries can be neatly marked off."

To know the chief rival attitudes towards life, as the history of human thinking has developed them, and to have heard some of the reasons they can give for themselves, ought surely to be considered an essential part of liberal education. Philosophy, indeed, in one sense of the term is only a compendious name for the spirit in education which the word 'college' stands for in America. Things can be taught in dry dogmatic ways or in a philosophic way. At a technical school a man may grow into a first-rate instrument for doing a certain job, but he may miss all the graciousness of mind suggested by the term 'liberal culture.' He may remain a cad, and not a gentleman, intellectually pinned down to his one narrow subject, literal, unable to suppose anything different from what he has seen, without imagination, atmosphere or mental perspective.

Philosophy, beginning in wonder, as Plato and Aristotle said, is able to fancy everything different from what it is. It sees the familiar as if it were strange, and the strange as if it were familiar. It can take things up and lay them down again. Its mind is full of air that plays round every subject. It rouses us from our native dogmatic slumber and breaks up our caked prejudices. Historically it has always been a sort of fecundation of four different human interests—science, poetry, religion, and logic—by one another. It has sought by hard reasoning for results emotionally valuable. To have some contact with it, to catch its influence, is thus good for both literary and scientific students. By its poetry it appeals to literary minds; but its logic stiffens them up and remedies their softness. By its logic it appeals to the scientific; but softens them by its other aspects, and saves them from too dry a technicality. Both types of student ought to get from philosophy a livelier spirit, more air, more mental background. "Hast any philosophy in thee, Shepherd?"—this question of Touchstone's is the one with which men should always meet one another. A man with no philosophy in him is the most inauspicious and unprofitable of all possible social mates.

Philosophy in the full sense is only *man thinking*, thinking about generalities rather than about particulars. But whether about generalities or particulars, man thinks always by the same methods. He observes, discriminates, generalizes, classifies, looks for causes, traces analogies, and makes hypotheses. Philosophy, taken as something distinct from science or from practical affairs, follows no method peculiar to itself. All our thinking to-day has evolved gradually out of primitive human thought, and the only really important changes that have come over its manner (as distinguished from the matters in which it believes) are a greater hesitancy in asserting its convictions, and the habit of seeking verification for them whenever it can.

It is obvious enough that if every step forward which philosophy makes, every question to which an accurate answer is found, gets accredited to science the residuum of unanswered problems will alone remain to constitute the domain of philosophy, and will alone bear her name. In point of fact this is just what is happening. Philosophy has become a collective name for questions that have not yet been answered to the satisfaction of all by whom they have been asked. It does not follow, because some of these questions have waited two thousand years for an answer, that no answer will ever be forthcoming. Two thousand years probably measure but one paragraph in that great romance of adventure called the history of the intellect of man. The extraordinary progress of the last three hundred years is due to a rather sudden finding of the way in which a certain order of questions ought to be attacked, questions admitting of mathematical treatment. But to assume, therefore, that the only possible philosophy must be mechanical and mathematical, and to disparage all inquiry into the other sorts of questions, is to forget the extreme diversity of aspects under which reality undoubtedly exists. To the spiritual questions the proper avenues of philosophic approach will also undoubtedly be found. They have, to some extent, been found already. In some respects, indeed, "science" has made less progress than "philosophy"—its most general conceptions would astonish neither Aristotle nor Descartes, could they revisit our earth. The composition of things from elements, their evolution, the conservation of energy, the idea of a universal determinism, would seem to them commonplace enough—the little things, the microscopes, electric lights, telephones, and details of the sciences, would be to them the awe-inspiring things. But if they opened our books on metaphysics, or visited a philosophic lecture room, everything would sound strange. The whole idealistic or "critical" attitude of our time would be novel, and it would be long before they took it in.

Many object that philosophy is dogmatic, and pretends to settle things by pure reason, whereas the only fruitful mode of getting at truth is to appeal to concrete experience. Science collects, classes, and analyzes facts, and thereby far outstrips philosophy. This objection is historically valid. Too many philosophers have aimed at closed systems, established *a priori*, claiming infallibility, and to be accepted or rejected only as totals. The sciences on the other hand, using hypotheses only, but always seeking to verify them by experiment and observation, open a way for indefinite self-correction and increase. At the present day, it is getting more and more difficult for dogmatists claiming finality for their systems, to get a hearing in educated circles. Hypothesis and verification, the watchwords of science, have set the fashion too strongly in academic minds.

Since philosophers are only men thinking about things in the most comprehensive possible way, they can use any method whatsoever freely. Philosophy must, in any case, complete the sciences, and must incorporate their methods.

One cannot see why, if such a policy should appear advisable, philosophy might not end by forswearing all dogmatism whatever, and become as hypothetical in her manners as the most empirical science of them all.

Others object that Philosophy is out of touch with real life, for which it substitutes abstractions. The real world is various, tangled, painful. Philosophers have, almost without exception, treated it as noble, simple, and perfect, ignoring the complexity of fact, and indulging in a sort of optimism that exposes their systems to the contempt of common men, and to the satire of such writers as Voltaire and Schopenhauer. The great popular success of Schopenhauer is due to the fact that, first among philosophers, he spoke the concrete truth about the ills of life.

This objection also is historically valid, but no reason appears why philosophy should keep aloof from reality permanently. Her manners may change as she successfully develops. The thin and noble abstractions may give way to more solid and real constructions, when the materials and methods for making such constructions shall be more and more securely ascertained. In the end philosophers may get into as close contact as realistic novelists with the facts of life.

In its original acceptation, meaning the completest knowledge of the universe, philosophy must include the results of all the sciences, and cannot be contrasted with the latter. It simply aims at making of science what Herbert Spencer calls a "system of completely unified knowledge." In the more modern sense, of something contrasted with the sciences, philosophy means "metaphysics." The older sense is the more worthy sense, and as the results of the sciences get more available for co-ordination, and the conditions for finding truth in different kinds of question get more methodically defined, we may hope that the term will revert to its original meaning. Science, metaphysics, and religion may then again form a single body of wisdom, and lend each other mutual support.

At present this hope is far from its fulfilment. I propose to take philosophy in the narrow sense of metaphysics, and to let both religion and the results of the sciences alone.

32

JOHN DEWEY
From Absolutism to Experimentalism

Before going to Johns Hopkins for graduate work, John Dewey (1859–1952) took a degree from the University of Vermont and taught high school. Influenced by his studies with Peirce, Stanley Hall, and G. S. Morris, he gave his Hegelian interests—the resolution of apparent experiential and conceptual conflicts in the constructive and constitutive activity of thought—a naturalistic and pragmatic twist. After teaching psychology and philosophy at the University of Michigan, he and George Herbert Mead moved to the University of Chicago, where their interdisciplinary work in pragmatic philosophy, psychology, and education led them to found an experimental elementary school. Dewey's influential *How We Think* (1910) and *Democracy and Education* (1916) developed a comprehensive theory of education that incorporated some of Peirce's epistemology, James' functionalist psychology, and Mead's social psychology.

After going to Columbia University in 1904, Dewey turned his attention to the logic of inquiry (*Essays in Experimental Logic* (1916) and *Logic: The Theory of Inquiry* (1938) treat inquiry as an instrumental activity directed to the resolution of experienced conflict. His philosophic scope included epistemology and metaphysics: *Human Nature and Conduct* (1922), *Experience and Nature* (1925). His naturalism extended to value theory: *Art and Experience* (1934), *A Common Faith* (1934), and *Theory of Valuation* (1939).

Dewey was politically active throughout his life. He took special interest in democratic theory and the pivotal role of education in the continuous extension of liberal democracy. He lectured in China and Japan, visited schools in the Soviet Union, helped found the New School for Social Research, and went to Mexico to review the procedures of the Trotsky trials.

From Absolutism to Experimentalism

In the late 'seventies, when I was an undergraduate, "electives" were still unknown in the smaller New England colleges. But in the one I attended, the University of Vermont, the tradition of a "senior-year course" still subsisted. This course was regarded as a kind of intellectual coping to the structure erected in earlier years, or, at least, as an insertion of the keystone of the arch. It included courses in political economy, international law, history of civilization (Guizot), psychology, ethics, philosophy of religion (Butler's *Analogy*), logic, etc., not history of philosophy, save incidentally. The enumeration of these titles may not serve the purpose for which it is made; but the idea was that after three years of somewhat specialized study in languages and sciences, the last year was reserved for an introduction into serious intellectual topics of wide and deep significance—an introduction into the world of ideas. I doubt if in many cases it served its alleged end; however, it fell in with my own inclinations, and I have always been grateful for that year of my schooling. There was, however, one course in the previous year that had excited a taste that in retrospect may be called philosophical. That was a rather short course, without laboratory work, in Physiology, a book of Huxley's being the text. It is difficult to speak with exactitude about what happened to me intellectually so many years ago, but I have an impression that there was derived from that study a sense of interdependence and interrelated unity that gave form to intellectual stirrings that had been previously inchoate, and created a kind of type or model of a view of things to which material in any field ought to conform. Subconsciously, at least, I was led to desire a world and a life that would have the same properties as had the human organism in the picture of it derived from study of Huxley's treatment. At all events, I got great stimulation from the study, more than from anything I had had contact with before; and as no desire was awakened in me to continue that particular branch of learning, I date from this time the awakening of a distinctive philosophic interest.

The University of Vermont rather prided itself upon its tradition in philosophy. One of its earlier teachers, Dr. Marsh, was almost the first person in the United States to venture upon the speculative and dubiously orthodox seas of German thinking—that of Kant, Schelling, and Hegel. The venture, to be sure, was made largely by way of Coleridge; Marsh edited an American edition of Coleridge's *Aids to Reflection*. Even this degree of speculative generalization, in its somewhat obvious tendency to rationalize the body of Christian theological doctrines, created a flutter in ecclesiastical dovecots. In particular, a controversy was carried on between the Germanizing rationalizers and the orthodox representatives of the Scottish school of thought through the representatives of the latter at Princeton. I imagine—although it is a very long time since I have had any contact with this material—that the controversy still provides data for a section, if not a chapter, in the history of thought in this country.

Although the University retained pride in its pioneer work, and its atmosphere was for those days theologically "liberal"—of the Congregational type—the teaching of philosophy had become more restrained in tone, more influenced by the still dominant Scotch school. Its professor, Mr. H. A. P. Torrey, was a man of genuinely sensitive and cultivated mind, with marked esthetic interest and taste, which, in a more congenial atmosphere than that of northern New England in those days, would have achieved something significant. He was, however, constitutionally timid, and never really let his mind go. I recall that, in a conversation I had with him a few years after graduation, he said: "Undoubtedly pantheism is the most satisfactory form of metaphysics intellectually, but it goes counter to religious faith." I fancy that remark told of an inner conflict that prevented his native capacity from coming to full fruition. His interest in philosophy, however, was genuine, not perfunctory; he was an excellent teacher, and I owe to him a double debt, that of turning my thoughts definitely to the study of philosophy as a life-pursuit, and of a generous gift of time to me during a year devoted privately under his direction to a reading of classics in the history of philosophy and learning to read philosophic German. In our walks and talks during this year, after three years on my part of high-school teaching, he let his mind go much more freely than in the classroom, and revealed potentialities that might have placed him among the leaders in the development of a freer American philosophy—but the time for the latter had not yet come.

Teachers of philosophy were at that time, almost to a man, clergymen; the supposed requirements of religion, or theology, dominated the teaching of philosophy in most colleges. Just how and why Scotch philosophy lent itself so well to the exigencies of religion I cannot say; probably the causes were more extrinsic than intrinsic; but at all events there was a firm alliance established between religion and the cause of "intuition." It is probably impossible to recover at this date the almost sacrosanct air that enveloped the idea of intuitions; but somehow the cause of all holy and valuable things was supposed to stand or fall with the validity of intuitionalism; the only vital issue was that between intuitionalism and a sensational empiricism that explained away the reality of all higher objects. The story of this almost forgotten debate, once so urgent, is probably a factor in developing in me a certain scepticism about the depth and range of purely contemporary issues; it is likely that many of those which seem highly important to-day will also in a generation have receded to the status of the local and provincial. It also aided in generating a sense of the value of the history of philosophy; some of the claims made for this as a sole avenue of approach to the study of philosophic problems seem to me misdirected and injurious. But its value in giving perspective and a sense of proportion in relation to immediate contemporary issues can hardly be overestimated.

I do not mention this theological and intuitional phase because it had any lasting influence upon my own development, except negatively. I learned the terminology of an intuitional philosophy, but it did not go deep, and in no way did it satisfy what I was dimly reaching for. I was brought up in a conventionally evangelical atmosphere of the more "liberal" sort; and the struggles that later arose between acceptance of that faith and the discarding of traditional and institutional creeds came from personal experiences and not from the effects of philosophical teaching. It was not, in other words, in this respect that philosophy either appealed to me or influenced me—though I am not sure that Butler's *Analogy*, with its cold logic and acute analysis, was not, in a reversed way, a factor in developing "scepticism."

During the year of private study, of which mention has been made, I decided to make philosophy my life-study, and accordingly went to Johns Hopkins the next year (1884) to enter upon that new thing, "graduate work." It was something of a risk; the work offered there was almost the only indication that there were likely to be any self-supporting jobs in the field of philosophy for others than clergymen. Aside from the effect of my study with Professor Torrey, another influence moved me to undertake the risk. During the years after graduation I had kept up philosophical readings and I had even written a few articles which I sent to Dr. W. T. Harris, the well-known Hegelian, and the editor of the *Journal of Speculative Philosophy*, the only philosophic journal in the country at that time, as he and his group formed almost the only group of laymen devoted to philosophy for non-theological reasons. In sending an article I asked Dr. Harris for advice as to the possibility of my successfully prosecuting philosophic studies. His reply was so encouraging that it was a distinct factor in deciding me to try philosophy as a professional career.

The articles sent were, as I recall them, highly schematic and formal; they were couched in the language of intuitionalism; of Hegel I was then ignorant. My deeper interests had not as yet been met, and in the absence of subject-matter that would correspond to them, the only topics at my command were such as were capable of a merely formal treatment. I imagine that my development has been controlled largely by a struggle between a native inclination toward the schematic and formally logical, and those incidents of personal experience that compelled me to take account of actual material. Probably there is in the consciously articulated ideas of every thinker an over-weighting of just those things that are contrary to his natural tendencies, an emphasis upon those things that are contrary to his intrinsic bent, and which, therefore, he has to struggle to bring to expression, while the native bent, on the other hand, can take care of itself. Anyway, a case might be made out for the proposition that the emphasis upon the concrete, empirical, and "practical" in my later writings is partly due to considerations of this nature. It was a reaction against what was more natural, and it served as a protest and protection against something in myself which, in the pressure of the weight of actual experiences, I knew to be a weakness. It is, I suppose, becoming a commonplace that when anyone is unduly concerned with controversy, the remarks that seem to be directed against others are really concerned with a struggle that is going on inside himself. The marks, the stigmata, of the struggle to weld together the characteristics of a formal, theoretic interest and the material of a maturing experience of contacts with realities also showed themselves, naturally, in style of writing and manner of presentation. During the time when the schematic interest predominated, writing was comparatively easy; there were even compliments upon the clearness of my style. Since then thinking and writing have been hard work. It is easy to give way to the dialectic development of a theme; the pressure of concrete experiences was, however, sufficiently heavy, so that a sense of intellectual honesty prevented a surrender to that course. But, on the other hand, the formal interest persisted, so that there was an inner demand for an intellectual technique that would be consistent and yet capable of flexible adaptation to the concrete diversity of experienced things. It is hardly necessary to say that I have not been among those to whom the union of abilities to satisfy these two opposed requirements, the formal and the material, came easily. For that very reason I have been acutely aware, too much so, doubtless, of a tendency of other thinkers and writers to achieve a specious lucidity and simplicity by the mere process of ignoring considerations which a greater respect for concrete materials of experience would have forced upon them.

It is a commonplace of educational history that the opening of Johns Hopkins University marked a new epoch in higher education in the United States. We are probably not in a condition as yet to estimate the extent to which its foundation and the development of graduate schools in other universities, following its example, mark a turn in our American culture. The 'eighties and 'nineties seem to mark the definitive close of our pioneer period, and the turn from the civil war era into the new industrialized and commercial age. In philosophy, at least, the influence of Johns Hopkins was not due to the size of the provision that was made. There was a half-year of lecturing and seminar work given by Professor George Sylvester Morris, of the University of Michigan; belief in the "demonstrated" (a favorite word of his) truth of the substance of German idealism, and of belief in its competency to give direction to a life of aspiring thought, emotion, and action. I have never known a more single-hearted and whole-souled man— a man of a single piece all the way through; while I long since deviated from his philosophic faith, I should be happy to believe that the influence of the spirit of his teaching has been an enduring influence.

While it was impossible that a young and impressionable student, unacquainted with any system of thought that satisfied his head and heart, should not have been deeply affected, to the point of at least a temporary conversion, by the enthusiastic and scholarly devotion of Mr. Morris, this effect was far from being the only source of my own "Hegelianism." The 'eighties and 'nineties were a time of new ferment in English thought; the reaction against atomic individualism and sensationalistic empiricism was in full swing. It was the time of Thomas Hill Green, of the two Cairds, of Wallace, of the appearance of the *Essays in Philosophical Criticism*, cooperatively produced by a younger group under the leadership of the late Lord Haldane. This movement was at the time the vital and constructive one in philosophy. Naturally its influence fell in with and reinforced that of Professor Morris. There was but one marked difference, and that, I think, was in favor of Mr. Morris. He came to Kant through Hegel instead of to Hegel by way of Kant, so that his attitude toward Kant was the critical one expressed by Hegel himself. Moreover, he retained something of his early Scotch philosophical training in a common-sense belief in the existence of the external world. He used to make merry over those who thought the *existence* of this world and of matter were things to be proved by philosophy. To him the only philosophical question was as to the *meaning* of this existence; his idealism was wholly of the objective type. Like his contemporary, Professor John Watson, of Kingston, he combined a logical and idealistic metaphysics with a realistic epistemology. Through his teacher at Berlin, Trendelenburg, he had acquired a great reverence for Aristotle, and he had no difficulty in uniting Aristoteleanism with Hegelianism.

There were, however, also "subjective" reasons for the appeal that Hegel's thought made to me; it supplied a demand for unification that was doubtless an intense emotional craving, and yet was a hunger that only an intellectualized subject-matter could satisfy. It is more than difficult, it is impossible, to recover that early mood. But the sense of divisions and separations that were, I suppose, borne in upon me as a consequence of a heritage of New England culture, divisions by way of isolation of self from the world, of soul from body, of nature from God, brought a painful oppression—or, rather, they were an inward laceration. My earlier philosophic study had been an intellectual gymnastic. Hegel's synthesis of subject and object, matter and spirit, the divine and the human, was, however, no mere intellectual formula; it operated as an immense release, a liberation. Hegel's treatment of human culture, of institutions and the arts, involved the same dissolution of hard-and-fast dividing walls, and had a special attraction for me.

As I have already intimated, while the conflict of traditional religious beliefs with opinions that I could myself honestly entertain was the source of a trying personal crisis, it did not at any time constitute a leading philosophical problem. This might look as if the two things were kept apart; in reality it was due to a feeling that any genuinely sound religious experience could and should adapt itself to whatever beliefs one found oneself intellectually entitled to hold—a half unconscious sense at first, but one which ensuing years have deepened into a fundamental conviction. In consequence, while I have, I hope, a due degree of personal sympathy with individuals who are undergoing the throes of a personal change of attitude, I have not been able to attach much importance to religion as a philosophic problem; for the effect of that attachment seems to be in the end a subornation of candid philosophic thinking to the alleged but factitious needs of some special set of convictions. I have enough faith in the depth of the religious tendencies of men to believe that they will adapt themselves to any required intellectual change, and that it is futile (and likely to be dishonest) to forecast prematurely just what forms the religious interest will take as a final consequence of the great intellectual transformation that is going on. As I have been frequently criticized for undue reticence about the problems of religion, I insert this explanation: it seems to me that the great solicitude of many persons, professing belief in the universality of the need for religion, about the present and future of religion proves that in fact they are moved more by partisan interest in a particular religion than by interest in religious experience.

The chief reason, however, for inserting these remarks at this point is to bring out a contrast effect. Social interests and problems from an early period had to me the intellectual appeal and provided the intellectual sustenance that many seem to have found primarily in religious questions. In undergraduate days I had run across, in the college library, Harriet Martineau's exposition of Comte. I cannot remember that his law of "the three stages" affected me particularly; but his idea of the disorganized character of Western modern culture, due to a disintegrative "individualism," and his idea of a synthesis of science that should be a regulative method of an organized social life, impressed me deeply. I found, as I thought, the same criticisms combined with a deeper and more far-reaching integration in Hegel. I did not, in those days when I read Francis Bacon, detect the origin of the Comtean idea in him, and I had not made acquaintance with Condorcet, the connecting link.

I drifted away from Hegelianism in the next fifteen years; the word "drifting" expresses the slow and, for a long time, imperceptible character of the movement, though it does not convey the impression that there was an adequate cause for the change. Nevertheless I should never think of ignoring, much less denying, what an astute critic occasionally refers to as a novel discovery—that acquaintance with Hegel has left a permanent deposit in my thinking. The form, the schematism, of his system now seems to me artificial to the last degree. But in the content of his ideas there is often an extraordinary depth; in many of his analyses, taken out of their mechanical dialectical setting, an extraordinary acuteness. Were it possible for me to be a devotee of any system, I still should believe that there is greater richness and greater variety of insight in Hegel than in any other single systematic philosopher—though when I say this I exclude Plato, who still provides my favorite philosophic reading. For I am unable to find in him that all-comprehensive and overriding system which later interpretation has, as it seems to me, conferred upon him as a dubious boon. The ancient sceptics overworked another aspect of Plato's thought when they treated him as their spiritual father, but they were nearer the truth, I think, than those who force him into the frame of a rigidly systematized doctrine. Although I have not the aversion to system as such that is sometimes attributed to me, I am dubious of my own ability to reach inclusive systematic unity, and in consequence, perhaps, of that fact also dubious about my contemporaries. Nothing could be more helpful to present philosophizing than a "Back to Plato" movement; but it would have to be back to the dramatic, restless, cooperatively inquiring Plato of the *Dialogues*, trying one mode of attack after another to see what it might yield; back to the Plato whose highest flight of metaphysics always terminated with a social and practical turn, and not to the artificial Plato constructed by unimaginative commentators who treat him as the original university professor.

The rest of the story of my intellectual development I am unable to record without more faking than I care to indulge in. What I have so far related is so far removed in time that I can talk about myself as another person; and much has faded, so that a few points stand out without my having to force them into the foreground. The philosopher, if I may apply that word to myself, that I became as I moved away from German idealism, is too much the self that I still am and is still too much in process of change to lend itself to record. I envy, up to a certain point, those who can write their intellectual biography in a unified pattern, woven out of a few distinctly discernible strands of interest and influence. By contrast, I seem to be unstable, chameleon-like, yielding one after another to many diverse and even incompatible influences; struggling to assimilate something from each and yet striving to carry it forward in a way that is logically consistent with what has been learned from its predecessors. Upon the whole, the forces that have influenced me have come from persons and from situations more than from books—not that I have not, I hope, learned a great deal from philosophical writings, but that what I have learned from them has been technical in comparison with what I have been forced to think upon and about because of some experience in which I found myself entangled. It is for this reason that I cannot say with candor that I envy completely, or envy beyond a certain point, those to whom I have referred. I like to think, though it may be a defense reaction, that with all the inconveniences of the road I have been forced to travel, it has the compensatory advantage of not inducing an immunity of thoughts to experiences—which perhaps, after all, should not be treated even by a philosopher as the germ of a disease to which he needs to develop resistance.

While I cannot write an account of intellectual development without giving it the semblance of a continuity that it does not in fact own, there are four special points that seem to stand out. One is the importance that the practice and theory of education have had for me: especially the education of the young, for I have never been able to feel much optimism regarding the possibilities of "higher" education when it is built upon warped and weak foundations. This interest fused with and brought together what might otherwise have been separate interests—that in psychology and that in social institutions and social life. I can recall but one critic who has suggested that my thinking has been too much permeated by interest in education. Although a book called *Democracy and Education* was for many years that in which my philosophy, such as it is, was most fully expounded, I do not know that philosophic critics, as distinct from teachers, have ever had recourse to it. I have wondered whether such facts signified that philosophers in general, although they are themselves usually teachers, have not taken education with sufficient seriousness for it to occur to them that any rational person could actually think it possible that philosophizing should focus about education as the supreme human interest in which, moreover, other problems, cosmological, moral, logical, come to a head. At all events, this handle is offered to any subsequent critic who may wish to lay hold of it.

A second point is that as my study and thinking progressed, I became more and more troubled by the intellectual scandal that seemed to me involved in the current (and traditional) dualism in logical standpoint and method between something called "science" on the one hand and something called "morals" on the other. I have long felt that the construction of a logic, that is, a method of effective inquiry, which would apply without abrupt breach of continuity to the fields designated by both of these words, is at once our needed theoretical solvent and the supply of our greatest practical want. This belief has had much more to do with the development of what I termed, for lack of a better word, "instrumentalism," than have most of the reasons that have been assigned.

The third point forms the great exception to what was said about no very fundamental vital influence issuing from books; it concerns the influence of William James. As far as I can discover one specifiable philosophic factor which entered into my thinking so as to give it a new direction and quality, it is this one. To say that it proceeded from his *Psychology* rather than from the essays collected in the volume called *Will to Believe*, his *Pluralistic Universe*, or *Pragmatism*, is to say something that needs explanation. For there are, I think, two unreconciled strains in the *Psychology*. One is found in the adoption of the subjective tenor of prior psychological tradition; even when the special tenets of that tradition are radically criticized, an underlying subjectivism is retained, at least in vocabulary—and the difficulty in finding a vocabulary which will intelligibly convey a genuinely new idea is perhaps the obstacle that most retards the easy progress of philosophy. I may cite as an illustration the substitution of the "stream of consciousness" for discrete elementary states: the advance made was enormous. Nevertheless the point of view remained that of a realm of consciousness set off by itself. The other strain is objective, having its roots in a return to the earlier biological conception of the *psyche*, but a return possessed of a new force and value due to the immense progress made by biology since the time of Aristotle. I doubt if we have as yet begun to realize all that is due to William James for the introduction and use of this idea; as I have already intimated, I do not think that he fully and consistently realized it himself. Anyway, it worked its way more and more into all my ideas and acted as a ferment to transform old beliefs.

If this biological conception and mode of approach had been prematurely hardened by James, its effect might have been merely to substitute one schematism for another. But it is not tautology to say that James's sense of life was itself vital. He had a profound sense, in origin artistic and moral, perhaps, rather than "scientific," of the difference between the categories of the living and of the mechanical; some time, I think, someone may write an essay that will show how the most distinctive factors in his general philosophic view, pluralism, novelty, freedom, individuality, are all connected with his feeling for the qualities and traits of that which lives. Many philosophers have had much to say about the idea of organism; but they have taken it structurally and hence statically. It was reserved for James to think of life in terms of life in action. This point, and that about the objective biological factor in James's conception of thought (discrimination, abstraction, conception, generalization), is fundamental when the role of psychology in philosophy comes under consideration. It is true that the effect of its introduction into philosophy has often, usually, been to dilute and distort the latter. But that is because the psychology was bad psychology.

I do not mean that I think that in the end the connection of psychology with philosophy is, in the abstract, closer than is that of other branches of science. Logically it stands on the same plane with them. But historically and at the present juncture the revolution introduced by James had, and still has, a peculiar significance. On the negative side it is important, for it is indispensable as a purge of the heavy charge of bad psychology that is so embedded in the philosophical tradition that it is not generally recognized to be psychology at all. As an example, I would say that the problem of "sense data," which occupies such a great bulk in recent British thinking, has to my mind no significance other than as a survival of an old and outworn psychological doctrine—although those who deal with the problem are for the most part among those who stoutly assert the complete irrelevance of psychology to philosophy. On the positive side we have the obverse of this situation. The newer objective psychology supplies the easiest way, pedagogically if not in the abstract, by which to reach a fruitful conception of thought and its work, and thus to better our logical theories—provided thought and logic have anything to do with one another. And in the present state of men's minds the linking of philosophy to the significant issues of actual experience is facilitated by constant interaction with the methods and conclusions of psychology. The more abstract sciences, mathematics and physics, for example, have left their impress deep upon traditional philosophy. The former, in connection with an exaggerated anxiety about formal certainty, has more than once operated to divorce philosophic thinking from connection with questions that have a source in existence. The remoteness of psychology from such abstractions, its nearness to what is distinctively human, gives it an emphatic claim for a sympathetic hearing at the present time.

In connection with an increasing recognition of this human aspect, there developed the influence which forms the fourth heading of this recital. The objective biological approach of the Jamesian psychology led straight to the perception of the importance of distinctive social categories, especially communication and participation. It is my conviction that a great deal of our philosophizing needs to be done over again from this point of view, and that there will ultimately result an integrated synthesis in a philosophy congruous with modern science and related to actual needs in education, morals, and religion. One has to take a broad survey in detachment from immediate prepossessions to realize the extent to which the characteristic traits of the science of to-day are connected with the development of social subjects—anthropology, history, politics, economics, language and literature, social and abnormal psychology, and so on. The movement is both so new, in an intellectual sense, and we are so much of it and it so much of us, that it escapes definite notice. Technically the influence of mathematics upon philosophy is more obvious; the great change that has taken place in recent years in the ruling ideas and methods of the physical sciences attracts attention much more easily than does the growth of the social subjects, just because it is farther away from impact upon us. Intellectual prophecy is dangerous; but if I read the cultural signs of the times aright, the next synthetic movement in philosophy will emerge when the significance of the social sciences and arts has become an object of reflective attention in the same way that mathematical and physical sciences have been made the objects of thought in the past, and when their full import is grasped. If I read these signs wrongly, nevertheless the statement may stand as a token of a factor significant in my own intellectual development.

In any case, I think it shows a deplorable deadness of imagination to suppose that philosophy will indefinitely revolve within the scope of the problems and systems that two thousand years of European history have bequeathed to us. Seen in the long perspective of the future, the whole of western European history is a provincial episode. I do not expect to see in my day a genuine, as distinct from a forced and artificial, integration of thought. But a mind that is not too egotistically impatient can have faith that this unification will issue in its season. Meantime a chief task of those who call themselves philosophers is to help get rid of the useless lumber that blocks our highways of thought, and strive to make straight and open the paths that lead to the future. Forty years spent in wandering in a wilderness like that of the present is not a sad fate—unless one attempts to make himself believe that the wilderness is after all itself the promised land.

33

GEORGE SANTAYANA
My Host the World

The son of a Spanish father and a Boston mother, George Santayana (1863–1952) came to the United States as a child. After attending the Boston Latin School and Harvard University, he went to Germany to study Plato and idealism. On returning to Harvard, he worked with William James and wrote a thesis on Lotze. He remarked that James had succeeded in making him a naturalist without making him a pragmatist. Remnants of his Platonic studies are manifest in his early work, *The Sense of Beauty* (1896) and *The Life of Reason* (1905–1906), in which he developed the view that artistic creativity is the primary human activity. He regarded society, religion, and even science and philosophy are expressions of that exuberance. In his four-volume *The Realms of Being* (1927–1940) he attempted to reconcile his naturalism with Platonic idealism, analyzing the relation among (what he called) the four realms of being: essence, matter, spirit, and truth.

Santayana taught at Harvard until 1912, when he retired to live in England, Paris, and Rome. Besides occasionally writing poetry, he also wrote a much acclaimed novel, *The Last Puritan* (1935), a subtle and nuanced account of the social and intellectual life of Boston Brahmins.

Persons and Places

The great master of sympathy with nature, in my education, was Lucretius. Romantic poets and philosophers, when they talk of nature, mean only landscape or other impressions due to aerial perspectives, sensuous harmonies of colour or form, or vital intoxications, such as those of riding, sea-faring, or mountain-climbing. Nature is loved for heightening self-consciousness and prized for ministering to human comfort and luxury, but is otherwise ignored as contemptible, dead, or non-existent. Or when people's temper is hardy and pugnacious, they may require nature as a buffer on which to rain their mighty blows and carve their important initials. Where human strength comes from or what ends human existence might serve, they neither know nor care.

The spirit in me felt itself cast upon this social and political world somewhat like Robinson Crusoe upon his island. We were both creatures of the same Great Nature; and my world, in its geography and astronomy, like Robinson Crusoe's island, had much more massive and ancient foundations than the small utterly insecure waif that had been wrecked upon it. In its social and political structure, however, my world was more like Crusoe's energetic person: for my island was densely inhabited: an ugly town, a stinted family, a common school; and the most troublesome and inescapable of its denizens was the particular body in which my spirit found itself rooted; so rooted that it became doubtful whether that body with its feelings and actions was not my true self, rather than this invisible spirit which they oppressed. I seemed to be both; and yet this compulsive and self-tormenting creature called "Me" was more odious and cruel to the "I" within than were the sea and sky, the woods and mountains, or the very cities and crowds of people that this animal "Me" moved among: for the spirit in me was happy and free ranging through that world, but troubled and captive in its close biological integument.

This is the double conflict, the social opposition and the moral agony, that spirit suffers by being incarnate; and yet if it were not incarnate it could not be individual, with a situation in space and time, a language and special perspective over nature and history: indeed, if not incarnate, spirit could not *exist* at all or be the inner light and perpetual witness of *life* in its dramatic vicissitudes.

If it be the fate of all spirit to live in a special body and a special age, and yet, for its vocation and proper life, to be addressed from that centre to all life and to all being, I can understand why I have been more sensible to this plight and to this mission than were most of my contemporaries. For by chance I was a foreigner where I was educated; and although the new language and customs interested me and gave me no serious trouble, yet speculatively and emotionally, especially in regard to religion, the world around me was utterly undigestible. The times also were moving, rapidly and exultingly, towards what for me was chaos and universal triviality. At first these discords sounded like distant thunder. Externally they were not yet violent; the world smiled in my eyes as I came to manhood, and the beauties and dignity of the past made the present unimportant. And as the feeling of being a stranger and an exile by nature as well as by accident grew upon me in time, it came to be almost a point of pride; some people may have thought it an affectation. It was not that; I have always admired the normal child of his age and country. My case was humanly unfortunate and involved many defects; yet it opened to me another vocation, not better (I admit no absolute standards) but more speculative, freer, juster, and for me happier.

I had always dreamt of travel, and it was oftenest in the voluntary, interested, appreciative rôle of the traveller that I felt myself most honest in my dealings with my environment. The world was My Host; I was a temporary guest in his busy and animated establishment. We met as strangers; yet each had generic and well-grounded ideas of what could be expected of the other. First impressions made these expectations more precise; the inn was habitable; the guest was presumably solvent. We might prove mutually useful. My I lost and I could become friends, diplomatically; but we were not akin in either our interests or our powers. The normal economy of an innkeeper, though incidentally and in a measure it supplies the wants of his guests, knows nothing of their private moral economy. Their tastes in wines, in service, or in music may entirely outrun or contradict his long-established practice, which he will impose on his guests with all the authority of a landlord; and there may not be another inn in the place, or only worse ones. The guest has no right to demand what is not provided. He must be thankful for any little concessions that may be made to his personal tastes, if he is tactful and moderate in his requirements, pays his bills promptly and gives decent tips.

Such at least was the case in the nineteenth century when the world made itself pleasant to the traveller; and not to rich travellers only but to the most modest, and even to the very poor in their little purchases and popular feasts. Personal freedom produced a certain dignity and good humour even in bargaining; for to buy and sell, to patronise a shop or a boarding-house, was an act of kindness; and bills, at least in civilly commercial England, were always receipted "with thanks." Having lived a peaceful independent life, free from hardship or misfortune, I have found it easy to conform externally with the mechanism of society. Matter has been kind to me, and I am a lover of matter. Not only aesthetically but dynamically, as felt by Lucretius, nature to me is a welcome presence; and modern progress in mechanical invention and industrial luxury has excited joyously my materialistic imagination, as it did prophetically that of Bacon. Moreover, I inherited from my father a bond with matter which Bacon and Lucretius probably did not feel: the love of employing leisure in small mechanical occupations. I should never have read and written so much if the physical side of these employments had not been congenial to me and rich with a quiet happiness. Any common surroundings and any commonplace people pleased me well enough; it was only when sugary rapture was demanded about them or by them, as happened almost everywhere in my youth, that my stomach rose in radical protest. Then I discovered how much the human world of my time had become the enemy of spirit and therefore of its own light and peace.

How had this happened? Not at all as lovers of antiquity or of the middle ages seem to think, because of mechanical inventions or natural sciences or loss of Christian faith. These transformations might all have occurred in the normal growth of society. Variety in cultures is not due to aberrations any more than is the variety of animal species. But there may be aberration in any species or any culture when it becomes *vicious;* that is, when it forms habits destructive of its health and of its ability to prosper in its environment. Now modern sciences and inventions are not vicious in this sense; on the contrary, they bring notable additions to human *virtù* . And I think that the Renaissance, with the historical learning and humanism which it fostered, was also a great gain for human happiness and self-knowledge. Of this the surface of the modern world during my youth gave continual evidence, in spite of an undercurrent of unrest and disaffection sometimes heard rumbling below. "My Host's" establishment made a brave appearance; and I was particularly conscious of many new facilities of travel, breadth of information, and cosmopolitan convenience and luxury. Though there was no longer any dignity in manners, or much distinction in costume, fashion had not lost all its charm. In literature and the fine arts talent could give pleasure by its expertness, if not by its taste or savour. I have described how in Boston and in England I sometimes sipped at the rim of the plutocratic cup; and this was a real pleasure, because beneath the delicacy of the material feast there was a lot of shrewd experience in that society, and of placid kindness.

There was another cosmopolitan circle, however, less select and less worldly, but no less entertaining and no less subject to fashion and to ironical gossip, the Intellectuals, into whose company I was sometimes drawn. I was officially one of them, yet they felt in their bones that I might be secretly a traitor. "Ah, yes," cried a distinguished Jesuit recently when I was casually mentioned, "he is the *poetical* atheist." And an Italian professor, also a Catholic but tinged with German idealism, remarked of me: "the trouble with him is that he has never succeeded in outgrowing materialism." Finally, a faithful diehard of British psychologism, asked why I was overlooked among contemporary philosophers, replied: "Because he has no originality. Everything in him is drawn from Plato and Leibnitz." This critical band is democratic in that it recognises no official authority and lets fluid public opinion carry the day; yet it is, on principle, in each man, private and independent in judgment. Few, however, have much time to read originals or to study facts. Leaders and busybodies must obey their momentum. A personal reaction on what other people say is socially sufficient; it will do for the press; and it will corroborate the critic's opinion in his own eyes.

I cannot overcome a settled distrust of merely intellectual accomplishment, militant in the void. I prefer common virtues and current beliefs, even if intellectually prejudiced and simple, when the great generative order of nature has bred them, and lent them its weight and honesty. For I do not rebel in the least at political and moral mutations when this same generative order brings them about spontaneously; for it is then on the side of change that clear intelligence discerns the lesser danger and the wider interests. I should have loved the Gracchi; but not the belated Cato or the belated Brutus. All four were martyrs; but the first two spoke for the poor, for the suffering half of the people, oppressed by a shortsighted power that neglected its responsibilities; while the last two were conceited idealogues, jealous of their traditional rights, and utterly blind to destiny. If I were not too old and could venture to write in French, I should compose a short history of *Les Faux Pas de la Philosophie*; by which title I should not refer to *innocent* errors, with which all human speculation must be infected, nor to the symbolic or mythological form of the wisest wisdom, but only to militant heresies and self-contradictions due to wilful conceit, individual or tribal, verbal or moral; and there is little in European philosophy that is not infected with these *unnecessary* errors. Let the reader compose his own catalogue of these blind alleys explored by the ancients and by the moderns; since this is a biographical book, I will limit myself to the first and principal *Faux Pas* that the world has seemed to me to have taken in my time.

The contemporary world has turned its back on the attempt and even on the desire to live reasonably. The two great wars (so far) of the twentieth century were adventures in enthusiastic unreason. They were inspired by unnecessary and impracticable ambitions; and the "League" and the "United Nations," feebly set up by the victors, were so irrationally conceived that they at once reduced their victory to a stalemate. What is required for living rationally? I think the conditions may be reduced to two: First, self-knowledge, the Socratic key to wisdom; and second, sufficient knowledge of the world to perceive what alternatives are open to you and which of them are favourable to your true interests.

Now the contemporary world has plenty of knowledge of nature for its purposes, but its purposes show a positively insane abandonment of its true interests. You may say that the proletariat knows its interests perfectly; they are to work less and to earn more. Those are indeed its interests so long as it remains a proletariat: but to be a proletariat is an inhuman condition. Proletarians are human beings, and their first interest is to have a home, a family, a chosen trade, and freedom in practising it. And more particularly a man's true interest may exceptionally be not to have those things, but to wander alone like the rhinoceros; or perhaps to have a very special kind of home, family and occupation. There must be freedom of movement and vocation. There must be *Lebensraum* for the spirit.

There have always been beggars and paupers in the world, because there is bound to be a margin of the unfit, too bad or too good to keep in step with any well organised society; but that the great body of mankind should sink into a proletariat has been an unhappy effect of the monstrous growth of cities, made possible by the concentration of trade and the multiplication of industries, mechanised, and swelling into monopolies.

The natural state of mankind, before foreign conquerors dominate it or native ideologues reform it, is full of incidental evils; prophets have ample cause for special denunciations and warnings; yet there is, as in all animal economy, a certain nucleus of self-preserving instincts and habits, a normal constitution of society. Nature with its gods is the landlord of whose fields and woods they are local and temporary tenants; and with this invincible power they make prudent and far-seeing covenants. They know what is for their good and by what arts it might be secured. They live by agriculture, the hunting or breeding of animals, and such domestic arts as their climate and taste lead them to cultivate; and when a quarrel arises among them, or with strangers, they battle to preserve or to restore their free life, without more ambitious intentions. They are materially and morally rooted in the earth, bred in one land or one city. They are *civilised*. Wandering nations, with nothing of their own and working havoc wherever they go, are *barbarians*. Such "barbarians" were the proletariat of antiquity. When they occupied some civilised region without exterminating the natives, and established in the old strongholds a permanent foreign domination, they became half-civilised themselves, without shedding altogether the predatory and adventurous practices of their ancestors. This is the compound origin and nature of modern Western governments.

Varied, picturesque, and romantic mixtures of civilisation beneath and barbarism above have filled the history of Christendom, and produced beautiful transient arts, in which there was too little wisdom and too much fancy and fashion: think of Gothic architecture, or of manners, dress, poetry, and philosophy from the middle ages to our day. Civilisation had become more enterprising, plastic, and irresponsible, while barbarism seemed to retreat into sports, and into legal extravagances in thought and action. Intellectual chaos and political folly could thus come to co-exist strangely with an irresistible dominance of mechanical industry. The science that served this industrial progress by no means brought moral enlightenment. It merely enlarged acquaintance with phenomena and enabled clever inventors to construct all sorts of useful or superfluous machines. At first perhaps it was expected that science would make all mankind both rich and free from material cares (two contradictory hopes) and would at the same time enlighten them at last about the nature of things, including their own nature, so that adequate practical wisdom would be secured together with fabulous material well-being.

This is the dream of the moderns, on which I found My Host boastfully running his establishment. He expected his guests also to act accordingly and to befuddle and jollify one another, so that all should convince themselves that they were perfectly happy and should advertise their Host's business wherever they went. Such forced enterprise, forced confidence, and forced satisfaction would never have sprung from domestic arts or common knowledge spontaneously extended. It was all artificial and strained, marking the inhuman domination of some militant class or sect. This society lacked altogether that essential trait of rational living, to have a clear, sanctioned, ultimate aim. The cry was for vacant freedom and indeterminate progress: *Vorwärts*! Avanti! Onward! Full speed ahead! without asking whether directly before you was not a bottomless pit.

This has been the peculiar malady of my times. I saw the outbreak of it in my boyhood, and I have lived to see what seem clear symptoms of its end. The Great Merchants of my parents' youth had known nothing of it on their blue-sea voyages round Cape Horn or the Cape of Good Hope. Their good hope had been to amass a great fortune in fifteen or twenty years, and return home to bring up a blooming family in splendour and peace. They foresaw an orderly diffused well-being spreading out from them over all mankind. The fountains of happiness were ready to flow in every heart and mind if only people were suffered to have their own way materially and socially. That the masses would crowd out, exclude, indoctrinate, enslave, and destroy one another could not cross their genial and innocent minds, as they skimmed those immense oceans in their tight, strictly disciplined, white-sailed little craft.

Alas! The healthy growth of science and commerce had been crossed, long before the rise of the Great Merchants, by an insidious moral and political revolution. From the earliest times there have been militant spirits not content with inevitable changes and with occasional wars between neighbouring states, not usually wars of conquest or eternal hatred, but collisions in readjusting the political equilibrium between nations when their actual relations were no longer the same. Indeed, the tragic causes of conflict and ruin in civilizations are fundamentally internal to each society. A whole city or state may sometimes be destroyed, like Carthage: but history, then, comes to an end for that particular society, and the others continue their course as if their vanished rival had never existed. This course may be cut short, however, by internal disruption and suicidal revolutions. Every generation is born as ignorant and wilful as the first man; and when tradition has lost its obvious fitness or numinous authority, eager minds will revert without knowing it to every false hope and blind alley that had tempted their predecessors long since buried under layer upon layer of ruins. And these eager minds may easily become leaders; for society is never perfect; grievances and misfortunes perpetually breed rebellion in the oppressed heart; and the eloquent imagination of youth and of indignation will find the right words to blow the discontent, always smouldering, into sudden flame. Often things as they are become intolerable; there must be insurrection at any cost, as when the established order is not only casually oppressive, but ideally perverse and due to some previous epidemic of militant madness become constitutional. Against that domination, established in wilful indifference to the true good of man and to his possibilities, any political nostrum, proposed with the same rashness, will be accepted with the same faith. Thus the blind in extirpating the mad may plant a new madness.

That this is the present state of the world everyone can see by looking about him, or reading the newspapers; but I think that the elements in this crisis have been working in the body-politic for ages; ever since the Reformation, not to say since the age of the Greek Sophists and of Socrates. For the virulent cause of this long fever is subjectivism, egotism, conceit of mind. Not that culture of the conscience and even the logical refinements of dialectic are anything but good for the mind itself and for moral self-knowledge, which is one of the two conditions that I have assigned to political sanity; but the same logical arts are fatal if they are used to construct, by way of a moral fable, an anthropomorphic picture of the universe given out for scientific truth and imposed on mankind by propaganda, by threats, and by persecution. And this militant method of reforming mankind by misrepresenting their capacities and their place in the universe is no merely ancient or mediaeval delusion. It is the official and intolerant method of our most zealous contemporary prophets and reformers. Barbarism has adopted the weapons of flattery and prophecy. Merciless irrational ambition has borrowed the language of brotherly love.

The very fact, however, that these evils have deep roots and have long existed without destroying Western civilisation, but on the contrary have stimulated its contrary virtues and confused arts—this very fact seems to me to counsel calmness in contemplating the future. Those who look for a panacea will not find it. Those who advise resignation to a life of industrial slavery (because spiritual virtues may be cultivated by a slave, like Epictetus, more easily perhaps than by rich men) are surrendering the political future to an artificial militant regime that cannot last unaltered for a decade anywhere, and could hardly last a day, if by military force it were ever made universal. The fanaticism of all parties must be allowed to burn down to ashes, like a fire out of control. If it survives, it will be only because it will have humanised itself, reduced its dogmas to harmless metaphors, and sunk down a tap-root, to feed it, into the dark damp depths of mother earth. The economy of nature includes all particular movements, combines and transforms them all, but never diverts its wider processes to render them obedient to the prescriptions of human rhetoric. Things have their day, and their beauties in that day. It would be preposterous to expect any one civilisation to last forever.

Had it happened in my time (as by chance it did happen) that my landlord should give me notice that he was about to pull down his roof over my head, I might have been a little troubled for a moment; but presently I should have begun to look for other lodgings not without a certain curious pleasure, and probably should have found some (as I did, and better ones) in which to end my days. So, I am confident, will the travelling Spirit do—this ever-renewed witness, victim, and judge of existence, divine yet born of woman. Obediently it will learn other affections in other places, unite other friends, and divide other peoples; and the failure of over-exact hopes and overweening ambitions will not prevent spirit from continually turning the passing virtues and sorrows of nature into glimpses of eternal truth.

34

BERTRAND RUSSELL
Why I Became a Philosopher

Bertrand Russell (1872–1970) was the (secular) godson of John Stuart Mill and the grandson of Lord John Russell, who introduced the Reform Bill of 1832. Orphaned at an early age, his education was directed by his grandmother, who had him privately tutored until he went to Cambridge to do mathematics and philosophy. After rejecting the influence of the British idealism of McTaggart and Bradley, he focused on mathematics and the philosophy of logic (*Principles of Mathematics*, 1903). With A. N. Whitehead, he wrote the seminal formalization of the unity of logic and mathematics, *Principia Mathematica* (1910–1913). Remarkably capable of self-criticism, Russell continuously developed and changed his views. Having started as a realist (*Principles of Mathematics*, 1903), he came to think of that position as vacuous. His theory of description and logically proper names eventually led him to logical atomism ("On Denoting," 1905) and logical constructionism (*Our Knowledge of the External World* (1914)). When he was appointed as a lecturer at Cambridge in 1910, his interest in empiricist epistemology led him to attempt to construct a modified version of phenomentalism, one that could support a sophisticated physics. But the theory of constitutive sensibilia developed in *Our Knowledge of the External World* was replaced by a theory of constitutive complex events in *The Analysis of Matter* (1927). Russell's foundationalist views were again modified in *Human Knowledge: Its Scope and Limits* (1948): the direct realism of perceptual knowledge was replaced by fallibilism.

Russell's interest in ethics extended to political and social activism. He ran for Parliament in 1907, supported women's suffrage, and founded a progressive experimental school in 1931. Imprisoned for his pacifism in 1918, Russell was dismissed from Trinity College for atheism and radical socialist views. He originally supported the Bolshevik revolution, but he returned from a visit to Soviet Union in 1920 as a severe critic of Russian communism (*The Theory and Practise of Bolshevism*, 1920). He abandoned his pacifism to support World War II and spent 1938–1944 in the United States, where he wrote *An Inquiry into Meaning and Truth* (1940) and his money-earning potboiler, *A History of Western Philosophy* (1945). In 1940, a prospective appointment at CCNY was, to his amusement, rescinded on the charge that he was "an enemy of religion and morality." Remaining politically active, he participated in the antinuclear movement, questioned the Warren Commission's report on the Kennedy assassination, and joined Sartre in organizing the Vietnam war crimes tribunal.

Besides some short stories, Russell also wrote numerous autobiographical essays: *Portraits from Memory* (1956), *My Philosophical Development* (1959), and a long essay in *The Philosophy of Bertrand Russell*, edited by Paul Schlipp (1963).

The Philosophy of Bertrand Russell

MY MENTAL DEVELOPMENT

My mother having died when I was two years old, and my father when I was three, I was brought up in the house of my grandfather, Lord John Russell, afterwards Earl Russell. Of my parents, Lord and Lady Amberley, I was told almost nothing—so little that I vaguely sensed a dark mystery. It was not until I was twenty-one that I came to know the main outlines of my parents' lives and opinions. I then found, with a sense of bewilderment, that I had gone through almost exactly the same mental and emotional development as my father had.

It was expected of my father that he should take to a political career, which was traditional in the Russell family. He was willing, and was for a short time in Parliament (1867–68); but he had not the temperament or the opinions that would have made political success possible. At the age of twenty-one he decided that he was not a Christian, and refused to go to Church on Christmas Day. He became a disciple, and afterwards a friend, of John Stuart Mill, who, as I discovered some years ago, was (so far as is possible in a non-religious sense) my godfather. My parents accepted Mill's opinions, not only such as were comparatively popular, but also those that still shocked public sentiment, such as women's suffrage and birth control. During the general election of 1868, at which my father was a candidate, it was discovered that, at a private meeting of a small society, he had said that birth control was a matter for the medical profession to consider. This let loose a campaign of vilification and slander. A Catholic Bishop declared that he advocated infanticide; he was called in print a "filthy foul-mouthed rake;" on election day, cartoons were exhibited accusing him of immorality, altering his name to "Vice-count Amberley," and accusing him of advocating "The French and American system." By these means he was defeated. The student of comparative sociology may be interested in the similarities between rural England in 1868 and urban New York in 1940. The available documents are collected in *The Amberley Papers*, by my wife and myself. As the reader of this book will see, my father was shy, studious, and ultra-conscientious—perhaps a prig, but the very opposite of a rake.

My father did not give up hope of returning to politics, but never obtained another constituency, and devoted himself to writing a big book, *Analysis of Religious Belief*, which was published after his death. He could not, in any case, have succeeded in politics, because of his very exceptional intellectual integrity; he was always willing to admit the weak points on his own side and the strong points on that of his opponents. Moreover his health was always bad, and he suffered from a consequent lack of physical vigour.

My mother shared my father's opinions, and shocked the 'sixties by addressing meetings in favour of equality for women. She refused to use the phrase "women's rights," because, as a good utilitarian, she rejected the doctrine of natural rights.

My father wished my brother and me to be brought up as free thinkers, and appointed two free thinkers as our guardians. The Court of Chancery, however, at the request of my grandparents, set aside the will, and I enjoyed the benefits of a Christian upbringing.

In 1876, when after my father's death, I was brought to the house of my grandparents, my grandfather was eighty-three and had become very feeble. I remember him sometimes being wheeled about out-of-doors in a bath-chair, sometimes in his room reading Hansard (the official report of debates in Parliament). He was invariably kind to me, and seemed never to object to childish noise. But he was too old to influence me directly. He died in 1878, and my knowledge of him came through his widow, my grandmother, who revered his memory. She was a more powerful influence upon my general outlook than any one else, although, from adolescence onward, I disagreed with very many of her opinions.

My grandmother was a Scotch Presbyterian, of the border family of the Elliots. Her maternal grandfather suffered obloquy for declaring, on the basis of the thickness of the lava on the slopes of Etna, that the world must have been created before B.C. 4004. One of her great-grandfathers was Robertson, the historian of Charles V.

She was a Puritan, with the moral rigidity of the Covenanters, despising comfort, indifferent to food, hating wine, and regarding tobacco as sinful. Although she had lived her whole life in the great world until my grandfather's retirement in 1866, she was completely unworldly. She had that indifference to money which is only possible to those who have always had enough of it. She wished her children and grandchildren to live useful and virtuous lives, but had no desire that they should achieve what others would regard as success, or that they should marry "well." She had the Protestant belief in private judgment and the supremacy of the individual conscience. On my twelfth birthday she gave me a Bible (which I still possess), and wrote her favourite texts on the fly-leaf. One of them was "Thou shalt not follow a multitude to do evil;" another, "Be strong, and of a good courage; be not afraid, neither be Thou dismayed; for the Lord Thy God is with thee whithersoever thou goest." These texts have profoundly influenced my life, and still seemed to retain some meaning after I had ceased to believe in God.

At the age of seventy, my grandmother became a Unitarian, at the same time, she supported Home Rule for Ireland, and made friends with Irish Members of Parliament, who were being publicly accused of complicity in murder. This shocked people more than now seems imaginable. She was passionately opposed to imperialism, and taught me to think ill of the Afghan and Zulu wars, which occurred when I was about seven. Concerning the occupation of Egypt, however, she said little, as it was due to Mr. Gladstone, whom she admired. I remember an argument I had with my German governess, who said that the English, having once gone into Egypt, would never come out, whatever they might promise, whereas I maintained, with much patriotic passion, that the English never broke promises. That was sixty years ago, and they are there still.

My grandfather, seen through the eyes of his widow, made it seem imperative and natural to do something important for the good of mankind. I was told of his introducing the Reform Bill in 1832. Shortly before he died, a delegation of eminent nonconformists assembled to cheer him, and I was told that fifty years earlier he had been one of the leaders in removing their political disabilities. In his sitting-room there was a statue of Italy, presented to my grandfather by the Italian Government, with an inscription: "A Lord John Russell, L'Italia Riconoscente;" I naturally wished to know what this meant, and learnt, in consequence, the whole saga of Garibaldi and Italian unity. Such things stimulated my ambition to live to some purpose.

My grandfather's library, which became my schoolroom, stimulated me in a different way. There were books of history, some of them very old; I remember in particular a sixteenth-century Guicciardini. There were three huge folio volumes called *L'Art de vérifier les dates*. They were too heavy for me to move, and I speculated as to their contents; I imagined something like the tables for finding Easter in the Prayer-Book. At last I became old enough to lift one of the volumes out of the shelf, and I found, to my disgust, that the only "art" involved was that of looking up the date in the book. Then there were *The Annals of Ireland* by the Four Masters, in which I read about the men who went to Ireland before the Flood and were drowned in it; I wondered how the Four Masters knew about them, and read no further. There were also more ordinary books, such as Machiavelli and Gibbon and Swift, and a book in four volumes that I never opened: *The Works of Andrew Marvell Esq. M.P.* It was not till I grew up that I discovered Marvell was a poet rather than a politician. I was not supposed to read any of these books; otherwise I should probably not have read any of them. The net result of them was to stimulate my interest in history. No doubt my interest was increased by the fact that my family had been prominent in English history since the early sixteenth century. I was taught English history as the record of a struggle against the King for constitutional liberty. William Lord Russell, who was executed under Charles II, was held up for special admiration, and the inference was encouraged that rebellion is often praiseworthy.

A great event in my life, at the age of eleven, was the beginning of Euclid, which was still the accepted textbook of geometry. When I had got over my disappointment in finding that he began with axioms, which had to be accepted without proof, I found great delight in him. Throughout the rest of my boyhood, mathematics absorbed a very large part of my interest. This interest was complex: partly mere pleasure in discovering that I possessed a certain kind of skill, partly delight in the power of deductive reasoning, partly the restfulness of mathematical certainty; but more than any of these (while I was still a boy) the belief that nature operates according to mathematical laws, and that human actions, like planetary motions, could be calculated if we had sufficient skill. By the time I was fifteen, I had arrived at a theory very similar to that of the Cartesians. The movements of living bodies, I felt convinced, were wholly regulated by the laws of dynamics; therefore free will must be an illusion. But, since I accepted consciousness as an indubitable datum, I could not accept materialism, though I had a certain hankering after it on account of its intellectual simplicity and its rejection of "nonsense." I still believed in God, because the First-Cause argument seemed irrefutable.

Until I went to Cambridge at the age of eighteen, my life was a very solitary one. I was brought up at home, by German nurses, German and Swiss governesses, and finally by English tutors; I saw little of other children, and when I did they were not important to me. At fourteen or fifteen I became passionately interested in religion, and set to work to examine successively the arguments for free will, immortality, and God. For a few months I had an agnostic tutor with whom I could talk about these problems, but he was sent away, presumably because he was thought to be undermining my faith. Except during these months, I kept my thoughts to myself, writing them out in a journal in Greek letters to prevent others from reading them. I was suffering the unhappiness natural to lonely adolescence, and I attributed my unhappiness to loss of religious belief. For three years I thought about religion, with a determination not to let my thoughts be influenced by my desires. I discarded first free will, then immortality; I believed in God until I was just eighteen, when I found in Mill's *Autobiography* the sentence: "My father taught me that the question 'Who made me'? cannot be

answered, since it immediately suggests the further question 'Who made God'?"
In that moment I decided that the First-Cause argument is fallacious.

During these years I read widely, but as my reading was not directed, much
of it was futile. I read much bad poetry, especially Tennyson and Byron; at last,
at the age of seventeen, I came upon Shelley, whom no one had told me about.
He remained for many years the man I loved most among great men of the past.
I read a great deal of Carlyle, and admired *Past and Present*, but not *Sartor Re-
sartus*. "The Everlasting Yea" seemed to me sentimental nonsense. The man with
whom I most nearly agreed was Mill. His *Political Economy, Liberty*, and *Subjection of Women* influenced me profoundly. I made elaborate notes on the whole
of his *Logic*, but could not accept his theory that mathematical propositions are
empirical generalizations, though I did not know what else they could be.

All this was before I went to Cambridge. Except during the three months when
I had the agnostic tutor mentioned above, I found no one to speak to about my
thoughts. At home I concealed my religious doubts. Once I said that I was a
utilitarian, but was met with such a blast of ridicule that I never again spoke of
my opinions at home.

Cambridge opened to me a new world of infinite delight. For the first time I
found that, when I uttered my thoughts, they seemed to be accepted as worth
considering. Whitehead, who had examined me for entrance scholarships, had
mentioned me to various people a year or two senior to me, with the result that
within a week I met a number who became my life-long friends. Whitehead, who
was already a Fellow and Lecturer, was amazingly kind, but was too much my
senior to be a close personal friend until some years later. I found a group of
contemporaries, who were able, rather earnest, hard-working, but interested in
many things outside their academic work—poetry, philosophy, politics, ethics,
indeed the whole world of mental adventure. We used to stay up discussing till
very late on Saturday nights, meet for a late breakfast on Sunday, and then go
for an all-day walk. Able young men had not yet adopted the pose of cynical
superiority which came in some years later, and was first made fashionable in
Cambridge by Lytton Strachey. The world seemed hopeful and solid; we all felt
convinced that nineteenth-century progress would continue, and that we ourselves should be able to contribute something of value. For those who have been
young since 1914 it must be difficult to imagine the happiness of those days.

Among my friends at Cambridge were McTaggart, the Hegelian philosopher;
Lowes Dickinson, whose gentle charm made him loved by all who knew him;
Charles Sanger, a brilliant mathematician at College, afterwards a barrister,
known in legal circles as the editor of Jarman on Wills; two brothers, Crompton
and Theodore Llewelyn Davies, sons of a Broad Church clergyman most widely
known as one of "Davies and Vaughan," who translated Plato's *Republic*. These
two brothers were the youngest and ablest of a family of seven, all remarkably
able; they had also a quite unusual capacity for friendship, a deep desire to be
of use to the world, and unrivalled wit. Theodore, the younger of the two, was
still in the earlier stages of a brilliant career in the government service when he
was drowned in a bathing accident. I have never known any two men so deeply
loved by so many friends. Among those of whom I saw most were the three
brothers Trevelyan, great-nephews of Macaulay. Of these the oldest became a
Labour politician and resigned from the Labour Government because it was not
sufficiently socialistic; the second became a poet and published, among other
things, an admirable translation of Lucretius; the third, George, achieved fame as

an historian. Somewhat junior to me was G. E. Moore, who later had a great influence upon my philosophy.

The set in which I lived was very much influenced by McTaggart, whose wit recommended his Hegelian philosophy. He taught me to consider British empiricism "crude," and I was willing to believe that Hegel (and in a lesser degree Kant) had a profundity not to be found in Locke, Berkeley, and Hume, or in my former pope, Mill. My first three years at Cambridge, I was too busy with mathematics to read Kant or Hegel, but in my fourth year I concentrated on philosophy. My teachers were Henry Sidgwick, James Ward, and G. F. Stout. Sidgwick represented the British point of view, which I believed myself to have seen through; I therefore thought less of him at that time than I did later. Ward, for whom I had a very great personal affection, set forth a Kantian system, and introduced me to Lotze and Sigwart. Stout, at that time, thought very highly of Bradley; when *Appearance and Reality* was published, he said it had done as much as is humanly possible in ontology. He and McTaggart between them caused me to become a Hegelian; I remember the precise moment, one day in 1894, as I was walking along Trinity Lane, when I saw in a flash (or thought I saw) that the ontological argument is valid. I had gone out to buy a tin of tobacco; on my way back, I suddenly threw it up in the air, and exclaimed as I caught it: "Great Scott, the ontological argument is sound." I read Bradley at this time with avidity, and admired him more than any other recent philosopher.

After leaving Cambridge in 1894, I spent a good deal of time in foreign countries. For some months in 1894, I was honorary attaché at the British Embassy in Paris, where I had to copy out long dispatches attempting to persuade the French Government that a lobster is not a fish, to which the French Government would reply that it was a fish in 1713, at the time of the Treaty of Utrecht. I had no desire for a diplomatic career, and left the Embassy in December, 1894. I then married, and spent most of 1895 in Berlin, studying economics and German Social Democracy. The Ambassador's wife being a cousin of mine, my wife and I were invited to dinner at the Embassy; but she mentioned that we had gone to a Socialist meeting, and after this the Embassy closed its doors to us. My wife was a Philadelphia Quaker, and in 1896 we spent three months in America. The first place we visited was Walt Whitman's house in Camden, N.J.; she had known him well, and I greatly admired him. These travels were useful in curing me of a certain Cambridge provincialism; in particular, I came to know the work of Weierstrass, whom my Cambridge teachers had never mentioned. After these travels, we settled down in a workman's cottage in Sussex, to which we added a fairly large work-room. I had at that time enough money to live simply without earning, and I was therefore able to devote all my time to philosophy and mathematics, except the evenings, when we read history aloud.

In the years from 1894 to 1898, I believed in the possibility of proving by metaphysics various things about the universe that religious feeling made me think important. I decided that, if I had sufficient ability, I would devote my life to philosophy. My fellowship dissertation, on the foundations of geometry, was praised by Ward and Whitehead; if it had not been, I should have taken up economics, at which I had been working in Berlin. I remember a spring morning when I walked in the Tiergarten, and planned to write a series of books in the philosophy of the sciences, growing gradually more concrete as I passed from mathematics to biology; I thought I would also write a series of books on social and political questions, growing gradually more abstract. At last I would achieve a Hegelian synthesis in an encyclopaedic work dealing equally with theory and practice. The scheme was inspired by Hegel, and yet something of it survived the change in my philosophy. The moment had had a certain importance: I can still, in memory, feel the squelching of melting snow beneath my feet, and smell the damp earth that promised the end of winter.

During 1898, various things caused me to abandon both Kant and Hegel. I read Hegel's *Greater Logic*, and thought, as I still do, that all he says about mathematics is muddle-headed nonsense. I came to disbelieve Bradley's arguments against relations, and to distrust the logical bases of monism. I disliked the subjectivity of the "Transcendental Aesthetic." But these motives would have operated more slowly than they did, but for the influence of G. E. Moore. He also had had a Hegelian period, but it was briefer than mine. He took the lead in rebellion, and I followed, with a sense of emancipation. Bradley argued that everything common sense believes in is mere appearance; we reverted to the opposite extreme, and thought that *everything* is real that common sense, uninfluenced by philosophy or theology, supposes real. With a sense of escaping from prison, we allowed ourselves to think that grass is green, that the sun and stars would exist if no one was aware of them, and also that there is a pluralistic timeless world of Platonic ideas. The world, which had been thin and logical, suddenly became rich and varied and solid. Mathematics could be *quite* true, and not merely a stage in dialectic. Something of this point of view appeared in my *Philosophy of Leibniz*. This book owed its origin to chance. McTaggart, who would, in the normal course, have lectured on Leibniz at Cambridge in 1898, wished to visit his family in New Zealand, and I was asked to take his place for this course. For me, the accident was a fortunate one.

The most important year in my intellectual life was the year 1900, and the most important event in this year was my visit to the International Congress of Philosophy in Paris. Ever since I had begun Euclid at the age of eleven, I had been troubled about the foundations of mathematics; when, later, I came to read philosophy, I found Kant and the empiricists equally unsatisfactory. I did not like the synthetic *a priori*, but yet arithmetic did not seem to consist of empirical generalizations. In Paris in 1900, I was impressed by the fact that, in all discussions, Peano and his pupils had a precision which was not possessed by others. I therefore asked him to give me his works, which he did. As soon as I had mastered his notation, I saw that it extended the region of mathematical precision backwards towards regions which had been given over to philosophical vagueness. Basing myself on him, I invented a notation for relations. Whitehead, fortunately, agreed as to the importance of the method, and in a very short time we worked out together such matters as the definitions of series, cardinals, and ordinals, and the reduction of arithmetic to logic. For nearly a year, we had a rapid series of quick successes. Much of the work had already been done by Frege, but at first we did not know this. The work that ultimately became my contribution to *Principia Mathematica* presented itself to me, at first, as a parenthesis in the refutation of Kant.

In June 1901, this period of honeymoon delight came to an end. Cantor had a proof that there is no greatest cardinal; in applying this proof to the universal class, I was led to the contradiction about classes that are not members of themselves. It soon became clear that this is only one of an infinite class of contradictions. I wrote to Frege, who replied with the utmost gravity that *"die Arithmetik ist ins Schwanken geraten."* At first, I hoped the matter was trivial and could be easily cleared up; but early hopes were succeeded by something very near to despair. Throughout 1903 and 1904, I pursued will-o'-the wisps and made no progress. At last, in the spring of 1905, a different problem, which proved soluble, gave the first glimmer of hope. The problem was that of descriptions, and its solution suggested a new technique.

Scholastic realism was a metaphysical theory, but every metaphysical theory has a technical counterpart. I had been a realist in the scholastic or Platonic sense; I had thought that cardinal integers, for instance, have a timeless being. When integers were reduced to classes of classes, this being was transferred to classes. Meinong, whose work interested me, applied the arguments of realism to descriptive phrases. Everyone agrees that "the golden mountain does not exist" is a true proposition. But it has, apparently, a subject, "the golden mountain," and if this subject did not designate some object, the proposition would seem to be meaningless. Meinong inferred that there is a golden mountain, which is golden and a mountain, but does not exist. He even thought that the existent golden mountain is existent, but does not exist. This did not satisfy me, and the desire to avoid Meinong's unduly populous realm of being led me to the theory of descriptions. What was of importance in this theory was the discovery that, in analysing a significant sentence, one must not assume that each separate word or phrase has significance on its own account. "The golden mountain" can be part of a significant sentence, but is not significant in isolation. It soon appeared that class-symbols could be treated like descriptions, i.e., as non-significant parts of significant sentences. This made it possible to see, in a general way, how a solution of the contradictions might be possible. The particular solution offered in *Principia Mathematica* had various defects, but at any rate it showed that the logician is not presented with a complete *impasse*.

The theory of descriptions, and the attempt to solve the contradictions, had led me to pay attention to the problem of meaning and significance. The definition of "meaning" as applied to words and "significance" as applied to sentences is a complex problem, which I tried to deal with in *The Analysis of Mind* (1921) and *An Inquiry into Meaning and Truth* (1940). It is a problem that takes one into psychology and even physiology. The more I have thought about it, the less convinced I have become of the complete independence of logic. Seeing that logic is a much more advanced and exact science than psychology, it is clearly desirable, as far as possible, to delimit the problems that can be dealt with by logical methods. It is here that I have found Occam's razor useful.

Occam's razor, in its original form, was metaphysical: it was a principle of parsimony as regards "entities." I still thought of it in this way while *Principia Mathematica* was being written. In Plato, cardinal integers are timeless entities; they are equally so in Frege's *Grundgesetze der Arithmetik*. The definition of cardinals as classes of classes, and the discovery that class-symbols could be "incomplete symbols," persuaded me that cardinals as entities are unnecessary. But what had really been demonstrated was something quite independent of metaphysics, which is best stated in terms of "minimum vocabularies." I mean by a "minimum vocabulary" one in which no word can be defined in terms of the others. All definitions are theoretically superfluous, and therefore the whole of any science can be expressed by means of a minimum vocabulary for that science. Peano reduced the special vocabulary of arithmetic to three terms; Frege and *Principia Mathematica* maintained that even these are unnecessary, and that a minimum vocabulary for mathematics is the same as for logic. This problem is a purely technical one, and is capable of a precise solution.

There is need, however, of great caution in drawing inferences from minimum vocabularies. In the first place, there are usually, if not always, a number of different minimum vocabularies for a given subject-matter; for example, in the theory of truth-functions we may take "not-p or not-q" or "not-p and not-q" as undefined, and there is no reason to prefer one choice to the other. Then again there is often a question as to whether what seems to be a definition is not really an empirical proposition. Suppose, for instance, I define "red" as "those visual sensations which are caused by wave-lengths of such and such a range of frequencies." If we take this as what the word "red" means, no proposition containing the word can have been known before the undulatory theory of light was known and wavelengths could be measured; and yet the word "red" was used before these discoveries had been made. This makes it clear that in all every-day statements containing the word "red" this word does not have the meaning assigned to it in the above definition. Consider the question: "Can everything that we know about colours be known to a blind man?" With the above definition, the answer is yes; with a definition derived from every-day experience, the answer is no. This problem shows how the new logic, like the Aristotelian, can lead to a narrow scholasticism.

Nevertheless, there is one kind of inference which, I think, can be drawn from the study of minimum vocabularies. Take, as one of the most important examples, the traditional problem of universals. It seems fairly certain that no vocabulary can dispense wholly with words that are more or less of the sort called "universals." These words, it is true, need never occur as nouns; they may occur only as adjectives or verbs. Probably we could be content with one such word, the word "similar," and we should never need the word "similarity." But the fact that we need the word "similar" indicates some fact about the world, and not only about language. What fact it indicates about the world, I do not know.

Another illustration of the uses of minimum vocabularies is as regards historical events. To express history, we must have a means of speaking of something which has only happened once, like the death of Caesar. An undue absorption in logic, which is not concerned with history, may cause this need to be overlooked. Spatio-temporal relativity has made it more difficult to satisfy this need than it was in a Newtonian universe, where points and instants supplied particularity.

Thus, broadly speaking, minimum vocabularies are more instructive when they show a certain kind of term to be indispensable than when they show the opposite.

In some respects, my published work, outside mathematical logic, does not at all completely represent my beliefs or my general outlook. Theory of knowledge, with which I have been largely concerned, has a certain essential subjectivity; it asks "how do *I* know what I know?" and starts inevitably from personal experience. Its data are egocentric, and so are the earlier stages of its argumentation. I have not, so far, got beyond the earlier stages, and have therefore seemed more subjective in outlook than in fact I am. I am not a solipsist, nor an idealist; I believe (though without good grounds) in the world of physics as well as in the world of psychology. But it seems clear that whatever is not experienced must, if known, be known by inference. I find that the fear of solipsism has prevented philosophers from facing this problem, and that either the necessary principles of inference have been left vague, or else the distinction between what is known by experience and what is known by inference has been denied. If I ever have the leisure to undertake another serious investigation of a philosophical problem, I shall attempt to analyse the inferences from experience to the world of physics, assuming them capable of validity, and seeking to discover what principles of inference, if true, would make them valid. Whether these principles, when discovered, are accepted as true, is a matter of temperament; what should not be a matter of temperament should be the proof that acceptance of them is necessary if solipsism is to be rejected.

I come now to what I have attempted to do in connection with social questions. I grew up in an atmosphere of politics, and was expected by my elders to take up a political career. Philosophy, however, interested me more than politics, and when it appeared that I had some aptitude for it, I decided to make it my main work. This pained my grandmother, who alluded to my investigation of the foundations of geometry as "the life you have been leading," and said in shocked tones: "O Bertie, I hear you are writing *another* book." My political interests, though secondary, nevertheless, remained very strong. In 1895, when in Berlin, I made a study of German Social Democracy, which I liked as being opposed to the Kaiser, and disliked as (at that time) embodying Marxist orthodoxy. For a time, under the influence of Sidney Webb, I became an imperialist, and even supported the Boer War. This point of view, however, I abandoned completely in 1901; from that time onwards, I felt an intense dislike of the use of force in human relations, though I always admitted that it is sometimes necessary. When Joseph Chamberlain, in 1903, turned against free trade, I wrote and spoke against him, my objections to his proposals being those of an internationalist. I took an active part in the agitation for Women's Suffrage. In 1910, *Principia Mathematica* being practically finished, I wished to stand for Parliament, and should have done so if the Selection Committee had not been shocked to discover that I was a free thinker.

The first world war gave a new direction to my interests. The war, and the problem of preventing future wars, absorbed me, and the books that I wrote on this and cognate subjects caused me to become known to a wider public. During the war I had hoped that the peace would embody a rational determination to avoid future great wars; this hope was destroyed by the Versailles Treaty. Many of my friends saw hope in Soviet Russia, but when I went there in 1920 I found nothing that I could like or admire. I was then invited to China, where I spent nearly a year. I loved the Chinese, but it was obvious that the resistance to hostile militarisms must destroy much of what was best in their civilization. They seemed to have no alternative except to be conquered or to adopt many of the vices of their enemies. But China did one thing for me that the East is apt to do for Europeans who study it with sensitive sympathy: it taught me to think in long stretches of time, and not to be reduced to despair by the badness of the present. Throughout the increasing gloom of the past twenty years, this habit has helped to make the world less unendurable than it would otherwise have been.

In the years after my return from China, the birth of my two older children caused me to become interested in early education, to which, for some time, I devoted most of my energy. I have been supposed to be an advocate of complete liberty in schools, but this, like the view that I am an anarchist, is a mistake. I think a certain amount of force is indispensable, in education as in government;

but I also think that methods can be found which will greatly diminish the necessary amount of force. This problem has both political and private aspects. As a rule, children or adults who are happy are likely to have fewer destructive passions, and therefore to need less restraint, than those who are unhappy. But I do not think that children can be made happy by being deprived of guidance, nor do I think that a sense of social obligation can be fostered if complete idleness is permitted. The question of discipline in childhood, like all other practical questions, is one of degree. Profound unhappiness and instinctive frustration is apt to produce a deep grudge against the world, issuing, sometimes by a very roundabout road, in cruelty and violence. The psychological and social problems involved first occupied my attention during the war of 1914–18; I was especially struck by the fact that, at first, most people seemed to enjoy the war. Clearly this was due to a variety of social ills, some of which were educational. But while individual parents can do much for their individual children, large-scale educational reform must depend upon the state, and therefore upon prior political and economic reforms. The world, however, was moving more and more in the direction of war and dictatorship, and I saw nothing useful that I could do in practical matters. I therefore increasingly reverted to philosophy, and to history in relation to ideas.

History has always interested me more than anything else except philosophy and mathematics. I have never been able to accept any general schema of historical development, such as that of Hegel or that of Marx. Nevertheless, general trends can be studied, and the study is profitable in relation to the present. I found much help in understanding the nineteenth century from studying the effect of liberal ideas in the period from 1814 to 1914. The two types of liberalism, the rational and the romantic, represented by Bentham and Rousseau respectively, have continued, ever since, their relations of alternate alliance and conflict.

The relation of philosophy to social conditions has usually been ignored by professional philosophers. Marxists are interested in philosophy as an *effect*, but do not recognize it as a *cause*. Yet plainly every important philosophy is both. Plato is in part an effect of the victory of Sparta in the Peloponnesian war, and is also in part among the causes of Christian theology. To treat him only in the former aspect is to make the growth of the medieval church inexplicable. I am at present writing a history of western philosophy from Thales to the present day, in which every important system is treated equally as an effect and as a cause of social conditions.

My intellectual journeys have been, in some respects, disappointing. When I was young I hoped to find religious satisfaction in philosophy; even after I had abandoned Hegel, the eternal Platonic world gave me something non-human to admire. I thought of mathematics with reverence, and suffered when Wittgenstein led me to regard it as nothing but tautologies. I have always ardently desired to find some justification for the emotions inspired by certain things that seemed to stand outside human life and to deserve feelings of awe. I am thinking in part of very obvious things, such as the starry heavens and a stormy sea on a rocky coast; in part of the vastness of the scientific universe, both in space and time, as compared to the life of mankind; in part of the edifice of impersonal truth, especially truth which, like that of mathematics, does not merely describe the world that happens to exist. Those who attempt to make a religion of humanism, which recognizes nothing greater than man, do not satisfy my emotions. And yet

I am unable to believe that, in the world as known, there is anything that I can value outside human beings, and, to a much lesser extent, animals. Not the starry heavens, but their effects on human percipients, have excellence; to admire the universe for its size is slavish and absurd; impersonal non-human truth appears to be a delusion. And so my intellect goes with the humanists, though my emotions violently rebel. In this respect, the "consolations of philosophy" are not for me.

In more purely intellectual ways, on the contrary, I have found as much satisfaction in philosophy as any one could reasonably have expected. Many matters which, when I was young, baffled me by the vagueness of all that had been said about them, are now amenable to an exact technique, which makes possible the kind of progress that is customary in science. Where definite knowledge is unattainable, it is sometimes possible to prove that it is unattainable, and it is usually possible to formulate a variety of exact hypotheses, all compatible with the existing evidence. Those philosophers who have adopted the methods derived from logical analysis can argue with each other, not in the old aimless way, but cooperatively, so that both sides can concur as to the outcome. All this is new during my lifetime; the pioneer was Frege, but he remained solitary until his old age. This extension of the sphere of reason to new provinces is something that I value very highly. Philosophic rationality may be choked in the shocks of war and the welter of new persecuting superstitions, but one may hope that it will not be lost utterly or for more than a few centuries. In this respect, my philosophic life has been a happy one.

FROM WITTGENSTEIN TO APPIAH

35

LUDWIG WITTGENSTEIN
Logical Arrangements

Born in Vienna to a wealthy industrialist family, Ludwig Wittgenstein (1889–1951) was privately educated before he studied engineering in Berlin and Manchester. Having become interested in the philosophy of mathematics, he went to Cambridge to study with Bertrand Russell in 1912, who introduced him to G. E. Moore and J. M. Keynes. He began writing the *Tractatus Logico-Philosophicus* (1921), but, having given away his large inheritance, Wittgenstein decided to return to Austria, to serve as a soldier in World War I. He was held prisoner at Monte Casino. After the war, Wittgenstein taught in a rural elementary school from 1920 to 1926. He fell into a depression, gave up schoolteaching, became a gardener, and spent two years in Vienna designing a house for his sister. He became acquainted with Moritz Schlick and other members of the Vienna Circle. Renewing his interest in philosophy, Wittgenstein returned to Trinity College, Cambridge, in 1928.

The *Tractatus* presents a metaphysically oriented theory of language. "The world is everything that is the case," that is, it is composed of facts that can be expressed in truth-functional, propositional form. The underlying logical structure of all possible true propositions represents the logical structure of the world. For Wittgenstein, this meant that sentences which do not express facts—for instance, the "claims" of ethics and philosophy—are, strictly speaking, meaningless. Such "nontruths" are, like works of art, nevertheless serious matters for silent, mystical reflection.

Wittgenstein came to think that the *Tractatus* failed to capture the way that ordinary language expresses, and is embedded in practical activity. His early 1933 and 1935 lectures on the functions of language appeared in *Philosophical Remarks* and *The Blue and Brown Books*. When properly used in ordinary contexts, the ambiguities of ordinary speech need not be confusing or paradoxical: their meaning is expressed in their use. Traditional philosophy generates unresolvable problems (e.g. What is the relation between mind and body? Is the will free?) because it attempts a rational reconstruction of ordinary terms, taking them out of their functional practical contexts. Philosophy should turn to the task of dissolving the problems of traditional philosophy ... and leaving the world as it found it.

Struggling to formulate his new turn of thought, Wittgenstein went for a brief visit to the Soviet Union before retiring to work in an isolated hut in Norway. He was appointed to Moore's chair in philosophy in 1939, served as a medical orderly during the war, and returned to Cambridge in 1945. Finding professorial life in Cambridge unbearably artificial, he resigned his chair, and briefly lived in Ireland. He continued his philosophical work while spending his last years staying with friends in Cornell, Oxford, and Cambridge. Wittgenstein's later views were posthumously translated and edited by G. E. M. Anscombe as *The Philosophical Investigations* (1953). *On Certainty* was published in 1969.

Letters to Bertrand Russell

(Ludwig Wittgenstein: Cambridge Letters)

Dear Russell,

I hope you have got my letter which I wrote on the 16th. I left it in the Dining room of the boat and afterwards telephoned that it should be posted but I don't know with what effect. This is an ideal place to work in.—Soon after I arrived here I got a violent influenza which prevented me from doing any work until quite recently. Identity is the very Devil and *immensely important; very* much more so than I thought. It hangs—like everything else—directly together with the most fundamental questions, especially with the questions concerning the occurrence of the *same* argument in different places of a function. I have all sorts of ideas for a solution of the problem but could not yet arrive at anything definite. However I don't lose courage and go on thinking.—I have got two nice rooms here in the Postmaster's house and am looked after very well indeed. By the way—would you be so good and send me *two* copies of Moore's paper: "The Nature and Reality of Objects of Perception" which he read to the Aristotelian Soc[iety] in 1906. I am afraid I can't yet tell you the reason why I want *two* copies but you shall know it some day. If you kindly send the bill with them I will send the money immediately after receiving the Pamphlets.—As I hardly meet a soul in this place, the progress of my Norwegian is exceedingly slow; so much so that I have not yet learned a single swear-word. Please remember me to Dr and Mrs Whitehead and Erik if you see them. Write to me *SOON*.

Yours as long as E! L. W.

30.10.

I wrote this letter yesterday. Since then quite new ideas have come into my head; new problems have arisen in the theory of molecular prop[osition]s and the theory of inference has received a new and very important aspect. One of the consequences of my new ideas will—I think—be that the whole of Logic follows from one P.p. only!! I cannot say more about it at present.

L. W.

Dear Russell,

Many thanks for your letter. As you see, I am at home and *unfortunately* once again quite unproductive. I only hope the ideas will start to flow again when I go back into isolation. (I am staying here for about another eight or ten days.) As regards your American lecture-course, there was naturally no need at all, as far as *I'm* concerned, to mention my name. But—as you wish—. Here I feel different every day. Sometimes things inside me are in such a ferment that I think I'm going mad: then the next day I am totally apathetic again. But deep inside me there's a perpetual seething, like the bottom of a geyser, and I keep on hoping that things will come to an eruption once and for all, so that I can turn into a different person. I can't write you anything about logic today. Perhaps you regard this thinking about myself as a waste of time—but how can I be a logician before I'm a human being! *Far* the most important thing is to settle accounts with myself!

Yours ever
L. W.

Dear Russell,

Many thanks for your kind letter. It's *very* sad but I've once again no logical news for you. The reason is that things have gone terribly badly for me in the last weeks. (A result of my "holidays" in Vienna.) Every day I was tormented by a frightful *Angst* and by depression in turns and even in the intervals I was so exhausted that I wasn't able to think of doing a bit of work. It's terrifying beyond all description the kinds of mental torment that there can be! It wasn't until two days ago that I could hear the voice of reason over the howls of the damned and I began to work again. And *perhaps* I'll get better now and be able to produce something decent. But I *never* knew what it meant to feel only *one* step away from madness.—Let's hope for the best!—

Yes: Mörike really is a *great* poet and his poems are among the best things we have. But I am curious to know whether you will really enjoy him. After all, you don't enjoy Goethe and the beauty of Mörike's work is very closely related to that of Goethe's. But *if* you have *really* enjoyed Mörike, then just try Goethe's *Iphigenie*. Then perhaps you'll see the light.

Now for a question: isn't what the "principle of sufficient reason" (law of causality) says simply that space and time are relative? I now think this is quite obvious, because all the events which, according to this assertion, are not meant to be possible could only occur, if at all, in an absolute time and space. (Admittedly this wouldn't in itself be an adequate reason for my assertion.) But think of the case of a particle that is the only thing existing in the world and that has been at rest for all eternity and that suddenly, at time A, begins to move. Think of this and similar cases and you will see, I believe, that it is *not* an a priori insight that makes such events seem impossible to us *unless it is the case* that space and time are relative. Please write and tell me your opinion on this point.

All best wishes for your lecture-course in America! Perhaps it will give you at any rate a more favorable opportunity than usual to tell them your *thoughts* and not *just* cut and dried results. *That* is what would be of the greatest imaginable value for your audience—to get to know the value of *thought* and not that of a cut and dried result. Write to me soon and think of me when you read Mörike.

Yours ever
L. W.

Letter to Maynard Keynes

My Dear Keynes,

I am so sorry to have to trouble you with my own affairs at a time when you yourself are not too well. I want however to describe to you my present situation and ask you whether you can by any chance, in some way not too difficult for you, give me some advice or help. You know that by the annexation of Austria by Germany I have become a German citizen and, by the German laws; a German Jew (as three of my grandparents were baptised only as adults). The same, of course, applies to my brother and sisters (not to their children, *they* count as Aryans). As my people in Vienna are almost all retiring and very respected people who have always felt and behaved patriotically it is, on the whole, unlikely that they are at present in any *danger*. I have not yet heard from them since the invasion and there hasn't yet been time as they would wait in any case with giving me news until things had settled down a bit. I wrote to them a week ago saying that if they needed me I would come home any time. But I *believe* that they aren't going to call me and also that I couldn't at present do anything for them, except possibly cheering them up a little.—If however I went to Vienna now the consequences would be a) that my passport, being an Austrian one, would be taken away from me and b) that, in all likelihood, *no* passport would be given to me; as passports, except in very special cases, are not, I gather, issued to German Jews. I could therefore c)not leave Austria again and d) never again get a job.

My people, who were rich before the war, are still wealthyish and will probably, even when a lot will be taken away from them, still have enough money to keep me (and they would *gladly* do so) but I needn't say this would be the last thing that I'ld wish to happen.

I also must say that the idea of becoming (or being) a German citizen, even apart from all the nasty consequences, is *appalling* to me. (This may be foolish, but it just is so.)

For all these reasons I have now decided to try I) to get a University job at Cambridge, 2) to acquire British citizenship.

The thought of acquiring British citizenship had *occurred* to me before; but I have always rejected it on the ground: that I do not wish to become a sham-Englishman (I think you will understand what I mean). The situation has however entirely changed for me now. For now I have to choose between two new nationalities, one of which deprives me of *everything*, while the other, at least, would allow me to work in a country in which I have spent on and off the greater part of my adult life, have made my greatest friends and have done my best work.

Now if I wish to try to become naturalised here I'm afraid I have to make haste; one of the reasons being that (as Sraffa pointed out to me) it would be easier as long as I hold an Austrian passport. And this I might have to give up before so very long.

As to getting a job at Cambridge you may remember that I was an assistant faculty lecturer for 5 years, and that the regulations don't allow one to hold this job for more than 5 years. When my 5 years had expired the faculty allowed me to go on lecturing as before and they went on paying me as before. Now it is for *this* that I shall apply, for there is no other job vacant. I had, in fact, thought of doing so anyway; though not now, but perhaps next autumn. But it would be important now for me to get a job *as quickly as possible;* for a) it would help me in becoming naturalised and b) if I failed in this and *had* to become a German I would have more chance to be allowed out of Austria again on visiting my people if I had a *job* in England.

I have talked all this over with Sraffa yesterday. He is leaving today or tomorrow for Italy and I came here in a hurry from Dublin to see him and talk with him. He thought the right thing for me is to see a solicitor about becoming naturalized, one who is an expert in this kind of thing. Sraffa thought that you might possibly be able to tell me the right person or give me some sort of advice about the matter, or also about applying for a University job.

I want to add that I'm in no sort of financial difficulties. I shall have about 300 or 400 £ and can therefore easily hold out for another year or so.

Well, this is all. Forgive me for making you read this *long* letter; if indeed you ever get to this line.

I hope I may see you again before so *very* long. *Whatever* you may think about me or my problems I am

Yours ever
Ludwig

P.S. If my people wrote to me now that they wanted me at home I would, of course have to go. But, as I said, this is most unlikely.

Reflections on Life
(Notebooks, 1914–1916)

7.10.14

During the night we headed for Russia; barely any sleep, posted at the search-light, etc. We are soon to come under fire. The spirit with me. I'm icy cold—from the inside. I have a certain feeling: If I could only fall asleep again, before the affair begins—! Better to think. Worked a bit. I still keep failing to understand how to do my duty only because it is my duty, and to keep my whole person for the spiritual life. I may die in an hour, I may die in two hours, I may die in a month or in a couple of hours. I can't know when and can do nothing for or against it: *Thus is this life.* How must I therefore live, in order to exist in every moment? To live in the good and the beautiful, until life stops of its own accord.

I bought Nietzsche's [Werke] volume 8 and read around in it. I am strongly affected by his hostility to Christianity. For his writings also contain some truth. Certainly, Christianity is the only *certain* way to happiness. But how is it when someone scorns this happiness? Might it not be better to perish unhappily, in hopeless struggle with the external world? Only, such a life is without sense (*Sinnlos*). But why not lead a senseless life? Is such a life unworthy? How much is it in agreement with the strict solipsistic standpoint? But what must I do, in order for my life not to pass me by? To myself I must always be conscious of it—of the spirit.

29.7.16

Under fire yesterday. I lost heart. I had fear before death. I now so wish to live! And it is difficult to give up life when one has once so wanted it. That is even "sinful", unreasoning life, false life conception. I become from time to time an *animal*. Then I can think of nothing but eating, drinking, sleeping. Terrifying! And then I also suffer like an animal, without the possibility of inner deliverance. I am then at the mercy of my cravings and aversions: Then a genuine life can't be thought of.

1.8.16

How everything is the case, is God.
God is, how everything is the case.
Only from the consciousness of the *uniqueness of my life* arises religion—science—and art.

2.8.16

And this consciousness is life itself.
Can there be any ethics if there is no living being but myself?
If ethics is supposed to be something fundamental: Yes! (NB 79)

10.1.17
If suicide is allowed then everything is allowed.
If anything is not allowed then suicide is not allowed.
This throws a light on the nature of ethics, for suicide is, so to speak, the elementary sin (NB 91).

6.5.16
Life in constant danger. The night passed through the grace of God. From time to time I lost heart. That is the school of false life conceptions! Understand the people! Always, when you hate them, strive instead to understand them. Live in inner peace! How else do you come to inner peace? ONLY insofar as I live to please God. *Only* so is it possible to endure life. (GT 70)

At bottom the whole *Weltanschauung* of the moderns involves the illusion that the so-called laws of nature are explanations of natural phenomena.

In this way they stop short at the laws of nature as at something *impregnable* as those of former times did at God and fate.

And both are right and wrong. The old ones are indeed clearer in the sense that they acknowledge a clear terminus, while with the new system it is supposed to look as if *everything* had a reason. (NB 72)

11.6.16
What do I know about God and the purpose of life?
I know that this world exists.
That I am placed in it like my eye in its visual field.
That something about it is problematic, which we call its meaning (*Sinn*).
That this meaning (*Sinn*) does not lie in it but outside it.
That life is the world.
That my will penetrates the world.
That my will is good or evil.
Therefore that good and evil are somehow connected with the meaning (*Sinn*) of the world.
The meaning (*Sinn*) of life, i.e., the meaning (*Sinn*) of the world, we can call God.
And connect with this the comparison of God to a father.
To pray is to think about the meaning (*Sinn*) of life.
I cannot bend the happenings of the world to my will: I am completely powerless.
I can only make myself independent of the world—and so in a certain sense (*Sinn*) master—by renouncing any influence on happenings. (NB, pp. 72–3)
For it is a logical fact that wishing does not stand in any logical connexion with its own fulfillment. And it is also clear that the world of the happy is a *different* world from the world of the unhappy.
Is seeing an activity?
Is it possible to will good, to will evil, and not to will?
Or is only he happy who does *not* will?

"To love one's neighbor" would mean to will!
But can one wish and yet not be unhappy if the wish doesn't attain fulfillment? (And this possibility always exists.)
Is it, according to common conceptions, good to wish *nothing* for one's neighbor, neither good nor evil?

And yet it seems that not wishing is in a certain sense the only good.

Here I am still making crude mistakes! No doubt of that!

It is generally assumed that it is evil to wish the other to be unhappy. Can this be correct? Can it be worse than to wish him to be fortunate?

Here everything seems to turn, so to speak, on *how* one wishes.

It seems one can't say anything more than: Live in happiness!

The world of the happy is a different world from that of the unhappy.

The world of the happy is *a happy world*.

Then can there be a world that is neither happy nor unhappy? (NB 77D78)

If you want to say that I have no faith, you are completely right, only I didn't have it before either. It's indeed clear that the person who, so to speak, wants to invent a machine for becoming decent is a person with no faith. But what am I to do? *One thing is clear to me*: I am much too bad in being able to ruminate about myself, however, I shall either remain a swine-dog or else better myself, and that's that—not another word! Only no transcendental twaddle, when everything is as clear as a sock on the jaw (*Briefe*, p. 81 #87 to Engelmann, 16 January 1918).

On Solving Philosophical Problems
Tractatus Logico-Philosophicus

This book will perhaps only be understood by those who have themselves already thought the thoughts which are expressed in it—or similar thoughts . . .

If this work has a value it consists in two things. First that in it thoughts are expressed, and this value will be the greater the better the thoughts are expressed. The more the nail has been hit on the head.—Here I am conscious that I have fallen far short of the possible. Simply because my powers are insufficient to cope with the task.—May others come and do it better.

On the other hand the *truth* of the thoughts communicated here seems to me unassilable and definitive. I am, therefore, of the opinion that the problems have in essentials been finally solved. And if I am not mistaken in this, then the value of this work secondly consists in the fact that it shows how little has been done when these problems have been solved. Preface, *Tractatus*

5.621   The world and life are one.

5.63   I am my world. (The microcosm.)

6.4311   Death is not an event of life. Death is not experienced.

If by eternity is understood not endless temporal duration but timelessness, then he lives eternally who lives in the present.

Our life is endless in the way that our visual field is without limit.

6.4312   The temporal immortality of the human soul, that is to say, its eternal survival after death, is not only in no way guaranteed, but this assumption in the first place will not do for us what we always tried to make it do. Is a riddle solved by the fact that I survive for ever? Is this eternal life not as enigmatic as our present one?

Culture and Value

When you are philosophizing you have to descend into primeval chaos and feel at home there.

A philosopher is a man who has to cure many intellectual diseases in himself before he can arrive at the notions of common sense.

A present-day teacher of philosophy doesn't select food for his pupil with the aim of flattering his taste, but with the aim of changing it.

Nothing we do can be defended absolutely and finally. But only by reference to something else that is not questioned. I.e. no reason can be given why you should act (or should have acted) *like this*, except that by doing so you bring about such and such a situation, which again has to be an aim you *accept*.

Perhaps what is inexpressible (what I find mysterious and am not able to express) is the background against which whatever I could express has its meaning.

Working in philosophy—like work in architecture in many respects—is really more a working on oneself. On one's own interpretation. On one's way of seeing things. (And what one expects of them.)

A philosopher easily gets into the position of an incompetent manager who, instead of getting on with his *own* work and just keeping an eye on his employees to make sure they do theirs properly, takes over their work until one day he finds himself overloaded with other people's work, while his employees look on and criticize him.

Philosophers often behave like little children who scribble some marks on a piece of paper at random and then ask the grown-up "What's that?"—It happened like this: the grown-up had drawn pictures for the child several times and said: "this is a man", "this is a house", etc. And then the child makes some marks too and asks: what's *this* then?

36

MARTIN HEIDEGGER
My Way to Phenomenology

Before going to the University of Freiburg to study mathematics and philosophy, Martin Heidegger (1889–1976) attended a Jesuit seminary. At Freiburg, he worked with Husserl, who introduced him to phenomenology. In his first major book, *Being and Time* (1927), he followed Nietzsche and Kierkegaard in attempting to revise—and reverse—the history of philosophy, returning it to (what he took to be) its pre-Socratic mode. The question, "in what does the being of things that exist consist?," was to take a new turn. Although there is hardly a work of philosophy that is more abstract, more densely populated with technical ne-ologisms, Heidegger undertook to return "fallen," logocentric man back to the existential anxiety of the experience of finitude, his realization of his "nothing-ness," his "being-towards-death." Lured by science and technology, modern man has lost touch with the "everydayness" of existence, with "the Beingness of being, the ground...the clearing...in which existence reveals itself." Although every person is "thrown" into a specific time and condition, we define ourselves by questioning the meaning of our own existence.

After the publication of *Being and Time*, Heidegger succeeded Husserl as Professor at Freiburg in 1928. Increasingly, he found the "Volk Nationalism" of Germany—which he saw as a return to peasant simplicity—consonant with his critique of modern cosmopolitan society. Elected to the position of rector of the university in 1933, he became a member of the Nazi party and was instru-mental in stripping Husserl of his academic privileges. After a year in office, he retired from the rectorship and returned to his position as professor, but he remained a member of the party until 1945. Although he detached himself from his Nazi allegiance, he apparently never apologized for his treatment of Husserl and other Jewish university faculty.

Heidegger never finished the architectonic he set for himself in *Sein und Zeit*. His later works—essays on Hölderlin, art, metaphysics, technology—explore the ways in which language reveals—and obscures—"the ground and clearing of Being." He was impressed by, and declared himself to have found philosophic kinship with, Zen Buddhism.

On Being and Time

MY WAY TO PHENOMENOLOGY

My academic studies began in the winter of 1909–10 in theology at the University of Freiburg. But the chief work for the study in theology still left enough time for philosophy which belonged to the curriculum anyhow. Thus both volumes of Hus-serl's *Logical Investigations* lay on my desk in the theological seminary ever since my first semester there. These volumes belonged to the university library. The date due could be easily renewed again and again. The work was obviously of little in-terest to the students. But how did it get into this environment so foreign to it?

I had learned from many references in philosophical periodicals that Husserl's thought was determined by Franz Brentano. Ever since 1907, Brentano's dissertation. "On the manifold meaning of being since Aristotle" (1862) had been the chief help and guide of my first awkward attempts to penetrate into philosophy. The following question concerned me in a quite vague manner: If being is predicated in manifold meanings, then what is its leading fundamental meaning? What does Being mean? In the last year of my stay at the *Gymnasium*, I stumbled upon the book of Carl Braig, then professor for dogmatics at Freiburg University: "On Being. Outline of Ontology." It had been published in 1896 at the time when he was an associate professor at Freiburg's theological faculty. The larger sections of the work give extensive text passages from Aristotle, Thomas of Aquinas and Suarez, always at the end, and in addition the etymology for fundamental ontological concepts.

From Husserl's *Logical Investigations*. I expected a decisive aid in the questions stimulated by Brentano's dissertation. Yet my efforts were in vain because I was not searching in the right way. I realized this only very much later. Still, I remained so fascinated by Husserl's work that I read in it again and again in the years to follow without gaining sufficient insight into what fascinated me. The spell emanating from the work extended to the outer appearance of the sentence structure and the title page. On that title page I encountered the name of the publisher Max Niemeyer. This encounter is before my eyes as vividly today as then. His name was connected with that of "Phenomenology," then foreign to me, which appears in the subtitle of the second volume. My understanding of the term "phenomenology" was just as limited and vacillating as my knowledge in those years of the publisher Max Niemeyer and his work.

After four semesters I gave up my theological studies and dedicated myself entirely to philosophy. I still attended theological lectures in the years following 1911, Carl Braig's lecture course on dogmatics. My interest in, speculative theology led me to do this, above all the penetrating kind of thinking which this teacher concretely demonstrated in every lecture hour. On a few walks when I was allowed to accompany him, I first heard of Schelling's and Hegel's significance for speculative theology as distinguished from the dogmatic system of Scholasticism. Thus the tension between ontology and speculative theology as the structure of metaphysics entered the field of my search. . . .

Rickert dedicated the third fully revised edition of his work *The Object of Knowledge, Introduction to Transcendental Philosophy*, which was published the same year, "to my dear friend." The dedication was supposed to testify to the teacher's benefit derived from this pupil. Both of Emil Lask's writings—*The Logic of Philosophy and the Doctrine of Categories. A Study of the Dominant Realm of Logical Form* (1911) and *The Doctrine of Judgment* (1912)—themselves showed clearly enough the influence of Husserl's *Logical Investigations*.

[I tried] to delve into Husserl's work anew. However, my repeated beginning also remained unsatisfactory, because I couldn't get over a main difficulty. It concerned the simple question how thinking's manner of procedure which called itself "phenomenology" was to be carried out. What worried me about this question came from the ambiguity which Husserl's work showed at first glance.

The first volume of the work, published in 1900, brings the refutation of psychologism in logic by showing that the doctrine of thought and knowledge cannot be based on psychology. In contrast, the second volume, which was published the following year and was three times as long, contains the description of the acts of consciousness essential for the constitution of knowledge. So it is a psychology after all. What else is section 9 of the fifth investigation concerning "The Meaning of Brentano's Delimitation of 'psychical phenomena"? Accordingly, Husserl falls back with his phenomenological description of the phenomena of consciousness into the position of psychologism which he had just refuted. But if such a gross error cannot be attributed to Husserl's work, then what is the phenomenological description of the acts of consciousness? Wherein does what is peculiar to phenomenology consist if it is neither logic nor psychology? Does a quite new discipline of philosophy appear here, even one with its own rank and precedence?

I could not disentangle these questions. I remained without knowing what to do or where to go. I could hardly even formulate the questions with the clarity in which they are expressed here.

The year 1913 brought an answer. The *Yearbook for Philosophy and Phenomenological Investigation* which Husserl edited began to be published by the publisher Max Niemeyer. The first volume begins with Husserl's treatise *Ideas*.

"Pure phenomenology" is the "fundamental science" of philosophy which is characterized by that phenomenology. "Pure" means: "transcendental phenomenology." However, the "subjectivity" of the knowing, acting and valuing subject is posited as "transcendental." Both terms, "subjectivity" and "transcendental," show that "phenomenology" consciously and decidedly moved into the tradition of modern philosophy but in such a way that "transcendental subjectivity" attains a more original and universal determination through phenomenology. Phenomenology retained "experiences of consciousness" as its thematic realm, but now in the systematically planned and secured investigation of the structure of acts of experience together with the investigation of the objects experienced in those acts with regard to their objectivity.

In this universal project for a phenomenological philosophy, the *Logical Investigations*, too—which had so to speak remained philosophically neutral—could be assigned their systematic place. They were published in the same year (1913) in a second edition by the same publisher. Most of the investigations had in the meantime undergone "profound revisions." The sixth investigation, "the most important with regard to phenomenology" (preface to the second edition) was, however, withheld. But the essay "Philosophy as Exact Science" (1910–11) which Husserl contributed to the first volume of the new journal *Logos* also only now acquired a sufficient basis for its programmatical theses through the *Ideas*.

Even after the *Ideas* was published, I was still captivated by the never-ceasing spell of the *Logical Investigations*. That magic brought about anew an unrest unaware of its own reason, although it made one suspect that it came from the inability to attain the act of philosophical thinking called "phenomenology" simply by reading the philosophical literature.

My perplexity decreased slowly, my confusion dissolved laboriously, only after I met Husserl personally in his workshop.

Husserl came to Freiburg in 1916 as Heinrich Rickert's successor. Rickert had taken over Windelband's chair in Heidelberg. Husserl's teaching took place in the form of a step-by-step training in phenomenological "seeing" which at the same time demanded that one relinquish the untested use of philosophical knowledge. But it also demanded that one give up introducing the authority of the great thinkers into the conversation. However, the clearer it became to me that the increasing familiarity with phenomenological seeing was fruitful for the interpretation of Aristotle's writing, the less I could separate myself from Aristotle and the other Greek thinkers. Of course I could not immediately see what decisive consequences my renewed occupation with Aristotle was to have.

As I myself practiced phenomenological seeing, teaching and learning in Husserl's proximity after 1919 and at the same time tried out a transformed understanding of Aristotle in a seminar, my interest leaned anew toward the *Logical Investigations*, above all the sixth investigation in the first edition. The distinction which is worked out there between sensuous and categorial intuition revealed itself to me in its scope for the determination of the "manifold meaning of being."

Husserl watched me in a generous fashion, but at the bottom in disagreement, as I worked on the *Logical Investigations* every week in special seminars with advanced students in addition to my lectures and regular seminars. Especially the preparation for this work was fruitful for me. There I learned one thing—at first rather led by surmise than guided by founded insight: What occurs for the phenomenology of the acts of consciousness as the self-manifestation of phenomena is thought more originally by Aristotle and in all Greek thinking and existence as *aletheia*, as the unconcealedness of what is present, its being revealed, its showing itself. That which phenomenological investigations rediscovered as the supporting attitude of thought proves to be the fundamental trait of Greek thinking, if not indeed of philosophy as such.

The more decisively this insight became clear to me, the more pressing the question became: Whence and how is it determined what must be experienced as "the things themselves" in accordance with the principle of phenomenology? Is it consciousness and its objectivity or is it the Being of beings in its unconcealedness and concealment?

Thus I was brought to the path of the question of Being, illumined by the phenomenological attitude, again made uneasy in a different way than previously by the questions prompted by Brentano's dissertation. But the path of questioning became longer than I suspected. It demanded many stops, detours and wrong paths. What the first lectures in Freiburg and then in Marburg attempted shows the path only indirectly.

National Socialist Education*
(January 22, 1934)

German Volksgenossen! German Workers!

As Rector of the University, I cordially welcome you to our institution. This welcome will at the same-time be the beginning of our work together. Let us start by understanding clearly the significance of the fact that you, for whom the City of Freiburg has created jobs by emergency decree, are coming together with us in the largest lecture hall of the University.

What does this fact mean?

Because of novel and comprehensive measures on the part of the City of Freiburg you have been given work and bread has been put on your tables. You thereby

---

*An address given by Heidegger at Freiburg University to 600 beneficiaries of the National Socialist "labor service" *Arbeitsdienst* program (see note, p. 42). Published in *Der Alemann: Kampfblatt der Nationalsozialisten Oberbadens*, February 1, 1934.

enjoy a privileged position among the rest of the City's unemployed. But this preferential treatment means at the same time an obligation.

And your duty is to understand the creation of jobs, and to accept the work for which you are paid, in the way that the Führer of our new State demands. For the creation of jobs means not only the alleviation of external need, not only the elimination of inner discouragement or, indeed, despair; the creation of jobs means not only the *warding off* of that which burdens. The creation of jobs is at the same time, and in its essence, an act of *building up* and construction [*Aufbau und Bau*] in the new future of our Volk.

The creation of work must, first of all, make the unemployed and jobless *Volksgenosse* again *capable of existing* [*daseinsfähig*] in the State and for the State and thereby capable of existing for the Volk as a whole. The *Volksgenosse* who has found work should learn thereby that he has not been cast aside and abandoned, that he has an ordered place in the Volk, and that every service and every accomplishment possesses its own value that is fungible by other services and accomplishments. Having experienced this, he should win back proper dignity and self-confidence in his own eyes and acquire proper self-assurance and resoluteness in the eyes of his *Volksgenossen*.

The goal is: to become strong for a fully valid existence as a *Volksgenosse* in the German *Volksgemeinschaft*.

For this, however, it is necessary:

to know where one's place in the Volk is,

to know how the Volk is organized and how it renews itself in this organization,

to know what is happening with the German Volk in the National Socialist State,

to know in what a bitter struggle this new reality was won and created,

to know what the future recovery of the body of the Volk [*Volkskörper*] means and what it demands of each individual,

to know to what point urbanization has brought the Germans, how they would be returned to the soil and the country through resettlement,

to know what is entailed in the fact that 18 million Germans belong to the Volk but, because they are living outside the borders of the Reich, do not yet belong to the Reich.

Everyone of our Volk who is employed must *know for what reason* and *to what purpose* he is where he is. It is only through this living and ever-present *knowledge* that his life will be rooted in the Volk as a whole, and in its destiny. *Providing this knowledge is thus a necessary part of the creation of work;* and it is your right, but therefore also your obligation, to demand this knowledge and to endeavor to acquire it.

And now, your younger comrades from the *university* stand ready to help you acquire this knowledge. They are resolved to help that knowledge to become alive in you, to help it develop and grow strong and never again to slumber. They stand ready, not as "intellekshuals" ["*Gschtudierten*"] from the class of your "betters," but as *Volksgenossen* who have recognized their duty.

They stand ready, not as the "educated" vis-à-vis a class—indeed, a "lower class"—of *uneducated* individuals, but as comrades. They are prepared to listen to your questions, your problems, your difficulties, and your doubts, to think through them with you, and, in shared effort, to bring them to a clear and decisive resolution. What, therefore, is the significance of the fact that you are assembled here in the auditorium of the University with us?

This fact is a sign that a new, common will exists, the will to build *a living bridge* between the worker of the "hand" and the worker of the "head." Today, the will to bridge this gap is no longer a project that is doomed to failure. And why not? Because the whole of our German reality has been changed by the National Socialist State, with the result that our whole past way of understanding and thinking must also become different.

What we thought up to now when we used the words "knowledge" and "Wissenschaft" has taken on another significance.

What we meant up to now with the words "worker" and "work" has acquired another meaning.

"Wissenschaft" is not the possession of a privileged class of citizens, to be used as a weapon in the exploitation of the working people. Rather, Wissenschaft is merely the *more rigorous* and hence *more responsible* form of that knowledge which the entire German Volk must seek and demand for its own historical existence as a state [*sein eigenes geschichtlich-staatliches Dasein*] if it still wants to secure its continued existence and greatness and to preserve them in the future. *In its essence*, the knowledge of true Wissenschaft does *not* differ *at all* from the knowledge of the farmer, woodcutter, the miner, the artisan. For knowledge means: *to know one's way around* in the world into which we are placed, as a community and as individuals.

Knowledge means: in our decisions and actions *to be up* to the task that is assigned us, whether this task be to till the soil or to fell a tree or to dig a ditch or to inquire into the laws of Nature or to illumine the fatelike force of History.

Knowledge means: to be *master* of the situation into which we are placed.

What is decisive is not so much how varied our knowledge is and what quantity of things we know, but whether our knowledge has grown naturally out of and is directed towards our circle of existence [*ein ursprünglich gewachsenes und auf unseren Daseinskreis aussgerichtetes*] and whether, through our deeds and in our behavior, we take responsibility for what we know. We no longer distinguish between the "educated" and the "uneducated." And not because these are both the same, but because we no longer tie our estimation of a person to this distinction. We do, on the other hand, differentiate between *genuine knowledge* and *pseudo-knowledge*. Genuine knowledge is something that both the farmer and the manual laborer have, each in his own way and in his own field of work, just as the scholar has it in his field. And, on the other hand, for all his learning, the scholar can in fact simply be wasting his time in the idle pursuit of pseudo-knowledge.

If you are to become *ones who know* here, then that does not mean that you will be served up scraps of some "general education," as a charitable afterthought. Rather, *that knowledge* shall be awakened in you *by means of which you*—each in his respective class and work group—*can be clear and resolute Germans.*

Knowledge and the possession of knowledge, as National Socialism understands these words, does not divide into classes, but binds and unites *Volksgenossen* and social and occupational groups [*Stände*] in the one great will of the State.

Like these words "knowledge" and "Wissenschaft," the words "worker" and "work," too, have a transformed meaning and a new sound. The "worker" is not, as Marxism claimed, a mere object of exploitation. The workers [*Arbeiterstand*] are not the class of the disinherited who are rallying for the general class struggle. But labor is also not simply the production of goods for others. Nor is labor simply the occasion and the means to earn a living. Rather:

For us, "work" is the title of every well-ordered action that is borne by the responsibility of the individual, the group, and the State and which is thus of service to the Volk.

Work only exists where man's determination and perseverance are freely engaged in the assertion of will and the accomplishment of a task; *but there it exists everywhere.* Therefore, all work is, *as work*, something spiritual [*Geistiges*], for it is founded in the free exercise of expert knowledge and in the competent understanding of one's task; that is: it is founded in authentic knowledge [*eigentliches Wissen*]. The accomplishment of a miner is basically no less spiritual [*geistig*] than the activity of a scholar.

Worker and work, as National Socialism understands these words, does not divide into classes, but binds and unites *Volksgenossen* and the social and occupational groups into the one great will of the State.

The "workers" and "academics" [*die "wissenschaftlich Wissenden"*] are not opposites. Every worker is, in his own way, one who knows; and only as one who knows is he able to work at all. The privilege of work is denied the animal. And conversely: every person who acts knowingly and who makes decisions in and on the basis of Wissenschaft [*wissenschaftlich Entscheidender*] is a worker.

Letter to the Rector of Freiburg University, November 4, 1945

With reference to the Rector's letter of October 30, 1945, I request to be reinstated in my professorial duties (reintegration). I also remind you that on October 8, 1945, I submitted my request for emeritus status to the philosophy faculty. I ask that you convey this request to the proper authorities.

Regarding the reasons for and conditions of my entry into the Party on May 1, 1933, as well as my relations with the Party during the years 1933–1945, I wish to make the following observations:

I. THE RECTORSHIP, 1933–1934

In April 1933, I was unanimously elected Rector (with two abstentions) in a plenary session of the university and not, as rumor has it, appointed by the National Socialist minister. It was as a result of pressure from my circle of colleagues, and especially upon the urgent request of my predecessor [Wilhelm] von Möllendorff, that I consented to be a candidate for this election and agreed to serve. Previously I neither desired nor occupied an academic office. I never belonged to a political party nor maintained a relation, either personal or substantive, with the NSDAP or with governmental authorities. I accepted the rectorship reluctantly and in the interest of the university alone.

However, I was nevertheless absolutely convinced that an autonomous alliance of intellectuals [*der Geistigen*] could deepen and transform a number of essential elements of the "National Socialist movement" and thereby contribute in its own way to overcoming Europe's disarray and the crisis of the Western spirit. Three [sic] addresses by a man of no lesser rank than Paul Valéry ("The Crisis of Spirit," "The Politics of Spirit," "Our Sovereign Good," "The Balance of Intelligence") constitute sufficient proof of the seriousness, concern, and profundity with which the destiny of the West became an object of reflection outside of Germany during these years. Also, insofar as the will manifested by the free choice of the preponderant majority of the German people affirmed the labor of reconstruction in a National Socialist direction, I viewed it as necessary and feasible to join in at the university level in order to remedy in a consistent and effective manner the general confusion and threat that weighed against the West. And it is precisely because in the realm of the sciences and of spirit so-called "impossible" persons strove to assert their power and influence on the "movement" that it seemed to me necessary to emphasize essentially spiritual goals and horizons and to try, on the basis of Western responsibility, to further their influence and reality. I explained my intentions with sufficient clarity in my rectoral address, "The Self-Assertion of the German University" (1933). If I may be permitted to explain the basic spiritual tenor of the address from a twofold perspective: with reference to the essential task of spirit, it says: "And the spiritual world of a people is neither the superstructure of a culture, nor an attestation of practical knowledge and values. . . . The greatness of a Volk is guaranteed by its spiritual world alone." For those who know and think, these sentences express my opposition to [Alfred] Rosenberg's conception, according to which, conversely, spirit and the world of spirit are merely an "expression" and emanation of racial facts and of the physical constitution of man. According to the dogma of "politicized science," which was then propagated by the National Socialist student organizations, the sciences should serve as a model for vocational goals, and the value or the lack of value of knowledge should be measured according to the needs of "life." In response, the address clearly and unambiguously has this to say: "Knowledge does not stand in the service of the professions, but the reverse: the professions effectuate and administer this highest, essential knowledge of the Volk concerning its entire Dasein." "The university" is "the locus of spiritual legislation." All of those who are capable of substantive thought [*sachliche Denken*] will be able to judge whether the essence of the university can be thought in a more exalted manner than here. And whether the essence of the various fields of knowledge has, from a spiritual standpoint, been defined in a more clear or categorical fashion than in this formulation: "The departments are only departments if they are deployed in a power of spiritual legislation that is rooted in a capacity consistent with their essence, in order that they might transform the force of Dasein which besieges *them* into a *single* spiritual world of the Volk."

In the spirit of this address, I tried, following the irremediably disruptive summer semester of revolution [in 1933] and despite the many setbacks experienced thus far, in the initial months of the 1933–34 winter semester to keep the business of the university going. It was clear for me that to act in the middle of the frictions of real life was not possible without compromise and concessions in unessential matters. But I was equally convinced, especially following Hitler's May 1933 speech asking for peace, that my basic spiritual position and my conception of the task of the university could be reconciled with the political will of those in power.

The practical efforts of the winter semester failed. During the few days of Christmas vacation I realized that it was a mistake to believe that, from the basic spiritual position that was the result of my long years of philosophical work, I could immediately influence the transformation of the bases—spiritual or non-spiritual—of the National Socialist movement. At the beginning of 1934 I decided to abandon my duties at the end of the semester. The increasing hostility of the minister to my work as rector manifested itself in practice by the summons to replace the deans of the divisions of law and medicine (professors Wolf and von Möllendorff) because they were politically unacceptable. I refused to acquiesce in this demand and handed in my resignation. (I refused equally to assist in the traditional ceremony of the inauguration of my successor, who was installed by force and acclaimed as the first National Socialist rector. I gave as my explanation that there was nothing to "hand over" since the new rector was chosen and nominated by the government.)

II. MY ENTRY INTO THE PARTY

A short while after I took control of the rectorship the district head presented himself, accompanied by two functionaries in charge of university matters, to urge me, in accordance with the wishes of the minister, to join the Party. The minister insisted that in this way my official relations with the Party and the governing organs would be simplified, especially since up until then I had had no contact with these organs. After lengthy consideration, I declared myself ready to enter the Party in the interests of the university, but under the express condition of refusing to accept a position within the Party or working on behalf of the Party either during the rectorship or afterward. These conditions were accepted by the leader of the district, and I adhered to them strictly thereafter.

III. MY LATER RELATION TO THE PARTY

My membership [in the Party] resulted in practically no advantages as far as the facilitation of my administrative duties was concerned. I was never invited to meetings of the district leadership. University personnel began to mistrust me. After my resignation from the rectorship it became clear that by continuing to teach, my opposition to the principles of the National Socialist world-view would only grow. There was little need for me to resort to specific attacks; it sufficed for me to express my fundamental philosophical positions against the dogmatism and primitivism of Rosenberg's biologism. I found myself in an essentially different situation from that of other representatives of scientific disciplines, where there was neither immediately nor in principle a need to formulate fundamental metaphysical positions; and this is precisely what I did during all of my hours in the classroom. Since National Socialist ideology became increasingly inflexible and increasingly less disposed to a purely philosophical interpretation, the fact that I was active as a philosopher was itself a sufficient expression of opposition. During the first semester that followed my resignation I conducted a course on logic and under the title, the doctrine of *logos*, treated the essence of language. I sought to show that language was not the biological-racial essence of man, but conversely, that the essence of man was based in language as a basic reality of *spirit*. All intelligent students understood this lecture as well as its basic intention. It was equally understood by the observers and informers who then gave reports of my activities to [Ernst] Krieck in Heidelberg, to [Alfred] Bäumler in Berlin, and to Rosenberg, the head of National Socialist scientific services. Thereafter there began a malicious polemic against my thought and person in *Volk im Werden*, a review edited by Krieck. During the journal's twelve years in print, there hardly appeared an issue that didn't contain some heinous and misleading point about my thought. All these declarations emanating from the Part press were made in the same tone whenever I lectured before scholarly organizations, in my lectures on "The Origins of the Work of Art," or on "The Metaphysical Foundations of the Modern Picture of the World." No member of the Freiburg University faculty was defamed to such a degree during the years 1933–34 in newspapers and journals, and, in addition, in the journal of the Hitler Youth, *Will and Power*.

Beginning in 1936 I embarked on a series of courses and lectures on Nietzsche, which lasted until 1945 and which represented in even clearer fashion a declaration of spiritual resistance. In truth, it is unjust to assimilate Nietzsche to National Socialism, an assimilation which—apart from what is essential—ignores his hostility to anti-Semitism and his positive attitude with respect to Russia. But on a higher plane, the debate with Nietzsche's metaphysics is a debate with *nihilism* as it manifests itself with increased clarity under the political form of fascism.

The Party functionaries also took note of the spiritual resistance of my courses on Nietzsche, which led to measures such as the following:

In 1934, I was excluded, at Rosenberg's urging, from the German delegation of the International Congress of Philosophy. I was also excluded in 1937 from the German delegation at the Descartes conference in Paris, which was also an international philosophical conference (although the French for their part twice expressly requested that I attend). The reedition of my work, *Kant and the Problem of Metaphysics*, which originally appeared in 1929 and which was out of print as of 1931, and which contained a refutation of philosophical anthropology, was also banned at the instigation of the same office. From 1938 on, one could no longer cite my name nor evaluate my works as a result of secret instructions given to journal editors. I cite one such directive dating from 1940, which was revealed to me in confidence by friends:

"Martin Heidegger's essay, "Plato's Concept of Truth," to appear soon in the Berlin journal, *Jahrbuch für geistige Überlieferung*, edited by Helmut Küper, may be neither reviewed nor cited. Heidegger's participation in this number of the journal, which otherwise may be reviewed, should not be mentioned." (Z.D. *165/ 34*. Edition No. 7154)

The publication of this essay, which was accepted by the editor for a special edition to be sold in bookstores, was forbidden. The same thing occurred with my contribution to a volume commemorating Hölderlin, which had to appear in a separate edition.

Whereas my name and writings have been passed over in silence in Germany, where it has been impossible for me to publish individual works—in 1943 three small lectures appeared in secret, without ever being cited in any bibliography—during the war I was on many occasions invited for propagandistic ends to give lectures in Spain, Portugal, and Italy. I formally refused these strange invitations by making it known that I was not disposed to lend my name abroad for purposes of propaganda while I was not allowed to publish my writings in my own country.

The German Institute of Paris utilized the same methods as the Ministry of Foreign Affairs. In a collection entitled *Friedrich Hölderlin*, which was published in 1943 in Paris, it reproduced my lecture, "Hölderlin and the Essence of Poetry," which appeared in 1936 and was translated into French in 1938, in the same translation and *without my knowledge*, and without the permission of the French translator. This arbitrary publication occurred despite the fact that I had already declined the offer to participate in a review published by the same institute.

I also demonstrated publicly my attitude toward the Party by not participating in its gatherings, by not wearing its regalia, and, as of 1934, by refusing to begin my courses and lectures with the so-called German greeting [*Heil Hitler!*].

There was nothing special about my spiritual resistance during the last eleven years. However, if crude claims continue to be advanced that numerous students had been "enticed" toward "National Socialism" by my year as rector, justice requires that one at least recognize that between 1934 and 1944 thousands of students were trained to reflect on the metaphysical basis of our age and that I opened their eyes to the world of spirit and its great traditions in the history of the West.

Martin Heidegger

Translated by Richard Wolin

37

RUDOLPH CARNAP
Autobiography

Rudolph Carnap (1891–1970) studied philosophy at the University of Jena, got his degree in 1921, and went to teach at the University of Vienna in 1926. With other members of the Vienna Circle—which at various times included Moritz Schlick, Hans Reichenbach, and Otto Neurath—Carnap became engaged in the programs of (what came to be called) logical positivism or logical empiricism. He helped develop and refine the verification criterion of meaning, according to which the meaning of a sentence is given by the conditions under which it would be true. The strict verification criterion was later revised as a probabilistic theory of degrees of confirmation. A good deal of the work of the Vienna Circle originally appeared in *Erkenntnis*, a journal founded by Carnap and Reichenbach in 1930. Carnap's first major work, *The Logical Construction of the World*, was published in 1928; it was followed by *The Logical Syntax of Language* (1934).

Carnap left Germany for the United States in 1935 where he taught at the University of Chicago until 1952. During that time, he was among the general editors of the *International Encyclopedia of the Unified Sciences*, a series of monographs on scientific method in the natural and social sciences. Turning his attention to semantics, he wrote *Introduction to Semantics* (1942) and *Meaning and Necessity* (1947). In 1954, Carnap went to UCLA, where he returned to his earlier interest in probability theory. Most of his essays on that subject appeared in *Studies in Inductive Logic and Probability* (1971, 1980).

Although his semantics led him to regard value theory and the greater part of traditional metaphysics and epistemology, as empty of cognitive content, Carnap thought the philosophical work of clarifying concepts—exposing vagueness and obfuscation—has significant moral and political importance.

I
The Development of My Thinking

MY STUDENT YEARS

I was born in 1891 in Ronsdorf near Barmen, in Northwest Germany. My father, Johannes S. Carnap, came from a family of poor weavers, but had in a long, industrious life acquired a prosperous and respected position. The forebears of my mother, Anna Carnap nee Dörpfeld, were teachers, pastors, and peasants. When I was a child, my mother worked for years on a large book describing the life, work, and ideas of her late father, the teacher and pedagogical author, Friedrich Wilhelm Dörpfeld. I was fascinated by the magical activity of putting thought on paper, and I have loved it ever since.

My parents were deeply religious; their faith permeated their whole lives. My mother used to impress upon us that the essential in religion was not so much the acceptance of a creed, but the living of the good life; the convictions of another were for her morally neutral, as long as he sought seriously for the truth. This attitude made her very tolerant toward people with other beliefs.

When my sister and I reached school age, my mother, having been a teacher, obtained permission to teach us herself at home. She did so for three years, but for only an hour each day. She did not believe much in the quantity of material learned; she aimed rather at helping us to acquire a clear and interconnected knowledge of each item and, above all, to develop the ability to think for ourselves.

After the death of my father in 1898 we moved to Barmen. I attended the *Gymnasium*, whose curriculum was based on the classical languages. The subjects I liked most were mathematics, which attracted me by the exactness of its concepts and the possibility of proving results by mere thinking, and Latin with its rational structure.

In 1909 we moved to Jena. From 1910 to 1914 I studied at the Universities of Jena and Freiburg/i.B. First I concentrated on philosophy and mathematics; later, physics and philosophy were my major fields. In the selection of lecture courses I followed only my own interests without thinking about examinations or a professional career. When I did not like a lecture course, I dropped it and studied the subject by reading books in the field instead.

Within the field of philosophy, I was mainly interested in the theory of knowledge and in the philosophy of science. On the other hand, in the field of logic, lecture courses and books by philosophers appeared to me dull and entirely obsolete after I had become acquainted with a genuine logic through Frege's lectures. I studied Kant's philosophy with Bruno Bauch in Jena. In his seminar, the *Critique of Pure Reason* was discussed in detail for an entire year. I was strongly impressed by Kant's conception that the geometrical structure of space is determined by the form of our intuition. The after-effects of this influence were still noticeable in the chapter on the space of intuition in my dissertation, *Der Raum* (written in 1920, see the next section).

On the whole, I think I learned much more in the field of philosophy by reading and by private conversations than by attending lectures and seminars.

I greatly enjoyed the study of mathematics. In contrast to the endless controversies among the various schools of philosophy, the results in mathematics could be proven exactly and there was no further controversy. But the most fruitful inspiration I received from university lectures did not come from those in the fields of philosophy proper or mathematics proper, but rather from the lectures of Gottlob Frege (1848–1925) on the borderlands between those fields, namely, symbolic logic and the foundations of mathematics.

In the advanced course on *Begriffsschrift*, Frege explained various applications, among them some which are not contained in his publications, e.g., a definition of the continuity of a function, and of the limit of a function, the distinction between ordinary convergence and uniform convergence. All these concepts were expressible with the help of the quantifiers, which appear in his system of logic for the first time. He gave also a demonstration of the logical mistake in the ontological proof for the existence of God.

Although Frege gave quite a number of examples of interesting applications of his symbolism in mathematics, he usually did not discuss general philosophical problems. It is evident from his works that he saw the great philosophical importance of the new instrument which he had created, but he did not convey a clear impression of this to his students. Thus, although I was intensely interested in his system of logic, I was not aware at that time of its great philosophical significance. Only much later, after the first world war, when I read Frege's and Russell's books with greater attention, did I recognize the value of Frege's work not only for the foundations of mathematics, but for philosophy in general.

In the summer semester of 1914 I attended Frege's course, *Logik in der Mathematik*. Here he examined critically some of the customary conceptions and formulations in mathematics. He deplored the fact that mathematicians did not even seem to aim at the construction of a unified, well-founded *system* of mathematics, and therefore showed a lack of interest in foundations. He pointed out a certain looseness in the customary formulation of axioms, definitions, and proofs, even in works of the more prominent mathematicians. As an example he quoted Weyerstrass' definition: "A number is a series of things of the same kind" ("... *eine Reihe gleichartiger Dinge"*). He criticized in particular the lack of attention to certain fundamental distinctions, e.g., the distinction between the symbol and the symbolized, that between a logical concept and a mental image or act, and that between a function and the value of the function. Unfortunately, his admonitions go mostly unheeded even today.

Among the empirical sciences physics was for me the most attractive. I was strongly impressed by the fact that it is possible to state laws with exact numerical relations by which events can be generally described and thus explained, and future events predicted.

I was also interested in other fields of knowledge. I read books in many fields and pondered whether to study some of them more thoroughly. But psychology was the only field in which I attended courses and seminars and did a little experimental work. What was disturbing to me in all fields of empirical science except physics, was the lack of clarity in the explanation of the concepts and in the formulation of the laws, and the great number of insufficiently connected facts.

During my pre-university years I had gradually begun to doubt the religious doctrines about the world, man, and God. As a student I turned away from these beliefs more deliberately and definitely. Under the influence of books and conversations with friends, I recognized that these doctrines, if interpreted literally, were incompatible with the results of modern science, especially with the theory of evolution in biology and determinism in physics. The freethinker movement in Germany was at that time mainly represented by the *Monistenbund* (Society of Monists). I studied eagerly the works of the leaders of this movement, e.g., the zoologist Ernst Haeckel and the prominent chemist Wilhelm Ostwald. Although most of these books could not be regarded as serious philosophical writings but belonged rather to popular literature, and from the point of view of the theory of knowledge their formulations seemed to me often quite primitive, I was nevertheless in sympathy with their insistence that the scientific method was the only method of obtaining well-founded, systematically coherent knowledge and with their humanist aim of improving the life of mankind by rational means.

The transformation of my basic beliefs occurred however not suddenly, but in a gradual development. First the supernatural features in the doctrines of religion disappeared. Christ was regarded not as divine, but as a man among men, distinguished as an important leader in the development of humane morality. Later the idea of God as a personal, though immaterial being, interfering in the course of nature and history in order to reward and punish, was abandoned and replaced by a kind of pantheism. This conception had certain Spinozist features, which came to me less from the works of Spinoza himself than from those of men like Goethe, whose work, personality, and *Lebensweisheit* (wisdom of life) I esteemed very highly. Since my pantheism was thus more influenced by poetical than by philosophical works, it had more an ethical than a theoretical nature; that is to say, it was more a matter of the attitude toward the world and fellow human beings than of explicitly formulated doctrines. Later I became more and more convinced that pantheism, if taken not as an emotional-ethical attitude but as a doctrine, could not be scientifically grounded, inasmuch as the events in nature, including those in man and society as a part of nature, can be explained by the scientific method without the need of any idea of God.

Together with the belief in a personal God, I abandoned also the belief in immortality as the survival of a personal, conscious soul. The main factor in this development was a strong impression of the continuity in the scientific view of the world. Man has gradually developed from lower forms of organisms without sudden changes. All mental processes are intimately connected with the brain; how can they continue when the body disintegrates? Thus I arrived gradually at a clear naturalistic conception: everything that happens is part of nature, man is a higher form of organism and dies like all other organisms. There remained the question of an explanation of the historical fact that the belief in one or several gods and in immortality was very widespread in all known cultures. This, however, was not a philosophical problem but a historical and psychological one. I gradually found an answer based on anthropological results concerning the historical evolution of religious conceptions. Much later I gained important insights into the development of the individual's picture of the world through the results of Freud's investigations and in particular his discovery of the origin of the conception of God as a substitute for the father.

Since I experienced the positive effect of a living religion in the lives of my parents and in my own life during childhood, my respect for any man whose character I esteem highly is not diminished by the fact that he embraces some form of religion, traditional or otherwise. At the present stage of development of our culture, many people still need religious mythological symbols and images. It seems to me wrong to try to deprive them of the support they obtain from these ideas, let alone to ridicule them.

An entirely different matter is the question of theology, here understood as a system of doctrines in distinction to a system of valuations and prescriptions for life. Systematic theology claims to represent knowledge concerning alleged beings of a supernatural order. A claim of this kind must be examined according to the same rigorous standards as any other claim of knowledge. Now in my considered opinion this examination has clearly shown that traditional theology is a remnant of earlier times, entirely out of line with the scientific way of thinking in the present century. Any system of traditional theological dogmas can usually be interpreted in many different ways. If they are taken in a direct and literal sense, for example, based on a literal interpretation of statements in the Bible or other "holy scriptures," then most of the dogmas are refuted by the results of science. If, on the other hand, this crude literal interpretation is rejected and instead a refined reformulation is accepted which puts theological questions outside the scope of the scientific method, then the dogmas have the same character as statements of traditional metaphysics. As I shall explain later, I came in my philosophical development first to the insight that the main statements of traditional metaphysics are outside the realm of science and irrelevant for scientific knowledge, and later to the more radical conviction that they are devoid of any cognitive content. Since that time I have been convinced that the same holds for most of the statements of contemporary Christian theology.

The transformation and final abandonment of my religious convictions led at no time to a nihilistic attitude towards moral questions. My moral valuations were afterwards essentially the same as before. It is not easy to characterize these valuations in a few words, since they are not based on explicitly formulated principles, but constitute rather an implicit lasting attitude. The following should therefore be understood as merely a rough and brief indication of certain basic features. The main task of an individual seems to me the development of his personality and the creation of fruitful and healthy relations among human beings. This aim implies the task of co-operation in the development of society and ultimately of the whole of mankind towards a community in which every individual has the possibility of leading a satisfying life and of participating in cultural goods. The fact that everybody knows that he will eventually die, need not make his life meaningless or aimless. He himself gives meaning to his life if he sets tasks for himself, struggles to fulfill them to the best of his ability, and regards all the specific tasks of all individuals as parts of the great task of humanity, whose aim goes far beyond the limited span of each individual life.

The outbreak of the war in 1914 was for me an incomprehensible catastrophe. Military service was contrary to my whole attitude, but I accepted it now as a duty, believed to be necessary in order to save the fatherland. Before the war, I, like most of my friends, had been uninterested and ignorant in political matters. We had some general ideals, including a just, harmonious and rational organization within the nation and among the nations. We realized that the existing political and economic order was not in accord with these ideals, and still less the customary method of settling conflicts of interests among nations by war. Thus the general trend of our political thinking was pacifist, anti-militarist, anti-monarchist, perhaps also socialist. But we did not think much about the problem of how to implement these ideals by practical action. The war suddenly destroyed our illusion that everything was already on the right path of continuous progress.

THE BEGINNING OF MY WORK IN PHILOSOPHY (1919–1926)

After the war, I lived for a while in Jena, and then in Buchenbach near Freiburg/ i.B. In this period, I first passed my examinations, and then I began my own research in philosophy, first in relative isolation, but later in contact with Reichenbach and others who worked in a similar direction. This period ended in 1926, when I went to Vienna and joined the Vienna Circle.

Before the war I had studied according to my own interests without any clear practical plans. I had the idea that some day I would be a university teacher, but I had not decided whether in philosophy or in physics. When I came back from more than four years of service in the war, I was still equally interested in both fields. However, I now saw clearly that I did not wish to do experimental work in physics, because my inclination and abilities were purely theoretical. Therefore I tried to combine my interests in theoretical physics and philosophy.

The largest part of my philosophical work from 1922 to 1925 was devoted to considerations out of which grew the book, *Der logische Aufbau der Welt* [1928–1].

Inspired by Russell's description of the aim and the method of future philosophy, I made numerous attempts at analyzing concepts of ordinary language relating to things in our environment and their observable properties and relations, and at constructing definitions of these concepts with the help of symbolic logic. Although I was guided in my procedure by the psychological facts concerning the formation of concepts of material things out of perceptions, my real aim was not the description of this genetic process, but rather its rational reconstruction—i.e., a schematized description of an imaginary procedure, consisting of rationally prescribed steps, which would lead to essentially the same results as the actual psychological process. Thus, for example, material things are usually immediately perceived as three-dimensional bodies; on the other hand, in the systematic procedure they are to be constructed out of a temporal sequence of continually changing forms in the two-dimensional visual field. At first I made the analysis in the customary way, proceeding from complexes to smaller and smaller components, e.g., first from material bodies to instantaneous visual fields, then to color patches, and finally to single positions in the visual field. Thus the analysis led to what Ernst Mach called the elements. My use of this method was probably influenced by Mach and phenomenalist philosophers. But it seemed to me that I was the first who took the doctrine of these philosophers seriously. I was not content with their customary general statements like "A material body is a complex of visual, tactile, and other sensations", but tried actually to construct these complexes in order to show their structure. For the description of the structure of any complex, the new logic of relations as in *Principia Mathematica* seemed to me just the required tool. While I worked on many special problems, I was aware that this ultimate aim could not possibly be reached by one individual, but I took it as my task to give at least an outline of the total construction and to show by partial solutions the nature of the method to be applied.

A change in the approach occurred when I recognized, under the influence of the Gestalt psychology of Wertheimer and Köhler that the customary method of analyzing material things into separate sense-data was inadequate—that an instantaneous visual field and perhaps even an instantaneous total experience is given as a unit, while the allegedly simple sense-data are the result of a process of abstraction. Therefore I took as elements total instantaneous experiences (*Elementarerlebnisse*) rather than single sense-data. I developed a method called "quasi-analysis", which leads, on the basis of the similarity-relation among experiences, to the logical construction of those entities which are usually conceived as components. On the basis of a certain primitive relation among experiences, the method of quasi-analysis leads step by step to the various sensory domains—first to the visual domain, then to the positions in the visual field, the colors and their similarity system, the temporal order, and the like. Later, perceived things in the three-dimensional perceptual space are constructed, among them that particular thing which is usually called my own body, and the bodies of other persons. Still later, the so-called other minds are constructed; that is to say, mental states are ascribed to other bodies in view of their behavior, in analogy to the experience of one's own mental states.

Leaving aside further details of the system, I shall try to characterize one general feature of it that seems to me important for the understanding of my basic attitude towards traditional philosophical ways of thinking. Since my student years, I have liked to talk with friends about general problems in science and in practical life, and these discussions often led to philosophical questions. My friends were philosophically interested, yet most of them were not professional philosophers, but worked either in the natural sciences or in the humanities. Only much later, when I was working on the *Logischer Aufbau*, did I become aware that in talks with my various friends I had used different philosophical languages, adapting myself to their ways of thinking and speaking. With one friend I might talk in a language that could be characterized as realistic or even as materialistic; here we looked at the world as consisting of bodies, bodies as consisting of atoms; sensations, thoughts, emotions, and the like were conceived as physiological processes in the nervous system and ultimately as physical processes. Not that the friend maintained or even considered the thesis of materialism; we just used a way of speaking which might be called materialistic. In a talk with another friend, I might adapt myself to his idealistic kind of language. We would consider the question of how things are to be constituted on the basis of the given. With some I talked a language which might be labelled nominalistic, with others again Frege's language of abstract entities of various types, like properties, relations, propositions, etc., a language which some contemporary authors call Platonic.

I was surprised to find that this variety in my way of speaking appeared to some as objectionable and even inconsistent. I had acquired insights valuable for my own thinking from philosophers and scientists of a great variety of philosophical creeds. When asked which philosophical positions I myself held, I was unable to answer. I could only say that in general my way of thinking was closer to that of physicists and of those philosophers who are in contact with scientific work. Only gradually, in the course of years, did I recognize clearly that my way of thinking was neutral with respect to the traditional controversies, e.g., realism vs. idealism, nominalism vs. Platonism (realism of universals), materialism vs. spiritualism and so on. When I developed the system of the *Aufbau,* it actually did not matter to me which of the various forms of philosophical language I used, because to me they were merely modes of speech, and not formulations of positions. Indeed, in the book itself, in the description of the system of construction or constitution, I used in addition to the neutral language of symbolic logic three other languages, in order to facilitate the understanding for the reader; namely, first, a simple translation of the symbolic formula of definition into the word language; second, a corresponding formulation in the realistic language as it is customary in natural science; and third, a reformulation of the definition as a rule of operation for a constructive procedure, applicable by anybody, be it Kant's transcendental subject or a computing machine.

The system of concepts was constructed on a phenomenalistic basis; the basic elements were experiences, as mentioned before. However, I indicated also the possibility of constructing a total system of concepts on a physicalistic basis. The main motivation for my choice of a phenomenalistic basis was the intention to represent not only the logical relations among the concepts but also the equally important epistemological relations. The system was intended to give, though not a description, still a rational reconstruction of the actual process of the formation of concepts. The choice of a phenomenalistic basis was influenced by some radical empiricist or positivist German philosophers of the end of the last century whom I had studied with interest, in the first place Ernst Mach, and further Richard Avenarius, Richard von Schubert-Soldern, and Wilhelm Schuppe. For the construction of scientific concepts on the phenomenal basis I found fruitful suggestions in the works of Mach and Avenarius, and, above all, in the logical constructions made by Russell. With respect to the problem of the basis, my attitude was again ontologically neutral. For me it was simply a methodological question of choosing the most suitable basis for the system to be constructed, either a phenomenalistic or a physicalistic basis. The ontological theses of the traditional doctrines of either phenomenalism or materialism remained for me entirely out of consideration.

This neutral attitude toward the various philosophical forms of language, based on the principle that everyone is free to use the language most suited to his purpose, has remained the same throughout my life. It was formulated as "principle of tolerance" in *Logical Syntax* and I still hold it today, e.g., with respect to the contemporary controversy about a nominalist or Platonic language. On the other hand, regarding the criticism of traditional metaphysics, in the *Aufbau* I merely refrained from taking sides; I added that, if one proceeds from the discussion of language forms to that of the corresponding metaphysical theses about the reality or unreality of some kind of entities, he steps beyond the bounds of science. I shall later speak of the development towards a more radical anti-metaphysical position.

THE VIENNA CIRCLE (1926–1935)

In the summer of 1924, through Reichenbach, I had become acquainted with Moritz Schlick. Schlick told me that he would be happy to have me as an instructor in Vienna. In 1925 I went for a short time to Vienna and gave some lectures in Schlick's Philosophical Circle. From the fall of 1926 to the summer of 1931 I was an instructor of philosophy at the University of Vienna.

For my philosophical work the period in Vienna was one of the most stimulating, enjoyable, and fruitful periods of my life. My interests and my basic philosophical views were more in accord with those of the Circle than with any group I ever found. From the very beginning, when in 1925 I explained in the Circle the general plan and method of *Der logische Aufbau*, I found a lively interest. When I returned to Vienna in 1926, the typescript of the first version of the book was read by the members of the Circle, and many of its problems were thoroughly discussed.

The task of fruitful collaboration, often so difficult among philosophers, was facilitated in our Circle by the fact that all members had a first-hand acquaintance with some field of science, either mathematics, physics or social science. This led to a higher standard in clarity and responsibility than is usually found in philosophical groups, particularly in Germany. Also, the members of the Circle were familiar with modern logic. This made it possible to represent the analysis of a concept or proposition under discussion symbolically and thereby make the arguments more precise. Furthermore, there was agreement among most of the members to reject traditional metaphysics. However, very little time was wasted in a polemic against metaphysics. The anti-metaphysical attitude showed itself chiefly in the choice of the language used in the discussion. We tried to avoid the terms of traditional philosophy and to use instead those of logic, mathematics, and empirical science, or of that part of the ordinary language which, though more vague, still is in principle translatable into a scientific language.

Characteristic for the Circle was the open and undogmatic attitude taken in the discussions. Everyone was willing constantly to subject his views to a reexamination by others or by himself. The common spirit was one of co-operation rather than competition. The common purpose was to work together in the struggle for clarification and insight.

In the Vienna Circle, a large part of Ludwig Wittgenstein's book *Tractatus Logico-Philosophicus* was read aloud and discussed sentence by sentence. Often long reflections were necessary in order to find out what was meant. And sometimes we did not find any clear interpretation. But still we understood a good deal of it and then had lively discussions about it. I had previously read parts of Wittgenstein's work when it was published as an article in Ostwald's *Annalen der Natur und Kulturphilosophie*. I found in it many interesting and stimulating points. But at that time I did not make the great effort required to come to a clear understanding of the often obscure formulations; for this reason I had not read the whole treatise. Now I was happy to see that the Circle was interested in this work and that we undertook to study it together.

Wittgenstein's book exerted a strong influence upon our Circle. But it is not correct to say that the philosophy of the Vienna Circle was just Wittgenstein's philosophy. We learned much by our discussions of the book, and accepted many views as far as we could assimilate them to our basic conceptions. The degree of influence varied, of course, for the different members.

For me personally, Wittgenstein was perhaps the philosopher who, besides Russell and Frege, had the greatest influence on my thinking. The most important insight I gained from his work was the conception that the truth of logical statements is based only on their logical structure and on the meaning of the terms. Logical statements are true under all conceivable circumstances; thus their truth is independent of the contingent facts of the world. On the other hand, it follows that these statements do not say anything about the world and thus have no factual content.

Another influential idea of Wittgenstein's was the insight that many philosophical sentences, especially in traditional metaphysics, are pseudo-sentences, devoid of cognitive content. I found Wittgenstein's view on this point close to the one I had previously developed under the influence of anti-metaphysical scientists and philosophers. I had recognized that many of these sentences and questions originate in a misuse of language and a violation of logic. Under the influence of Wittgenstein, this conception was strengthened and became more definite and more radical.

AMERICA (SINCE 1936)

A. My Life in the United States

In 1934 I became acquainted with two American philosophers who visited my friends in Vienna and afterwards visited me in Prague; Charles W. Morris of the University of Chicago, and W. V. Quine, of Harvard University. Both were strongly attracted by our way of philosophizing and later helped to make it known in America. Furthermore, both exerted themselves in order to make it possible for me to come to the United States. Harvard University invited me to participate in its Tercentenary Celebration, September 1936. The University of Chicago asked me to teach there in the Winter Quarter of 1936, and later offered me a permanent position, which I held from the fall of 1936 until 1952. I was very happy to remain permanently in America and, in 1941, I became a citizen of the United States. I was not only relieved to escape the stifling political and cultural atmosphere and the danger of war in Europe, but was also very gratified to see that in the United States there was a considerable interest, especially among the younger philosophers, in the scientific method of philosophy, based on modern logic, and that this interest was growing from year to year.

In Princeton I had some interesting talks with Einstein, whom I had known personally years before. Although a short time before he had suffered a serious illness and looked pale and aged, he was lively and cheerful in conversation. He liked to make jokes and would then burst into hearty laughter. For me personally these talks were impressive and valuable, particularly because they reflected not only his great mind but also his fascinating human personality. Most of the time I listened to him and observed his gestures and his expressive face; only occasionally I indicated my opinion.

Once Einstein said that the problem of the Now worried him seriously. He explained that the experience of the Now means something special for man, something essentially different from the past and the future, but that this important difference does not and cannot occur within physics. That this experience cannot be grasped by science seemed to him a matter of painful but inevitable resignation. I remarked that all that occurs objectively can be described in science; on the one hand the temporal sequence of events is described in physics; and, on the other hand, the peculiarities of man's experiences with respect to time, including his different attitude towards past, present, and future, can be described and (in principle) explained in psychology. But Einstein thought that these scientific descriptions cannot possibly satisfy our human needs; that there is something essential about the Now which is just outside of the realm of science. We both agreed that this was not a question of a defect for which science could be blamed, as Bergson thought. I did not wish to press the point, because I wanted primarily to understand his personal attitude to the problem rather than to clarify the theoretical situation. But I definitely had the impression that Einstein's thinking on this point involved a lack of distinction between experience and knowledge. Since science in principle can say all that can be said, there is no unanswerable question left. But though there is no theoretical question left, there is still the common human emotional experience, which is sometimes disturbing for special psychological reasons.

On one occasion Einstein said that he wished to raise an objection against positivism concerning the question of the reality of the physical world. I said that there was no real difference between our views on this question. But he insisted that he had to make an important point here. Then he criticized the view, going back to Ernst Mach, that the sense data are the only reality, or more generally, any view which presumes something as an absolutely certain basis of all knowledge. I explained that we had abandoned these earlier positivistic views, that we did no longer believe in a "rockbottom basis of knowledge"; and I mentioned Neurath's simile that our task is to reconstruct the ship while it is floating on the ocean. He emphatically agreed with this metaphor and this view. But then he added that, if positivism were now liberalized to such an extent, there would no longer be any difference between our conception and any other philosophical view. I said that there was indeed no basic difference between our conception and his and other scientists' in general, even though they often formulate it in the language of realism; but that there was still an important difference between our view and that of those traditional philosophical schools which look for an absolute knowledge.

At another time, Einstein raised a fundamental problem concerning the concept formation in contemporary physics, namely the fact that magnitudes of two entirely different kinds are used, those with continuous scales and those with discrete scales. He regarded this combination of heterogeneous concepts as intolerable in the long run. In his view, physics must finally become either pure field physics with all magnitudes having continuous scales, or else all magnitudes, including those of space and time, must be discrete. At the present time it is not yet possible to foresee which of these two forms will develop. For a pure field physics there is among others the great difficulty of explaining why electric charges do not occur in all possible values but only as multiples of the elementary charge. Then he mentioned the problem of explaining, on the basis of fundamental laws, which presumably would be symmetrical with respect to positive and negative electricity, the fact that all atomic nuclei must have a positive charge. Perhaps originally both kinds of nuclei did actually occur, but finally the positive ones devoured the others, at least in our part of the universe. (This assumption was confirmed after Einstein's death by the discovery of anti-protons.)

Once I referred in a talk with Einstein to the strong conformism in the United States, the insistence that the individual adjust his behavior to the generally accepted standards. He agreed emphatically and mentioned as an example that a complete stranger had written him that he ought to have his hair cut: "Don't forget that you now live in America."

In 1953, when Reichenbach's creative activity was suddenly ended by his premature death, our movement lost one of its most active leaders. But his published work and the fruit of his personal influence live on. In 1954 I accepted the chair which he had occupied at the University of California at Los Angeles. I was happy to see how much the spirit of scientific philosophy was alive among the philosophers at this university.

B. The Situation of Philosophy in the United States

In Vienna, there were rarely philosophical discussions with colleagues outside of our Circle. In Prague I had even fewer opportunities for discussions with philosophers, especially because there I did not belong to the Philosophical Division (i.e., the Humanities), but to the Division of the Natural Sciences. It is only when I came to live in the United States and was a member of a philosophy department, that I had frequent and close contact with other philosophers. In Chicago we had not only private conversations, but also discussions in the Department Seminar for faculty members and Ph.D. candidates, and very extensive oral examinations for the Ph.D. degree, which were attended by the entire department staff.

In this section I wish to make some remarks, mainly meant for philosophically interested readers in other countries, about the state of philosophy as I found it in the United States and especially in Chicago, and my personal reactions to it.

The contrast to the situation of philosophy in Central Europe, in particular in Germany, was remarkable and for me very heartening. Modern logic, almost unknown among philosophers in Germany, was here regarded by many as an important field of philosophy and was taught at some of the leading universities. The Association for Symbolic Logic and its *Journal* were founded in 1936. During the past twenty years, while I could observe the development, the recognition of modern logic became more and more widespread. The possibility of its application for the clarification of philosophical problems is by now widely recognized at least in principle, and the majority of philosophers understand at least the elementary parts of symbolic logic. It is true that only a minority make active use of this method, and there is still disagreement as to the range of its useful application; but at least this question is seriously discussed by all sides.

In 1936, when I came to this country, the traditional schools of philosophy did not have nearly the same influence as on the European continent. The movement of German idealism, in particular Hegelianism, which had earlier been quite influential in the United States, had by then almost completely disappeared. Neo-Kantian philosophical conceptions were represented here and there, not in an orthodox form but rather influenced by recent developments of scientific thinking, much like the conceptions of Cassirer in Germany. Phenomenology had a number of adherents mostly in a liberalized form, not in Husserl's orthodox form, and even less in Heidegger's version.

Most influential were those philosophical movements which had an empiricist tendency in a wide sense. Pragmatic ways of thinking, mostly in the version derived from John Dewey, were widely represented both among philosophers and in the movement of progressive education, which had won great influence on the methods practically applied in public schools. Many philosophers called themselves realists; their conception came from the movements of Critical Realism and of Neo-Realism, which had arisen in the beginning of this century as a reaction against the formerly strong idealism, and which therefore also had an empiricist tendency. Most of the followers of the movements mentioned rejected metaphysics and emphasized the importance of scientific ways of thinking for the solution of all theoretical problems. In the last twenty years, the ideas of analytic philosophy gained more and more acceptance, partly through the influence of logical empiricism, and also through that of the British movement stemming from G. E. Moore and Wittgenstein.

Thus I found in this country a philosophical atmosphere which, in striking contrast to that in Germany, was very congenial to me. Under the strong impression of this contrast, I expected perhaps sometimes too much, so that I became unduly impatient when I saw that philosophical thinking was still lagging far behind science even in this country with the most advanced development of philosophy.

In order to be more concrete I should like to make some remarks about the state of philosophy at the place where I spent most of my time and could observe it most closely, namely in the Department of Philosophy at the University of Chicago. These remarks are not meant as an objective report, but rather as a description of my personal impressions and feelings about what appeared to me as strengths or weaknesses in the situation. In this department great emphasis was placed on the history of philosophy. More frequently than in most other universities of the country, Ph.D. theses were based on a thorough knowledge of the philosophical sources in Greek and Latin of ancient and medieval times. The methodological attitude toward the history of philosophy which the students learned was characterized by a thorough study of the sources and by emphasis on the requirement that the doctrine of a philosopher must be understood immanently, that is, from his own point of view, inasmuch as a criticism from outside would not do justice to the peculiarity of the philosopher in question and his place in the historical development. This education in historical carefulness and a neutral attitude seemed to me useful and proper for the purpose of historical studies, but not sufficient for training in philosophy itself. The task of the history of philosophy is not essentially different from that of the history of science. The historian of science gives not only a description of the scientific theories, but also a critical judgment of them from the point of view of our present scientific knowledge. I think the same should be required in the history of philosophy. This view is based on the conviction that in philosophy, no less than in science, there is the possibility of cumulative insight and therefore of progress in knowledge. This view, of course, would be rejected by historicism in its pure form.

One of the most striking examples of this cultural lag in contemporary philosophy seemed to me a lecture given by Mortimer Adler as a visitor in the Department Seminar. He declared that he could demonstrate on the basis of purely metaphysical principles the impossibility of of man's descent from "brute", i.e., subhuman forms of animals. I had of course no objection to someone's challenging a widely accepted scientific theory. What I found startling was rather the kind of arguments used. They were claimed to provide with complete certainty an answer to the question of the validity or invalidity of a biological theory, without making this answer dependent upon those observable facts in biology and paleontology, which are regarded by scientists as relevant and decisive for the theory in question.

In some philosophical discussion meetings I had the weird feeling that I was sitting among a group of medieval learned men with long beards and solemn robes. This feeling was perhaps further strengthened when I looked out of the window at the other university buildings with their medieval Gothic style. I would perhaps dream that one of my colleagues raised the famous question of how many angels could dance on the point of a needle. Or I might imagine that the colleagues who were sitting around me were not philosophers but astronomers and that one of them proposed to discuss the astrological problem whether it was more favorable for the character and fate of a person if the planet Mars stood in Taurus or in Virgo at the hour of his birth. I heard myself expressing a humble doubt whether this problem fitted well into the twentieth century. But then I heard the imaginary astronomical colleagues declaring that we must be open-minded and never exclude by personal prejudice any question from the discussion.

Of course, there were also times when I told myself not to be too impatient. It was clear anyhow that for thousands of years philosophy had been one of the most tradition-bound fields of human thinking. Philosophers, like anybody else, tend to follow the customary patterns of thinking; even movements which regard themselves as very revolutionary, such as existentialism as a philosophical doctrine (in distinction to existentialism as an attitude in life), are often basically merely a modification of an ancient metaphysical pattern, namely a certain feeling or attitude toward the world in a pseudo-theoretical disguise. I often see also the brighter aspects of the picture. It is encouraging to remember that philosophical thinking has made great progress in the course of two thousand years through the work of men like Aristotle, Leibniz, Hume, Kant, Dewey, Russell, and many others, who were basically thinking in a scientific way. Personally I regard myself as very fortunate to be living in a country with the greatest progress in philosophical thinking and to be working together with friends on the basis of a common philosophical attitude. Above all I am gratified by the fact that many young people of the generation now growing up show promise of working in philosophy in a way which will tend to diminish the cultural lag.

II
Philosophical Problems

In this part I shall report more systematically on my philosophical activities from the Vienna period to the present time. In each section, a certain problem or complex of problems will be dealt with. Although the order is roughly determined by the time at which the problem became prominent in my thinking, the considerations, discussions and publications on which I shall report in each of the sections often continued through many years, so that certain sections will overlap chronologically.

PSEUDO PROBLEMS IN PHILOSOPHY

During the time while I was writing the *Logischer Aufbau*, I arrived more and more at a neutral attitude with respect to the language forms used by the various philosophical schools, e.g., the phenomenalistic language about sense data and the realistic language about perceptible things and events in the so-called external world. This neutral attitude did not mean, however, that I regarded the differences between the various language forms as unimportant. On the contrary, it seemed to me one of the most important tasks of philosophers to investigate the various possible language forms and discover their characteristic properties. While working on problems of this kind, I gradually realized that such an investigation, if it is to go beyond common-sense generalities and to aim at more exact results, must be applied to artificially constructed symbolic languages. The investigation of versions of the ordinary word language, corresponding to various philosophical points of view, may certainly be useful, but only as a preparation for the more exact work on artificial language systems. Only after a thorough investigation of the various language forms has been carried through, can a well-founded choice of one of these languages be made, be it as the total language of science or as a partial language for specific purposes. . . .

Even in the pre-Vienna period, most of the controversies in traditional metaphysics appeared to me sterile and useless. When I compared this kind of argumentation with investigations and discussions in empirical science or in the logical analysis of language, I was often struck by the vagueness of the concepts used and by the inconclusive nature of the arguments. I was depressed by disputations in which the opponents talked at cross purposes; there seemed hardly any chance of mutual understanding, let alone of agreement, because there was not even a common criterion for deciding the controversy. . . .

The most decisive development in my view of metaphysics occurred later, in the Vienna period, chiefly under the influence of Wittgenstein. I came to hold the view that many theses of traditional metaphysics are not only useless, but even devoid of cognitive content. . . .

Unfortunately, following Wittgenstein, we formulated our view in the Vienna Circle in the oversimplified version of saying that certain metaphysical theses are "meaningless". This formulation caused much unnecessary opposition, even among some of those philosophers who basically agreed with us. Only later did we see that it is important to distinguish the various meaning components, and therefore said in a more precise way that such theses lack cognitive or theoretical meaning. They often have other meaning components, e.g., emotive or motivative ones, which, although not cognitive, may have strong psychological effects. . . .

PHYSICALISM AND THE UNITY OF SCIENCE

I explained earlier that we had regarded the theses of phenomenalism, materialism, realism and so on in their traditional forms as pseudo-theses. On the other hand, we believed that we obtained fruitful philosophical problems if we directed our attention not to the traditional ontological problems, but rather to the question, either theoretical or practical, concerning the corresponding language forms.

In our discussions we were especially interested in the question of whether a phenomenalistic language or a physicalistic language was preferable for the purposes of philosophy. By a phenomenalistic language we meant one which begins with sentences about sense data, such as "there is now a red triangle in my visual field." The sentences of the physicalistic language or thing-language speak of material things and ascribe observable properties to them, e.g., "this thing is black and heavy". . . . I believed that the task of philosophy consists in reducing all knowledge to a basis of certainty. Since the most certain knowledge is that of the immediately given, whereas knowledge of material things is derivative and less certain, it seemed that the philosopher must employ a language which uses sense-data as a basis. In the Vienna discussions my attitude changed gradually toward a preference for the physicalistic language. Against the conception that this language may serve as a total language for all knowledge, sometimes the objection was raised that on a physicalistic basis it is impossible to reach the concepts of psychology. But I did not find this argument convincing. In the *Logischer Aufbau* I had indicated the possibility of taking a physicalistic basis instead of the phenomenalistic one actually used in the book. Furthermore, I had explained the construction of concepts concerning other minds (*"das Fremdpsychische"*) on the basis of the observed behavior of other human bodies; these considerations refute the objection mentioned above, and offer the possibility of choosing either the one or the other basis. . . .

In my view, one of the most important advantages of the physicalistic language is its intersubjectivity, i.e., the fact that the events described in this language are in principle observable by all users of the language.

In our discussions the principle of the unity of science became one of the main tenets of our general philosophical conception. This principle says that the different branches of empirical science are separated only for the practical reason of division of labor, but are fundamentally merely parts of one comprehensive unified science. This thesis must be understood primarily as a rejection of the prevailing view in German contemporary philosophy that there is a fundamental difference between the natural sciences and the *Geisteswissenschaften* (literally "spiritual sciences", understood as the sciences of mind, culture, and history, thus roughly corresponding to the social sciences and the humanities). In contrast to this customary view, Neurath maintained the monistic conception that everything that occurs is a part of nature, i.e., of the physical world. I proposed to make this thesis more precise by transforming it into a thesis concerning language, namely, the thesis that the total language encompassing all knowledge can be constructed on a physicalistic basis. . . .

VALUES AND PRACTICAL DECISIONS

In our discussions in the Vienna Circle we were much concerned with clarifying the logical nature of value statements. We distinguished between absolute or unconditional value statements, e.g., one that says that a certain action is morally good in itself, and relative or unconditional value statements, e.g., one saying that an action is good in the sense of being conductive toward reaching certain aims. Statements of the latter kind are obviously empirical, even though they may contain value terms like "good". On the other hand, absolute value statements that speak only about what ought to be done are devoid of cognitive meaning according to the empiricist criterion of significance. They certainly possess non-cognitive meaning components, especially emotive or motivating ones, and their effect in education, admonition, political appeal, etc., is based on these components. But, since they are not cognitive, they cannot be interpreted as assertions. The fact that they are often expressed, not in the most appropriate form as imperatives such as "love thy neighbor", put in the grammatical form of declaratives sentences such as "it is thy duty to love thy neighbor," has misled many philosophers to consider them as assertive, cognitive sentences.

This result of a logical analysis of value statements and the controversies concerning them may appear as a purely academic matter without any practical interest. But I have found that the lack of distinction between factual questions and pure value questions leads to confusions and misunderstandings in discussions of moral problems in personal life or of political decisions. If the distinction is clearly made, the discussion will be more fruitful, because with respect to the two fundamentally different kinds of questions the approach most appropriate to each will be used; thus for factual questions arguments of factual evidence will be offered; whereas persuasion, educational influence, appeal, and the like will be brought to bear upon decisions concerning pure value questions.

My view that the practical effect of our own thesis is similarly limited, seems to be supported by the fact that there is no agreement on it even among empiricists who share the same basic philosophical position. The thesis of the non-cognitive character of value statements is accepted by most of those who regard themselves as belonging to the movement of logical empiricism, but it is rejected by most of those empiricists who regard themselves as pragmatists or who are at least strongly influenced by Dewey's philosophy. It seems to me that the divergence in this point between the two groups of empiricists is theoretically interesting and should lead to further thorough discussions, but is relatively unimportant in its influence on practical life. In my personal experience I do not know of any case in which the difference in attitude between an empiricist of the first group and one of the second group with respect to a moral problem ever arose from the difference in their philosophical positions concerning the nature of value statements.

The view that recognition of the non-cognitive nature of value statements is either conducive to or symptomatic of a loss of interest in moral or political problems seems clearly refuted by my own experience. I have maintained the thesis for about thirty years. But throughout my life, from my childhood to the present day, I have always had an intense interest in moral problems, both those concerning the life of individuals and, since the First World War, those of politics. I have not been active in party politics, but I was always interested in political principles and I have never shied away from professing my point of view. All of us in the Vienna Circle took a strong interest in the political events in our country, in Europe, and in the world. These problems were discussed privately, not in the Circle which was devoted to theoretical questions. I think that nearly all of us shared the following three views as a matter of course which hardly needed any discussion. The first is the view that man has no supernatural protectors or enemies and that therefore whatever can be done to improve life is the task of man himself. Second, we had the conviction that mankind is able to change the conditions of life in such a way that many of the sufferings of today may be avoided and that the external and the internal situation of life for the individual, the community, and finally for humanity will be essentially improved. The third is the view that all deliberate action presupposes knowledge of the world, that the scientific method is the best method of acquiring knowledge and that therefore science must be regarded as one of the most valuable instruments for the improvement of life. In Vienna we had no names for these views; if we look for a brief designation in American terminology for the combination of these three convictions, the best would seem to be "scientific humanism".

I shall now try to indicate more concretely, beyond these general principles, the views about ends and means which I have held at least since the Vienna time, if not earlier, and which I still hold today. A number of my friends in the Vienna Circle probably shared these views in their essential features; but in detail, naturally, there were important differences. It was and still is my conviction that the great problems of the organization of economy and the organization of the world at the present time, in the era of industrialization, cannot possibly be solved by "the free interplay of forces", but require rational planning. For the organization of economy this means socialism in some form; for the organization of the world it means a gradual development toward a world government. However, neither socialism nor world government are regarded as absolute ends; they are only the organizational means which, according to our present knowledge, seem to give the best promise of leading to a realization of the ultimate aim. This aim is a form of life in which the well-being and the development of the individual is valued most highly, not the power of the state. Removing the obstacles, the main causes of suffering, such as war, poverty, disease, is merely the negative side of the task. The positive side is to improve and enrich the life of the individuals and their relations in family, friendship, professional work, and community. Enrichment of life requires that all individuals be given the possibility to develop their potential abilities and the opportunity to participate in cultural activities and experiences. If we look at the problem from the point of view of this aim, we shall recognize the dangers lying in the constant increase in the power of the state; this increase is necessary because the national states must fuse into larger units and the states must take over many functions of the economy. Therefore it will be of prime importance to take care that the civil liberties and the democratic institutions are not merely preserved but constantly developed and improved. Thus one of the main problems, perhaps the most important and the most difficult one after the terribly urgent problem of the avoidance of atomic war, is the task of finding ways of organizing society which will reconcile the personal and cultural freedom of the individual with the development of an efficient organization of state and economy.

38

JEAN-PAUL SARTRE
Self-Portrait at Seventy

While studying at l'École Normale Supérieure and teaching at a lycée, J.-P. Sartre (1905–1980) immersed himself in reading Hegel, Husserl, Heidegger, and Marx. During World War II, He was active in the Resistance and spent a year in prison. He joined the, group that founded and edited *Les Temps Modernes* in 1945. In his early work—phenomenological studies of the imagination and self-consciousness (*The Imagination*, 1936, and *Transcendence of the Ego*, 1937)—Sartre argued that consciousness has no essence: it is a radically free activity, choosing to define and redefine itself. In *Being and Nothingness* (1943) he analyzed "the self" as a "for-itself," a being actively engaged in self-conscious awareness that is also, at the same time, passively observing itself as an object in the world, an "in-itself." While the self has no essential attributes, it affirms itself to be this or that ("a writer," "a Jew," "sad," "dreamy"). Although it is also capable of realizing itself as nothing ("no-thing"), the self nevertheless *is* a writer, a French Jew, melancholy. Bad faith is the human condition. Against the background of this theory Sartre wrote *Anti-Semite and Jew* (1948).

Sartre increasingly turned to Marxism and to describing the role of "the look of the Other" in the constitution of the self. Many of these explorations appeared in the form of fiction (*Nausea*, 1938; *Dirty Hands*, 1948; *No Exit*, 1944), an autobiography (*Words*, 1963), and literary studies (on Faulkner, Baudelaire, Genet, and a three-volume study of Flaubert, *The Family Idiot*, 1971–1972). He struggled to reconcile his existentialism with his neo-Marxism in *Critique of Dialectical Reason* (1958–1959). Politically active throughout his life, he joined Russell in organizing the Vietnam war crimes tribunal. Sartre was awarded—and declined—the Nobel Prize for literature in 1964; he had also refused to accept the French Legion of Honor.

Self-Portrait at Seventy in *Life/Situations*

From the very beginning my family filled me with the feeling that I was a valuable child. Yet at the same time I had the sense of my own contingency, which somewhat undermined the idea of value, because value is a whole whirlwind that presupposes ideologies and alienations, while contingency is a plain reality. But I discovered a dodge: to attribute value to myself because I had a sense of contingency when others did not. So I became the man who talked about contingency and consequently, the man who had invested his value in searching for the sense and significance of it. All that is very clear.

I did not come from a family where the relation between money and work was clearly understood as something hard, painful.

My grandfather worked a great deal, but he worked with writing, and for me it was fun to do nothing but read and write. There were books in his workroom, and he wrote, he had fun. I had seen the proofs he was correcting; it amused me.

And then he talked to people; he gave them German lessons. And all that was earning him money. As you can see, the relation between work and money was not distinct.

Later, when I myself wrote, there was absolutely no relation between the money I received and the books I wrote. I did not understand it, since I believed that the value of a book was established over the course of centuries. As a consequence, the money that my books earned for me was itself a sort of contingent sign. You might say that the first relation between money and my life endured. It is a stupid relation.

There was my work, my way of living, my efforts which I enjoyed—for I have always been happy when I am writing. And my position as professor, which was somewhat tied to all that, did not annoy me. I liked what I was doing.

I was in the habit of writing alone and reading alone, and I still think that real intellectual work demands solitude. I am not saying that some intellectual work—even writing books—cannot be undertaken by several people. But I do not see how two or three people can perform real intellectual work of the kind that leads both to a *written* work and to philosophical reflections. At the present time, with our current methods of thought, the unveiling of a thought before an object implies solitude. . . .

Writing is born of secrecy. But we should not forget that it either tries to hide this secrecy and to lie (in which case it is without interest) or to give a glimpse of this secrecy, even to try and expose it by showing what the writer is in relation to others—and in this case it approaches the translucence that I want. . . .

What spoils relations among people is that each keeps something hidden from the other, holds something secret, not necessarily from everyone, but from the person he is speaking to at the moment.

I think transparency should always be substituted for secrecy. I can imagine the day when two men will no longer have secrets from each other, because no one will have any more secrets from anyone, because subjective life, as well as objective life, will be completely offered up, given. It is impossible to accept the fact that we yield our bodies as we do and yet keep our thoughts hidden, since for me there is no basic difference between the body and the consciousness.

We yield our bodies to everyone, even beyond the realm of sexual relations: by looking, by touching. You yield your body to me, I yield mine to you: we each exist for the other, as body. But we do not exist in this same way as consciousness, as ideas, even though ideas are modifications of the body.

If we truly wished to exist for the other, to exist as body, as body that can continually be laid bare—even if this never actually happens—our ideas would appear to others as coming from the body. Words are formed by a tongue in the mouth. All ideas would appear in this way, even the most vague, the most fleeting, the least tangible. There would no longer be the hiddenness, the secrecy which in certain centuries was identified with the honor of men and women, and which seems very foolish to me. . . .

The desire for glory is the effect of the fear of death and contingency, the gratuitousness of existence . . . One is always unjustified. . . . Glory is an idea inherent in literature. A boy who immersed himself in literature around 1910 found in the books he read a whole literary ideology dating from the last century and forming a set of imperatives, what I called "literature to be done." . . . It took me quite a long time to get rid of it.

The chief obstacle to [the kind of] transparency that can set aside glory [are] distrust, ignorance and fear. [They keep us] from being confidential with one another, or confidential enough. Personally, moreover, I do not express myself on all subjects with the people I meet. But I try to be as translucent as possible, because I feel that this dark region that we have within ourselves, which is at once dark for us and dark for others, can only be illuminated for ourselves in trying to illuminate it for others. As with other people, there is a depth of dark-ness within me that does not allow itself to be expressed.

There is always a kind of small fringe of things that are not said, that do not want to be said, but that want to be known, known by me. One can't say every-thing. But I think that later people will talk about themselves more and more, and it will bring about a great change. Moreover, I think this change is linked to a real revolution.

A man's existence must be entirely visible to his neighbor, whose own exis-tence must be entirely visible in turn, before true social harmony can be estab-lished. This cannot be realized today, but I think that it will in the future, once there has been a change in the economic, cultural, and affective relations among men. It will begin with the eradication of material scarcity—which, as I showed in the *Critique of Dialectical Reason*, is for me the root of the antagonisms, past and present, among men.

In the future there will doubtless be other antagonisms which I cannot imagine now, which no one can imagine. But they will not be an obstacle to a form of sociality in which each person will give himself completely to someone else, who will likewise give himself completely. Such a society, of course, would have to be worldwide, for if there remained inequalities and privileges anywhere in the world, the resulting conflicts would little by little take over the whole social body.

It is very hard to know who a work belongs to. It belongs to the author, and at the same time it belongs to the reader—these facts are difficult to reconcile. And then, the reader rarely acknowledges it to be his, while the writer believes that it is his. As for me, I think that a man's work belongs to him until his conscious death—meaning either his real death in consciousness and in body, or the death of his consciousness through madness, if it is irreversible. But as long as he is alive, the work he has written belongs to him. It especially belongs to him if it is not finished, because theoretically he might amuse himself by going on with it. . . .

I know that an image of me exists, but it is the image other people have of me and not my own. I don't know what my own is; I don't think about myself very much, not about myself as an individual. When I do think reflexively, the ideas I have would apply to anyone.

I became interested in myself at about the age of nineteen, and afterwards I was looking much more for generalities when I was observing myself and digging around in my conscience in order to write *Imagination*. As for *The Words*, it was a matter of understanding my childhood, understanding a former self, in order to grasp how I had become what I was at the time I was writing. But many more books would have been needed to explain where I am at the moment.

I am trying to explain how things have changed, how certain events have affected me. I don't believe that a man's history is written in his infancy. I think there are other very important periods where things are added: adolescence, youth, and even maturity. What I see most clearly in my life is a break dividing it into two almost completely distinct periods. Being in the second period, I can hardly recognize myself anymore as I was in the first, before the war and just after it.

[Just now] I have for the most part been talking about my private life as if it were separate from the rest—from my ideas, the books I've published, my political beliefs, my actions, what one could call my public life. Yet we know that this distinction between private and public life does not really exist, that it is pure illusion, a hoax. That is why I can't claim to have a private life, I mean a hidden, secret life, and that is also why I am answering your questions freely. Yet in this so-called "private" life there are contradictions which stem from the present state of relations between people and which, as I said to you before, in some sense force us to be secretive and even to lie. But one's existence forms a whole which cannot be split up. Our lives inside and outside, subjective and objective, personal and political—all necessarily awake echoes in one another because they are aspects of one and the same whole, and one can only understand an individual, whoever he may be, by seeing him as a social being. Every man is political. But I did not discover that for myself until the war, and I did not truly understand it until 1945.

Before the war I thought of myself simply as an individual. I was not aware of any ties between my individual existence and the society I was living in. At the time I graduated from the Ecole normale, I had based an entire theory on that feeling. I was a "man alone," an individual who opposes society through the independence of his thinking but who owes nothing to society and whom society cannot affect, because he is free. That was the evidence on which I based everything I believed, everything I wrote, and everything I did in my life before 1939. During the whole period before the war I had no political opinions, and of course I did not vote. I was very interested in the political speeches of Nizan, who was a Communist, but I also listened to Aron and other Socialists. As for me, I felt that what I had to do was write, and I absolutely did not see writing as a social activity.

I thought the bourgeois were skunks, and I thought I could support this judgment, so I did not hesitate to address those very bourgeois in order to drag them through the mud. *Nausea* is not exclusively an attack against the bourgeoisie, but in large part it is: look at the pictures in the museum. . . . In some sense *Nausea* is the literary culmination of the "man alone" theory. I did not manage to go beyond that position, even though I already glimpsed its limitations. I condemned the bourgeois as skunks and tried to justify my existence, at the same time attempting to define for the solitary individual the conditions for an existence without illusions. To tell the truth about existence and to strip the pretenses from bourgeois lies was one and the same thing, and that was what I had to do in order to fulfill my destiny as a man, because I had been created in order to write.

As for the rest, I mean my private life, I felt that it should be filled with pleasures. I assumed that like everyone, I would have troubles descending on me without any chance of avoiding them, but on the whole mine would be a life of pleasure: women, good food, traveling, friendships . . . Of course, I was a teacher, because I had to earn a living. But I did not hate teaching, not at all, even though I found it very unpleasant to become an adult with all the responsibilities of an adult. In about 1935 I went through a sort of depression which lasted several months and which I interpret now more or less as an identity crisis connected with this passage into adult life. But finally I managed to reduce to a minimum the social obligations that go along with being a teacher, and that worked out very well. So, as I say, that is how I saw my life: primarily to write, and along with that to have a pleasant existence.

Starting in 1936, certain political events began to make me see that that was not all. First, the Popular Front—which we had admired from afar, as Castor has said. We saw the lines of the Popular Front marching past as we stood on the sidewalk, and our friends were in those lines. We were on the outside, separate from them, and we felt it. All the same, it forced us to emerge from our absolute indifference, since we were wholeheartedly in favor of the Popular Front. But I did nothing that could have caused me to consider myself one of its supporters. Then in 1938, at the time of the Munich crisis, the social movement developed; things began to accelerate. At the time of Munich I was torn between my individual pacifism and my anti-Nazi feelings. Yet for me, at least, anti-Nazi feelings were already becoming predominant.

Nazism seemed to us like the enemy force which wanted to fight us, fight the French people. And that feeling came on top of an experience which, though I had not yet realized it, was not simply an individual experience but a social one: my impressions when I had lived in Nazi Germany for a year in 1933. I had known Germans, I had talked to them, I had seen Communists hiding from the Nazis. At the time I did not think this was important on a political level, but actually it was already affecting what I was thinking and experiencing. Nazi Germany simply put me into a rage, and there was Doumergue in France—who was a sort of good-natured fascist—and the leagues, the Croix-de-Feu, and so on. Some time after my return I adopted an antifascist position, obviously without any practical consequences. I was comfortably installed as an antibourgeois and individualist writer.

What made all this fall apart was that one day in September 1939, I received a mobilization slip and had to go to a barracks in Nancy to join other men I didn't know who had been mobilized as I had been. This was what made the social aspect enter my mind. I suddenly understood that I was a social being when I saw myself torn from where I was, taken away from the people who mattered to me, and put on a train going someplace I didn't want to go, with other fellows who didn't want to go any more than I did, who were still in civilian clothes like me, and who like me were asking why they had ended up there. When I looked at these fellows, as I passed them in the barracks where I was pacing back and forth not knowing what to do, I saw something they had in common in spite of their differences, something I shared. They were no longer simply like the people I had known in my *lycée* a few months before, when I did not yet suspect that they and I were social individuals. Until then I had thought I was above everyone else. Through this mobilization I had to encounter the negation of my freedom in order to become aware of the weight of the world and my ties with all the others and their ties with me.

The war really divided my life in two. It started when I was thirty-four years old and ended when I was forty, and that really was the transition from youth to maturity. At the same time, the war revealed certain aspects of myself and of the world to me. For example, that was when I experienced the profound alienation of captivity. It was also when I had relations with people, with the enemy—the real enemy, not the adversary who lives in the same society as you or who attacks you verbally, but the enemy who can have you arrested and thrown in prison by making a brief gesture to some armed men.

At that time I was also conscious of an oppressed, battered, but still existing social order, a society that was democratic to the very degree that it was oppressed and destroyed. I knew that we were fighting to preserve its value, hoping that it would be reborn after the war. It was then, if you like, that I abandoned my prewar individualism and the idea of the pure individual and adopted the social individual and socialism. That was the turning point of my life: before and after. And at least until the war, Marxism remained something which bothered me, which hurt me, which showed me that I didn't know everything, far from it, and that I had to learn. And I couldn't manage to learn. At one point, in Le Havre, I read some works by Marx or on Marx. But I couldn't remember them; I couldn't see what their meaning was.

During the war, during the Occupation, when I was part of a resistance group in which there were Communists, Marxism began to seem powerful to me.

I remained close to the Communists, but my ideas weren't the same as theirs, and they knew it. They made use of me without becoming too involved, and they suspected that if something like Budapest happened, I would quit—which I did. My ideas were more or less formed; I didn't abandon them while I was involved with the Communists. And I took them up again and developed them in the *Critique of Dialectical Reason*.

As for 1968, yes, it was important for everyone, and particularly for me. The reason I had become involved with the Communists was that there was nothing further to the left before 1968 except the Trotskyists, who were really unhappy Communists. If there had been a left-wing movement after the war, I would have joined it immediately.

I think the essential aspects of Marxism are still valid: the class struggle, surplus value, and so on. It was the element of power contained in Marxism that was taken up by the Soviets. As a philosophy of power, I think Marxism showed what it was made of in Soviet Russia. Today I feel, as I try to suggest in *On a raison de se révolter*, that another way of thinking is necessary. We must develop a way of thinking which takes Marxism into account in order to go beyond it, to reject it and take it up again, to absorb it. That is the condition for arriving at a true socialism.

My [political] statements are never very optimistic, because in each social event that is important to us, that touches us, I see the contradictions—either manifest or hardly noticeable yet. I see the mistakes, the risks, everything that can prevent a situation from going in the direction of freedom. And there I am pessimistic because each time, the risks are in fact enormous. Looking at everything generally, I say to myself: Either man is finished (and in that case not only is he finished, but he has never existed—he will have been no more than a species, like the ant) or else he will adapt by bringing about some form of libertarian socialism. When I think about individual social acts, I tend to think man is finished. But if I consider all the conditions necessary for man to exist at all, I tell myself that the only thing to do is to point out, emphasize, and support with all one's strength whatever aspects of a particular political and social situation can produce a society of free men. If one does not do that, one is in effect agreeing that man is a piece of shit.

If I were convinced that any fight for freedom was necessarily doomed to failure, there would be no sense in fighting. No, if I am not completely pessimistic it is primarily because I sense in myself certain needs which are not only mine but the needs of every man. To express it another way, it is the experienced certainty of my own freedom, to the extent that it is everyone's freedom, which gives me at the same time the need for a free life and the certainty that this need is felt in a more or less clear, more or less conscious way by everyone.

The coming revolution will be very different from the previous ones. It will last much longer and will be much harsher, much more profound. I identify myself with the revolutionary battles being fought throughout the world. There will be advances and retreats, limited successes and reversible defeats, in order finally to bring into existence a new society in which all the powers have been done away with because each individual has full possession of himself. Revolution is not a single moment in which one power overthrows another; it is a long movement in which power is dismantled. Nothing can guarantee success for us, nor can anything rationally convince us that failure is inevitable. But the alternatives really are socialism or barbarism. . . .

Socialism is not a certainty, it is a value: it is freedom choosing itself as a goal. . . .

And how can we lay the foundations for the future reality? Nothing allows me to do it. I am sure of one thing—that we must make a radical politics. But I am not sure that it will succeed, and there faith enters in. I can understand my refusals, I can demonstrate the reasons for refusing this society, I can show that it is immoral—that it is made not for people but for profit and that therefore it must be radically changed. All this is possible and does not imply faith, but action. All I can do as an intellectual is try to win over as many people as I can—that is, the masses—to radical action for changing society. That is what I have tried to do, and I cannot say either that I have succeeded or that I have failed, since the future is undecided.

39

SIMONE DE BEAUVOIR
Writing a Life of Writing

Simone de Beauvoir (1908–1986) studied philosophy at L'Ecole Normale Supérieure and the Sorbonne. Like many other intellectuals of the time, she taught in a lycée. Influenced by Husserl and Heidegger, she wrote a phenomenological study of the experience of radical freedom (*The Ethics of Ambiguity*, 1949). She preferred to express her philosophical views in works of fiction: *She Came to Stay* (1943), *All Men Are Mortal* (1946), and *The Mandarins* (1954). Active in the Resistance, she wrote political essays, increasingly turning her attention to feminist theory. Her groundbreaking *The Second Sex* (1949) influenced feminist thinking around the world. She later turned to writing autobiography, using her life as an example of the complex situation of politically active intellectual women who are also fully engaged daughters and lovers (*Memoirs of a Dutiful Daughter*, 1958; *The Prime of Life*, 1960; *The Force of Circumstance*, 1963). Reflecting on the death of her mother, she began to write about ageing: *The Coming of Age* (1970) and *All Said and Done* (1972). She continued to write political essays, many of them severely critical of the United States (*America Day by Day*, 1948).

The Prime of Life in *Living/Writing*

To divide one's life up into sections is an arbitrary process. But the year 1929 obviously opened a new era for me: from it date the end of my formal education, my economic emancipation, my departure from home, the breaking up of old friendships, and my first meeting with Sartre. In 1939 my existence was upset in an equally radical fashion. History took hold of me, and never let go thereafter; and I threw myself totally and permanently into a life of literature. An epoch was ending. [I had been] dominated by two preoccupations: to live fully, and to achieve my still theoretical vocation as a writer—that is to say, to find the point at which literature could best enter my life.

A full life, above all. Whatever one does, naturally, one is alive; but there is more than one way of unifying the moments in time through which one passes: by subordinating them to some specific action, for instance, or projecting them into a work of art. My own particular enterprise was the development of my life, which I believed lay in my own hands. It had to satisfy two requirements, which in my optimism I treated as identical: it must make me happy, and put the whole world at my disposal. Unhappiness, I thought, would have given me a contaminated view of reality. Since my intimacy with Sartre guaranteed my happiness, I was mainly concerned to cram in as rich a harvest of experience as I could. My discoveries did not follow a straight, clear line, as they had done during my childhood, and I did not get that feeling of steady day-by-day progress; but in their muddled, disorderly way they quite overwhelmed me. I was facing up to real flesh-and-blood *things*, and found unsuspected qualities about them besides those I had anticipated while still shut away in my cage. We have seen how earnestly I pursued my investigations. I long cherished the illusion that *my* rational mind could grasp the absolute truth of things, and mine alone—with a possible exception in favor of Sartre. Obviously I was aware that people existed who could understand a picture or a sonata better than I could; but in a confused way it seemed to me that the moment any object became absorbed into my own life, it took on a specially privileged sort of luminosity. A landscape was virgin of all mortal gaze till *I* had set eyes on it.

Until I was thirty I felt myself to be better informed than the young, and younger than the old, the first being too scatterbrained and the second too staid. In me alone did existence organize itself in truly exemplary fashion, with every little detail profiting from such perfection. As a consequence it was as important for the universe as it was for me that I should know all of it. Enjoyment took second place to this self-perpetuating mandate that was laid upon me.

Granted the infinite immensity of such a task, it is not surprising that I was ceaselessly caught up by various projects: each conquest was one stage further on my journey. This characteristic is not, however, wholly explicable in terms of the vast field I had set myself to cover, since today, though I have given up all hope of exhausting it, I am very little changed in myself, and still full of projects. The idea of contingency terrifies me; by filling the future with demands and appeals and expectations, I inject an element of determinism into the present. Yet, as I have said, I knew moments of respite, when scheming was replaced by contemplation. Such occasions, when the cares of my existence were lost in the fullness of that universal state with which I merged myself, offered priceless recompense.

The working plan which Sartre and I were pursuing for the annexation of the world around us did not fit in with those patterns and taboos established by society. Very well, then; we rejected the latter, on the supposition that man would have to create his world over again from scratch. And yet our life, like that of all *petits bourgeois* intellectuals, was in fact mainly characterized by its *lack* of reality. We had a profession, which we pursued in the correct manner, but which did not detach us from our own verbal universe. On an intellectual plane we were both honest and conscientious: as Sartre said to me one day, we had a genuine sense of the truth (as opposed to the bulk of the bourgeoisie and the entire fashionable world, whose approach to truth is utterly unreal); though this was a step in the right direction, it did not in any way imply that we possessed *a true sense of reality*. Like every bourgeois, we were sheltered from want; like every civil servant, we were guaranteed against insecurity. Furthermore, we had no children, no families, no responsibilities: we were like elves. There was no intelligible connection between the work we did (which was on the whole enjoyable and not in the least exhausting) and the money we got for it, which seemed to lack all proper substance. Since we had no position to keep up, we spent it in a capricious fashion: sometimes it lasted us till the end of the month, sometimes not. Such mishaps did not tell us the truth about our economic position, which we contrived to ignore; we flourished, in fact, like the lilies of the field, and circumstances fostered our illusions. We were bursting with good health, and our bodies objected to no demands we made on them unless we pushed things to extremes: the fact that we could ask a lot in this quarter compensated us for the slenderness of our resources. We had seen as much of the world as any rich person might do—simply because we were quite prepared to sleep out of doors, eat in cheap cafés, and travel on foot. In one sense we earned our pleasures, by paying a price for them which other people would have found intolerable; but the fact that we *could* earn them in this fashion was one of our lucky breaks. [Sartre and I] had each in our own way been pursuing a dream. I still wanted my life to be "a lovely story that became true as I told it to myself," and touched it up improvingly here and there in the telling. I loaded my life for two or three years with symbols and myths. Afterward I gave up fantasy, though I failed to shake off those puritanical and moralizing tendencies which prevented me from seeing people as they really are. Nor could I break free from my universalist abstractions; I remained riddled with bourgeois idealism and aestheticism. Above all, my emotionally ambivalent obsession with happiness blinded me to political realities. This blindness, however, was not peculiar to me; it was a characteristic and almost universal failing of the period. No one possessed the necessary equipment to grasp the over-all pattern of this new world then coming about, which could not be understood at all except in its totality. Nevertheless I carried my rejection of History and its dangers to extraordinary lengths.

In that case, it might be asked, what value is there in the experiences I have now related? Sometimes they seem wrapped in such layers of ignorance and dishonesty that I can feel nothing but contempt for this part of my past life. When I looked at the Umbrian landscape, it gave me a unique and unforgettable moment; but in fact Umbria itself eluded me. What I contemplated were mere tricks of light and shade, what I told myself was the old myth: I failed to see the harshness of the soil, and the joyless lives of the peasants who work it. Doubtless there is such a thing as the truth of appearances—granted, that is, that one recognizes appearances as such, which was not so in my case. I was greedy for knowledge, but let myself be satisfied with false lures.

All the same, any balanced reckoning of these years shows, I think, a vast amount on the credit side: so many books and pictures, so many new towns, new faces, new ideas, such a wealth of feelings and emotions! Not everything was false. If error is marred truth, and truth can only be realized through the development of its imperfect manifestations, it becomes clear that reality can reach us even through a fog of obscurity and muddle. Such culture as I had acquired, inadequate though it might be, was essential for this filtering process. The fact that we had very little idea what to do with the information we amassed did not make its collection any the less valuable per se. What leads me to treat our divagations with a certain degree of indulgence is the fact that not even our firmest convictions ever held us back: the future remained open, truth still enjoyed a reprieve.

In any case, even if we had been more clear-headed than we were, our lives would hardly have differed, since we were less concerned to plot our exact position than to move forward. The very confusion against which I struggled goaded me on irresistibly toward the goal I had long since set myself: the writing of books.

Here, then, was the second of my problems, inextricably bound up with the first. In order to lead a satisfying life I *had* to give pride of place in it to literature. During my adolescence and early maturity my vocation, though sincere, had lacked fulfillment: I had contented myself with the statement that I wanted to be a writer. Now the problem was to find out both *what* I wanted to write about, and to what extent I could actually do so: action was called for. This took me some time. Long ago I had sworn to complete my great, all-revealing work at the age of twenty-two; yet when I embarked upon the first of my published novels,

She Came to Stay, I was already thirty. In the family and among my childhood friends the whisper went around that I was a *fruit sec;* my father remarked irritably that if I had something inside me, why couldn't I hurry up and get it out? But I wasn't impatient myself. I knew that creating a first book out of nothing—or at least entirely from one's own resources—and making it stand up against anything, was a task that, exceptional luck apart, demanded endless time and labor, a long process of trial and error. Writing, I told myself, is a profession that can only be learned by writing. All the same, ten years is a long time, and during that period I covered reams of *paper* with my handwriting. I do not believe that my lack of experience can suffice to explain so prolonged a failure: I was hardly more professional when I began writing *She Came to Stay.* Must I, then, admit that whereas previously I had nothing to say, I had now "found a subject"? But the world is always there around one: what does that word "nothing" *mean* then? How, why, and in what circumstances does a situation present itself to the writer as "something to say"?

Literature is born when something in life goes slightly adrift. In order to write the first essential condition is that *reality should no longer be taken for granted; only* then can one both perceive it, and make others do so. When I struggled free of the boredom and slavery of my childhood years, I was overwhelmed, stunned, blinded with sheer happiness. How could I ever have found in this blissful condition the urge to escape from it? My schemes of work remained futile dreams till the day came when that happiness was threatened, and I rediscovered a certain kind of solitude in anxiety. Have I ever written that women were the same as men? Have I ever claimed that I, personally, was not a woman? On the contrary, my main purpose has been to isolate and identify my own particular brand of femininity. I received a young lady's education, and when my studies were finished, my position was still that of any woman in a society where the sexes are divided into two embattled castes. In a great many ways I reacted like the woman I was: what distinguishes my thesis from the traditional one is that, as far as I am concerned, femininity is neither a natural nor an innate entity, but rather a condition brought about by society, on the basis of certain physiological characteristics. For reasons which I have set forth in some detail in *The Second Sex,* women experience a greater need for a stable firmament above their heads than men do; they are not endowed with the temper that makes explorers, in the sense that Freud used the word. They are averse to questioning the fundamental premises of existence, or to organizing and controlling the world. Therefore it suited me to live with a man whom I regarded as my superior; my ambitions, though stubbornly held, were nevertheless timid; and though public affairs might interest me, I could not regard them as my personal concern. Yet as I have made clear, I attached small importance to the actual conditions of my life: nothing, I believed, could impede my will. I did not deny my femininity, any more than I took it for granted: I simply ignored it. I had the same freedoms and responsibilities as men did. I was spared the curse that weighs upon most women, that of dependence—and whether they are afflicted by it, adapt themselves to it, or treat it as a subject for self-congratulation, in the last resort it still remains a curse; since I wrote *The Second Sex* my conviction on this point has merely been strengthened. To earn one's living is not an end in itself, but it is the only way to achieve securely based inner independence. [During the Occupation] not only time but space had contracted. Paris had occupied the center of a world which for the larger part lay open to my curiosity; but now France was Occupied Territory, and cut off from the rest of the globe. Italy and Spain, which we had loved so dearly, were now our enemies. Between us and America dark, fiery storm clouds lay, and the only voice which reached us from beyond our frontiers was that of the B.B.C. We were stifling under a blanket of ignorance.

At least, as the year went by, I no longer found myself an isolated case. My emotions and expectations and anxieties and rebellious instincts were all shared with a multitude of people. They were anonymous and faceless, but present all about me, both externally and within my own mind: it was they who, through the beating of my heart, were stirred to passion or hatred. Never before, I realized, had I known what hatred really was: the objects of my rage had been more or less abstract entities. But now I recognized its flavor, and focused it with especial violence against those of our enemies whom I knew most about. Pétain's speeches had a more inflammatory effect on me than Hitler's; and while I condemned all collaborators, I felt a sharply defined and quite excruciating personal loathing for those of my own kind who joined their ranks—intellectuals, journalists, writers. When artists or men of letters went to Germany to assure the conquerors of our spiritual loyalty, I felt I had been personally betrayed.

Fear, rage, and blind impotence: these were the foundations on which my life now developed. But there were also flickers of hope, and so far I had not suffered directly from the war: I had not, for instance, lost one of my nearest or dearest. Sartre had returned from captivity, with neither his health nor his good spirits impaired; it was impossible to be depressed for long in his company. However restricted the area in which we found ourselves enclosed, his inquisitiveness and enthusiasm would animate every last corner of it. Here we were in Paris, with its village-like streets and great country skies, and so many people all around us—so many faces, so many adventures, such a lot still to see and understand and love! I no longer experienced any feeling of security, any overwhelming sensations of elated joy; but my day-to-day mood was one of gayness, and I often reflected that, despite everything, this obstinate gaiety was still a kind of happiness.

The war changed my attitude to everything; it had radically transformed the objects of my attention: the skies over Paris (and Breton villages, women's mouths and children's eyes.) After June, 1940, I no longer recognized anything—objects, people, seasons, places, even myself. The age I lived in, which for ten years had revolved on a firm axis, now abruptly shifted out of orbit and dragged me with it. Without even quitting the streets of Paris, I found myself more *dépaysée* now than I would have done after crossing the high seas in the old days. With all the naiveté of a child who believes in the absolute vertical, I thought that there was an absolute truth governing the world. This truth might still be half buried under some matrix that the years would slowly wear away, or which might be shattered suddenly by the impact of the revolution, but *substantially it did exist*. In the peace which had been granted us, justice and reason worked like a yeast. I built my happiness on firm ground and beneath immutable constellations.

What a misapprehension this was! It was not a fragment of eternity I had lived through but a transitory period, the prewar years. The earth turned, and revealed another of its faces to me. Violence and injustice were let loose, with every kind of folly, scandal, and horror. Not even victory would turn back the clock and revive the old order that had been temporarily disrupted: it ushered in a new era, the postwar period. No blade of grass in any meadow, however I looked at it, would ever again be what it had been. The ephemeral was my lot. And down the stream of Time, History bore its vast jumble of incurable ills, its brief moments of glory.

Yet now, at the end of August, 1944, I contemplated the future with some confidence. History was not my enemy since, in the last resort, my hopes had been fulfilled. Indeed, it had just bestowed on me the most poignant joy I had ever experienced. How fond I had been, on my travels, of slipping away and losing myself among trees and rocks; and yet I shook off my own personality even more radically when I plunged into the hurly-burly of daily happenings. All Paris was incarnate in me, and I recognized myself in every face I saw. I was stunned by the sheer intensity of my own presence: through some miraculous communal intimacy it extended my awareness till it encomassed every other living soul. I seemed to have grown wings; henceforth I would soar above the narrow confines of my personal life and float in the empyrean that was all mankind. My happiness would reflect the magnificent adventure of a world creating itself afresh. I was not forgetting its darker side; but that moralistic streak I have mentioned helped me to face it. To act in concert with all men, to struggle, to accept death if need be, that life might keep its meaning—by holding fast to these precepts, I felt, I would master that darkness whence the cry of human lamentation arose.

Or would I? Those suffering voices pierced my barricades and threw them down. It was impossible for me to return to my former optimistic outlook: defeat and shock and horror can neither be made good nor left behind. That at least I knew, and would never forget. Never again would I slip back into the fantasies of a divided mind, by which for years on end I had contrived, or imagined I had, to bend the universe to serve my will. I remained indifferent to many things that most people take seriously; but my life ceased to be a game, I knew what my roots were, and I no longer pretended that I could escape my own human condition. Instead I endeavored to bear it. Henceforth I took reality at its proper weight and valuation. At times I found it repugnant to accept it. By renouncing my illusions, I had also lost my intransigence and my pride: that is perhaps the greatest change that took place in me, and sometimes I regretted it bitterly. Despite all the deaths that lay behind me, despite all my anger and rebelliousness, I had re-established myself in the condition of happiness. Of all the blows I had endured, none had broken me. I had survived; indeed, I was unscathed. What thoughtlessness, what inconsistency!—yet neither less nor worse than other people's; and so in feeling ashamed of myself I also felt shame for them. Yet I bore my unworthiness so lightly that, save at rare and fleeting moments, I was not even conscious of it.

This shock, this defeat that I was up against—now refusing to accept, now acknowledging its presence, at times irritated by my own docility, and on other occasions upholding it—had a specific name: death. Never did my own death, or other people's, obsess me so violently as during those years. Now is the appropriate time to discuss this preoccupation of mine.

From the time I knew I was mortal I found the idea of death terrifying. Even when the world was at peace and my happiness seemed secure, my fifteen-year-old self would often turn giddy at the thought of that utter nonbeing—*my* utter nonbeing—that would descend on its appointed day, for ever and ever. This annihilation filled me with such horror that I could not conceive the possibility of facing it coolly: what people called "courage" I could only regard as blind frivolousness. I would add, however, that neither during this period nor in the years that followed did I show myself exceptionally pusillanimous. When I put on skis or tried to swim I lacked boldness, it is true: I never dared to move really fast on a snow-slope, or to get out of my depth in water. Being physically clumsy, I was afraid of breaking a leg, or choking, of being obliged to call other people to my assistance: death did not enter into it. On the other hand, I felt no qualms about scaling precipitous mountains, in espadrilles, or working my way across stretches of screes or firn where one false step might well have cost me my life. The morning I fell from a very considerable height and ended up in the bed of a stream, I simply thought, in an interested way: Well, that's that; these things do happen. I had the same reaction when a fall from my bicycle stunned me; that is, I observed with great detachment this unforeseen but by and large normal event, that is, my death. In both cases I was caught unawares; I don't know how I would have behaved if I had been faced with a really serious danger and my imagination had had time to get to work on it. I have never had the occasion to take the relative measure of my cowardice and my courage. The raids on Paris and Le Havre did not make me lose any sleep; but then the risks I ran were minimal. What *is* certain is that, granted the actual circumstances in which I was variously placed, fear never stopped my taking any particular course. My optimism acted as a check against excessive precautions; besides, I did not even fear the prospect of death, insofar as it was bound to arise in my life at a certain moment. It would be the final point of life for me, true, but still a *part* of life; and on the occasions when I believed myself face to face with it, I surrendered myself calmly to this lively adventure, never giving a thought to the void that yawned for me on the farther side. What I rejected, with all my heart and soul, was the horror of that endless night, which, since it did not exist, would never *be* horrible, but held infinite horror for me, who *did* exist. I could not bear to think of myself as finite and ephemeral, a drop of water in the ocean; at times all my endeavors seemed vanity, happiness became a false lure, and the world wore the mocking, illusory mask of Nothingness.

Because I accepted it in my heart without any feeling of shock, I realized that one *could* defy it: a few years more or less matter little when set against the freedom and peace of mind one achieves the moment one stops running away from death. There were phrases that I had always regarded as hollow and meaningless, the truth of which I now discovered in the most intimate fashion: you must accept death when there is no other means of preserving your life; or, death is not always an absurd and lonely accident, but sometimes creates living bonds with other people, and then it has both meaning and justification. A little later I thought I had had the experience of what death was like, and had discovered that it was, precisely, nothing at all. At some point I ceased to be afraid of it, and even to think about it.

40

TAKATURA ANDO
A Philosopher in the Midst of War

Takatura Ando (1911–), who taught at the University of Kyoto, studied in Europe with Moritz Schlick. His Japanese translation of Moritz Schlick's *Fragen der Ethik* was published in 1967. Written during World War II, Ando's *Aristotle's Theory of Practical Cognition* was translated and published in 1958. His major work on metaphysics was translated into English as *Metaphysics: A Critical Survey of Its Meaning* (1963).

Philosophy as a Refuge From War
Aristotle's Theory of Practical Cognition

AUTHOR'S FOREWORD

In publishing this book, I cannot prohibit myself of reminding the days and nights when it was written. In that era of worldwide madness, Aristotle's philosophy was the only refuge wherein my depressed mind could come to life. It was written bit by bit under all desperate circumstances throughout the war time. My heart was set on the completion of this work while the fate allowed me to live. It was nearly carried out by the end of the war. Having no hope of survival, I buried my manuscript in the earth, without however any expectance of a better lot for it.

The situation grew worse and worse. Towns and cities were burnt and perished day by day. There remained only few of them. In a summer night of 1944, an inauspicious siren blew as if pronouncing our end. I let my wife take refuge with the child, and lied alone on the ground beside the hole in which my manuscript was stored. The blue sky was scattered with twinkling stars, and the buzzying of air corps came far over from the depth of serene night. I was gazing the stars with resignation and despise to human nature, but the corps passed over my head without making any attack. Few minutes later, the sky grew red near the horizont, and I found that the victim of that night was the unfortunate neibourghing city. After few days the citizens of Hirosima and Nagasaki met the atmost misery in the history. The war was over, and I survived with my manuscript.

Since that time I tried to publish this manuscript only in vain. At last, I came to the idea to translate it in English and show to Sir W. D. Ross. When this idea was realized, to my great joy, he gave me a letter full of favour. He acknowledged that he was in the same opinion with regard to many of my arguments, and guaranteed that my treatise would be able to contribute to modern study of Aristotle.

Being much encouraged by this letter and following his advice, I engaged in revising my English by the aid of Dr. S. Nivison of Stanford University. Prof. Ross and Dr. Nivison helped me also in searching a publisher in England and in America, though this attempt did not succeed.

I am firmly convinced of my being the most fortunate fellow who lived under that starly heaven, not only to enjoy again the Lipton tea, which I sadly dreamed in that dreary nights, but also to get the favour of an eminent British scholar, not only to taste again California raisons that I despairingly desired in that weary days, but also to receive kindness of an excellent American scholar.

I debt my English also to my previous colleague Mr. Tyuzo Utidate, who read through my manuscript and gave many advices. My special thanks are due to Prof. John D. Goheen of Stanford University, who paid warm attention to my work and gave me some help. I am grateful to Miss Musako Iwai for her assistance.

As regards English rendering of the text, I owes much to Oxford translations and Hick's De Anima.

Kyoto, 1958

41

HANS-GEORG GADAMER
Philosophical Apprenticeships

A student of Natorp and Heidegger at Marburg, Hans-Georg Gadamer (1900–) has been professor of philosophy at the University of Heidelberg since 1949. His first book, *Plato's Dialectical Ethics* (1931), announced one of the major themes of his later work: the role of dialogue in the tasks of hermeneutic interpretation. Critical of Heidegger's rejection of the history of philosophy of as merely logocentric, he thought that "the return to being" is best expressed in the continuity of a tradition of dialogic interpretation. In *Truth and Method* (1960) and *Philosophical Hermeneutics* (1967–1972) Gadamer argue that art should replace natural science as the model for understanding in the human sciences because works of art are inexhaustibly open to interpretation. Like genuine conversation, the "dialogue" between an interpreter and a work of art transforms the interpreter's self-understanding.

Habermas has criticized Gadamer for a conservatism that seems implicit in treating dialogue as a hermeneutic interpretation of the past, rather than as political deliberation about the future. Gadamer replied that he was engaged in explicating the conditions for the possibility of any communication—conservative or revolutionary. In *Dialogue and Deconstruction* (1989) Gadamer attacked (what he saw as) Derrida's claim that perceptive interpretation undermines itself by revealing its own critical deconstruction.

On the Origins of Philosophical Hermeneutics

Many have seen and continue to see in hermeneutic philosophy a repudiation of methodical rationality. Many others misuse the term and that to which it refers by seeing in it a new methodological doctrine that they then use to legitimate methodological unclarity or ideological concealment. This is especially the case now that hermeneutics has become fashionable and every interpretation wants to call itself "hermeneutical." Still others, who belong to the camp of the critique of ideology, do recognize truth in the term, but only a half-truth. It is well and good, they say, to recognize the prejudgmental significance of tradition, but the decisive dimension is missing, namely the critical and emancipatory reflection that serves in practice to liberate us from it.

Perhaps it would help clarify matters if I present the motivation behind my approach as it actually developed. It might thereby become clear that the method fanatics and the radical ideology critics are the ones who do not reflect enough. The former treat the uncontested rationality of trial and error as if it were the *ultima ratio* of human reasonability. The latter recognize the ideological bias of this kind of rationality but then do not give a sufficient accounting for the ideological implications of their own ideology critique.

As I was attempting to develop a philosophical hermeneutic, it followed from the previous history of hermeneutics that the interpretive (*verstehenden*) sciences provided my starting point. But to these was added a hitherto neglected supplement. I am referring to the experience of art. For both art and the historical sciences are modes of experiencing in which our own understanding of existence comes directly into play. Heidegger's unfolding of the existential structure of understanding provided conceptual help in dealing with the problematic of *Verstehen*, now posed in its proper scope. He formerly called this the "hermeneutic of facticity," the self-interpretation of factual human existence, the existence that was there for the finding. My starting point was thus the critique of Idealism and its Romantic traditions. It was clear to me that the forms of consciousness of our inherited and acquired historical education—aesthetic consciousness and historical consciousness—presented alienated forms of our true historical being. The primordial experiences that are transmitted through art and history are not to be grasped from the points of view of these forms of consciousness. The calm distance from which a middle-class educational consciousness takes satisfaction in its educational achievements misunderstands how much we ourselves are immersed in the game [*im Spiele*] and are the stake in this game. So from the perspective of the concept of *play* [*des Spieles*] I tried to overcome the illusions of self-consciousness and the prejudices of Consciousness-Idealism. Play is never a mere object but rather has an existence for the one who plays along, even if only as a spectator. The unsuitability of the concepts of subject and object, which Heidegger had shown in his treatment of the question of being [*Sein*] in *Being and Time*, here let itself be demonstrated concretely. What in Heidegger's thinking had led to "the turn," I for my part attempted to describe as the horizon experience of our self-understanding, as the "effective historical consciousness" that is more being than being conscious. What I thereby formulated was not strictly a task for the methodical *praxis* of art history and historical scholarship, nor did it apply in the first instance to the consciousness of method in these disciplines; rather, it applied exclusively or preeminently to the philosophical idea of grounding an argument. To what extent is method a guarantor of truth? Philosophy must demand of science and method that they recognize their own particularity in the context of human *Existenz* and its reasonableness.

In the end the undertaking was obviously itself conditioned by an effective history and rooted in a very definite German philosophical and cultural heritage. Nowhere so strongly as in Germany had the so-called human sciences united in themselves scientific and orienting functions. Or better: Nowhere else had they so consistently concealed the orienting, ideological determination of their interests behind the method-consciousness of their scientific procedure. The indissoluble unity of all human self-knowledge expressed itself more clearly elsewhere: in France in the broad conception of *lettres*, in English-speaking countries in the newly assimilated conception of the humanities. Implied in the recognition of an effective historical consciousness was above all a rectification of the self-conception of the historic human sciences, and this also included art scholarship.

But with this the dimensions of the problem were by no means fully measured. There is something like a hermeneutical problematic in the natural sciences too. Their way is not simply that of the progress of their methods, as Thomas Kuhn has shown in an argument corresponding in its truth to insights that Heidegger had implied in his "The Age of the World Picture" and in his interpretation of Aristotle's *Physics*. The "paradigm" is of decisive importance for both the employment and the interpretation of methodical research and is obviously not itself the simple result of such research. Galileo would have called it a *mente concipio*.

Behind this, however, a much broader dimension opens up, one that is rooted in a fundamental linguisticality or language-relatedness. In all recognition of the world and orientation in the world, the element of understanding is to be worked out, and with this the universality of hermeneutics is to be demonstrated. Of course, the fundamental linguisticality of understanding cannot possibly mean that all experiencing of the world takes place only as language and in language. All too well known are those prelinguistic and metalinguistic dawnings, dumb-nesses, and silences in which the immediate meeting with the world expresses itself. And who would deny that there are real conditions to human life? There are such things as hunger and love, work and domination, which themselves are not speech and language but which circumscribe the space within which speaking-with-each-other and listening-to-each-other can take place. There is no dispute that it is precisely such preformations of human opinion and speech that make hermeneutic reflection necessary. In respect to a hermeneutic oriented toward Socratic conversation, it goes without saying that *doxa* is not knowledge and that the seeming agreement in which we live and speak quasi-consciously is no real agreement. But even the exposing of the illusory, as done in Socratic dialogue, completes itself only in the element of linguisticality. Dialogue lets us be certain of possible assent, even in the wreckage of agreement, in misunderstanding, and in the famous admission of ignorance. The communality that we call human rests on the linguistic constitution of our life-world. Every attempt to bring suit against distortions of interhuman understanding on the basis of critical reflection and argumentation confirms this communality.

Thus the hermeneutic aspect itself cannot remain limited to the hermeneutic sciences of art and history, nor to intercourse with "texts," and also not, by extension, to the experience of art itself. The universality of the hermeneutic problem, already recognized by Schleiermacher, has to do with the universe of the reasonable, that is, with anything and everything about which human beings can seek to reach agreement. Where reaching an understanding [*Verständigung*] seems to be impossible, because we "speak different languages," hermeneutics is still not at an end. Here the hermeneutic task poses itself in its full seriousness, namely as the task of finding a common language. But the common language is never a fixed given. Between speaking beings it is a language-at-play, one that must first warm itself up so that understanding can begin, especially at the point where different points of view seem irreconcilably opposed. The possibility of reaching an agreement between reasonable beings can never be denied. Even relativism, which seems rooted in the multiplicity of human languages, was already known to Heraclitus. The adult learning a foreign language and the child first learning to speak signify not just an appropriation of the means of producing understanding. Rather, this kind of learning by appropriation depicts a kind of preschematization of possible experience and its first acquisition. Growing into a language is a mode of gaining knowledge of the world. Not just such "learning," however, but all experience realizes itself in ongoing communicative improvement of our knowledge of the world. We live in traditions, and these are not a fragment of our world-experience, not a matter of "cultural transmissions" emerging from texts and monuments and communicating a meaning that is linguistically composed and historically documented. Rather, it is the world itself that is communicatively experienced and constantly given over to us as an infinitely open task. It is not the world of a first day but one that is always already handed down to us. In all those places where something is experienced, where unfamiliarity is overcome and what occurs is the shedding of light, the coming of insight, and appropriation, what takes place is the hermeneutic process of translation into the word and into the common consciousness. Even the monological language of modern science wins social reality only by this means.

In respect to our philosophical tradition, we must come to terms with the same hermeneutical task. Philosophizing does not begin at some zero point but must think and speak with the language we already possess. As in the days of the ancient Sophists, so today, this means leading a language, estranged from its native sense of saying something, back to the common way of saying things and to the communality that supports this way of saying.

The Aristotelian program of a practical science seems to me to present the only scholarly model according to which the interpretive sciences can be thought out. For in hermeneutical reflection on the conditions of understanding, it turns out that their possibilities articulate themselves in a consciousness that formulates itself in language and does not begin with nothing or end in infinity. Aristotle shows that practical reason and practical insight do not possess the "teachability" of science but rather win their possibility in *praxis* itself, and that means in the inner linkage of ethics. This is worth remembering. The model of practical philosophy must take the place of a *theoria* whose ontological legitimation may be found only in an *intellectus infinitus* that is unknown to an existential experience unsupported by revelation. This model must also be held out as a contrast to all those who bend human reasonableness to the methodical thinking of "anonymous" science. In opposition to the perfecting of the logical self-understanding of science, this seems to me to be the authentic task of philosophy and is so precisely in the face of the practical meaning of science for our life and survival.

But "practical philosophy" is more than a mere methodical model for the hermeneutic sciences. It is also something like its substantive foundation. The special feature of method in practical philosophy is only the result of the "practical reasonability" that Aristotle worked out in its conceptual peculiarity. Its structure is completely ungraspable from the modern concept of science. Even the dialectical fluidity that was won for traditional concepts through Hegel and that served to renew some of the old truths of practical philosophy, threatens a new, impenetrable dogmatism of reflection. The concept of reflection that lies at the heart of ideology critique implies an abstract concept of coercion-free discourse, one that loses sight of the authentic conditions of human *praxis*. I had to reject this as an illegitimate transference of the therapeutic situation of psychoanalysis. In the field of practical reason, there is no analogy to the knowing analyst who can guide the productive, reflective achievement of the analysand. In the question of reflection, it seems to me that Brentano's distinction, traceable to Aristotle, of the reflective awareness of objectivating reflection is superior to the heritage of German Idealism.

Insofar as they are my constant companions, I have been formed more by the Platonic dialogues than by the great thinkers of German Idealism. The dialogues provide unique company. However much we, instructed by Nietzsche and Heidegger, like to take the anticipatoriness [*Vorgreiflichkeit*] of Greek conceptualization from Aristotle to Hegel and up to modern logic to be a border on the other side of which our questions have no answers and our intentions remain unsatisfied, the art of Platonic dialogue also anticipates this seeming superiority, which we take to be our possession from our Judeo-Christian heritage. Certainly it is none other than Plato, with his doctrine of ideas, his dialectic of ideas, his mathematization of physics, and his intellectualization of what we would call ethics, who laid the foundation for the metaphysical conceptualization of our tradition. But simultaneously he limited all his pronouncements by means of mimicry, and just as Socrates with customary irony knew how to reach his ends with his conversation partners, so Plato with his art of dialogue-poetry knew how to strip his reader of his supposed superiority. The task is not to philosophize with Plato but to criticize Plato. Criticizing Plato is perhaps as simple-minded as it is to hold it against Sophocles that he is not Shakespeare. This may seem paradoxical, but only to someone who is blind to the philosophical relevance of Plato's poetic imagination.

Of course one must first learn to read Plato's writings as mimicry. In the literal sense they are "loaded" speeches. In them is confided for the first time what Socrates actually intends with an art of refutation that too often works sophistically and drives opponents into the worst of entanglements. Yes, if human wisdom were such that it could pass from one to the other as water can be led from one vessel to another over a strand of wool . . . (*Symposium*, 175d). But this is not the way of human wisdom. A knowledge of our own ignorance is what human wisdom is. The other person with whom Socrates carries on his conversation is convicted of his own ignorance by means of his "knowledge." This means that something dawns upon him about himself and his life of illusions. Or to put it in the bold manner of Plato's *Seventh Letter*: Not only his argument, but also his soul is refuted. This also holds for the boys who believe in their friends but still do not know what friendship is (*Lysis*). It holds for the famous generals, who believe that they embody the virtues of soldiers (*Laches*), or the ambitious statesmen who claim to possess a knowledge superior to all other knowledge (*Charmides*). It holds just as much for all those who follow professional doctrines of knowledge, and in the final analysis it holds for the most ordinary of citizens, who must believe in himself and make others believe that he is a just person in his capacity as salesman, dealer, banker, or craftsman. But obviously it is not a specialized knowledge that is in question here. It is another mode of knowing beyond all the special claims and competence of a knowing superiority, beyond all of the otherwise known *technai* and *epistemai*. This other form of knowing intends a "turn to the ideas" that lie behind all exposures of pretentious knowing.

But even this does not mean that in the end Plato has a doctrine that one can learn, a doctrine of ideas. And if he criticizes this doctrine in his *Parmenides*, this does not mean that he had at that time begun to doubt it. The adoption of "ideas" did not so much signal a doctrine as a direction for questioning, whose implications it was then the task of philosophy, meaning Platonic dialectic, to develop and discuss. Dialectic is the art of carrying on a conversation, and this includes the conversation with oneself and the following out of the agreement reached with oneself. That is the art of thinking. But this is an art of raising questions about what one actually intends with what one thinks and says. With this one sets out on a way. Better, with this one is already on the way. For there is something like a natural human facility for philosophy. Our thinking does not come to a grinding halt because some thinker has framed a system about this or that. Thinking always points beyond itself. Platonic dialogue has an expression for this; it refers to the one, the being, the good that presents itself in the order of the soul, the political constitution, or the nature of the world.

42

HANNAH ARENDT
Thinking Through the Good Life

Having studied with Heidegger and Jaspers at Marburg, Freiburg, and Heidelberg, Hannah Arendt (1906–1975) emigrated to France in 1933 and then, in 1941, to the United States, where she taught at the New School for Social Research. Influenced by Greek and Roman political theory, she became a critic of totalitarianism and (what she thought of as) defective democracies. She described a form of civic life that accords primacy to the *praxis* of shared, deliberative political activity as an essential expression of human nature (*The Origins of Totalitarianism* 1951; *The Human Condition*, 1958; *Between Past and Future*, 1968.) Profoundly affected by the rise of fascism, she attempted to explain how ordinary people living in a highly developed culture could have lapsed into the barbarism of the Holocaust. In *Eichmann in Jerusalem* (1963) Arendt describes the banal, unnoticed, incremental steps that allow an Eichmann to think of himself as merely doing his duty. Precisely because not paying attention—deflecting reflection and self-criticism—is a perfectly normal psychological pattern, the "banality of evil" can occur anywhere, anytime. Arendt also wrote on Kant (1982) and Augustine (1996). She also occasionally wrote produced biographical studies of courageous and original thinkers who seemed marginal in their time (*Men in Dark Times* 1968, and *Rachel Vernhagen: The Life of a Jewish Woman*, 1974. Her ambitious work in philosophical psychology, *The Life of the Mind* (1977), characterized varieties of mental activity, distinguishing instrumental calculation from genuinely civic thought and contemplation. A good deal of her philosophical correspondence with Heidegger and Jaspers has been published posthumously, as was her more personal correspondence with Mary MacCarthy (*Between Friends*, 1995).

On Humanity in Dark Times: Thoughts about Lessing

I explicitly stress[ed] my membership in the group of Jews expelled from Germany at a relatively early age because I wish to anticipate certain misunderstandings which can arise only too easily when one speaks of humanity. In this connection I cannot gloss over the fact that for many years I considered the only adequate reply to the question, Who are you? to be: A Jew. That answer alone took into account the reality of persecution. As for the statement with which Nathan the Wise (in effect, though not in actual wording) countered the command: "Step closer, Jew"—the statement: I am a man—I would have considered as nothing but a grotesque and dangerous evasion of reality.

Let me also quickly clear away another likely misunderstanding. When I use the word "Jew" I do not mean to suggest any special kind of human being, as though the Jewish fate were either representative of or a model for the fate of mankind. (Any such thesis could at best have been advanced with cogency only during the last stage of Nazi domination, when in fact the Jews and anti-Semitism were being exploited solely to unleash and keep in motion the racist program of extermination. For this was an essential part of totalitarian rule. The Nazi movement, to be sure, had from the first tended toward totalitarianism, but the Third Reich was not by any means totalitarian during its early years. By "early years" I mean the first period, which lasted from 1933 to 1938.) In saying, "A Jew," I did not even refer to a reality burdened or marked out for distinction by history. Rather, I was only acknowledging a political fact through which my being a member of this group outweighed all other questions of personal identity or rather had decided them in favor of anonymity, of namelessness. Nowadays such an attitude would seem like a pose. Nowadays, therefore, it is easy to remark that those who reacted in this way had never got very far in the school of "humanity," had fallen into the trap set by Hitler, and thus had succumbed to the spirit of Hitlerism in their own way. Unfortunately, the basically simple principle in question here is one that is particularly hard to understand in times of defamation and persecution: the principle that one can resist only in terms of the identity that is under attack. Those who reject such identifications on the part of a hostile world may feel wonderfully superior to the world, but their superiority is then truly no longer of this world; it is the superiority of a more or less well-equipped cloud-cuckoo-land.

When I thus bluntly reveal the personal background of my reflections, it may easily sound to those who know the fate of the Jews only from hearsay as if I am talking out of school, a school they have not attended and whose lessons do not concern them. But as it happens, during that selfsame period in Germany there existed the phenomenon known as the "inner emigration," and those who know anything about that experience may well recognize certain questions and conflicts akin to the problems I have mentioned in more than a mere formal and structural sense. As its very name suggests, the "inner emigration" was a curiously ambiguous phenomenon. It signified on the one hand that there were persons inside Germany who behaved as if they no longer belonged to the country, who felt like emigrants; and on the other hand it indicated that they had not in reality emigrated, but had withdrawn to an interior realm, into the invisibility of thinking and feeling. It would be a mistake to imagine that this form of exile, a withdrawal from the world into interior realm, existed only in Germany, just as it would be a mistake to imagine that such emigration came to an end with the end of the Third Reich. But in that darkest of times, inside and outside Germany the temptation was particularly strong, in the face of a seemingly unendurable reality, to shift from the world and its public space to an interior life, or else simply to ignore that world in favor of an imaginary world "as it ought to be" or as it once upon a time had been.

There has been much discussion of the widespread tendency in Germany to act as though the years from 1933 to 1945 never existed; as though this part of German and European and thus world history could be expunged from the textbooks; as though everything depended on forgetting the "negative" aspect of the past and reducing horror to sentimentality. (The world-wide success of *The Diary of Anne Frank* was clear proof that such tendencies were not confined to Germany.) It was a grotesque state of affairs when German young people were not allowed to learn the facts that every schoolchild a few miles away could not help knowing. Behind all this there was, of course, genuine perplexity. And this very incapacity to face the reality of the past might possibly have been a direct heritage of the inner emigration, as it was undoubtedly to a considerable extent, and even more directly, a consequence of the Hitler regime—that is to say, a consequence of the organized guilt in which the Nazis had involved all inhabitants of the German lands, the inner exiles no less than the stalwart Party members and the vacillating fellow travelers. It was the fact of this guilt which the Allies simply incorporated into the fateful hypothesis of collective guilt. Herein lies the reason for the Germans' profound awkwardness, which strikes every outsider, in any discussion of questions of the past. How difficult it must be to find a reasonable attitude is perhaps more clearly expressed by the cliché that the past is still "unmastered" and in the conviction held particularly by men of good will that the first thing to be done is to set about "mastering" it. Perhaps that cannot be done with any past, but certainly not with the past of Hitler Germany. The best that can be achieved is to know precisely what it was, and to endure this knowledge, and then to wait and see what comes of knowing and enduring.

Perhaps I can best explain this by a less painful example. After the First World War we experienced the "mastering of the past" in a spate of descriptions of the war that varied enormously in kind and quality; naturally, this happened not only in Germany, but in all the affected countries. Nevertheless, nearly thirty years were to pass before a work of art appeared which so transparently displayed the inner truth of the event that it became possible to say: Yes, this is how it was. And in this novel, William Faulkner's *A Fable*, very little is described, still less explained, and nothing at all "mastered"; its end is tears, which the reader also weeps, and what remains beyond that is the "tragic effect" or the "tragic pleasure," the shattering emotion which makes one able to accept the fact that something like this war could have happened at all. I deliberately mention tragedy because it more than the other literary forms represents a process of recognition. The tragic hero becomes knowledgeable by reexperiencing what has been done in the way of suffering, and in this *pathos*, in resuffering the past, the network of individual acts is transformed into an event, a significant whole. The dramatic climax of tragedy occurs when the actor turns into a sufferer; therein lies its peripeteia, the disclosure of the dénouement. But even non-tragic plots become genuine events only when they are experienced a second time in the form of suffering by memory operating retrospectively and perceptively. Such memory can speak only when indignation and just anger, which impel us to action, have been silenced—and that needs time. We can no more master the past than we can undo it. But we can reconcile ourselves to it. The form for this is the lament, which arises out of all recollection. It is, as Goethe has said (in the Dedication to *Faust*):

> *Der Schmerz wird neu, es wiederholt die Klage*
> Des Lebens labyrinthisch irren Lauf.

> (Pain arises anew, lament repeats
> Life's labyrinthine, erring course.)

The tragic impact of this repetition in lamentation affects one of the key elements of all action; it establishes its meaning and that permanent significance which then enters into history. In contradistinction to other elements peculiar to action—above all to the preconceived goals, the impelling motives, and the guiding principles, all of which become visible in the course of action—the meaning of a committed act is revealed only when the action itself has come to an end and become a story susceptible to narration. Insofar as any "mastering" of the past is possible, it consists in relating what has happened; but such narration, too, which shapes history, solves no problems and assuages no suffering; it does not master anything once and for all. Rather, as long as the meaning of the events remains alive—and this meaning can persist for very long periods of time—"mastering of the past" can take the form of ever-recurrent narration. The poet in a very general sense and the historian in a very special sense have the task of setting this process of narration in motion and of involving us in it. And we who for the most part are neither poets nor historians are familiar with the nature of this process from our own experience with life, for we too have the need to recall the significant events in our own lives by relating them to ourselves and others. Thus we are constantly preparing the way for "poetry," in the broadest sense, as a human potentiality; we are, so to speak, constantly expecting it to erupt in some human being. When this happens, the telling-over of what took place comes to a halt for the time being and a formed narrative, one more item, is added to the world's stock. In reification by the poet or the historian, the narration of history has achieved permanence and persistence. Thus the narrative has been given its place in the world, where it will survive us. There it can live on—one story among many. There is no meaning to these stories that is entirely separable from them—and this, too, we know from our own, non-poetic experience. No philosophy, no analysis, no aphorism, be it ever so profound, can compare in intensity and richness of meaning with a properly narrated story.

I seem to have digressed from my subject. The question is how much reality must be retained even in a world become inhuman if humanity is not to be reduced to an empty phrase or a phantom. Or to put it another way, to what extent do we remain obligated to the world even when we have been expelled from it or have withdrawn from it? For I certainly do not wish to assert that the "inner emigration," the flight from the world to concealment, from public life to anonymity (when that is what it really was and not just a pretext for doing what everyone did with enough inner reservations to salve one's conscience), was not a justified attitude, and in many cases the only possible one. Flight from the world in dark times of impotence can always be justified as long as reality is not ignored, but is constantly acknowledged as the thing that must be escaped. When people choose this alternative, private life too can retain a by no means insignificant reality, even though it remains impotent. Only it is essential for them to realize that the realness of this reality consists not in its deeply personal note, any more than it springs from privacy as such, but inheres in the world from which they have escaped. They must remember that they are constantly on the run, and that the world's reality is actually expressed by their escape. Thus, too, the true force of escapism springs from persecution, and the personal strength of the fugitives increases as the persecution and danger increase.

At the same time we cannot fail to see the limited political relevance of such an existence, even if it is sustained in purity. Its limits are inherent in the fact that strength and power are not the same; that power arises only where people act together, but not where people grow stronger as individuals. No strength is ever great enough to replace power; wherever strength is confronted by power, strength will always succumb. But even the sheer strength to escape and to resist while fleeing cannot materialize where reality is bypassed or forgotten—as when an individual thinks himself too good and noble to pit himself against such a world, or when he fails to face up to the absolute "negativeness" of prevailing world conditions at a given time. How tempting it was, for example, simply to ignore the intolerably stupid blabber of the Nazis. But seductive though it may be to yield to such temptations and to hole up in the refuge of one's own psyche, the result will always be a loss of humanness along with the forsaking of reality.

Thus, in the case of a friendship between a German and a Jew under the conditions of the Third Reich it would scarcely have been a sign of humanness for the friends to have said: Are we not both human beings? It would have been mere evasion of reality and of the world common to both at that time; they would not have been resisting the world as it was. A law that prohibited the intercourse of Jews and Germans could be evaded but could not be defied by people who denied the reality of the distinction. In keeping with a humanness that had not lost the solid ground of reality, a humanness in the midst of the reality of persecution, they would have had to say to each other: A German and a Jew, and friends. But wherever such a friendship succeeded at that time (of course the situation is completely changed, nowadays) and was maintained in purity, that is to say without false guilt complexes on the one side and false complexes of superiority or inferiority on the other, a bit of humanness in a world become inhuman had been achieved.

Dedication to Karl Jaspers

Lieber verehrtester,[1]

Thank you for permitting me to dedicate this little book to you, and thank you, too, for the opportunity to say to you what I have to say on its publication in Germany.

For it is not an easy thing for a Jew to publish in Germany today, even if he is a German-speaking Jew. In the face of what has happened, the appealing opportunity to write in one's own language again counts for very little, although this is the only return home from exile that one can never entirely ban from one's dreams. But we Jews are not or are not any longer exiles and hardly have a right to such dreams. Quite apart from how our expulsion appears and is understood in the context of German or European history, the fact of our expulsion itself forced us at first to look back on our own history, in which expulsion appears not as a unique and unusual phenomenon but as a familiar and repeated one.

This understanding of the present in the light of the past proved, of course, to be illusory. Recent years have taught us things we could in no way document as events that had repeated themselves in our history. Never before had we been faced with a determined effort to eradicate us, and we never seriously considered such a possibility. In view of the annihilation of one-third of the world's Jewish population and almost three-fourths of European Jewry, the catastrophes the Zionists were predicting before Hitler came to power look like tempests in a teapot.

But to say this is no way makes a publication of this kind easier to understand or better understood. It seems clear to me that the majority of both Germans and Jews will find it difficult to regard any Jew who wants to speak to Germans in Germany or, as I am doing in this book, to speak to Europeans as anything but a scoundrel or a fool. This has nothing whatever to do with the question of guilt or responsibility. I speak here only of factual matters as I see them, because one should never stray from the basis of fact without knowing what one is doing and why.

None of the following essays was, I hope, written without awareness of the facts of our time and without awareness of the Jewish fate in our century. But I believe and hope that I have not in any of them taken up a position on the basis of those facts alone, that I have not accepted the world created by those facts as necessary and indestructible. Without your philosophy and without the fact of your existence, both of which became much more vivid to me than ever before in the long years when the madness at loose in the world separated me completely from you, I could never have summoned up such a willed independence of judgment and a conscious distance from all fanaticisms, however attractive these may have seemed and however frightening the isolation, in every sense, that threatened to follow as a consequence of my position.

What I learned from you and what helped me in the ensuing years to find my way around in reality without selling my soul to it the way people in earlier times sold their souls to the devil is that the only thing of importance is not philosophies but the truth, that one has to live and think in the open and not in one's own little shell, no matter how comfortably furnished it is, and that necessity in whatever form is only a will-o'-the-wisp that tries to lure us into playing a role instead of attempting to be a human being. What I have personally never forgotten is your attitude—so difficult to describe—of listening, your tolerance that is constantly ready to offer criticism but is as far removed from skepticism as it is from fanaticism; ultimately, it is simply the realization of the fact that all human beings are rational but that no human being's rationality is infallible.

Back then, I was sometimes tempted to imitate you, even in your manner of speech, because that manner symbolized for me a human being who dealt openly and directly with the world, a human being without ulterior motives. I had little idea at that time how difficult it would be at a later one to find people without ulterior motives, little idea that a time would come when what reason and clear, illuminating attentiveness required of us would appear to be presumptuous, even profligate, optimism. For among the facts of this world we live in today is a fundamental mistrust between peoples and individuals that did not and could not disappear with the Nazis because it is rooted in the overpowering evidence of our experience. It is consequently almost impossible for us Jews today not to ask any German we happen to meet: What did you do in the twelve years from 1933 to 1945? And behind that question lie two unavoidable feelings: a harrowing uneasiness at placing on another human being the inhuman demand to justify his existence and the lurking suspicion that one is face to face with someone who worked in a death factory or who, when he learned something about the monstrous crimes of the government, responded with: You can't make an omelet without breaking eggs. That a person didn't have to be a born murderer to have done the first of these things, or a hired accomplice, indeed, not even a convinced Nazi, to have said the second is precisely the unsettling reality that can so easily tempt us to generalize.

The factual territory onto which both peoples have been driven looks something like this: On the one side is the complicity of the German people, which the Nazis consciously planned and realized. On the other side is the blind hatred, created in the gas chambers, of the entire Jewish people. Unless both peoples decide to leave this factual territory, the individual Jew will no more be able to abandon his fanatical hatred than will the individual German be able to rid himself of the complicity imposed upon him by the Nazis.

The decision to leave this territory completely behind us and to renounce completely the laws that it would impose on our actions is difficult to make. It arises from the insight that something has happened in the past that was not just bad or unjust or cruel, but something that should never under any circumstances have been allowed to happen. That was not the case for as long as the Nazi regime remained within certain limits and as long as a Jew could shape his behavior according to the rules that apply under the conditions of a normal and understood hostility between two peoples. At that time there was still a factual basis on which one could rely without becoming inhuman. One could defend oneself as a Jew because one had been attacked as a Jew. National concepts and national membership still had a meaning; they were still elements of a reality within which one could live and move. In the context of such a world, a world still intact despite all the hostility in it, the possibility of communication between peoples and individuals remains. We are spared that blind and eternal hatred that inevitably seizes us if we accept the consequences of the facts the Nazis created.

But the fabrication of corpses goes beyond hostility and cannot be comprehended by political categories. In Auschwitz, the factual territory opened up an abyss into which everyone is drawn who attempts after the fact to stand on that territory. Here, the reality of the politicians of *Realpolitik*, under whose spell the majority of the peoples always and naturally falls, has become a monster that could only urge us to perpetuate annihilation the way the Nazis continued to produce corpses in Auschwitz.

If the factual territory has become an abyss, then the space one occupies if one pulls back from it is, so to speak, an empty space where there are no longer nations and peoples but only individuals for whom it is now not of much consequence what the majority of peoples, or even the majority of one's own people, happens to think at any given moment. If these individuals who exist today in all the peoples and in all the nations of the world are to reach understanding among themselves, it is essential that they learn not to cling frantically any longer to their own national pasts—pasts that explain nothing anyhow, for Auschwitz can no more be explained from the perspective of German history than from Jewish history—that they don't forget that they are only chance survivors of a deluge that in one form or another can break over us again any day, and that they therefore may be like Noah in his ark; and finally that they must not yield to despair or scorn for humankind but be thankful that there are quite a few Noahs floating around out there on the world's seas trying to bring their arks as close together as they can.

As you said in Geneva, "We live as if we stood knocking at gates that are still closed to us. Today something may perhaps be taking place in the purely personal realm that cannot yet found a world order because it is only given to individuals, but which will perhaps someday found such an order when these individuals have been brought together from their dispersion."

With that hope and with that intent, I feel the publication of this book in Germany is justified. And in any case, your life and your philosophy provide us with a model of how human beings can speak with each other, despite the prevailing conditions of the deluge.

New York, May 1947

Thinking as the Life of the Mind

The title I have given this lecture series, *The Life of the Mind*, sounds pretentious, and to talk about Thinking seems to me so presumptuous that I feel I should start less with an apology than with a justification. No justification, of course, is needed for the topic itself, especially not in the framework of eminence inherent in the Gifford Lectures. What disturbs me is that *I* try my hand at it, for I have neither claim nor ambition to be a "philosopher" or be numbered among what Kant, not without irony, called, *Denker von Gewerbe* (professional thinkers). The question then is, should I not have left these problems in the hands of the experts, and the answer will have to show what prompted me to venture from the relatively safe fields of political science and theory into these rather awesome matters, instead of leaving well enough alone.

Factually, my preoccupation with mental activities has two rather different origins. The immediate impulse came from my attending the Eichmann trial in Jerusalem. In my report of it I spoke of "the banality of evil." Behind that phrase, I held no thesis or doctrine, although I was dimly aware of the fact that it went counter to our tradition of thought—literary, theological, or philosophic—about the phenomenon of evil. Evil, we have learned, is something demonic; its incarnation is Satan, a "lightning fall from heaven" (Luke 10:18), or Lucifer, the fallen angel ("The devil is an angel too"—Unamuno) whose sin is pride ("proud as Lucifer"), namely, that *superbia* of which only the best are capable: they don't want to serve God but to be like Him. Evil men, we are told, act out of envy; this may be resentment at not having turned out well through no fault of their own (Richard III) or the envy of Cain, who slew Abel because "the Lord had regard for Abel and his offering, but for Cain and his offering he had no regard." Or they may be prompted by weakness (Macbeth). Or, on the contrary, by the powerful hatred wickedness feels for sheer goodness (Iago's "I hate the Moor: my cause is hearted"; Claggart's hatred for Billy Budd's "barbarian" innocence, a hatred considered by Melville a "depravity according to nature"), or by covetousness, "the root of all evil" (*Radix omnium malorum cupiditas*). However, what I was confronted with was utterly different and still undeniably factual. I was struck by a manifest shallowness in the doer that made it impossible to trace the uncontestable evil of his deeds to any deeper level of roots or motives. The deeds were monstrous, but the doer—at least the very effective one now on trial—was quite ordinary, common-place, and neither demonic nor monstrous. There was no sign in him of firm ideological convictions or of specific evil motives, and the only notable characteristic one could detect in his past behavior as well as in his behavior during the trial and throughout the pre-trial police examination was something entirely negative: it was not stupidity but *thoughtlessness*. In the setting of Israeli court and prison procedures he functioned as well as he had functioned under the Nazi regime but, when confronted with situations for which such routine procedures did not exist, he was helpless, and his cliché-ridden language produced on the stand, as it had evidently done in his official life, a kind of macabre comedy. Clichés, stock phrases, adherence to conventional, standardized codes of expression and conduct have the socially recognized function of protecting us against reality, that is, against the claim on our thinking attention that all events and facts make by virtue of their existence. If we were responsive to this claim all the time, we would soon be exhausted; Eichmann differed from the rest of us only in that he clearly knew of no such claim at all.

It was this absence of thinking—which is so ordinary an experience in our everyday life, where we have hardly the time, let alone the inclination, to *stop* and think—that awakened my interest. Is evil-doing (*the sins of omission*, as well as the sins of *commission*) possible in default of not just "base motives" (as the law calls them) but of any motives whatever, of any particular prompting of interest or volition? Is wickedness, however we may define it, this being "determined to prove a villain," *not* a necessary condition for evil-doing? Might the problem of good and evil, our faculty for telling right from wrong, be connected with our faculty of thought? To be sure, not in the sense that thinking would ever be able to produce the good deed as its result, as though "virtue could be taught" and learned—only habits and customs can be taught, and we know only too well the alarming speed with which they are unlearned and forgotten when new circumstances demand a change in manners and patterns of behavior. (The fact that we usually treat matters of good and evil in courses in "morals" or "ethics" may indicate how little we know about them, for morals comes from *mores* and ethics from *ēthos*, the Latin and the Greek words for customs and habit, the Latin word being associated with rules of behavior, whereas the Greek is derived from habitat, like our "habits.") The absence of thought I was confronted with sprang neither from forgetfulness of former, presumably good manners and habits nor from stupidity in the sense of inability to comprehend—not even in the sense of "moral insanity," for it was just as noticeable in instances that had nothing to do with so-called ethical decisions or matters of conscience.

The question that imposed itself was: Could the activity of thinking as such, the habit of examining whatever happens to come to pass or to attract attention, regardless of results and specific content, could this activity be among the conditions that make men abstain from evil-doing or even actually "condition" them against it? (The very word "con-science," at any rate, points in this direction insofar as it means "to know with and by myself," a kind of knowledge that is actualized in every thinking process.) And is not this hypothesis enforced by everything we know about conscience, namely, that a "good conscience" is enjoyed as a rule only by really bad people, criminals and such, while only "good people" are capable of having a bad conscience?

With the rise of the modern age, thinking became chiefly the handmaiden of science, of organized knowledge; and even though thinking then grew extremely active, following modernity's crucial conviction that I can know only what I myself make, it was Mathematics, the non-empirical science par excellence, wherein the mind appears to play only with itself, that turned out to be the Science of sciences, delivering the key to those laws of nature and the universe that are concealed by appearances. If it was axiomatic for Plato that the invisible eye of the soul was the organ for beholding invisible truth with the certainty of knowledge, it became axiomatic for Descartes—during the famous night of his "revelation"—that there existed "a fundamental accord between the *laws* of nature [which are concealed by appearances and deceptive sense perceptions] and the laws of mathematics"; that is, between the laws of discursive thinking on the highest, most abstract level and the laws of whatever lies behind mere semblance in nature. And he actually believed that with this kind of thinking, with what Hobbes called "reckoning with consequences," he could deliver certain knowledge about the existence of God, the nature of the soul, and similar matters. . . .

What are we "doing" when we do nothing but think? The philosopher, to the extent that he is a philosopher and not (what of course he also is) "a man like you and me," withdraws from the world of appearances, and the region he then moves in has always, since philosophy's beginning, been described as the world of the few. This age-old distinction between the many and the "professional thinkers" specializing in what was supposedly the highest activity human beings could attain to—Plato's philosopher "shall be called the friend of the god, and if it ever is given to man to put on immortality, it shall be given to him"—has lost its plausibility, and this is the second advantage in our present situation. If, as I suggested before, the ability to tell right from wrong should turn out to have anything to do with the ability to think, then we must be able to "demand" its exercise from every sane person, no matter how erudite or ignorant, intelligent or stupid, he may happen to be. Kant—in this respect almost alone among the philosophers—was much bothered by the common opinion that philosophy is only for the few, precisely because of its moral implications, and he once observed that "stupidity is caused by a wicked heart." This is not true: absence of thought is not stupidity; it can be found in highly intelligent people, and a wicked heart is not its cause; it is probably the other way round, that wickedness may be caused by absence of thought. In any event, the matter can no longer be left to "specialists" as though thinking, like higher mathematics, were the monopoly of a specialized discipline.

NOTE

1. Published in German as "Zueignung an Karl Jaspers" in *Sechs Essays*, Heidelberg, 1948. English translation by Robert and Rita Kimber.

43

ISAIAH BERLIN
My Intellectual Path

Born in Riga, Latvia, Isaiah Berlin (1909–1997) immigrated to Britain in 1920. With the exception of a period during which he served as an attaché at the British embassy in Washington, D.C. during World War II, he spent the greater part of his life in Oxford. A critic of historical determinism, moral relativism, and all forms of totalitarianism, Berlin wrote numerous essays on such political theorists as Machiavelli, Vico, Herder, le Maistre, Marx, and Sorel.

Berlin's influential "Two Concepts of Liberty" (1958) distinguishes the liberal "negative" liberty of Mill and Herzen from the "positive" liberty of Rousseau, Hegel, and Marx. The former argues for limiting the power of authority to constrain individual choice and action. In the name of assuring the development of human potentialities, the adherents of "positive" liberty are willing to grant authority to those who would promote (what they consider) the conditions for rational autonomy. Berlin argues that the movement toward positive liberty is a movement toward totalitarianism (*The Crooked Timber of Humanity*, 1990).

Berlin's papers on liberty were followed by a series of essays arguing for the irreducible plurality of incommensurable values and ends, many of which—like the pursuit of both radical liberty and equality, or the assurance of both justice and mercy—undermine one another. In *The Hedgehog and the Fox* (1953) he expands on the difference between two types of temperaments. The likes of Aristotle, Shakespeare, and Joyce celebrate the variety of life and the likes of Plato and Dostoyevsky long for unity and simplification. The hope of reconciling the plurality of values and modes of life in one life—or even in the aims of a culture or political system—is utopian. They remain in constant dynamic tension with one another (*The Sense of Reality*, 1996). Berlin greatly influenced Stuart Hampshire, Charles Taylor, Richard Wollheim, and Bernard Williams.

My Intellectual Path

I

OXFORD PHILOSOPHY BEFORE THE SECOND WORLD WAR

My interest in philosophical issues started when I was an undergraduate at Oxford in the late 1920s and early 1930s, because philosophy was part of the course which at that time a great many students in Oxford pursued. As a result of a continuing interest in this field I was appointed in 1932 to teach philosophy, and my views at that time were naturally influenced by the kind of discussions that my philosophical contemporaries held in Oxford. There were plenty of other issues in philosophy, but as it happens the topics which my colleagues and I concentrated on were the fruits of a return to empiricism which began to dominate British philosophy before the First World War, under the influence mainly of two celebrated Cambridge philosophers, G. E. Moore and Bertrand Russell.

VERIFICATIONISM

The first topic which occupied our attention in the middle and late 1930s was the nature of meaning—its relation to truth and falsehood, knowledge and opinion, and in particular the test of meaning in terms of the verifiability of the propositions in which it was expressed. The impulsion towards this topic came from the members of the Vienna School, themselves disciples of Russell and greatly influenced by thinkers such as Carnap, Wittgenstein and Schlick. The fashionable view was that the meaning of a proposition was the way in which it was verifiable—that if there was no way whatever of verifying what was being said, it was not a statement capable of truth or falsehood, not factual, and therefore either meaningless or a case of some other use of language, as seen in commands or expressions of desire, or in imaginative literature, or in other forms of expression which did not lay claim to empirical truth.

I was influenced by this school in the sense of being absorbed in the problems and theories which it generated, but I never became a true disciple. I always believed that statements that could be true or false or plausible or dubious or interesting, while indeed they did relate to the world as empirically conceived (and I have never conceived of the world in any other way, from then to the present day), were nevertheless not necessarily capable of being verified by some simple knock-down criterion, as the Vienna School and their logical positivist followers asserted. From the beginning I felt that general propositions were not verifiable in that way. Statements, whether in ordinary use or in the natural sciences (which were the ideal of the Vienna School), could be perfectly meaningful without being strictly verifiable. If I said 'All swans are white', I would never know if I knew this about all the swans there were, or whether the number of swans might not be infinite; a black swan no doubt refuted this generalisation, but its positive verification in the full sense seemed to me unattainable; nevertheless it would be absurd to say that it had no meaning. The same was true about hypothetical propositions, and still more so about unfulfilled hypotheticals, of which it was plainly paradoxical to maintain that they could be shown to be true or false by empirical observation; yet they were clearly meaningful.

I thought of a great many other statements of this kind, which clearly had meaning in the full sense of the word, but whose meaning escaped the narrow criterion proposed, that of direct empirical observation—the world of the senses. Consequently, though I took a lively part in these discussions (indeed, what later came to be called Oxford Philosophy began in my rooms in the evenings, at gatherings attended by such later celebrated philosophers as A. J. Ayer, J. L. Austin and Stuart Hampshire, influenced as they all were by Oxford empiricism, and to some degree by Oxford realism—that is, the belief that the external world is independent of human observers), nevertheless I remained a heretic, though a friendly one. I have never departed from the views I held at that time, and still believe that while empirical experience is all that words can express—that there is no other reality—nevertheless verifiability is not the only, or indeed the most plausible, criterion of knowledge or beliefs or hypotheses. This has remained with me for the rest of my life, and has coloured everything else that I have thought.

Another topic which I offered for the attention of my young colleagues was the status of such propositions as "This pink (shade) is more like this vermilion than it is like this black." If generalised, it was clear that this was a truth which no experience was likely to refute—the relations of visible colours being fixed. At the same time the general proposition could not be called a priori because it did not proceed formally from any definitions, and did not therefore belong to the formal disciplines of logic or mathematics, in which alone a priori propositions, then regarded as tautologies, belong. So we had found a universal truth in the empirical sphere. What were the definitions of 'pink', 'vermilion' and the rest? They had none. The colours could be recognised only by looking, so that their definitions were classified as ostensive, and from such definitions nothing logically followed. This came close to the old problem of Kant's synthetic a priori propositions, and we discussed this and its analogues for many months. I was convinced that my proposition was, if not strictly a priori, self-evidently true, and that its contradictory was not intelligible. Whether my colleagues ever raised the matter again I do not know, but the topic entered formally into the discussions held by us at the time. It corresponded to a view of Russell's embodied in a work called *The Limits of Empiricism*.

PHENOMENALISM

The other main topic that my contemporaries discussed was phenomenalism— that is, the question of whether human experience was confined to that provided by the senses, as was taught by the British philosophers Berkeley and Hume (and in some of their writings by Mill and Russell), or whether there existed a reality independent of sensible experience. For some philosophers, like Locke and his followers, there was such a reality, although it was not directly accessible to us— a reality which caused the sensible experiences which are all that we can directly know. Other philosophers held that the external world was a material reality which could be perceived directly, or misperceived as the case might be: this was called realism, as opposed to the view that our world was entirely created by human faculties—reason, imagination and the like—which was called idealism, in which I never believed. I have never believed in any metaphysical truths—whether rationalist truths, as expounded by Descartes, Spinoza, Leibniz and, in his own very different fashion, Kant, or the truths of (objective) idealism, the fathers of which are Fichte, Friedrich Schelling and Hegel, who still have their disciples. Thus meaning, truth and the nature of the external world were the topics which I thought about, and to some extent wrote about—and some of my views on them have been published.

One of the intellectual phenomena which made the greatest impact on me was the universal search by philosophers for absolute certainty, for answers which could not be doubted, for total intellectual security. This from the very beginning appeared to me to be an illusory quest. No matter how solidly based, widespread, inescapable, 'self-evident' a conclusion or a direct datum may seem to be, it is always possible to conceive that something could modify or indeed upset it, even if one cannot at the moment imagine what this might be. And this suspicion that a great deal of philosophy was set on an illusory path later came to dominate my ideas in a quite new and different connection.

While thus engaged in teaching and discussing the kind of philosophy I have outlined, I was commissioned to write a biography of Karl Marx. Marx's philosophical views never appeared to me to be particularly original or interesting, but my study of his views led me to investigate his predecessors, in particular the French *philosophes* of the eighteenth century—the first organised adversaries of dogmatism, traditionalism, religion, superstition, ignorance, oppression. I acquired an admiration for the great task which the thinkers of the French Ency-clopaedia had set themselves, and for the great work which they did to liberate men from darkness—clerical, metaphysical, political and the like. And although I came in due course to oppose some of the bases of their common beliefs, I have never lost my admiration for and sense of solidarity with the Enlightenment of that period: what I came to be critical of, apart from its empirical shortcomings, are some of its consequences, both logical and social; I realised that Marx's dog-matism, and that of his followers, in part derived from the certainties of the eighteenth-century Enlightenment.

II
HISTORY OF IDEAS' AND POLITICAL THEORY

During the War I served as a British official. When I came back to Oxford to teach philosophy, I became preoccupied with two central problems. The first was mo-nism—the central thesis of Western philosophy from Plato to our day—and the second, the meaning and application of the notion of freedom. I devoted a good deal of time to each, and they shaped my thought for a good many years to come.

MONISM

Dazzled by the spectacular successes of the natural sciences in their own century and its predecessors, men such as Helvétius, Holbach, d'Alembert, Condillac, and propagandists of genius such as Voltaire and Rousseau, believed that, pro-vided the right method was discovered, truth of a fundamental kind could be uncovered about social, political, moral and personal life—truth of the kind that had scored such triumphs in the investigations of the external world. The En-cyclopaedists believed in scientific method as the only key to such knowledge; Rousseau and others believed in eternal truths discovered by introspective means. But however they differed, they belonged to a generation which was con-vinced that it was on the path to the solution of all the problems that had plagued mankind from its beginnings.

A wider thesis underlay this: namely, that to all true questions there must be one true answer and one only, all the other answers being false, for otherwise the questions cannot be genuine questions. There must exist a path which leads clear thinkers to the correct answers to these questions, as much in the moral, social and political worlds as in that of the natural sciences, whether it is the same method or not; and once all the correct answers to the deepest moral, social and political questions that occupy (or should occupy) mankind are put together, the result will represent the final solution to all the problems of existence. Of course, we may never attain to these answers: human beings may be too confused by their emotions, or too stupid, or too unlucky, to be able to arrive at them; the answers may be too difficult, the means may be lacking, the techniques too com-plicated to discover; but however this may be, provided the questions are gen-uine, the answers must exist. If we do not know, our successors may know; or perhaps wise men in antiquity knew; and if they did not, perhaps Adam in Paradise knew; or if he did not, the angels must know; and if even they do not know, God must know—the answers must be there.

If the answers to social, moral and political questions are discovered, then, knowing them for what they are—the truth—men cannot fail to follow them, for they would have no temptation to do otherwise. And so a perfect life can be conceived. It may not be attainable, but in principle the conception must be capable of being formed—indeed, the possibility of discovering the only true answers to the great questions must in principle be believed in.

This creed was certainly not confined to the thinkers of the Enlightenment, though the methods recommended by others differ. Plato believed that mathematics was the route to truth, Aristotle, perhaps, that it was biology; Jews and Christians sought the answers in sacred books, in the pronouncements of divinely inspired teachers and the visions of mystics; others believed that the laboratory and mathematical methods could settle things; still others believed, like Rousseau, that only the innocent human soul, the uncorrupted child, the simple peasant would know the truth—better than the corrupt inhabitants of societies ruined by civilisation. But what they all agreed about, as did their successors after the French Revolution, who may have supposed the truth more difficult to obtain than their more naïve and optimistic predecessors, was that the laws of historical development could be—and by then had been—discovered, that the answers to the questions of how to live and what to do—morality, social life, political organisation, personal relationships—are all capable of being organised in the light of the truths discovered by the correct methods, whatever those may be.

This is a *philosophia perennis*—what men, thinkers, have believed from the pre-Socratics to all the reformers and revolutionaries of our own age. It is the central belief on which human thought has rested for two millennia. For if no true answers to questions exist, how can knowledge ever be attainable in any province? This was the heart of European rational, and indeed spiritual, thought for many ages. No matter that people differ so widely, that cultures differ, moral and political views differ; no matter that there is a vast variety of doctrines, religions, moralities, ideas—all the same there must somewhere be a true answer to the deepest questions that preoccupy mankind.

I do not know why I always felt sceptical about this almost universal belief, but I did. It may be a matter of temperament, but so it was.

GIAMBATTISTA VICO

What first shook me was my discovery of the works of the eighteenth-century Italian thinker Giambattista Vico. He was the first philosopher, in my view, to have conceived the idea of cultures. Vico wanted to understand the nature of historical knowledge, of history itself: it was all very well to lean on the natural sciences as far as the external world was concerned, but all they could provide us with was an account of the behaviour of rocks or tables or stars or molecules. In thinking about the past, we go beyond behaviour; we wish to understand how human beings lived, and that means understanding their motives, their fears and hopes and ambitions and loves and hatreds—to whom they prayed, how they expressed themselves in poetry, in art, in religion. We are able to do this because we are ourselves human, and understand our own inner life in these terms. We know how a rock, or a table, behaves because we observe it and make conjectures and verify them; but we do not know why the rock wishes to be as it is—indeed, we think it has no capacity for wishing, or for any other consciousness. But we do know why we are what we are, what we seek, what frustrates us, what expresses our inmost feelings and beliefs; we know more about ourselves than we shall ever know about rocks or streams.

True knowledge is knowledge of why things are as they are, not merely what they are; and the more we delve into this, the more we realise that the questions asked by the Homeric Greeks are different from the questions asked by the Romans, that the questions asked by the Romans differ from those asked in the Christian Middle Ages or in the seventeenth-century scientific culture or Vico's own eighteenth-century days. The questions differ, the answers differ, the aspirations differ; the use of language, of symbols, differs; and the answers to one set of questions do not answer, do not have much relevance to, the questions of other cultures. Of course Vico was a pious Roman Catholic, and he believed that the Church alone could provide the answers. But be that as it may, it did not prevent him from formulating the original idea that cultures differ, that what matters to a fifth-century Greek is very different from what matters to a Red Indian or a Chinese or a scientist in an eighteenth-century laboratory; and therefore their outlooks differ, and there are no universal answers to all their questions. Of course there is a common human nature, otherwise men in one age could not understand the literature or the art of another, or, above all, its laws, about which Vico, as a jurist, knew most. But that did not prevent there being a wide variety of cultural experience, so that activity of one kind was relevant to activity of some other kind within a single culture, but did not share such close links with the parallel activity in another culture.

J. G. HERDER

Then I read a far more relevant thinker, namely the German philosopher and poet Johann Gottfried Herder. Herder was not the first (his teacher, Johann Georg Hamann, has that honour) to deny the doctrine of his French contemporaries that there are universal, timeless, unquestionable truths which hold for all men, everywhere, at all times; and that the differences are simply due to error and illusion, for the truth is one and universal—'quod ubique, quod semper, quod ab omnibus creditum est'. Herder believed that different cultures gave different answers to their central questions. He was more interested in the humanities, the life of the spirit, than in the external world; and he became convinced that what was true for a Portuguese was not necessarily true for a Persian. Montesquieu had begun to say this kind of thing, but even he, who believed that men were shaped by environment, by what he called 'climate', was in the end a universalist—he believed that the central truths were eternal, even if the answers to local and ephemeral questions might be different. Herder laid it down that every culture possesses its own 'centre of gravity'; each culture has its own points of reference; there is no reason why these cultures should fight each other—universal toleration must be possible—but unification was destruction. Nothing was worse than imperialism. Rome, which crushed native civilisations in Asia Minor in order to produce one uniform Roman culture, committed a crime. The world was a great garden in which different flowers and plants grew, each in its own way, each with its own claims and rights and past and future. From which it followed that no matter what men had in common—and of course, again, there was a common nature to some degree—there were no universally true answers, as valid for one culture as for another.

Herder is the father of cultural nationalism. He is not a political nationalist (that kind of nationalism had not developed in his time), but he believed in the independence of cultures and the need to preserve each in its uniqueness. He believed that the desire to belong to a culture, something that united a group or a province or a nation, was a basic human need, as deep as the desire for food or drink or liberty; and that this need to belong to a community where you understood what others said, where you could move freely, where you had emotional as well as economic, social and political bonds, was the basis of developed, mature human life. Herder was not a relativist, though he is often so described: he believed that there were basic human goals and rules of behaviour, but that they took wholly different forms in different cultures, and that consequently, while there may have been analogies, similarities, which made one culture intelligible to another, cultures were not to be confused with each other—mankind was not one but many, and the answers to the questions were many, though there might be some central essence to them all which was one and the same.

ROMANTICISM AND ITS OFFSPRING

This idea was developed further by the romantics, who said something wholly new and disturbing: that ideals were not objective truths written in heaven and needing to be understood, copied, practised by men; but that they were created by men. Values were not found, but made; not discovered, but generated—that is what some of the German romantics certainly believed, as against the objectivist, universalising tendency of the superficial French. Uniqueness mattered. A German poet writes poetry in German, in language which, in the course of writing, he to some degree creates: he is not simply a writer in German. The German artist is a maker of German paintings, poems, dances—and so in all other cultures. A Russian thinker, Alexander Herzen, once asked, 'Where is the song before it is sung?' 'Where indeed? 'Nowhere' is the answer—one creates the song by singing it, by composing it. So, too, life is created by those who live it, step by step. This is an aesthetic interpretation of morality and of life, not an application of eternal models. Creation is all.

From this sprang all kinds of diverse movements—anarchism, romanticism, nationalism, Fascism, hero-worship. I make my own values, maybe not consciously: and besides, who is 'I'? For Byronic romantics, 'I' is indeed an individual, the outsider, the adventurer, the outlaw, he who defies society and accepted values, and follows his own—it may be to his doom, but this is better than conformity, enslavement to mediocrity. But for other thinkers 'I' becomes something much more metaphysical. It is a collective—a nation, a Church, a Party, a class, an edifice in which I am only a stone, an organism of which I am only a tiny living fragment. *It* is the creator; I myself matter only in so far as I belong to the movement, the race, the nation, the class, the Church; I do not signify as a true individual within this super-person to whom my life is organically bound. Hence German nationalism: I do this not because it is good or right or because I like it—I do it because I am a German and this is the German way to live. So also modern existentialism—I do it because I commit myself to this form of existence. Nothing makes me; I do not do it because it is an objective order which I obey, or because of universal rules to which I must adhere; I do it because I create my own life as I do; being what I am, I give it direction and I am responsible for it. Denial of universal values, this emphasis on being above all an element in, and loyal to, a super-self, is a dangerous moment in European history, and has led to a great deal that has been destructive and sinister in modern times; this is where it begins, in the political ruminations and theories of the earliest German romantics and their disciples in France and elsewhere.[1]

I never for a moment accepted the idea of these super-egos, but I recognised their importance in modern thought and action. Slogans like 'Not I but the Party', 'Not I but the Church', 'My country right or wrong, but my country' have inflicted a wound on the central faith of human thought as I outlined it above—that the truth is universal, eternal, for all men at all times—from which it has never recovered. Mankind not as an object but as a subject, an ever-moving spirit, self-creating and self-moving, a self-composed drama in many acts, which, according to Marx, will end in some kind of perfection—all this issues from the romantic revolution. While I reject this huge metaphysical interpretation of human life *in toto*—I remain an empiricist, and know only what I am able to experience, or think I could experience, and do not begin to believe in supra-individual entities—nevertheless I own that it made some impact on me, in the following way.

PLURALISM

I came to the conclusion that there is a plurality of ideals, as there is a plurality of cultures and of temperaments. I am not a relativist; I do not say 'I like my coffee with milk and you like it without; I am in favour of kindness and you prefer concentration camps'—each of us with his own values, which cannot be overcome or integrated. This I believe to be false. But I do believe that there is a plurality of values which men can and do seek, and that these values differ. There is not an infinity of them: the number of human values, of values which I can pursue while maintaining my human semblance, my human character, is finite—let us say 74, or perhaps 122, or 26, but finite, whatever it may be. And the difference this makes is that if a man pursues one of these values, I, who do not, am able to understand why he pursues it or what it would be like, in his circumstances, for me to be induced to pursue it. Hence the possibility of human understanding.

I think these values are objective—that is to say, their nature, the pursuit of them, is part of what it is to be a human being, and this is an objective given. The fact that men are men and women are women and not dogs or cats or tables or chairs is an objective fact; and part of this objective fact is that there are certain values, and only those values, which men, while remaining men, can pursue. If I am a man or a woman with sufficient imagination (and this I do need), I can enter into a value-system which is not my own, but which is nevertheless something I can conceive of men pursuing while remaining human, while remaining creatures with whom I can communicate, with whom I have some common values—for all human beings must have some common values or they cease to be human, and also some different values else they cease to differ, as in fact they do.

That is why pluralism is not relativism—the multiple values are objective, part of the essence of humanity rather than arbitrary creations of men's subjective fancies. Nevertheless, of course, if I pursue one set of values I may detest another, and may think it is damaging to the only form of life that I am able to live or tolerate, for myself and others; in which case I may attack it, I may even—in extreme cases—have to go to war against it. But I still recognise it as a human pursuit. I find Nazi values detestable, but I can understand how, given enough misinformation, enough false belief about reality, one could come to believe that they are the only salvation. Of course they have to be fought, by war if need be, but I do not regard the Nazis, as some people do, as literally pathological or insane, only as wickedly wrong, totally misguided about the facts, for example in believing that some beings are subhuman, or that race is central, or that Nordic races alone are truly creative, and so forth. I see how, with enough false education, enough widespread illusion and error, men can, while remaining men, believe this and commit the most unspeakable crimes.

If pluralism is a valid view, and respect between systems of values which are not necessarily hostile to each other is possible, then toleration and liberal consequences follow, as they do not either from monism (only one set of values is true, all the others are false) or from relativism (my values are mine, yours are yours, and if we clash, too bad, neither of us can claim to be right). My political pluralism is a product of reading Vico and Herder, and of understanding the roots of romanticism, which in its violent, pathological form went too far for human toleration.

So with nationalism: the sense of belonging to a nation seems to me quite natural and not in itself to be condemned, or even criticised. But in its inflamed condition—my nation is better than yours, I know how the world should be shaped and you must yield because you do not, because you are inferior to me, because my nation is top and yours is far, far below mine and must offer itself as material to mine, which is the only nation entitled to create the best possible world—it is a form of pathological extremism which can lead, and has led, to unimaginable horrors, and is totally incompatible with the kind of pluralism which I have attempted to describe.

It may be of interest to remark, incidentally, that there are certain values that we in our world accept which were probably created by early romanticism and did not exist before: for example, the idea that variety is a good thing, that a society in which many opinions are held, and those holding different opinions are tolerant of each other, is better than a monolithic society in which one opinion is binding on everyone. Nobody before the eighteenth century could have accepted that: the truth was one and the idea of variety was inimical to it. Again, the idea of sincerity, as a value, is something new. It was always right to be a martyr to the truth, but only to the truth: Muslims who died for Islam were poor, foolish, misled creatures who died for nonsense; so, for Catholics, were Protestants and Jews and pagans; and the fact that they held their beliefs sincerely made them no better—what was important was to be right. In discovering the truth, as in every other walk of life, success was what was important, not motive. If a man says to you that he believes that twice two is seventeen, and someone says, 'You know, he doesn't do it to annoy you, he doesn't do it because he wants to show off or because he has been paid to say it—he truly believes, he is a sincere believer', you would say, 'This makes it no better, he is talking irrational nonsense.' That is what Protestants were doing, in the view of Catholics, and vice versa. The more sincere, the more dangerous; no marks were given for sincerity until the notion that there is more than one answer to a question—that is, pluralism—became more widespread. That is what led value to be set on motive rather than on consequence, on sincerity rather than on success.

The enemy of pluralism is monism—the ancient belief that there is a single harmony of truths into which everything, if it is genuine, in the end must fit. The consequence of this belief (which is something different from, but akin to, what Karl Popper called essentialism—to him the root of all evil) is that those who know should command those who do not. Those who know the answers to some of the great problems of mankind must be obeyed, for they alone know how society should be organised, how individual lives should be lived, how culture should be developed. This is the old Platonic belief in the philosopher-kings, who were entitled to give orders to others. There have always been thinkers who hold that if only scientists, or scientifically trained persons, could be put in charge of things, the world would be vastly improved. To this I have to say that no better excuse, or even reason, has ever been propounded for unlimited despotism on the part of an élite which robs the majority of its essential liberties.

Someone once remarked that in the old days men and women were brought as sacrifices to a variety of gods; for these, the modern age has substituted new idols:-isms. To cause pain, to kill, to torture are in general rightly condemned; but if these things are done not for my personal benefit but for an-ism—socialism, nationalism, Fascism, Communism, fanatically held religious belief, or progress, or the fulfilment of the laws of history—then they are in order. Most revolutionaries believe, covertly or overtly, that in order to create the ideal world eggs must be broken, otherwise one cannot obtain the omelette. Eggs are certainly broken—never more violently or ubiquitously than in our times—but the omelette is far to seek, it recedes into an infinite distance. That is one of the corollaries of unbridled monism, as I call it—some call it fanaticism, but monism is at the root of every extremism.

FREEDOM

Political freedom is a topic to which I devoted two lectures during the 1950s. The later of these, entitled 'Two Concepts of Liberty',[2] inaugurated my Oxford Professorship, and its gist was to distinguish between two notions of liberty (or freedom—the terms are used interchangeably), negative and positive. By negative liberty I meant the absence of obstacles which block human action. Quite apart from obstacles created by the external world, or by the biological, physiological, psychological laws which govern human beings, there is lack of political freedom—the central topic of my lecture—where the obstacles are man-made, whether deliberately or unintentionally. The extent of negative liberty depends on the degree to which such man-made obstacles are absent—on the degree to which I am free to go down this or that path without being prevented from doing so by man-made institutions or disciplines, or by the activities of specific human beings.

It is not enough to say that negative freedom simply means freedom to do what I like, for in that case I can liberate myself from obstacles to the fulfillment of desire simply by following the ancient Stoics and killing desire. But that path, the gradual elimination of the desires to which obstacles can occur, leads in the end to humans being gradually deprived of their natural, living activities: in other words, the most perfectly free human beings will be those who are dead, since then there is no desire and therefore no obstacles. What I had in mind, rather, was simply the number of paths down which a man can walk, whether or not he chooses to do so. That is the first of the two basic senses of political freedom.

Some have maintained, against me, that freedom must be a triadic relationship: I can overcome or remove or be free from obstacles only in order to do something, to be free to perform a given act or acts. But I do not accept that. The basic sense of unfreedom is that in which we ascribe it to the man in jail, or the man tied to a tree; all that such a man seeks is the breaking of his chains, escape from the cell, without necessarily aiming at a particular activity once he is liberated. In the larger sense, of course, freedom means freedom from the rules of a society or its institutions, from the deployment against one of excessive moral or physical force, or from whatever shuts off possibilities of action which otherwise would be open. This I call 'freedom from'.

The other central sense of freedom is freedom *to*: if my negative freedom is specified by answering the question 'How far am I controlled?', the question for the second sense of freedom is 'Who controls me?' Since we are talking about man-made obstacles, I can ask myself 'Who determines my actions, my life? Do I do so, freely, in whatever way I choose? Or am I under orders from some other source of control? Is my activity determined by parents, schoolmasters, priests, policemen? Am I under the discipline of a legal system, the capitalist order, a slave-owner, the government (monarchical, oligarchic, democratic)? In what sense am I master of my fate? My possibilities of action may be limited, but how are they limited? Who are those who stand in my way, how much power can they wield?'

These are the two central senses of 'liberty' which I set myself to investigate. I realised that they differed, that they were answers to two different questions; but, although cognate, they did not in my view clash—the answer to one did not necessarily determine the answer to the other. Both freedoms were ultimate human ends, both were necessarily limited, and both concepts could be perverted in the course of human history. Negative liberty could be interpreted as economic *laissez-faire*, whereby in the name of freedom owners are allowed to destroy the lives of children in mines, or factory-owners to destroy the health and character of workers in industry. But that was a perversion, not what the concept basically means to human beings, in my view. Equally it was said that it is a mockery to inform a poor man that he is perfectly free to occupy a room in an expensive hotel, although he may not be able to pay for it. But that, too, is a confusion. He is indeed free to rent a room there, but has not the means of using this freedom. He has not the means, perhaps, because he has been prevented from earning more than he does by a man-made economic system—but that is a deprivation of freedom to earn money, not of freedom to rent the room. This may sound a pedantic distinction, but it is central to discussions of economic versus political freedom.

The notion of positive freedom has led, historically, to even more frightful perversions. Who orders my life? I do. I? Ignorant, confused, driven hither and thither by uncontrolled passions and drives—is that all there is to me? Is there not within me a higher, more rational, freer self, able to understand and dominate passions, ignorance and other defects, which I can attain to only by a process of education or understanding, a process which can be managed only by those who are wiser than myself, who make me aware of my true, 'real', deepest self, of what I am at my best? This is a well-known metaphysical view, according to which I can be truly free and self-controlled only if I am truly rational—a belief which goes back to Plato—and since I am not perhaps sufficiently rational myself, I must obey those who are indeed rational, and who therefore know what is best not only for themselves but also for me, and who can guide me along lines which will ultimately awaken my true rational self and put it in charge, where it truly belongs. I may feel hemmed in—indeed, crushed—by these authorities, but that is an illusion: when I have grown up and have attained to a fully mature, 'real' self, I shall understand that I would have done for myself what has been done for me if I had been as wise, when I was in an inferior condition, as they are now.

In short, they are acting on my behalf, in the interests of my higher self, in controlling my lower self; so that true liberty for the lower self consists in total obedience to them, the wise, those who know the truth, the élite of sages; or perhaps my obedience must be to those who understand how human destiny is made—for if Marx is right, then it is a Party (which alone grasps the demands of the rational goals of history) which must shape and guide me, whichever way my poor empirical self may wish to go; and the Party itself must be guided by its far-seeing leaders, and in the end by the greatest and wisest leader of all.

There is no despot in the world who cannot use this method of argument for the vilest oppression, in the name of an ideal self which he is seeking to bring to fruition by his own, perhaps somewhat brutal and *prima facie* morally odious, means (*prima facie* only for the lower empirical self). The 'engineer of human souls', to use Stalin's phrase,[3] knows best; he does what he does not simply in order to do his best for his nation, but in the name of the nation itself, in the name of what the nation would be doing itself if only it had attained to this level of historical understanding. That is the great perversion which the positive notion of liberty has been liable to: whether the tyranny issues from a Marxist leader, a king, a Fascist dictator, the masters of an authoritarian Church or class or State, it seeks for the imprisoned, 'real' self within men, and 'liberates' it, so that this self can attain to the level of those who give the orders.

This goes back to the naïve notion that there is only one true answer to every question: if I know the true answer and you do not, and you disagree with me, it is because you are ignorant; if you knew the truth, you would necessarily believe what I believe; if you seek to disobey me, this can be so only because you are wrong, because the truth has not been revealed to you as it has been to me. This justifies some of the most frightful forms of oppression and enslavement in human history, and it is truly the most dangerous, and, in our century in particular, the most violent, interpretation of the notion of positive liberty.

This notion of two kinds of liberty and their distortions then formed the centre of much discussion and dispute in Western and other universities, and does so to this day.

DETERMINISM

My other lecture on freedom was entitled 'Historical Inevitability'.[4] Here I stated that determinism was a doctrine very widely accepted among philosophers for many hundreds of years. Determinism declares that every event has a cause, from which it unavoidably follows. This is the foundation of the natural sciences: the laws of nature and all their applications—the entire body of natural science— rest upon the notion of an eternal order which the sciences investigate. But if the rest of nature is subject to these laws, can it be that man alone is not? When a man supposes, as most ordinary people do (though not most scientists and philosophers), that when he rises from the chair he need not have done so, that he did so because he chose to do so, but he need not have chosen—when he supposes this, he is told that this is an illusion, that even though the necessary work by psychologists has not yet been accomplished, one day it will be (or at any rate in principle can be), and then he will know that what he is and does is necessarily as it is, and could not be otherwise. I believe this doctrine to be false, but I do not in this essay seek to demonstrate this, or to refute determinism— indeed, I am not sure if such a demonstration or refutation is possible. My only concern is to ask myself two questions. Why do philosophers and others think that human beings are fully determined? And, if they are, is this compatible with normal moral sentiments and behaviour, as commonly understood?

My thesis is that there are two main reasons for supporting the doctrine of human determinism. The first is that, since the natural sciences are perhaps the greatest success story in the whole history of mankind, it seems absurd to suppose that man alone is not subject to the natural laws discovered by the scientists. (That, indeed, is what the eighteenth-century *philosophes* maintained.) The question is not, of course, whether man is wholly free of such laws—no one but a madman could maintain that man does not depend on his biological or psychological structure or environment, or on the laws of nature. The only question is: Is his liberty totally exhausted thereby? Is there not some corner in which he can act as he chooses, and not be determined to choose by antecedent causes? This may be a tiny corner of the realm of nature, but unless it is there, his consciousness of being free, which is undoubtedly all but universal—the fact that most people believe that, while some of their actions are mechanical, some obey their free will—is an enormous illusion, from the beginnings of mankind, ever since Adam ate the apple, although told not to do so, and did not reply, 'I could not help it, I did not do it freely, Eve forced me to do it.'

The second reason for belief in determinism is that it does devolve the responsibility for a great many things that people do on to impersonal causes, and therefore leaves them in a sense unblameworthy for what they do. When I make a mistake, or commit a wrong or a crime, or do anything else which I recognise, or which others recognise, as bad or unfortunate, I can say, 'How could I avoid it?—that was the way I was brought up' or 'That is my nature, something for which natural laws are responsible' or 'I belong to a society, a class, a Church, a nation, in which everyone does it, and nobody seems to condemn it' or 'I am psychologically conditioned by the way in which my parents behaved to each other and to me, and by the economic and social circumstances in which I was placed, or was forced into, not to be able to choose to act otherwise' or, finally, 'I was under orders.'

Against this, most people believe that everyone has at least two choices that he can make, two possibilities that he can realise. When Eichmann says 'I killed Jews because I was ordered to; if I had not done it I would have been killed myself?' one can say 'I see that it is improbable that you would have chosen to be killed, but in principle you could have done it if you had decided to do it— there was no literal compulsion, as there is in nature, which caused you to act as you did.' You may say it is unreasonable to expect people to behave like that when facing great dangers: so it is, but however unlikely it may be that they should decide to do so, in the literal sense of the word they *could* have chosen to do so. Martyrdom cannot be expected, but can be accepted, against whatever odds—indeed, that is why it is so greatly admired.

So much for the reasons for which men choose to embrace determinism in history. But if they do, there is a difficult logical consequence, to say the least. It means that we cannot say to anyone, 'Did you have to do that? Why need you have done that?'—the assumption behind which is that he could have refrained, or done something else. The whole of our common morality, in which we speak of obligation and duty, right and wrong, moral praise and blame—the way in which people are praised or condemned, rewarded or punished, for behaving in a way in which they were not forced to behave, when they could have behaved otherwise—this network of beliefs and practices, on which all current morality seems to me to depend, presupposes the notion of responsibility, and responsibility entails the ability to choose between black and white, right and wrong, pleasure and duty; as well as, in a wider sense, between forms of life, forms of government, and the whole constellations of moral values in terms of which most people, however much they may or may not be aware of it, do in fact live.

If determinism were accepted, our vocabulary would have to be very, very radically changed. I do not say that this is impossible in principle, but it goes further than what most people are prepared to face. At best, aesthetics would have to replace morality. You can admire or praise people for being handsome, or generous, or musical—but that is not a matter of their choice, that is 'how they are made'. Moral praise would have to take the same form: if I praise you for saving my life at your own risk, I mean that it is wonderful that you are so made that you could not avoid doing this, and I am glad that I encountered someone literally determined to save my life, as opposed to someone else who was determined to look the other way. Honourable or dishonourable conduct, pleasure-seeking and heroic martyrdom, courage and cowardice, deceitfulness and truthfulness, doing right against temptation—these would become like being good-looking or ugly, tall or short, old or young, black or white, born of English or Italian parents: something that we cannot alter, for everything is determined. We can hope that things will go as we should like, but we cannot do anything towards this—we are so made that we cannot help but act in a particular fashion. Indeed, the very notion of an act denotes choice; but if choice is itself determined, what is the difference between action and mere behaviour?

It seems to me paradoxical that some political movements demand sacrifices and yet are determinist in belief. Marxism, for example, which is founded on historical determinism—the inevitable stages through which society must pass before it reaches perfection—enjoins painful and dangerous acts, coercion and killing, equally painful at times both to the perpetrators and to the victims; but if history will inevitably bring about the perfect society, why should one sacrifice one's life for a process which will, without one's help, reach its proper, happy destination? Yet there is a curious human feeling that if the stars in their courses are fighting for you, so that your cause will triumph, then you should sacrifice yourself in order to shorten the process, to bring the birth-pangs of the new order nearer, as Marx said, But can so many people be truly persuaded to face these dangers, just to shorten a process which will end in happiness whatever they may do or fail to do? This has always puzzled me, and puzzled others.

All this I discussed in the lecture in question, which has remained controversial, and has been much discussed and disputed, and is so still.

THE PURSUIT OF THE IDEAL

There is one further topic which I have written about, and that is the very notion of a perfect society, the solution to all our ills. Some of the eighteenth-century French *philosophes* thought the ideal society they hoped for would inevitably come; others were more pessimistic and supposed that human defects would fail to bring it about. Some thought that progress towards it was inexorable, others that only great human effort could achieve it, but might not do so. However this may be, the very notion of the ideal society presupposes the conception of a perfect world in which all the great values in the light of which men have lived for so long can be realised together, at least in principle. Quite apart from the fact that the idea had seemed Utopian to those who thought that such a world could not be achieved because of material or psychological obstacles, or the incurable ignorance, weakness or lack of rationality of men, there is a far more formidable objection to the very notion itself.

I do not know who else may have thought this, but it occurred to me that some ultimate values are compatible with each other and some are not. Liberty, in whichever sense, is an eternal human ideal, whether individual or social. So is equality. But perfect liberty (as it must be in the perfect world) is not compatible with perfect equality. If man is free to do anything he chooses, then the strong will crush the weak, the wolves will eat the sheep, and this puts an end to equality. If perfect equality is to be attained, then men must be prevented from outdistancing each other, whether in material or in intellectual or in spiritual achievement, otherwise inequalities will result. The anarchist Bakunin, who believed in equality above all, thought that universities should be abolished because they bred learned men who behaved as if they were superior to the unlearned, and this propped up social inequalities. Similarly, a world of perfect justice—and who can deny that this is one of the noblest of human values?—is not compatible with perfect mercy. I need not labour this point: either the law takes its toll, or men forgive, but the two values cannot both be realised.

Again, knowledge and happiness may or may not be compatible. Rationalist thinkers have supposed that knowledge always liberates, that it saves men from being victims of forces they cannot understand; to some degree this is no doubt true, but if I know that I have cancer I am not thereby made happier, or freer—I must choose between always knowing as much as I can and accepting that there are situations where ignorance may be bliss. Nothing is more attractive than spontaneous creativity, natural vitality, a free flowering of ideas, works of art— but these are not often compatible with a capacity for careful and effective planning, without which no even moderately secure society can be created. Liberty and equality, spontaneity and security, happiness and knowledge, mercy and justice—all these are ultimate human values, sought for themselves alone; yet when they are incompatible, they cannot all be attained, choices must be made, sometimes tragic losses accepted in the pursuit of some preferred ultimate end. But if, as I believe, this is not merely empirically but conceptually true—that is, derives from the very conception of these values—then the very idea of the perfect world in which all good things are realised is incomprehensible, is in fact conceptually incoherent. And if this is so, and I cannot see how it could be otherwise, then the very notion of the ideal world, for which no sacrifice can be too great, vanishes from view.

To go back to the Encyclopaedists and the Marxists and all the other movements the purpose of which is the perfect life: it seems as if the doctrine that all kinds of monstrous cruelties must be permitted, because without these the ideal state of affairs cannot be attained—all the justifications, of broken eggs for the sake of the ultimate omelette, all the brutalities, sacrifices, brain-washing, all those revolutions, everything that has made this century perhaps the most appalling of any since the days of old, at any rate in the West—all this is for nothing, for the perfect universe is not merely unattainable but inconceivable, and everything done to bring it about is founded on an enormous intellectual fallacy.

NOTES

1. The romantics viewed their notion of self-moving centres of historical activity, thrusting forward on their own terms, as ultimately subjective. These were arbitrary entities—whether Byronic, somewhat satanic figures at war with society, or heroes who mould around themselves groups of followers (robbers, in the case of Schiller's play) or entire nations (Lycurgus, Moses—nation-builders so much admired by Machiavelli—to whom there are certainly modern parallels)—

creating in accordance with freely invented patterns. This view was sternly opposed by such thinkers as Hegel and Marx, who taught, each in his own fashion, that progress must conform to the iron laws of historical development—whether material development, as in Marx, or spiritual, as in Hegel. Only thus can the emancipation of human powers from irrational drives be achieved, and a reign be ushered in of total justice, freedom, virtue, happiness and harmonious self-realisation. This idea of inexorable progress is inherited from the Judaeo-Christian tradition, but without the notions of the inscrutable divine will or the Last Judgement of mankind—the separation of the satisfactory sheep from the unsatisfactory goats—conducted after death.

2. Delivered in 1958, and available in two collections of essays by the author: *Four Essays on Liberty* (London and New York, 1969) and *The Proper Study of Mankind* (see p. ix above, note I).

3. Stalin used the phrase 'engineers of human souls' in a speech on the role of Soviet writers made at Maxim Gorky's house on 26 October 1932, recorded in an unpublished manuscript in the Gorky archive—K. L. Zelinsky, 'Vstrecha pisatelei s I. V. Stalinym' ('A meeting of writers with I. V. Stalin')—and published for the first time, in English, in A. Kemp-Welch, *Stalin and the Literary Intelligentsia, 1928–39* (Basingstoke and London, 1991), pp. 128–31: for this phrase see p. 131 (and, for the Russian original, 'inzhenery chelovecheskikh dush', I. V. Stalin, *Sochineniya* (Moscow, 1946–67), vol. 13, p. 410). Ed.

4. Delivered in 1953, and also included both in *Four Essays on Liberty* and in *The Proper Study of Mankind*.

44

G.E.M. ANSCOMBE
My Interests in Philosophy

After studying at Oxford, G.E.M. Anscombe (1919–2001) came to know and to be influenced by Wittgenstein. Her *Intention* (1957) framed the questions and the terminology of subsequent work in the philosophy of mind. It addresses such questions as: What are the criteria for the identity of actions and intentions? What role do an agent's reasons and justifications play in identifying her intentions? What is the structure and aim of practical reasoning? Her influential essay "What's Wrong with Modern Moral Philosophy?" (1958) mounts a formidable critique of contemporary moral evaluation. Instead of taking the agent's future-oriented deliberative point of view, they mistakenly adopt the position of an omniscient judge, evaluating the consequences of an action, all things considered. Anscombe also wrote on moral and political issues. She opposed granting President Truman an honorary degree at Oxford on the grounds that he ordered the bombing of Hiroshima and Nagasaki. She produced classical essays against abortion, contraception, homosexuality and euthanasia.

As one of Wittgenstein's literary executors, Anscombe translated and co-edited *Philosophical Investigations* (1958) and some of his posthumous works. Her *Introduction to Wittgenstein's "Tractatus"* (1959) was a turning point in the interpretation of that difficult work. With Peter Geach, she wrote *Three Philosophers* (1961). Her *Collected Philosophical Papers* (1981) include essays on Aristotle on metaphysics, and epistemology.

Causes and Beliefs
Introduction in *Collected Papers*

My first strenuous interest in philosophy was in the topic of causality. I didn't know that what I was interested in belonged to philosophy. As a result of my teen-age conversion to the Catholic Church—itself the fruit of reading done from twelve to fifteen—I read a work called *Natural Theology* by a nineteenth-century Jesuit.[1] I read it with great appetite and found it all convincing except for two things. One was the doctrine of *Scientia media*, according to which God knew what anybody would have done if, e.g., he hadn't died when he did. This was a part of theodicy, and was also the form in which the problem of counter-factual conditionals was discussed. I found I could not believe this doctrine: it appeared to me that there was not, quite generally, any such thing as what would have happened if what did happened had not happened, and that in particular there was no such thing, generally speaking, as what someone would have done if . . . and certainly that there was no such thing as how someone would have spent his life if he had not died a child. I did not know at the time that the matter was one of fierce dispute between the Jesuits and the Dominicans, who took rather my own line about it. So when I was being instructed a couple of years later by a Dominican at Oxford, Fr. Richard Kehoe, and he asked me if I had any difficulties, I told him that I couldn't see how that stuff could be true. He was obviously amused and told me that I certainly didn't have to believe it, though I only learned the historical fact I have mentioned rather later.

But it was the other stumbling block that got me into philosophy. The book contained an argument for the existence of a First Cause, and as a preliminary to this it offered a proof of some 'principle of causality' according to which anything that comes about must have a cause. The proof had the fault of proceeding from a barely concealed assumption of its own conclusion. I thought that this was some sort of carelessness on the part of the author, and that it just needed tidying up. So I started writing improved versions of it; each one satisfied me for a time, but then reflection would show me that I had committed the same fault. I don't think I ever showed my efforts to anyone; I tore them up when I found they were no good, and I went round asking people *why*, if something happened, they would be sure it had a cause. No one had an answer to this. In two or three years of effort I produced five versions of a would-be proof, each one of which I then found guilty of the same error, though each time it was more cunningly concealed. In all this time I had no philosophical teaching about the matter; even my last attempt was made before I started reading Greats at Oxford. It was not until then that I read Hume and the discussion in Aquinas, where he says that it isn't part of the concept of *being* to include any relation to a cause. But I could not understand the grounds of his further claim, that it *is* part of the concept of *coming into being*.

The other central philosophical topic which I got hooked on without even realizing that it was philosophy, was perception. I read a book by Fr. Martin D'Arcy, S.J., called *The Nature of Belief*[2] and got just that out of it. I was sure that I saw objects, like packets of cigarettes or cups or . . . any more or less substantial thing would do. But I think I was concentrated on artefacts, like other products of our urban life, and the first more natural examples that struck me were 'wood' and the sky. The latter hit me amidships because I was saying dogmatically that one must know the category of object one was speaking of— whether it was a colour or a kind of stuff, for example; *that* belonged to the logic of the term one was using. It couldn't be a matter of empirical discovery that something belonged to a different category. The sky stopped me.

For years I would spend time, in cafés, for example, staring at objects saying to myself: 'I see a packet. But what do I really see? How can I say that I see here anything more than a yellow expanse?' While still doing Honour Mods, and so not yet having got into my undergraduate philosophy course, I went to H. H. Price's lectures on perception and phenomenalism. I found them intensely interesting. Indeed, of all the people I heard at Oxford, he was the one who excited my respect; the one I found worth listening to. This was not because I agreed with him, indeed, I used to sit tearing my gown into little strips because I wanted to argue against so much that he said. But even so, what he said seemed to me to be absolutely about the stuff. The only book of his that I found so good was *Hume's Theory of the External World* which I read straight on from first sentence to last. Again, I didn't agree with some of it; he offered an amended account of identity to rewrite Hume, in a way that seemed to me to miss the force of Hume's thoughts about identity as seeming to be "midway betwixt unity and diversity": he wanted to amend Hume into starting with the idea that identity really belonged just to atomic sense-impressions—which won't work because "every sense-impression contains temporal parts"; and then changing to the conception of "identical" as applying always to a *whole*, having temporal parts or spatial parts or both, and never to a single indivisible entity, if such there be. That is, he wanted to smooth Hume out. But he was really writing about the stuff itself, even if one did not accept his amendment. It was he who had aroused my intense interest in Hume's chapter "On scepticism with regard to the sense".

I always hated phenomenalism and felt trapped by it. I couldn't see my way out of it but I didn't believe it. It was no good pointing to difficulties about it, things which Russell found wrong with it, for example. The strength, the central nerve of it remained alive and raged achingly. It was only in Wittgenstein's classes in 1944 that I saw the nerve being extracted, the central thought "I have got *this*, and I define 'yellow' (say) as *this*" being effectively attacked.—At one point in these classes Wittgenstein was discussing the interpretation of the sign-post, and it burst upon me that the way you go by it is the final interpretation. At another I came out with "But I still want to say: Blue is there." Older hands smiled or laughed but Wittgenstein checked them by taking it seriously, saying "Let me think what medicine you need. . . . Suppose that we had the word 'painy' as a word for the property of some surfaces." The 'medicine' was effective, and the story illustrates Wittgenstein's ability to understand the thought that was offered to him in objection. One might protest, indeed, that there is *this* wrong with Locke's assimilation of secondary qualities to pain: you can sketch the functioning of "pain" as a word for a secondary quality, but you can't do the reverse operation. But the 'medicine' did not imply that you could. If "painy" were a possible secondary quality word, then wouldn't just the same motive drive me to say: "Painy is there" as drove me to say "Blue is there"? I did not mean " 'Blue' is the name of *this* sensation which I am having," nor did I switch to that thought . . .

War and Morality
Introduction in *Collected Philosophical Papers*

Some of [my papers] were written for the general public, for ordinary philosophical meetings or for philosophical journals. Others were composed to express an explicitly Catholic view; indeed they were mostly written for meetings of Catholics or were addressed to a Catholic readership. This accounts for a difference of assumptions. For, addressing Catholics or writing expressly as a Catholic, I would assume a certain background of common belief and faith, and might or might not discuss these in their problematic aspects. There is one paper which straddles the two classifications. It is the part which I wrote of a pamphlet called "The Justice of the Present War Examined", the second part of which was written by my friend Norman Daniel. We were both undergraduates at Oxford at the time and we gave our pamphlet an extra description as expressing a 'Catholic view'; we got it on sale in Oxford bookshops and, I think, in one or two London ones. Soon the University Chaplain sent for Norman Daniel and told him the Archbishop of Birmingham wanted us to withdraw it: we had no right to call it 'Catholic' without getting an *imprimatur*. (Bishops *seemed* to have much more authority in those days.) We obeyed: we thought the demand wrong and unreasonable, but the authority of one's ordinary involved the right to exercise such control. Some notice of the pamphlet had got into the press, and it seems this had alarmed the Archbishop.

This pamphlet has a certain historical interest: it shows some truths which it was possible to judge about the war already in the autumn of 1939. When in 1956 I opposed the conferment of an honorary degree by Oxford University on

Mr Truman, Mr Goodhart, then Master of University College, sneered at my 'hind-sight' about the conduct of the war by the massacre of civilian populations: the pamphlet shows that this was already seen by us as what was going to happen, and as lying in the intentions of our rulers, in 1939.—My remarks about the 'injustice' of the Treaty of Versailles were, I fear, a mere repetition of the common propaganda of the day. I hadn't read the treaty and had no right to echo that widely purveyed opinion.

"War and Murder" was written for a collection of Catholic essays and is writ-ten in a tone of righteous fury about what passed for thinking about the destruc-tion of civilian populations. I don't much like it, not because I disagree with its sentiments but because, if I was torn by a *saeva indignatio*, I wish I had the talent of Swift in expressing it.

I would have said I got interested in political philosophy in the 1970s, simply out of an interest in the concept of murder. 'Murder' is a moral action concept of great complexity, and one cannot give an account of it without discussing both whether its definition *includes* its wrongfulness, and *also* whether and why cap-ital punishment and some other deliberate killings under the authority of the state do not fall under the concept 'murder'. But I see the seeds of my interest in political theory were there in the writings about war, though I did not then refer to civil authority in a questioning or even enquiring spirit.

In general, my interest in moral philosophy has been more in particular moral questions than in what is now called 'meta-ethics'. So far as general questions of moral theory have interested me, I have thought them closely tied up with prob-lems of action-description and unsettlable without help from philosophy of mind. Some of these papers represent a struggle to treat all deliberate action as a matter of acting on a calculation how to obtain one's ends. I have now become rather doubtful about this. Of course, it is always possible to force practical rea-sons into this mould, constructing descriptions of ends like "not infringing the regulations about traffic lights", "observing the moral law", "being polite", "play-ing a game according to its rules", and so on. But it now seems to me that there is a contrast between such constructed descriptions of ends, and the means—ends calculations which really do—at least implicitly—take their starting point from some objective which one has. Certain considerations put before me by my friend Georg Henrik von Wright have led me to think this; but I have no full-fledged thoughts on the subject, and what I publish is, I think, all written under the older conception.

My first paper on contraception, "Contraception and Chastity," excited attack from my colleagues Bernard Williams and Michael Tanner, as well as some friendlier criticism from Peter Winch. . . . That [paper] has the historical interest of being delivered before *Humanæ Vitae* came out. In it I wished my audience to draw for itself what seemed to me the obvious conclusion: namely that you might as well accept any sexual goings-on, if you accepted contraceptive inter-course. At that time this was denied by the 'Catholic' defenders of contraception, though it has since been cheerfully embraced. I also thought then that the pro-motion of contraception by having public clinics might prevent the far worse business of widespread abortion. This used to be argued; but I very soon came to think it an illusion. Only in countries where abortion was already much prac-tised, and contraceptives not easy to get, did a new availability of contraceptives reduce abortion; and the reduction was only temporary. Abortion has indeed now come to be regarded as a long-stop for unwanted conceptions and a desirable means of population control. One could say: if you want to promote abortion, promote contraception. We now live in a kind of madness on these themes, in which vocal people at large are completely thoughtless about the awful consequences of *far less than reproducing* the parental generation, where it has itself been a large one. Our schools are already suffering, as professional teachers know, and what they can offer in the way of specialist teaching, such as the teaching of music, for example, is being cut down. Nor is it difficult to smell prospective murder in the air: so far, we have the murder of defective infants, but among young doctors we hear mutterings about the senile occupancy of valuable beds. These are likely to be echoes of what is said among the older members of the profession.

Notes from a Conversation

[The following consists of notes from a conversation between Mary Mothersill and Elizabeth Anscombe. Mothersill asked Anscombe about her conversion to Catholicism and its influence on her philosophical work.]

[My] family was not devout nor even particularly concerned about religious matters. In 1934 when [I was] 15, and had just passed [my] O levels, [I] spent the summer with an aunt and uncle in Normandy. There [I] read George Bernard Shaw—mostly the prefaces—and Proust and assorted works by G. K. Chesterton. In the course of reading one of these, *The Everlasting Man*, it came to [me] that [I] believed in God and ought to pray. [I] asked a local priest what steps one took to become a Catholic and he gave [me] an address in Alencon, birthplace of the Carmelite nun, Saint Therese famous for her "the little way"—a plan for Christians whereby you don't try for grand achievements but concentrate on small acts of charity.

[My] daughter Mary asked . . . if [I] had ever felt there was a tension between [my] philosophical commitments and [my] religious beliefs. [The answer is:] No, and [what's more] there couldn't be.

Mothersill asked: "Aside from *Intention* what is the single work you would most like to be remembered for?" Anscombe replied: "My Introduction to Wittgenstein's *Tractatus Logico-Philosophicus.*

NOTES

1. Bernard Boedder, SJ, *Natural Theology* (New York, 1902).
2. Martin D'Arcy, SJ, *The Nature of* Belief (London, 1931).

45

KWAME ANTHONY APPIAH
The Many Sources of Philosophic Reflection

Descended from two great clans—the Asante kings of (what is now) Ghana and the family of Sir Stafford Cripps—Kwame Anthony Appiah (1954–) was educated in Ghana and Cambridge. Having previously taught at Duke, Cornell, Yale and Harvard, he is presently a professor at Princeton University. Appiah has written numerous essays in the philosophy of language (*Necessary Conditionals*, 1985, *For Truth in Semantics*, 1986). Besides being a philosopher, Appiah is also an astute historian and anthropologist. Reflecting on the scope of his family— spanning Lebanon, Norway, Kenya, Thailand, Nigeria, and England—he argues against racial and cultural essentialism on the grounds that the history of marriages, trade, conquests, and migrations has thoroughly mixed and enriched races and cultures. His *In My Father's House: Africa in the Philosophy of Culture* (1992) documents the complex varieties of African cultures and their histories. While recognizing the political utility of the rhetoric of identity, the book also analyzes its dangers. With Amy Guttman, Appiah is the author of *Color Conscious: The Political Morality of Race* (1996). With Henry Louis Gates Jr. he is the editor of *Africana: Encyclopedia of the African and African-American Experience* (1999). His novel *Avenging Angel* was published in 1990 and reissued in 1991.

Preface to *In My Father's House*

My first memories are of a place called "Mbrom," a small neighborhood in Kumasi, capital of Asante, as that kingdom turned from being part of the British Gold Coast colony to being a region of the Republic of Ghana. Our home was opposite my grandparent's house—where scores of her kinsfolk and dependents lived under the direction of my stepgrandmother, "Auntie Jane," who baked bread for hundreds of people from Mbrom and the surrounding areas—down the street from many cousins of various, usually obscure, degrees of affinity. Near the center of the second largest city in Ghana, behind our hibiscus hedge in the "garden city of West Africa," our life was essentially a village life, lived among a few hundred neighbors; out from that village we went to the other little villages that make up the city.

We could go higher up the hill, to Asante New Town, to the palace of the Asante king, Prempeh II, whose first wife, my great-aunt, always called me "Akroma-Ampim" (the name of our most illustrious ancestor) or "Yao Antony" (the name of the great-uncle and head of the family from whom I acquired my anglicized name, "Anthony"). Or we could travel in another cultural direction to the campus of the Kwame Nkrumah University of Science and Technology— known always as "Tech"—where I went to primary school, and where many of my friends' parents were professors.

Some worlds—the world of the law courts where my father went, dressed in his dark European suits, carrying the white wig of the British barrister (which he wore after independence as in the colonial period), a rose from the garden (my mother's garden) always in his buttonhole; the world of parliament, where he went in the first years I can remember, an opponent now of his old friend Nkrumah—some worlds we knew of only because our parents spoke of them. Others—the world of the little church, Saint George's, where we went to Sunday school with Baptists and Copts and Catholics and Methodists and Anglicans, from other parts of the country, other parts of the continent, other parts of the world—we knew inside and out, knew because they were central to our friendships, our learning, our beliefs.

In our house, my mother was visited regularly by Muslim Hausa traders from what we called (in a phrase that struck my childhood ear as wonderfully mysterious, exotic in its splendid vagueness) "the North." These men knew she was interested in seeing and, sometimes, in buying the brass weights the Asante had used for weighing gold; goldweights they had collected from villages all over the region, where they were being sold by people who had no use for them anymore, now that paper and coin had replaced gold dust as currency. And as she collected them, she heard more and more of the folklore that went with them; the proverbs that every figurative goldweight elicited; the folktales, *Ananseasɔm*, that the proverbs evoked. My father told us these Ananse stories, too, some of them picked up when he was a political prisoner under Nkrumah (there was little else to do in prison but spin yarns). Between his stories and the cultural messages that came with the goldweights, we gathered the sort of sense of a cultural tradition that comes from growing up in it. For us it was not Asante tradition but the webwork of our lives. We loved the stories—my sisters now read the ones that my mother has published to my nephews in Gaberone and in Lagos; my godchildren read them here in America—and we grew to love the goldweights and the carvings that the traders brought.

And the family we grew into (an "extended" family, our English friends would have said, though we would have thought of their conceptions of family as "contracted") gave us an immense social space in which to grow.

But we also went from time to time to my mother's native country, to England, to stay with my grandmother in the rural West Country, returning the visits she had made to us. And the life there—perhaps this is only because it is also part of my earliest memories—seems, at least now, to have been mostly not too different. My grandmother lived next door to my aunt (my mother's sister) and her family, in the village where my aunt was born, just as my father lived next to his father. And so, by an odd cultural reversal, my father lived opposite and close to his patrilineal kin (in matrilineal Asante), while my aunt and her children lived next to their matrilineal kin (in patrilineal England). But it was my father's matriclan and my English grandfather's matriclan—descendants of the eight sisters, of whom one was my great-grandmother—that I came to know best over the years.

If my sisters and I were "children of two worlds," no one bothered to tell us this; we lived in one world, in two "extended" families divided by several thousand miles and an allegedly insuperable cultural distance that never, so far as I can recall, puzzled or perplexed us much. As I grew older, and went to an English boarding school, I learned that not everybody had family in Africa and in Europe; not everyone had a Lebanese uncle, American and French and Kenyan and Thai cousins. And by now, now that my sisters have married a Norwegian and a Nigerian and a Ghanaian, now that I live in America, I am used to seeing the world as a network of points of affinity.

This book is dedicated to nine children—a boy born in Botswana, of Norwegian and Anglo-Ghanaian parents; his brothers, born in Norway and in Ghana; their four cousins, three boys in Lagos, born of Nigerian and Anglo-Ghanaian parents, and a girl in Ghana; and two girls, born in New Haven, Connecticut, of an African-American father and a "white" American mother. These children, my nephews and my godchildren, range in appearance from the color and hair of my father's Asante kinsmen to the Viking ancestors of my Norwegian brother-in-law; they have names from Yorubaland, from Asante, from America, from Norway, from England. And watching them playing together and speaking to each other in their various accents, I, at least, feel a certain hope for the human future.

These children represent an eye to posterity, but this book is also dedicated to my father, who died while I was revising the final manuscript and became the closest of my ancestors. Long before he fell ill, I had decided to name this book for him: it was from him, after all, that I inherited the world and the problems with which this book is concerned. From him I inherited Africa, in general; Ghana, in particular; Asante and Kumasi, more particularly yet; his Christianity (his and my mother's) gave me *both* the biblical knowledge that means that for me the phrase "in my father's house . . ." must be completed "there are many mansions," *and* the biblical understanding that, when Christ utters those words at the Last Supper, he means that there is room enough for all in heaven; *his* Father's house. Even my father, who loved Ghana as much as anyone, would, of course, have resisted the assimilation of Ghana to heaven; though he might have been tempted to claim that the Kumasi of his youth was as close to heaven as anywhere on earth. But he would not deny—no one who knows these places could deny—that there is plenty of room in Africa, in Ghana, even in Asante, for all sorts and conditions of men and women; that at each level, Africa is various.

Two other crucial intellectual legacies from my father inform this book. One is his Pan-Africanism. In 1945 my father was with Nkrumah and Du Bois at the Pan-African Congress in Manchester; in 1974 he was one of the very few from the 1945 congress (he himself met no other) who attended the congress, hosted by Julius Nyerere, in Dar es Salaam. By then Du Bois and Nkrumah were gone: in 1972 my father had gone to Guinée to negotiate the return of Nkrumah's body for a Ghanaian state funeral; his office, in those days, in Christiansborg Castle in Accra, was a few short steps from Du Bois's grave. My father was, I think, as complete a Pan-Africanist as either of them; yet he also taught us, his children, to be as completely untempted by racism as he was. And he was able, despite his antiracism—despite what I am inclined to call his complete unracism, since racism was never a temptation he had to resist—to find it natural, when he was a delegate from Ghana to the UN to seek solidarity in Harlem, where he went to church most Sundays and made many lifelong friends. My father is my model for the possibility of a Pan-Africanism without racism, both in Africa and in its diaspora—a concrete possibility whose conceptual implications this book is partly intended to explore.

The second legacy is my father's multiple attachment to his identities: above all as an Asante, as a Ghanaian, as an African, and as a Christian and a Methodist. I cannot claim to participate fully in any of these identities as he did; given the history we do not share, he would not have expected me to. But I have tried in this book, in many places, to examine the meaning of one or another, and, by the end, all of these identities, and to learn from his capacity to make use of these many identities without, so far as I could tell, any significant conflict.

I could say more about my father's multiple presences in this book; but, in the end, I would rather that the book should show what I have learned from him than that I should catalog my debts at the start.

I say all this in part because in thinking about culture, which is the subject of this book, one is bound to be formed—morally, aesthetically, politically, religiously—by the range of lives one has known. Others will disagree with much that I have to say, and it is right that those who disagree, as those who agree with me, should know, as we say in America, "where I am coming from." This is especially important because the book is about issues that are bound to be deeply personally important for anyone with my history; for its theme is the question how we are to think about Africa's contemporary cultures in the light both of the two main external determinants of her recent cultural history—European and Afro-New World conceptions of Africa—and of her own endogenous cultural traditions. I believe—this is one of the central goals of the academy, which is my vocation—that we should think carefully about the issues that matter to us most. When I argue that ideological decolonization is bound to fail if it neglects either endogenous "tradition" or exogenous "Western" ideas, and that many African (and African-American) intellectuals have failed to find a negotiable middle way, I am talking about friends and neighbors and I am talking about how *we* deal with *our* shared situation. It would be foolhardy to suppose and unpersuasive to claim that in such a situation it is always one's dispassionate reason that triumphs, that one can pursue the issues with the impartiality of the disinterested. Precisely because I am aware of these other forces, I expect that sometimes along the way my history has not only formed my judgment (which I delight in) but distorted it (which, of course, I do not); to judge whether it has, you will need to know something of that history, and I want you to know, not least because only through the responses of readers will *I* learn of my distortions.

But it is also important to testify, I think, to the practical reality of the kind of intercultural project whose theoretical ramifications I explore in these essays: to show how easy it is, without theory, without much conscious thought, to live in human families that extend across the boundaries that are currently held to divide our race. It may help to have a thumb-nail sketch of the territory that lies before us.

Africa's intellectuals have long been engaged in a conversation with each other and with Europeans and Americans, about what it means to be African. At the heart of these debates on African identity are the seminal works of politicians, creative writers, and philosophers from Africa and her disapora. In this book, I draw on the writings of these African and African-American thinkers to explore the possibilities and pitfalls of an African identity in the late twentieth century.

The essays fall into four clusters, and, as I look over them with hindsight, I detect a central preoccupation in each.

In the two opening essays, which form the first cluster, I explore the role of racial ideology in the development of Pan-Africanism. I argue that the idea of the Negro, the idea of an African race, is an unavoidable element in that discourse, and that these racialist notions are grounded in bad biological—and worse ethical—ideas, inherited from the increasingly racialized thought of nineteenth-century Europe and America.

The next two essays are united in asking how questions about African identity figure in African literary life; and they do so by exploring the ideas of critics and literary theorists in Chapter 3 and of a major writer—Wole Soyinka—in Chapter 4. The burden of these essays is that the attempt to construct an African literature rooted in African traditions has led both to an understating of the diversity of African cultures, and to an attempt to censor the profound entanglement of African intellectuals with the intellectual life of Europe and the Americas.

The pair of chapters that follows—cluster three—is motivated by an essentially philosophical preoccupation with the issues of reason and modernity. In thinking about modern African philosophy and "traditional" religion, I rely on a view of the central role of reason in African life before and after colonialism; and I suggest a view of modernization in Africa that differs, as a result, from the standard Weberian view. The upshot here is not so easily reduced to a formula: but my theme is that an ideal of, reasonableness (conceived, in a specific sense, transculturally) has a central role to play in thinking about Africa's future. To one side lies parochialism; to the other, false claims to universality.

The final set of chapters raise more explicitly questions of politics and identity. I trace the art market and some contemporary novels to the emergence of an unsentimental form of African humanisms that can undergird our resistance to tyranny. I explore the meaning of the African nation-state and the forms of social organization that both challenge and enable it. I take up in a more theoretical way the general question of identities—racial, ethnic, national, Pan-African—and what the power of identities at each of these levels reveals about the possibilities for politics and the role of intellectuals in political life.

It is in this political sphere that so many of the issues raised in this book come together. Rejecting the rhetoric of descent requires a rethinking of Pan-Africanist politics; literature and its criticism are more explicitly preoccupied in Africa than in Europe and North America with political questions; and modernization and its meaning are the major policy questions facing our political institutions. Naturally, therefore, there is no easy separation of the issues; and naturally, also, political questions surface again and again throughout the book. More surprising, I think, is the persistent recurrence of questions of race; of the racialist history that has dogged Pan-Africanism from its inception.

But, that said, I would want to resist the reduction of this book to a single theme. For the situation of the African intellectual is as complex and multifarious a predicament as a human being can face in our time, and in addressing that situation I would not want to bury the many stories in a single narrative. This claim has become a postmodernist mannerism: but it strikes me as, in fact, also a very old and sane piece of wisdom. Wittgenstein used to quote Bishop Butler's remark that "everything is what it is and not another thing." There is a piece of Akan wordplay with the same moral "Esono Esono, na Esono sosono," . . . which being translated reads "The elephant is one thing and the worm another."

Credits

The publisher and editor gratefully acknowledge permission to reprint the material in this book from the following copyright holders:

1. Plato: "A Philosopher Educates a Tyrant," in *Complete Works*, edited by John Cooper, 1997. Reprinted by permission of Hackett Publishing Company. All rights reserved.
2. Seneca: *Letters from a Stoic*, translated by Robin Campbell, Penguin, 1969, 36–38, 96–99, 162, 172–176. Reprinted by permission of Penguin, UK.
3. Augustine: "The Happy Life," in *Selected Writings*, edited by Mary Curd, Paulist Press, 1984; *Against the Academicians*, edited by Peter King, Hackett, 1995. Reprinted by permission. All rights reserved; *The Essential Augustine*, edited by Vernon Bourke, Hackett, 1974. Reprinted by permission. All rights reserved; *Nicene and Post-Nicene Fathers*, vol. 1, edited by Philip Schaff, Hendrickson Publishers, 1994; two letters to St. Jerome (sections of letters XXVIII, LXXXII), in *The Letters of St. Augustine*, edited by John Leinenweber, Triumph Books, 1992.
4. Al Ghazali: "The Rescuer from Error," in *University Library of Autobiographies*, vol. 2, *The Middle Ages and Their Autobiographies*, edited by Charles J. Bushnell, Tyler Daniels Co., 1918.
5. Abelard and Héloïse: "Abelard's "Confessions of Faith," in *The Letters of Abelard and Héloïse*, translated by Betty Radice, Penguin, 1975. Reprinted by permission of Penguin UK.
6. Moses Maimonides: *A Guide for the Perplexed*, translated by Shlomo Pines. Reprinted by permission of the University of Chicago Press.
7. Francis Bacon: *Selected Philosophical Works*, edited by Rose-Mary Sargent, Hackett, 1999; *The Works of Francis Bacon*, vol. 8, edited by James Spedding, Robert Leslie Ellis, and Douglas Denon Heath, *Translations of the Philosophical Works*, Taggard & Thompson, 1943; "Letter to Lord Burghley" [1592] and "A Letter to Lancelot Andrewes" [1687], *The Oxford Authors Series*, edited by Brian Vickers, Oxford University Press, 1996.
8. René Descartes: "Discourse on Method," in *The Philosophical Writings of Descartes*, vol. 1, translated by John Cottingham, Robert Stoothoff, and Dugald Murdoch, Cambridge University Press, 1985. Reprinted by permission; "Observations," "Adrien Baillet," in *La vie de Monsieur Descartes*, 1691 translation, Jacob Dreyfack, from Ferdinand Alquie, *Oeuvre Philosophiques*, vol. 1, Garnier, 1963; "Letters to Elizabeth," in *The Philosophical Writings of Descartes*, vol. 3, translated by John Cottingham, Robert Stoothoff, Dugald Murdoch, and Anthony Kenney, Cambridge University Press, 1991. Reprinted by permission.
9. Blaise Pascal: *Pensées/The Provincial Letters*, Modern Library, 1941. Copyright © 1950 by Pantheon Books, Inc. Reprinted by permission of Pantheon, a division of Random House, Inc.
10. Thomas Hobbes: "To the Right and Honourable William, Earl of Newcastle," epistle dedicatory, in *The Elements of Law*, edited by Ferdinand Tönnies, Cambridge at the University Press, 1928, pp. xvii–xviii; epistle dedicatory and author's preface to the reader, in *De Cive*, edited with an introduction by Sterling P. Lamprecht, Appleton-Century-Crofts, 1949, pp. 1–18;"Hobbes's Verse Autobiography," in *Leviathan*, edited and with an introduction and notes by Edwin Curley, Hackett, 1994, pp. 1–5; selection from Aubrey's *Life of Hobbes*.
11. Baruch Spinoza: "On the Emendation of the Intellect," in *The Collected Works of*

Spinoza, translated by Edwin Curley, Princeton University Press, 1985. Reprinted by permission; *The Letters*, translated by Samuel Shirley, with an introduction and notes by Steven Barbone, Lee Rice, and Jacob Adler, Hackett, 1995. Reprinted by permission. All rights reserved.

12. John Locke: "The Epistle to the Reader," in *An Essay Concerning Human Understanding*, vol. 1, edited by Alexander Campbell Fraser, Clarendon, 1894; H. R. Fox Bourne, *The Life of John Locke*, Scientia Verlag Aalen, 1969, 1:358–365; Fox Bourne quotes Peter King, Lord Chancellor (1698), Extracts from his Correspondence and Commonplace Books, 1829, 1830; "My Epitaph."

13. Gottfried Wilhelm Leibniz: *Philosophical Essays*, edited and translated by Roger Ariew and Daniel Garber, Hackett, 1989. Reprinted by permission. All rights reserved; letters to Thomas Hobbes, Simon Foucher, Gabriel Wagner, in *Philosophic Papers and Letters,* edited by Leroy Loemker Dordrecht, Reidel Publishing, 1969–1976.

14. George Berkeley: "The Analyst," Berkeley's Rough Draft of the Introduction to the *Principles of Human Knowledge,* first published 1734; "Introduction to Principles of Human Knowledge," *The Works of George Berkeley,* D.D., formerly Bishop of Cloyne, including posthumous works, etc.; w/account of life by Alexander Campbell Fraser, vol. 1, Clarendon, 1901; *Three Dialogues between Hylas and Philonous*, Hackett, 1979. Reprinted by permission; *The Works of George Berkeley, Bishop of Cloyne*, edited by A. A. Luce and T. E. Jessop, vol. 1, Nelson, 1979. Philosophical Commentaries from Notebook B.

15. David Hume and Adam Smith: *A Treatise on Human Nature*, edited by L. A. Selby-Bigge, Clarendon, 1958; *The Letters of David Hume*, vol. 1, edited by J.Y.T. Greig, Garland, 1983; "To JJ Rousseau," "To Adam Smith," and "To the Comtesse de Boufflers," in *The Letters of David Hume*, edited by J.Y.T Greig, Clarendon, 1932, pp. 28–36, 171–173; Hume, "My Own Life" and "Letter from Adam Smith to Wm. Strahan," in *Essays: Moral, Political, and Literary*, edited by Eugene Miller, Liberty Fund, 1985, pp. xxxi–xlix.

16. Giambattista Vico: *The Autobiography of Giambattista Vico*, translated by Max Harold Fisch and Thomas Goddard Bergin, Great Seal Books, Cornell University Press, 1975. Used by permission of Cornell University Press.

17. Voltaire: *The Portable Voltaire*, edited by Ben Ray Redman, Viking Penguin, 1949. Used by permission of Viking Penguin, a division of Penguin Putnam Inc.

18. Jean-Jacques Rousseau: *Citizen of Geneve (Selections from the Letters of J.J. Rousseau)*, translated by Charles W. Hendel, Oxford University Press, 1937. Reprinted by permission of Oxford University Press; *The Reveries of the Solitary Walker*, translated by Charles E. Butterworth, Hackett, 1992. Reprinted by permission. All rights reserved.

19. Denis Diderot: *The Encyclopedia: Selections,* edited and translated by Stephen J. Gendzier, Harper Torchbooks/Harper & Row, 1967. Reprinted by permission; *Rameau's Nephew and Other Works*, translated by Jacques Barzun and Ralph H. Bowen, Library of Liberal Arts/Bobbs-Merrill. Reprinted by permission of Jacques Barzun and Writers' Representatives Inc.

20. Immanuel Kant: *Prolegomena to Any Future Metaphysics,* translated by Lewis Beck, Liberal Arts Press, 1950. Copyright © 1950 by Lewis Beck. Reprinted by permission; *The Critique of Pure Reason,* translated by Paul Guyer and Allen Wood, Cambridge University Press, 1998. Reprinted by permission; *Critique of Practical Reason and Other Works,* translated by T. K. Abbott, Longmans, Green, 1873, pp. 260–262; *Philosophical Correspondence, 1759–1799*, edited and translated by Arnulf Zweig, Cambridge University Press, 1999. Reprinted by permission. *Fragments* translated by Ernst Gassiner in his *Rousseau, Kant, Goethe: Two Essays*, Princeton University Press, 1945, pp. 1–2. Reprinted by permission.

21. Johann Gottfried von Herder: "Journal of my Voyage, 1969," in *J. G. Herder on Social and Political Culture*, edited by F. M. Barnard, Cambridge University Press, 1969. Reprinted by permission.

22. Johann Gottlieb Fichte: *Fichte: Early Philosophical Writings*, edited and translated by Daniel Breazeale, Cornell University Press, 1988. Reprinted by permission of Cornell

University Press; *Introduction to Wissenschaftslehre (1797–1800)*, edited and translated by Daniel Brealzeale, Hackett, 1994. Reprinted by permission.

23. Georg Wilhelm Friedrich Hegel: *Encyclopedia of the Social Sciences: The Logic of Hegel*, translated by William Wallace, Oxford University Press, 1892, pp. 19–21, 127–128 (and introduction); *Philosophy of Mind*, translated by A. V. Miller, Clarendon, 1971, pp. 1–2, 265–266; *Hegel: The Essential Writings*, edited by Frederick G. Weiss, Harper and Row, 1974; *Phenomenology of Spirit*, translated by A. V. Miller, Oxford University Press, 1977, preface and introduction, pp. 1–3, 7–8, 12, 14, 22–23, 41–45. Reprinted by permission; *Hegel: The Letters*, translated by Clark Butler and Christiane Seiler, Indiana University Press, 1984. Reprinted by permission of Indiana University Press.

24. Arthur Schopenhauer: *The World as Will and Representation*, translated by E.F.J. Payne, vol. 1, 1958. Reprinted by permission of Dover Publications Inc.; *Essays and Aphorisms*, edited by R. J. Hollingdale, Penguin, 1970, pp. 41–44, 117–121. Copyright © 1977 by R. J. Hollingdale. Reprinted by permission of Penguin UK.

25. Jeremy Bentham: "Preface: An Introduction to the Principles of Morals and Legislation," reprinted in *A Bentham Reader*, edited by Mary Peter Mack, Pegasus/Western, 1969, pp. 78–81, 84–89; *The Works of Jeremy Bentham*, edited by John Bowring, vols. 8, 10, Russell and Russell, 1962, *The Rationale of Reward*, Robert Howard, 1830, pp. 205–207, 214–215; Mill on Bentham: *Dissertations and Discussions* from *The Westminster Review*, August 1838, reprinted in *Mill's Essays on Literature and Society*, edited by J. B. Schneewind, Collier & Macmillan, 1965.

26. John Stuart Mill: *The Earlier Letters of John Stuart Mill, 1812–1848*, edited by Francis E. Mineka, University of Toronto Press/Routledge & Kegan Paul, 1963, with an introduction by F. A. Hayek; *On the Logic of the Moral Sciences* (*A System of Logic, Book VI*), edited by Henry Magid, Bobbs-Merrill, 1965; *Mill's Essays on Literature and Society*, edited by J. B. Schneewind, Collier & Macmillan, 1965, pp. 548–550; "Inaugural Address at the University of St. Andrews" (1867); *On Liberty*, edited by Gertrude Himmelfarb, Penguin, 1959–1974; *The Autobiography of John Stuart Mill*, Humphrey Milford/Oxford University Press, 1924–1940, with a preface by Harold J. Laski; *The Autobiography of John Stuart Mill*, Columbia University Press, 1924.

27. Søren Kierkegaard: *The Point of View for My Work as an Author*, translated by Walter Lowrie, Harper & Row, 1962. Reprinted by permission of HarperCollins Publishers Inc.

28. Karl Marx: preface to "A Contribution to the Critique of Political Economy" (1859); "Letter to Arnold Ruge" (1843); "Introduction to Critique of Hegel's Philosophy of Right" (1843); "Theses on Feuerbach" (1845); reprinted from *The Marx-Engels Reader*, 2d ed., edited by Robert Tucker, Norton, 1972. Reprinted by permission of W. W. Norton & Company, Inc.; preface to the first edition of the first volume of *Capital* (1887); "V.I. Lenin, Article on Karl Marx" (1914) from *Collected Works*, vol. 21:46–50; reprinted from *Karl Marx and Frederick Engels: Selected Works* International Publishers/New World Paperbacks, 1968.

29. Frederick Nietzsche: "Letters," from *The Portable Nietzsche*, edited by Walter Kaufman. Translation copyright © 1954 by The Viking Press, renewed © 1982 by Viking Penguin Inc. Used by permission of Viking Penguin, a division of Penguin Putnam Inc.; from "Ecce Homo," in *Basic Writings of Nietzsche*, translated by Walter Kaufmann, Modern Library/Random House, 1966. Copyright © 1967 by Walter Kaufman. Reprinted by permission of Random House Inc.

30. Charles Sanders Peirce: *The Collected Papers of Charles Sanders Peirce*, edited by Charles Hartshorne and Paul Weiss, vol. 1, *Principles of Philosophy*, Harvard University Press, 1931; vol. 2, *Elements of Logic*, Harvard University Press, 1932. Reprinted by permission of Harvard University Press.

31. William James: "The Sentiment of Rationality," in *Mind*, 1879; "The Moral Philosopher and the Moral Life," *International Journal of Ethics*," 1891, reprinted in *Essays in Pragmatism;* "Philosophy and Its Critics," in *Some Problems in Philosophy*, 1911.

32. John Dewey: "From Absolutism to Experimentalism," in *The Collected Works of John Dewey: The Later Works, 1925–1953*, vol. 5, *1929–1930,* edited by Jo Ann Boydston, Southern Illinois University Press. Reprinted by permission of Southern Illinois University Press.

33. George Santayana: "My Host the World," in *Persons and Places: The Background of My Life*, Charles Scribners, 1944. Copyright © 1944 by Charles Scribners and Sons. Reprinted by permission of MIT Press.

34. Bertrand Russell: *The Philosophy of Bertrand Russell*, vol. 5, edited by Paul Arthur Schlipp, Library of Living Philosophers, 1946.

35. Ludwig Wittgenstein: *Ludwig Wittgenstein: Cambridge Letters* [correspondence with Russell, Keynes, et al.], edited by Brian McGuiness and G. H. von Wright, Blackwell, 1995, pp. 45–46; 55; 66, 69–70; 85–86; 199–200; 205–207; 293–295; 315–317; *Geheime Tagebücher (1914–1916),* edited by Wilhelm Baum, Thuria & Kant, 1991; manuscript translated by Juliet Floyd, 1 page; *Notebooks 1914–1916,* edited by G.dH. von Wright and G.E.M. Anscombe, Blackwell, 1973. Reprinted by permission of Blackwell Publishers and the University of Chicago Press; *Tractatus Logico-Philosophicus* (1922), translated by David Pears and Brian McGuiness, Routledge & Kegan Paul, 1961; three paragraphs from the preface to *Tractatus;* 5.621, 5.63, 6.4311, 6.4312; *Culture and Value,* edited by G. H. von Wright, translated by Peter Winch, University of Chicago Press, 1977–1980.

36. Heidegger: "My Way to Phenomenology," in *On Time and Being*, by Martin Heidegger, translated by Joan Stambaugh, Harper Torchbooks/Harper & Row, 1941. Reprinted by permission of HarperCollins Publishers, "*National Socialist Education* address," and "Letter," in *The Heidegger Controversy: A Critical Reader,* edited by Richard Wolin, Columbia University Press, 1991, pp. 55–59, 61–66.

37. Rudolf Carnap: *The Philosophy of Rudolf Carnap*, edited by Paul Arthur Schlipp, Open Court, 1963. Reprinted by permission of Open Court Publishing Company, a division of Carus Publishing Company, Peru, Illinois.

38. Jean-Paul Sartre: *Life/Situations: Essays Written and Spoken*, translated by Paul Auster and Lydia Davis, Random House, 1977. Reprinted by permission of Pantheon Books, a division of Random House, Inc.; "Self-Portrait at Seventy," *Le Nouvel Observateur*, 1975.

39. Simone de Beauvoir: *The Prime of Life*, translated by Peter Green, World, 1962. Copyright © 1976 by Harper & Row Publishers. Reprinted by permission.

40. Takatura Ando: preface to *Aristotle's Theory of Practical Cognition*, 2d ed., Inuzukatyo Syugakuin (Kyoto), 1958; reprint, The Hague: M. Nijhoff, 1965.

41. Hans-Georg Gadamer: *Philosophical Apprenticeships*, translated by Robert R. Sullivan, MIT Press, 1985. Copyright © by Robert R. Sullivan. Reprinted by permission of MIT Press.

42. Hannah Arendt: "Dedication to Karl Jaspers," in *Essays in Understanding, 1930–1954*, Harcourt Brace, 1994; "On Lessing," in *Men in Dark Times*, Harcourt Brace and World, 1968, pp. 17–23. Reprinted by permission of Harcourt Brace & Company; *The Life of the Mind: Thinking*, Harcourt Brace Jovanovich, 1977, pp. 3–5, 7, 13.

43. G.E.M. Anscombe: *The Collected Philosophical Papers of G.E.M. Anscombe,* vol. 2, *Metaphysics and the Philosophy of Mind*, 1981; vol. 3, *Ethics, Religion, and Politics*, 1981. Reprinted by permission of Blackwell Publishers; "Notes from a Conversation between Mary Mothersill and Elizabeth Anscombe," typescript. Courtesy of Mary Mothersill.

44. Isaiah Berlin: *My Intellectual Path*, from *The Power of Ideas*. Copyright cW 1998 The Isaiah Berlin Literary Trust and Henry Hardy. Reprinted by permission.

45. Kwame Anthony Appiah: preface to *In My Father's House: Africa in the Philosophy of Culture*, Oxford University Press. Copyright © 1992 by Kwame Anthony Appiah. Reprinted by permission.